WEAPONS & WARFARE

WEAPONS & WARFARE

REVISED EDITION

Volume 1

ANCIENT AND MEDIEVAL WEAPONS AND WARFARE (TO C. 1500)

Editor
JOHN POWELL
Oklahoma Baptist University

SALEM PRESS
Pasadena, California   Hackensack, New Jersey

Editorial Director: Christina J. Moose
Acquisitions Manager: Mark Rehn
Acquisitions Editor: Steven L. Danver/Mesa Verde Publishing
Editorial Assistant: Brett S. Weisberg
Research Supervisor: Jeffry Jensen
Photo Editor: Cynthia Breslin Beres
Production Editor: Joyce I. Buchea
Graphics and Design: James Hutson
Layout: Mary Overell

Cover images: The Granger Collection, New York; Library of Congress;
©iStockphoto.com/(Craig DeBourbon, Ian Ilott, Melissa Madia, Adam James Kazmierski)

Library of Congress Cataloging-in-Publication Data

Weapons & warfare / editor, John Powell. — Rev. ed.
    p. cm.
Includes bibliographical references and index.
    ISBN 978-1-58765-594-4 (set : alk. paper) — ISBN 978-1-58765-595-1 (v. 1 : alk. paper) —
ISBN 978-1-58765-596-8 (v. 2 : alk. paper) — ISBN 978-1-58765-597-5 (v. 3 : alk. paper)
1. Military weapons—History. 2. Military art and science—History. I. Powell, John, 1954-
II. Title: Weapons and warfare.
    UF500.W48 2010
    623.409—dc22
                                                                        2009050491

CONTENTS
ANCIENT AND MEDIEVAL WEAPONS AND WARFARE TO C. 1500

PUBLISHER'S NOTE

Originally published in 2002 in two volumes, the three-volume *Weapons and Warfare: Revised Edition* is designed to meet the needs of students seeking information about weaponry, tactics, and models of warfare from ancient times to the present, worldwide. Written with the needs of both students and nonspecialists in mind, the articles contained in this set present clear discussions of the topics, explaining any terms or references that may be unfamiliar. The focus on the technical and strategic development of weapons and tactics, more than on a narrative chronological history of events, allows students of history, political science, and technology to gain a broad understanding of both the scientific and the strategic advances made over time and geography. The new third volume adds the essential dimension of placing these topics in broad cultural, sociopolitical, and ethical contexts.

The expanded edition covers all topics included in the original two-volume edition and adds 58 new essays and appendixes, along with 22 heavily revised and expanded essays and appendixes. In addition to the new and revised text, all previous entries have been fully updated: Bibliographies have been expanded to add recent scholarship, and "Films and Other Media" sections have been expanded or added where they were missing before. The new third volume adds a fresh dimension, offering social, cultural, ethical, and political perspectives on warfare and weaponry.

Scope and Coverage

Weapons and Warfare, Revised Edition offers 141 essays (56 completely new) and 7 appendixes (2 completely new). In the first two volumes, these are arranged chronologically within thematic groupings. Hence, volume 1, *Ancient and Medieval*, first covers "Weapons and Forces" for the period ("Clubs, Maces, and Slings" through "Warships and Naval Warfare"), followed by sections of essays on "The Ancient World" and then "The Medieval World."

Similarly, volume 2 covers "Weapons and Forces" ("Swords, Daggers, and Bayonets" through "Naval Development: The Age of Propulsion"), followed by sections addressing modern warfare, from "Western Warfare in the Age of Maneuver" through "Warfare in the Global Age." Each "Weapons and Forces" section covers weapons and strategies, while the rest of the essays examine specific cultures and empires in terms of their weapons and methods of warfare as well as their military achievements.

Volume 3, *Warfare: Culture and Concepts*, presents 35 overviews (34 of them new) of the way warfare, weapons, and military history have been expressed socially, politically, and in the arts, addressing not only these societal aspects of warfare but also "behind the battlefield" theories, strategies, and policies. These overviews are followed by a section of Research Tools consisting of 7 appendixes; 2 new appendixes have been added as valuable teaching tools: "War Films" and "War Literature." A comprehensive Subject Index ends this final volume.

Organization and Format

The essays in these volumes are organized into three essay types:

- *Weapons Overviews* are organized with sections on "Nature and Use" and "Development" of each weapons type. The first section describes the basic concepts behind this category of weapon and details the ways these weapons were used during the period in question; the second section follows their evolution over the period, paying special attention to key developments. Secondary sources for further study are listed in the "Books and Articles" sections that close the Weapons Overviews.
- *Historical Overviews*: In volumes 1 and 2, Weapons Overviews are followed by chronologically and geographically arranged sections cov-

ering major historical periods and civilizations and their contributions to military weapons, technologies, and strategies. These Historical Overviews contain subsections covering "Political Considerations" (where relevant), "Military Achievement," "Weapons, Uniforms, and Armor," "Military Organization," and "Doctrine, Strategy, and Tactics." The worldwide geographical scope of the set is truly evident in these overviews, which include essays on Eastern and Southern Asia, the Middle East and Africa, and the Americas, as well as Europe. The historical range of the set is equally clear, covering the evolution of warfare from the time of the earliest Mesopotamian empires into the third millennium.

Historical Overviews also feature a unique section headed "Ancient [or Medieval or Contemporary] Sources," which summarizes for both students and researchers the primary sources upon which historians have drawn, in concert with other evidence (archaeological, for example), to form their understanding of the military history in question. These sections are invaluable for further in-depth research, and they provide an essential complement to the following section, "Books and Articles," a bibliography of secondary sources listing the most authoritative and editorially vetted print resources for understanding the warfare of the period or civilization at hand.

- *Culture and Concepts Overviews:* Finally, the new third volume's Culture and Concept Overviews approach warfare and weaponry from several different perspectives: sociological, geographical, cultural, political, ethical, religious, tactical, and strategic. These essays provide the perspectives from which the other essays can be understood in a broader context. Each begins with an "Overview" (definition) of coverage, followed by a summary of its "Significance" in regard to warfare and then a complete historical overview, with subsections reviewing the "Ancient World," "Medieval World," and "Modern World."

SPECIAL FEATURES

Volume 3 ends with a set of valuable research tools, beginning with two new appendixes: an annotated list of "War Films" and an annotated list of "War Literature." These are arranged chronologically by war, for use in teaching. The annotations guide students and teachers with regard to the novels' or films' usefulness in historical study (and where they may fall short, as well). Other research tools in this section include a Lexicon of military terms (expanded), an annotated list of Military Theorists (expanded), a Time Line (expanded), a Bibliography (expanded), and an updated list of Web Sites. A comprehensive and fully cross-referenced Subject Index rounds out the set.

The essays are accompanied by more than 70 time lines, lists of "Turning Points" that bring to readers' attention the key battles, inventions, and other events bearing on the technology or civilization covered. These are joined by 251 photographs and artists' renderings depicting the weapons discussed, as well as maps that direct readers to the geographic areas inhabited or conquered by the empires, civilizations, and cultures discussed.

USAGE NOTES

The names of wars and battles and the names of military leaders and other personages vary from resource to resource and from country to country, depending on variables such as political perspective, the different methods of transcribing non-Roman languages, and customary usage over the years. In these volumes, the names that are used in the essays, along with dates of events and for persons' life spans, are those that, over time, have proved to be the appellations, spellings, and renderings most familiar to the general English-speaking audience. Chinese names have generally been given in their Pinyin form, with Wade-Giles transliterations cross-referenced in the index.

Sources consulted to confirm these data are recognized as authoritative and hinge on a consensus of the most trusted available. Birth and death years follow the first mentions of key personages' names where appropriate, and titles of works are introduced using their original dates of appearance (or publication in the modern world), along with original-language titles where available. Key foreign terms are introduced in italics where they are defined, and all wars and battles are accompanied by their years (or date spans) of occurrence upon first mention in each essay.

ACKNOWLEDGMENTS

This revised edition of *Weapons and Warfare* owes a debt to many participating consultants and contributors. Chief among these is John Powell, Professor of History at Oklahoma Baptist University, who conceived of the first edition and continued his role as the chief creative force for this revised edition, including coverage, arrangement, and design of the essays and all supplemental features of the set. Both as a respected historian with specializations in modern Britain and as a longtime classroom teacher, he provided invaluable input on what works best for teaching the curriculum—not only military history but also related curricula involving cultural studies and perspectives.

Steven L. Danver of Mesa Verde Publishing commandeered the revised edition's acquisitions and revisions. Managing editor of *Journal of the West* and a visiting professor of history in Seaver College at Pepperdine University, Dr. Danver earned his doctorate in history at the University of Utah, concentrating on the history of American Indian peoples and the American West.

More than 100 contributors, including historians, political scientists, and other academicians, have lent their knowledge and insight to this project, and without their expertise the significant revisions of the essays, as well as the new contributions, would not have been possible. Their names and academic affiliations appear on the following pages.

CONTRIBUTORS

Donna Alvah
St. Lawrence University

Stephen J. Andrews
*Midwestern Baptist Theological
Seminary*

James A. Arieti
Hampden-Sydney College

John H. Barnhill
Houston, Texas

Frederic J. Baumgartner
*Virginia Polytechnic Institute &
State University*

Alvin K. Benson
Utah Valley University

Wayne H. Bowen
Ouachita Baptist University

Denvy A. Bowman
Coastal Carolina University

Stefan M. Brooks
Lindsey Wilson College

Dino E. Buenviaje
University of California, Riverside

Bryan Buschner
New Mexico State University

Joseph P. Byrne
Belmont University

Laura M. Calkins
Independent Scholar

Douglas Campbell
Independent Scholar

J. Nathan Campbell
Episcopal School of Dallas

John Casey
Columbia College Chicago

Frederick B. Chary
Indiana University Northwest

Michael Coker
South Carolina Historical Society

Justin Corfield
Geelong Grammar School

Thomas I. Crimando
*State University of New York,
College at Brockport*

Kenneth P. Czech
St. Cloud State University

Everett Dague
Benedictine College

John Daley
Pittsburg State University

Steven L. Danver
Pepperdine University

John Coleman Darnell
Yale University

Touraj Daryaee
*California State University,
Fullerton*

Benedict E. DeDominicis
Catholic University of Korea

Bruce J. DeHart
*University of North Carolina at
Pembroke*

Jeffrey Dippmann
Central Washington University

Paul W. Doerr
Acadia University

Charles Mayer Dupier, Jr.
Cumberland College

Richard D. Fitzgerald
Onondaga Community College

Andrew Reynolds Galloway
St. Philip's College

K. Fred Gillum
Independent Scholar

Robert F. Gorman
*Texas State University,
San Marcos*

Oliver Griffin
Weber State University

Gavin R. G. Hambly
University of Texas at Dallas

Christopher Howell
Red Rocks College

Charles F. Howlett
Molloy College

George Hoynacki
Merrimack College

Steven Isaac
Northwestern College

Robert Jacobs
Central Washington University

Lance Janda
Cameron University

Phyllis G. Jestice
University of Southern Mississippi

J. E. Kaufmann
Palo Alto Junior College

Jerry Keenan
Longmont, Colorado

Paul Bentley Kern
Indiana University Northwest

Martin Kich
*Wright State University—
Lake Campus*

Jacob P. Kovel
University of Kansas

Mark S. Lacy
University of Wisconsin, Madison

John W. I. Lee
*University of California,
Santa Barbara*

Keith A. Leitich
Independent Scholar

Van Michael Leslie
Union College

Eric v.d. Luft
*College of Saint Rose,
Gegensatz Press*

Joseph M. McCarthy
Suffolk University

Michael J. McGrath
Georgia Southern University

James R. McIntyre
Moraine Valley Community College

Carl Henry Marcoux
University of California, Riverside

Thomas C. Maroukis
Capital University

Jennifer P. Mathews
Trinity University

Timothy May
*North Georgia College and State
University*

Ruben G. Mendoza
*California State University,
Monterey Bay*

Elizabeth L. Meyers
Independent Scholar

Gregory Moore
Notre Dame College

R. Scott Moore
Indiana University of Pennsylvania

John Morello
DeVry University

Walter Nelson
RAND Corporation

Caryn E. Neumann
Miami University of Ohio

Scott Allen Nollen
Mobile, Alabama

Oladele A. Ogunseitan
University of California, Irvine

R. K. L. Panjabi
*Memorial University of
Newfoundland*

Robert J. Paradowski
Rochester Institute of Technology

Brian A. Pavlac
King's College

Alan P. Peterson
Gordon College

Aaron Plamondon
University of Calgary

Mark Polelle
University of Findlay

John Powell
Oklahoma Baptist University

Steven J. Ramold
Eastern Michigan University

Eugene L. Rasor
Emory & Henry College

Kevin B. Reid
Henderson Community College

Burnam W. Reynolds
Asbury College

Edward J. Rielly
Saint Joseph's College of Maine

Charles W. Rogers
*Southwestern Oklahoma State
University*

Charles Rosenberg
Milwaukee, Wisconsin

Alison Rowley
Duke University

Scott M. Rusch
University of Pennsylvania

Elizabeth D. Schafer
Loachapoka, Alabama

Carl Otis Schuster
Honolulu, Hawaii

James P. Sickinger
Florida State University

David Silbey
Bowdoin College

Michael J. Siler
*California State University,
Los Angeles*

Andrew C. Skinner
Brigham Young University

Roger Smith
Portland, Oregon

Larry Smolucha
Aurora University

Sonia Sorrell
Pepperdine University

James Stanlaw
Illinois State University

Arthur K. Steinberg
Salisbury, North Carolina

Geoff Stewart
University of Western Ontario

Cameron Sutt
Austin Peay State University

Ghada Talhami
Lake Forest College

James N. Tallon
Lewis University

Cassandra Lee Tellier
Capital University

Contributors

Jachin W. Thacker
Western Kentucky University

William T. Walker
Chestnut Hill College

David Westwood
MLRS Books

Chris Thomas
Texas A&M University

Kathy Warnes
Allendale, Michigan

John D. Windhausen
Saint Anselm College

Louis P. Towles
Southern Wesleyan University

Andrew J. Waskey
Dalton State College

Michael Witkoski
University of South Carolina

Nicolas G. Virtue
University of Western Ontario

Thomas Weiler
University of Bonn

Helen M. York
University of Maine

LIST OF ILLUSTRATIONS, MAPS, AND TIME LINES

Volume 1

ALPHABETIZED INDEX OF ESSAYS

CATEGORIZED INDEX OF ESSAYS

CUTTING WEAPONS

ECONOMICS AND TRADE

EIGHTEENTH AND NINETEENTH CENTURIES (1700'S AND 1800'S)

EUROPE AND MEDITERRANEAN

MIDDLE EAST

MILITARY THEORY

MORALITY, ETHICS, AND JUSTICE

WEAPONS & WARFARE

WEAPONS AND FORCES

CLUBS, MACES, AND SLINGS

Dates: To c. 1500 C.E.

NATURE AND USE

Clubs, maces, and slings, originally appearing in primitive times, are alike in their antiquity and concussive effect. Clubs are stout sticks, weighted at the striking end and usually made of hardwood, although bone, horn, and stone were also used. Clubs, the oldest weapons, have taken many forms throughout history. As small personal weapons, less than 2 feet in length, they could be thrust into belts and carried anywhere. Larger war clubs—from 2 to 3 feet in length—were wielded with one hand, and very large clubs, from 3 to 6 feet in length, were used with both hands. Shafts could be straight or curved, with cylindrical, ball-shaped, or broad, flat heads. Shaft edges could be sharpened, knobbed, spiked, or fitted with naturally sharp items, such as shark's teeth, rays' tails, or obsidian blades.

Although hand weapons could be used with more accuracy and force than thrown ones, clubs meant for throwing were also used. These "throwing sticks" were usually 2 to 3 feet long and could be curved, such as the Australian boomerang, or could have a ball and handle, such as the African knobkerrie. Users of these weapons hoped either to kill an enemy outright by crushing its skull or to incapacitate it by breaking its bones or stunning it. The club has seen worldwide use among primitive tribal peoples and early civilizations, and simple forms were wielded by early hominids.

Developed from the club, the mace is a heavy weight attached to the end of a handle. Stone maces appeared during the seventh millennium B.C.E. in the Neolithic Near East, and their use spread into Europe, Egypt, and India, where they were employed into the early Bronze Age. A mace was made by inserting 2- to 3-foot-long handles into holes bored through stones that had been worked into spherical, or at least symmetrical, shapes. Maces with bronze or iron heads became popular during the medieval era

Greek slingers, circa 400 B.C.E.

3

(approximately 500-1500 C.E.), and their use spread from Central Asia and the Near East into Europe, the Far East, and North Africa. Although intended to injure people, maces were also designed to damage armor: smashing it with blunt heads, penetrating it with spiked or knobbed heads, or cutting it with flanged or winged heads. Maces could also be thrown, although this was an unusual usage. The military flail, which had mace heads or clubs attached by chains to the handle, also appeared during the medieval period but may have been more of a demolition device for siege warfare than a combat weapon, at least in Western Europe.

The sling was most likely a product of the Neolithic Near East (ninth millennium B.C.E.) but may have had earlier origins. It was probably derived from throwing stones whirled about by attached lashes; the South American *bolas* is an example. The most common sling, the hand sling, consisted of a 3-foot-long strap with a pouch in the center in which a missile, usually a stone, was placed. The user would take both ends of the sling in one hand, whirl the stone around quickly, and then let go of one end of the sling. The released stone would then fly toward its target. Hand slings—made of leather, wool, woven grasses, sinew, or human hair—have been used by many primitive peoples worldwide for hunting, warfare, and protection from predators. They were popular among civilized peoples in the Indus Valley, the Near East, Greece, Sicily, Spain and the Baleares, Celtic Europe, Mesoamerica, and the Andes.

TURNING POINTS

9th millen. B.C.E.	The sling makes its first known appearance.
7th millen. B.C.E.	The stone-head mace makes its first known appearance.
c. 2500 B.C.E.	Metal armor is developed in Mesopotamia, making the stone-headed mace obsolete.
c. 1000 B.C.E.	Metal-headed maces become common in Europe.
401 B.C.E.	Slings are used to great effect against the Persians at the Battle of Cunaxa, outranging Persian bows and arrows.
c. 31 B.C.E.	Specialist corps of slingers largely disappear from ancient armies.

Skilled slingers could hurl heavy stones to damage armor out to 15 yards, strike small targets with stones out to 30 yards, shatter skulls out to 50 yards, hit man-sized targets out to 180 yards, and throw light lead shot over 360 yards. In battle, slingers were employed to harass enemy formations before hand-to-hand combat began, to pursue routed foes, to ward off enemy cavalry and elephants, and to protect one's own troops from missile attacks. During sieges slingers provided covering fire, harassed working parties, and hurled incendiaries into buildings or siegeworks.

Another type of sling was the staff sling, apparently invented in the Roman Empire and used at sieges in medieval Europe. It was essentially a hand sling attached to a 4-foot staff. The user held the staff horizontally in both hands, then swung it upright, flinging the missile from the sling attached to the end of the staff.

DEVELOPMENT

The club's developmental history is largely lost, because of the perishability of wood. By approximately 50,000 B.C.E., humans had developed the creativity and skill to produce any of the many club designs found among modern tribal peoples. In combat, prehistoric hunter-gatherers and small groups of farmers and herders probably preferred, whenever possible, to ambush or raid their enemies, thereby avoiding the hazards of close combat made more dangerous by their lack of armor, numbers, and strong leadership. Clubs would have been used mainly to finish off wounded or trapped foes. In direct confrontations hunter-gatherers would have hurled missiles, including throwing sticks or slingstones, at one another from a safe distance, contenting themselves with low casualties.

As populations expanded in Neolithic Europe and in the Near East, more complex societies arose in which powerful chiefs led their war-

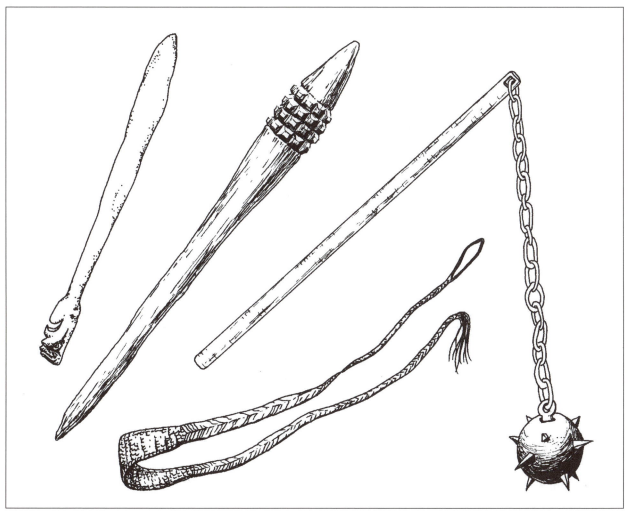

From left to right, an Iroquois club from eastern North America; an aboriginal throwing stick from northwestern Australia; a spiked Swiss "morning star" mace; and a braided sling from the Pacific Islands.

riors into close combat. This explains the appearance of the stone-headed mace and of new sling projectiles that were added to the usual water-worn stone. Worked spherical stone projectiles appeared by about 6000 B.C.E., kiln- or sun-hardened clay balls by about 5000 B.C.E., and biconical-shaped missiles by about 4000 B.C.E. Such aerodynamic shapes and regularized sizes allowed slingers to shoot farther and with more accuracy.

In open combat, warriors probably exchanged fire with slings and bows for some time before advancing to fight with spears, maces, and clubs, hurling throwing sticks as they neared their opponents. Piles of slingstones found in the destruction horizons of Neolithic and Chalcolithic settlements also indicate sling use in early siege warfare. Incendiary projectiles, in the form of heated clay shot or grasses plaited around stones, probably also made their initial appearances during Neolithic sieges.

As early civilizations developed in both hemispheres, so did armies. Units of like-armed men organized either as light infantry outfitted with missile weapons or as heavy infantry equipped with close combat weapons. Light infantry began battles by showering enemy formations with missiles, hoping to disrupt them. The heavy infantry then charged, fought the enemy infantrymen, and put them to flight, whereupon the light troops pursued. Slingers served as light troops in Bronze Age Mesopotamia, the Indus Valley, and Greece.

Throwing sticks were used in Mesopotamia until about 2000 B.C.E. and for another millennium in Egypt. Stone-headed maces played an important role in infantry combat in Old and Middle Kingdom Egypt (c. 3100 to 1674 B.C.E.), in Canaan during the same era, and in the Indus Valley's Harappan civilization (c. 2500 to 1750 B.C.E.). In the Americas, the Incas (c. 1200 to 1572 C.E.) used a combination of slingers, spearmen, and macemen, the maces having circular bronze heads with six points. The Aztecs of that era employed slingers and club bearers, some of whom utilized the *maquahuitl*, a powerful two-handed, obsidian-edged sword-club.

The stone-headed mace had virtually disappeared in Mesopotamia by approximately 2500 B.C.E., probably because the area's fierce military competition spurred the development of metal arms and armor. Bronze could be turned into sickle swords, socket axes, and other new weapons, while copper helmets backed with leather spread the impact of a club or stone macehead blow enough to prevent their wearers from being stunned or killed. By the time of the New Kingdom (c. 1570 to 1085 B.C.E.), Egypt had adopted armor as well. As armor and metal weapons became common, clubs and stone-headed maces disappeared. Maces with metal heads were used in the Incan Empire, and mace-like bronze weapons continued in use in Egypt. Bronze maceheads similar to medieval weapons have been discovered in Armenian tombs of the second half of the second millennium B.C.E. Maces had long been associated with authority: Narmer, one of the first Egyptian Pharaohs (c. 3100 B.C.E.), is depicted wielding a mace. Other evidence suggests that mace use was restricted to officers, such as those of the Neo-Assyrian Empire (911 to 612 B.C.E.), and kings, such as the Scythian monarchs (seventh to fourth centuries B.C.E.) for some two millennia.

It was not until the early Middle Ages that metal-headed maces became popular. Steppe nomads and Muslim warriors—Arabs, Iranians, Turks, Mongols—employed them as an important secondary weapon for their lance- or bow-armed cavalry, an alternative to the sword and ax. The Chinese, Indians, Byzantines, Russians, Eastern Europeans, and, after about 1000 C.E., Western Europeans then followed suit. Infantry only occasionally used maces, because foot soldiers could accomplish more with staff weapons. The mace was more useful to cavalry in easy reach of foot soldiers' heads. As long as mail or lamellar armor remained the norm, maces could be rather light, with rounded heads, either symmetrical or nonsymmetrical in form, or equipped with knobs or spikes. Flange-headed maces also appeared early and became common in Europe once plate armor came into use. However, lighter maces survived as emblems of authority. The club also survived as an ersatz weapon or police arm: William the Conqueror is depicted bearing one at Hastings, where he defeated the English in 1066 C.E. The club probably denoted William's rank, distinguishing him from lesser men carrying maces.

The sling enjoyed more common usage than the mace. David's slaying of Goliath is only the most famous use of the sling by the ancient Jews. The Neo-Assyrian Empire considered its slingers so valuable it armored them. Certain peoples were noted as skilled slingers. The Baleares, inhabiting the Balearic Islands off the coast of Spain in the western Mediterranean, used slings from childhood. They carried three slings of different sizes—short, medium, long—for various ranges. They could allegedly hurl stones weighing up to 14 ounces, smashing armor at close range. Assyrian slingstones, by contrast, averaged only 7 to 9.5 ounces in weight. Balearic slingers served with Hannibal (247-182 B.C.E.) and Julius Caesar (100-44 B.C.E.) and remained known into the Middle Ages for their skill with slings. Another noted group of slingers were the Greeks of Rhodes. During the Battle of Cunaxa (401 B.C.E.), slingers from Rhodes used lead shot to outrange Persian bows and slings—the latter with heavy stones—to help the Greek army make its escape.

Lead shot first appears in the late second millennium B.C.E. on Crete and Cyprus. Cast in molds and weighing 0.7 to 4.5 ounces, lead shot was often marked with insults, invocations, or identifications. It outranged clay or stone shot and was more difficult to see, and thus harder to dodge. It could bury itself in the target's flesh, requiring careful surgery to extract. In the second century B.C.E. the Greeks invented a sling that fired a *kestros*: a bolt with a pointed iron head 6 inches long, set in a winged wooden shaft 9 inches long. However, the use of the kestros never spread beyond Greece.

After the Pax Romana, a period of peace within the Roman Empire that began in approximately 31 B.C.E., specialist corps of slingers largely disappeared. The Imperial Roman army tried to compensate by training all recruits in use of the sling. It is unlikely, however, that men introduced to the weapon late and on a part-time basis became strong, accurate slingers.

The staff sling, easier to use than a hand sling, is a likely response to this situation. Although the sling never attained the popularity in medieval times that it enjoyed in antiquity, it remained in use in militias and peasant revolts. Monarchs such as King Frederick I Barbarossa of Germany (r. 1152-1190), King Edward I of England (r. 1272-1307), and Ottoman Sultan Mehmed II (r. 1451-1481) also recruited slingers to engage in siege warfare. In Spain the sling remained especially important: At the Battle of Nájera in 1367 C.E., for instance, English longbowmen suffered heavily from Spanish slingers before finally defeating them. Spaniards in turn suffered at the hands of Mesoamerican and Andean slingers. In various regions the weapon is still used by shepherds, sportsmen, hunters, and rioters.

BOOKS AND ARTICLES

DeVries, Kelly. *Medieval Military Technology*. Lewiston, N.Y.: Broadview Press, 1992.

Diagram Group. *The New Weapons of the World Encyclopedia: An International Encyclopedia from 5000 B.C. to the Twenty-first Century*. New York: St. Martin's Griffin, 2007.

Dupuy, R. Ernest, and Trevor N. Dupuy. "The Dark Ages: Battle-Ax and Mace, 800-1000." In *Encyclopedia of Military History from 3500 B.C. to the Present*. New York: Harper and Row, 1977.

Gabriel, Richard, and Karen Metz. *From Sumer to Rome: The Military Capabilities of Ancient Armies*. 1991. Reprint. New York: Greenwood Press, 2005.

Grant, R. G. *Warrior: A Visual History of the Fighting Man*. New York: DK, 2007.

Gurstelle, William. *The Art of the Catapult: Build Greek Ballistae, Roman Onagers, English Trebuchets, and More Ancient Artillery*. Chicago: Chicago Review Press, 2004.

Hogg, Oliver Frederick Gillilan. *Clubs to Cannon: Warfare and Weapons Before the Introduction of Gunpowder*. London: Duckworth, 1968.

Keeley, Lawrence H. *War Before Civilization: The Myth of the Peaceful Savage*. Oxford, England: Oxford University Press, 1996.

Nicolle, David. *A Companion to Medieval Arms and Armour*. Rochester, N.Y.: Boydell Press, 2002.

O'Connell, Robert L. *Soul of the Sword: An Illustrated History of Weaponry and Warfare from Prehistory to the Present*. New York: Free Press, 2002.

Woods, Michael, and Mary B. Woods. *Ancient Warfare: From Clubs to Catapults*. Minneapolis, Minn.: Runestone Press, 2000.

FILMS AND OTHER MEDIA

Arms in Action: Slings and Spears. Documentary. History Channel, 1999.

Conquest: Weapons of the Barbarians. Documentary. History Channel, 2003.

Scott M. Rusch

PICKS, AXES, AND WAR HAMMERS
Dates: To c. 1500 C.E.

NATURE AND USE

Picks, axes, and war hammers are shock weapons. Like all members of this weaponry class, they are designed to be held rather than thrown and to multiply the amount of force that can be brought to bear upon an opponent, while also extending the warrior's deadly range beyond the length of the arm.

Prehistoric picks, axes, and war hammers were variations on a single basic design. A wooden or bone haft, or handle, served as an extension of the user's arm, so that the bone, horn, wood, stone, or metal head could be swung through a larger arc, thus acquiring more speed than could be achieved with the arm alone. When the head struck an enemy, its speed and mass transferred sudden, intense pressure to a small area and thereby delivered a wound that could be either disabling or fatal, depending upon the part of the body struck. The three weapons differed only in the impacting surface delivering the force and the type of damage that ensued.

The pick had a pointed head and was meant to puncture. The natural and most force-efficient method for wielding the pick was an overhead stroke, which meant that the head, shoulders, and frontal chest cavity of the opponent were the primary targets. Slanting and even horizontal strokes to the body trunk, although more awkward to perform, could also cause deadly injuries. Furthermore, should the pick point pierce the chest cavity, even if the blow was not swiftly mortal, the small, deep wound that the pick head made was likely to become infected.

The ax-head was a wedge with a sharpened edge that ran parallel to the haft. The battle-ax almost invariably had a single leading edge rather than double blades. It was for cleaving, slicing, and cutting. Like the pick, the ax was most easily swung vertically, but it was a more versatile weapon because of its broad edge. Although the head and shoulders were the pri-

mary points of attack, the entire body, in fact, was at risk. If the ax-head had a sharpened rather than a blunt edge, slanting or horizontal strokes could do severe damage to the arms and legs, breaking bones or severing limbs entirely. Even a glancing blow or partial contact could open a long gash or slice and cause massive bleeding. Because of this utility, axes were nearly universally employed prehistoric weapons, from the first flint heads lashed onto sticks to such specimens as finely crafted North American tomahawks and ornately inlaid Scandinavian two-handed battle-axes.

The head of the war hammer, or war club, was blunt, often only a sturdy wooden knob or lump of stone, and its purpose was to shatter and crush. Although the war hammer could break leg, arm, and rib bones, the primary target areas were, again, the head and shoulders. A direct blow to the head killed by causing massive hemorrhaging even if the skull was not caved in, but even a light or partial impact was likely to stun, at the very least. Likewise, a blow to the shoulders, with their relatively delicate clavicles, could disable enemies and leave them unprotected against further attack. A variation on the war hammer, the mace, had short flanges or spikes protruding from its head. Thus, it pierced and tore the flesh as well as shattered bones.

The great advantages of shock weapons were their accuracy, power, and economy. Even an unskilled warrior was capable of swinging and striking home with a pick, ax, or club, whereas it took considerable training and skill to use successfully such stand-off weapons as javelins or bows. Moreover, unlike javelins and arrows, which once sent in flight were difficult to retrieve for reuse, shock weapons posed a threat as long as warriors had the strength to wield them. On the other hand, picks, axes, and war hammers were very short-ranged, seldom extending the warriors' effective battle reach more than twice that of the arm alone. The warrior, in close proximity to his enemy, was in imminent danger.

Combatants using shock weapons had to exploit these advantages while mitigating the disadvantages. Archaeological evidence, anthropological studies of nineteenth and twentieth century primitive societies, and surviving weapons reveal three often-employed tactical uses. Most often, battles opened with an exchange of fire from standoff weapons by the front ranks of opposing groups separated by an empty zone. If one group stopped fighting and fled, the second might pursue to kill or capture the enemy. The pursuers then used shock weapons after closing with the foe. Picks, axes, and war hammers also proved effective for fighting in confined spaces where standoff weapons were impractical: for example, a forest ambush or an assault on a fortified area. The weapons could be used to break apart defensive works and to destroy property as well as to harm people.

Last, shock weapons were occasionally used for close combat. A high degree of discipline is required for troops to meet face-to-face in a battle line, but by the Bronze Age, societies were sophisticated enough to support the requisite level of training, and this basic battle doctrine lasted into the Middle Ages. Engagements almost certainly began with exchanges of arrow or javelin fire, but then the front ranks of warriors advanced on each other until the lines collided, and warriors fought directly with shock weapons. In this hand-to-hand combat, comrades-in-arms had to be close to one another in the line, practically shoulder-to-shoulder, so that their sides were protected while they concentrated their attack on the enemy warriors directly in front of them.

Wood shields were developed to protect their fronts, and the initial clash involved each opponent striving to shatter the opponent's protection in order to force an opening for a killing blow. The side that succeeded in penetrating the line and dividing its enemy usually won the battle.

During the Iron Age, however, swords and lances increasingly became the main battle weapons. Axes, picks, and war hammers were used more and more as auxiliary weapons.

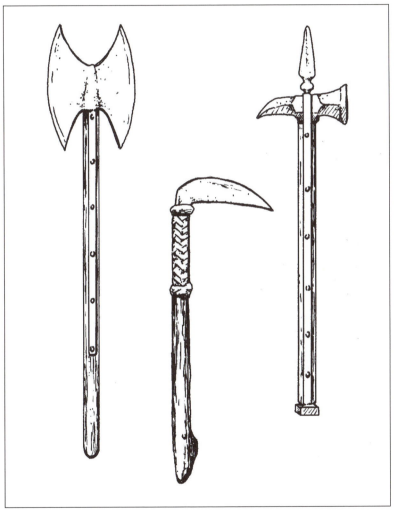

Kimberly L. Dawson Kurnizki

From left to right, an early sixteenth century battle-ax with a double-headed blade; an early Japanese pick with a stone blade bound to a wooden haft; and a late fifteenth century Italian war hammer with langets securing the head to the haft.

DEVELOPMENT

By about 1.5 million years before the present, the first small hand axes were being produced as part of the Acheulean tool tradition of the Lower Paleolithic era, the earliest part of the Old Stone Age. Probably first used as tools, these axes, or bifaces, were about 4 to 6 inches in length and were made by flaking both sides of a stone to form an edge. The affixation of this biface to a handle was an innovation of the Upper Paleolithic era (35,000 to 10,000 years ago), as was the development of hammers, an evolution of the simple club. The use of obsidian or flint, which could be chipped into a much sharper edge than could other types of rock, began during the Mesolithic, or Middle Stone Age, period in Europe (10,000 to 8,000 years ago). Likewise, picks probably began as simple sticks with pointed ends more or less perpendicular to the handle and evolved in tandem with the ax, as pointed rocks or horns were attached to handles. Picks, axes, and battle-hammers appear to have been employed as weapons generally throughout the pre-historic world during the Mesolithic period, depending only on the availability of suitable materials to make them. Isolated, preliterate cultures continued to use such weapons, in some cases, well into the twentieth century. Indeed, highly developed non-Western armies used such weapons—for example the Zulu knobkerrie, a short, heavy, wooden club that could be swung or thrown—to telling effect against Western forces with firearms through the nineteenth century.

The addition of the haft, or handle, to a shaped head was the key technological step in producing shock weapons. Three common methods of attachment developed: lashing the head into a wooden sleeve, as in the vee formed by two branches of a limb; binding the head into split wood; and inserting the head into a bone socket. Rawhide or animal tendons served as lashings. During the Neolithic period (8,000 to about 4,000 years ago), stone-workers learned to drill holes into flint by applying alternately heat and water. This process allowed them to insert a haft through the head and wedge it in firmly with shims, improving the strength of the ax.

With one face left blunt and the other shaped to either a point or a blade, the Neolithic weapons could function as combination hammer-axes or pick-axes. When artisans learned to grind the edge, rather than to form it by flaking off chips of flint, they were able to produce slimmer ax-heads with sharper edges, which enhanced the power of the weapons to pierce and slice. These finely wrought axes were valuable commodities. In some areas, notably prehistoric England, axes were highly prized for barter. In fact, archaeologists debate whether the axes were intended to be wielded or to serve strictly as a kind of currency, although they might well have served both functions.

Another innovation occurred when humans began to use copper to make ax-, pick-, hammer-, and mace-heads. The molten metal could be poured into a mold and, after cooling, cold-hammered and whetted to a fine edge. However, copper is soft and the edges quickly dulled. Bronze, an alloy of copper and tin, is much harder, and became the standard material for tools and weapons beginning about 3000 B.C.E. in the Near East. This technical advancement launched the Bronze Age. About 1600 B.C.E. Roman artisans began making tools and weapons from brass, a zinc-copper alloy harder and more durable than bronze. About 2500 B.C.E. in Sumer, craftspeople moved the socket holding the handle to the back of the ax-head, reducing its weight and giving the weapon better balance.

In Europe during the Neolithic period, maces were more common than axes, and at Çatalhüyük in modern Turkey, the site of a large Neolithic settlement, archaeologists uncovered copper maces dating from as early as 7000 B.C.E. Because they were difficult to make, these early copper maces may have been the weapons of leaders. An indication of their status appears in a small relief sculpture dating from around 3100 B.C.E., showing Menes (c. 3100-3000 B.C.E.), the first Pharaoh to rule all of Egypt, striking an enemy's head with a mace.

The advent of iron and steel made it possible to shape more elegantly flared, sharper ax-heads with thinner heads, as was true, for instance, with the two-handed Viking battle-ax. Maces became common weapons during the Middle Ages, whereas picks were relegated to use in warfare primarily for digging and breaking down defensive structures. These weapons became obsolete after the introduction of firearms, and by the beginning of the sixteenth century, European armies were unlikely to carry them into battle.

Books and Articles

"Anglo-Saxon Broadax." *Military History*, 24, no. 3 (May, 2007): 21.

Bennett, Matthew, et al. *Fighting Techniques of the Medieval World, A.D. 500 to A.D. 1500.* New York: St. Martin's Press, 2005.

Diagram Group. *The New Weapons of the World Encyclopedia: An International Encyclopedia from 5000 B.C. to the Twenty-first Century.* New York: St. Martin's Griffin, 2007.

Dupuy, R. Ernest, and Trevor N. Dupuy. "The Dark Ages—Battle-Ax and Mace: 800-1000." In *Encyclopedia of Military History from 3500 B.C. to the Present.* New York: Harper and Row, 1977.

Ferrill, Arther. *Origins of War: From the Stone Age to Alexander the Great.* Rev. ed. Boulder, Colo.: Westview Press, 1997.

Grant, R. G. *Warrior: A Visual History of the Fighting Man.* New York: DK, 2007.

Guilaine, Jean, and Jean Zammit. *The Origins of War: Violence in Prehistory.* Translated by Melanie Hersey. Malden, Mass.: Blackwell, 2005.

Hogg, Oliver Frederick Gillilan. *Clubs to Cannon: Warfare and Weapons Before the Introduction of Gunpowder.* London: Duckworth, 1968.

Keely, Lawrence H. *War Before Civilization.* New York: Oxford University Press, 1996.

Nicolle, David. *A Companion to Medieval Arms and Armour.* Rochester, N.Y.: Boydell Press, 2002.

Otterbein, Keith F. *How War Began.* College Station: Texas A&M University Press, 2004.

Films and Other Media

Barbarian Battle Tech. Documentary. History Channel, 2007.

The Dark Ages. Documentary. History Channel, 2007.

Roger Smith

BOWS AND ARROWS
Dates: To c. 1500 C.E.

NATURE AND USE

Bows and arrows are among the oldest and most popular weapons of all time. Although simple in design, their invention represented one of the most important technological innovations of primitive humans, one that allowed individuals to attack both animal and human targets with greater force, from longer range, and with a more rapid rate of fire than had been possible with the spear or other handheld projectiles. Bows and arrows were presumably first used for hunting, perhaps as early as 30,000 B.C.E., but Neolithic cave paintings show them deployed as weapons against other humans by about 10,000 B.C.E.

In its most basic form the bow consists of a shaft of wood with a string attached to both its ends. When this bowstring is drawn back, the energy of the archer's pull is transferred to the bending bow, and after the bowstring is released, this energy is channeled through the bowstring to project the arrow forward. The arrow's speed and distance depend on the flexibility of the bow; a stiffer bow requires more strength to string and shoot, but this added resistance translates into greater velocity and distance for the arrow itself.

The varieties of ancient bows were as numerous as the peoples who made them, but they generally fall into two categories. A self bow—also called a simple bow, stave bow, or longbow—was constructed from a single piece of wood, although bows of reed and other materials are known. They measured from 1.5 to more than 6 feet in length, and their effective range could extend to more than 200 yards. Self bows were extremely simple to make, but a suitable type of wood was required: Too pliant a wood packed little power, whereas one that was too stiff might break or prove difficult to use efficiently.

The second basic type of bow was the composite bow. It consisted of either a single piece or several pieces of wood glued together. This wooden core was reinforced by bone on the interior, or belly, and by sinew on the outside, or front, lending the bow greater elasticity. Composite bows were extremely strong and difficult to string, but they had an effective range of up to 300 yards, far greater than that of the self bow. They were also smaller and easier to carry, making them more versatile, especially for firing from horseback.

Arrows also came in different types, but their basic design was simpler and changed little over time. Ancient arrows typically consisted of two parts: a light, slender shaft of wood or reed and an arrowhead of stone, bone, or metal. Arrowheads could be flat, leaf-shaped, or triangular and were sometimes barbed. They were attached to their shafts either by a hollow socket, into which

TURNING POINTS

c. 10,000 B.C.E.	Bows and arrows appear as weapons in Neolithic cave paintings.
c. 2250 B.C.E.	A composite bow is depicted in Akkadian Stele of Naram-Sin.
c. 1600 B.C.E.	Chariot archers are increasingly used in warfare.
c. 400 B.C.E.	The development of the gastraphetes, or belly bow, allows the shooting of more powerful arrows.
53 B.C.E.	Parthian mounted archers defeat heavily armed Roman infantry at the Battle of Carrhae.
1346 C.E.	English longbowmen defeat French knights at Crécy, demonstrating the importance of archers to English warfare.
c. 14th-15th cent.	The increasing predominance of firearms in Europe results in the diminishing use of archers in warfare.

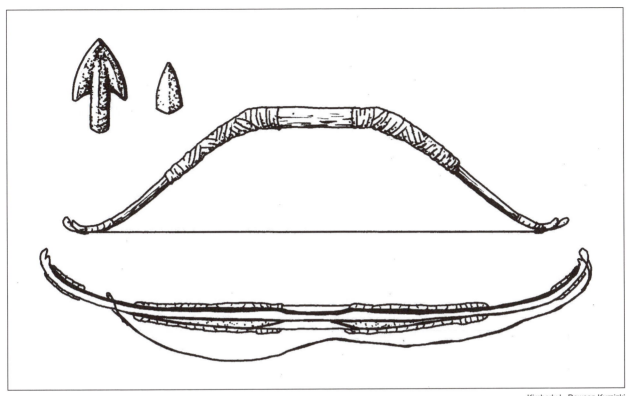

A simple bow, the joints bound with animal sinew, shown in both strung and unstrung positions. Also shown are barbed and leaf-shaped arrowheads.

the shaft was inserted, or by means of a tang, a flat projection that fit into a notch in the shaft itself. Feathers were frequently affixed to the opposite end of the shaft to maintain an arrow's speed and accuracy in flight.

Virtually all ancient civilizations, from China and the Near East to Greece and Rome, employed bows and arrows in some capacity. Archers were common in siege warfare, in which both attackers and defenders routinely harassed their opponents with volleys of arrows. Their use in battle, however, varied, seemingly along geographical lines. In Europe archers tended to be stationed on the wings, in front of, or behind a battle line of infantry or cavalry, and they tended to provide cover as these other forces prepared to engage the enemy at closer range. In the ancient Near East and Central Asia, however, bowmen on foot or horseback played a more decisive role in warfare; they made up the bulk of many armies and often determined the outcome of battle itself.

DEVELOPMENT

As noted above, bows and arrows appear as weapons in cave paintings of the late Neolithic period (8,000 to 4,000 years ago), although their use in combat may be much older. Surprisingly, however, evidence for archers in the warfare of early civilizations is sparse. The Sumerian hero Gilgamesh carried, along with several other weapons, a bow in the Gilgamesh epic (c. 2000 B.C.E.; English translation, 1917), and the so-called Stele of Naram-Sin (c. 2250 B.C.E.) shows the Akkadian king Naram-Sin (c. 2254-c. 2218) carrying what appears to be a composite bow. The Egyptians may have been the first to employ archers on a large scale. By 2000 B.C.E. their armies included a corps of Nubian archers, who presumably supported native Egyptian infantry armed with spears and daggers.

The bow and arrow acquired more importance when they were combined with the war chariot.

A Manchu bowman circa 1871.

(1274 B.C.E.), between the Egyptians and the Hittites. The significance of the bow in the latter battle is reinforced by wall carvings; an Egyptian relief commemorating the battle shows the Pharaoh Ramses II (c. 1300-1213 B.C.E.) standing on his chariot and shooting his bow, seemingly mowing down the opposing Hittites single-handedly.

Chariot archers survived into the first millennium B.C.E. under the Assyrians, who dominated the Near East from the ninth through the seventh centuries B.C.E., but bows and arrows also found greater use in other units. Assyrian infantry consisted primarily of archers wearing heavy armor, who released their arrows under the protection of body-sized shields held by attendants. More significant, the Assyrians were instrumental in developing cavalry, including mounted archers. Like their counterparts on foot, Assyrian horse archers worked in pairs, as one rider shot his arrows while a second held the archer's reins and a shield. The combination of foot and horse archers was also adopted by the Persians, who became the preeminent power in the Near East in the sixth century B.C.E. Their tactics are well illustrated at the Battle of Plataea (479 B.C.E.) during the Greco-Persian Wars (499-448 B.C.E.). At the start of the battle, Persian cavalry harassed the Greek infantry with a constant onslaught of missiles, while refusing to engage the Greeks at close range. The Persian infantry soon followed with its own barrage of arrows, which were unleashed from behind a shield wall. The intention, it seems, was to weaken the Greeks with missile weapons, so that the infantry could emerge from behind its shield wall and overcome the remnants of the Greek infantry with the spears and daggers they also carried.

The heavily armed Greek spearmen, however, proved superior to the lightly armed Persian archers at Plataea, and the Greek victory in the Greco-Persian Wars signaled the end of the archer's prominence in Near Eastern and Western warfare for several centu-

Chariots had been used as transport vehicles in Mesopotamia in the third millennium B.C.E., but by the sixteenth century B.C.E. they had become the preeminent weapon of war throughout the Near East and Egypt. The chariot functioned as a mobile firing platform, carrying a driver and archer armed with a composite bow. As the driver brought the chariot within range of opposing forces, the archer released his arrows, seeking to create confusion and disorder in the enemy line. In some armies archer-bearing chariots numbered in the thousands, and the union of bow, arrow, and chariot figured prominently at the Battles of Megiddo (1469 B.C.E.), between the Egyptians and a coalition of forces from the Levant, and Kadesh

ries. The Greeks were familiar with the bow and arrow; the Athenians had a contingent of archers at Plataea, and bowmen from the island of Crete were popular as mercenaries throughout the Mediterranean from the fifth century B.C.E. onward. Indeed, Alexander the Great (356-323 B.C.E.) utilized Cretan and Macedonian archers effectively throughout his conquest of the Persian Empire. The Greeks, however, despised the bow and arrow as cowardly and effeminate weapons, and archers generally played only a supporting role in combat.

The Romans, too, originally had little use for bows and arrows. They possessed no native archers of their own, and they relied on mercenaries or allies to supply archers when needed. Only as the nature of Rome's enemies changed in the first, second, and third centuries C.E. did archers take on an increasingly significant role in Rome's armies. Among these enemies were the Parthians, who in the second century B.C.E. had established an empire where the Persian Empire had once stood. The Parthians fought with composite bows on horseback and were best known for the so-called Parthian shot, in which Parthian horse archers would charge an enemy and, as soon as they released their arrows, would immediately reverse direction and ride quickly out of range of enemy missile fire. Such tactics proved highly successful at Carrhae (53 B.C.E.), where Parthian mounted archers annihilated seven Roman legions, approximately 40,000 men.

Developments in China mirrored those of the Near East and Europe. Archers on chariots were known as early as 1200 B.C.E., and they remained the elite weapon of war throughout most of the Zhou (Chou) Dynasty (1066-256 B.C.E.). Archers also served in Chinese infantry, but not until the fourth century B.C.E. did the Chinese begin to develop an effective cavalry. The incursions of nomadic horse archers from the steppes of Central Asia forced the Chinese to adopt their own mounted cavalry, which they did in the third, second, and first centuries B.C.E.

It was in the hands of nomadic peoples skilled in horsemanship that the bow and arrow achieved their greatest successes in warfare. Beginning in the seventh century B.C.E. the Iranian Plateau and Eurasian steppes produced several cultures whose movements threatened and sometimes overthrew the more sedentary civilizations of Europe, the Near East, and China. These peoples included the Scythians, Huns, Avars, and Turks, who shared with one another a life seemingly lived on horseback and a reliance on the composite bow. They wore little armor and were extremely mobile, and with their large numbers they could inflict heavy damage on an opposing force while avoiding direct contact against a more heavily armed foe. The most formidable of these horse archers were probably the Mongols, who emerged from Mongolia in the twelfth century C.E. Fighting on horseback and carrying one or more composite bows and sixty arrows, Mongol warriors were highly disciplined, and they used both mobility and deception to overwhelm their opponents. Under Mongol leader Genghis Khan (between 1155 and 1162-1227), Mongol armies swept across Asia and the Near East and into Europe. They established their own dynasty in China early in the thirteenth century, and by 1250 their empire stretched from Asia to Eastern Europe.

While Mongol horse archers were terrorizing Asia and Eastern Europe, the English were experimenting with the longbow, a development that changed the nature of Western warfare. Longbows had been known in Europe for centuries and had played no small role in the victory of William the Conqueror (c. 1028-1087) over the English at Hastings in 1066, but their role in battle was marginal until the English adopted the Welsh longbow in the twelfth century. Made from the wood of the yew tree, the Welsh longbow reached almost 6 feet in length and required considerable strength and skill to wield. It was also inexpensive, and, with training, common soldiers could learn to shoot with enough distance, speed, and power to penetrate even the thickest suits of knightly armor. Edward I (1239-1307) was the first English king to enlist large numbers of longbowmen (mostly Welshmen) in his armies, with whom he defeated the Scottish pikemen at Falkirk in 1298. During the fourteenth century, however, native English archers took up the longbow in greater numbers and proved their worth against heavily armored knights, especially during the Hundred Years' War against France (1337-1453). At Crécy (1346) the English longbowmen first routed the mercenary Genoese crossbowmen before wreaking havoc on successive charges of French cavalry, killing more than one thousand knights by the end of the battle. Similar charges by armored knights on horseback at Poitiers (1356) and on foot at Agincourt (1415) brought similar results, and helped hasten the end of the dominance of mounted cavalry in European warfare.

The rise of gunpowder ultimately brought about the demise of the bow and arrow in battle. That demise, however, did not occur overnight, and for centuries after the introduction of gunpowder (c. 1300), archers remained an important component of most armies. Only with the development of effective and reliable handheld firearms in the sixteenth century did bows and arrows become obsolete.

BOOKS AND ARTICLES

Bennett, Matthew, et al. *Fighting Techniques of the Medieval World, A.D. 500 to A.D. 1500.* New York: St. Martin's Press, 2005.

Bradbury, Jim. *The Medieval Archer.* Rochester, N.Y.: Boydell and Brewer, 1999.

Bradford, Alfred S. *With Arrow, Sword, and Spear: A History of Warfare in the Ancient World.* Illustrated by Pamela M. Bradford. Westport, Conn.: Praeger, 2001.

Diagram Group. *The New Weapons of the World Encyclopedia: An International Encyclopedia from 5000 B.C. to the Twenty-first Century.* New York: St. Martin's Griffin, 2007.

Drews, Robert. *The End of the Bronze Age: Changes in Warfare and the Catastrophe c. 1200 B.C.* Princeton, N.J.: Princeton University Press, 1993.

Ferrill, Arther. *The Origins of War.* Rev. ed. Boulder, Colo.: Westview Press, 1997.

Grant, R. G. *Warrior: A Visual History of the Fighting Man.* New York: DK, 2007.

Harding, Stephen. "The Deadly Dozen." *Military History* 26, no. 2 (June/July, 2009): 58.

Hardy, Robert. *The Longbow: A Social and Military History.* London: Bois d'Arc Press, 1998.

Hurley, Vic. *Arrows Against Steel: The History of the Bow.* New York: Mason/Charter, 1975.

Nicolle, David. *A Companion to Medieval Arms and Armour.* Rochester, N.Y.: Boydell Press, 2002.

Soar, Hugh D. H. *The Crooked Stick: A History of the Longbow.* Yardley, Pa.: Westholme, 2005.

FILMS AND OTHER MEDIA

Arms in Action: Bows. Documentary. History Channel, 1999.

Henry V. Feature film. BBC/Curzon/Renaissance, 1989.

Wild West Tech: Native American Tech. Documentary. History Channel, 2008.

James P. Sickinger

CROSSBOWS

Dates: To c. 1500 C.E.

NATURE AND USE

The crossbow was a handheld weapon consisting of a short bow made of either composite materials such as wood and horn, or iron, mounted on a stock, generally of wood. The bowstring was usually drawn by a type of mechanical device and fired by a trigger mechanism. The crossbow's missile, called a quarrel, or bolt, was short and heavy, designed to penetrate armor at close range. Various devices were employed to cock the bow, with its short limbs and heavy draw weight. The crossbow's power and short-range accuracy were counterbalanced by the length of time required to arm the weapon and its lack of range. Sometimes called arbalests, crossbows have been used as infantry weapons, and in heavier, more complicated versions as siege weapons.

Evidence points to the Chinese of the Shang Dynasty (1600-1066 B.C.E.) as the originators of the crossbow. Early missiles included stones and fire arrows. By the time of the Han Dynasty (206 B.C.E.-220 C.E.), crossbows had come into regular use among Chinese troops, particularly along the northwestern frontier. Soldiers stationed on the Great Wall could use the protection of the wall as they loaded and fired their bolts at invaders. Chinese crossbows featured bows of laminated bamboo, specially glued and covered with lacquered silk, which were fitted onto lacquered, wooden stocks. Chinese bolts were usually about 12 inches long with bronze heads capable of puncturing the quilted silk, padded leather, and metal armor of the era.

Another refinement was the repeating crossbow, fitted with a wooden, boxlike magazine holding from ten to twelve bolts and appearing in China in the first century C.E. The hinged magazine could be moved forward and back, thus serving as both a loading mechanism and a cocking device. Although the magazine increased the output of the archer, the magazine

system was awkward and time consuming to reload. There is evidence, however, that types of magazine-fed crossbows were still in use during the First Sino-Japanese War (1894-1895).

Crossbows spread from Asia to Europe at some unspecified date. The Romans used large, complex versions of the crossbow as siege engines capable of firing heavy missiles against walled cities. In terms of infantry use, however, fragments of tombstone carvings from Le Puy and Polignac-sur-Loire in France dating roughly from the fourth century C.E. indicate that Roman legions may also have had crossbowmen using a basic model of laminated wood with a manual cocking arrangement. There is no evidence to show that the Romans employed the weapon on a broad scale.

DEVELOPMENT

Although there have been allusions to the crossbow's use in fifth and sixth century England, the first Western written record of its use appears in a manuscript from 985 C.E. Derived from the Latin *arc*, or bow, and *ballista*, or missile thrower, the weapon became known as an *arcuballista*, or arbalest. Several eleventh century references note that William the Conqueror (c. 1028-1087) included crossbowmen in his Norman army, which invaded England in 1066. By the time of the Crusades of the eleventh through thirteenth centuries, crossbows had become a standard and valued part of European armies. Anna Comnena of Byzantium (1083-c. 1148) provided one of the most complete descriptions of Crusader crossbows, noting that soldiers had to strain with both arms to cock, or span, the bow.

Among the most proficient soldiers using crossbows were the Italians, particularly the Genoese. Hired as mercenaries by a variety of European crowned heads, Italian crossbowmen were noted for their accuracy in battle. Simple soldiers could be trained in the use of the crossbow in a matter of weeks, whereas longbow archers required years of strengthening and practice to become expert. The use of the crossbow allowed a common soldier with minimal training to dispatch a well-armored, professional knight. So devastating had the crossbow become in conflicts raging across Europe that Pope Innocent II (died 1143), at the Lateran Council (1139), prohibited their use. The prohibition did not extend, however, to use against infidels, and even in Europe the ban was generally ignored.

Although the crossbow had been used in the First (1095-1099) and Second Crusades (1145-1149), it had its greatest impact during the Third Crusade (1187-1192). King Richard I of England (1157-1199), a proponent of crossbow use and an accomplished marksman, was reported to have used the weapon to slay a Muslim archer high atop a wall during the Siege of Acre (1189-1191). In various skirmishes throughout the campaign, crossbowmen successfully defended supply routes and garrison posts. At the Battle of Arsuf (1191), Christian cross-bowmen wreaked havoc against the lightly armored Muslim bowmen of the sultan Saladin (1138-1193). Muslim arrows did not easily penetrate the thick felt overcoats and mail shirts of the Europeans, whereas the short, heavy quarrels pierced the light armor of Muslim soldiers and horses. At Jaffa (1192) crossbowmen played a key part in Richard s victory over a numerically superior force. Later, after returning to England, Richard was mortally wounded by a crossbow quarrel while laying siege to the castle of Chalus, in the Limousin, France (1199).

The cocking mechanisms of crossbows went through a variety of developments during the Middle Ages. Although dates of innovations are unknown, evidence shows the weapon's evolution. As armor increased in strength, crossbows increased in power. The simple method of cocking, or spanning, by hand was replaced with both a stirruplike device at the head of the stock and a pair of belt hooks known as the "belt and claw." By placing the bowstring in the hooks, and the foot in the stirrup, sufficient leverage and power could be exerted to cock the weapon.

With the desire to increase range, even more radical spanning devices were needed. The *arbalest à tour* utilized a pulley system hooked to the string rather than the belt claws. By drawing on the pulleys, the string could be more easily cocked. In the fifteenth century, a "screw and handle" device consisting of a threaded rod hooked to the string and cranked at the rear of the stock by a handle, created a powerful weapon. The "goat's foot lever" employed hinged double levers, which bent the bow and cocked the string. This system was particularly efficient in the lighter-weight crossbows favored by European cavalry. A French innovation called the *cranequin*, or ratchet winder, utilized a handle connected to a pair of cogs enclosed in a drumlike attachment hooked to the string by a rail. By cranking the handle in a circular motion, the rail drew the string to the cocked position.

TURNING POINTS

c. 1384-1122 B.C.E.	Crossbow is originated during China's Shang Dynasty.
10th-11th cent. B.C.E.	The crossbow makes its first European appearance, in Italy.
c. 206-220 B.C.E.	Crossbows come into regular usage during China's Han Dynasty.
1139 C.E.	The use of the crossbow in Christian Europe is prohibited by Pope Innocent II at the Lateran Council.
1191	Christian crossbowmen are instrumental in defeating Muslim warriors at the Battle of Arsuf during the Third Crusade.
1415	English longbowmen prove more effective than Genoese mercenary crossbowmen hired by the French at the Battle of Agincourt during the Hundred Years War.
c. 16th-17th cent.	Use of crossbows diminishes as firearms become more common.

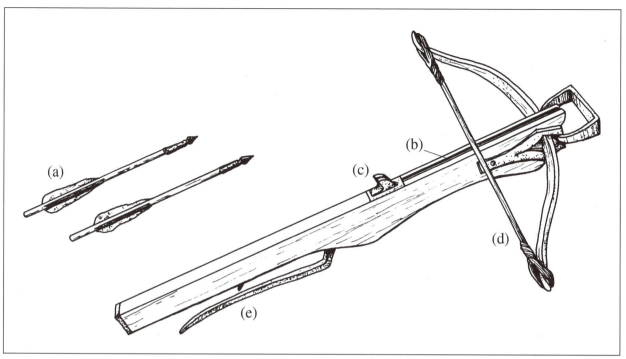

A crossbow shown with two quarrels, or bolts (a), which are fitted into the groove (b), with their butt ends against the nut (c) after the bowstring (d) has been drawn back and held by the nut. When ready to fire, the operator aims from the shoulder and presses the trigger (e) to release the bolt.

Each time a cranequin was used, however, it had to be removed in order to fire the crossbow and then reattached for reloading. Such a device was especially necessary as laminated bows were replaced with stiffer, more powerful metal limbs.

Perhaps the most complicated version of crossbow mechanisms was the windlass, or *moulinet*, system. A combination of fixed and free pulleys was attached to the stock of the bow, and the free-running pulleys hooked to the string. By inserting a foot into the stirrup to stabilize the weapon, crossbowmen would then crank a pair of handles engaging a windlass to wind the fixed pulleys. This marriage of pulleys and handles could span even the heaviest of crossbows used in besieging castles and other fortifications. As with the cranequin, however, the moulinet system had to be removed to shoot, thus creating a slow rate of fire.

As crossbows evolved, so too did quarrels. Wooden shafts fitted with iron heads remained the standard missile for centuries. Quarrels were usually from 9 to 12 inches long. To stabilize the quarrel in flight, fletchings of wood, leather, or feathers were used, although these were much shorter and shallower vanes than those of longbow arrows. With the development of mechanical spanning devices, all-metal bolts became the most lethal of projectiles, particularly when used on heavier crossbows.

In English and continental European armies, crossbowmen were generally placed in the front line of battle to pepper foes with their bolts. At the Battle of Taillebourg (1242), England's King Henry III (1207-1272) was defeated by French king Louis IX (1214-1270) even though the English counted some 700 crossbowmen in the infantry. During the Hundred Years' War (1337-1453), Genoese crossbowmen in the employ of the French dueled English longbow archers at Crécy (1346) and Agincourt (1415). In both engagements, the longbowmen prevailed with their greater range and accuracy.

Corps of crossbowmen were included in most European armies into the sixteenth century. At the Battle of Marignano (1515), a bodyguard of two hundred mounted crossbowmen helped Francis I (1494-1547) of France defeat the duke of Milan. When Spanish adventurer Hernán Cortés (1485-1547) trekked into Mexico (1521), he brought with him a company of arbalesters, as did Francisco Pizarro (c. 1478-1541) in his invasion of Peru (1524). As late as 1570, Spanish marines stationed aboard galleons were still armed with crossbows.

With the advent of gunpowder and handguns, the military use of the crossbow dwindled. By the seventeenth century, it had primarily become a tool for hunting and target practice. During World War I (1914-1918), medieval crossbows were stripped from armories and converted into grenade launchers for use in the trenches. More recently, some modern military special forces have adopted crossbow use for clandestine operations.

BOOKS AND ARTICLES

Bennett, Matthew, et al. *Fighting Techniques of the Medieval World, A.D. 500 to A.D. 1500.* New York: St. Martin's Press, 2005.

Brodie, Bernard. *From Crossbow to H-Bomb.* New York: Dell, 1962

Diagram Group. *The New Weapons of the World Encyclopedia: An International Encyclopedia from 5000 B.C. to the Twenty-first Century.* New York: St. Martin's Griffin, 2007.

Gardner, Charles W. "Weapon of Power: Slower than the Longbow, the Crossbow Offered Deadly, Accurate Simplicity." *Military History* 6, no. 3 (1989): 18, 70-74.

Heath, E. G. *The Grey Goose Wing.* Greenwich, Conn.: New York Graphic Society, 1971.

Hurley, Vic. *Arrows Against Steel: The History of the Bow.* New York: Mason Charter, 1975.

Nicolle, David. *A Companion to Medieval Arms and Armour.* Rochester, N.Y.: Boydell Press, 2002.

Nosov, Konstantin S. *Ancient and Medieval Siege Weapons: A Fully Illustrated Guide to Siege Weapons and Tactics.* Illustrated by Vladimir Golubev. Guilford, Conn.: Lyons Press, 2005.

Payne-Gallwey, Sir Ralph. *The Crossbow: Its Military and Sporting History, Construction. and Use.* 1903. Reprint. New York: Skyhorse, 2007.

FILMS AND OTHER MEDIA

Crossbow. Television series. Cinecom, 1987.

The Dark Ages. Documentary. History Channel, 2007.

Henry V. Feature film. BBC/Curzon/Renaissance, 1989.

Kenneth P. Czech

KNIVES, SWORDS, AND DAGGERS
Dates: To c. 1500 C.E.

NATURE AND USE

Almost every human culture and civilization in the world has used knives and daggers. A knife is one of the most basic tools, used for cutting any number of materials, from food to fibers. Knives were also used as weapons to kill humans. A dagger could be considered a long, double-edged knife, ranging from 15 to 50 centimeters and meant specifically as a weapon. Knives and daggers have two basic parts: first, the blade, a flat surface with one sharp edge or two, usually narrowing to a point; second, the hilt, covering the tang, which extends back from the blade, and providing a handhold. The hilt itself has two parts: the grip, perhaps with some sort of guard to protect the hand, and a pommel, which is a piece at the end of the grip to back up the hand and provide balance. For protection from the sharp blade, knives were carried in sheaths or scabbards while not in use.

Some knives were meant to be thrown. Otherwise knives and daggers were usually wielded either overhanded, with the blade extending down from the fist, or underhanded, with the blade sticking up from the fist. These weapons also had the advantage of concealment when worn underneath clothing. In the warfare of all but the most primitive societies, the knife or dagger was usually the weapon of last resort, after other weapons had been lost.

Most cultures have also developed swords, which could be considered extended daggers, with blades longer than 40 centimeters. Swords could, given their weight and length, more effectively hack, slash, puncture, or cut an enemy. Grooves in blades, or fullers, are often believed to have been channels to drain away blood but were usually built into the blade to add flexibility, lightness, and strength. The limited reach of the sword, compared to that of the spear or bow, often meant that it was a secondary weapon. Although rarely decisive in itself during battle, the sword was one of the most widely used weapons for close combat before 1500 C.E.

The history of knives, daggers, and swords has perhaps been more influenced by fashion than by application in warfare. These weapons and their sheaths have often been made with great care and decoration, conveying the status of their owners. The sword, especially, became a work of art, status symbol, magisterial emblem, and cult object. The right of knights or samurai to wear swords indicated their social positions, and men defended that rank in sword duels. In medieval Europe a squire was dubbed to knighthood with a sword blow, known as an accolade. Large ceremonial swords of state were carried in processions or displayed in court to illustrate a ruler's power over life and death. Swords or daggers also embodied religious significance, such as sacrificial daggers made of chalcedony used by the Aztecs for human sacrifice. The similarity of a sword's shape to that of a cross also lent it a Christian symbolism. Legends concerning Arthur's Excalibur and Roland's Durandal celebrated the sword in Europe, and many Japanese believed that certain old swords embody the spirits of Shinto deities.

DEVELOPMENT

The earliest humans made the first knives and daggers from stone, such as flint or obsidian. They shaped blades through "pressure flaking," banging pieces of stone against one another so that chips of stone broken off would leave a blade form behind. By the time of the agricultural cultures of the New Stone Age (Neolithic times), a grip made of wood or bone was then formed and attached with lime or binding to the tang. The peoples of the Americas and the Pacific rarely progressed beyond stone technology, and so did not develop significant swords. The Aztecs, however, may have been able to dominate their neighbors in the thirteenth century C.E. with the interesting sword-club, the *maquahuitl*, which set obsidian blades on either side of a wooden shaft. They also used special stone knives to cut out the hearts of human sacrificial victims.

The essential change came with the beginnings of metallurgy. Copper was the first metal to be used for knives, probably beginning around 4000 B.C.E. in the Middle East and East Asia. The invention of bronze, usually copper alloyed with tin, lcd to a great improvement in the strength and durability of weapons. In "grip-tongue" blades, whether cast in one piece or two, hilts were attached to the blade or reinforced with rivets. By the second millennium B.C.E. hilt and blade were forged from one piece of metal, with flanges between hilt and blade to protect the user's hand.

As blades began to get longer, the resulting weapons became known as swords. Some were curved, based on the sickle, an agricultural implement used for harvesting. Curved blades were better suited to cutting, whereas straight blades were better at hacking and thrusting. The Minoans and Mycenaeans of the Eastern Mediterranean from about 1400 to 1200 B.C.E. began to develop not only decorative long swords but also highly useful short swords. The curi-

ous "halberd" of the Early Bronze Age looked like a dagger set at right angles to a shaft, creating a kind of dagger-ax.

Swords became more lethal after smiths had mastered the use of iron, beginning around 900 B.C.E. Instead of being cast from liquid metal, iron weapons were beaten out of ingots heated in forges. Because the hardness of ancient iron varied considerably, a key development toward improving the swords was pattern welding, which was the combining or plaiting together of different strips of iron into formations or patterns. This technique blended the weaker and stronger parts of the iron into a more uniformly strong and flexible blade. Although ancient smiths might not have understood the scientific basis of making steel, iron hardened with carbon, many swordmakers developed techniques that guaranteed its use in the sword.

With the Iron Age, the sword became a standard, if not always decisive, weapon. In the Greeks' phalanx method of combat, the opposing formations of spear and shield were most important, but swords were used in close combat, often as a desperate measure. The hoplite sword, intended mainly for slashing, had a wide bulge about one-third of the way down from the point, narrowing to a waist until widening at the hilt again. Some Greeks also used a *kopis*, a heavy, single-edged, downward-curved sword.

The Roman legions made their short "Spanish" sword, the *gladius hispaniensis*, a more essential part of their fighting system. After weakening the enemy with thrown spears, they closed and smashed their large shields against their opponents. Then, while the enemy usually used an overhand sword blow, caught by the Roman shield, the Roman legionary would thrust his short, stabbing sword underneath into the stomach, where its long point could penetrate most linked armor. The Romans also carried fine daggers, but they seem not to have been used in battle. By the time of the early empire, the in-

North Wind Picture Archives via AP Images

A collection of Bronze Age Celtic swords.

fantry preferred the short, hacking, "Pompeian" sword. Beginning in the second century C.E., with the rise of cavalry, a more suitable, longer (80-centimeter), slashing sword, the *spatha*, began to dominate in the Roman armies. This sword was the ancestor of medieval European swords.

The Roman Empire was brought down by Germanic peoples using long swords. Through the early Middle Ages, the sword became the basic weapon of a warrior. Battle would often begin with a charge, on foot or on horseback, using spears or lances. Once those weapons were spent, however, the warriors would hack at their armored foes with swords. Axes and maces were also popular, as well as the *seax*, a heavy, single-edged, broad-bladed chopping sword which had evolved by 900 into the *scramasax*, a short chopping blade. With the rise of knighthood by the eleventh century, warfare with lances and swords allowed Europeans to push back their opponents in the Crusades. After armorers developed better armor to help knights survive in battle, swordsmiths devised blades that would break through metal. The falchion, a broad-bladed, cleaverlike sword addressed that need. Thirteenth century knights also began to use heavier and longer one-and-one-half-handed ("bastard") or two-handed swords. By 1500 infantry, especially the Swiss and German *Landsknechte*, had developed huge swords, up to 175 centimeters long.

Another solution to European plate armor was to emphasize the swords' thrusting ability. The blade became thicker and more rigid, so the user could pierce weaker joints in the armor. In order to improve grips on such swords, protective rings began to be added to the cross-guard. Guards became more elaborate, including a curved bar stretching from cross-guard back to pommel, while the blade became narrower and sharper at the point. Thus the modern rapier appeared, which began to dominate after 1500.

Daggers were worn by European warriors throughout the Middle Ages. Daggers played only a minor

TURNING POINTS

4000 B.C.E.	Copper is used to make the first metal knives, in Middle East and Asia.
2000 B.C.E.	First metal swords, made from bronze, appear.
900 B.C.E.	Smiths master the use of iron to make stronger, more lethal, swords.
100 C.E.	With the increasing use of cavalry in Roman warfare, the *spatha*, a longer, slashing sword becomes popular.
1300	Japanese craftsmen perfect the art of swordmaking, creating the *katana*, a curved sword used by samurai warriors.
1500	As European plate armor becomes more prevalent, the sharp, narrow rapier is developed to combat it.

role in combat, with one exception: Should a knight through exhaustion or wound be found on the ground, his enemy might dispatch him with a "misericord" dagger thrust through a chink in the armor. The popular late-medieval *baselard* and *rondel* daggers with their long, narrow blades were used for this purpose. The former had a curved cross-guard and pommel, whereas the latter had a disk-shaped guard and pommel. The rondel dagger also evolved into the Scottish dirk.

Sub-Saharan Africa was not using bronze weapons by the Bronze Age and began to use iron by the third century B.C.E. By the fourth century C.E., the use of iron tools and weapons had spread throughout the continent. A shortage of iron, however, meant that sub-Saharan peoples had to import many weapons from European and Islamic civilizations. In some cultures, the Kuba kingdom of the Congo, for instance, daggers and swords with unusual blade shapes acquired great cultural importance. Africans also developed a unique throwing knife, the *hunga-munga*, with several blades branching out at angles from a main shaft.

Islamic swords, whether Arab, Turk, Persian, or Indian, were often typified by the scimitar, a curved, single-edged blade meant for slashing, which developed in the eighth or ninth century C.E. Scimitars predominated by 1400 C.E. but never entirely replaced straight blades. Until the fifteenth century the city of Damascus not only made famous swords but also served as a trading center for weapons made else-

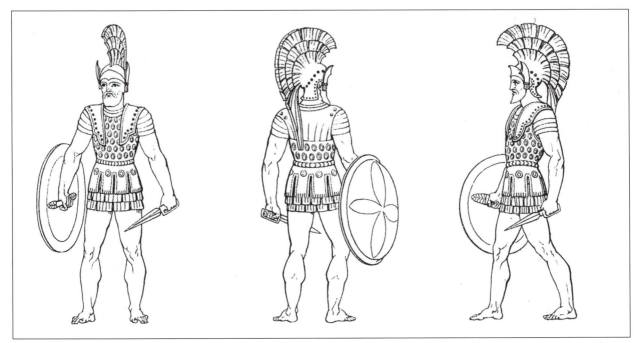

Etruscan warriors in uniform, armed with short swords and carrying shields for protection.

where. Persian weapons were famous for "watered" steel, in which the combination of higher and lower carbon content created a wavy pattern in the blade visible after an acid wash. Islamic dagger shapes varied widely according to region, although the *jambiya*, or curved ceremonial dagger, is most famous. Persian and Indian versions have a double curve. Interesting daggers from India included the Gurkha's *kukri*, with a downward-curved, single-edged, leaf-shaped blade, and the *katar*, or punch dagger. The unusual Malayan kris had a blade that could be wavy and widened from the point to a thick wedge at the hilt, which itself was set at an angle down from the blade. Throughout Southeast Asia, machetes, or parangs, were used as jungle knives for both clearing vegetation and fighting.

In China, straight bronze swords of various lengths dominated until the establishment of the Chinese Empire in the third century B.C.E. Iron weapons were then introduced, which led to long (90-centimeter) straight swords. Cavalry, charioteers, and infantry all used swords, although an important side weapon was also the dagger-ax. The scimitar-like cavalry

sword, probably introduced by Turkish peoples of Central Asia, became more popular after the eighth century C.E.

The high point of sword-making skill lay in Japan. Japanese swords were made with a highly sophisticated folding of metals: millions of times for the cutting edge, mere thousands for the spine. With polished blades and decorative hilt fittings, Japanese blades were unsurpassed in both beauty and lethality. The earliest swords in Japan, around 700 C.E., were based on straight Chinese blades. During the Heian period (794-1185 C.E.) the blades of the long *tachi* used by samurai horse warriors began to be curved. These types of swords were perfected in Japan during the late eighth and early ninth centuries. Although the primary weapon of the samurai was originally the bow, failed attempts by the Mongols to invade Japan in 1274 and 1283 C.E. led to a new emphasis on the sword in combat. In the fourteenth century the Soshu tradition of sword making was founded, creating the curved sword that became the *katana*. By the fifteenth century, the samurai warrior class had the sole right to carry swords, normally both the long sword, the katana, and the short sword, the *wakizashi*. The Japanese also had equally fine knives, ranging from the dagger, or *tanto*, carried with the swords, to smaller blades that fit into the scabbards of other weapons. Knives had various uses: as a replacement for chopsticks, for throwing at an enemy, for committing ritual suicide, or for giving the coup de grâce to an opponent.

Books and Articles

Bradford, Alfred S. *With Arrow, Sword, and Spear: A History of Warfare in the Ancient World.* Illustrated by Pamela M. Bradford. Westport, Conn.: Praeger, 2001.

Coe, Michael D., et al. *Swords and Hilt Weapons.* New York: Barnes and Noble Books, 1993.

Diagram Group. *The New Weapons of the World Encyclopedia: An International Encyclopedia from 5000 B.C. to the Twenty-first Century.* New York: St. Martin's Griffin, 2007.

Fischer, Werner, and Manfred A. Zirngibl. *African Weapons: Knives, Daggers, Swords, Axes, Throwing Knives.* Passau: Prinz-Verlag, 1978.

Levine, Bernard R., and Gerald Weland. *Complete Handbook of Knives, Swords, and Daggers.* New York: Barnes and Noble Books, 2004.

Molloy, Barry. "Martial Arts and Materiality: A Combat Archaeology Perspective on Aegean Swords of the Fifteenth and Fourteenth Centuries B.C." *World Archaeology* 40, no. 1 (March, 2008): 116.

Nicolle, David. *A Companion to Medieval Arms and Armour.* Rochester, N.Y.: Boydell Press, 2002.

Oakeshott, R. Ewart. *The Archaeology of Weapons: Arms and Armor from Prehistory to the Age of Chivalry.* Mineola, N.Y.: Dover, 1996.

_____. *Records of the Medieval Sword.* 1991. Reprint. Rochester, N.Y.: Boydell Press, 1998.

O'Connell, Robert L. *Soul of the Sword: An Illustrated History of Weaponry and Warfare from Prehistory to the Present.* New York: Free Press, 2002.

Thompson, Logan. *Daggers and Bayonets: A History.* Staplehurst, England: Spellmount, 1999.

Wagner, Eduard. *Swords and Daggers: An Illustrated Handbook.* Translated by Jean Layton. New York: Hamlyn, 1975. Reprint. Mineola, N.Y.: Dover, 2004

Warner, Gordon, and Donn F. Draeger. *Japanese Swordsmanship: Technique and Practice.* 2d ed. New York: Weatherhill, 1990.

Films and Other Media

Arms in Action: Swords. Documentary. History Channel, 1999.

Modern Marvels: Axes, Swords, and Knives. History Channel, 2008.

Samurai Sword. Documentary. Panther Productions, 1995.

Secrets of the Samurai Sword. Documentary. Public Broadcasting Service, 2008.

Brian A. Pavlac

Spears and Pole Arms

Dates: To c. 1500 C.E.

Nature and Use

The spear is among the simplest and most universal of early weapons: a simple penetrating point secured to a shaft that adds either aerodynamic qualities or leverage and distance from the target. Evidence for the manufacture and use of such weapons exists among every major population group in the world and stretches back to Paleolithic times. A basic spear consists of a long shaft of wood, bamboo, or iron with a sharpened head or point attached to one end. If the head is long and provided with a sharpened edge, the spear may be used as a slashing weapon. However, most spears were designed either to be hurled, as were javelins, or to be used as thrusting weapons held in one or both hands.

Used by infantry against other infantry or cavalry, pole arms encompass a range of weapons consisting of a long, sturdy pole, or haft, with a pointed, hooked, or edged blade attached to one end. The heads of these weapons—consisting of the blades plus the sockets and side braces used for attachment—varied in length and complexity. Hellenistic sarissas (*sarissophoroi*) and late medieval pikes were fairly simple iron spear points at the ends of 16- to 18-foot poles. Medieval and early modern halberds were complex combinations of thrusting points, blades, and hooks used to unseat horsemen. Some scholars categorize any thrusting spear as a pole arm, while others define pole arms as having specifically evolved during the Middle Ages from agricultural implements such as pruning hooks, axes, forks, and hammers. The widest variety of these latter weapons is to be found in the European and Mediterranean regions and in Japan.

Development

Early humans created the first spears by sharpening and later hardening in fire the ends of long, straight, wooden shafts. At some time people began to attach pointed heads of sharpened bone or flaked flint by notching the shaft end, inserting the flange, or tang, on the head behind the point, and lashing the two together. Javelins had light shafts and triangular or even barbed heads that helped the weapon remain in its victim. Prehistoric Europeans as well as peoples of the Americas, Oceania, and Asia also developed spear-throwers, which were short handles of carved horn, wood, or ivory cupped at one end. The cup held the butt of the shaft, and the handle acted as a lever or rigid sling that hurled the spear with greater accuracy and force than could an unaided human arm. Thrusting spears developed longer, leaf-shaped heads that could be more easily withdrawn after penetration.

Copper, and later bronze, spearheads first appeared in Mesopotamia and were used along with stone spearheads. Beaten or cast metal allowed for the creation of sockets behind the heads. These sockets could be as long as 2 feet, making for a more secure attachment than lashed tangs and reducing the likelihood of the shaft breaking. The heroes of Homer's epics the *Iliad* (c. 750 B.C.E.; English translation, 1611) and the *Odyssey* (c. 725 B.C.E.; English translation, 1614) fought their individual combats with two javelins with 6-inch heads, as well as stout 10-foot olive-wood spears with sharpened butts and 2-foot bronze heads with straight, rather than leaf-shaped, edges and a prominent median ridge running back from the tip.

Iron heads emerged in tenth century B.C.E. Greece and among the Celts of the Hallstatt culture (c. 700 B.C.E.). The latter created leaf-shaped heads with short wings, or lugs, at the base of the point to prevent overly deep penetration—perhaps a development from hunting practice. Later La Tène-era (c. 500-50 B.C.E.) graves contained heads that display a wide variety of shapes and sizes, including triangular, wavy-edged, and leaf-shaped. Celtic charioteers hurled

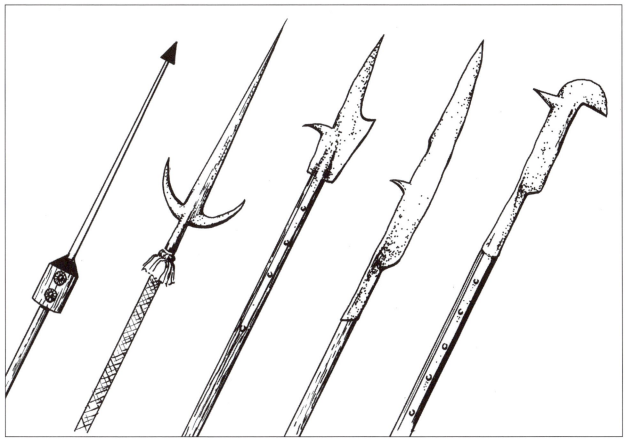

Kimberly L. Dawson Kurnizki

From left to right, a pilum, *with a leaf-shaped tip and an iron neck weakened to break on impact; a* corseque, *with a triangular blade and wings; a* halberd, *displaying a characteristically complex combination of thrusting points, blades, and hooks for unseating horsemen; a* glaive, *with a spike and a long, gently curving blade, like that of a knife or single-edged sword; and a* bill, *with a broad outward-curving blade for cutting or grabbing horsemen.*

iron-tipped javelins, as did eastern Mediterranean light infantry, or *akonistai*, at the beginning of Greece's classical period. Fifth century B.C.E. Greek hoplites, or infantry soldiers, fought with stout 9-foot spears in phalanxes several men deep. Vulnerable Persian infantry armed with shorter spears had to rely on archers. The armies of Alexander the Great, king of Macedonia from 336 to 323 B.C.E., and his successors also relied on phalanxes of spear-throwers in ranks of up to five men deep with ash-shafted sarissas of up to 21 feet in length. Some Hellenistic cavalry also used sarissas, while others wielded shorter spears for under- or overhand thrusting. The Roman victory

at Pydna (168 B.C.E.) ended the dominance of the sarissa.

The standard Roman javelin was the *pilum*. One third of its 5.5-foot length was a long iron neck with a leaf-shaped tip. To prevent the pilum from being hurled back, its wooden socket was weakened to break upon impact. Later, under Julius Caesar (100-44 B.C.E.), the iron neck was weakened so that it would bend after penetration and render the enemy's shield useless. From either the Sabines or the Celt-Iberians, the Romans borrowed the *verutum*, a curved-bladed javelin thrown with a leather sling, or *amentum*, that wrapped around the shaft. The verutum largely replaced the pilum in the second century C.E. The *falarica*, or Saguntine spear, was a javelin with a foot-long head of triangular section; balls of fiber soaked in pitch could be attached and ignited to make an incendiary missile.

In Asia, Tibetans wielded the *dung*, a spear 7 to 10 feet in length with a long, narrow, two-edged head on a socket. The shaft was often wrapped with iron bands, tipped at the butt end with an iron cap, and was used by cavalrymen for vaulting into the saddle. Japanese armies carried several types of pole weapons, beginning with the *take-yari* or *take-hoko* a 6.5- to 8-foot bamboo pole tipped with a simple jagged edge. The traditional *yari* usually had long tangs that attached either triangular or diamond-sectioned tips with pegs and metal collars, called *habaki*. Some heads were as long as short swords, and spear-fencing emerged as a respected martial art. Wings, hooks, and curved blades eventually were added, as in the forked or crescent-headed *sasumata* or the cross-shaped *maga-yari*. Other Japanese pole arms included the *ono*, a poleax with a hammer or peen opposite the blade, and the *kama-yari*, with a picklike head. Hafts were usually of wood, lacquered or plain, and sometimes wrapped in silk thread.

In Africa, native and Arab warriors hurled the 4-foot-long *assagai* or *zaghaya*, with a long, barbed lancet head whose tang was lashed to a wood or bamboo shaft. At lengths of up to 36 inches, the shorter javelin known as the *jarid*, or *djerid*, with its square-sectioned steel head was used in most Islamic-dominated areas.

In medieval Europe the use of the spear continued while other pole arms were developed. Frankish warriors borrowed the Roman pilum (*angon*), barbing the tip and sheathing nearly the entire shaft in iron. Frankish thrusting spears had leaf-shaped tips with short lugs or wings at the base. Scandinavians used a variety of spears, including those designed for slashing (*hoggspjot*), hurling (*gaflak*), and flinging with an amentum (*snoeris-spjot*). They also employed thrusting weapons with long spikes. Hundreds of iron heads with bronze or gold inlay and ashwood shafts of 6.5 to 11 feet have been found in Danish graves. Norse warriors often named their weapons, usually incorporating serpent imagery. European in-

fantry continued to use thick-shafted spears tipped with lugged, leaf-shaped, or triangular heads until well after 1500 C.E.

Stirrups and deep-welled saddles allowed cavalry to wield spears more effectively in both over- and underhand motions, as shown in images such as the Bayeux tapestry (c. 1080 C.E.), which depicts the Norman Conquest. The lance developed as a shock weapon couched close to the body for charging other cavalry. Roman and early Byzantine *cataphracts* lashed their long spears against their horses' necks, supporting the butt by a rope sling at the croup. In the high Middle Ages, the 9- to 11-foot-long shaft had uniform thickness and a small, leaf-shaped tip. Tournament jousters used a three-pronged tip, or *cronel*, designed to grab, rather than to penetrate, the opponent's shield or armor. Hilts were added in the fourteenth century to absorb recoil upon impact, and conical vamplates that also served to deflect the enemy's lance tip appeared in the fifteenth century. Jousting shafts composed of bundles of thin staves (*bourdonass*) designed to shatter upon impact replaced those of solid wood, and plate breast armor sported small brackets, called arrests, that cradled the butt of the knight's lance.

Infantry spears evolved in two directions after about 1200 C.E. On one hand, the sarissa emerged again as the pike, with its small diamond-sectioned head at the end of a 12- to 18-foot-long ash shaft. Phalanxes or squares of up to four effective men deep could withstand the most determined cavalry charge with their leveled weapons, as at Courtrai (1302 C.E.) and Bannockburn (1314 C.E.), but archers easily decimated the unprotected ranks at Falkirk (1298 C.E.). Nonetheless, armies of pikemen proved successful until effective firepower broke their ranks, as at Bicocca in 1522 C.E.

On the other hand, spears with short wings or lugs evolved into more complex thrusting weapons as the tips lengthened and the wings arced out from the base. The *langue-de-bœuf* (ox tongue) began as a long, two-edged blade with a short socket and no wings; in the fifteenth century wings were added, and the resulting weapon became known as the partisan. The Italian *corseque*, with a broad, triangular blade and generally longer wings evolved similarly. The wide, flat surfaces of the corseque served Renaissance decorators well, and the weapon ended up as the ceremonial weapon of bodyguards.

Although ancient Egyptians had fought with axlike blades attached to long poles, most slashing pole arms evolved from the agricultural implements that European peasants used to defend themselves against mounted warriors. The English bill, designed for pruning, consisted of a long and broad cleaverlike blade that curved outward at the top. It could strike downward or horizontally, and the hooked top could cut or grab mounted men. Iron sleeves that protected the shaft from blows gradually evolved, as did the blade's design. The fully developed bill of the fourteenth century sported a long, curved fluke on the backside, a pointed thrusting blade on the top, hooked and sharpened lugs at the base, and a peen or spike that projected perpendicularly from the haft, or pole. The top blade or spike could penetrate breastplates and the peen could penetrate helmets, while the fluke could hook and pull knights from horses or trip foot soldiers. The French *guisarme* retained more of the early bill's cutting edge, while the symmetrical Italian double-bill resembled a fleur-de-lis mounted on a long, broad leaf-shaped cutting blade.

Axes came with short or long hafts, and long hafts were favorites with the Norse, Russians, and Anglo-Saxons. Poleaxes developed in the later Middle Ages and were surmounted by long, straight, or curved Danish ax-heads, perhaps with rear-projecting flukes. When a thrusting point was added, in approximately 1300, a proper halberd was born. Swiss halberdiers slaughtered Austrian troops at Hildisrieden and at Sempach in 1386 and at Näfels in 1388, and later became the Pope's bodyguards. Various combinations of flukes, points, and blades often make differentiating between bills and halberds difficult, but the halberd is generally distinguishable by its salient convex ax-blade. The glaive, or broadsword, evolved during the fifteenth century from the long-hafted scythe, with its long, gently curving blade. The concave edge was inverted to convex, like that of a knife or single-edged sword, and spikes or flukes were added to the back of the blade. The *fauchard*, with its distinctive crescent fluke, derives from the glaive. The practical value of these weapons declined after the late fifteenth century, and bills, halberds, and glaives became highly decorated ceremonial weapons.

Other farm implements, including hammers, flails, and forks, were also mounted on poles for military use. Pole hammers might also sport hooked flukes or long spikes, whereas military forks with two tines were sometimes supplied with blades or hooks. Spiked maces with long hafts and even spiked balls with one long spike extending as a thrusting point also appeared on late medieval battlefields.

BOOKS AND ARTICLES

Bradford, Alfred S. *With Arrow, Sword, and Spear: A History of Warfare in the Ancient World.* Illustrated by Pamela M. Bradford. Westport, Conn.: Praeger, 2001.

Cundy, B. J. *Formal Variation in Australian Spear and Spearthrower Technology.* Oxford, England: B.A.R., 1989.

Diagram Group. *The New Weapons of the World Encyclopedia: An International Encyclopedia from 5000 B.C. to the Twenty-first Century.* New York: St. Martin's Griffin, 2007.

Grant, R. G. *Warrior: A Visual History of the Fighting Man.* New York: DK, 2007.

Knutsen, Roald, and Patricia Knutsen. *Japanese Spears: Polearms and Their Use in Old Japan.* Folkestone, Kent., England: Global Oriental, 2004.

Miller, Douglas. *The Swiss at War, 1300-1500.* Illustrated by Gerry Embleton. Botley, Oxford, England: Osprey, 1979.

Nicolle, David C. *Arms and Armour of the Crusading Era.* 2 vols. White Plains, N.Y.: Kraus International, 1988.

_____. *A Companion to Medieval Arms and Armour.* Rochester, N.Y.: Boydell Press, 2002.

O'Connell, Robert L. *Soul of the Sword: An Illustrated History of Weaponry and Warfare from Prehistory to the Present.* New York: Free Press, 2002.

Puricelli-Guerra, A. "The Glaive and the Bill." In *Art, Arms, and Armour*, edited by Robert Held. Chiasso, Switzerland: Acquafresca Editrice, 1979.

Santosuosso, Antonio. *Soldiers, Citizens, and the Symbols of War: From Classical Greece to Republican Rome, 500-167 B.C.* Boulder, Colo.: Westview Press, 1997.

Snook, George A. *The Halberd and Other European Pole Arms, 1300-1650.* Bloomfield, Ont.: Museum Restoration Service, 1998.

Spring, Christopher. *African Arms and Armour.* London: British Museum, 1993.

Swanton, M. J. *The Spearheads of the Anglo-Saxon Settlements.* London: Royal Archaeological Institute, 1973.

FILMS AND OTHER MEDIA

Arms in Action: Slings and Spears. Documentary. History Channel, 1999.

The Dark Ages. Documentary. History Channel, 2007.

Joseph P. Byrne

CHARIOTS

Dates: To c. 400 B.C.E.

NATURE AND USE

The chariot derived from the four-wheeled wagon, and was replaced by a two-wheeled vehicle after the original wagon was found to be too cumbersome for combat. While the precise origin of the chariot remains unknown, it is known that the Hyksos, of Semitic origin (c. 1700 B.C.E.), introduced the horse-drawn chariot during invasions of Egypt (c. 1674 B.C.E.). Hammurabi, ruler of the Amorite Dynasty (c. 1750 B.C.E.) in Mesopotamia, was driven from the Near Eastern sphere of power when conquered by the Hittites, a people from the northern mountain regions of modern Iran and Iraq whose spearmen fought from chariots. In Asia Shang Dynasty (1384-1122 B.C.E.) armies introduced the chariot to northern China in order to overrun the earlier Chou (Zhou) Dynasty (1122-221 B.C.E.).

The rapid development of the chariot, the breeding of horses, and the ability to control them with a bridle and bit allowed for efficient use of the chariot in battle. Chariots drawn by horses were yoked horizontally in pairs. Two wooden, Y-shaped forms attached to the yoke were fitted to the horses but limited the terrain over which they could be used effectively for battle. As chariot use increased, so did the need for professional charioteers and chariot-warrior teams, each consisting of a driver and an archer. The Hittites were credited with the expansion of the chariot crew to include a third man, the guard or shield bearer. The Hittites also used the chariot defensively against enemies. Reconstructions of early chariots found primarily in Egyptian tombs of New Kingdom (c. 1550 B.C.E.) kings reveal a hard, dense wood used to prevent cracking of the hub, an inflexible wood for the spokes, and a flexible wood for the wheel rim, or segments of the wheel rim, called fellies.

Initially, the chariot provided armies with speed and thus the potential for surprise attacks. This new form of attack forced military leaders to adopt new battle tactics. When integrated into the battlefield, the maneuverability of the chariot allowed the chariot-warrior to perform an outflanking maneuver. In early use, archers were able to use the chariot as a mobile platform from which to shoot. The mobility increased the damage inflicted on enemy troops and enabled chariot soldiers to chase down fleeing enemy soldiers.

In the Near East, the chariot became an effective offensive weapon. Often more disruptive than destructive, aggressively mobile chariot forces could gain control over the east-west and north-south trade routes to the sea, as well as inland access to natural resources, eliminating the need to mount an expensive army campaign.

Treaties formed with opposing enemies combining a large kingdom and vassal-states within one area of influence illustrate the important role chariots played in the history of the Near East. Even the show of force by aggressive chariot tactics helped to dissuade confederations in opposition.

Egyptian tomb paintings (c. 1700 B.C.E.) depicting the design and manufacture of early chariots show a vehicle with four-spoked wheels and a single axle centered under a single platform, on which the chariot driver stood directly over the axle. The light weight of wooden chariots provided Egyptians with needed mobility in battle. At approximately 1300 B.C.E., two changes in chariot design were made. The first innovation was an increase in the number of spokes, from four to six, in order to sustain a heavier weight on the wheels. The second was the relocation of the axle from the center of the chassis to the edge of the platform, which was open at the end of the chassis.

Early chariot tactics were immediate and intrusive; the charioteers would rapidly advance and encircle the enemy at a distance of approximately 100

TURNING POINTS

c. 1674 B.C.E.	The Hyksos people introduce the horse-drawn chariot during invasions of Egypt.
c. 1300 B.C.E.	Chariot design undergoes major innovations, with an increase in the number of spokes and the relocation of axles.
c. 1122 B.C.E.	Shang Dynasty armies introduce the chariot to northern China in warfare against the Chou Dynasty.
c. 546 B.C.E.	Persian king Cyrus the Great uses chariots to great advantage at the Battle of Thymbra.
c. 401 B.C.E.	Charioteers are overwhelmed by more flexible cavalry in the Battle of Cunaxa, ending the dominance of chariots in warfare.

yards and then use the chariot as a mobile platform from which the archer would shoot. This method permitted both speed and a greater ability to maneuver on the battlefield than had war wagons or troops on foot. The result left an enemy defenseless to form a counterattack.

In a two-wheeled, four-spoked Greek chariot, there was a chariot-warrior group of two: the driver and the archer. The two-wheeled Greek chariot did not provide an archer with protective cover, and no spear-throwing could be accommodated in the two-wheeled chassis, or in the battle strategy, without bringing the chariot to a stop. The open-framed chassis had bentwood rods with leather sheets stretched between them. These light chariots allowed for side screens but required the attachment of metal plates for protective purposes. The characteristically curved draught-pole, connecting the yoke to the chassis, was supported at the yoke end by a leather swathe and then continued back to the protective chassis screen.

DEVELOPMENT

The component parts of the chariot—wheels, draught-pole and yoke, chassis, and fittings for harnessing—developed independently in different regions. Wheels were made either as a single unit or as segments of smaller pieces of wood, often fastened together with

leather. The spoke wheel derived from the earlier three-part wheel. Implementation of the hub permitted a lighter-weight chariot with the spoke used to disperse the weight density. Spoke wheels were more expensive to produce than were the earlier three-part wheels, and their production demanded a higher level of technology, as well as a skilled work force. The finished wheel consisted of a hub to hold the axle, as well as sockets for each spoke end.

To lessen the stress of the chariot's dispersed weight, spokes were of precisely equal lengths. The spoke was trimmed to fit, like a dowel, into the hub holes and wheel rims. Egyptian spokes were carved separately to fit the hub hold and were connected by mortise-and-tenon joints borrowed from Old Kingdom furniture-making techniques. Bent wood, in either single pieces or segments, heated to form the circular shape, was used for the wheels. In Bohemia, the Rhineland, and possibly India, the spoke was held together with overlapping metal strips wrapped to envelop the join. In Shang Dynasty China (1384-1122 B.C.E.), chariots utilized a spoke wheel. Both six- and eight-spoked wheels were used in the Near East (c. 1900 B.C.E.), and the six-spoked wheel was standard for Hittite- and Syrian-designed chariots (c. 1400 B.C.E.).

Unlike Egyptian chariots, the Greek light chariot rotated on a fixed axle held by a metal linchpin. Iron linchpins coated with bronze were used in the Celtic chariot. The Greeks used a four-horse chariot team, which continued to be employed by the Etruscans (c. 900 B.C.E.) and the Northern Europeans. After the fall of the Roman Empire, little is known about medieval chariots until the twelfth century. Apart from new technology evidenced by a lathe-turned and mortised hub, chariots of this period do not show much technical innovation. Instead, a series of wheeled vehicles served mainly as carting or farm vehicles and, in battle, moved men and weapons.

Iron Age wheelmakers often lined wheel hubs with bronze and then fitted them with an iron collar.

Roman designs introduced a gear-like set of rods made of wood to form channels inside the hub or to turn between the hub and axles.

The harness remained unimproved beyond the yoke until the twelfth century introduction of the traction harness. In Han Dynasty China (207 B.C.E.-222 C.E.) and in third century C.E. Persia, girth bands were developed to harness horses without choking them. The leather breast band fell horizontally to respond to the horizontal pull of the horse.

During the second millennium B.C.E., the horse-drawn light chariot provided armies with new mobility and speed. In early battles, chariots were used to create confusion in enemy ranks in preparation for coordinated chariot and cavalry charges. In China (c. 1400 B.C.E.) the chariot was a mobile command post. Chariots and cavalry were used on flanks or sometimes in front with the objective of outflanking the enemy and gaining rear access to the enemy's

vulnerable infantry. At the Battle of Thymbra (546 B.C.E.), Persian king Cyrus the Great used the chariot to take advantage of gaps in the Lydian chariot wings.

Once coordinated teams of chariots and cavalry organized, the role of the chariot diminished, especially in difficult terrain. Charioteers formed elite corps in Near Eastern and Egyptian armies for nearly a thousand years. In Greece, however, where the terrain varied, cavalry replaced the chariot. The Hellenic army consisted of a line of infantry, known as hoplites, in a formation of eight-deep units. The hoplites advanced with the object of smashing through the enemy's front line. Flanking the hoplites were armed spearmen with javelins and shields. The success of the Greek system depended on the hoplites' ability to penetrate the enemy's front line so that in retreat the enemy would be vulnerable to Greek missile weapons. Apart from the two classes of Greek

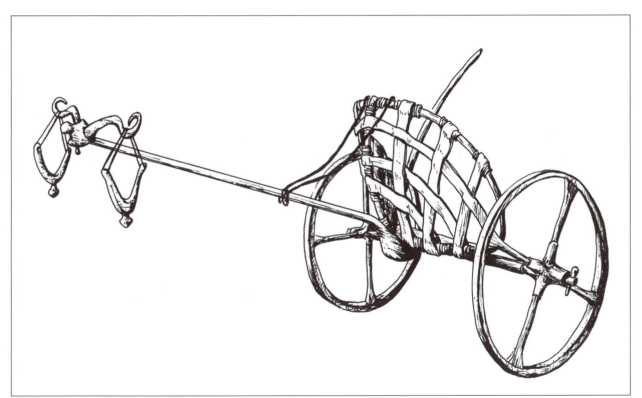

Kimberly L. Dawson Kurnizki

A two-wheeled, four-spoked Bronze Age chariot constructed with bent wood, showing the Y-shaped forms that fitted the pair of horses to the yoke.

infantrymen, hoplites and spearmen, there was no cavalry force, nor was the composite bow used extensively in conjunction with chariot attacks. With these battle tactics, the need for chariots disappeared.

The characteristics of the Greek fighting style were established in the decisive Battle of Cunaxa (401 B.C.E.), in which Persian prince Cyrus the Younger attempted to seize the throne from his brother Artaxerxes II (r. 404-359/358 B.C.E.). The hoplites easily dispersed the Persian infantry and drove Cyrus's forces off the battlefield, killed him, and isolated the Greek infantry in Cyrus's employ. Here the cavalry replaced the chariot because the cavalry could exploit tactical maneuvers on the battlefield and added a flexibility not possible with the chariot. The lesson was not lost on the Macedonian army led by Philip II (382-336 B.C.E.).

Philip's Macedonian army formed a core around the "Companion cavalry." This group numbered about two thousand, and Philip added about six thousand other armed cavalry from previously conquered Near Eastern groups. This cavalry was joined by an infantry of about twenty-five thousand men divided into three main groups: the phalanx, a highly trained group twice as deep as the earlier hoplite formation that provided freedom of movement on the battlefield; the *hypaspistai*, or hypaspists, a secondary shield-bearing corps of soldiers similar to those of the phalanx; and a group of lightly armed soldiers equipped with javelins and bows. Because these forces were effective against chariots and horses, the art of chariots soon disappeared from battle formations and became limited to observation posts or command posts.

BOOKS AND ARTICLES

Bilson, Frank. *Crossbows*. New York: Hippocrene Books, 1975.

Bryce, Trevor. *Hittite Warrior*. Illustrated by Adam Hook. Botley, Oxford, England: Osprey, 2007.

Cotterell, Arthur. *Chariot: From Chariot to Tank, the Astounding Rise and Fall of the World's First War Machine*. Woodstock, N.Y.: Overlook Press, 2005.

Crouwel, J. H. *Chariots and Other Means of Land Transport in Bronze Age Greece*. Drawings by J. Morel. Amsterdam: Allard Pierson Museum, 1992.

Fields, Nic. *Bronze Age War Chariots*. Botley, Oxford, England: Osprey, 2006.

Gabriel, Richard A. "Chariotry." In *The Ancient World*. Westport, Conn.: Greenwood Press, 2007.

Harding, Stephen. "The Deadly Dozen." *Military History* 26, no. 2 (June/July 2009): 58.

Littauer, M. A., and J. H. Crouwel. *Chariots and Related Equipment from the Tomb of Tut'ankhamen*. Oxford, England: Griffith Institute, 1985.

_____. *Selected Writings on Chariots and Other Early Vehicles, Riding and Harness*. Edited by Peter Raulwing. Boston: Brill, 2002.

Shaw, Ian. *Egyptian Warfare and Weapons*. Risborough, Buckinghamshire, England: Shire, 1991.

Yadin, Yigeah. *The Art of Warfare in Biblical Lands*. 2 vols. New York: McGraw-Hill, 1963.

FILMS AND OTHER MEDIA

Ben Hur. Feature film. Metro-Goldwyn-Mayer, 1959.

Modern Marvels: Barbarian Battle Tech. Documentary. History Channel, 2008.

Elizabeth L. Meyers

FIREARMS AND CANNON
Dates: To c. 1500 C.E.

NATURE AND USE

The first precise recipe for gunpowder, a Chinese invention dating to before 1000 C.E., is found in a work from 1044. Long before it gained any military significance, gunpowder was used for holiday displays of colored smoke and fireworks. The earliest evidence of gunpowder weapons is a set of figurines dating from 1128 found in a cave. One figure holds a device that appears to be a potbellied vase with a blast of fire coming out, within which is a disk that probably was intended to portray a ball. Further evidence from Chinese records and art indicates that gunpowder weapons were in widespread use by 1280. These weapons seem to have included the three essential elements of true gunpowder weapons: a metal barrel, an explosive powder similar in chemical makeup to that of black powder, and a projectile that filled the barrel in order to take full advantage of the propellant blast.

The consensus among historians is that the Mongols carried gunpowder westward from China in the thirteenth century, but there is no agreement on whether gunpowder weapons were brought to Europe with the powder. The first European mention of gunpowder was by thirteenth century scientist and educator Roger Bacon (1220-1292), who recorded a recipe in 1267. His term, "fire for burning up the enemy," suggests that Bacon regarded gunpowder as an incendiary, not a propellant. Late thirteenth century gunpowder recipes called for saltpeter, sulfur, and charcoal in the propor-

tion of six parts saltpeter for every one part each of sulfur and charcoal—a more explosive combination than that used by the Chinese and therefore better for projectile weapons. There is no convincing evidence for the existence of such weapons before 1326, although several earlier sources have been interpreted as referring to them.

Although a reference to the making of gunpowder artillery found in a 1326 document from Florence is widely accepted as the first reliable mention, it is less informative than an illustrated English manuscript from the following year. This illustration shows a large pot-bellied vessel lying on its side on a table

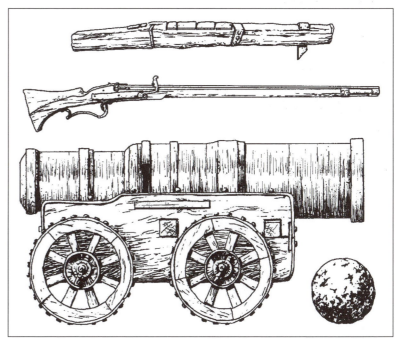

Kimberly L. Dawson Kurnizki

From top to bottom, a harquebus, the first effective matchlock firearm, dating from around 1470; a more evolved matchlock musket, dating from around 1600; a muzzle-loading bombard, known as "Mons Meg," dating from around 1440.

with a large bolt projecting from its mouth, which is aimed at the gate of a walled place. Behind the device stands an armored man with a heated poker, which he is about to put to its touch hole. Such a device became known as *pot de fer* (iron pot). As that illustration reveals, these early gunpowder weapons were largely associated with sieges. The first definitive mention of them in action came from a siege of Tournai (1340). Whether the English deployed cannon in the Battle of Crécy (1346), the first decisive battle in the Hundred Years' War, is disputed, but they did use them at the Siege of Calais (1346-1347).

In field warfare, early gunpowder weapons—both firearms and artillery—lacked the technical quality to compete effectively with longbows and crossbows. Their weight, unreliability, inaccuracy, and slow rate of fire made them inferior in most respects to traditional combat weapons for more than a century after 1327. In sieges, however, these defects were less problematic. The cannonball's flat trajectory assured that the ball would strike low against the high walls of medieval fortifications and be more likely to open a breach than would mechanical artillery, which had a high trajectory. The first known instance of gunpowder artillery bringing a siege to a successful end occurred in 1377 at Odruik, the Netherlands.

By the late fourteenth century, the size of gunpowder artillery had increased greatly. Huge bombards—so called because their hewn stone cannonballs buzzed like bumblebees when fired—reached twenty tons in weight. Balls weighed as much as one thousand pounds, a weight attributed to the balls fired by the largest bombard used by the Turks against Constantinople in 1453. Although a direct hit from a ball of that weight had a good chance of collapsing a wall, bombards were extremely difficult to move, and the amount of gunpowder they required was expensive and difficult to procure. Smaller pieces of artillery went by names such as *ribauld* and *serpentine*.

In Bohemia military leader Jan Žižka (c. 1360-1424) used small cannon in the Hussite Wars (1419-1434) against the forces of the Bohemian king Sigismund (1368-1437). Forced to fight German knights with poorly trained foot soldiers, Žižka developed the *Wagenburg*, a defensive line of wagons. On some were placed small cannon, and on others, men with firearms. The Germans on horseback presented large targets for the inaccurate gunpowder weapons in use, and the smoke and noise of the weapons frightened their horses. Some of the Hussites' primitive firearms had hooks attached that fit over the upper edge of the wagons' sideboards to absorb the recoil and provide a steady base for firing. It has been suggested that the term "harquebus," the common word for the first effective firearms, came from the German for such hook guns.

DEVELOPMENT

It is difficult to date the development of effective firearms because most of the people who created and used the new weapons were illiterate and did not leave written records. A chronology of firearm technology depends on a few surviving examples, as well as drawings and sketches that are not detailed enough to show the changes involved. Corned powder, which provided greater explosive power than did earlier serpentine powder, appeared around 1420. Corned powder produced higher muzzle velocities and could fire balls capable of penetrating the plate armor worn by the knights who were the mainstay of most fifteenth cen-

TURNING POINTS

1044 B.C.E.	The first precise recipe for gunpowder is given, in a Chinese work.
1340 C.E.	The first definitive use of gunpowder weapons is made at the Siege of Tournai.
1346-1347	Cannons are deployed by the English at the Siege of Calais.
1377	The first siege won by cannon is ended at Odruik, the Netherlands.
c. 1420	Corned powder and matches are developed.
1503	The first effective use of the combination of firearms and pikes, a formation called the "Spanish Square," is made at the Battle of Cerignola.

tury armies. Higher muzzle velocity, however, could be achieved only with a barrel longer than that of the hand-cannon. Because of such defects, hand-cannons were not competitive with bows until 1450. By then gunsmiths had found the right compromise between ballistic performance and weight by fitting hand-cannons with barrels of about 40 inches in length. The first known illustration of a long-barreled firearm shows it being used for duck hunting. Hunting requirements often produced technological changes that later appeared in weapons.

Another innovation toward more effective firearms was the match-string; soaked in saltpeter, it burned slowly but with enough heat to touch off gunpowder. The match also was developed sometime around 1420, replacing the clumsy and unreliable burning stick. The match, however, created the same problem for its users as had the burning stick: It had to be held in one hand and touched down into the chamber to fire the powder. That meant that only one hand could be used to hold the piece, butted up against the chest, not the shoulder. Too large a charge of powder could result in a broken breastbone. The solution was the matchlock. The matchlock evolved in Germany to include springs, a trigger, and a clamp for holding a smoldering match so that when the trigger was pulled, the match's burning tip was thrust into the powder and touched it off. After the shoulder stock, borrowed from the crossbow, was added to reduce the impact of the recoil from the greater muzzle velocity, the firearm was made up of the proverbial lock, stock, and barrel.

The users of the matchlock device found that coarse powder often failed to ignite and fine powder often created too forceful a recoil. The innovative solution to this problem was to place a small pan filled with fine powder behind the chamber of the barrel and to put coarse powder in the chamber. The match touched off the fine powder in the pan, blowing flame through a small hole into the chamber, igniting the coarser powder there, and firing off the ball. Often, however, the powder in the pan ignited with fire and sparks without touching off the powder in the chamber.

The harquebus, as the first matchlock firearm became known, was developed by 1460, but its impact

A harquebusier with both sword and harquebus.

on the battlefield was slow to appear. As a smoothbore weapon, it was inherently inaccurate: The spin of a ball tumbling down a smoothbore barrel is determined by the last point on the barrel the ball touches as it leaves the muzzle. The user has no idea what direction the spin will cause the ball to take; balls fired from smoothbore weapons never have the same trajectories. Consequently, the harquebus was reasonably accurate for only a short distance, before the un-

Frederick Ungar Publishing Co.

An artist's woodcut rendition of movable sixteenth century mortars.

controlled spin took over. The impact of the ball on its target, even an armored cavalryman, was great at close range, but that advantage was largely negated by the long time it took to reload a harquebus. If the harquebusier missed the charging knights with his first shot or if he had a misfire—a common occurrence with the harquebus—they would be on top of him before he could reload. Before the seventeenth century invention of the paper cartridge that combined a ball and a measured amount of powder, reloading a harquebus, even under the best conditions, took well over a minute. In the confusion and disorder of a battlefield, especially with lance-wielding knights bearing down, many harquebusiers took several minutes to reload or were never able to reload and fire a second time. Compared to longbows, the early harquebus performed poorly in reliability, rate of fire, and accuracy.

The harquebus found its first niche as a siege weapon, where it replaced the crossbow. Firearms were good weapons for urban militias guarding city walls across Europe. A minimal amount of training was required to use the harquebus effectively on walls, and, although the weapon was more expensive than the crossbow, it was still affordable to the arti-

sans and merchants who belonged to the urban militias. The harquebus was probably introduced to the field armies, which doubled as siege forces, in the context of sieges.

The harquebus served for a time as a useful weapon for defending a fortification, but improvements in gunpowder artillery quickly negated the defensive advantage. Because late medieval iron casting produced a poor product, barrels made of cast iron frequently burst, killing gunners and bystanders. Pieces of better quality were made by forging iron bars arranged in a circle and banded by hot metal hoops that tightened down as they cooled. These hooped bombards were the weapons first associated with the name "cannon," which came from a Latin word for "tube." Early cannons, with short barrels and large muzzles, used stone balls. Smaller pieces often were equipped with breech pans, which were loaded in advance and were set in the piece in rapid succession for firing. Another solution to the poor quality of pieces made with cast iron was to use bronze instead. Europeans were familiar with the casting of bronze bells, and that technology was easily transferred to the making of weapons. The use of bronze allowed gunmakers to manufacture long-barreled pieces with smaller muzzles—called culverins, from a French word for serpent—that were capable of using iron or lead balls. The French led in the development of high-quality culverins and of the gun carriage, with high wheels and long tail, that defined gun carriages until the nineteenth century. With an artillery train of some eighty bronze culverins on mobile carriages, French king Charles VIII (r. 1483-1498) had great success in reducing Italian fortifications during the initial phase of the Italian Wars of 1494-1559. In the Battle of Fornovo (1495) the French artillery also played a significant role as an effective field weapon.

During the wars in Italy after 1494, field armies began to include harquebusiers. At the Battle of Cerignola (1503) in the French-Spanish war over Naples, the Spanish commander Gonzalo Fernández de Córdoba (1453-1515) devised a way to make effective use of harquebusiers by digging trenches in front of their lines. This action transformed the battlefield into a fort and imitated a siege, a situation in which the harquebus had long proven itself. Harquebus fire raked the French forces as they approached the Spanish trenches. Over the next twenty years, the Spanish rapidly increased the number of handgunners in their forces and developed the infantry formation called the "Spanish Square," in which pikemen and harquebusiers provided mutual support for each other. It remained the dominant infantry system until the beginning of the Thirty Years' War in 1618.

BOOKS AND ARTICLES

Buchanan, Brenda, ed. *Gunpowder: The History of an International Technology*. Bath, England: Bath University Press, 1996.

Chase, Kenneth. *Firearms: A Global History to 1700*. New York: Cambridge University Press, 2003.

DeVries, Kelly. *Guns and Men in Medieval Europe, 1200-1500: Studies in Military History and Technology*. Burlington, Vt.: Ashgate/Variorum, 2002.

Diagram Group. *The New Weapons of the World Encyclopedia: An International Encyclopedia from 5000 B.C. to the Twenty-first Century*. New York: St. Martin's Griffin, 2007.

Hall, Bert. *Weapons and Warfare in Renaissance Europe*. Baltimore: Johns Hopkins University Press, 1997.

Lu, Gwei-Djen, et al. "The Oldest Representation of a Bombard." *Technology and Culture* 29 (1988): 594-605.

Lugs, Jaroslav. *Firearms Past and Present: A Complete Review of Firearms Systems and Their Histories*. 2 vols. London: Grenville, 1973.

Nosov, Konstantin S. *Ancient and Medieval Siege Weapons: A Fully Illustrated Guide to Siege Weapons and Tactics*. Illustrated by Vladimir Golubev. Guilford, Conn.: Lyons Press, 2005.

Partington, J. R. *A History of Greek Fire and Gunpowder*. 1960. Reprint. Baltimore: Johns Hopkins University Press, 1999.

Pauly, Roger. *Firearms: The Life Story of a Technology*. Westport, Conn.: Greenwood Press, 2004.

FILMS AND OTHER MEDIA

Arms in Action: The First Firearms. Documentary. History Channel, 1999.

Modern Marvels: Cannons. Documentary. History Channel, 2002.

Tales of the Gun. Documentary series. History Channel, 2005.

Frederic J. Baumgartner

ANCIENT FORTIFICATIONS

Dates: To c. 500 C.E.

NATURE AND USE

Fortifications are structures built by human beings for the purpose of warding off attacks by hostile animals or humans. In the broadest sense, fortifications can be forms of protection, such as armor, inoculation, or even insect repellent, worn by an individual to protect against harm. Fortifications can also be communal defenses, such as forts, moats, walls, or the "strategic missile defense," a proposed network of satellites positioned in outer space to protect against attacking ballistic missiles. In the study of warfare, "fortifications" generally refers to temporary or permanent communal defenses against attacks by human enemies. Temporary fortifications for immediate use in battles or other engagements are called "field fortifications" to distinguish them from permanent structures such as castles, stone walls, and forts.

DEVELOPMENT

In Neolithic times, small villages were located either on high ground or in barely accessible areas reached only with considerable difficulty. Where nature did not provide a barrier to intruders, human ingenuity placed trenches, palisades, or moats over which bridges could be placed or removed. These three types of defenses, when intended to protect against other humans, were the first military fortifications.

It seems likely that permanent fortifications evolved in response to the settling of agricultural communities. Early fortifications did not require much sophistication, because threats came mainly from weak and desperate nomadic individuals or from small raiding parties. Jericho—an agricultural community in the Jordan Valley north of the Dead Sea, settled in part because of its celebrated spring,

which provides a thousand gallons of water every minute—is believed to have been the first town to build an encircling fortification, around the fifth millennium B.C.E. The town was surrounded by a stone circle and a massive tower, also of stone, that enabled lookouts to spot potential enemies long before they arrived. It is not currently known whether there were such fortifications in the Old Kingdom of Egypt, though fortifications on a large scale would certainly have required an advanced degree of political organization.

In an era when the principal weapons were spears, swords, and arrows, permanent fortifications were an effective defense against swift and vigorous frontal attack. The safest and most effective means of conquest was by siege: an attack on or blockade of a city or castle, in which the inhabitants would be starved, frightened, or bored into submission. The Trojan War (c. 1200-1100 B.C.E.) was basically a ten-year siege of Troy by the Greeks. Legend indicates that after such a long period of time, Troy would not have fallen but for the Greek stratagem of the Trojan horse. The Trojan horse was a large, hollow, wooden horse placed outside the Trojan gates. The Trojans were deceived into tearing down their own gates so that the horse, and the Greeks hidden within it, could enter.

The difficulty of a successful siege lay in maintaining an army in the field for a sustained length of time. Without regular supplies, the army laying siege would be compelled to withdraw, especially if the besieged party had, as in the case of Jericho, access to water and food. Even if the fortification could hold out, a siege might end if there were a betrayal, stirred by civil strife or bribery.

Assyrian reliefs show that by 850 B.C.E., the principles of fortress building were already in place. Portrayals of military camps of the period show them as round and reveal curtain walls, or protective walls between gates or bastions; loopholes, small holes for shooting arrows; parapets, guarding walls at the edge or terraces of a building; crenelation, or repeated depressed openings; strong, fortified gates; and towers or bastions, projections from the curtain walls. With all these defenses, no part of the wall went unobserved or undefended. As more and more of the world became civilized, city walls became regular parts of landscapes. Rare was the city, such as Sparta or Rome for a good part of its history, that could boast of its security with an absence of walls. It was a glaring indication of Rome's decline when, in the third century C.E., Aurelian built new walls for the imperial capital. When siege equipment, such as battering rams and catapults, came into use in the West, walls were thickened and made higher, and deeper moats were dug to provide further protection. Eventually, as better organization and more money became available, empires were able to construct monumental fortifications such as the Great Wall of China, built in the third century B.C.E. during the Qin (Ch'in) Dynasty (221-206 B.C.E.) and Hadrian's Wall in northern England, built on the orders of the Roman emperor Hadrian around 122-136 C.E. These fortifications were the greatest military structures of the ancient world.

AFRICA

Egypt is a land blessed with natural defenses. To the west of the Nile Valley lies the immense Libyan Desert, to the east, the Arabian Desert. To the south are the high rocky ledges of the Nile River cataracts and, to the north, the Mediterranean Sea. Beyond the cataracts to the south was Nubia, a land inhospitable to agriculture but valuable for its copper, gold, semiprecious stones, and exotic animals. Here, during the Middle Kingdom (c. 2000 B.C.E.), Egypt set up a system of forts to protect its conquests of Nubia. These fortifications stretched for 250 miles between the first and fourth cataracts and gave protection to the settled areas of both

river and desert. They were constructed close enough to one another that communication by fire or smoke signals was possible. The first forts, in Lower Nubia, close to the first cataract, seem to have been planned to support the agricultural communities living along the banks of the Nile; the later forts, in less civilized areas to the south, probably were established to serve as a military line marking the southern frontier of Egypt. Garrisons were maintained to administer, rule, and protect the populations, and perhaps also to intimidate them into continued submission to the central authority.

ASIA

Sumeria, the world's oldest known civilization, was located in southern Mesopotamia, the fertile land between the Tigris and Euphrates Rivers. The Sumerians created walled communities at the foothills of the Mesopotamian alluvial plain. By about 3000 B.C.E., the Sumerians were building independent cities, among which Ur, Uruk, and Kish were the most prominent. These cities did not at first have walls, perhaps suggesting an absence of warfare. However, peace did not last, and between 3100 and 2300 B.C.E.,

TURNING POINTS

c. 5000 B.C.E.	The city of Jericho becomes arguably the first town to be fortified with a stone wall.
1204-1194 B.C.E.	The fortified city of Troy is besieged by the Greeks for ten years and falls only after succumbing to the Greek deception tactic of the Trojan Horse placed outside the city's gates.
850 B.C.E.	The principles of fortress-building are evidenced in an Assyrian relief sculpture.
4th-3d cent. B.C.E.	Mediterranean city-states undertake massive building of walls during a period of warfare.
214 B.C.E.	Chinese emperor Qin Shuangdi orders that the many portions of the Great Wall be joined to form a unified boundary.
c. 122-136 C.E.	Hadrian's Wall is constructed in northern England, marking the northernmost border of Roman Empire.
370	Rome rebuilds its walls as protection against barbarian invasions.

The Great Wall of China, which traverses a distance of 4,160 kilometers and is the largest defensive barrier in the history of humankind, was built to defend China against Mongol invaders.

war seems to have been a regular part of life and death. By 2700 B.C.E., the city of Uruk had erected walls of about 5 miles in length. The Akkadian king Sargon (c. 2334-2279 B.C.E.), one of the first great Mesopotamian leaders, conquered Sumeria and upper Mesopotamia and may have organized the various fortified communities he encountered into an interconnected whole. Rock sculptures depicting Sargon's grandson Naram-Sin (c. 2261-2224 B.C.E.) seem to show well-defined fortifications, as well as some of the methods of siegecraft, particularly the breaching and scaling of city walls.

The ancient Mesopotamian city of Babylon, capital of the Babylonian Empire first established in the early eighteenth century B.C.E., serves as an excellent example of a city well fortified for defense. The ancient account by the historian Herodotus (c. 484-424

B.C.E.) tells of a wall 15 miles long, 85 feet thick, and 335 feet high, surrounded by a broad, deep moat. Queen Nitocris, he adds, altered the straight-flowing Euphrates so that boats sailing to Babylon would pass the city three times before flowing through a tunnel under the wall and into the city itself. The same queen diverted the river and excavated a huge lake in order to slow the river's course, again giving Babylonians time to prepare a defense. The Persian king Cyrus the Great (c. 601-590 to c. 530 B.C.E.) conquered the city by diverting the river from its course and then marching his soldiers over the drained riverbed and through the wall. A generation later, around 520 B.C.E., when Babylon rebelled against the Persian king Darius I the Great (550-486 B.C.E.) and appeared likely to withstand a protracted siege, the city was taken by trickery, when one of Darius's men, pretending to be a defector to Babylon, opened the gates to the Persians.

The walls of Babylon required immense size to resist siege engines, battering rams, scaling ladders, siege towers, and catapults. Powerful battering rams are depicted in a Mesopotamian palace relief sculpture dated to 883-859 B.C.E. A mobile siege tower has been dated to 745-727. The biblical book of Chronicles speaks of King Uziah's stone-throwing machines, which protected Jerusalem, although most historians believe this reference to be an anachronism inserted by a later writer. These sorts of weapons did not come into widespread use in Europe until the fourth century B.C.E.

Fortified cities appeared later in China than in Egypt, sometime during the Shang Dynasty (c. 1523-1027 B.C.E.). Because the land did not provide trees, earthen walls were used there instead. The Great Wall, perhaps the world's most famous fortification, was made by connecting many small, local walls that had been constructed previously by regional rulers. The line of the wall kept changing until, by the third century B.C.E., it lay on the border between the agricultural areas, where irrigation was possible, and the unsettled pastoral lands, where nomadic life predominated. The line of the wall varied as it moved north to enclose the Ordos plateau or extended toward the west to the Tibetan plateau. The wall was relocated as changes in climate, landscape, and population caused shifts in the frontier between civilized and uncivilized regions. In the end, the length of the wall, with all its extensions and branches, was nearly 4,000 miles.

The wall's purpose is ambiguous: It may have been principally to keep the population in or to keep marauders out. Only a wealthy and powerful bureaucracy could have afforded to build and maintain such a structure. Only a well-organized army would have dared to oppose it. That China did not rely on the wall for its sole defense is clear from the fact that the Chinese never tore down the walls around the cities where irrigated farming communities had developed. Yet the wall must have intimidated any nomads contemplating attacks upon the awesome might of the wall's builder.

EUROPE

The earliest defensive structures in Europe seem to have been built in about 2200 B.C.E. in Britain, perhaps as early agricultural communities began to wage war with one another for resources or political power. In Dorset, a gate with massive timber posts 5 feet across has been dated from this time.

The Greek city-states that developed during the barbarous period known as the Greek Dark Age (about 1100-900 B.C.E.) at first fortified only an acropolis, a citadel located on a hill used as a refuge in times of war. Poverty was surely the reason for the limited defense; walls were expensive, and a sparsely populated agricultural society would not have been able to afford them. In the flush of success after the Greco-Persian Wars, however, the Athenian general and statesman Themistocles (c. 524-c. 460 B.C.E.) persuaded his fellow Athenians to rebuild the city's walls and its harbor, known as the Piraeus. About three decades later, his successor, Pericles (c. 495-

AP/Wide World Photos

The remains of a Roman fort along Hadrian's Wall, showing a vaulted underground room, in Northumbria, England.

HADRIAN'S WALL IN ROMAN BRITAIN, C. 122-136 C.E.

Roman Place Names	Modern Cities
Camulodunum	Colchester
Deva	Dover
Eburacum	York
Isca Silurum	Caerleon, Wales
Lindum	Lincoln
Londinium	London
Verulamium	St. Albans

as strong as any found in later times. These fortresses possessed multiple walls that provided mutual cover, so that if the exterior walls were scaled by invading enemies, the enemies would find themselves trapped between the scaled exterior wall and additional interior walls.

The account by ancient Greek historian Thucydides (c. 459-402 B.C.E.) of the Spartan siege of Plataea (429-427 B.C.E.) is perhaps the most revealing ancient account of siege warfare before the adoption in Greece of sophisticated siege engines. It also illustrates the use of field fortifications. While the Plataeans themselves were enclosed behind their walls, the Spartans worked continuously for seventy days to put up a palisade, or fence of stakes, made from fruit trees. They added timber and laid it in a lattice to support a mound of wood, earth, and stones. For their part, the Plataeans built up their wall opposite the mound to a great height, protecting it with hides against hostile burning arrows. In addition, they pulled down part of the wall where the Spartan mound abutted so that they could carry its dirt into their city, thus forestalling the mound's growth. The Spartans took the countermeasure of twisting clay in wattles of reeds to prevent the soil from being carried away, and the Plataeans responded by digging a tunnel under their wall to the mound and using it to carry away more mound material. The Plataeans also built a crescent wall inside their outer wall, so that if the first wall were taken, the enemy would have to begin anew with a fresh mound. When some simple siege engines and an attempt to burn the city also failed, the Spartans built a wall, or circumvallation, around Plataea and left a small force to continue the siege. After two years, the Plataeans ran out of provisions and surrendered to the Spartans, who killed them all.

Macedonian conqueror Alexander the Great (356-323 B.C.E.) conducted at least twenty sieges during his conquests, succeeding under the most difficult of circumstances. His 332 B.C.E. victory at Tyre, an island fortress that he attacked by means of a mole constructed from the shore to the island, and that against Prince Ariamazes of Sogdiana, whose mountain fortress Alexander captured in 328 B.C.E. by means of mountaineers from above, are perhaps his most splen-

429 B.C.E.), persuaded them to build the Long Walls between Athens and the harbor, so that even during a long siege the city would have access to supplies from the sea. Battles in Greece traditionally had been fought outside the cities. However, during the Peloponnesian Wars (431-404 B.C.E.) and increasingly throughout the fourth century B.C.E., cities themselves were targeted directly. Throughout the Hellenic world, cities used their wealth to expand their fortifications, so that by the third century B.C.E., places such as Rhodes and Pergamum had fortresses

did triumphs over seemingly insurmountable fortifications.

In Roman mythology, Romulus and Remus, the twin sons of Mars, the Roman god of war, founded the city of Rome. After a quarrel, Romulus supposedly killed Remus and built walls around the city. However, whatever walls Rome may have had in its early period were insufficient to keep out the Celts, who sacked the city in 390 B.C.E. Although this attack may have had a psychological impact on the city of Rome, it seems to have had no major political results. A few years later, the Romans built a massive wall, parts of which still stand. As Rome grew, however, it gave up its walls, so proud of its might and its policy of offensive preemptive strikes against enemies that it felt no need to fortify the city. During the Empire, Rome rarely faced enemies capable of organizing the siegecraft and supplies that would allow them to undertake long sieges against the well-stocked Roman garrisons. The would-be challengers functioned at little more than a tribal level and could not afford fortifications that would have been able to withstand the imperial army.

Toward the end of the third century C.E., Emperor Aurelian (c. 215-275) fortified Rome with a wall 12 miles around and 40 feet high, a structure that no doubt protected the citizens against the increasingly frequent barbarian forays into Roman territory, but the perceived need of which foreshadowed the precarious state of the Roman Empire. Cities in Gaul and Spain were also fortified with walls from this time, though at a fairly slow pace. Rome accelerated its building of chains of forts along the North Sea and Atlantic coasts, but when these frontier defenses were overcome by the Huns, the empire lay vulnerable.

To maintain their empire, the Romans built a system of forts, first in open territory, for the purpose of controlling the surrounding countryside, and later on hilltops where there were extensive views for keeping watch. It is likely that a coherent imperial policy dictated a standard form of forts and their distances from one another. In general, Rome used a cordon system of forts and watchtowers without running barriers.

It is believed that a Roman army on the march erected a temporary camp every night. As part of their individual equipment, soldiers carried stakes with which to construct a palisade on top of a bank of earth, which was made by digging a ditch around the camp and piling the earth on the inside perimeter. Although Flavius Vegetius Renatus, a late fourth century C.E. Roman military theorist, lamented in his time the fact that soldiers no longer carried the tools or were trained to construct such camps, by Vegetius's time, Rome's military was used primarily for defense and its system of permanent forts was already in place.

THE AMERICAS

The principal weapons used in the Mayan lowlands, which were populated as early as 1000 B.C.E., seem to have been spears, though clubs and knives were also used. Because these weapons did not pose the same dangers as did arrows or other projectiles, Mesoamerican fortifications did not need overlapping fields of vision. Thus, walls projecting outward from the main fortress—an identifying characteristic of forts in Europe and Asia—were unnecessary. As a result, it is at times difficult to identify certain archaeological sites as fortifications. What appear from the bottom of a mountain looking upward to be walled fortifications may appear from above to be terraced retaining walls. One might wonder whether the appearance as a fortification was designed to discourage would-be attackers or merely was a result of construction methods and topology. Although these questions cannot be answered, freestanding walls with moats in front of them do suggest strongly that these structures were fortifications. The fighting among early American peoples was intense and continuous, and its aim seems to have been, not the death, but the capture of the enemy for sacrificial purposes.

Before 600 B.C.E., there do not seem to have been major permanent fortifications, but, from 600 to 300 B.C.E., as dispersed settlements were replaced by larger societies, more hilltop sites were constructed. Lowland fortifications, generally embankments surrounded by ditches, seem not to have been very intimidating structures, but perhaps were adequate to the military requirements of those early periods. Inhabitants of Mexico's Valley of Oaxaca developed probably the most complex Mesoamerican culture in the centuries before the Christian era. Its religious center, Monte Albán, rose on a series of hills. Monte Albán was fortified around 200 B.C.E. with an earthen wall of 1.8 miles, a height of between 10 and 13 feet, and a width at its greatest of 60 feet. A large reservoir was also built that could hold enough water to sustain a siege of several years. In short, it was a structure that was as well suited for its purposes as some of the contemporaneous fortresses elsewhere in the world.

BOOKS AND ARTICLES

Brice, Martin Hubert. *Forts and Fortresses: From the Hillforts of Prehistory to Modern Times, the Definitive Visual Account of the Science of Fortification.* New York: Facts On File, 1990.

Ferrill, Arther. *The Origins of War.* Rev. ed. Boulder, Colo.: Westview Press, 1997.

Johnson, A. *Roman Forts of the First and Second Centuries A.D. in Britain and the German Provinces.* New York: St. Martin's Press, 1983.

Johnson, Stephen. *The Roman Forts of the Saxon Shore.* New York: St. Martin's Press, 1976.

Konstam, Angus. *The Forts of Celtic Britain.* Illustrated by Peter Bull. Botley, Oxford, England: Osprey, 2006.

McNicoll, A. *Hellenistic Fortifications from the Aegean to the Euphrates.* Oxford, England: Clarendon Press, 1997.

Rocca, Samuel. *The Forts of Judaea, 168 B.C.-A.D. 73: From the Maccabees to the Fall of Masada.* Illustrated by Adam Hook. Botley, Oxford, England: Osprey, 2008.

Southern, P., and K. R. Dixon. *The Late Roman Army.* New Haven, Conn.: Yale University Press, 1996.

Toy, Sidney. *A History of Fortification from 3000 B.C. to A.D. 1700.* London: Heinemann, 1955.

Waldron, Arthur. *The Great Wall of China: From History to Myth.* New York: Cambridge University Press, 1989.

Winter, F. E. *Greek Fortifications.* Toronto: University of Toronto Press, 1971.

FILMS AND OTHER MEDIA

Arms in Action: Castles and Sieges. Documentary. History Channel, 1999.

Hadrian's Wall: Edge of the Empire. Documentary. Cromwell Productions, 1999.

Modern Marvels: Forts. Documentary. History Channel, 2006.

Modern Marvels: The Great Wall of China. Documentary. History Channel, 2005.

James A. Arieti

MEDIEVAL FORTIFICATIONS
Dates: c. 500-1500 C.E.

NATURE AND USE

In even the earliest and most primitive societies, the need to stave off attackers led to the construction of defensive physical structures. The variety of such responses naturally became ever more diverse as groups worldwide had to meet the intersecting challenges of the foe, their own resources, climatic and geographical constraints, and anticipated forms of organized violence. Fortification is thus any construction, permanent or transitory, earthen, organic, or stone, designed to shield defenders from an attacker while those defenders either await help or resist assaults themselves. Even with the rather limitless bounds of human ingenuity, fortifications nonetheless tend to fall within four somewhat interrelated categories: refuges, strongholds, fortified lines or zones, and urban walls.

DEVELOPMENT

By 500 C.E., each type of fortification had appeared numerous times in human conflicts. A stronghold differs from a refuge in that it is a place that hosts an active defense; from its walls, defenders may launch offensive sallies. The refuge, by contrast, is primarily defensive, a place to wait out the enemy in such a position of strength that the enemy will forgo the costs of attack. The final types of military architecture are even less distinct; city walls are in one sense fortified lines. Here, though, the concern is with those fortified zones meant to secure the peace of whole regions.

All types appeared concurrently and in overlapping cycles of need and development worldwide before Europe's medieval period. The Roman Empire had its own strategic mix of city walls, fortified frontiers, and the near-instant fortress otherwise known as an encamped army. After the Empire's fall in Western Europe, its legacy continued in the walls that surrounded many cities, the fortified zones of northern England and the Rhine and Danube Rivers, and the defenses of Constantinople, which stymied and stupefied many an invader. In Asia the tradition of long walls was already centuries old, having been initiated by the first Qin emperor in 221 B.C.E. In the Americas, the lack of metallic technology severely constrained the forms warfare might take; moreover, the earliest Mayan societies may well have not had, in the traditional Western sense, cities to defend. In sub-Saharan Africa and Australasia, the archaeologi-

TIME LINE

c. 757-796	Offa's Dyke is built in the kingdom of Mercia to protect the kingdom's Welsh border.
880's	King Alfred the Great begins constructing a series of *burhs*, or garrisons, to defend Wessex from Vikings.
990's	The first stone keeps appear in northwestern Europe.
1066	Rapid proliferation of motte-and-bailey castles follows the Norman Conquest of England.
1196-1198	King Richard I of England builds Château Gaillard with three baileys, which had to be captured before the castle could be taken, serving as multiple lines of defense.
1277-1297	King Edward I of England builds a series of ten Welsh castles, with an implicitly offensive function as continuances of the king's campaigns.
1494	Charles VIII's invasion of Italy confirms the obsolescence of high medieval defenses.

cal record has been less forthcoming. Doubtless, the inhabitants shaped earth as needed into ditches and ramparts, the latter surmounted even today by thorny hedges, known as *bomas* or *zarebas*, to keep out predators.

FORTIFIED LINES

Despite the remaining fortifications that surrounded them, the Europeans of the Germanic West had difficulty reaching the level of defensive sophistication of the Roman Empire. Even with the extant physical reminders of the Roman fortified lines, especially Hadrian's Wall in Britain, they declined to maintain such lines and delayed a long time building their own. Perhaps they saw little point to such defenses, which had failed to keep them out of the Roman heartlands. The permeability of such zones has raised a number of debates as to their real purpose, and whether they were meant to prevent invasion, to slow invaders, or to keep internal populations within limits. The Saxons, who invaded Britain after the 450's, found the defenses of the Saxon Shore did little to slow their conquest. To the north Hadrian's Wall likewise hindered the Picts little in their raids.

Hadrian's Wall stretched for 117 kilometers across northern England, ranging in thickness from 2.3 to 3 meters and averaging a height of from 5 to 6 meters. The wall was part of the Roman strategy of defense in depth. In the absence of manned watchtowers and fortified camps to the rear, the Saxons were hardly set to use the wall to its best advantage. Even so, the wall did form, in its less than pristine state, something of a hindrance to the return of raiders northward. Northumbrian pursuers could count on it slowing marauders if those raiders tried to get their spoils through or over the fortifications.

It would appear that Offa's Dyke, built during the reign (757-796) of that Mercian king, was meant to achieve an effect along the Welsh border similar to that of Hadrian's Wall. An earthen rampart 18 meters wide formed in part by the ditches that bracket it, Offa's Dyke meandered for 192 kilometers through regions that had little in the way of leftover Roman defenses or roads. There was little hope of keeping out

Welsh raiders, especially since the dyke was virtually unmanned. Again, though, its physical bulk would slow the exodus of such raiders, especially if they were driving stolen livestock, permitting Mercian forces to catch up with the marauders. In addition, the dyke provided a roadway that cut across the ranges and rivers of the Welsh marches, thus easing both the report of such raids and the speed of reaction.

The impassability of terrain might make fortified lines not only a cost-prohibitive measure but also a rather unnecessary one. In Mesoamerica contending empires could keep invaders at bay simply by blocking well-established paths. In the absence of siege equipment and draft animals, such structures would not have needed much complexity to be effective. In Europe fortified bridges developed not only to secure lines of communication and transport but also to block the progress of Viking raiders up the river systems. Thus a number of such bridges controlled the rivers below Paris after the 880's to prevent direct access or indirect efforts by portage. When Vikings actually did besiege Paris in 885, it took them over four months just to reach the city.

The most famous and latest of all fortified lines are of course those of China. The Great Wall is not actually a single wall curling along China's northern borders, nor does its current condition date back to 221 B.C.E. The earliest (Qin) walls were earthen, tamped down by forced labor between retaining wooden walls that connected watchtowers. The actual remains of this wall are now in the realm of conjecture. The current masonry walls—which are actually many sets of walls, not always connected, and not one continuous line—date from the Ming Dynasty (1368-1644) emperors, who reigned after the expulsion of the Mongol Dynasty. The facts of these fortifications are impressive: 2,400 kilometers in length, 7.6 meters high at a minimum, often 9 meters wide, and sometimes scaling 70-degree slopes. Like their European counterparts, however, they proved less than impermeable, again raising the question of whether the walls were more clearly intended to keep the native population contained within and untainted by exterior contact.

As the Germanic groups, especially the Franks, entered the deteriorating Roman Empire, they brought a new structure to the landscape: the private fortress. Although these small refuges, which utilized so little stone, have left few archaeological remains, contemporaries noted their appearance in rural and isolated areas. Most important, commentators of the day stressed the remoteness or inaccessibility of such sites. Because of the new inhabitants' rudimentary technology, these protocastles relied on their physical surroundings to deter would-be invaders. On isolated summits, crowning precipitous sites, these forts gave some protection to the rural regions of Gaul and Visigothic Spain; their small size and private ownership, however, limited their value as refuges for a harried populace. Instead, the later Frankish kings found them to be troublesome centers of resistance, because it was so difficult to bring an army to bear on such places.

The situation differed in eighth and ninth century Anglo-Saxon England, especially Wessex. By the 870's, after Viking invaders had occupied much of England and pushed into Wessex, King Alfred the Great (r. 871-899) secured a truce after his victory at Edington (878). During the cessation of active campaigning, Alfred devised a sophisticated defensive strategy centered upon thirty-three refuges. These *burhs*, as they were called, were scattered over the kingdom, seldom more than a day's ride apart, and usually near major transportation routes. Often quite sizable and well provisioned, the burhs were meant both to house a large garrison and to provide ample room into which a refugee population might flee. Alfred's strategy, which would prove successful in 896, was to have

The twelfth century attack and defense of a city wall, with numerous types of siege engines in use.

the population and movable wealth protected in the burhs while he shadowed the invading Vikings with the Wessex army. By hampering the Vikings' ability to forage or pillage, Alfred simply made his kingdom an uninviting prospect to Viking plunderers.

These fortifications did not have to be terribly complex, because the Vikings had little in the way of siege weaponry. Nonetheless, Alfred's administration prepared the burhs well, as is known from a document called the *Burghal Hidage* (c. 920), which lists them. By dividing the resources of the kingdom into units called hides, each of which was sufficient to provide one man for burh garrisons, the Anglo-Saxons assigned enough hides to each burh to assure that its walls were defended by one man for every 1.3 meters. Because some burhs had circumferences of over one mile, this meant that Viking invaders had to sense the sizable numbers of uncowed foes they left in their wake as they bypassed the burhs. The burhs themselves were formidable: The first barrier was an exterior ditch perhaps more than 30 meters wide and sometimes as deep as 8 meters; an earthen bank came next, reaching up to 3 meters in height; timber defenses surmounted this ringwork in most cases, but stone walls were put in place at major sites, especially those that housed the royal mints. Many burhs took advantage of natural defenses, such as swamps and rivers, whereas others were built upon the remains of previous Roman fortifications.

The advantages offered by burhs or even the most simple defenses naturally drew people to those fortified locales. This rationale appears to explain the growth of the stone enclosures at Great Zimbabwe centuries later. The original impetus for the southern African plateau's settlement remains debated, but the availability of iron doubtless held part of the appeal. At all three parts of the site, the most restricted sites are those where archaeology has found iron stores or iron-working tools. Between 1100 and 1500, the Great Enclosure was built, with walls of quarried granite about 10 meters and without any mortar, encompassing first a hilltop and later a site across a small valley. Early in the twentieth century, the archaeological record at Great Zimbabwe was greatly altered or nearly destroyed, and the reason for the site's abandonment by 1700 is unknown. However, no one has supposed a victory by besiegers.

STRONGHOLDS

The transition in Europe from simple refuges to castles came with the motte-and-bailey structure, whose origins lie in the tenth and eleventh centuries. The heart of this fortification was the motte, a steeply conical mound surrounded by a ditch and crowned by a timber palisade. Within this enclosure, a wooden tower originally rose, most often on stilts. The bailey was a secondary enclosure at the base of the motte, somewhat kidney-shaped as it fit alongside the motte. Separated from the motte by ditches and protected by its own palisade and ditches, the bailey formed a living area and an extra line of defense. From the bailey, a bridge either spanned the ditch on a more convenient gradient to the motte's gate or reached only to steps cut into the motte's steep slope. If the bailey became lost to attackers, the bridge was easily disposable. The quick proliferation of the motte-and-bailey lay in its most basic advantage: It provided a maximum amount of defense at the lowest cost of construction. Moreover, it was possible to build one within days.

In addition to its defensive capabilities, the motte-and-bailey had an offensive potential. As an easily built, forward base for troops, mottes were useful in subduing hostile regions. One of the earliest builders of mottes, Fulk III (c. 970-1040), the count of Anjou, used castles to push his borders farther toward Normandy. In turn, the Normans learned from this tactic and applied it most dramatically in the conquest of England. William the Conqueror (c. 1027-1087) built motte-style fortifications immediately upon his arrival in England, a fact graphically illustrated in the Bayeux tapestry. After his victory at the Battle of Hastings (1066), William and his chief followers brought the whole of England under control by establishing motte castles at crucial points throughout the kingdom. After the transition to stone castles became widespread in the twelfth century, many mottes did not have the stability to support massive keeps as replacements for the wooden towers. Instead, the palisade was rebuilt as a "shell keep," so that the weight of the new masonry was dispersed over the mound.

Although the use of timber castles continued into the thirteenth century, the transition to stone appears to have begun in the late tenth or early eleventh century, owing in part to the innovations of Fulk III. Some scholars have convincingly argued that the bulky, rectangular towers at Langeais and Montbazon, reaching to 16 and 30 meters high respectively, were Fulk's constructions and that Fulk may well have been responsible for a number of other stone castles in the region. Not surprisingly, many of the stone castles surrounding Anjou date from soon after this period, as Fulk's rivals and successors imitated his new building program. These new keeps, or donjons, were massive, multistoried edifices that could house many troops. Fulk's two towers had walls between 1.5 and 3 meters thick and up to 30 meters high. The White Tower in London, begun by William the Conqueror, had walls as thick as 4.5 meters and as tall as 27 meters, with the corner turrets reaching above that height. It comprised 30 square meters, and the keep at Colchester was even larger.

The new preference for such expensive and mammoth constructions physically reflected the increasing wealth of the feudal nobility as principalities such as Anjou, Normandy, and of course, England, stabilized. The ability of these lords to command greater resources also meant they could put better-equipped armies into the field. Thus the siege weapons of antiquity, which had never completely been forgotten, began reappearing: battering rams, ballistae, onagers, and later, the trebuchet, as well as the old standby, fire. Successful defense against these weapons required the use of stone. The spread of castles was dramatic: The French province of Poitou had only three castles before the Viking incursions, but at least thirty-nine castles dotted the province by 1100. No archaeological evidence has been found of castles in the northwestern region of Maine before 900; two centuries later there were sixty-two. Other regions saw similar levels of castle-building. Such numbers do not take into account fortified residences, which lacked the defensive power of castles.

The intensified wealth and warfare of Europe did not account alone for the spread of more sophisticated defenses; inspiration came also from Constantinople and the Muslim fortresses taken only with the greatest effort during the First Crusade (1095-1099).

The earliest castles that the Crusaders built were the rectangular keeps to which they had been accustomed in Europe, but the needs of these exposed states and sites soon mandated a change. Larger complexes became the rule in order to house both greater garrisons and the supplies necessary so that such a force could hold out, possibly for years, until relief could arrive from other allies or from Europe. Saphet had a garrison of between 1,650 and 2,000 men, while Margat's 1,000 defenders were supposed to be able to hold out for five years; the cisterns at Sahyun held ten million liters of water. These fortresses reflected Byzantine reliance on high, massive walls studded with towers to provide enfilading fire. These walls could actually be built more quickly than one of the rectangular keeps; moreover, they provided space for vitally necessary cisterns and reservoirs. Some castles still had keeps, but these were a final defensive point rather than the primary one.

The most famous of the Crusader castles is Krak des Chevaliers, which remains impressive even in its ruined state. Occupying a hilltop in Syria that had formerly been a Muslim stronghold, it began with the advantage of difficult access. Its outer wall was added in the 1200's even as the inner defenses were strengthened. This wall encompassed an area of 210 by 140 meters and had both semicircular towers and machicolations, or openings in the overhanging battlements that protected defenders who fired missiles, rolled stones, or dropped combustibles upon attackers at the wall's base. In forested Europe machicolations were only slowly adopted, because wooden overhangs, or hoardings, were so easily built for the same purpose. The higher inner circuit of walls could complement the outer defense with missile fire. Two towers flanked the small gate, which gave access either to the forecourt or to a series of gateways that protected the entrance into the fortress proper. The inner wall, or *enceinte*, was anchored by five large towers. In addition to these defenses, a massive talus, or sloped base, made the walls on the southern and eastern sides virtually impervious to mining and scaling ladders. Apart from its defensive function, the castle's increased lower bulk also protected Krak des Chevalier from the earthquakes that had damaged it in the mid-twelfth century. In later centuries, Japanese castles would also contend with natural catastrophe. Below the talus was an artificial reservoir, and granaries and armories lined the walls. Little wonder, then, that the Mamlūk armies that took Krak in 1271 opted to trick the defenders into surrendering rather than risk an unsuccessful siege.

The lessons learned in the Middle East soon wrought changes in the structure of castles in Europe. Circular towers came to predominate, as castle builders realized that square angles gave attackers extra blind spots to exploit; more important, curved surfaces resisted the projectiles of pregunpowder artillery better than flat ones. King Richard I (1157-1199) of England, also known as Richard the Lion-Heart, would apply this principle liberally at his "saucy cas-

tle," the Château Gaillard, where the exterior wall of the inner bailey had a rippled surface. Although keeps continued to be built, including the huge circular donjon at Coucy, which was 31 meters in diameter, the emphasis moved to multiple lines of defense. Gaillard had three baileys to be captured before attackers faced the keep. Barbicans appeared as new fortifications in front of gateways that provided further fire support for this weakest point in a wall. Concentric walls, with the second overtopping the first considerably, became the new fashion in fortification; towers often broke the continuity of such wall-walks so that one portion of the walls could be lost without losing the entire circuit.

The most distinctive examples of concentric cas-

Krak des Chevaliers, in modern Syria, the most famous of the Crusader castles.

tles were Edward I's (1239-1307) Welsh castles, ten fortresses built between 1277 and 1297. Like their motte-and-bailey predecessors and the Crusader outposts, they had an implicitly offensive function, as their dominating presence and garrisons were meant as continuances of the English king's campaigns. Edward turned primarily to Master James of St. George, a Savoyard architect, to oversee the project. The show of strength may have been as much in the swift construction of the expensive castles as in the high curtain walls pierced with arrow slits, protective drum towers at each angle, and heavily defended gateways. Only one of these castles had a keep, so the emphasis was on the concentric walls. The inner walls loomed high over the outer walls, so that defenders could fire missiles from both. At Harlech and Beaumaris, the successive gates were sandwiched between flanking towers, whereas the entry itself went through a passage. Attackers within the passage would find themselves at the mercy of archers firing through *meurtrières*, or murder-holes.

Although castles would appear during Japan's Sengoku, or Warring States, period (1477-1601), they differed markedly from European models in both geographical and cultural considerations. A typical *hirojiro*, or lowland fortress, had a broad stone base with a curving face which, it was hoped, would offset the threats of earthquake or rain-sodden soil giving way. The towering superstructures above this foundation were actually lightweight wood and plaster, again so built as to survive repeated tremors. Despite the immensity and complexity of Japanese castles, they were rarely the focus of battle, because samurai preferred to display their prowess in the field against individual foes. Such battles also had the advantage of leaving intact buildings to the victor. The Japanese reluctance to adopt Western styles of warfare also meant that artillery had a minimal impact on Japanese castles until the 1800's.

In very different circumstances, the Maoris of New Zealand likewise showed a predilection for ritual combat and the preservation of defenses. The Maori *pa*, the first evidences of which date to 900, seem similar to the motte-and-bailey. At their height, such strongholds often occupied hilltops with difficult access; a wooden palisade surrounded the summit, with ditches in front and embankments within that allowed defenders to hurl weapons upon attackers. The wall was regularly pierced with openings, so defenders could jab spears at those trying to scale the palisade. Close by was a less fortified village whose residents would retreat into the pa when warned by alarms. Long sieges, however, were rare. Attackers would challenge defenders to come out before the pa and engage in single or group combat. If the defenders declined, then a frontal assault might ensue, with the intent of capturing without destroying the fortification and its supplies.

WALLED CITIES

The defensive importance of cities marked both the beginning and the end of the medieval period. The Romans left a legacy of urban fortification: In Gaul alone, nearly 90 of the 115 cities received new walls, smaller in circumference but imposing still with their 10-meter height, 4-meter width, and foundations reaching from 4 to 5 meters underground. These defenses usually withstood Germanic assaults with ease but were rendered irrelevant if the walls were breached by trickery or treachery. Although rare, a long siege likewise could succeed by starving towns into submission. These conditions held true throughout the Merovingian period also, and one is reminded that the Crusaders only gained Antioch through bribery. During the Carolingian period, defenses were often neglected or even quarried for other projects, but repairs began anew with the Viking invasions. As towns grew in wealth and population from the 1100's onward, they had to erect new defenses to safeguard both. This would occur all over Europe, but the most striking example may well be the double curtain at Carcassonne, in southern France, which incorporated lessons learned from the cities of the eastern Mediterranean.

The techniques adopted by European cities may be highlighted by comparison with contemporary settlements in Mesoamerica. Maya centers show remarkable stonework, but it appears that these sites functioned more as royal residences and religious sites than as economic centers. Thus, the majority remained unfortified. Other sites, such as Becán or Mayapán, did have enclosing ditches, large embankments, and wooden palisades, and a few had stone walls topped again by palisades. Sometimes these defensive lines surrounded only core areas of the city. In all cases, however, this military architecture remained rather simple, because besiegers could bring so little weaponry to bear against it.

In Europe, though, the pendulum of innovation was already swinging away from the high walls of concentric castles and cities. Gunpowder artillery may have been present by 1340, and it made itself felt at the Siege of Calais from 1346 to 1347. Gunpowder weapons became increasingly refined, until they became the primary means of siege warfare. In the early 1400's the English used them successfully against both Scottish and French cities. More dramatically, in 1453 the land walls of Constantinople were breached by Turkish bombards after a millennium of successful defense. The high walls of medieval fortification were now considered a liability, but they could not easily be abandoned. At first, many curtain walls were pierced to admit cannons to be fired outward, but this had limited success. Outworks began to appear so that defenders could keep besiegers distant with their own cannons. These low-profile embankments foreshadowed the future of fortification. Military architects began to propose a new style of defense: low-profile, wide walls that could hold artillery, even wider ditches to distance besieging artillery, and still more outworks, or bastions, to provide flanking fire. Italian cities were the first to adopt this new form of siege warfare. When French king Charles VIII (1470-1498) invaded Italy in 1494, his artillery made a shambles of the medieval defenses in his way, and the Italians adopted the new techniques.

BOOKS AND ARTICLES

Brice, Martin Hubert. *Forts and Fortresses: From the Hillforts of Prehistory to Modern Times, the Definitive Visual Account of the Science of Fortification.* New York: Facts On File, 1990.

DeVries, Kelly. *Medieval Military Technology.* Lewiston, N.Y.: Broadview Press, 1992.

Higham, Robert, and Philip Barker. *Timber Castles.* London: Batsford, 1992.

Hill, David, and Alexander R. Rumble, eds. *The Defence of Wessex: The Burghal Hidage and Anglo-Saxon Fortifications.* New York: St. Martin's Press, 1996.

Jones, Richard L. C. "Fortifications and Sieges in Western Europe, c. 800-1450." In *Medieval Warfare: A History*, edited by Maurice Keen. New York: Oxford University Press, 1999.

Kaufmann, J. E., and H. W. Kaufmann. *The Medieval Fortress: Castles, Forts, and Walled Cities of the Middle Ages.* New York: Da Capo Press, 2004.

Kenyon, John. *Medieval Fortifications.* New York: St. Martin's Press, 1990.

Konstam, Angus. *British Forts in the Age of Arthur.* Illustrated by Peter Dennis. Botley, Oxford, England: Osprey, 2008.

Lepage, Jean-Denis. *Castles and Fortified Cities of Medieval Europe: An Illustrated History.* Jefferson, N.C.: McFarland, 2002.

Nosov, Konstantin S. *Medieval Russian Fortresses, A.D. 862-1480.* Illustrated by Peter Dennis. Botley, Oxford, England: Osprey, 2007.

Rogers, Randall. *Latin Siege Warfare in the Twelfth Century.* Oxford, England: Clarendon Press, 1992.

FILMS AND OTHER MEDIA

Arms in Action: Castles and Sieges. Documentary. History Channel, 1999.

Castle. Documentary. Public Broadcasting Service, 2000.

Nova: Medieval Siege. Documentary. Public Broadcasting Service, 2004.

Steven Isaac

SIEGES AND SIEGECRAFT
ANCIENT AND MEDIEVAL
Dates: c. 7000 B.C.E.-1500 C.E.

NATURE AND USE

Siege warfare is the art of taking a fort or fortified city. In a passive siege, the besiegers attempted to starve the defenders by sealing off the city or fort from the outside world by circumvallation, which means encircling with a wall or rampart. Active siege tactics assaulted the fortifications by attempting to go over, through, or under the wall. The main weapons and tools for an active siege were ladders for climbing walls, drills and battering rams for punching through walls, and spades for undermining walls. Catapults and siege towers provided support.

Fortifications go back at least to Neolithic times. Seven thousand years B.C.E., the inhabitants of Jericho constructed massive fortifications that included a stone wall 3 meters thick and 4 meters high, a moat 3 meters deep and 9 meters wide, and a stone tower 8.5 meters high and 10 meters in diameter. By the time of the early civilizations in Mesopotamia and Egypt, the art of fortification had already been well developed. Walls featured balconies that allowed defenders to shoot straight down at the enemy, as well as towers and bastions from which defenders could rake besiegers with flanking fire. Gates were the most vulnerable points in a wall, and ancient architects spared no effort to secure them. Pilasters, bastions, towers, and balconies protected them. Metal plating covered the gates to prevent fire. Narrow, winding entryways made it more difficult for attackers to enter the city if they succeeded in breaking through the gate.

Although besiegers undoubtedly circumvallated cities almost from the beginning of siege warfare, the ancient Greek historian Thucydides (c. 459-402 B.C.E.) provides the first detailed account of the construction of a wall of circumvallation in the Siege of Plataea by Sparta and Thebes (429-427 B.C.E.) at the beginning of the Peloponnesian War (431-404 B.C.E.). A mile in circumference, it was a double wall

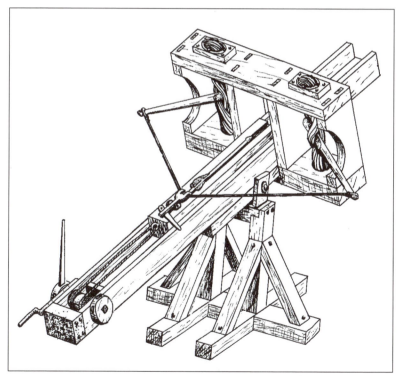

The Roman ballista, circa 50 B.C.E., a two-armed torsion weapon used to hurl large arrows or stones.

with space between in which to quarter troops. It took two and a half months to build. Battlements and towers strengthened the wall, and the digging of clay for the bricks left a moat on both sides. Plataea was thoroughly isolated but it held out for two and one-half years, revealing the weakness of passive sieges.

To shorten sieges, more aggressive methods were necessary. Escalade, or scaling, was perhaps the earliest means of overcoming fortified walls. A twenty-seventh century B.C.E. Egyptian wall painting at Dehashe shows soldiers trying to pry the gate open with poles while assault teams attack the wall with scaling ladders and archers attempt to drive the defenders from the wall. Escalade was not effective, however, against walls higher than 10 meters. The long ladders needed to scale greater heights were unwieldy and collapsed under the weight of too many soldiers climbing them.

Because walls in ancient Egypt and Mesopotamia rose as high as 20 meters, means other than escalade were necessary to assault them, and battering rams soon came into use. An Egyptian palette dating from around 3000 B.C.E. shows creatures that may be symbolic of battering rams attacking a wall. More clearly, a twentieth century B.C.E. Egyptian wall painting depicting a siege shows three men protected by a mobile hut using a long beam to pry stones from the wall. By the eighteenth century B.C.E. the Assyrians were deploying battering rams in integrated assault tactics that included the use of not only rams but also siege towers, siege ramps, and sapping, a method of undermining walls. Lack of remaining evidence precludes a clear picture of the earliest Assyrian rams, which were probably prying devices used to dislodge bricks from walls. It is not until the Neo-Assyrian Empire in the ninth century B.C.E. that Assyrian rams are seen in palace wall paintings. Assyrian emperor Ashurnasirpal II (r. 883-859 B.C.E.) deployed huge rams that required six wheels for support. A domed turret from which archers could fire protected the front of the ram, and wicker shields also covered the sides and front. The machine was about 5 meters long and from 2 to 3 meters high. The battering pole hung like a pendulum from a rope attached to the roof. It had a metal blade at the end, which the crew could jam between bricks to pry them loose from the wall.

The wheels provided mobility, but the ram was so heavy it was difficult to maneuver. Future Assyrian emperors sacrificed weight for mobility, but Tiglath-pileser III (r. 745-727 B.C.E.) used lighter four-wheeled rams that were more maneuverable.

Siege towers were in use in both Egypt and Mesopotamia at least by the early second millennium B.C.E. They rested on wheels or rollers and could be pushed forward into position, providing a means of crossing the wall by dropping a boarding bridge from the tower to the wall. They also gave archers and slingers a better angle of fire to drive the defenders off the wall.

The construction of siege ramps goes back to the third millennium B.C.E. Siege ramps helped attackers cross walls and provided a means of bringing battering rams across moats, outer walls, or slopes at the base of the wall known as glacis. They allowed attackers to attack the wall toward the top, where it was thinner than at the base. Ancient Babylonian mathematics problems show that engineers could calculate how long it would take them to construct a ramp. If these problems reflect reality, the Babylonians could build a ramp to the top of a 22-meter wall in five days with 9,500 men working at the task.

By at least the early second millennium B.C.E. Mesopotamian engineers had developed the art of collapsing walls by sapping. Sapping involved either boring through a wall or undermining it. To undermine a wall, sappers dug a tunnel and then set the support beams on fire to collapse both the tunnel and the wall above. The depth of the tunnel had to be exactly right; if it was too shallow, the weight of the wall might collapse the tunnel on top of the sappers, if it was too deep, it would not collapse when the support beams were burned.

The Assyrians were the first to develop tactically integrated siege armies. Siege warfare was like a giant construction project. The construction of siege towers and siege ramps and the undermining of walls required large amounts of manpower and the ability to organize labor. Assyrian siege armies deployed a variety of skilled troops—sappers, archers, slingers, assault troops, and battering ram crews—and Assyrian commanders knew how to coordinate them toward a common tactical purpose.

DEVELOPMENT

The most important development in siege warfare was the invention of the catapult. The first catapult was probably invented by an unknown craftsman under the employ of the Greek tyrant Dionysius I of Syracuse (r. 405-367 B.C.E.). Dionysius had brought a large number of craftsmen from Sicily, Italy, and Greece to Syracuse to manufacture arms for his war against the Carthaginians in Sicily. One of them devised the *gastraphetes*, or belly bow, which is considered the first catapult. The archer could, by bracing the bow against his stomach, use both hands to pull back a slider with more strength than he could muster with one arm. A trigger, when pulled, then released the arrow. These catapults helped Dionysius take the city of Motya, a formidable Carthaginian stronghold on the west coast of Sicily, in 397 B.C.E. It is probable that winches were added to the gastraphetes early on to pull back the slider with mechanical power.

The next step in the development of catapults was the application of torsion power in which ropes were wound tightly with a windlass. The sudden release of the tension released a powerful burst of energy. Little is known about the origins of the torsion catapult. The Macedonian king Philip II (382-336 B.C.E.) used arrow-shooting torsion catapults that may have been invented by his engineers. Philip's son Alexander the Great (356-323 B.C.E.) deployed stone-throwing torsion catapults in the Siege of Halicarnassus in 334 B.C.E. Catapults more often strengthened the defense than the offense. For example, in the Roman Siege of Syracuse in 213 B.C.E. the Syracusans used catapults of various sizes to keep Roman ships away from their walls.

In Hellenistic times, siege warfare became more technical and the equipment more complicated. The Macedonian commander Demetrius

Poliorcetes (336-283 B.C.E.) employed a huge siege tower called a *helepolis*, literally translated as "taker of cities," at the Siege of Rhodes in 305 B.C.E. Protected by iron plates, the tower rose nine stories and was large enough to carry catapults. Twelve hundred men pushed it forward on its eight iron-rimmed wheels. The helepolis provided cover for two gigantic rams. When the helepolis advanced, the Rhodians were able to knock loose some of its iron plating with stone-throwing catapults and set it on fire with flaming arrows shot from catapults. After repairs, Demetrius attacked again. The huge rams did batter down a part of the Rhodian wall, but Demetrius failed to take the city and, in the end, his acceptance of a negotiated end to the siege was a testimony to the difficulty of capturing a well-defended city.

Although the siege equipment of republican Rome was somewhat haphazard, siege machinery was a regular part of the Roman imperial army's equipment. Each legion was equipped with ten catapults as well as engineers and sappers. A Roman battering ram was a heavy beam with an iron head in the shape of a ram's head. The Romans used all sizes of cata-

TURNING POINTS

c. 7000 B.C.E.	The inhabitants of Jericho construct massive fortifications around their city.
c. 1900 B.C.E.	Primitive battering rams are depicted in Egyptian wall paintings.
c. 1700 B.C.E.	Assyrians employ integrated siege tactics with rams, towers, ramps, and sapping.
c. 429-427 B.C.E.	A wall of circumvallation is used in the Siege of Plataea by Sparta and Thebes at the beginning of the Peloponnesian War.
c. 399 B.C.E.	The catapult is invented at Syracuse under Dionysius I, significantly advancing the art of siege warfare.
334 B.C.E.	Alexander the Great uses stone-throwing torsion catapults at the Siege of Halicarnassus.
305-304 B.C.E.	Macedonians employ a huge siege tower known as a helepolis during the Siege of Rhodes.
70 C.E.	Romans employ catapults during their Siege of Jerusalem.
1304	English king Edward I employs thirteen trebuchets at the Siege of Stirling

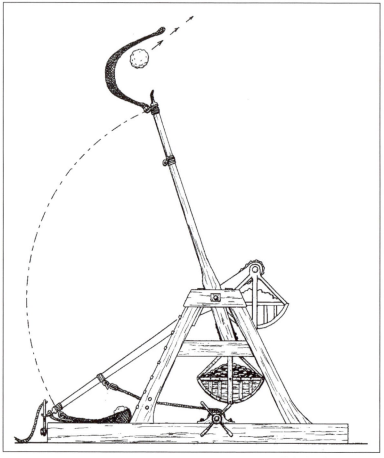

Kimberly L. Dawson Kurnizki

A drawing of a trebuchet, after Sir Ralph Payne-Gallwey (1842-1916), A Summary of the History, Construction, and Effects in Warfare of the Projectile-Throwing Engines of the Ancients *(1907). Such siege weapons of antiquity reappeared throughout the medieval period, as the building of castles proliferated.*

Medieval siege warfare evolved little from that of ancient times. The outstanding medieval innovation was the trebuchet, a stone-throwing catapult powered by a counterweight. The throwing arm rested on a pivot so that the end with the counterweight was shorter than the end throwing the missile. When released, the counterweight forced the short end down, lifting the long end with enough force to hurl a stone a considerable distance. The earliest trebuchets used men for counterweights. Several men would simultaneously pull on ropes with all their weight to force down the short end and propel the stone. By the early thirteenth century trebuchets with much heavier dead weights required fifty men to operate them and were capable of throwing a 100-kilogram stone about 150 meters. The biggest Roman catapults could throw a 30-kilogram stone about 225 meters.

Large trebuchets were expensive and relatively rare. In the Siege of Holyrood (1296) the English king Edward I (1239-1307) deployed three trebuchets, which threw 158 large stones in three days. In 1304 he used thirteen trebuchets to throw 600 stones during the Siege of Stirling.

Despite the impressive array of siege machinery, the reduction of powerfully fortified cities remained difficult throughout ancient and medieval times. Sieges were often time-consuming and expensive. Well-defended, well-provisioned cities could hold out for months or even years. Ancient armies fed themselves by foraging, and when they stopped moving, they soon exhausted food supplies in their immediate area, presenting siege commanders with difficult logistical problems. Siege armies labored in unhealthy circumstances. The disposal of human and animal waste was difficult. Disease was a major killer.

pults. In general Romans seemed to have called their smaller catapults *scorpions* and the larger ones *ballistae*, but there was no real consistency in the terminology. Later the word "onager" came into use to describe large catapults. "Onager" means "ass," and the catapults were so called because of the way the rear kicked up, like that of a donkey, when they were fired. Ancient historian Flavius Josephus (c. 37-c. 100 C.E.) claimed that Roman catapults were capable of throwing 25-kilogram stones to a distance of 366 meters at the Siege of Jerusalem in 70 C.E., although he probably exaggerated their range.

Against this background, psychological warfare was of great importance. Siege commanders tried to intimidate cities into surrendering by offering relatively lenient terms but threatening dire consequences if resisted. The common practices of sacking, rape, transportation, enslavement, and massacre added credibility to the threats.

Ruse and treachery were the preferred means of taking a city. The legend of the Trojan horse reflected the reality that often the only way to gain entry to a city was by trickery. The ancient historian Herodotus (c. 484-424 B.C.E.) tells the story of Zopyrus, a fanatically loyal Persian soldier who mutilated himself so that he could pose as an aggrieved deserter in order to gain entry to Babylon, which was under siege by the Persian emperor Darius (550-486 B.C.E.). Once in the city, Zopyrus opened the gate to the Persians.

Sieges placed cities under great stress, and siege commanders attempted to exploit any social or political fault lines in the hope that traitors would betray the city. This ploy was especially useful in Greek siege warfare. During the Peloponnesian War (431-404 B.C.E.), more cities fell by betrayal than by any other means.

The introduction of gunpowder in the fourteenth century brought an end to a long epoch in siege warfare, which had changed little since ancient times. By the fifteenth century cannon were a regular part of siege warfare for which stone walls were no match. Thus the ancient art of fortification was revolutionized and, with it, the art of siegecraft.

BOOKS AND ARTICLES

Anglim, Simon, et al. "Siege Warfare." In *Fighting Techniques of the Ancient World, 3,000 B.C.-500 A.D.: Equipment, Combat Skills, and Tactics.* New York: St. Martin's Press, 2002.

Bradbury, Jim. *The Medieval Siege.* Woodbridge, England: Boydell Press, 1992.

Campbell, Duncan B. *Ancient Siege Warfare: Persians, Greeks, Cathaginians, and Romans, 546-146 B.C.* Illustrated by Adam Hook. Botley, Oxford, England: Osprey, 2004.

_____. *Besieged: Siege Warfare in the Ancient World.* Botley, Oxford, England: Osprey, 2006.

Corfis, Ivy A., and Michael Wolfe, eds. *The Medieval City Under Siege.* Rochester, N.Y.: Boydell Press, 1995.

DeVries, Kelly. *Guns and Men in Medieval Europe, 1200-1500: Studies in Military History and Technology.* Burlington, Vt.: Ashgate/Variorum, 2002.

Gabriel, Richard A. "Siegecraft and Artillery." In *The Ancient World.* Westport, Conn.: Greenwood Press, 2007.

Kern, Paul Bentley. *Ancient Siege Warfare.* Bloomington: Indiana University Press, 1999.

Marsden, E. W. *Greek and Roman Artillery.* Oxford, England: Clarendon Press, 1969.

Yadin, Yigael. *The Art of Warfare in Biblical Lands in the Light of Archeological Discovery.* London: McGraw-Hill, 1963.

FILMS AND OTHER MEDIA

Arms in Action: Castles and Sieges. Documentary. History Channel, 1999.

Nova: Medieval Siege. Documentary. Public Broadcasting Service, 2004.

Paul Bentley Kern

ARMIES AND INFANTRY
ANCIENT AND MEDIEVAL
Dates: c. 2500 B.C.E.-1400 C.E.

NATURE AND USE

Infantry is that part or those parts of an army trained and organized to fight on foot with handheld weapons. Foot soldiers have formed the largest component of most armies throughout history. Infantry forces are attested in ancient Mesopotamia, Egypt, Assyria, Greece, Rome, and China, where they were used both in battle and in assaulting and defending fortified positions.

Infantry forces were termed either "light" or "heavy," according to the weapons carried and armor worn by individual foot soldiers. Light infantrymen were equipped with little if any armor, and they used missile weapons such as javelins, bows, and slings to engage the enemy from a distance. Because of their greater mobility, light infantry units were effective in rugged terrain and using guerrilla tactics, but lightly armed soldiers could also be deployed as skirmishers fighting in front of or along the flanks of heavy infantry. Heavy infantrymen usually wore heavy defensive armor, carried weapons suited for close combat, such as swords and spears, and fought in dense, compact units. They were most effective in pitched battles fought on open plains.

In loosely organized armies foot soldiers often relied more on numerical superiority than on tactical maneuvering, achieving victory by simply overwhelming enemy forces. Infantrymen were most effective, however, when deployed in organized formations. The phalanx and the legion are the best known formations from ancient and medieval times. The phalanx was a square or rectangular formation in which foot soldiers stood shoulder to shoulder in files several ranks deep. When the soldiers of the front line locked their shields together, they presented an impenetrable wall capable of withstanding charges by chariots, cavalry, and even other infantry. On the attack members of a phalanx wielded either thrusting spears or pikes, and a well-disciplined phalanx could overrun many types of opposition. The phalanx was utilized with great success in antiquity by the ancient Greek city-states and the Macedonian Empire. In the fourteenth and fifteenth centuries Swiss pikemen readopted the phalanx to defeat mounted knights.

The legion was the basic infantry formation of the Roman army. Its size varied over time, but during the third and second centuries B.C.E. it consisted of 4,000 to 5,000 men, mostly heavy infantry. Legionaries wore a helmet and carried a tall body shield called the *scutum*. They carried a javelin (*pilum*) and sword (*gladius*) as close-combat weapons. Unlike the phalanx, the legion did not fight in a single massed formation. Each legion was subdivided into several smaller tactical units usually deployed in three lines that attacked in successive waves. Mobile and flexible, the Roman legion proved to be the preeminent infantry force of the ancient world.

DEVELOPMENT

Written records of battles from ancient Egypt and the kingdoms of the Middle East frequently mention infantry, but it is difficult to determine what role foot soldiers played and how important they were in combat. The Sumerian Stela of the Vultures, dating from about 2500 B.C.E., depicts spearmen in a phalanx-like formation, but during the second millennium B.C.E. infantry may have fought primarily as skirmishers in support of chariots. One theory holds that the foot soldiers rose in prominence only around 1200 B.C.E., when "barbarian" tribes, fighting on foot and armed with javelins and long swords, overran many of the kingdoms of the ancient Middle East. A similar transition away from chariot warfare to infantry began to occur in China in the fifth century B.C.E.

The Assyrians organized their infantry into specialized units in the early first millennium B.C.E., but the armies of the ancient Greek city-states were the first to rely almost exclusively on soldiers fighting on foot. Around 700 B.C.E. they began to deploy infantrymen called hoplites in densely packed phalanxes. Each hoplite wore a bronze helmet, corselet, and greaves, or shin guards. He carried a circular shield for protection and used a thrusting spear as his primary weapon. The phalanx was suited to the small plains of Greece, and in battle it attacked in tight formation. As they neared the enemy, hoplites in the front ranks of the phalanx raised their shields and spears and jabbed at their opponents, while those in the rear pushed on the backs of those ahead of them. Hoplite battles resembled shoving matches, as a phalanx sought to overwhelm its opponent by its momentum. The success of the phalanx ultimately depended on the cohesion of its members.

The superiority of the Greek hoplite army was demonstrated first at the Battle of Marathon (490 B.C.E.), where the Athenian hoplite phalanx charged and defeated a numerically superior but more lightly armed Persian force. A second Persian campaign against Greece met a similar fate during the Greco-Persian Wars (499-448 B.C.E.). Spartan hoplites held the narrow pass of Thermopylae (480 B.C.E.) for several days against vastly superior Persian numbers, and at Plataea (479 B.C.E.) a hoplite army drawn from Sparta, Athens, and other Greek city-states defeated the Persians decisively. Greek hoplites remained the elite warriors of the Mediterranean world for nearly a century and a half.

TURNING POINTS

c. 1200 B.C.E.	The use of the chariot in warfare declines and foot soldiers increasingly come into use, as "barbarian" tribes, fighting on foot and armed with javelins and long swords, overrun many ancient Middle Eastern kingdoms.
c. 700 B.C.E.	Tight-formation hoplite tactics, well-suited to the small plains of the ancient Greek city-states, are first introduced in Greece.
c. 350 B.C.E.	Philip II of Macedon develops the Macedonian phalanx and adopts the use of the sarissa, a pike of nearly 15 feet in length wielded with two hands.
58-45 B.C.E.	Julius Caesar employs independently operating cohorts in the Gallic Wars and the Roman Civil Wars against Pompey.
3d-4th cent. C.E.	Despite the increasing role of cavalry due to barbarian influence, infantry remains the dominant component of the Roman legions.
476	The Sack of Rome by barbarians brings about an "age of cavalry," during which foot soldiers play a diminished role in warfare.
1298	The English army uses the longbow to great effect against the Scots at Falkirk.
14th cent.	An "infantry revolution" spurred by the greater use of the pike and bow, takes place in Europe.
1315	Swiss pikemen begin a string of victories against mounted knights by defeating the Austrians at Morgarten.

The prominence of infantry battle in Greek warfare declined somewhat during the Peloponnesian Wars (431-404 B.C.E.), which pitted the naval strength of Athens against the land-based power of Sparta. Few infantry battles were fought, and the war was ultimately decided at sea. Decisive hoplite battles did take place during the fourth century B.C.E., but new developments changed the face of Greek warfare. At Lechaeum (390 B.C.E.), on the Gulf of Corinth, a force of peltasts, light infantry armed with javelins, decimated a Spartan regiment and illustrated the vulnerability of heavy infantry to light-armed troops. At Leuctra (371 B.C.E.) the Theban commander Epaminondas (c. 410-362 B.C.E.) employed novel tactics to defeat the Spartan phalanx. Epaminondas strengthened the left wing of the Theban phalanx to a depth of fifty men and charged the Spartans at an oblique angle. The weight of the Theban left flank ripped through the Spartan line, and the supremacy of the Spartan hoplite was ended forever.

More significant were the innovations of Philip II of Macedon (382-336 B.C.E.), who reformed the Macedonian army, including its infantry. Philip increased the depth of the Macedonian phalanx and reduced the size of the shield carried by its members. He also armed his infantry with sarissas, pikes nearly 15 feet in length and, unlike the spears of the Greek hoplites, wielded with two hands. At Chaeronea (338 B.C.E.) Philip combined the new Macedonian phalanx with his cavalry to rout a hoplite army of Thebans and Athenians. Philip's son, Alexander the Great (356-323 B.C.E.), employed similar combinations of infantry and cavalry charges at Granicus (334 B.C.E.), Issus (333 B.C.E.), and Gaugamela (331 B.C.E.) to break the Persian army and conquer the Persian Empire. The size of the Macedonian phalanx grew in the armies of the Hellenistic kingdoms founded after Alexander's death, but infantry was increasingly used in conjunction with other forces, including chariots and elephants.

As the Greeks and Macedonians employed phalanx tactics, the Romans developed a style of infantry warfare based on the legion. The legion evolved over the course of the Roman conquest of Italy in the fifth and fourth centuries B.C.E. Its heavy infantrymen were deployed in three lines, each made up of ten units called maniples. In battle the first line of maniples, the *hastati*, advanced first. When they neared the enemy they released their javelins and then drew their swords and charged, seeking to take advantage of the confusion caused by their missiles. If the hastati failed to defeat the enemy, they were joined by the second line of maniples, the *principes*, which used similar tactics. The third line of maniples, the *triarii*, were armed as spearmen, and they engaged only when the situation became critical.

With their legionary tactics, the Romans overcame the peoples of Italy and the western Mediterranean. Roman legions, however, were not invincible, and the Roman infantry met defeat in battles against Pyrrhus

Kimberly L. Dawson Kurnizki

A Greek hoplite, circa 700 B.C.E., wearing a bronze helmet, corselet, and shin guards, and carrying a circular shield and a thrusting spear.

and in the Second Punic War (219-202 B.C.E.) against the Carthaginian general Hannibal (247-182 B.C.E.). The Romans were able to draw on enormous reserves of manpower to replenish their losses, and they learned from their defeats. They lost battles but won wars. In the second century B.C.E. the experience gained by decades of fighting in Italy helped Roman infantrymen defeat the Macedonian phalanx in the Second and Third Macedonian-Roman Wars (200-196 B.C.E., 172-167 B.C.E.). Thus, although the Macedonian phalanx initially carried all before it at the Battle of Pydna (168 B.C.E.), it lost cohesion as it advanced, allowing Roman legionaries to pour into gaps in its line and cut down the Macedonians at close range with their swords.

The Roman legion underwent further reforms during the second century B.C.E., and by the time of the general Gaius Marius (157-86 B.C.E.) ten cohorts had replaced the thirty maniples as the legion's tactical units. With the change to cohorts the distinctions between hastati, principes, and triarii disappeared, so that all legionaries were armed and fought in the same fashion. The legion continued to deploy for battle in three lines, with four cohorts in the first line and three cohorts in the second and third, but this arrangement could be varied, and unlike maniples, individual cohorts could operate independently. Julius Caesar (100-44 B.C.E.) employed cohorts very effectively in the Gallic Wars (58-51 B.C.E.) and in the Roman Civil Wars against Pompey (49-45 B.C.E.).

Under the Roman Republic, the infantry of Rome's legions was an offensive force. With the establishment of the Empire, Roman infantry forces acquired a defensive role. Rome's legions manned the frontiers of the Roman Empire and engaged in few pitched battles in the first few centuries C.E. The size of the legion decreased, and legionaries discarded their heavy armor and adopted missile weapons. Cavalry acquired a more important role in Rome's armies as a result of barbarian incursions across the Empire's borders during the third and fourth centuries C.E. Infantry remained the dominant component of the legion into the fourth and fifth centuries C.E., and in pitched battle Roman foot soldiers were vastly superior to their barbarian counterparts, as demonstrated in 357 C.E., for example, at

Strasbourg, then called Argentoratum. Even the defeat of the Roman army at Adrianople (378 C.E.) was due largely to the flight of the Roman cavalry, not to the weakness of its infantry. After that point, however, foot soldiers became increasingly dependent on mounted soldiers, and cavalry gradually assumed a more decisive role.

The millennium following the fall of the Roman Empire is sometimes labeled an age of cavalry. Although cavalry charges often determined the outcome of battle, it would be a mistake to discount altogether the importance of foot soldiers in this period. Frankish armies fought on foot well into the time of Charlemagne (742-814 C.E.), and Anglo-Saxon armies in England relied on foot soldiers up until the Battle of Hastings (1066 C.E.). Well-disciplined infantry could also withstand a charge of mounted knights, as did the Milanese at Legnano (1176 C.E.). Something of an infantry revolution, however, took place in the fourteenth century, spurred in part by the greater use of the pike and bow. At Courtrai (1302 C.E.) Flemish infantry, armed with pikes, withstood a charge of French cavalry and then slaughtered the knights who had fallen from their mounts. In 1314 English cavalry suffered a similar fate against the Scottish pikemen at Bannockburn. Use of the crossbow, capable of piercing the armor of a mounted knight, had also begun to challenge the supremacy of cavalry during the twelfth century, but the longbow proved more effective in terms of cost, rate of fire, range, and accuracy. By the late thirteenth century a majority of English foot soldiers carried the longbow, and their large numbers proved decisive against the Scots at Falkirk (1298), and later in the Hundred Years' War (1337-1453) against the French at Crécy (1346), Poitiers (1356), and Agincourt (1415).

The most significant infantry innovation was the development of the Swiss phalanx. Swiss infantrymen wore little armor and carried no shields, but they carried either a pike 18 feet in length or a halberd, both of which were wielded with deadly effect. After infantrymen in the outer ranks of the phalanx delivered the initial blows with their pikes, soldiers armed with halberds emerged from the phalanx and engaged enemy cavalry and foot soldiers at close quarters. When harassed on all sides by cavalry, the Swiss phalanx could also adopt a "hedgehog" formation, with pikes turned outward in all directions. A string of Swiss victories over mounted knights began early in the fourteenth century at Morgarten (1315) and by the end of the fifteenth century, European monarchs were either recruiting Swiss infantrymen into their armies or modeling their own infantry units after the Swiss. Infantry had again come to dominate Western warfare.

BOOKS AND ARTICLES

Darnell, John Coleman, and Colleen Manassa. *Tutankhamun's Armies: Battle and Conquest During Ancient Egypt's Late Eighteenth Dynasty*. Hoboken, N.J.: John Wiley and Sons, 2007.

Dawson, Doyne. *The First Armies*. London: Cassell, 2001.

DeVries, Kelly. *Infantry Warfare in the Early Fourteenth Century: Discipline, Tactics, and Technology*. Woodbridge, England: Boydell Press, 1996.

Drews, Robert. *The End of the Bronze Age: Changes in Warfare and the Catastrophe c. 1200 B.C.* Princeton, N.J.: Princeton University Press, 1993.

Gabriel, Richard A. *The Great Armies of Antiquity*. Westport, Conn.: Praeger, 2002.

Gush, George. *Renaissance Armies, 1480-1650*. Cambridge: P. Stephens, 1982.

Hanson, Victor. *The Western Way of War: Infantry Battle in Classical Greece*. 2d ed. Berkeley: University of California Press, 2000.

Head, Duncan. *Armies of the Macedonian and Punic Wars, 359 B.C. to 146 B.C.: Organisation, Tactics, Dress, and Weapons*. Drawings by Ian Heath. Goring-by-Sea, West Sussex, England: Wargames Research Group, 1982.

Heath, Ian. *Armies of the Middle Ages: Organisation, Tactics, Dress, and Weapons*. Goring-by-Sea, West Sussex, England: Wargames Research Group, 1982.

Katcher, Philip R. N. *Armies of the American Wars, 1753-1815*. New York: Hastings House, 1975.

Lepage, Jean-Denis. *Medieval Armies and Weapons in Western Europe: An Illustrated History*. Jefferson, N.C.: McFarland, 2005.

Marshall, Christopher. *Warfare in the Latin East, 1192-1291*. New York: Cambridge University Press, 1992.

Prestwich, Michael. *Armies and Warfare in the Middle Ages: The English Experience*. New Haven, Conn.: Yale University Press, 1996.

Sage, Michael M. *The Republican Roman Army: A Sourcebook*. New York: Routledge, 2008.

Santosuosso, Antonio. *Soldiers, Citizens, and the Symbols of War: From Classical Greece to Republican Rome, 500-167 B.C.* Boulder, Colo.: Westview Press, 1997.

Wise, Terence. *Armies of the Crusades*. Color plates by G. A. Embleton. Botley, Oxford, England: Osprey, 1978.

FILMS AND OTHER MEDIA

Henry V. Feature film. BBC/Curzon/Renaissance, 1989.

In Search of History: The Roman Legions. Documentary. History Channel, 1996.

Modern Marvels: Battle Gear. Documentary. History Channel, 2008.

Weapons at War: Infantry. Documentary. History Channel, 1992.

James P. Sickinger

CAVALRY
ANCIENT AND MEDIEVAL
Dates: To c. 1500 C.E.

NATURE AND USE

Historically, cavalries were military forces that traveled and fought on horseback, unlike mounted infantrymen, who traveled on horseback but fought on foot, and charioteers, who fought from carts pulled by horses. Cavalry was less expensive and more mobile than was chariotry and could move two to three times faster than could infantry, covering at least 30 to 40 miles a day for an indefinite period. The physically and psychologically imposing combination of man and horse made resistance difficult for foot soldiers.

Cavalry in antiquity fell into two basic categories: light cavalry, unarmored or lightly armored men on small, swift ponies or horses, and heavy cavalry, moderately or heavily armored men on large, sometimes armored, horses. The principal cavalry weapons were the composite bow, javelin, and lance. Almost every cavalryman used at least one of these weapons; light cavalrymen emphasized the bow or javelin and heavy cavalry the lance. However, many other combinations of weapons were used. On the march, light cavalry would scout ahead, protect the flanks and rear of their army, and raid enemy forces. In camp, at sieges, or on garrison duty, cavalry would patrol and undertake escort duties. In battle, light cavalry would ride at the enemy, fire missiles, and then gallop out of the range of return fire. Skilled horse archers could turn in their saddles and fire while withdrawing, a maneuver known as the Parthian shot, for the Parthians (third century B.C.E.), a nomad steppe people who perfected the technique. Heavy cavalry would mass and charge enemy forces, hoping to rout them. If this happened, the light cavalry would pursue. If things went badly, the light cavalry would instead try to cover the retreat of friendly forces. Finally, cavalry and mounted infantry used the horse's high march rate to perform raids. After short-range raids, the raiders quickly returned to the safety of their border forts. In long-distance raids, traversing hundreds of miles of enemy territory, the raiders used speed and unexpected movements to avoid interception.

The first known cavalry appeared in the Near East, around 1200 B.C.E., after the collapse of the Bronze Age civilizations there. Armies dominated by cavalry were fielded by Eurasian steppe nomad groups, such as the Cimmerians, Scythians, Sarmatians, Huns, Avars, Turks, and Mongols. Combined forces of cavalry and infantry were fielded by the agricultural peoples of Europe, Asia, and North Africa, notably the Assyrians, Achaemenid Persians, Greeks, Macedonians, Celts, Spaniards, Numidians, Carthaginians, Romans, Chinese, and Indians. Cavalry enjoyed a dominant position in the armies of many peoples, beginning with the Parthians and Sāsānian Persians and continuing with the Byzantines, Arabs, Russians, and medieval Europeans.

DEVELOPMENT

The horse was first domesticated and ridden six thousand years ago by the Sredni Stog culture of the North Pontic region in the modern Ukraine. The development of horseback riding and, several centuries later, the wheeled cart allowed nomads to exploit the resources of the prairie steppe that runs from Hungary past the Ural and Altai Shan Mountains of Central Asia to Mongolia and Manchuria in the east. Because chariotry preceded cavalry everywhere in the Bronze Age, the first mounted warriors probably fought dismounted, adopting the chariot because it allowed

TURNING POINTS

c. 4000 B.C.E.	Horses are first domesticated and ridden by people of the Sredni Stog culture.
c. 900 B.C.E.	Cavalry begins to compete with chariotry as a method of warfare in the Neo-Assyrian Empire.
c. 4th cent. B.C.E.	Earliest known stirrups, made from leather or wood, are used by the Scyths.
c. 3d cent. B.C.E.	The Parthians, a steppe nomad people, perfect the Parthian shot, fired backward from the saddle while in retreat.
333 B.C.E.	Alexander the Great uses combined infantry and cavalry forces to route the Persian cavalry at the Battle of Issus.
53 B.C.E.	Parthian horsemen devastate the Roman legions at the Battle of Carrhae.
50 B.C.E.-50 C.E.	The earliest horseshoes are made in Gaul.
400	Horseshoes come into general use throughout Europe.
1100	European knights adopt the use of the couched lance, which provides more force than previous hand-thrust weapons.
1260	Mongol warriors are defeated at the Battle of Ain Jalut by Mamlūk slave cavalry, trained by the Egyptians to steppe nomad levels.

them to fight on foot, as they were accustomed, and leaving control of the horses to the charioteers. Armed riders are depicted in late Bronze Age (c. 1550-1200 B.C.E.) Greek, Egyptian, and Near Eastern art, but they appear sitting "donkey seat," on the animal's rump, not up on its shoulders: an inefficient position that is also harmful to the horse. It is likely such riders were only scouts or messengers, armed for self-defense.

After the collapse of the Greek and Near Eastern Bronze Age civilizations (around 1200 B.C.E.), cavalry gradually began to replace chariotry. The process is clearly depicted in reliefs of the Neo-Assyrian Empire (911-612 B.C.E.). The earliest cavalrymen, of the ninth century B.C.E., unarmored and still sitting donkey seat, were chariot riders on horseback. The "chariot warrior" wielded a bow, and the accompanying "charioteer" managed the reins of both his own and the bowman's horses and carried a shield and spear for self-defense. By the mid-eighth century

B.C.E., each horseman controlled his own mount, sat on the horse's withers, used lances as well as bows, and, in some cases, wore lamellar corselets as body armor. By the end of the eighth century B.C.E., corseleted cavalrymen equipped with both bows and lances appeared, supported by horse archers. Half a century later, horses were outfitted with cloth armor similar to that of chariot horses.

CAVALRY ACCOUTREMENTS

Like most cultures in and after the ninth century B.C.E., the Sredni Stog culture managed its horses by directly controlling their heads, using reins connected to bits held in place in the horses' mouths by antler cheekpieces attached to bridles. Even this was not always necessary; the Numidians, raised on horseback, controlled their small, swift, and obedient Libyan steeds with only a stick or cord around the neck. Throughout the first millennium B.C.E., most horsemen rode either bareback or seated upon a saddle cloth. The first saddles, consisting of a pad with two cushions resting on either side of the horse's spine and held on by a girth, appeared around 400 B.C.E., used by nomads in the Altai Shan Mountains of central Asia. It took five centuries for saddles to become commonplace. Whips or goads were favored by Asian horsemen, but spurs were used in Greece during the fifth century B.C.E. and in Celtic lands soon afterward.

To protect horses' hooves from the wet conditions of the northwestern European climate, the Celts began making horseshoes. The earliest horseshoes were made in Gaul between 50 B.C.E. and 50 C.E., and horseshoes also enjoyed some popularity in Roman Britain. Elsewhere in the Roman Empire, temporary "hipposandals" of woven grass or leather and metal predominated. Horseshoes did not come into general use until after 400 C.E.

The earliest known stirrups, made of leather straps

or wood, or featuring metal hooks, appear in Scythian contexts in the fourth century B.C.E. and in India around the end of the first millennium B.C.E. Although stirrups may have been a necessity for the heaviest cavalry forces, they were rarely depicted in art of the period, perhaps because men reared in the saddle found the use of stirrups embarrassing. Only in fourth century C.E. China was the full metal stirrup adopted; by the seventh century C.E. it had made its way west with the Avars. Although none of the aforementioned inventions can be demonstrated clearly to have had a decisive impact upon cavalry operations during the first millennium C.E., they must have made the creation of mounted forces easier for peoples unaccustomed to riding, such as the Chinese and the Franks.

By around 1100 C.E., Western European knights had discovered the use of the couched lance. Held onto the horse by a high saddle and stirrups, the knight could hold the lance firmly under his arm, adding far more force to the blow than any thrust by hand could do. However, because the massed charge of Western European knights had long been considered irresistible by their Byzantine and Arab foes, the couched lance would seem to be only a tactical refinement, not a decisive advance.

CAVALRY DEVELOPMENT IN CIVILIZED NATIONS

There were two general lines of development in cavalry: that of the civilized nations of the Mediterranean and that of the steppe nomads and those who imitated them. For the first group, the problem was in integrating cavalry into armies that were composed predominantly of infantry. The Achaemenid Persians, who reigned from 560 to 330 B.C.E., followed the Assyrians' example and used light foot archers

Kimberly L. Dawson Kurnizki

A Parthian horse archer of the third century B.C.E. practicing the Parthian shot, a maneuver in which the rider turns in his saddle and fires while withdrawing.

and spearmen with missile-armed cavalry that did not try to charge massed infantry forces. This combination worked well in the Near East but failed in offensives against the Greeks and the steppe nomads.

The Greeks themselves came to realize by the fourth century B.C.E. the value in the coordinated use of heavy and light infantry and cavalry together. Macedonian conqueror Alexander the Great (356-323 B.C.E.) used this strategy in the eventual defeat of the Achaemenid Persians. Alexander's heavy, pike-armed infantry provided a solid base, and the light-infantry provided missile fire wherever needed. Thessalian light cavalry, armed with javelins, guarded his left flank, and other light cavalry were positioned on the far right flank. The elite Companion heavy lancers and supporting *hypaspist* infantry massed farther in on the right. At both Issus (333 B.C.E.) and Gaugamela (331 B.C.E.), after the other units had drawn out the enemy, the Companions charged into the Persian left flank cavalry, ruptured the enemy line, and then rallied and charged into the enemy flanks and rear, achieving the victory in both battles.

Alexander's "combined arms" approach was adopted by the Carthaginians and, eventually, by the Romans as well, after the Carthaginian general Hannibal (247-182 B.C.E.) had demonstrated its effectiveness. Although the Romans experimented with heavy cavalry, they generally preferred light cavalry, relying upon their superb legion infantry for shock action.

CAVALRY DEVELOPMENT AMONG STEPPE NOMADS

The second main line of cavalry development occurred among the steppe nomad peoples, who enjoyed far more pasturage than did the peoples of Western Europe, the Mediterranean region, and China. Because the steppe nomads spent so much time on horseback, their armies were dominated by cavalry, a tactical development imitated by Iranian monarchies and Chinese dynasties. The Cimmerians, a people who inhabited southern Russia and were driven to Turkey by the Scythians in the eighth century B.C.E., were the earliest known steppe nomad horse archers. As evidenced by later steppe nomad tactics, these people probably stressed hit-and-run

attacks from front, flanks, and rear by small, scattered bodies of horse, using feigned retreats and ambushes to draw out and destroy enemy forces. As the Cimmerians passed over the Caucasus in the eighth century B.C.E., they wrecked kingdoms throughout Anatolia before finally being destroyed. Their Scythian and Sarmatian successors fielded both light-armed horse archers and heavy cavalry, equipped with lances and armor covering man and, often, horse as well. Such heavy cavalrymen, called *cataphracts* by the Greeks, would charge and rout enemy forces already weakened by the horse archers' attacks. The Parthians, a steppe people who seized Persia from the Macedonians, exploited the matchless advantages of Iran's wide pasturelands and unique Nisaean breed of horse—larger and better bred to carry weight than most steppe or western animals—to field numerous cataphract and horse archer units. The effectiveness of the Parthian force was displayed in 53 B.C.E., when a Roman army under Marcus Licinius Crassus (115-53 B.C.E.) invaded Parthian territory at Carrhae. Commanded by a noble known as Surenas, the Parthians lured Crassus into open desert terrain, where Parthian horse archers shot his infantry to pieces. When Crassus's Gallic horses charged to drive them off, the cataphracts countercharged and crushed them. The Roman army was destroyed, and Crassus killed.

THE RISE AND FALL OF CAVALRY

Parthia, not Rome, influenced the development of cavalry over the next millennium. In the late Roman Empire and its Byzantine successor in the East, the balance tilted in favor of the horse, with infantry forming a defensive body in battle and serving chiefly as a refuge for the cavalry. Others who adopted this pattern were the Indians; the Chinese; the Arabs, who quickly moved from camels to horses; and, more gradually, the European peoples as well. Whether the adoption of saddle and stirrup drove this development, or was driven by it, is unclear. Heavy cavalry service eventually became a justification for aristocratic political power and encouraged cavalry's growing predominance. However, large infantry forces were still needed, if only for siege warfare. Thus, aside from cavalry raids such as the long-distance *chevauchées* of the Hundred Years' War (1337-1453 C.E.), offensive operations necessarily tied cavalry to an infantry pace. The Mongols under Genghis Khan (died 1227 C.E.) solved this problem: Their armies of highly trained, fast-moving horse archers and cataphract lancers simply rounded up local peasants by the thousands and forced them to perform siege warfare duties. The epitome of steppe nomad armies, the Mongols were hindered only by environmental factors and internal political problems until they suffered their first defeat in 1260 C.E. at Ain Jalut, Israel, at the hands of the Mamlūks, Egyptian slave cavalry, trained to steppe nomad levels. Toward 1500 C.E., infantrymen began to return to prominence in Europe; notable examples are the English longbowmen, Swiss pikemen, and Hussite *Wagenburg* soldiers. The development of gunpowder artillery and firearms ultimately spelled the end of cavalry dominance in Europe and, eventually, everywhere that European armies marched.

BOOKS AND ARTICLES

DeVries, Kelly. *Medieval Military Technology*. Lewiston, N.Y.: Broadview Press, 1992.

Drews, Robert. *Early Riders: The Beginnings of Mounted Warfare in Asia and Europe*. New York: Routledge, 2004.

Ellis, John. *Cavalry: The History of Mounted Warfare*. New York: G. P. Putnam's Sons, 1978. Reprint. Barnsley, England: Pen and Sword, 2004.

Gabriel, Richard A. "Cavalry." In *The Ancient World*. Westport, Conn.: Greenwood Press, 2007.

Gaebel, Robert E. *Cavalry Operations in the Ancient Greek World*. Norman: University of Oklahoma Press, 2002.

Gillmor, Carroll. "Cavalry, Ancient and Medieval." In *The Reader's Companion to Military History*, edited by Robert Cowley and Geoffrey Parker. Boston: Houghton Mifflin, 1996.

Hyland, Ann. *The Warhorse, 1250-1600*. Stroud, Gloucestershire, England: Sutton, 1998.

Morillo, Stephen. "The 'Age of Cavalry' Revisited." In *The Circle of War in the Middle Ages: Essays on Medieval Military and Naval History*, edited by Donald J. Kagay and L. J. Andrew Villalon. Rochester, N.Y.: Boydell Press, 1999.

O'Connell, R. L. *Ride of the Second Horseman: The Birth and Death of War*. Oxford, England: Oxford University Press, 1995.

Sidnell, Philip. *Warhorse: Cavalry in Ancient Warfare*. New York: Hambledon Continuum, 2006.

Sinclair, Andrew. *Man and Horse: Four Thousand Years of the Mounted Warrior*. Stroud, Gloucestershire, England: Sutton, 2008.

Smith, Gene. *Mounted Warriors: From Alexander the Great and Cromwell to Stewart, Sheridan, and Custer*. Hoboken, N.J.: Wiley, 2009.

Vuksic, V., and Z. Grbasic. *Cavalry: The History of a Fighting Elite, 650 B.C.-A.D. 1914*. New York: Sterling, 1993.

FILMS AND OTHER MEDIA

The True Story of Hannibal. Documentary. History Channel, 2004.

Scott M. Rusch

WARSHIPS AND NAVAL WARFARE

Dates: To c. 1200 C.E.

NATURE AND USE

From ancient times, the principal warship of the Mediterranean Sea was the oared galley, which was used to ram and sink opposing ships. The galley typically had fore and aft decked platforms with a lower, usually open, area for the rowers. The galley was built using a "shell-first" construction, in which the planks of the galley's hull were edge joined with mortise-and-tenon joints, to which a system of frames was later inserted. Joints typically were made out of oak for strength, and the other sections were constructed from lighter woods, such as pine or fir, for speed. From the bow of the vessel at its waterline projected a sharp beak, or ram, usually made of bronze, which was used to puncture the sides of opposing ships and cause them to sink.

Control of the sea and protection of merchant shipping were important for many Mediterranean civilizations. Although the Phoenicians and Etruscans previously had developed navies to defend their trading interests, the Greek city-state of Athens was the first to actively use its navy in efforts toward imperial expansion. Even a largely land-based power such as Rome was eventually forced to develop a navy to deal with naval threats such as the Carthaginians and the Vandals.

The oared galley also predominated in the Atlantic Ocean for many centuries. Raiders such as the Vikings used their oared galleys, known as longships, to make raids along the coast of Europe. In response to the more strenuous maritime conditions along the

A Greek trireme, which employed three banks of rowers to achieve the superior speed, handling, and power that enabled Athens's growth as an imperial power in the mid-fifth century B.C.E.

coast of northern Europe, these vessels did not use mortise-and-tenon joints, but instead were clinker-built. Clinker-built construction, sometimes called clench-built construction, is a method of shipbuilding in which overlapping planks are fastened to one another using wooden pins, called treenails, or iron clench nails. Next, a form of caulking, consisting of animal hair dipped in pitch to prevent leaking, is placed in the seams between the planks.

The oared galley remained the dominant warship until the development of the cog in the thirteenth century C.E. The cog was a large merchant vessel associated with the development of the Hanseatic League, a commercial union of German, Dutch, and Flemish towns. It had very high sides and a flat bottom and was propelled by a single square sail. Although the cog was a poor sailer, its high sides offered protection against smaller oared vessels, such as the Viking longships. The addition of fighting castles at the bow and stern allowed the vessel to be used to fight wars and blockade towns. The cog was soon replaced, however, by the carrack, a sailing ship with multiple masts and a combination of square and lateen, or tri-

angular, sails. The carrack was a very efficient sailing vessel that became popular in both the Atlantic and the Mediterranean. After cannons were added to the carrack, many Western European countries utilized the vessel to become worldwide naval powers.

DEVELOPMENT

The Greek civilization was one of the first to develop naval power. The first Greek warships, consisting of a single level of oarsmen with one rower per oar, were called *triacontors* and *pentecontors* (thirty- and fifty-oared ships). By the end of the eighth century B.C.E., a second level of rowers was added, in an effort to improve the vessel's speed and to increase the force of the collision between the vessel's ram and the opposing ship. After the addition of a third row of oarsmen in the late seventh century B.C.E., the resulting vessel was known as a trireme. According to the Greek historian Thucydides (c. 459-c. 402 B.C.E.), the trireme was invented by a Corinthian named Ameinocles. However, other ancient sources credit

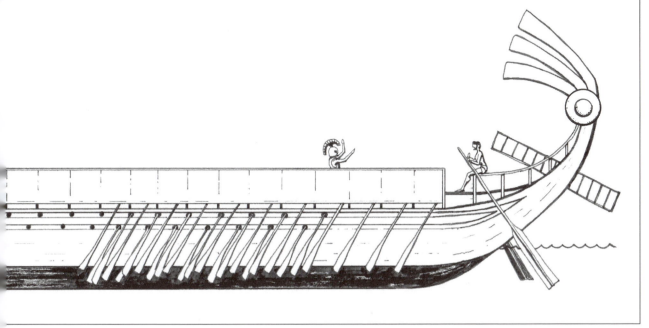

Kimberly L. Dawson Kurnizki

TURNING POINTS

c. late 7th cent. B.C.E.	The Greeks develop the trireme, a large ship powered by three rows of oarsmen.
c. mid-5th cent. B.C.E.	Athens establishes itself as a major naval power in the Mediterranean.
c. 4th cent. B.C.E.	Onboard catapults are added to ships, effectively rendering them as floating siege engines.
c. 3d cent. B.C.E.	Romans utilize the corvus, a nautical grappling hook, allowing sailors to board and capture opposing vessels.
674-678 C.E.	Greek fire, a flammable liquid, is used by the Byzantines against Arab ships during the Siege of Constantinople.
mid-13th cent.	The cog, with high sides that offer protection against other vessels, is developed in Northern Europe.
mid-14th cent.	The carrack, an efficient sailing ship with multiple masts, becomes popular in Atlantic and Mediterranean waters.

the Sidonians with the innovation. Because only the wealthiest cities could afford to build and maintain a trireme, these vessels were not used extensively for several centuries, after which the Phoenicians and Egyptians began to incorporate triremes into their fleets. It was during Athens's growth as an imperial power in the mid-fifth century B.C.E. that the superior speed, handling, and power of the trireme firmly established its position as the premier warship.

The design of the trireme slowly evolved during the Hellenistic Age into that of a much larger and bulkier vessel. To increase the ship's speed and power, extra men were added to each bank of oars, leading to quadriremes and quinqueremes. A quadrireme was not a vessel with four banks of oars, as the prefix "quad-" suggests, but rather it was a trireme with a top row of oars with two oarsmen to each oar and two lower rows of oars, each manipulated by one man. A quinquereme, also known as a *pentereis*, or a "five," had two rows of oars manned by two men and one row manned by one. The new configuration of oars and oarsmen brought about several changes in the design of the vessel's hull, among which was its increased breadth. The longer oar length changed the

stroke of the oarsmen. Because a seated stroke did not allow the full power of the oar to be utilized, a full stroke had to be performed from a standing position by the man on the inside end, as the oar rose and fell during the course of one revolution. More room between decks was also needed, as the men were standing instead of sitting. These adjustments led to larger and larger ships.

CONSTRUCTION OF LARGE SHIPS

Among the most important reasons for the construction of larger ships were technological advances in weaponry. The torsion catapult had been invented around 400 B.C.E. but did not play an important role until the campaigns of Alexander the Great (356-323 B.C.E.). A logical next step was the mounting of catapults on board galleys to use against other ships, as seen in the famous battle for Cyprus between Demetrius Poliorcetes (336-283 B.C.E.) and Ptolemy in 306 B.C.E. To mount the catapult, a larger ship and a sturdier deck, to absorb the weapon's recoil, were needed. Because smaller ramming ships were easy prey for long-range weapons, warships were built larger to offer protection from aerial bombardment. As the ships became larger, however, their mobility was retarded. This gigantism saw the construction of "sixteens," "twenties," and "thirties," and culminated in the huge ship constructed by Ptolemy IV around 200 B.C.E., which was referred to in the ancient literature as a "forty."

When Demetrius Poliorcetes attacked Rhodes in 305 B.C.E., he was forced to experiment with new naval tactics, in response to the strength of the city's defenses. To attack the harbor, he built a floating siege machine that was mounted on the hulls of two cargo ships. He constructed four towers, or "penthouses," for use against the harbor's fortifications. These penthouses were taller than the city's harbor towers and permitted arrows and javelins to be directed at the defenders manning the harbor towers. Demetrius

Poliorcetes also planked over several of his lighter boats, into which he placed archers and catapults, who fired through ports that could be opened and closed.

During the First Punic War (264-241 B.C.E.) Rome found that, despite the strength of its army, its Carthaginian opponent was a superior naval power. In response, the Romans utilized the *corvus*, or raven, a nautical grappling hook. This device was simply a long, spiked gangplank mounted on the bow of a Roman warship and dropped onto the deck of a Carthaginian ship, securing the two ships together and allowing a Roman contingent to board and capture the opposing vessel.

After its final defeat of Carthage in the second century B.C.E., the Roman navy began a slow decline in strength. The only real need for a continued naval presence was the protection of merchant ships, especially the annual grain ships coming from Egypt, from piracy. The large quadremes and quinqueremes of the Hellenistic Age were phased out, and smaller, faster ships better able to combat the pirates were increasingly produced. New vessels, such as the *liburnian* and the *dromon*, were introduced into the Imperial fleet and soon replaced the trireme as the main warship of the Roman navy.

THE DROMON

The dromon was built for a specific purpose: to combat a different type of enemy than had the trireme, which was typically used against other triremes in pitched naval contests. During the years of the Roman Empire, vessels became smaller and faster. A military vessel was needed that could catch these smaller vessels and still be powerful enough to fight in large-scale naval battles against organized opponents. The dromon, with its various capabilities, was the solution. It was fast—in fact, its name means "runner" in Greek—yet it was still large enough to carry the weapons required during large naval conflicts.

Perhaps the best-known offensive weapon of the Byzantine fleet was "Greek fire," invented by a Syrian, Callinicus, in Constantinople and used in 674-678 C.E. during the first Arab siege of Constantinople. Greek fire was a flammable liquid that would supposedly burn even in water. It was shot through a metal tube, or siphon, onto enemy ships, causing them to catch fire. Most Byzantine ships had a siphon, protected by the forecastle, mounted at the bow. Larger vessels sometimes had siphons mounted on each side of the ship, as well as small siphons that could be used for boarding actions or for repelling boarders. Although the Byzantines zealously guarded the secret makeup of Greek fire, the Arabs eventually produced a similar flammable liquid in the ninth century C.E.

Dromons also carried other offensive weapons, for both long-distance attacks and close ship-to-ship action. They had large crossbows, known as *toxoballistrai*, mounted on deck. Small catapults capable of launching stones or pots containing vipers, scorpions, quicklime, or Greek fire were also used. Deck crews were armed with bows and crossbows. For close work, cranes were used to drop heavy stones onto and hopefully through the decks of opposing ships.

Byzantine naval supremacy remained unchallenged until the seventh century reign of the Byzan-

North Wind Picture Archives via AP Images

The sea battle at Actium, 31 B.C.E.

tine emperor Heraclius (c. 575-641). In 626 C.E., a Persian army and an Avar fleet threatened Constantinople, but the Byzantines destroyed the Avar ships, forcing the besiegers to withdraw. Soon afterward, the Arabs, realizing the importance of naval power, developed a fleet based upon the Byzantine model and began to challenge the Byzantines for control of the Mediterranean. This fleet proved to be quite successful, defeating the Byzantines in 655 C.E. at Lycia (Dhat al-Sawari), off the Syrian coast. In 717 C.E. Constantinople was attacked by a large Arab flotilla,

but the Byzantines were able to destroy the attacking fleet with Greek fire, lifting the siege and allowing Emperor Leo III (c. 680-741) to drive off the Arabs.

Although the Byzantines were successful in fending off Arab attacks on Constantinople, they were less successful in 1204 C.E. during the Fourth Crusade. In a carefully planned amphibious assault using both soldiers and warships, the Crusaders were able to capture the city that had withstood capture for nearly nine hundred years.

BOOKS AND ARTICLES

Anglim, Simon, et al. "Naval Warfare." In *Fighting Techniques of the Ancient World, 3,000 B.C.-500 A.D.: Equipment, Combat Skills, and Tactics*. New York: St. Martin's Press, 2002.

Casson, Lionel. *The Ancient Mariners: Seafarers and Sea Fighters of the Mediterranean in Ancient Times*. London: V. Gollancz, 1960.

_____. *Ships and Seamanship in the Ancient World*. Baltimore: Johns Hopkins University Press, 1971.

Fernández-Armesto, Felipe. "Naval Warfare After the Viking Age, c. 1100-1500." In *Medieval Warfare: A History*, edited by Maurice Keen. New York: Oxford University Press, 1999.

Fields, Nic. *Ancient Greek Warship, 500-322 B.C.* Illustrated by Peter Bull. Botley, Oxford, England: Osprey, 2007.

Gardiner, Robert, ed. *The Age of the Galley: Mediterranean Oared Vessels Since Pre-classical Times*. London: Conway Maritime Press, 1995.

Lewis, Archibald, and Timothy J. Runyan. *European Naval and Maritime History, 300-1500*. Bloomington: Indiana University Press, 1985.

McGrail, Sean. *Ancient Boats in North-West Europe: The Archaeology of Water Transport to A.D. 1500*. New York: Longman, 1987.

Morrison, J. S., J. F. Coates, and N. B. Rankov. *The Athenian Trireme*. 2d ed. Cambridge, England: Cambridge University Press, 2000.

Nelson, Richard Bruce. *Warfleets of Antiquity: Ships, Crews, Tactics, and Campaigns of Greek, Persian, Carthaginian, Hellenic, Roman, Celtic, Germanic, Scandinavian, and Byzantine Fleets*. Illustrations by P. W. Norris. Goring by Sea, England: Wargames Research Group, 1973.

Nicholson, Helen J. "Naval Warfare." In *Medieval Warfare: Theory and Practice of War in Europe, 300-1500*. Basingstoke, England: Palgrave Macmillan, 2004.

Throckmorton, Peter. *The Sea Remembers*. New York: Weidenfeld and Nicolson, 1987.

Thubron, Colin. *The Ancient Mariners*. Alexandria, Va.: Time-Life Books, 1981.

Tilley, Alec. *Seafaring on the Ancient Mediterranean: New Thoughts on Triremes and Other Ancient Ships*. Oxford, England: John and Erica Hedges, 2004.

FILMS AND OTHER MEDIA

Warship. Documentary. Public Broadcasting Service, 2002.

R. Scott Moore

THE ANCIENT WORLD

VIOLENCE IN THE PRECIVILIZED WORLD

Dates: To c. 4000 B.C.E.

OVERVIEW

Traditionally, historians distinguish between violence perpetrated by individuals against other individuals and group violence perpetrated against other individuals or groups. Organized, lethal group violence among social groups is "warfare," as in the modern "gang wars" concept. In historic times group violence became associated with the progression toward organized state warfare from more individualistic forms of violence in the precivilized world. In the twenty-first century, archaeological researchers have challenged the traditional border between precivilized group violence and civilized warfare. Evidence from the Stone Age, before 4000 B.C.E., shows the existence of episodic group violence that can be construed as warfare. The main issue is how researchers define and interpret evidence of violence and warfare in the precivilized world.

SIGNIFICANCE

The lack of technological advancement in the precivilized world led to the view that warfare of the time was also relatively "undeveloped." In 1949, Harry Holbert Turney-High developed the influential concept of a "military horizon" for what he termed the "primitive warfare" of the precivilized world. This view led military historians to focus on state-level warfare after 4000 B.C.E., while anthropologists focused on modern tribal conflict. Present-day archaeologists have accumulated enough data on the period that scholars now believe that warfare episodes did occur in the precivilized world, sometimes with more deadly results than are seen in modern wars. This challenges the traditional evolutionary model of warfare, which views ancient peoples as engaging in individual violence and small blood feuds, with complex warfare emerging only after states developed larger populations and more sophisticated war technologies.

SCHOLARSHIP

Turney-High's work *Primitive War*, first published in 1949, relied on anthropological studies of modern tribes such as the Zulus and Apaches, which were heavily affected by colonialism and technology. In the 1960's, anthropologists such as Margaret Mead (1901-1978) challenged the earlier model, noting the difficulties of applying data from the "ethnographic present" of modern cultures to a far different ancient world. Mead even claimed to have found Pacific island tribes that did not know of war. This fueled the academic nature-versus-nurture debate on the origins of war: Were early peoples inherently warlike, or is warlike behavior a learned trait?

Cultures such as the Maya and the Pueblo peoples of the American Southwest were put forth as peaceful examples, whereas the Spartans and Aztecs were cited as warlike. Some researchers claimed that war was common in the distant past, whereas others argued that war is a relatively recent phenomenon. The debate continues as archaeologists uncover increasing evidence of group violence in the precivilized world. When did war begin? Have human beings always been violent? How should violence and war be defined? The answers to such questions have much to do with the interpretive worldviews of the scholars and researchers who explore these topics.

EVIDENCE

Evidence of the ancient presence of violence and war in human life comes primarily from skeletal remains and human-made artifacts, geographical features, architecture, and iconography created before 4000 B.C.E. Some of the best evidence is provided by groups of skeletons with ellipsoid cranial fractures, embedded projectiles, and decapitation marks found along with associated artifacts such as maces, spears, sling balls, and arrowheads in the context of defensively built or located architecture. Such forms of evidence are rarely found all together at sites dating to before 4000 B.C.E., perhaps indicating how rare actual battle was at that time.

The various kinds of evidence tend to be found in differing combinations. Evidence exists of mass death by violence in Egypt by 7000 B.C.E.; of the building of walls, towers, and other defensive locations as well as the use of maces and slings in the Levant and Turkey by 6000 B.C.E.; and of the construction of elevated forts with moats, baffled gates, and palisades in China by 5000 B.C.E. All of the mentioned forms of evidence—including battle scenes on cylinder seals—can be found in Sumer by 4000 B.C.E., indicating that by that time warfare was clearly under way.

The existing evidence concerning human violence has spawned debate among researchers such as Lawrence H. Keeley, R. Brian Ferguson, and Steven A. LeBlanc concerning the best ways in which to define, identify, and interpret the relationship between group violence and war. When is group violence a battle? Does the definition of warfare need to include the existence of battles? Is evidence of the threat of "coercive force" expressed in architecture, weaponry, and the like enough to indicate the presence of war? What if the evidence is limited to a few times and places? Researchers point to the lack of skeletal marks left on many remains in modern warfare when individuals perish from soft-tissue trauma. They note also that modern military systems have armies, soldiers, and fortifications that will never be involved in any battle deaths, yet no one doubts these are associated with war. Is specialization by the individual, the weapon, and the architecture the key? This is a debate that will not die down anytime soon.

VIOLENCE VS. WARFARE

The growing body of archaeological evidence has led to renewed interest in the relationship between ancient violence and warfare, and in the question of the nature of warfare in the precivilized world. It has been suggested that several "origins" for war are associated with specialization in violence, one taking the form of sporadic outbreaks of war among specialized Stone Age hunter-gatherers as settlements emerged and another being the outbreaks related to the first formations of states after 4000 B.C.E. This possibility fits well with the episodic nature of the available archaeological evidence. As the great philosopher of war Carl von Clausewitz (1780-1831) noted, war is the province of violence; it is the nature of the relationship between violence and war in the Stone Age with which archaeologists now grapple.

BOOKS AND ARTICLES

Carman, John, and Anthony Harding. *Ancient Warfare: Archaeological Perspectives*. Stroud, Gloucestershire, England: Sutton, 1999.

Ehrenreich, Barbara. *Origins and History of the Passions of War*. New York: Holt Metropolitan Books, 1997.

Ferguson, R. Brian. "Archaeology, Cultural Anthropology, and the Origins and Intensifications of War." In *The Archaeology of Warfare: Prehistories of Raiding and Conquest*, edited by Elizabeth N. Arkush and Mark W. Allen. Gainesville: University Press of Florida, 2006.

Gat, Azar. *War in Human Civilization*. New York: Oxford University Press, 2008.

Guilain, Jean. *The Origins of War: Violence in Prehistory*. Hoboken, N.J.: Wiley-Blackwell, 2005.

Keeley, Lawrence H. *War Before Civilization: The Myth of the Peaceful Savage*. New York: Oxford University Press, 1996.

Kelly, Raymond. *Warless Societies and the Origins of War*. Ann Arbor: University of Michigan Press, 2000.

LeBlanc, Steven A., with Katherine E. Register. *Constant Battles: The Myth of the Peaceful, Noble Savage*. New York: St. Martin's Press, 2003.

O'Connell, Robert. *Ride of the Second Horseman: The Birth and Death of War*. New York: Oxford University Press, 1995.

Otterbein, Keith. *How War Began*. College Station: Texas A&M University Press, 2004.

Peterson, Dale, and Richard Wrangham. *Demonic Males: Apes and the Origins of Human Violence*. Boston: Mariner Books, 1997.

Turney-High, Harry Holbert. *Primitive War: Its Practices and Concepts*. 2d ed. Columbia: University of South Carolina Press, 1971.

Christopher Howell

THE ANCIENT WORLD

WORLD

EGYPT AND THE MIDDLE EAST

CITY-STATES AND EMPIRES THROUGH OLD BABYLON

Dates: c. 3500-1595 B.C.E.

MILITARY ACHIEVEMENT

The evolution of warfare in ancient Mesopotamia led to the creation of large and powerful empires in the Near East, the weapons and formations of which influenced classical civilization. Historians believe that the beginnings of organized warfare coincided with the dawn of written history in both Mesopotamia and Egypt, probably independently of each other. Around 4000 B.C.E. the Sumerians, a people of unknown ethnic origin, settled in southern Mesopotamia, building their cities and fortifications from mud bricks. They failed to create a stable, unified kingdom and lived in a cluster of independent city-states, such as Ur, Kish, Lagash, Erech, Suruppack, Larsa, and Umma, and constantly warred with each other for supremacy over the region.

The first steps toward unity were taken in southern Mesopotamia when King Lugalzaggesi (r. c. 2375-2350 B.C.E.) of Uruk created a temporary Sumerian Empire by subduing his rivals and ultimately establishing nominal control over all of Mesopotamia, as well as parts of Syria and Asia Minor. He was defeated by the Akkadian king, Sargon the Great (c. 2334-2279 B.C.E.), who led a Semitic band of warriors in conquest of Sumer, unifying upper and lower Mesopotamia and creating the first real empire in history, which lasted nearly three hundred years. In thirty-four major battles, Sargon used new technology to establish a domain that stretched eventually from the Mediterranean Sea to the Persian Gulf. Akkadian civilization eventually succumbed to an invasion of barbarous mountain dwellers from the east called the Gutians, who were victorious not because of their superior technology but because of their intensity in combat. Some time after 2100 B.C.E., the Sumerians reasserted their supremacy over southern Mesopotamia, which precipitated a renaissance of Sumerian culture and control in the area that lasted for approximately two hundred years.

After the beginning of the second millennium B.C.E. a new Semitic race of people, the Babylonians, perhaps from the area of modern Syria, rose to prominence in Mesopotamia. With its capital established at the city-state of Babylon, the whole region once again became unified under the rule of the powerful Babylonian leader Hammurabi (c. 1810-1750 B.C.E.), the famous lawgiver, warrior, and strategist.

Hammurabi's death was followed by a number of revolts that led to the rapid disintegration of his king-

TURNING POINTS

c. 3200 B.C.E.	The Bronze Age is inaugurated in Mesopotamia as new metal technology allows more lethal weapons and more effective armor.
c. 2500 B.C.E.	The Sumerian phalanx is first employed.
c. 2300 B.C.E.	After the composite bow is introduced by Sargon the Great, the use of the Sumerian phalanx declines.
c. 2100 B.C.E.	The Sumerians reassert their supremacy over southern Mesopotamia, precipitating a renaissance of Sumerian culture and control that lasts for approximately 200 years.
c. 1810 B.C.E.	Neo-Babylonian leader Hammurabi unifies Mesopotamian region under his rule and establishes capital at the city-state of Babylon.
1595 B.C.E.	Mesopotamian Empire falls to the Kassites.

SUMER AND AKKAD, C. 4000-2000 B.C.E.

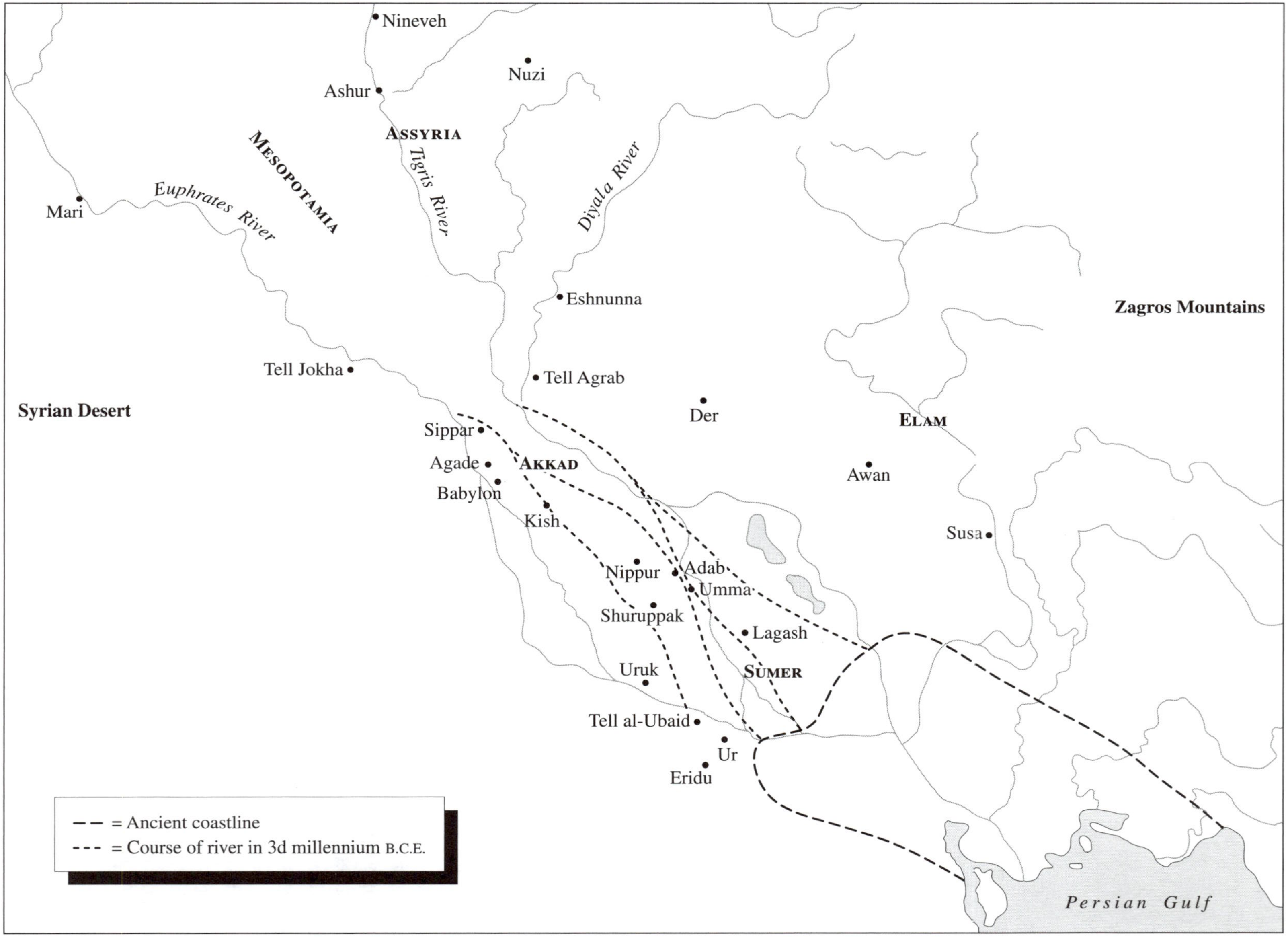

Zagros Mountains

Persian Gulf

ELAM

Susa •

Awan •

SUMER

Lagash •

Umma •
Adab •

Der •

Nippur •
Shuruppak •

Ur •
Eridu •

Uruk •

Tell al-Ubaid •

Diyala River

Eshnunna •

Tell Agrab •

AKKAD

Kish •

Nuzi •

Sippar •
Agade •
Babylon •

ASSYRIA

Tigris River

Nineveh •

Ashur •

MESOPOTAMIA

Tell Jokha •

Euphrates River

Syrian Desert

Mari •

— — = Ancient coastline

- - - = Course of river in 3d millennium B.C.E.

dom. In the late seventeenth century B.C.E. the Hittite Empire, centered in Asia Minor, began expanding with the aid of early iron technology. In 1595 B.C.E. Mesopotamia fell to the Kassites and entered into a long period of lethargy.

WEAPONS, UNIFORMS, AND ARMOR

Ancient weapons in Mesopotamia can be divided into two categories: shock weapons, for striking the enemy in hand-to-hand combat, and missile weapons, for shooting or throwing at the enemy. The earliest weapons were crafted from stone and included the mace and the stone ax. The inauguration in Mesopotamia of the Bronze Age (c. 3200 B.C.E.), so called for the introduction of new metal technology, was roughly contemporaneous with the beginnings of city-state civilization and ushered in the use of metal weapons, making warfare much more lethal than it had been previously. The use of metal transformed shock weapons. Brittle stones were unsuited to producing lasting sharp edges used for striking opposing combatants. The introduction of metal helmets, shields, and body armor with bronze scales eliminated the effectiveness of the mace in favor of the battle-ax and metal-tipped spear. A helmet excavated from one of the richly adorned graves at the Royal Cemetery of Ur and dating from 2600 to 2400 B.C.E. was made of electrum, a gold and silver alloy, and hammered into shape from the inside.

The chariot appeared much earlier in Mesopotamia than elsewhere. Although it was in wide use as early as 3000 B.C.E., it was not the highly mobile, two-man, two-wheeled vehicle that appeared only after centuries of development. The war chariot of Sumer was a large, heavy, rather clumsy four-wheeled vehicle that carried a driver, a warrior, and two

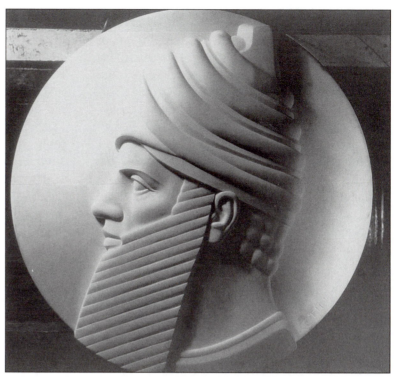

A relief of Hammurabi, the powerful Babylonian leader who united the Babylonian kingdom and codified its laws.

shield-bearers commissioned to protect the warrior. The chariot warrior was armed with a spear, sometimes a battle-ax, but not a bow, which was used earlier and more regularly in other Near Eastern cultures, particularly in Egypt, and arrived in Sumer only much later. Akkadian warriors under Sargon introduced Mesopotamia to the use of the composite bow, which provided this force with the necessary margin of superiority over the Sumerians. The bow fell into disuse until it began to be employed again during the reunification of Mesopotamia under Hammurabi.

MILITARY ORGANIZATION

The Sumerian Stela of the Vultures, an artifact of singular importance dating from approximately 2500 B.C.E., supplies information about the organization and formation of combatants into fighting units in

Mesopotamia. This limestone victory monument depicts King Eannatum of Lagash leading his troops into battle. The warrior-hero stands at the head of his advancing army, which is composed of a cadre of infantrymen packed shoulder to shoulder behind a barrier of interlocking, handheld rectangular shields, wearing matching helmets and presenting a hedgehog formation of protruding spears. In other words, the infantry forms a genuine, full-fledged phalanx. This depiction is significant because it constitutes evidence that the phalanx was used two thousand years before it was implemented by the Greeks, and it emphasizes the importance of Sumerian military developments, which are often overlooked in the history of weapons and warfare. The Sumerian phalanx seems to have been a full-blown innovation rather than a product of an evolutionary technological process.

Additionally, the Stela of the Vultures depicts all of the phalangite infantrymen as outfitted and protected in the same fashion but distinct in dress from the single warrior-leader placed in front to direct the shock troops. Although the egalitarian outfitting of troops is certainly predicated on the practical demands of the type of close-arm combat tactics employed in Mesopotamia, it also suggests to scholars that regalia determined one's standing and social status as well as the expectations and presumed responsibilities of office.

The campaign of Sargon the Great, empowered by the new technology used by his Akkadian bowmen against the Sumerian leader Lugalzaggesi of Uruk, is regarded as the factor responsible for the disappearance of the Sumerian phalanx. Sargon's empire consisted of a small warrior class living off the work of a few artisans and craftsmen and a large peasantry.

North Wind Picture Archives via AP Images

A mounted Babylonian warrior carrying a sword, spear, and bow and arrow.

DOCTRINE, STRATEGY, AND TACTICS

Very little is known about the roles played by individual kings or commanders. The first organized battles in Mesopotamia occurred before 3500 B.C.E., when smaller groups armed only with crude stone weapons and without protective armor clashed with one another for control of food sources and land. Although cultures coalesced and armies increased in size, any cogent doctrine of warfare or sophisticated strategies seem to have been lacking. The key to effective combat was to find and kill the enemy's leader. If the king and his retainers were destroyed, so would be their army's chances for victory. With the development of city-states and walled towns in early Mesopotamia, siege warfare became increasingly important. The subjugation of all city-states and towns became the common goal of every competing army seeking to control the entire area. Warfare in early Mesopotamia was more frequent and less decisive strategically than in other parts of the ancient world precisely because of the constant intramural wars of the competing city-states. With the establishment of the first empires in Mesopotamia, warfare became directed outward, toward the conquest of neighboring peoples and adjacent lands. For the most part Sumerian, Akkadian, and Babylonian styles of war remained confrontational, geared toward the frontal assault. This type of warfare, along with the types of weapons associated with such fighting, tended to emphasize the need for, and the prestige attached to, the attributes of bravery and physical prowess.

Because chariots in early Mesopotamia were not very mobile, they probably were not used in the same tactical way as were later two-man chariots. Later chariots could be deployed in quick shock attacks against an enemy's flank and in fighting against other chariots. However, the early four-man chariots had to be drawn by asses because they were so cumbersome and, consequently, had to be maneuvered very close to enemy fortifications and forces in order to deliver any kind of effective firepower. Sources seem to agree that the early Mesopotamian chariots had little effective use as tools of destruction. They did, however, serve as instruments of intimidation, or for bringing a leader to a battlefield.

ANCIENT SOURCES

The Sumerians kept records on clay tablets inscribed in cuneiform. One of the most famous stories from this culture, the Gilgamesh epic (c. 2000 B.C.E.; English translation, 1917), describes the life of Gilgamesh of Uruk, an actual person around whom legends formed and who may be regarded as the first military hero in Near Eastern literature, serving as a model for warriors who followed. Gilgamesh was armed with a battle-ax bearing an actual name, "Might of Heroism," the first in a long line of titled weapons in the ancient world. The Gilgamesh epic also indicates that before the Mesopotamian warrior-leader decided to go into battle, he put the question before an assembly of the warrior class.

For the most part, however, information on warfare during the Sumerian period has come from images recovered by archaeologists. The Standard of Ur, found in the Royal Cemetery at Ur and now in the British Museum, has clear images of a variety of soldiers, demonstrating their armor and weaponry, as well as of five chariots. Indeed it is from this one find that much knowledge of warfare involving Ur comes. Some old weapons have also been recovered, and there are also surviving stelae.

Various artifacts, including the Stela of the Vultures, uncovered by the work of archaeologists, present visual images of ancient weapons and methods of war. Although physical evidence from the Akkadian period is slim, two cuneiform fragments depict the use of the composite bow, which scholars have hypothesized was made by carefully laminating bone, sinew, and keratin to a wooden core to create a weapon with tremendously magnified power.

BOOKS AND ARTICLES

Crawford, Harriet. *Sumer and the Sumerians*. New York: Cambridge University Press, 2004.

Ferrill, Arthur. *The Origins of War: From the Stone Age to Alexander the Great*. New York: Thames and Hudson, 1986.

Gabriel, Richard A., and Karen S. Metz. *From Sumer to Rome: the Military Capabilities of Ancient Armies*. New York: Greenwood Press, 1991.

Humble, Richard. *Warfare in the Ancient World*. London: Weidenfeld and Nicolson, 1980.

Laffont, Robert. *The Ancient Art of Warfare*. Greenwich, Conn.: New York Graphic Society, 1966.

O'Connell, Robert L. *Of Arms and Men: A History of War, Weapons, and Aggression*. New York: Oxford University Press, 1990.

Wise, Terence. *Ancient Armies of the Middle East*. New York: Osprey, 1981.

Yadin, Yigael. *The Art of Warfare in Biblical Lands*. Vol. 1. New York: McGraw-Hill, 1963.

FILMS AND OTHER MEDIA

The Kings: From Babylon to Baghdad. Docudrama. History Channel, 2004.

Andrew C. Skinner

THE HITTITES
Dates: c. 1620-1190 B.C.E.

MILITARY ACHIEVEMENT

The Hittites ruled a powerful empire in Asia Minor and northern Syria during the seventeenth to twelfth centuries B.C.E. One of their primary military achievements was in establishing a sphere of political influence in the Near East. Another was their creation of a professional army, in conjunction with refinements in siege warfare and the training of horses for use with the lightweight, single-axle chariot.

Weakened by royal family infighting, the Hittite Empire militarily secured by Mursilis I (r. c. 1620-c. 1590 B.C.E.) was in disarray two hundred years later when Suppiluliumas I (r. c. 1380-1346 B.C.E.) ascended to the throne. Hittite domination of central Anatolia, Syria, and territory stretching as far as the Amorite capital of Babylon was no longer assured.

Toward the mid-fourteenth century B.C.E., the Hittite capital of Hattusas (modern Bogazk) was threatened, apparently with the assistance of the Hurrians of the Mitanni kingdom and of the Syrians at Aleppo. Around 1370 B.C.E., the Hittites under the leadership of Suppiluliumas I set out to reestablish their hold on Syria. The initial campaign against the Mitanni kingdom, a 300-mile march and attack on the Syrian kingdom's northwest corner, was unsuccessful. A second campaign (c. 1367 B.C.E.) took the Mitanni Nuhasse neighbor. A third (c. 1365 B.C.E.) resulted in Hittite control of Isuwa in northeast Anatolia. The fourth campaign advanced to threaten the southern Mitanni capital of Wassukkani. In 1366 B.C.E., Suppiluliumas captured Kadesh (Qadesh) in western Syria. Finally, in c. 1350 B.C.E., he succeeded in taking Carchemish, an important and strategic trade route on the west bank of the Euphrates River.

Suppiluliumas's military success reunited the Hittite Empire but introduced a third military power into the balance of the two dominant military forces in the Near East, Mesopotamia, and Egypt. Mursilis II (r. c. 1345-c. 1320 B.C.E.) the heir to Suppiluliumas's expansionist policy, passed the Hittite Empire to his son, Muwatallis (r. c. 1320-c. 1294 B.C.E.). Over time, a growing internal unrest, stimulated partly by allied Mitanni and Assyrian forces, caused uprisings but received little response from the Hittite leader. Consequently, the Assyrians reconquered the region in a unified and formal manner. The Hittites, harassed by requests for defensive assistance from their allies, but irritated by the sporadic raids made by their nominal vassal states, set out to reestablish Suppiluliumas's imperial holdings. The Hittites, rather than fight with their allies, the Assyrians, elected to engage the Egyptians in battle at Kadesh in Syria.

After about 1190 B.C.E., the Hittites faded as a major political and military power in the Near East. As the Assyrian Empire continued to expand systematically, the Hittite Empire eventually collapsed.

WEAPONS, UNIFORMS, AND ARMOR

The principal weapons used by the Hittites in battle were the bow and arrow, ax, and spear. The chariot was also used defensively. Suppiluliumas's strengths were his strategic tactics, his patience, and his ability to extract from defeat the seeds for future victory. His first defeat by the Mitanni illustrates his use of the chariot as a strategic weapon rather than a fighting wagon.

The Hittite spear, known from illustrations found at Egyptian ruins, consisted of a pointed metal blade attached to a wooden shaft with leather wrappings. Originally, the blade was made of copper, then bronze, and finally iron. The spear's structure consisted of a socket for the blunt blade end reinforced with leather strips attached to the wooden shaft. The spear shaft, for cutting and slashing, was fitted to maximize damage to the enemy in hand-to-hand combat. Although

A depiction of a relief on a wall at Giaur-Kala in modern Turkmenistan, showing two Hittite soldiers.

the spear has its advantages as a thrown weapon, there are no illustrations of Hittites actually using a spear offensively in this way. Instead, the spear seems to have been used primarily for defensive purposes, such as to guard the driver and bowman in the three-man chariot crew.

The design of both the ax and the battle-ax forms the shape of a human arm attached to a shaft. The flanged hand-end of the ax is flared in long bronze fingerlike forms. In hand-to-hand combat, the sharp-edged wrist section could not be grasped without cutting through the enemy's hand. The ax's extended, clawlike frontal section made it possible to slice through the neck of the enemy. In addition, the thumblike portion of the ax, just before the shaft, functioned as a hook for gouging. The dagger differs

in design, with a shorter, double-edged blade for use in hand-to-hand combat.

Body armor worn by the Hittites consisted of 4.5-inch bronze plates bound together with linen or leather to form a small breast jacket. The jacket was made originally to protect the chariot driver and crew. A relief found in Luxor, Egypt, detailing the Battle of Kadesh (1274 B.C.E.) shows the Hittite infantry wearing ankle-length skirts made of leather without any metal plating. Because infantrymen required mobility, the metal plating may have been eliminated and the protective metal plates replaced with leather.

Hittite infantrymen were armed with javelins intended to be thrown either while on the run or from a stationary position. The lance was the traditional Hittite weapon for the chariot crew. Their use in battle is not recorded visually in the Luxor relief. Although Ramses II made claim that the Hittites were unable to use either their bows or their javelins because his chariots charged through their lines, thereby preventing a frontal assault, it is questionable whether such a tactic was actually used. The statement suggests that the throwers may have been not in the chariots but rather on foot, in retreat, or unable to immobilize the Egyptian chariots. Such a thesis implies that the throwers either were separated from their chariot crew or were in disarray.

Although the physical evidence indicates that bows and arrows tipped in bronze were used as a major weapon in conjunction with the Hittite chariotry, there is little evidence that archers were used with chariots. Evidence for Hittite bowmen in action is scarce. Only Muwatallis, the king of the Hittites, is depicted in the Luxor reliefs in a chariot with an archer and bowcase. These reliefs show the Hittites with a defensive force and the Egyptian army with offensive weapons. Ironically, the intended purpose of this work was to show the heroic and invincible Egyptian Pharaoh in the face of Hittite aggression. Contradictory information is contained in the Abydos inscriptions, where the Egyptian king records "killing horses, capturing chariots, bows, swords, all weapons of warfare."

The simple but sturdy Hittite chariot provided the army with an effective battlefield vehicle. The chariot design enabled the Hittites to retain flexibility and mobility in battle and to carry a three-man crew, consisting of driver, archer, and spear bearer.

The typical offensive use of the chariot by the Hittites was to taunt and encircle the enemy at a distance. After the chariot's forward advance toward the enemy, the infantry might advance using lances to inflict damage. The Hittite strategy suggests an emphasis on a defensive use of the chariot against an offensive line. Once the enemy line was broken by the chariotry, the Hittite infantry could strike effectively.

MILITARY ORGANIZATION

Upon his ascension to the Hittite throne in about 1380, Suppiluliumas I inherited an empire frayed by Hittite vassal-states. To restore the Hittite kingdom, he reinforced and restored the decaying fortifications of the Hittite capital, Hattusas, constructing a massive wall to encircle the city's vulnerable perimeter. Suppiluliumas also reorganized the professional Hittite army, which recruited and enlisted infantrymen. The infantry provided the Hittites with a regular standing army that could be increased as needed by vassal treaty. The infantry did not contain the protectorate citizens or native Hittite populations. Supposedly, the use of vassal-state infantry eliminated the need for mercenaries, although Egyptian sources suggest otherwise, listing a great number of mercenaries in the Hittite ranks.

Instructional specifics about the training of Hittite soldiers are scarce. It is thought that special locales or training camps existed and that training consisted of drill practice. A Hittite king might bring several army divisions with him on a campaign, depending on the conflict. Hittite strategy originally focused on fast-attack troops but quickly shifted to siege warfare, in which support troops and supply lines for men and horses were more crucial than battlefield encounters to the success of the siege.

For strategic purposes, the basic military unit was a platoon of fifty infantrymen under the command of the king. These infantry units were reinforced with elite troops or chariot warriors. Decision making about battlefield tactics seems to have been left to the king alone. Acknowledged credit for battle success would lie respectively with the gods, the king, and then the king's generals. The different locations of unit types within the camp demonstrate a similar hierarchical arrangement.

Two principles defined the organization of the king's troops: chariotry and infantry. Within the reign of Suppiluliumas the leaders of each learned to work with the ten vassal-states. Although military professionals were incorporated into the Hittite army, they nonetheless remained identified with their individual vassal-states.

The Hittites had four types of troops: infantry, chariotry, outpost garrison, and elite guard. The sizes of the units are difficult to establish from existing descriptions, but evidence suggests that a division might have equaled about 5,000 men, a company about 250, a platoon approximately 50, and a squad as many as 10. In the Hittite military hierarchy, the king was the leader. Two generals represented the two protectorates, and they were followed in command by the generals of the vassal-states. Combat officers consisted of a platoon leader, garrison-troop leader, squad leaders, and the infantry and chariot soldiers.

The location of the Hittite capital shows the depth of Hittite defensive fears. The capital, Hattusas, was founded around 2000 B.C.E. within a natural defensive perimeter: a downward slope to the north, a dangerous gorge to the east, and a deep valley to the west.

The defensive fortifications of the upper city were located on the highest ground and designed of smooth rock to prevent an assault force from scaling the walls. Along the outer wall, there is another, inner wall. Parapets with round crenellations and high towers between them provided windows that allowed soldiers to survey the surroundings, guarding from attack. The massive walls were punctuated with several towers flanked by gateways. On the south, the outer wall was reached by a steep, sloping staircase defended from the ramparts. Between the outer and inner fortification walls, a ramp was built to inhibit free access. The main gateway was flanked with stone carved towers, double locking doors, and windows to decrease potential assaults.

Access to the city could be gained through an underground postern, or back gate, about 230 feet long. It served a defensive military purpose by preventing massed groups from assaulting the city from beneath. The postern also had an offensive use, allowing Hittite soldiers to enter and leave the city undetected during a siege.

DOCTRINE, STRATEGY, AND TACTICS

Hittite strategy consisted of two parts: a military strategy for battle and a diplomatic strategy for treaties. The strategic weakness of the Hittite Empire is demonstrated by their treaties, of which the Hittites made two types: a treaty of parity with their two protectorate allies and a treaty of vassal-states. The Hittite treaty made the Hittites vulnerable to the petty raids and complaints of vassal-states. The other two major powers, Mesopotamia and Egypt, could leverage their treaties, but the Hittite treaty with vassal-states necessitated immediate response to calls for help by the vassal-states. If the Hittite Empire did not respond, it would be considered disinterested or too weak.

Egypt's sovereignty over the region during the second millennium B.C.E. reached from Canaan and the Levantine ports and the cities that bordered on the inland routes from Megiddo in modern Israel to the lands of the Hittite, Mitanni, and Babylonian kingdoms. Because control of the region was important to Egypt's continued trade with Near Eastern partners, Egypt kept pressure on the cities of Palestine simultaneously with the Hittites. Complaints contained in ancient letters indicate one catalyst for renewed hostilities: the emergence of the Amurru kingdom as a power. The nineteenth Hittite Dynasty witnessed renewed military activity throughout the region, threatening Hittite national unity and international expansionist policies. The result for both the Egyptians and the Hittites was the loyalty of Canaan and control of the Orontes Valley for trade with Syrian ports. The Egyptian campaigns of Sety I (c. 1306-1290) attempted to restore Egyptian hegemony in Canaan and the Amurru kingdom, which stood on the Hittite boundary. However, Sety succeeded only in Palestine. After the Egyptian king Ramses II (c. 1300-1213) ascended the throne, the provocation remained unresolved, and Ramses systematically began to retake control of Hittite territories along the Palestinian coastal plain to Byblos.

The Hittite strategy for the battle was designed to delude the Egyptians into thinking that the Hittite army was encamped beyond the city of Kadesh when they were hidden behind it, to the north. Ramses II, leading four divisions of his army—Amon, Re, Ptah, and Sutekh—made an unimaginable frontal attack for the city, leading the Amon division ahead of the other three divisions. The Hittite leader, Muwatallis, advanced around Kadesh on the west, while his chariots attacked the Re division from the south. Although the two armies were of virtually equal strength, Ramses was cut off from the rest of his army, with only one division.

In the Egyptian records, the Egyptians claim victory but it is possible that the Egyptians were prevented from recovering sufficient strength to oust the Hittites from Kadesh. The cunning strategy used by the Hittites demonstrates a keen understanding of the chariot's potential for subterfuge, coupled with speed and mobility.

ANCIENT SOURCES

Although many cuneiform tables survive from the Hittites, most of these are to do with the administration of their empire, and few have any bearing on their military strengths. Some archaeological work at Boghazköy has unearthed statuettes and bas-reliefs, but the vast majority of our information on the Hittite soldiers comes from bas-reliefs and carvings in Egypt, where they are shown battling the Egyptians. The best known of these is at Abu Simbel, and there are also others at Luxor, Abydos, and the Ramesseum, the funerary temple of Ramses II in western Thebes, which all record strategic details of the Battle of Kadesh.

The reliefs reveal the strategy of Ramses: to penetrate as far as possible into enemy territory and to set up his offensive position before the city. The reliefs at Luxor illustrate Ramses' arrival and camp, and the Hittite ruse and subsequent surprise attack through the camp shield barriers. Ramses' counterattack, depicted on the walls of the Ramesseum, illustrates his second strategy: to make a full-force, frontal attack into the enemy lines. The Hittite charioteers were more intent on plundering the Egyptian camp than on fighting, and the Hittite forces fell into disarray. They were then chased by the Egyptians into retreat.

None of the Egyptian reliefs, however, shows the capture of Kadesh or Hittite surrender. Ramses claimed victory less for Egypt than for himself. There is some validity to his claim. After his army had fled, it was Ramses' leadership that sustained the Egyptian forces on the battlefield. Traditionally, historians interpret the outcome of the battle as a draw.

These ancient sources are significant in that they provide the names of ally groups, terminology for weapons, the organization and identification of types of soldier units and chariot warriors, and insight into strategies. The Hittites' use of subterfuge reveals an awareness of the tactical offensive role of the chariot in warfare.

BOOKS AND ARTICLES

Gurney, O. R. *The Hittites*. Rev. ed. London: Penguin, 1990.

Healy, Mark. *Qadesh 1300 B.C.* New York: Osprey, 1993.

Kitchen, K. A. *Pharaoh Triumphant: The Life and Times of Ramesses II, King of Egypt*. Warminster, England: Aris and Phillips, 1982.

Murname, W. *The Road to Kadesh: A Historical Interpretation of the Battle Reliefs of King Sety I at Karnak*. Chicago: University of Chicago Press, 1985.

Nossov, Konstantin. *Hittite Fortifications c. 1659-700 B.C.* New York: Osprey, 2008.

Wise, Terence. *Ancient Armies of the Middle East*. New York: Osprey, 1981.

Yadin, Y. *The Art of Warfare in Biblical Lands*. 2 vols. New York: McGraw-Hill, 1963.

FILMS AND OTHER MEDIA

Empire of the Hittites. Parts 5/6 of *In Search of the Trojan War*. Documentary. British Broadcasting Corporation, 1985.

The Hittites: A Civilization That Changed the World. Docudrama. Cinema Epoch, 2004.

Elizabeth L. Meyers

THE ASSYRIANS
Dates: c. 1950-612 B.C.E.

POLITICAL CONSIDERATIONS

Assyria was the ancient name of the area surrounding the upper Tigris River and its principal tributaries, the Greater Zab and the Lesser Zab, in northern Iraq. From an early period the people living there, the Assyrians, adopted many cultural features of the more civilized Sumerians of the lower Tigris and Euphrates River valleys, including cuneiform writing and a "hydraulic civilization," which required irrigation to take advantage of the available fertile alluvial plain. Although food could be produced locally, virtually all metals, luxury goods, and horses had to be imported or seized from surrounding mountains to the north and east, in modern Turkey and Iran, where the Assyrians frequently faced invasion from hostile tribes. The Assyrians needed to secure defensible borders beyond their homeland, and thus became intimately linked to the material prosperity of their empire.

Assyrian history can be divided into three periods. The empire first rose to power during the Old Empire period (1950-1500 B.C.E.). After the death of Shamshi-Adad I (r. c. 1813-1781 B.C.E.), Assyrian rule declined, leading to annexations by the Mitanni and to the revival of city-states, including Arrapha, Erbil, Ashur, and Ninevah. The Middle Empire period (c. 1500-900 B.C.E.) witnessed the rebirth of Assyrian domination. Ashur-uballit I (r. c. 1365-1330 B.C.E.) drove the Mitanni from Assyria and laid the foundations for further expansion. The Assyrians of the middle period reached their peak under Tiglath-pileser I (1115-1077 B.C.E.), who briefly expanded the empire as far as the Mediterranean Sea. After the death of Tiglath-pileser I, incursions of Aramaeans and dynastic struggles led to an alliance with Babylon and a retreat to the traditional Assyrian homeland.

MILITARY ACHIEVEMENT

Assyria's greatest era of military expansion came during the late imperial period (c. 900-600 B.C.E.). Ashur-dan II (934-912 B.C.E.) reestablished control of his kingdom, and his four successors all pushed forward Assyrian borders and expanded control of valuable trade routes. Under Ashurnasirpal II (r. 883-859 B.C.E.), the Assyrians crossed the Euphrates River, forcing most of the Aramaean, Phoenician, and neo-Hittite kings as far as the Mediterranean Sea, the Taurus and Zagros Mountains, and the Armenian Highlands to pay tribute. Reflecting the importance of these new borders, Ashurnasirpal II moved the Assyrian capital to Calah, modern Nimrud, nearer to the front. Shalmaneser III (r. 858-824 B.C.E.) waged almost continual war during his reign. Although he maintained Assyrian dominance in northern Syria, he was defeated at Karkar in central Syria (853 B.C.E.) by a coalition of Syro-Palestinian kings that included Ahab (r. c. 874-c. 853 B.C.E.) of Israel. Shalmaneser III failed on five occasions to subdue Damascus and southern Syria but did manage to subdue Tyre, Sidon, and Israel.

After eighty years of domestic turmoil, Tiglath-pileser III (r. 745-727 B.C.E.) reestablished control over the Assyrian homeland and initiated the campaigns that destroyed the independence of the kings of Syria and Israel. Between 743 and 732 he drove the Urartians back into the Taurus Mountains and captured Damascus. In 729 he conquered Babylon. Israel was finally subdued during the first year of the reign of Sargon II (r. 721-705 B.C.E.), and Jerusalem, the capital of the southern Israelite kingdom of Judah, was unsuccessfully besieged by Sargon's son Sennacherib (r. 704-681 B.C.E.). The last great Assyrian king, Ashurbanipal (r. 668-627 B.C.E.), completed the conquest of Egypt that had been under-

An Assyrian battle scene at the palace of Ashurnasirpal.

taken by his father. Continually harassed by the Elamites in the east (modern Iran), in 639 he led a massive campaign of extermination. The Assyrian Empire had never been greater, stretching from Thebes in southern Egypt to Tarsus in Asia Minor, to Babylonia in the south, and to Elam in the east. In less than thirty years, however, overextension, harsh treatment of subject peoples, and a disastrous struggle with the Medes led to the conquest of Nineveh (612 B.C.E.) by a combined army of Medes and Babylonians and to the final destruction of the Assyrian Empire. The Hebrew prophet Nahum (fl. seventh century B.C.E.) echoed the common sentiment of all Near Eastern peoples when he said, "All who hear the news of you clap their hands at your downfall, for who has not felt your unrelenting cruelty?"

WEAPONS, UNIFORMS, AND ARMOR

Assyria's offensive power initially rested upon development and use of the war chariot. Their vehicles evolved from the more mobile two-man chariot, used for reconnaissance, communication, and combat, to the heavy, four-horse, four-man chariot common during Ashurbanipal's reign. By the time the empire fell, cavalry units had taken over many of the duties of the chariots, which were then being used principally as firing platforms for archers and as shock vehicles in frontal attacks. Effective use of the chariot in combat was limited to flat or nearly flat terrain, making it less valuable as Assyria expanded into surrounding mountainous terrain.

The first record of Assyrian cavalry units is found in the ninth century B.C.E., when riders were deployed in pairs, with one man holding the reins of both mounts while the other fired a bow. As riders gained expertise, each horse and rider became an autonomous unit, with riders carrying long lances. By the seventh century B.C.E., the cavalry had largely displaced the chariot as the mobile force of the military, and horsemen were typically armed with both bows and lances. Riders covered their torsos with lamellar armor, consisting of bronze plates stitched to a leather underjacket, whereas fabric armor was used to protect their mounts.

ASSYRIA AND BABYLONIA, 600-500 B.C.E.

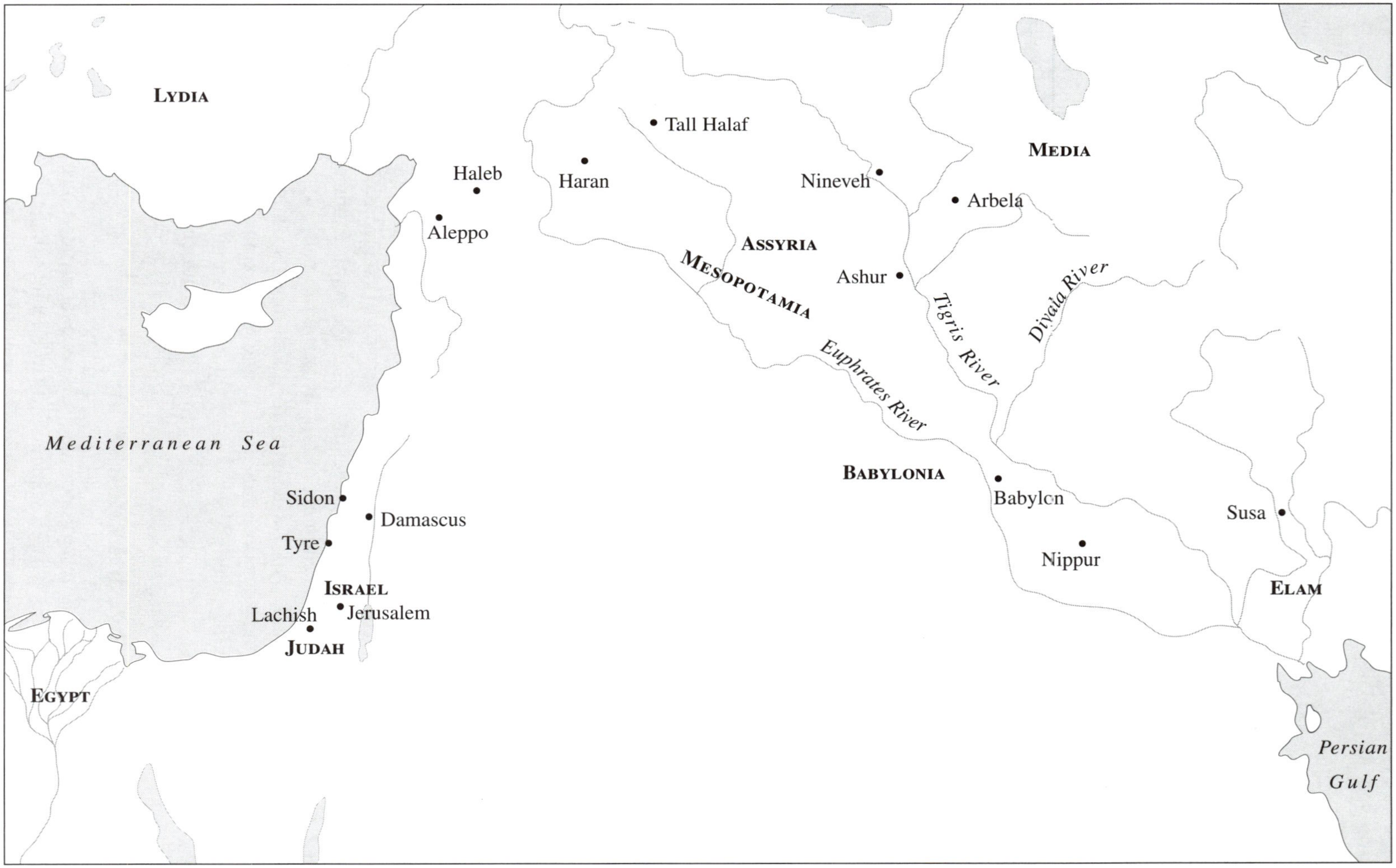

LYDIA

MEDIA

Susa •

ELAM

Persian Gulf

Arbela •

Nippur •

Babylon •

Diyala River

Nineveh •

Ashur •

ASSYRIA

Tigris River

BABYLONIA

• Tall Halaf

MESOPOTAMIA

Euphrates River

• Haran

Haleb •

Aleppo •

Damascus •

Sidon •

Tyre •

ISRAEL

• Jerusalem

Lachish •

JUDAH

Mediterranean Sea

EGYPT

The bow and arrow and the lance were the most common weapons among infantry units, but slings, knives, and swords were also utilized. In the late imperial period, archers were deployed in pairs, with one man serving as a shieldbearer. Shields made from plaited reeds were often taller than a man and curved at the top to deflect incoming arrows. Both simple and compound bows were used, with ranges of between 250 and 650 meters. The bow used by particular units was often linked to the ethnicity of the unit. Records indicate, for instance, that there were distinctive Akkadian, Assyrian, and Cimmerian bows. Tiglath-pileser III introduced both the lance-spear, for close-order thrusting, and lamellar armor, known among elite infantry units as the *zuku sa sheppe*. Ordinary units and native levies had only a helmet and shield for their personal protection.

In an age during which the art of fortification was highly developed, the Assyrians were innovators in siegecraft and siege organization. They built movable wooden towers covered by dampened leather hides, which enabled expert archers to clear the parapets above while troops below worked to undermine the walls. They sometimes used a swinging "ram" to batter the walls and sometimes a ram with a wide, iron blade that would be inserted between stones and rocked in order to pry the stones apart.

MILITARY ORGANIZATION

Assyrian military success owed much to superior preparation, which allowed large armies to be quickly assembled. Shalmaneser III, for instance, reportedly invaded Syria in 845 B.C.E. with 120,000 troops. Marshaling cities were kept in readiness to receive corn, oil, battle equipment, and troops in preparation for a new campaign, thus enabling forces to be quickly organized and provisioned. This led to the creation of Ashurnasirpal's Greater Assyria, a large area of northern Mesopotamia that could be controlled by relatively short campaigns and raids. In keeping with the agricultural basis of society, campaigning was seasonal, with conscripts called to arms by July, shortly after harvest.

Despite successes, more extensive campaigns, attrition, and battle losses made campaigning under the old system difficult. Tiglath-pileser III initiated important military reforms that created the most efficient army of the ancient world until the rise of Rome, enabling emperors to vastly increase the size of the empire. Instead of calling up agricultural workers during the summer, he introduced a standing army and personal bodyguard that was augmented as necessary by contingents raised in the provinces and levies drawn from vassal states. The Assyrian army may have been the first in which ethnic units were integrated largely on a basis of equality, though they frequently performed functions for which they were already expertly prepared.

On campaign, the Assyrian king frequently led the army, but sometimes he delegated authority to senior field marshals, known as *turtans*. Below these wing commanders, rank designations indicated control of 1,000, 500, or 100 troops. Although much remains unknown about Assyrian military organization, it is clear that it enabled the Assyrians to create the first

TURNING POINTS

1950-1500 B.C.E.	Assyrians first rise to power during the Old Empire period.
c. 1500-900 B.C.E.	During their Middle Empire period, the Assyrians drive the Mitanni from Assyria, laying foundations for further expansion.
c. 1000 B.C.E.	Iron begins to replace bronze in the making of weapons in Assyria.
900-600 B.C.E.	Assyria undergoes Late Empire period, its greatest era of military expansion.
745-727 B.C.E.	After years of domestic turmoil, Tiglath-Pileser III reestablishes control over Assyrian homeland and institutes military reforms.
721 B.C.E.	Sargon II conquers Israel.
612 B.C.E.	Assyrian city of Nineveh is conquered by Medes and Babylonians, marking the final destruction of the Assyrian Empire.

army capable of sustained, long-distance campaigning. An efficient system of supply depots, transport columns, and bridging trains enabled the Assyrian army to advance as rapidly as any army before the modern industrial age, fighting effectively at distances of up to 300 miles from their base of operations.

Assyria's unmatched striking capability was based upon its chariot force, which enabled it to wage lightning attacks across the plains of Mesopotamia and Syria, shocking enemy troops and paving the way for the lancers and archers of the infantry. From the ninth century onward, the cavalry became increasingly important, sometimes operating in units of 1,000 or more and eventually replacing the charioteers as the mobile arm of the military. This dependence upon cavalry forced the Assyrians to remain militarily aggressive in order to provide a continuous stream of remounts that could come only from capture, tribute payments, or taxation.

DOCTRINE, STRATEGY, AND TACTICS

Given the lack of geographical barriers, Assyria's grand strategy was to wage offensive wars that would push Assyrian boundaries far beyond the cities of the Tigris River Valley. As a part of this plan, terror was used as a deliberate tactic. The ultimate goal was to secure *adu*, or "pacts of loyalty," which required payment of tribute. If enemies refused to submit, it was not uncommon for all men, women, and children in a resisting city to be killed. Assyrians commonly laid waste to enemy lands, destroying granaries and irrigation systems and cutting down orchards. Surrounding territories would then be annexed, with native populations deported to distant cities.

Although all the Assyrian commanders were undoubtedly ferocious, some were recorded as being far more so than others. Tiglath-pileser III, in 744 B.C.E., for instance, was involved in the deporting of 65,000 people from Iran. Two years later, he resettled 30,000 Syrians in the Zagros Mountains of Persia. The use of deportation, torture, and other forms of terror was designed both to convince enemies to surrender and to deter future rebellious activity among conquered peoples. Tributary (vassal) states were allowed to maintain considerable autonomy, especially in the area of religion, whereas annexed territories, with imported foreign populations, were forced to worship Ashur and treated in every way as Assyrians.

As the power of the state grew, Assyrian strategy involved building a series of fortresses in annexed territories, and these would ensure control of trade routes. Control of roads enhanced trade and brought valuable commodities to a land that was not rich in natural resources, whereas fortresses were used as bases from which tribute raids could be launched into surrounding areas.

In terms of tactics, Assyria deployed infantry, cavalry, and charioteers in combined operations. Skirmishers, archers, and slingshot specialists harassed and demoralized opponents in the opening rounds of conflict. Infantry, armed with their lances, swords, and daggers, followed with a frontal assault against enemy lines. Cavalry and chariots would ideally provide the decisive thrust from the flanks or from the center of the Assyrian army toward a weak point in the enemy line. After the horses and chariots charged, a rout of the enemy could often be expected. However, if the forces were evenly matched, the cavalry and chariot charges might well be indecisive and yield a chaotic melee rather than a decisive victory.

ANCIENT SOURCES

There are extensive written records on campaigns of the late imperial period. The most important Assyrian sources include the annals of the Assyrian kings, which provide campaigning records; and many inscribed carvings and palace reliefs uncovered principally in Nineveh, Lachish, and other cities of the Assyrian homeland. Outside Assyria, victorious kings erected stelae, or carved stone pillars, on which they recorded their victories and reminded subjugated peoples of their tributary status. Hayim Tadmor has edited *The Inscriptions of Tiglath-pileser III* (2007), which contains much of military interest.

One of the most accessible sources of ancient information regarding the Assyrians is from the Old Testament of the Bible, principally in the books of 2 Kings, 2 Chronicles, Isaiah, and Hosea. There are also scattered references to Assyrian warfare in Sumerian and Greek sources, including those of Herodotus (c. 484-c. 424 B.C.E.) and Flavius Josephus (c. 37-c. 100 C.E.).

However, the most important sources on the Assyrian armies are not written, but bas-reliefs from Nineveh, many of which are held at the British Museum, London. These depict warriors, chariots, and even entire battle scenes such as that showing the siege of the city of Lachish by Sennacherib in 701 B.C.E.

BOOKS AND ARTICLES

Bradley, James Parker. *The Mechanics of Empire: The Northern Frontier of Assyria as a Case Study in Imperial Dynamics*. Helsinki: Neo-Assyrian Text Corpus Project, 2001.

Chapman, Cynthia R. *The Gendered Language of Warfare in the Israelite-Assyrian Encounter*. Winona Lake, Ind.: Eisenbrauns, 2004.

Gallagher, William R. *Sennacherib's Campaign in Judah*. Leiden, Netherlands: E. J. Brill, 1999.

Gwaltney, William C., Jr. "Assyrians." In *Peoples of the Old Testament World*, edited by Alfred J. Hoerth et al. Grand Rapids, Mich.: Baker Books, 1994.

Healy, Mark. *The Ancient Assyrians*. New York: Osprey, 1991.

Postgate, Nicholas. *The Land of Assur and the Yoke of Assur: Studies on Assyria, 1971-2005*. Oxford: Oxbow, 2007.

Saggs, Harry W. F. *The Might That Was Assyria*. London: Sidgwick and Jackson, 1984.

Yamada, Shigeo. *The Construction of the Assyrian Empire: A Historical Study of the Inscriptions of Shalmaneser II Relating to the Campaigns in the West*. Leiden, Netherlands: E. J. Brill, 2000.

FILMS AND OTHER MEDIA

Iraq: Stairway to the Gods. Documentary. Coronet Films and Video, 1973.

Mark Polelle and John Powell

THE CHALDEANS

Dates: 626-539 B.C.E.

MILITARY ACHIEVEMENT

The Chaldeans, or Neo-Babylonians, are credited with destroying the Assyrian Empire and establishing a new one in the Near East that was responsible for sacking Jerusalem, razing the Jewish temple located there, and destroying and deporting the kingdom of Judah in 586 B.C.E. The Chaldean culture was known not for military innovation but rather for honing previously used policies, weapons, and tactics in campaigns and battles that were fought over most of the ancient Near East.

During the period of Assyrian domination in the Near East (1300-700 B.C.E.), a new group of Semitic desert dwellers infiltrated southern Mesopotamia and established a culture that came to be known as Chaldean, named after the dominant tribe, the Kaldu. Discontent within the Assyrian Empire grew steadily during the reign of Ashurbanipal (r. 668-627 B.C.E.), the last great king of ancient Assyria. After his death, an imperial governor named Nabopolassar Nebuchadnezzar (r. 626-605 B.C.E.), a member of the Kaldu tribe, became leader of the insurrection. In 626 B.C.E., after a year of guerrilla war, Nabopolassar Nebuchadnezzar ascended the throne of the city-state of Babylon, inaugurated the Eleventh Babylonian dynasty, and established the Chaldean or Neo-Babylonian kingdom, to distinguish it from the Old Babylonian Empire of Hammurabi's (c. 1810-1750 B.C.E.) day.

For twelve years, from 626 to 614 B.C.E., war between the Chaldean, or Neo-Babylonian, kingdom and the remnants of the Assyrian Empire consisted of a series of battles over control of a network of fortified cities and towns in southern Mesopotamia, in modern-day Iraq. The Assyrians made an alliance with the Egyptians, who had become alarmed at the successes of the Chaldeans and of the Medes in what is now Iran. In 615 B.C.E. the Medes invaded Assyria and one year later captured the important city of Ashur. Significant emphasis was given by the Chaldeans to what might be termed coalition warfare in its early stages of development, and an alliance between the Chaldeans and the Medes was forged when Nabopolassar Nebuchadnezzar and the Median ruler Cyaxares (r. 625-585 B.C.E.) met under the walls of Ashur after the Median victory.

In 612 B.C.E. Nabopolassar Nebuchadnezzar led a final assault against Assyria's main city, Nineveh. Although it was strongly fortified, the city fell after a two-month siege, and, for all intents and purposes, the empire fell with it. In 610 B.C.E. the Medes and the Neo-Babylonians marched against Harran to the north and took it. The last of the Assyrian pretenders to the throne disappeared. The Medes did not lay claim to any part of the empire they helped to overthrow. Apparently content with their share of the booty, they withdrew to the east and turned their attention toward Armenia and Asia Minor. The Neo-Babylonians built their empire on the ruins of the Assyrian Empire, though they did not repair much of the damage they had inflicted.

After his final victory over the Assyrians, the aging Nabopolassar Nebuchadnezzar relied increasingly on his son, Nebuchadnezzar II (c. 630-562 B.C.E.) for the conduct of military operations. In 607 B.C.E. the crown prince attacked the Egyptian stronghold of Carchemish on the northern Euphrates River, routed the Egyptian army under Pharaoh Necho II (r. 610-595 B.C.E.), and gained military and economic control over areas to the west of Mesopotamia. However, just as all of Syria-Palestine now lay open to the Chaldeans, Nabopolassar Nebuchadnezzar died and Nebuchadnezzar II had to return to Babylon. He was crowned king in 605 B.C.E. For the next seven years he found himself quelling rebellion after rebellion in both Mesopotamia and Syria-Palestine. During the winter of 598 B.C.E. the king of Judah refused to pay

F. R. Niglutsch

Chaldean king Nebuchadnezzar II directs operations against rebellious Jews in 586 B.C.E., capturing and looting the capital of Jerusalem, destroying the Jewish temple, and rounding up and deporting thousands of Jews to Babylon.

tribute, forcing Nebuchadnezzar II to march on the kingdom's capital, Jerusalem, subjugating the city and installing a new king, Zedekiah.

Eleven years later, the kingdom of Judah was again at the center of rebellion against the Neo-Babylonian Empire. Nebuchadnezzar II personally directed operations against the rebellious Jews. In 586 B.C.E., after a siege of eighteen months, Jerusalem was captured, the city looted, the Jewish temple destroyed, and thousands of Jews rounded up and deported to Babylon. Thus, 135 years after thousands of citizens of the Northern Kingdom of Israel were deported by the Assyrians, thousands more Jews were once again carried away out of their lands in one of history's monumental turning points, the Babylonian Exile. One of the last actions of Nebuchadnezzar II in

Syria was the siege of the coastal town of Tyre, which lasted thirteen years. A fragmentary text now housed in the British Museum alludes to a Neo-Babylonian campaign against Pharaoh Ahmose II (570-526 B.C.E.) in 568 B.C.E., but it cannot be determined if the Neo-Babylonians ever actually set foot in the Nile Valley.

The last years of Nebuchadnezzar II's reign are obscure and seem to have ended amid internal chaos. His son, Evil-Merodach (died 560 B.C.E.), of Old Testament fame, ruled for only two years (561-560 B.C.E.). After another four years of political instability, the Babylonians installed Nabonidus (r. 556-539 B.C.E.) on the throne. A government official of Aramaean origin, Nabonidus was the last king of an independent Babylon. In 539 B.C.E. the founder of the Achaemenid Dynasty and first king of the Persian

Empire, Cyrus the Great (c. 601 to 590-c. 530 B.C.E.), conquered the Neo-Babylonian Empire.

WEAPONS, UNIFORMS, AND ARMOR

The Chaldeans do not appear to have been innovators in weapons development; they used the weapons of their immediate predecessors in Mesopotamia, including spears, daggers, and battle-axes. They also employed the composite bow first developed by Akkadian king Sargon the Great (c. 2334-2279 B.C.E.) and reintroduced by Hammurabi of the Old Babylonian Empire.

Babylonian infantry units are described fighting with metal helmets and carrying lances and wooden clubs. Friezes and reliefs show that the mace, though one of the oldest weapons employed in the Near East, was still being used in the seventh century B.C.E. Weapons used by the Neo-Babylonians were the product of the Iron Age technological revolution. By 900 B.C.E. smiths throughout the Near East had learned how to combine carbon with red-hot iron to produce carburized, or steel-like, iron weapons. Biblical as well as Babylonian texts imply the unmatched virtues of such weapons, referring to both their hardness and their sharpness. Other important pieces of equipment used in Neo-Babylonian warfare included scaling ladders, used in siege operations against walled cities, and war chariots.

MILITARY ORGANIZATION

Neo-Babylonian armies pursued their grand strategy by organizing together troops with different kinds of weapons and different tactical objectives: infantry units armed with spears and clubs, cavalry warriors on horseback, charioteers, and siege units that also included scaling parties composed of archers. Their strategy was to overwhelm the enemy. Although the Greek historian Herodotus (c. 484-424 B.C.E.) later indicated that the greatest of the Median kings, Cyaxares, was the first ruler who divided his troops into companies and distinct bodies of spearmen, archers, and others, all evidence indicates that Nabopolassar Nebuchadnezzar would have known of this well-coordinated, systematic arrangement of troops long before he formed his alliance with the Median ruler.

The Chaldeans undoubtedly followed the example of their predecessors, the Assyrians, in collecting horses for their cavalry troops from the many villages specifically cultivated for that purpose in Mesopotamia. Characteristic chariots of the period were large-wheeled, maneuverable, high-platformed vehicles accommodating three or four persons: a driver, an archer, and one or two shield bearers to protect them. Late seventh century B.C.E. reliefs show chariots being preceded by two archers mounted on horseback, with slingers ahead of them.

DOCTRINE, STRATEGY, AND TACTICS

Because the major cities and towns in the Near East were walled, strongly fortified complexes by the time the Neo-Babylonians appeared on the scene, siege warfare was the dominant tactical principle employed in the seventh and sixth centuries B.C.E. The first-attacked cities in a region were usually those that supported the most important city, the capital, because of their strategic military value, their economic importance,

TURNING POINTS

1300-700 B.C.E.	Semitic desert dwellers infiltrate southern Mesopotamia to establish Chaldean culture during period of Assyrian domination in Near East.
626 B.C.E.	Nabopolassar Nebuchadnezzar leads revolt against Assyrian rule and establishes Chaldean, or Neo-Babylonian, kingdom.
587-586 B.C.E.	Nebuchadnezzar II uses siege warfare to conquer Jerusalem.
539 B.C.E.	Chaldean Empire is conquered by Persian king Cyrus the Great.

and their symbolic value. These cities were usually of religious importance, because they were the home of either a region's patron deity or priestly class, or both. The capital city of a kingdom or group of people was often reserved for the final siege, because it was the most strongly fortified of the cities, and also because it could be greatly weakened in both supply and morale by the loss of its network of supporting towns.

A specific purpose of the siege was the attempt to starve the holdouts into submission, as in the Siege of Jerusalem (586 B.C.E.). Information about an opponent's troop strength, tactical weaknesses, fortifications, and other areas of possible exploitation was obtained either by spies who infiltrated the enemy camp or by internal informers. Once a city was captured, further resistance was often preempted by razing its walls. The rebuilding of a city's walls was usually regarded as a symbol of renewed revolt. The Neo-Babylonians also applied the policy of torching conquered cities. Modern archaeological excavations in Jerusalem attest to a great conflagration that swept over the whole city but that was especially prominent in the residential district, data which harmonizes well with the report presented in the Bible's Book of 2 Kings (25:9).

Campaign plans of the Neo-Babylonian military machine were often based on tradition and long-established patterns of warfare. The Neo-Babylonian conquest of Syria-Palestine followed much the same strategy and order employed by the Assyrians more than a century earlier. Like the Assyrians before them, the Neo-Babylonians also used the policy of deportation of vanquished foes with great effectiveness, especially as a tool of psychological warfare to break the will and ability of opponents to recombine against their oppressors.

Alliance warfare was an important strategy to the Chaldeans, or Neo-Babylonians, in their conquest of Assyria and the establishment of their own empire. Royal marriages during war sometimes sealed coalition agreements, as when Nabopolassar Nebuchadnezzar's son, Nebuchadnezzar II, was wed to Amytis, the daughter of the Median ruler, Cyaxares. From that point on, the Chaldeans and the Medes fought side by side and the fate of the Assyrians was sealed.

ANCIENT SOURCES

Perhaps the most valuable resource regarding Neo-Babylonian warfare is a series of ancient texts collectively translated and known in English as *The Babylonian Chronicle* (1887). Begun in 626 B.C.E., the same year Nabopolassar Nebuchadnezzar ascended the throne of Babylon, this record describes the many wars and campaigns of the Chaldeans and allows military historians to follow, almost day by day, the history of the Neo-Babylonian Empire. It includes invaluable accounts of the fall of Nineveh and other Assyrian cities.

The Hebrew Bible, or Old Testament, also provides important commentary on the strategy and tactics used by the Neo-Babylonians and reports on their destruction of various cities both in Syria-Palestine and Mesopotamia. For example, Nahum (3:1-7) preserves not only the sense of vengeance unleashed during the destruction of Nineveh but also the tools of war in use:

> Cursed be the city of blood, full of lies, full of violence. . . . The sound of the whip is heard, the gallop of horses, the rolling of chariots. An infinity of dead, the dead are everywhere! My anger is on thee, Nineveh, saith Jehovah. . . . I will show thy nakedness to the nations and thy shame to the kingdoms. And then it will be said: Nineveh is destroyed! Who will mourn her?

Other important sources on Chaldean or Neo-Babylonian warfare include the writings of classical authors as well as Flavius Josephus's (c. 37-c. 100 C.E.) *Antiquitates Judaicae* (93 C.E.; *The Antiquities of the Jews*, 1773).

BOOKS AND ARTICLES

Arnold, Bill T. *Who Were the Babylonians?* Boston: Brill, 2005.

Bahrani, Zainab. *Rituals of War: The Body and Violence in Mesopotamia.* New York: Zone Books, 2008.

Bradford, Alfred S. "The Medes and Chaldeans." In *With Arrow, Sword, and Spear: A History of Warfare in the Ancient World.* Illustrated by Pamela M. Bradford. Westport, Conn.: Praeger, 2001.

Ferrill, Arther. *The Origins of War.* Rev. ed. Boulder, Colo.: Westview Press, 1997.

Roux, Georges. *Ancient Iraq.* 3d ed. New York: Penguin Books, 1992.

Sack, Ronald H. *Images of Nebuchadnezzar: The Emergence of a Legend.* 2d rev. and expanded ed. Selinsgrove, Pa.: Susquehanna University Press, 2004.

Smith, Scott S. "Nebuchadnezzar's Military Achievements Made His Name—and That of His Native Babylon—Legend." *Military History* 20, no. 5 (December, 2003): 20.

Wiseman, D. J. *Nebuchadrezzar and Babylon.* New York: Oxford University Press, 1987.

Yadin, Yigael. *The Art of Warfare in Biblical Lands.* Vol. 2. New York: McGraw-Hill, 1963.

FILMS AND OTHER MEDIA

Ancient Mesopotamia. Documentary. Phoenix Learning Group, 2008.

Andrew C. Skinner

THE HEBREWS

Dates: c. 1400 B.C.E.-73 C.E.

POLITICAL CONSIDERATIONS

The history of the Hebrew people contains a large number of military campaigns and battles. The biblical stories of the walls of Jericho falling down and of David standing against Goliath with a slingshot are familiar ones to many people. These are, however, only two of many well-known war stories from the Bible. Initially, warfare was one of the methods the Israelites employed to first settle a homeland. The location of that homeland, the strategic Syro-Palestinian corridor, guaranteed that they would be engaged in continual warfare, trying to secure the land and to protect themselves from invasions from Mesopotamia and Egypt.

MILITARY ACHIEVEMENT

The first military engagements of the Hebrew people of the late Bronze Age were wars of conquest. These included, in Transjordan, the defeat of Sihon, king of Heshbon, and Og, king of Bashan, and the campaign against Midian, both of which are described in the biblical Book of Numbers. Later, Joshua ben Nun accomplished the occupation of Canaan, the Hebrew "promised land" west of the Jordan, through three strategic military actions, all of which are described in the biblical Book of Joshua. First, the Hebrews crossed the Jordan River opposite Jericho into the heart of the land,

capturing Jericho, Ai, and Bethel. Second, a coalition of kings from five Canaanite city-states in the south were defeated and routed in battle at Gibeon, and a number of cities of the southern Shephelah were taken or destroyed. Finally, a league of Canaanite kings under the leadership of Jabin, king of Hazor, were defeated in battle at the "waters of Merom," in

ISRAEL AND JUDAH, C. 900 B.C.E.

105

northern Galilee, and their cities were taken by the Israelites (Joshua 11). These achievements were accomplished with a unified militia of Israelite tribes.

Although the unified strategy of Joshua ben Nun succeeded in defeating the coalition of forces capable of threatening Israel's position in Canaan, the task of mopping up fell to individual tribes at the beginning of the Iron Age (1200-1000 B.C.E.). The lack of tribal unity within the Israelite confederacy during this period allowed a resurgence of Canaanite power and the emergence along the Mediterranean coast of the Philistines, one group from among the earlier invading Sea Peoples that had been repulsed from Egypt by Ramses III (r. 1184-1153 B.C.E.) around 1168 B.C.E. According to extrabiblical records, the Philistines held a well-deserved reputation for martial skill and organization. In addition, they controlled a monopoly on iron metallurgy. Owing to these factors, the Israelite leaders, the judges Samuel and Saul, found themselves fighting defensive engagements. The lack of tribal unity also contributed to a period of civil war, described in the biblical Book of Judges.

After consolidating his reign in Judah and Israel,

David (c. 1030-c. 962 B.C.E.) besieged and captured the Jebusite city of Jerusalem around 1000 B.C.E., making it the capital of his kingdom, as described in the biblical Book of 2 Samuel. After the Philistines heard that David had been made king of Israel, they moved to attack, but were defeated by David in the Valley of Rephaim and pursued to Gezer. David then campaigned to expand his kingdom, conquering the Moabites, Edomites, Ammonites, Aramaeans, and others. He instituted a standing army and placed garrisons throughout his growing empire. By such means he gained control of the trade along the Kings Highway east of the Jordan as well as the Via Maris, a lowland passage running through Israel to Damascus. Israel reached the zenith of its military and political power under David. Solomon (c. 991-930 B.C.E.), David's heir, maintained the same control and reigned from the great bend of the Euphrates to Elat on the Red Sea.

During the years of the divided monarchy, the southern kingdom of Judah and the northern kingdom of Israel were reduced to fighting each other in civil war or supporting each other in defensive battles against outside invasion. Two particular examples of the latter stand out. In 853 B.C.E. Ahab (c. 874-c. 853 B.C.E.), king of Israel, joined other small Canaanite and Syrian kingdoms in a coalition against Shalmaneser III (r. 858-824 B.C.E.), king of Assyria. Ahab was able to field 2,000 chariots and 18,000 infantrymen, some of them probably from Judah. The coalition met Shalmaneser III at Karkar in the Orontes Valley and stopped his advance. In 725 B.C.E. Shalmaneser V (r. 726-722 B.C.E.) laid siege to Samaria, the capital of Israel. Although the city held out for several years, it finally surrendered, and the kingdom of Israel disintegrated.

Judah remained a vassal-state of Assyria. However, at the end of the eighth century B.C.E. King Hezekiah of Judah (r. c. 715-c. 686 B.C.E.) revolted along with rulers of other

North Wind Picture Archives via AP Images

Hebrew leader Joshua ben Nun begins the occupation of Canaan, the Hebrew "promised land" west of the Jordan, with the taking of Jericho.

smaller kingdoms. The Neo-Assyrian king Sennacherib's (r. 704-681 B.C.E.) response was brutal. Every town in Judah was captured, and in 701 B.C.E. Sennacherib trapped Hezekiah in Jerusalem. In response to the Assyrian threat, Hezekiah reorganized the army, refortified Jerusalem, and redirected its water source, constructing the Siloam tunnel to bring water into the city. Sennacherib failed in his siege and returned to Assyria, where he was assassinated. The kingdom of Judah lasted until 587 B.C.E., when Jerusalem fell to the Neo-Babylonians.

For several centuries after the fall of Jerusalem the Hebrews were subject to foreign masters. Successively conquered by Babylon, Assyria, Persia, and Greece, they generally cooperated with rulers who tolerated their religious practices. Despite the pacifist strains of Isaiah and other prophets, the Jews could be quite bellicose in defending their religion. When Alexander the Great (356-323 B.C.E.) conquered Judea, he did not interfere with Jewish worship. However, one of his successors, Antiochus IV Epiphanes (c. 215-164 B.C.E.), decided to impose Greek culture on subject peoples, and around 167 B.C.E. constructed a statue of Zeus in the Holy Temple of Jerusalem, forbidding such practices as circumcision and the observance of the Sabbath. Rebellion again broke out in 167 B.C.E. under the Maccabees, a priestly family. The uprising began as a guerrilla war, but Judas Maccabeus (died 160 B.C.E.) organized the army along the old traditional lines. Fighting with small outnumbered forces, Judas proved to be a brilliant tactician accomplishing many difficult military feats. Judas and his brothers liberated Jerusalem and established a new independent Jewish state, with the kings and high priests both coming from the Maccabee family. Once independent, the Maccabees continued to wage war in Samaria, Transjordan, and among the descendants of the Edomites, forcing them to convert to Judaism. They also suppressed Jews who adopted Greek values and practices. For all

TURNING POINTS

c. 13th cent. B.C.E.	The Hebrews conquer Transjordan and Canaan under the leadership of Joshua.
1000-990 B.C.E.	David consolidates the reign of Judah and Israel and defeats neighboring kingdoms of Moab, Edom, Ammon, and Aramaea, among others.
705-701 B.C.E.	Judean king Hezekiah leads rebellion against Assyrian domination.
587 B.C.E.	Jerusalem falls to the Neo-Babylonians.
167-161 B.C.E.	Judas Maccabeus leads campaigns against Greek rule.
39-37 B.C.E.	Herod is named king of Judea by the Roman Senate and leads campaigns to establish his kingdom.
66-70 C.E.	The Jews wage war against the Romans.
70	Jerusalem falls to the Romans.
73	The stronghold of Masada falls to the Romans after a three-year siege.

their militarism, the Maccabees refused to fight on the Sabbath.

The later Maccabees allied with Rome and allowed Judea to fall under Roman control. Initially, the Romans tolerated the religion of Jews who did not challenge Roman authority. Jews were allowed to live and prosper throughout the empire, especially in Alexandria and Rome. The Roman Senate designated Herod the Great (r. 37-4 B.C.E.) king of Judea, but he had to fight for every inch of his kingdom. In the winter of 39 B.C.E. Herod returned to Palestine with the help of the Roman army. By 37 B.C.E. Herod had taken Jerusalem. Five years later Herod defeated the Nabateans and annexed a portion of their territory. Finally, by 20 B.C.E. Herod's kingdom had almost reached the size of that of David and Solomon.

Commonly, the Romans permitted conquered peoples to continue worshiping their gods, providing they acknowledged the Roman gods, including Caesar. However, monotheistic Judaism did not allow this accommodation, and guerrilla movements to resist Rome emerged in Judea. The Romans executed Jewish prophets and messiahs who challenged them. Among them may have been Jesus of Nazareth. One party, the Zealots, committed to purging Judea of all pagan elements, allegedly kidnapped and killed Jews

Getty Images

David, the Hebrew king of Judah and Israel, who besieged and captured the Jebusite city of Jerusalem and made it the capital of his kingdom.

who cooperated with Rome. In 66 C.E. the Jews revolted against Rome. The rebels set up a government in Jerusalem and divided the country into seven military districts. The emperor Nero (37-68 C.E.) sent his best general, Vespasian (9-79 C.E.), to quell the uprising. Vespasian systematically defeated the rebels until the Jews held only Jerusalem and the territory surrounding the city. Vespasian returned to Rome to be crowned emperor, leaving his son Titus (39-81 C.E.) in charge of the Siege of Jerusalem. By August 30, 70 C.E., Titus had taken the entire population of Jerusa-

lem captive and leveled its buildings to the ground. A small group of rebels fled to the stronghold at Masada. They lasted until 73 C.E., when the Romans breached the walls. Approximately 960 defenders at Masada committed suicide during the night rather than surrender to the Romans.

WEAPONS, UNIFORMS, AND ARMOR

A wide range of offensive and defensive weapons are mentioned in biblical texts. None of these are in essence unique to the Israelite soldier. By the time of the Iron Age, the Hebrew soldier employed the same weaponry used in the surrounding ancient Near Eastern area.

The most practical offensive weapon was the small sword or dagger. It was fewer than 50 centimeters in length and generally used in short-range, hand-to-hand combat. The sword was carried in a sheath attached to the belt. The Israelites also used javelins and lances. The most significant long-range offensive weapon, however, was the bow and arrow. Arrowheads were first made of bronze and later iron. They were designed to pierce armor. David used a sling against Goliath, and soldiers from the tribe of Benjamin developed a deadly accuracy with this weapon.

The most common defensive arm, the leather buckler or shield, could be made in several sizes. Body armor, coats of mail, and helmets were available although probably were not common until the time of David. The defenders of Lachish, besieged by the forces of Sennacherib in 701 B.C.E., are shown wearing bronze helmets in the famous Assyrian bas-relief in the palace of Sennacherib at Nineveh.

MILITARY ORGANIZATION

At the end of the Bronze Age, military service was a part of the life of every capable male. Although some exceptions were granted, as described in the biblical Book of Deuteronomy, the survival of the nation as a whole depended upon the tribal fighting units that could be called up for battle as needed. These forces were voluntary and functioned on an as-needed basis. Soldiers returned to their homes and fields after the war.

A major change took place during the monarchy. Saul (r. c. 1020-1000) was the first to begin to recruit a more permanent army. David developed his own personal bodyguard and a professional army including several mercenaries. The Hebrew army was divided into units of 1,000 commanded by a leader. These units could be further divided into smaller groups of 100 and 50. Solomon was the first to establish a strong chariot force. Chariots were effective on the open plain, but they proved useless in the mountain terrain of much of Palestine.

DOCTRINE, STRATEGY, AND TACTICS

The early Hebrew army did not seem to do well in pitched battles on open terrain. Usually outnumbered, they were far more effective when they employed guerrilla tactics. Some of these included feints, decoys, ambushes, and diversionary maneuvers. Night movements and night attacks were also used. The Hebrews also developed a battle cry that would frighten or dishearten the enemy.

David instituted a particular military and political doctrine that provided great wealth for himself and his son Solomon. Even later, when the kings of Israel and Judah also followed this doctrine, political power and prosperity followed. First, David sought peace between Israel and Judah. Second, he exercised a strong hand in matters east of the Jordan. His plan was to subjugate the Aramaeans, Ammonites, Moabites, and Edomites, and thus to control the trade along the Kings Highway in Transjordan. Finally, David opened trade relations with the maritime nation of Hiram of Tyre (r. 969-936 B.C.E.).

ANCIENT SOURCES

A fair knowledge of the military achievements of the nations of the ancient Near East is revealed by the numerous paintings, drawings, reliefs, and inscriptions left behind. Even peace treaties describe the titles and functions of individuals in the army. The famous Assyrian bas-relief of the siege of Lachish was at Nineveh and is now held at the British Museum. It has a detailed depiction of Hebrew soldiers. However, information about the military organization of Israel from 1400 B.C.E. to the first century C.E. is not so complete.

The Hebrew Bible, or Old Testament, remains the primary resource for understanding the military achievements of the Hebrew people. Although there are extensive references to battles, the Bible is not a military history. Flavius Josephus, in his *Bellum Judaicum* (75-79 C.E.; *History of the Jewish War*, 1773), wrote about the Revolt of 66-70 C.E., in which he participated, later supporting the Romans. He later wrote *Antiquitates Judaicae* (93 C.E.; *The Antiquities of the Jews*, 1773). However, these books must be supplemented with archaeological and epigraphic discoveries from elsewhere in Egypt, Mesopotamia, and Palestine. Many of these are included in J. B. Pritchard's edited collection, *Ancient Near Eastern Texts Relating to the Old Testament* (1969).

BOOKS AND ARTICLES

Aharoni, Yohanan, and Michael Avi-Yonah. *The Macmillan Bible Atlas*. 3d ed. New York: Macmillan, 1993.

Bright, John. *A History of Israel*. 4th ed. Louisville, Ky.: Westminster John Knox Press, 2000.

Chapman, Cynthia R. *The Gendered Language of Warfare in the Israelite-Assyrian Encounter.* Winona Lake, Ind.: Eisenbrauns, 2004.

De Vaux, Roland. *Ancient Israel: Its Life and Institutions.* Grand Rapids, Mich.: Wm. B. Eerdmans, 1997.

Gabriel, Richard. *The Military History of Ancient Israel.* Westport, Conn.: Praeger, 2003.

Gonen, R. *Weapons of the Ancient World.* London: Cassell, 1975.

Herzog, Chaim, and Mordechai Gichon. *Battles of the Bible.* London: Weidenfeld and Nicolson, 1978.

Kelle, Brad. *Ancient Israel at War, 853-586 B.C.* New York: Osprey, 2007.

Pritchard, J. B., ed. *Ancient Near Eastern Texts Relating to the Old Testament.* Princeton, N.J.: Princeton University Press, 1969.

Yadin, Yigael. *The Art of Warfare in Biblical Lands in the Light of Archaeological Study.* 2 vols. New York: McGraw-Hill, 1963.

FILMS AND OTHER MEDIA

Masada. Television miniseries. ABC, 1981.

Moses the Lawgiver. Television miniseries. 1975.

The Myth of Masada. Film. Humanities and Science/Arkios Productions, 1993.

The Ten Commandments. Film. Paramount, 1956.

Stephen J. Andrews

THE EGYPTIANS

Dates: c. 3000-30 B.C.E.

MILITARY ACHIEVEMENT

The Egyptian Empire was one of the longest-lasting in the ancient world, and it was largely kept together by military force rather than diplomacy. Its great wealth encouraged invasions such as those by the Hyksos, the Hittites, and the Sea Peoples. Later it was to face far greater threats from the Macedonians, and later still the Romans.

To combat these ever-present threats, the Egyptians did maintain a large army and navy. However, the chief innovations of Egyptian military thought were more in strategy and tactics than in weapons development. Although Egyptian military armaments remained relatively unchanged for millennia, the Egyptians' emphasis on indirect engagement and speed of movement—more than cultural conservatism—accounts for this lack of innovation.

Egyptian armies, from an early period, enlisted large numbers of foreign troops, foremost among whom were Nubian auxiliaries, renowned for their archery skills. The geology of southern Egypt, and the southern armies' use of Nubian troops, who were adept at desert warfare, led to wars of maneuver in the desert. Predynastic Period (c. 5300-3000 B.C.E.) and First Intermediate Period (c. 2160-2055 B.C.E.) forces used desert roads in order to outflank Nile Valley opponents. This emphasis on an indirect approach, and the Egyptians' apparent preference for projectile weapons and battles of speed, led to an increasing reliance on foreign troops during the first millennium B.C.E., as foreign troops became increasingly important. From the reign of Ptolemy IV Philopator (r. 221-205 B.C.E.), Egyptian soldiers were armed and trained in Hellenistic fashion.

WEAPONS, UNIFORMS, AND ARMOR

The bow was the most important weapon in the Egyptian arsenal. Early ones were the simple bow with animal horns as the tip elements. The composite bow appeared in Egypt during the Second Intermediate Period (c. 1650-1550 B.C.E.) and became increasingly popular during the New Kingdom (c. 1550-1069 B.C.E.), partly in response to the increased use of body armor by many of Egypt's enemies. The bows of Libyan auxiliaries were small composite bows;

A nineteenth century representation of an Egyptian chariot team of driver and archer.

Nubian troops preferred the self bow. New Kingdom Egyptian chariots served as mobile archery platforms.

Pointed, and sometimes barbed, Egyptian arrows caused deep wounds. Broad, and sometimes flat-tipped, Egyptian arrows caused stunning injuries. Arrow tips were made from flint, horn, wood, and bone; copper tips had appeared by the time of the Middle Kingdom (c. 2055-1650 B.C.E.), and bronze tips by the time of the New Kingdom. There is slight evidence for the use of poisoned arrows. Arrows were carried in quivers; primarily during the Middle Kingdom bows and arrows together were at times held within a sleevelike quiver, open at each end.

Slings are attested, and surviving images have slingers appearing in the crows' nests of Egyptian warships. Late Coptic sources portray Egyptian women as adept at the use of the sling. The Egyptians also employed throw sticks in combat.

Spears appeared early in the Egyptian arsenal, both long, thrusting spears and short, stabbing spears. By the time of the Nineteenth Dynasty (1295-1186 B.C.E.) two spears had appeared in the arsenal of Egyptian chariot soldiers, to be used if the chariot became disabled. Throwing spears are also attested. New Kingdom troops at times carried both spear and battle-ax, possibly throwing spears prior to closing with axes.

Battle-axes, with blades of stone, copper, or bronze as technology evolved, were the preferred close-combat weapons. Early metal battle-axes had rounded blades. From the time of the Second Intermediate Period the standard shape was a long, roughly rectangular blade, convex on the cutting edge, with slightly concave sides. New Kingdom Libyan auxiliaries carried battle-axes with archaic, rounded blades.

The mace administered the coup de grâce to the heads of the mortally wounded, the origin of the pharaonic image of the ruler smiting the enemies of Egypt. Apparently common in earlier Egyptian forces as actual weapons with pear- and disc-shaped heads, the mace is rarely depicted outside smiting scenes and royal regalia. The mace becomes more visible in later New Kingdom scenes, in which it is larger, with a curved blade attached, beginning at the base of the mace head and coming to a point beyond the top of the mace head. The weight of the mace was apparently intended to help the blade pierce body armor.

A variety of staves and clubs were employed. A First Intermediate Period warrior refers to a staff of copper, perhaps a metal-sheathed staff, and fighting rods are relatively common in Ramessid Period (1295-1069 B.C.E.) battle scenes. These weapons, like the biblical "rod of iron," delivered crushing blows and became more prevalent during the later New Kingdom as a means of combating armored foes. Nubian foes and allies of the Egyptians often wielded wooden clubs with relatively narrow handles, swelling below the tip.

Soldiers carried daggers of various lengths, which could be used to remove a hand, or the phallus of an uncircumcised foe, from each slain enemy, a well-attested New Kingdom practice that allowed an accurate estimate of the strength of enemy forces. The slashing scimitar appeared in Egypt during the New Kingdom; mounted troops developed long, stabbing rapiers. Long swords and body armor appeared with Mediterranean mercenaries during the New Kingdom.

As in hunting, so in warfare, dogs frequently accompanied Egyptian soldiers into battle. Old Kingdom (c. 2686-2125 B.C.E.) and Middle Kingdom desert rangers often appeared with their dogs, usually basenjis. During the New Kingdom greyhound- and saluki-like hounds became more common in battle scenes. Ramses II (c. 1300-1213 B.C.E.) was accompanied into battle by a pet "battle-lion."

Early shields depicted on the Hunters Palette, a stone carving from the Predynastic Period, were small and irregular, perhaps made from turtle shells, like some more recent shields of Red Sea nomads. Shields during the Early Dynastic Period (c. 3000-2686 B.C.E.) were often large; tall, full-coverage shields are known from the time of the Middle Kingdom. Shields became smaller during the New Kingdom, rounded at the top and square at the bottom. During the New Kingdom they were often covered in animal hide, often with a metal boss in the upper middle. During melees New Kingdom soldiers often slung their shields over their shoulders with a diagonal strap, protecting their backs and necks while freeing both hands. At the end of the New Kingdom period, Mediterranean mercenaries introduced round shields into the Egyptian arsenal.

The chariot appeared in Egypt's arsenal at the beginning of the Eighteenth Dynasty (1550-1295 B.C.E.) and presumably had entered the land during the Second Intermediate Period, when the Hyksos, an Eastern Mediterranean maritime power, dominated northern Egypt. Egyptian chariots were light, usually with a rear-mounted wheel, and carried a driver and an archer. Horses wore protective armor, or bardings. Egypt's opponents followed this pattern until the Hittites, under pressure from heavily armored troops in their western marches, adopted a heavier chariot with three occupants, used for rapid transport of infantry rather than for archery. Egyptian chariotry did not adopt such a response to the rise of heavy infantry. Runners accompanied chariots; many were foreign mercenaries who protected the chariots and horses and attempted to capture those of the enemy.

The earliest Egyptian chariots had wheels with four spokes. During the middle of the Eighteenth Dynasty, six spokes became standard. Egyptian chariots had a cab with a D-shaped floor plan; a curved wooden banister at waist level in front stretched back and down to the rear floor. The light bodies could be partially closed with wood or leather sidings. Floors of rope or leather mesh absorbed the shock of rough terrain. Side-mounted cases held bows and arrows and, from the time of the Nineteenth Dynasty, spears.

The infrequently attested use of mounted troops was primarily as reconnaissance patrols and couriers.

OLD KINGDOM EGYPT, C. 2686–C. 2125 B.C.E.

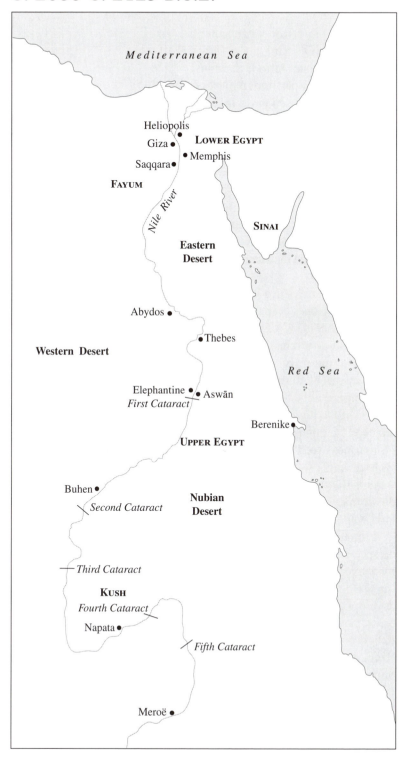

Many of these cavalry troopers were Nubians. Roads and remount stations were maintained for these patrols.

Wheeled siege ladders appeared during the late Old Kingdom and the First Intermediate Period. Sapping is attested, often performed by soldiers with hand weapons. In one Middle Kingdom scene, three men within a protective testudo siege engine work a long pole, similar to a crowbar, against the walls of a fortress. The use of sloping glacis at the bases of fortress walls by the time of the Middle Kingdom suggests the use of similar sapping, and would also have deterred the use of battering rams.

Supposed evidence for stone-throwing machines from the Twenty-fifth Dynasty (747-656 B.C.E.) is based on faulty translations. Siege ramps, apparently of earth and wood, with platforms for archers and slingers, are attested. When the Nubian ruler Piye (747-716 B.C.E.) attacked Memphis by land and river, his marines used their ships' spars to scale the river walls of the city, and the construction of a siege ramp held down many of the defenders of the land walls.

Climate and Egyptian emphasis on speed of movement and flanking maneuvers through the deserts flanking the Nile Valley discouraged the development of body armor. A metal breast protector appears in a Middle Kingdom scene, but during the Old Kingdom and Middle Kingdom the only garments common on soldiers' torsos were crossed textile bands. Quilted and leather protection for the torso appeared during the New Kingdom, usually in the form of bands wrapped around the chest and over one shoulder. Textile or leather shirts with

EIGHTEENTH DYNASTY EGYPT, C. 1550-1295 B.C.E.

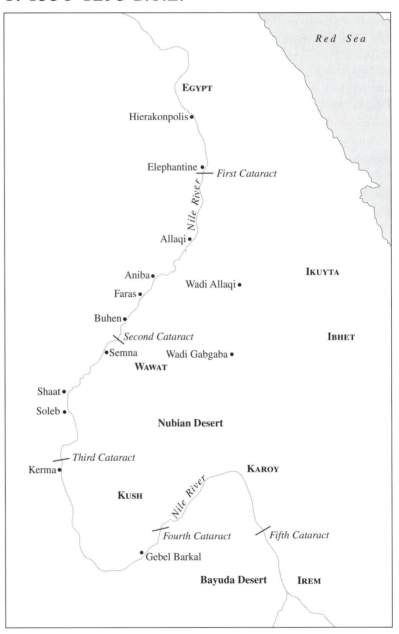

metal and leather scale armor also appeared during the New Kingdom, primarily providing protection for chariot warriors. During the New Kingdom, Mediterranean pirates and mercenaries in Egyptian service began to wear significant metal body armor;

however, it is unclear to what extent native troops adopted such armor.

Nubian auxiliaries wore leather sporrans, or pouches, during both the First Intermediate Period and Middle Kingdom. Large, heart-shaped, quilted sporrans appeared during the New Kingdom. These elements of clothing appear to have functioned as protection for the groin area. Soldiers often wore a leather overkilt, cut to have the appearance of a leather net with a seat patch.

Middle Kingdom soldiers, as revealed by mummified remains at Deir el-Bahri, a temple site on the west bank of the Nile near Thebes, wore their hair thick and greased, forming a natural protection against blows to the head and neck. Textile head coverings are well attested, and there is sporadic evidence for helmets during the New Kingdom.

MILITARY ORGANIZATION

Early Egyptian forces were divided between infantry and archers; during the New Kingdom the chief divisions were between chariotry and foot soldiers. The smallest independently operating units appear to have been of ten men, with a squad leader; during the New Kingdom the smallest units appear to have been fifty men. The New Kingdom saw the emergence of a complex military hierarchy. Armies were equipped by various temples, institutions that fulfilled many important economic functions in Egypt. The four armies of Ramses II (r. 1279-1213 B.C.E.) at Kadesh were named for four deities. Mercenaries were important, and there were early units of Nubian troops, usually archers. Libyans and Mediterranean mercenaries and pirates were also important. Each independently operating unit had at least one scribe. During the Ptolemaic (332-30 B.C.E.) and Roman (30 B.C.E.-395 C.E.) periods, Hellenistic and Roman military practices supplanted earlier Egyptian practices.

DOCTRINE, STRATEGY, AND TACTICS

As the primary role for the Egyptians was defense, fortified positions first appeared during the Predy-

nastic Period. During the Middle Kingdom, a series of fortresses, watch posts, and patrol roads created an elaborate system of defense in depth at the Second Cataract of the Nile in Nubia, the southern boundary of direct Egyptian control and influence in the south. The complexity and extent of this system presaged later Roman achievements. Roman border defenses, and their Egyptian precursors, consisted of three types: defense by client states, with lightly defended legionary camps; perimeter defense; and defense in depth. Perimeter defense involved main fortresses behind outer defenses, with patrol roads and watchtowers stretching back to the fortresses. In defense in depth, larger and more heavily fortified fortresses were intended to stand alone in areas periodically overrun by foes.

Middle Kingdom Egyptian forts in Nubia developed in almost the opposite way. Initially they were well-fortified outposts in a perimeter defense, part of an elaborate system of patrol roads and watch posts, befitting their location in the low desert plain. Later Middle Kingdom forts on the southern end of the Second Cataract were, like later Roman fortresses, heavily fortified, with spur walls for enfilading fire, atop granite outcroppings, a response to the rise of the powerful Kerman state in Nubia. The Middle Kingdom fortresses in Nubia were supply depots and strongholds allowing the extension of Egyptian patrols into the far south.

By the time of Thutmose II (r. 1492-1479 B.C.E.) there were client states in Nubia, and the New Kingdom fortress of Buhen was less heavily defended, like the later Roman fortresses of the perimeter defense system. During the New Kingdom Egypt had a *foederati*-like arrangement with more developed Nubian client states. Nubia was important to Egypt as a source of military manpower, and the point of origin or transshipment of many goods, including gold and incense.

A network of patrol roads, camps, and watch posts stretched through the Western Desert during the Middle Kingdom, and the Theban Seventeenth Dynasty (c. 1580-1550 B.C.E.) maintained and elaborated upon certain elements of this system. Fortresses also guarded the eastern Nile Delta; a Middle Kingdom fortress in the Wadi an-Naṭrūn implies a similar line guarding the Western Delta. During the reign of Ramses II a line of fortresses guarded the approach to the Delta between the Mediterranean coast and the Qattara Depression.

Chariotry dominated late Bronze Age battlefields, on which the vehicles initially served as mobile archery platforms. A reliance on the expensive chariot arm was possible only for the wealthiest states of the ancient Near East, allowing those states to rely on small, elite forces, a desirable situation for complex societies in which labor was needed in many fields. Chariotry was ineffective against massed barbarian infantry and unsuited to mountainous or forested terrain. In battles in which chariotry was the principal arm, infantry provided support. At the Battle of Kadesh (1274 B.C.E.) under Ramses II, an infantry division assured the Egyptians' tactical success.

Unlike the Nubians, the Egyptians never permanently occupied Asia. In the northeast, Egypt supported the lesser of two conflicting powers, thereby seeking to create buffer states that, with Egyptian aid, might oppose a third power, but could not alone pose a threat to Egypt.

Amphibious infantry landings are known from the late Old Kingdom and the First Intermediate Period. During the Seventeenth Dynasty, Kamose (r. 1555-1550 B.C.E.) employed warships in three lines ahead, the central line breaking the enemy line and flanking lines preventing enemy escape. Kamose could thereby break the line of the Hyksos battle squadron and capture its merchant fleet. Thutmose III (r. 1479-1425 B.C.E.) constructed ships in sections on the Mediterranean coast and transported them overland for an amphibious attack on the Euphrates.

When invasions of marauding Sea Peoples occurred during the reign of Ramses III (r. 1184-1153 B.C.E.), various ships, including smaller Nile warships, protected the Nile Delta. Archers and grappling hooks and lines for capsizing enemy warships were the main offensive weapons. Large ships filled with troops appear to have broken the formations of the attacking enemy. Smaller vessels, able to operate in the treacherous areas of sandbanks near the mouths of the Nile, completed the destruction of the enemy. Ramming apparently was not practiced until the Ptolemaic and Roman periods.

Considering the importance of religion in Egyptian culture, it is to be expected that religion should serve military purposes as well. The names of foreign and domestic foes were written on small, usually clay images of bound enemies, and buried in execration rituals. Warfare was equated with hunting, both activities asserting Egyptian authority and control over chaotic forces and contributing to the proper order of the cosmos.

ANCIENT SOURCES

The considerable accomplishments of the ancient Egyptians in the realm of tactics must be reconstructed from much disparate and indirect evidence, and the lack of any true military treatise from ancient Egypt means that much information has been lost. Military scribes kept daybook accounts of expeditions, excerpts of which appeared occasionally in inscriptions, such as those of Thutmose III at Karnak. The ancient Egyptians stressed the timeless importance of events and of history as festival, an emphasis leading to a lack of what might be considered truly historical accounts of military activities.

However, although these manuscripts have not survived, there are numerous scenes and inscriptions recounting military activity which do survive, the earliest from the late Gerzean Period (c. 3500-3200 B.C.E.). Some actually show the recording of military events, and there are many bas-reliefs showing chariots, soldiers and ships.

In addition, many actual weapons, and even some chariots, have survived. Some of those, such as the throwing sticks in the tomb of Tutankhamen of the Eighteenth Dynasty, were clearly decorative, but there are also swords, knives, and bows that do survive, from the tomb of Tutankhamen, and from archaeological sites both much older and more recent than the Eighteenth Dynasty. Other information comes from bodies and skeletons, some of which show the effects of Egyptian weaponry.

Some contemporary written accounts exist from non-Egyptian sources. These include the Bible, which mentions the Egyptians in the Book of Exodus and other parts. Herodotus, in his *Historiai Herodotou* (c. 424 B.C.E.; *The History*, 1709), provides some descriptions of the Egyptians in battle. There are far more extensive written sources from the Hellenistic period from the works of Arrian, the *Anabasis Alexandri* (early second century C.E.; *The Campaigns of Alexander*, 1893), and also from the writings of Plutarch (c. 100 C.E.).

BOOKS AND ARTICLES

Drews, Robert. *The End of the Bronze Age*. Princeton, N.J.: Princeton University Press, 1993.

Fields, Nic. *Bronze Age War Chariots*. New York: Osprey, 2006.

Healy, Mark. *Armies of the Pharaohs*. New York: Osprey, 1992.

_____. *New Kingdom Egypt*. New York: Osprey, 1992.

_____. *Qadesh, 1300 B.C.* New York: Osprey, 1993.

Shaw, Ian. *Egyptian Warfare and Weapons*. Princes Risborough, England: Shire, 1991.

Spalinger, Anthony John. *Aspects of the Military Documents of the Ancient Egyptians*. New Haven, Conn.: Yale University Press, 1982.

Wachsmann, Shelley. *Seagoing Ships and Seamanship in the Bronze Age Levant*. College Station: Texas A&M University Press, 1998.

Yadin, Yigael. *The Art of Warfare in Biblical Lands in the Light of Archaeological Study*. New York: McGraw-Hill, 1963.

FILMS AND OTHER MEDIA

Antony and Cleopatra. Film. Transac, 1972.

Cleopatra. Film. Twentieth Century-Fox, 1963.

Egypt Golden Empire. Documentary. Lion Television, 2001.

The Egyptian. Film. Twentieth Century-Fox, 1954.

Ramses: Favorite of the Gods. Documentary. Time-Life Video, 1997.

John Coleman Darnell

THE PERSIANS
Dates: To 651 C.E.

MILITARY ACHIEVEMENT

The Persians were an Iranian-speaking, Indo-European people. As described in both the *Rigveda* and the *Avesta*, the sacred texts of Hinduism and Zoroastrianism respectively, warriors played an important part in Persian society. The warrior class, from which chiefs and kings were chosen, was second in status only to that of the priests. However, these religious texts, written by priests, may overemphasize the importance of the priest class within Persian society. Horses were important to the Persians, who used them effectively against both the native inhabitants of the Iranian plateau and their Mesopotamian neighbors, especially the Assyrians, whose military technology was the most advanced in the world in the first millennium B.C.E. Ancient Persian history can be divided into three periods: the Achaemenid Persian period (550-330 B.C.E.), the Hellenic and Parthian period (330 B.C.E.-224 C.E.), and the Sāsānian period (224-651 C.E.).

ACHAEMENID PERSIAN PERIOD

The Achaemenid Persians achieved supremacy by 550 B.C.E. after their leader, Cyrus the Great (r. 550-529 B.C.E.), had conquered the Iranian plateau, Mesopotamia, Levant, and Anatolia. The Achaemenid Persians defeated their cousins, the Medes, who had previously defeated the Assyrians. Cyrus's successors, Cambyses II (r. 529-522 B.C.E.) and Darius I (r. 522-486 B.C.E.), conquered Egypt, Nubia, Libya, and Central Asia, forming the largest empire known to the world at that time. The Achaemenid Persian Empire was matched only by that of Alexander the Great (356-323 B.C.E.), who later conquered the Persian Empire. For two centuries the Persians maintained a vast empire with a large army requiring a large administrative apparatus. Only the Greeks were able to resist the Persians, and the struggle between the two civilizations became a focal point of Greek and Western historiography.

HELLENIC AND THE PARTHIAN PERIOD

After the Greek conquest of Persia in 330 B.C.E., Seleucus I (between 358 and 354-281 B.C.E.), one of Alexander's generals, took over the Asiatic portion of the Persian Empire and formed the Seleucid Dynasty. The Seleucid Empire centered on Syria and extended, at its peak, from the Mediterranean Sea to as far east as India's Indus Valley. By 238 B.C.E. an Iranian group known as the Parthians had established themselves in the eastern portion of the Persian Empire, in the area that encompasses the modern Iranian province of Khurāsān and part of southern Turkmenistan. Because the Parthians were a nomadic group, the cavalry remained the most important aspect of the Persian army during this period. The Parthians were able to defend themselves against the Roman forces, defeating the Romans in several key battles.

SĀSĀNIAN PERIOD

The Sāsānian Dynasty was established in 224 C.E. by Ardashīr I (r. c. 224-241 C.E.), who revived the Achaemenid religious tradition of Zoroastrianism and made it the official religion. From the outset of their reign, the Sāsānian were able to defeat the Romans and all other competing forces in Southwest Asia. The Sāsānian controlled Central Asia, the Iranian Plateau, and Mesopotamia, and made major incursions into Syria. Throughout the third century they repeatedly defeated Roman forces, killing one emperor, capturing another, and forcing a third to pay a ransom for the safety of his army. Seventh century Sāsānian forces conquered Palestine, Egypt, and Anatolia, laying siege to the Byzantine capital, Constantinople. For four centuries, the Sāsānian successfully defended their empire from invasions by the Turkic tribes and the Kushāns from the east, the Ro-

The Persian forces of Darius I the Great employ elephants in battle against the forces of Alexander the Great at Gaugamela (331 C.E.).

mans, Byzantines, and Arabs from the west, and the nomadic tribes from the north.

WEAPONS, UNIFORMS, AND ARMOR

The sacred Zoroastrian text, the *Avesta*, mentions weapons and war sporadically. Certain Zoroastrian gods, such as Wahrām, had been worshiped by the military since well before the time of the Achaemenid Persians. Wahrām, whose name means "offensive victory," could take on many forms, mainly those of fierce beasts. The goddess Anahitā was another deity from whom the Persians sought aid in bat-

tle against their enemies. Prayers were usually accompanied with sacrifices and ritual acts.

Greek and Iranian sources indicate that the elite Persian forces wore long, draped robes with trousers, as well as coats of mail covering their chests. The Greek historian Xenophon (430-354 B.C.E.) states that Persian cavalry forces carried javelins and wore breastplates, armor, and helmets. Xenophon also mentions various standards, or banners carried in battle, specifically the royal standard, a spread-winged eagle on a shield.

The Persian infantry wore loose tunics with corselets of metal scales underneath for protection from spear thrusts. They wore felt hoods and helmets

PERSIAN EMPIRE, C. 500 B.C.E.

= Areas within the Persian Empire

Taxila

GANDHARA
Kabul

INDUS

Maracanda (Samarqand)

PERGANA

SOGDIANA

BACTRIA
Bactria

GEDROSIA

Sea of Oman

MARGIANA
Merv

ARIA

PARTHIA

Aral
Sea

Persepolis
Shiraz
PERSIS

Rai (Tehran)

MEDIA

Caspian Sea

Ecbatana

Babylon Susa
Nippur ELAM

Persian Gulf

Gaugamela

BABYLONIA

ARMENIA

Nineveh
Nisibis

ASSYRIA

Damascus

Pontus Euxinus

CAPPADOCIA

Gordium
PHRYGIA

LYDIA

Sardis

IONIA

THRACE

Ephesus

GREECE

Sidon
Tyre
Jerusalem

Red Sea

Memphis

EGYPT

Mediterranean Sea

Cyrene

LIBYA

for head protection and carried short swords, lances with wooden shafts and metal points, quivers full of arrows with bronze or iron points, bows with ends shaped like animals' heads, and wicker shields of different shapes.

Greek sources tend to exaggerate the numbers of Persian forces, with estimates ranging from 900 thousand to 5 million. The main reason for such exaggeration was to boast the Greeks' ability to repel Achaemenid aggression during the Greco-Persian Wars (499-448 B.C.E.). The Persian navy, stationed at Cilicia on the Mediterranean coast, was composed mainly of foreigners, such as the Phoenicians, Greeks, and Egyptians. The mercenary status of the Persian navy was a reason for its defeat against the Greek navy; when the war became difficult or its outcome unsure, the Persian naval commanders either retreated or left altogether. The lack of a competent naval force would be a major reason that the Achaemenid Persians were ultimately unsuccessful against the Greek city-states.

MILITARY ORGANIZATION

The success of the Persian military was based on the capability of its military leaders and its army. Greek sources provide ample information on the composition of the Persian army, especially during the Greco-Persian Wars. The Persian nomadic forces that conquered the Medes were turned into organized standing forces composed of both Persians and Medians. These forces consisted of both cavalry, which included chariots, horses, and camels, and infantry, which included lance bearers and bowmen. As more people, including Greeks, Lydians, and Mesopotamians, were incorporated into the Persian Empire, they were also brought into the army. Greek mercenaries were used from the time of Cambyses in the sixth century B.C.E.

The Persian army's sophisticated training regiment of elite forces was drawn from the ranks of the nobility. In a system resembling that of the Spartans, who trained soldiers from youth, the Persians selectively trained certain youths, who passed required tests, to be warriors. According to Greek sources, the youths who were accepted into warrior society were taught various athletic, farming, and craft skills. As they matured, they were trained in the military arts, such as archery, spear and javelin throwing, and marching. In addition to these elite warrior forces, there were special forces composed of hardened warriors who acted as a sort of secret service.

The Persian army was divided according to the decimal system, in units of tens, hundreds, and thousands. Greek sources mention an elite Persian force known as the Immortals, composed of ten thousand men and so called because previously selected men waited to fill the places of casualties in battle. The Immortals reportedly included spearmen of Persian nobility: one thousand in the cavalry and ten thousand in the infantry. Of these ten thousand infantrymen, one thousand had golden pomegranates instead of spikes on the butt-ends of their spears. They marched in two sections, one ahead of and the other behind the remaining nine thousand Immortals, whose spears had silver pomegranates.

After 238 B.C.E. when the Parthians came to dominate the Persian Empire, the heavily armored cavalry, known as *cataphracts*, became the elite forces of the army. The extremely accurate mounted bowmen of the Parthian cavalry repeatedly defeated the Romans with their famed maneuvering techniques. The most famous of these techniques, riding a horse while shooting arrows backward, came to be known as the Parthian shot. Parthian horses were covered with mail to protect them from attacks by Roman infantrymen. Another unit of lighter, more mobile cavalry also carried bows and arrows. At the Battle of Carrhae in 53 B.C.E., Roman troops under the general Crassus were destroyed by the Parthian cavalry, which harassed the Roman infantry until it broke ranks, at which point the Parthian cavalry pursued and cut the Roman foot soldiers to pieces. People from other regions were also used in the Parthian forces as either light cavalry or infantry. The infantry was the second group of the army and it was usually considered to be weak and untrained and less reliable in wars.

In the fourth century C.E. Roman soldier and historian Ammianus Marcellinus (c. 330-395) described the Persian cavalry as clad in body armor, mailed

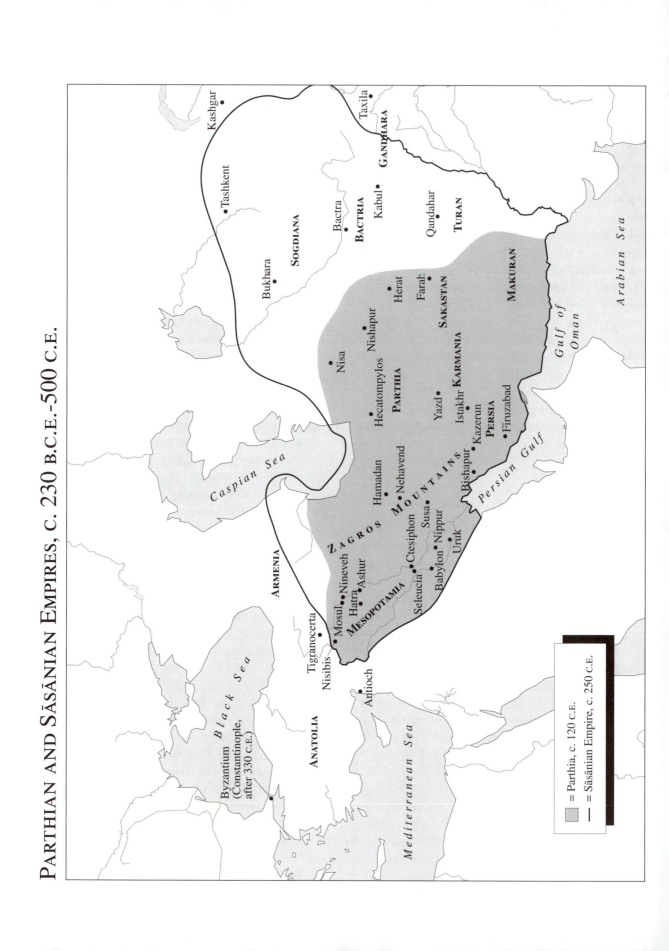

PARTHIAN AND SĀSĀNIAN EMPIRES, C. 230 B.C.E.–500 C.E.

Kashgar

Taxila

GANDHARA

Tashkent

Bactra

Kabul

Qandahar

BACTRIA

TURAN

SOGDIANA

Bukhara

MAKURAN

Herat

Farah

Nisa

Nishapur

SAKASTAN

Arabian Sea

Hecatompylos

KARMANIA

Yazd

Istakhr

PARTHIA

Kazerun

PERSIA

Firuzabad

Gulf of Oman

Caspian Sea

Hamadan

Nehavend

Bishapur

ZAGROS MOUNTAINS

Susa

Persian Gulf

Ctesiphon

Nippur

Mosul Nineveh

Seleucia

Babylon

Uruk

Hatrā Ashur

MESOPOTAMIA

ARMENIA

Tigranocerta

Nisibis

Antioch

ANATOLIA

Black Sea

Byzantium (Constantinople, after 330 C.E.)

Mediterranean Sea

= Parthia, c. 120 C.E.

= Sāsānian Empire, c. 250 C.E.

coats, breastplates, leg armor plates, and helmets with holes only for the eyes. The Persian cavalry horses were also covered with armor. The grotto of King Xusrō II (590-628 C.E.) at Tāq-i Bustān in northern Persia represents the culmination of the advancement in armor. The Persian weapons, based on the descriptions of Muslim historians, included swords, lances, shields, maces, battle-axes, clubs, bow cases containing two bows with their strings, thirty arrows, and two plaited cords. By the sixth century the chancery of warriors set a stable stipend for cavalry. It was from among these soldiers that the the Immortals, the elite corps of the Achaemenid Persians, were chosen. Their leader was probably the *puštigbān-sālar*, or "commander of the royal guard."

There was also a light cavalry composed of mercenaries or tribespeople in the empire, including the Dailamites, Gīlānīs, Georgians, Armenians, Turks, Arabs, Kushāns, Khazars, and Hephthalites. The other form of cavalry used in wars were the elephant corps, or *pīl-bānān*. Ammianus Marcellinus described the elephants as having awful figures and savage, gaping mouths. They looked like walking towers and scarcely could be endured by the faint-hearted. According to Muslim historians, elephants were used as early as the third century C.E. by the Sāsānians, who used them to raze such cities as Hatra. Sāsānian king Pīrōz I (r. 457/459-484 C.E.) used fifty elephants in his campaign against the Ephthalites in the fifth century. Elephants were again used against the Arabs in the seventh century.

The infantry, or *paygān*, was headed by the *paygān-sālar*, or "commander of the infantry." Infantrymen were fitted with shields and lances. Behind them in formation were the archers, who actually started the war with volleys of shots into the enemy camp before the cavalry charged. The *Strategikon* (c. 580 C.E.; English translation, 1984) of Flavius Tiberius Mauricius (c. 539-602 C.E.), a Byzantine emperor who reigned from 582 to 602 C.E., gives detailed information on the differences in strategies between the Persian and the Roman soldiers, as well as the intricacies and differences in their weapons and their uses. Naturally the cavalry and infantry forces required a huge logistical apparatus that was sustained by conscripts from the general population. These forces prepared food, repaired weapons, tended to the wounded, and established camps, among other tasks. The Sāsānians also utilized Roman techniques in the use of siege weapons including ballistae, battering rams, moving towers, and catapults. The Sāsānian navy had been instrumental from the beginning of the Sāsānian period, when the founder of the Sāsānian Persian dynasty, Ardašīr I (r. 224-241), conquered the Arab side of the Persian Gulf. The control of the Persian Gulf was necessary both militarily and economically, to make it safe from piracy and Roman encroachment. Based on the accounts of Muslim historians, it appears that the Persian ships held one hundred men but were not very important to the military.

Other Persian titles and classifications are from later sources that describe several other military positions, including commander of the forts, warden of marches, the hereditary title of the general of Tus, in northeastern Persia, and the army general. The warrior estate also had a designated Zoroastrian fire temple known as Adur Gušnasp. This fire temple was at Šīz, in northwestern Persia, where the king and the warriors went to worship. Rulers such as the Sāsānian king Bahrām V, or Bahrām Gūr (fl. fifth century C.E.), sent the booty of jewelry to be hung in the Zoroastrian fire temple after defeating the Turks in his campaign against them. Ardashīr I also made offerings—the heads of rebels—to the fire temple of Anāhīd.

During the Sāsānian period the warrior class formed the second tier of the social structure; the function of the warrior was to protect the empire and its subjects. There were several divisions within the military, and within the cavalry and infantry. As clergy attended seminaries, the soldiers attended academies where they were trained in the military sciences. The alliance between the priests and the warriors was of paramount importance; the idea of *ērān-sahr*, which had manifested itself under the Sāsānian as that of a set territory ruled by the warrior aristocracy, had been developed and revived by Zoroastrian priests. Under the Zoroastrian religion, which was made the official state religion during the Sāsānian period, church and state were considered inseparable from each other. In reality, however, each group attempted to impose its will on the other, and this long battle caused the final fragmentation and the weakening of the Persian Empire.

DOCTRINE, STRATEGY, AND TACTICS

Although Achaemenid Persian forces were superior on the ground, their weakness was on the seas, where they mainly employed mercenary forces. At the battles, it was the norm for the king to be present to watch over the battle lines and to engage in battle as well. Before each individual battle a council decided the plan and the strategy the forces would follow. In terms of the military attack, the foot soldiers and the foot archers were stationed in the front and in the middle, flanked by the cavalry and the armed forces. To begin the war, the archers began sending volleys of arrows toward the enemy, then the spearmen and the cavalry came into action. These tactics were successful against the people of the Near East, but they did not crush the Greeks, who, with their hoplite forces, were able to withstand the Persians. Man-to-man combat was also known, and it was a sign of heroic deed to defeat one's enemy in this manner. Cyrus

the Younger (c. 424-401 B.C.E.), versed in the Greek tactics, was able to strengthen the Persian military capabilities by enlisting Greek hoplite forces into his army. This group was aided by a heavily armored but ineffective cavalry. Xenophon mentions the Persian cavalry kept their seat only through the pressure of their knees, indicating that they lacked stirrup and saddle.

During the Sāsānian period, there existed manuals of warfare that have since been lost. Portions, however, remain extant in Middle Persian and Arabic texts. The Middle Persian text known as the *Dīnkart* (ninth century C.E.; acts of religion) contains a section devoted to the military. This manual informed soldiers about tactics and rations for food, methods for dealing with war prisoners, and the positions for specific forces. For example, the text mentions that the cavalry should be in front and that left-handed archers should be put on the left flank to defend the army. The center should be on an elevated place, where the army commander could be supported by the infantry. The army should also be placed with the sun and the wind at their backs to blind and hamper the capability of the enemy.

ANCIENT SOURCES

Sources for the earliest history of the Persians come from the sacred book of the Zoroastrians, the *Avesta*, in which references to combat and weapons are made. The Old Persian sources of the Achaemenid period also give some terminology on weapons, but the Greek sources furnish much more. Herodotus (c. 484-424 B.C.E.), Xenophon, and Strabo (64 or 63-after 23 B.C.E.) are the chief Greek sources, providing many details of the Persian army and their tactics. For the Hellenic and the Parthian period classical authors such as Herodian (third century C.E.), Pliny (23-79 C.E.), and Plutarch (c. 46-after 120) are the major sources. For the Sāsānian period, there are a variety of sources not limited to the classical authors. Among the Greek and Latin sources, Ammianus Marcellinus is quite informative on Persian siege tactics, armor, and military. Sāsānian sources such as the *Dīnkart* are primary sources, whereas the Arabic and Persian sources after the seventh century C.E. give much information; the best of these is Abū Jaʿfar Muḥammad ibn Jarīr al-Ṭabarī's *Taʾrīkh al-rusul wa al-mulūk* (872-973; *The History of al-Ṭabarī*, 1985-1999, 39 volumes).

BOOKS AND ARTICLES

Briant, P. "The Achaemenid Empire." In *War and Society in the Ancient and Medieval Worlds*, edited by K. Raaflabu and N. Rosenstein. Cambridge, Mass.: Harvard University Press, 1999.

Campbell, Duncan B. *Ancient Siege Warfare: Persians, Greeks, Cathaginians, and Romans, 546-146 B.C.* Illustrated by Adam Hook. Botley, Oxford, England: Osprey, 2004.

De Souza, Philip. *The Greek and Persian Wars, 499-386 B.C.* New York: Routledge, 2003.

Farrokh, Kaveh. *Sassanian Elite Cavalry, A.D. 224-642.* Illustrated by Angus McBride. Botley, Oxford, England: Osprey, 2005.

―――――. *Shadows in the Desert: Ancient Persia at War.* Botley, Oxford, England: Osprey, 2007.

Ferrill, Arther. "Assyria and Persia: The Age of Iron." In *The Origins of War: From the Stone Age to Alexander the Great.* Rev. ed. Boulder, Colo.: Westview Press, 1997.

Gabriel, Richard A. "Persia and the Art of Logistics, 546-330 B.C.E." In *The Great Armies of Antiquity.* Westport, Conn.: Praeger, 2002.

Rung, Eduard. "War, Peace, and Diplomacy in Graeco-Persian Relations from the Sixth to the Fourth Century B.C." In *War and Peace in Ancient and Medieval History*, edited by Philip de Souza and John France. New York: Cambridge University Press, 2008.

Santosuosso, Antonio. *Soldiers, Citizens, and the Symbols of War: From Classical Greece to Republican Rome, 500-167 B.C.* Boulder, Colo.: Westview Press, 1997.

Sekunda, Nicholas. *The Persian Army, 560-330 B.C.* Illustrated by Simon Chew. Botley, Oxford, England: Osprey, 1992.

Shahbazi, A. "Army in Pre-Islamic Iran." In *Encyclopaedia Iranica*, edited by Ehsan Yarshater. Vol. 2. London: Routledge and Kegan Paul, 1985.

Wiesehöfer, J. *Ancient Persia.* London: I. B. Taurus, 1996.

FILMS AND OTHER MEDIA

Decisive Battles: Thermopylae. Documentary. History Channel, 2005.

Greek and Persian Wars. Documentary. Cromwell Productions, 2009.

Iran: The Forgotten Glory. Documentary. Mystic Films, 2009.

Touraj Daryaee

THE ANCIENT WORLD

WORLD

EUROPE AND THE MEDITERRANEAN

Greek Warfare to Alexander

Dates: c. 1600-336 b.c.e.

Military Achievement

The period from 1600 to 336 b.c.e. saw the emergence in Greece of four distinct ways of war. The first of these, Mycenaean chariot warfare, did not survive past about 1100 b.c.e. It was succeeded by an infantry-based system of individual combat, often called "heroic" because of its prominence in Homer's *Iliad* (c. 750 b.c.e.; English translation, 1611) and *Odyssey* (c. 725 b.c.e.; English translation, 1614). This system in turn gave way to the close-order infantry warfare of classical Greece. A fourth way of war, the combined arms system developed by the Macedonians in the mid-fourth century b.c.e., ultimately overcame the classical Greeks and provided the basis for the conquests of Alexander the Great.

Mycenaean civilization, named after the citadel of Mycenae in southern Greece, emerged about 1600 b.c.e. and reached its height between 1400 and 1200 b.c.e. Mycenaean monarchs ruled from fortified royal palaces, which were economic as well as political and religious centers. Palaces flourished at Mycenae, Pylos, Tiryns, Thebes, and elsewhere on mainland Greece, as well as at Knossos on the island of Crete. These citadels shared a common culture but were not politically unified. Mycenaean society was hierarchical and bureaucratic; professional scribes used clay tablets and a script called Linear B to track everything that entered or left the palaces. Although little conclusive evidence survives, it appears that Mycenaean armies relied heavily on chariots, perhaps supported by infantry. As in the contemporary Egyptian and Hittite military systems, these chariots probably served as mobile fighting platforms for aristocratic archers and spearmen.

For uncertain reasons, Mycenaean civilization began to collapse around 1250 b.c.e. Indeed, there were upheavals throughout the Mediterranean at this time; the fictional story of the Trojan War reflects later poetic memories of these disturbances. In mainland Greece, the palaces were burned, the countryside was depopulated, and Linear B script disappeared. The chariot forces, dependent on logistical support from the palaces, also declined. Consequently, foot soldiers seem to have gained greater prominence in late Mycenaean warfare. By 1100 b.c.e., however, the great Mycenaean centers and the military system they supported had disappeared completely.

The centuries (1100-750 b.c.e.) following the destruction of Mycenaean civilization are often designated the Greek Dark Age. As petty chieftains replaced Mycenaean kings, warfare became sporadic and local, in the form of raids for booty and individual duels between aristocratic champions. The Homeric poems suggest that Dark Age or heroic warriors preferred spears to swords; spears could be thrown from a distance or used hand to hand. Archery, however, was disdained as barbaric and unfair. Chariots may have continued in limited use, perhaps as transports to and from battle. Eventually aristocrats also began to fight from horseback, as cavalry. Yet the most significant military development of the Dark Age was metallurgical: By 900 b.c.e., iron weapons were in widespread use.

By 800 b.c.e. Greece was recovering from the Dark Age. Renewed commerce with the wider Mediterranean world led around 750 b.c.e. to the introduction of the alphabet. During the eighth century b.c.e., increased population and prosperity throughout Greece fostered the rise of the polis, or city-state. A polis (plural, poleis) was a self-governing political unit with a defined territory. Eventually there were more than a thousand poleis in Greece, each one with its own laws, calendar, and military organization. Athens and Sparta, the best known of these states, were exceptionally large in territory and population. Most other poleis were relatively small, with perhaps a few hundred citizens each. Polis governments came

ATHENIAN EMPIRE, FIFTH CENTURY B.C.E.

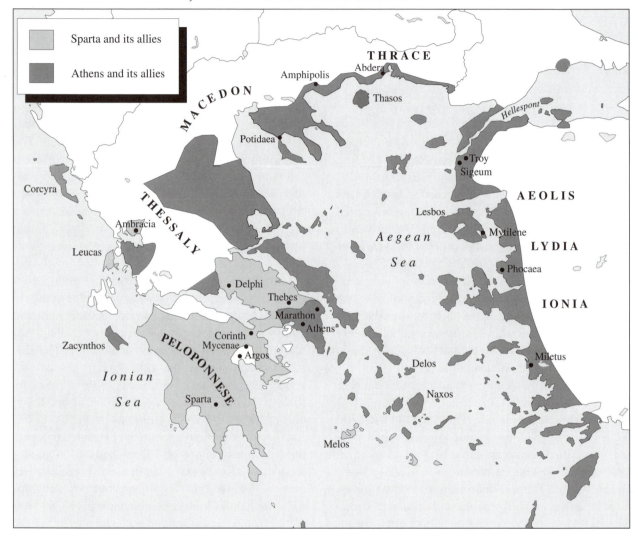

in many forms, but all included an assembly of adult male citizens and a council of elders. Political rights and military service were closely linked, so the new emphasis on community over individualism soon transferred into warfare. By about 650 B.C.E. a communal way of war, the hoplite system, had supplanted the individual aristocratic fighting of the Dark Age.

The hoplite was a heavily armored spearman who fought alongside his fellow citizens in a close-order formation called a phalanx. Because hoplites were required to provide their own equipment, most hop-

lites were middle-class farmers who could afford metal arms and armor. Because citizen farmers could not spare time for extensive training, hoplites were militia, rather than professional, forces. Battles were limited, ritualized affairs, fought on the borderlands between poleis during lulls in the agricultural schedule. There was little in the way of tactics or strategy: Opposing phalanxes lined up against each other on flat open ground, listened to speeches and performed sacrifices, then marched forward against each other. Inevitably one side won the shoving match that followed. Although the losers broke and ran, the victors usually preferred to strip the enemy dead, erect a trophy, and head home. Pursuit after battle was rare. Hoplite warfare, then, did not often result in the complete subjugation of the losing opponent.

The great achievement of the hoplite system was not so much military as political. Hoplite warfare demanded teamwork. There was no room for displays of individual heroism. The communal structure of the phalanx thus reinforced the community spirit of the polis. The hoplite system also helped confine the destructiveness of war to decisive single-day struggles that would not interfere with farming. It therefore gave middle-class agrarians a monopoly on organized violence. Aristocrats were relegated to the cavalry, which usually played only a minor battlefield role. Poor men who could not afford arms and armor were left out of battle altogether, unless they served as slingers or rock throwers.

Sparta was the exception to the hoplite rule. Threatened by military defeat and internal disorder during the mid-seventh century B.C.E., the Spartans responded by turning their state into an armed camp. Spartan boys began military training at age seven. For most of their adult lives, even when married, they lived in sex-segregated barracks rather than private homes. Girls also received military training. Adult male Spartan citizens, or Spartiates, practiced almost constantly for war, giving Sparta the only professional phalanx in all of Greece. Unlike the militiamen of other city-states, Spartan hoplites marched in step to the sound of flutes and could carry out complex tactical maneuvers. This drill and discipline made the Spartan army invincible on the battlefield. Yet in order to free its citizens for war, Sparta's economy had to rely on the labor of helots, serfs who worked the land for their Spartiate masters. Fear of helot revolts often kept the Spartan army at home, thus inhibiting Spartan control of the whole Greek world.

For more than two centuries, the hoplite reigned supreme on Greek battlefields. The Greco-Persian Wars (499-448 B.C.E.) reinforced Greek beliefs in their own military superiority. At the Battle of Marathon in 490 B.C.E., for example, some 10,000 Athenian and Plataean hoplites routed about 25,000 lightly armed Persian invaders. Even the Greek defeat at Thermopylae (480 B.C.E.), where 300 Spartiates held

off perhaps 70,000 Persians for several days, represented in some sense a victory for the hoplite system. To the Greeks, Thermopylae showed that only treachery and vastly superior numbers could overwhelm free citizens fighting in a hoplite phalanx.

In the last half of the fifth century B.C.E. the hoplite way of war confronted several challenges. In particular, during the Greco-Persian Wars several city-states had developed fleets of oared galleys called triremes. Athens took the lead in naval warfare and by 450 B.C.E. had a skilled professional fleet numbering two hundred ships, the best and largest in the Greek world. Navies added strategic mobility to the military equation. No longer were battles confined to the borderlands between neighboring poleis. Fleets could now launch amphibious assaults hundreds of miles away from their home cities.

To take advantage of this mobility, a new type of soldier began to appear: the peltast. The original peltasts were Thracian mercenaries equipped with a small shield, or *peltē*, in Greek; later the term "peltast" denoted a wide variety of lightly armored foot soldiers equipped primarily with javelins. Peltasts fought in loose skirmishing formation. Although they could not confront a phalanx head-on, they were more mobile than heavily armored hoplites and so excelled at quick attacks in difficult terrain. Other light infantry, including slingers and archers, also became more common.

The long and agonizing Peloponnesian War (431-404 B.C.E.), fought between opposing coalitions led by Athens and Sparta, clearly demonstrated the effects of these military innovations. Near Pylos in 425 B.C.E., for instance, an amphibious assault by Athenian peltasts and other light infantry overwhelmed Spartiate hoplites stationed on the rocky island of Sphakteria. The next year, at Amphipolis in northern Greece, the Spartan general Brasidas used a surprise attack combining hoplites, peltasts, and cavalry to rout a superior Athenian force. In this period, battle lost its limited and ritual character, and fighting occurred instead in both summer and winter, in both rain and snow, at night, on mountains, and even inside cities. The growing importance of fleets and light troops, in sum, was bringing an end to the agrarian monopoly on organized violence.

The Peloponnesian War also spurred the growth of military professionalism. Commanders, once amateurs, became skilled tacticians through constant campaigning. Some states imitated Sparta by drilling units of picked troops—*epilektoi*, in Greek—to provide a trained corps for their phalanx militias. Along with growing professionalism, the economic devastation caused by the war prompted many men to seek employment outside Greece. By the end of the fifth century, tens of thousands had enlisted as mercenaries with the Persian army in Asia Minor. In fact, twelve thousand of these soldiers supported the Achaemenid prince Cyrus the Younger (c. 424-401 B.C.E.) during his abortive attempt to usurp the Persian throne (401 B.C.E.).

Although shaken, the hoplite system was not totally overthrown by the Peloponnesian War. Indeed, its best practitioners, the Spartans, took comfort in the fact that they had triumphed in the major phalanx clashes of the conflict. During the Corinthian War (395-386 B.C.E.), though, Spartan military confidence suffered when a Spartan unit was attacked and nearly destroyed near Corinth by Athenian troops under the general Iphicrates (c. 410-353 B.C.E.) Iphicrates is said to have trained his hoplites as peltasts, lightening their armor and lengthening their spears.

The real blow came in 371 B.C.E., when the Thebans defeated the Spartans in a pitched hoplite battle at Leuctra. The Theban commander, Epaminondas (c. 410-362 B.C.E.), took advantage of many of the military innovations of the preceding century. He deployed cavalry and light troops to screen his advance and protect his flanks and used his force of picked troops, the Sacred Band, to spearhead his hoplite assault. Epaminondas also drew up the left wing of his phalanx fifty men deep; the usual depth was eight men. The Thebans easily crushed the much thinner opposing Spartan wing. For the first time in centuries, a Spartan army had been defeated in hoplite battle; the era of Spartan invincibility was over.

Thus by the mid-fourth century B.C.E. the classical Greek way of war had undergone many modifications. Nonetheless, as long as the polis remained the characteristic Greek political organization, the hop-

lite phalanx of citizen militia persisted. Ultimately, a fourth military system evolved to challenge the phalanx. It arose not in the poleis, but in Macedon, a region of northern Greece long considered a backwater.

Philip II of Macedon (382-336 B.C.E.), father of Alexander the Great (356-323 B.C.E.), came to the throne in 359 B.C.E. He inherited a kingdom in crisis; Illyrian invaders had just smashed the Macedonian army, killing King Perdiccas III, Philip's brother. Macedon was large and populous but in danger of being dismembered by its neighbors. To save his monarchy, Philip reformed his army. He began by creating a new mass infantry force. These soldiers, peasants rather than middle-class agrarians, fought as a phalanx but wore significantly less armor than hoplites. They carried a long pike, the sarissa, rather than the hoplite spear. Philip also reorganized Macedon's aristocratic cavalry, equipping it with lances and training it for mounted charges. In battle, cavalry and infantry functioned as hammer and anvil. The sarissa phalanx, with its hedgehog of pikes, would pin the enemy in place until the cavalry could charge a flank or other vulnerable spot. Specialized troops, including archers, light cavalry, slingers, and spearmen, protected the army's flanks, screened infantry advances, and conducted reconnaissance before battles. Finally, Philip created a corps of engineers and a siege train, enabling the Macedonians to capture fortified cities.

The new Macedonian army, then, was a true combined arms force. Many of its elements had surfaced before in Greek warfare—Philip reputedly drew inspiration from both Iphicrates and Epaminondas—but they had never been fully developed. Only a large monarchy such as Macedon, not a traditional polis, could afford to maintain such an army. Philip himself added the final ingredient to the Macedonian way of war. A master diplomat, he combined intrigue and negotiation with swift military strikes. By 348 B.C.E., Macedon not only had recovered from crisis but also reigned supreme in northern Greece. Philip then moved gradually south, threatening the independence of the city-states. After much squabbling, Athens and its allies took the field against the Macedonians. The two sides met at Chaeronea in 338 B.C.E., the citizen phalanx against Philip's new model army. First the Macedonian infantry pinned their hoplite opponents. Then Philip's cavalry, led by his eighteen-year-old son Alexander, charged through a gap in the line and fell on the Greek rear. The Greeks broke and ran. Only the Theban Sacred Band stood its ground and fought to the death. The day of the independent polis and its citizen militia hoplites was over; the ascendancy of Macedon's military system was just beginning.

Philip never lived to enjoy the fruits of his victories. He was assassinated in 336 B.C.E., bringing his son Alexander III, known as Alexander the Great, to the Macedonian throne. Within two years, Alexander would embark on a journey of world conquest that eventually took him to the banks of the Indus River. Alexander's conquests, though, owed at least part of their success to the professional combined arms approach created by Philip II. The Macedonian way of war would reign supreme in the eastern Mediterranean until the second century B.C.E., when the successors of Alexander confronted the legions of Republican Rome.

WEAPONS, UNIFORMS, AND ARMOR

The earliest Mycenaean weapons, dating from the sixteenth century B.C.E., include long rapiers, daggers, large spearheads, and arrows of bronze, flint, or obsidian. Bows were of the simple, noncomposite type. Slings were certainly deployed in this period and in all following ones. Little evidence for armor exists, although small metal discs found in early graves at Mycenae may be the remnants of otherwise perishable leather or fabric armor. The famous boar's tusk helmet, known from Homer's *Iliad* as well as from Mycenaean art, was also in use during this period. Artistic representations show two kinds of large shield: an oblong "tower" shield and the more common "figure eight," both of animal hide with metal reinforcement. Neither type had handles. Instead the shield was suspended by a shoulder strap, so a warrior could easily throw it over his back to protect a retreat.

Both weapons and armor improved during the height of Mycenaean power. Sword redesign eliminated weak tangs and provided better hand guards. A new large spearhead, some 50 centimeters long, appeared by the fifteenth century B.C.E.; its ribbed blade ran straight into its socket for greater strength. Composite bows, a borrowing from Minoan Crete, also came into use. Bronze body armor made its debut in the late fifteenth century B.C.E. An example from Dendra, constructed of overlapping metal plates with greaves and a high neck, seems designed for chariotborne use. A boar's tusk helmet accompanies the Dendra armor; at Knossos and elsewhere conical bronze helmets have appeared. Shields became less popular; the "figure eight" type especially became more a ritual than a military item.

Striking changes in weapons and armor accompanied the last years of Mycenaean power. Between 1250 and 1150 B.C.E., long thrusting swords gave way to new types, shorter and stouter, with strong hilts and flat, straight-edged blades. The so-called

TURNING POINTS

1400-1200 B.C.E.	Mycenaean civilization flourishes, with a wealth of political, economic, and religious centers.
1200-1100 B.C.E.	Mycenaean order collapses during a period of upheaval.
1100-750 B.C.E.	In the period known as the Greek Dark Age, petty chieftains replace the Mycenaean kings.
c. 900 B.C.E.	Iron weapons become increasingly popular.
750-650 B.C.E.	Hoplite armor and tactics are developed.
499-448 B.C.E.	The Persian Wars are fought between Persia and the Greek city-states.
431-404 B.C.E.	The Peloponnesian Wars are fought between Athens and Sparta.
371 B.C.E.	Thebes defeats Sparta at Leuctra, ending Spartan supremacy in hoplite warfare.
338 B.C.E.	The Macedonian army of Philip II defeats Athens at Chaeronea.

THE PELOPONNESIAN WARS

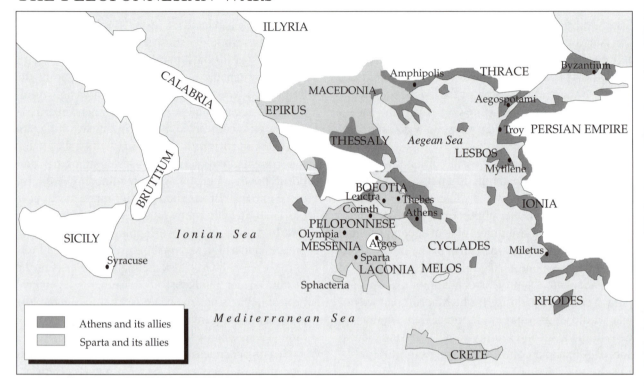

Griffzungenschwert, most distinctive of these types, was mass-produced and widely distributed. Examples appear in central Europe, Cyprus, the Levant, and Egypt as well as in Greece. Spearheads became smaller and less ornate, and spears began to be equipped with end spikes. Late Mycenaean arrowheads were invariably bronze and joined with a tang instead of slotted into shafts, like earlier arrowheads. Art of the period shows soldiers wearing reinforced leather or fabric, rather than bronze armor. Contemporary helmets may also have been made of reinforced hide rather than metal. Small circular or elliptical shields with handgrips appear alongside this armor.

Dark Age weaponry made a major shift from bronze to iron. Lighter, tougher and sharper than bronze, iron came into widespread use during the eleventh century B.C.E. The late Mycenaean Griffzungenschwert sword, translated into iron, remained common in the early Dark Age, but in the ninth and eighth centuries, shorter, broader swords appeared.

Spearheads, often with wide leaf blades, initially remained bronze but became iron by the tenth century B.C.E. Dark Age graves often included multiple spearheads but no swords, perhaps reflecting the long-range warfare in Homer. The paucity of early Dark Age arrowhead finds also reflects the Homeric disdain for archery. Only on Crete did long, tanged arrowheads remain relatively common. Extremely little evidence exists for early Dark Age metal armor, although there may have been perishable leather or fabric armor. Metal corselets reappeared in Greece around 800 B.C.E. Conical metal helmets, with transverse or fore-and-aft crests, resurfaced around the same time. Artistic representations reveal the presence of cavalry throughout the later Dark Age; little evidence exists for the continued battlefield use of chariots.

New types of arms and armor accompanied the development of the hoplite phalanx during the eighth century B.C.E. Hoplites took their name from the *hoplon*, a large, round shield of leather or bronze-covered wood, some 3 feet in diameter. The hoplon boasted an armband, or *porpax*, as well as a handgrip, or *antilabē*, making it far easier to handle. Shields might have borne either a state emblem or individual insignia. Hoplite equipment also included a bronze helmet, greaves, and corselet. The most common helmet was the Corinthian, beaten from a single piece of metal and offering all-around protection at the expense of vision and hearing. The hoplite's main weapon, the spear, or *doru*, was roughly 6 feet long, with a bronze point and end spike. A variety of short swords served as secondary weapons. Among these was the single-edged *machaira*, a machete-like slashing blade. Over time the hoplite panoply got lighter. By the fifth century B.C.E., greaves were discarded, leather and fabric composite corselets often substituted for bronze, and metal helmets sometimes replaced with felt ones. Although Spartiates all wore red cloaks, no polis army had standardized equipment or a real uniform.

Peltasts wore little or no armor and carried light animal-hide shields. Often they attached a throwing-loop to their javelins for increased range. Greek archers generally used a short, weak bow to shoot bronze- or iron-tipped arrows. The recurved Scythian type arrow was known but not widely used. Slingers, their weapons made of gut or sinew, often outranged archers. They used stones or almond-shaped lead bullets as ammunition. Classical Greek cavalry was weak and suited mostly for pursuit. Horsemen carried javelins and wore light armor; they had no stirrups.

In the fourth century B.C.E., Macedonian phalangites usually wore only light fabric or leather armor. Their pike, or sarissa, required both hands, so they carried a small light shield on a neck strap. Like the hoplite spear, the sarissa had a bronze tip and end spike. Both cavalry and infantry versions of the sarissa existed; the infantry version was 12 to 15 feet long, and the cavalry type relatively shorter. As shock troops, Macedonian cavalry often wore metal armor. They were expert lancers even without the aid of stirrups.

MILITARY ORGANIZATION

Virtually nothing is known about Mycenaean military organization. Linear B tablets from Pylos suggest an army divided into ten units with attached officers. The tablets also mention an official called the *lawagetas* ("people-leader"), who might have been the kingdom's wartime commander. Dark Age military structure remains similarly obscure. Chieftains together with clansmen and retainers probably fought as loose warrior bands.

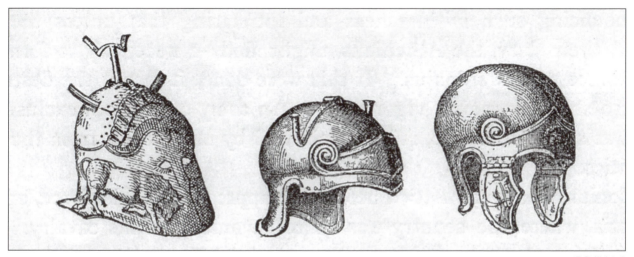

F. R. Niglutsch

Some Athenian helmets.

In the hoplite era, each polis had its own military structure, usually reflecting its civic organization. At Athens, for example, the phalanx was divided into ten tribal regiments or *phylai* (singular *phylē*), also called *taxeis* (singular *taxis*). The phylē or taxis was not a tactical unit, and it varied in strength according to the number of men called up for any given campaign. Athens's cavalry was also divided into ten tribal regiments. The early Athenian army was commanded by its *polemarchos*, or war leader; later a board of ten elected generals (*stratēgoi*, singular *stratēgos*) took over.

The Spartan phalanx possessed a defined tactical organization, but its details remain disputed. According to Thucydides, it consisted of seven *lochoi* (singular *lochos*), each divided into four *pentēkostyes* (singular *pentēkostys*) of 128 men apiece. The pentēkostys in turn comprised four *enoomotiai* (singular *enoomotia*) of 32 men apiece. Xenophon in contrast describes an army of six *morai* (singular *mora*), each containing four lochoi of 128 men. These lochoi mustered only two pentēkostyes of two enoomotiai apiece. Thucydides and Xenophon agree that each subunit had its own regular officers. The army as a whole was commanded by Sparta's two kings.

During the fifth and fourth centuries B.C.E., a number of states experimented with units of picked troops, or *epilektoi*. Their size varied; the most famous of these elite units, the Theban Sacred Band, comprising 150 pairs of homosexual lovers, was maintained at state expense. Greek mercenaries in Asia Minor, perhaps following Persian military principles, were regularly organized into lochoi of one hundred men each. These lochoi were independent tactical and administrative units, with regular officers, called *lochagoi* (singular *lochagos*).

The basic unit of the Macedonian phalanx was the *syntagma* of 256 men, comprising 16 files of 16 men apiece. Macedonian syntagmata were maneuverable tactical units, with regular officers. Cavalry was organized into squadrons of two hundred horsemen called *ilai* (singular *ilē*). Units of elite infantry and cavalry functioned as vanguards in battle. Macedonian kings bestowed the coveted status of "Companions" (*hetairoi*) on both horse and foot soldiers in order to reward and encourage valor.

DOCTRINE, STRATEGY, AND TACTICS

Nothing certain can be said of Mycenaean or Dark Age military doctrine. The essential doctrine of the hoplite system, however, is clear: to engage in decisive phalanx battle. This principle undergirded Greek warfare from the rise of the polis on through the fourth century B.C.E. Its rationale was as much political as military: Short, decisive clashes kept war limited and allowed farmers to devote maximum time to agriculture. As long as hoplite warfare depended on mutual agreement to fight, moreover, strategy was not an issue.

The Peloponnesian War did see the development of Greek strategy. Athens, a sea power, sought to avoid hoplite battle by relying on its navy. Sparta, supreme on land, undertook annual invasions of Athenian territory in a fruitless attempt to lure the Athenian phalanx out to battle. These disparate strategies ensured that although neither side lost, neither side won a clear victory. Attempts in the middle years of the war by both belligerents to break the deadlock failed. Although each side had minor successes in the other's territory, neither side could win the war unless it beat the other at its own game. Ultimately the Spartans did exactly this. They deployed their own fleet, defeated Athens at sea, and blocked the city's grain imports. The Athenians could have prevented this outcome, but they overconfidently squandered much of their naval strength in a failed attempt to capture the island of Sicily.

As with strategy, there was not much to traditional hoplite tactics. Commanders were aware that advancing phalanxes tended to drift to the right, each man trying to get behind the shield of the man next to him, and they sometimes took measures to forestall this. The Spartans, with their intricate tactical organization, were able to maneuver effectively on the battlefield. This ability won them the day on several occasions. Otherwise, the main tactic of phalanx battle, even for the Spartans, was head-on collision. The development of light troops in the late fifth century B.C.E. gave impetus to flanking movements and surprise attacks. Using hit-and-run tactics, peltasts, slingers, and spearmen could discomfit the traditional phalanx. Greek armies, though, still relied on

F. R. Niglutsch

Use of the Macedonian phalanx during the Battle of the Carts (mid-fourth century B.C.E.).

hoplites to strike the decisive blow. Two strategies for increasing the strength of this blow were a deeper phalanx—the tactic of Epaminondas at Leuktra—and the use of picked troops.

On the battlefield, the combined arms tactics of the Macedonians gave them a decisive edge over even the best Greek troops. Perhaps more important, though, was Macedon's consistent strategy. From his accession, Philip proceeded methodically first to stabilize his kingdom, then to subjugate its neighbors, and finally to consolidate power over all Greece. Unlike the Greeks, the Macedonians were not tied to the doctrine of decisive battle. Indeed, Philip achieved some of his major victories through diplomacy and political intrigue.

The Macedonians also made logistics a keystone of strategy. The hoplite system gave little consideration to the requirements of extended campaigning. Traditional phalanx clashes, after all, occurred close to home. Furthermore, classical hoplites went to battle followed by slave servants bearing rations and equipment. When hoplites deployed far afield, as in the Peloponnesian War, they could usually depend on a fleet to carry supplies. The Macedonians, on the other hand, learned to conduct extended land campaigns without naval supply. Philip eliminated slave porters and made his troops travel light. He successfully employed coercion to ensure that food supplies would be ready and waiting when his troops entered new territory. Just as he trained Alexander's army, Philip developed the logistical and strategic thought that made feasible his son's conquests.

ANCIENT SOURCES

For all periods of Greek warfare from 1600 to 336 B.C.E., archaeological excavation provides the basic evidence for Greek arms and armor. A. M. Snodgrass, in *Arms and Armor of the Greeks* (1999), collects this evidence in a format accessible to nonspecialists. For the late Bronze Age, excavated Linear B tablets from Mycenae, Pylos, and elsewhere furnish information about the military organization and equipment of the Mycenaean kingdoms.

The *Iliad* (c. 750 B.C.E.; English translation, 1611) and *Odyssey* (c. 725 B.C.E.; English translation, 1614), epic poems ascribed to Homer, are among the earliest literary sources for information about Greek warfare. Scholars continue to debate the veracity of Homeric descriptions of warfare; most would agree that the poems reflect the battle conditions of the Greek Dark Age rather than those of the Mycenaean period.

In his *Historiai Herodotou* (c. 424 B.C.E.; *The History*, 1709), Herodotus (c. 484-424) recounts the major land and naval battles of the Persian Wars. Likewise, Thucydides (c. 459-402 B.C.E.) narrates the course of the long and agonizing Peloponnesian Wars. Both Herodotus and Thucydides provide useful information on Greek strategies, tactics, and military organization during the fifth century B.C.E.

The works of the Athenian author Xenophon (431-354 B.C.E.) are essential for any understanding of Greek warfare. In addition to a memoir of his experiences as a mercenary commander during 401-399, *Kurou anabasis* (*Anabasis*, 1623; also known as *Expedition of Cyrus* and *March Up Country*), Xenophon composed a history of Greece, *Ellīnika*, also known as *Helenica* (*History of the Affairs of Greece*, 1685), and technical treatises on the cavalry, horsemanship, and hunting. His *Lakedaimoniōn politeia* (*Polity of the Lacedaemonians*, 1832; also known as *Constitution of Sparta*) describes Spartan army organization and training in the fourth century B.C.E.

Finally, the Roman magistrate and writer known as Arrian (c. 89-155 C.E.), produced several texts that furnish important evidence for the organization, equipment, and tactics of the Macedonian army. These texts include a history of the campaigns of Alexander as well as a tactical manual.

BOOKS AND ARTICLES

Anderson, J. K. *Military Theory and Practice in the Age of Xenophon*. Berkeley: University of California Press, 1970.

De Souza, Philip, and Waldemar Heckel. *The Greeks at War: From Athens to Alexander*. Botley, Oxford, England: Osprey, 2004.

Ducrey, Pierre. *Warfare in Ancient Greece*. Translated by Janet Lloyd. New York: Schocken Books, 1986.

Everson, Tim. *Warfare in Ancient Greece: Arms and Armour from the Heroes of Homer to Alexander the Great*. Stroud, Gloucestershire, England: Sutton, 2004.

Ferrill, Arther. *The Origins of War*. Rev. ed. Boulder, Colo.: Westview Press, 1997.

Hanson, Victor Davis. *The Western Way of War: Infantry Battle in Classical Greece*. 2d ed. Berkeley: University of California Press, 2000.

Hanson, Victor Davis, and John Keegan, eds. *The Wars of the Ancient Greeks: And Their Invention of Western Military Culture*. London: Cassell, 1999.

Kern, Paul Bentley. *The Greeks in Ancient Siege Warfare*. Bloomington: Indiana University Press, 1999.

Lendon, J. E. *Soldiers and Ghosts: A History of Battle in Classical Antiquity*. New Haven, Conn.: Yale University Press, 2005.

Montagu, John Drogo. *Greek and Roman Warfare: Battles, Tactics, and Trickery*. St. Paul, Minn.: MBI, 2006

Raaflaub, Kurt A., ed. *War and Peace in the Ancient World*. Malden, Mass.: Blackwell, 2007.

Rawlings, Louis. *The Ancient Greeks at War*. Manchester, England: Manchester University Press, 2007.

Sage, Michael M. *Warfare in Ancient Greece: A Sourcebook*. New York: Routledge, 1996.

Santosuosso, Antonio. *Soldiers, Citizens, and the Symbols of War: From Classical Greece to Republican Rome, 500-167 B.C.* Boulder, Colo.: Westview Press, 1997.

FILMS AND OTHER MEDIA

Decisive Battles: Gaugamela. Documentary. History Channel, 2005.

Greek and Persian Wars. Documentary. Cromwell Productions, 2009.

In Search of the Trojan War. Documentary. British Broadcasting Corporation, 1985.

Troy. Feature film. Warner Bros., 2005.

John W. I. Lee

GREEK AND HELLENISTIC WARFARE FROM ALEXANDER TO ROME

Dates: 336-30 B.C.E.

POLITICAL CONSIDERATIONS

In the early fourth century B.C.E., Greece did not exist as a unified nation but as a number of separate, often hostile, city-states struggling among themselves for power. Although the major cities of Sparta, Thebes, and Athens had warred against each other for control of the Hellenic peninsula, none had been able to establish permanent dominance. Despite their mutual antagonism, all of these separate political entities still identified themselves as "Greek," based on their shared history, traditions, and customs. To the ancient Greeks, other cultures or nationalities were, of necessity, barbarian and inferior. This categorization extended not only to the Celts, the Gauls, other aggressive tribes to the north, and radically different cultures to the east but also to other kingdoms, such as Macedonia, that shared much of their culture with Greece. It is ironic, therefore, that the greatest Greek empire of all time arose from the marginally barbarian region of Macedonia.

Claiming Greek status through alleged descent from the legendary Greek hero Heracles, Philip II of Macedonia began his rise to dominance in 352 B.C.E. and by 348 B.C.E. ruled all of Greece north of Thermopylae. Using a combination of wealth and political savvy backed by military strength, Philip eventually defeated the combined armies of the Greeks at Chaeronea in 338 B.C.E., ending the era of the independent Greek city-state. Despite his victory and his obvious leadership qualities, Philip was never entirely accepted as an authentic Greek. In an attempt to win favor with Athenians and other Greek elites, he announced an invasion of Persia to liberate the Greek cities seized by the Persians during the previous century. Philip's plans were cut short by his assassination in 336 B.C.E. Philip's son, Alexander, only twenty-two years old when he assumed the Macedonian throne, inherited his father's army, his uneasy relationship with the Greeks, and his dreams of empire.

MILITARY ACHIEVEMENT

Military empires never last forever. Like human beings, empires come into being, grow, mature, falter, and eventually perish. In little more than a decade, from 332 to 323 B.C.E., the empire of Alexander the Great of Macedonia grew to encompass most of the known world. After Alexander's death this vast empire splintered, fracturing into smaller kingdoms that struggled for power among themselves, eventually to be defeated one after another by the legions of the expanding Roman Empire.

Inspired by the idealized heroes of Homer's epic poems, Alexander utilized both strategy and charismatic personal leadership to effect an unbroken string of major victories. The Battle of the Granicus River in 334 B.C.E., fought near the ancient ruins of Troy, was the first of three major battles between Alexander the Great and the Persian Empire. After Alexander defeated the Persians and a large force of Greek mercenaries led by Memnon of Rhodes, city after city opened to him. In 333 B.C.E., Alexander's army and the Persian forces of Darius met at Issus, in what is now coastal Turkey. The Persians' left wing collapsed under an assault from Alexander's cavalry, the Persian line was flanked, and the Persian emperor, Darius the Great, fled.

After being crowned Pharaoh in Egypt, Alexander returned to the Persian campaign. In 331 B.C.E., Darius positioned his scythed chariots on flat ground near Gaugamela. As the Macedonians seized reins and slew horses and charioteers, Darius was pushed off the edge of the plain onto uneven ground. Darius fled again, only to be assassinated by one of his own couriers. In the succeeding three years, Alexander's army completed the conquest of the Iranian plateau. By 326 B.C.E., Alexander had reached the Hydaspes River in Punjab, India, where he defeated Porus and his war elephants in battle. Porus surrendered and pledged allegiance to Alexander.

If not the greatest military commander in the ancient world, Alexander was one of the best. He was the son of one of the great military leaders of the ancient world and the pupil of Aristotle, one of the greatest philosophers and teachers of the ancient world. He inherited a great army and made it greater. Under his leadership, his armies conquered Persia, Anatolia, Syria, Phoenicia, Judea, Gaza, Egypt, Bactria, and Mesopotamia. Toward the end of his short life, he pushed the boundaries of his empire as far as India.

As in any extended empire, however, vastness worked against him. As Alexander acquired new territories, his men remained farther from home with every march and with every victorious battle. Hence, although Alexander wanted to continue eastward to the Great Outer Sea and the very ends of the earth, he was forced to turn back. After surviving twelve years of battle, Alexander the Great died in bed at his palace in Babylon in June, 323 B.C.E., either as a result of being poisoned or from disease. When asked on his deathbed to whom his empire should be given, he has famously been quoted as saying, "To the strongest."

After his death, his empire was ripped apart by various factions attempting to be the strongest. In creating his own great empire, Alexander had destroyed the older, more stable empire of the Achaemenids, creating a vacuum of power ultimately to be filled by new rival kingdoms, all founded by members of Alexander's inner circle of commanders, the Diadochi. These successors murdered Alexander's son, broke pacts, and allowed a weakened Macedonia to be attacked by tribes of Gauls from the north. Antigonus I Monophthalmos and his descendants dominated the old kingdom of Mac-

edon, and most of the old Greek city-states, until they were defeated at the Battle of Pydna in 168 B.C.E. The Attalid kingdom that ruled Pergamon ceded it to the Roman Republic in 133 to avoid a war of succession. The last remnants of the Seleucid Empire, formerly encompassing Babylonia and the eastern part of Alexander's empire, were absorbed by Rome in 63 B.C.E. After Ptolemy and his descendants were accepted as successors to the ancient Pharaohs, their empire was finally conquered by Octavian (later Augustus) in 30 B.C.E. The reign of the last of the Hellenistic empires ended, and with it died Alexander's dreams of a pan-Hellenistic world.

Like the lingering aftershocks after a major earthquake, the empires of Alexander's successors could never rival the original. Yet the fact that they persisted for nearly three centuries, from 336 to 30 B.C.E., is a testament to the legacy of this great military commander and to the Hellenistic way of war.

Weapons, Uniforms, and Armor

Although the ascendance of the Macedonian forces, especially under Alexander, was based on decisive generalship and intelligent use of cavalry, the emblematic weapon of the Macedonian infantry was the *sarissa*, a weighted and double-pointed, iron-tipped pike more than eighteen feet in length. Jutting forward from the Macedonian phalanx, the weapons of the first five rows of men all projected beyond the leading edge of the formation. With five spear points bristling in front of each phalangite, the massed sarissa could be a formidable offensive weapon, particularly if the entire phalanx advanced down an

Turning Points

399 B.C.E.	Dionysius I of Syracuse sponsors catapult research.
338 B.C.E.	Philip II of Macedon defeats united Greek army at Chaeronea.
333 B.C.E.	Alexander defeats main army of Darius III at Issus.
332 B.C.E.	Alexander the Great begins Siege of Tyre.
331 B.C.E.	Alexander defeats main army of Darius III at Gaugamela.
197 B.C.E.	Romans defeat main army of Philip V at Cynoscephalae.

CLASSICAL GREECE, FIFTH CENTURY B.C.E.

EPIRUS

Ionian Sea

THESSALY

Pharsalus

MACEDONIA

Methone
Pydna

Therma

Amphipolis
Apollonia

Mende

THRACE

Thasos
Samothrace

Proponti s

Byzantium
Chalcedon

LEMNOS

Aegean Sea

Antissa

Mytilene

LESBOS

Smyrna

IONIA
Colophon

Teos

Ephesus

Magnesia

Miletus

CARIA

Halicarnassus

RHODES

KARPATHOS

Cos

Samos

CHIOS

IKARIA

Mykonos

NAXOS

Minoa

PAROS

Ios

THERA

AETOLIA

Delphi

BOEOTIA

Thebes
Chaeronea
Plataea

Chalcis
Eretria

EUBOEA

ATTICA

Athens

Megara

Corinth

CEOS

Sicyon

Elis

Olympia

ARCADIA

Mantinea

Mycenae
Argos

Sparta

LACONIA

MESSENIA

Pylos

Melos

CRETE

Knossos
Gortyn

incline, lending momentum to the push, or charge. Defensively, the *saurotēr*, the counterweighted spike at the rear, could be planted in the ground to fend off an attack. Since phalangist troops used both hands to wield the heavy sarissa, they bore shields on their left arms on straps or harnesses. In close formation, each shield protected the man to the left, an arrangement covering most of the phalanx in a "shield wall" but leaving the extreme right open to a flanking attack. If the phalanx became scattered, the secondary weapon was a short sword.

Later Hellenistic infantry of the period used the *doru*, a shorter spear; curved short swords distinguished as the *kopis* and the *machaira*, depending on the direction of curve; and the *xiphos*, a double-edged sword. Defensive equipment included metallic or nonmetallic breastplates, leather shields covered in thin metal sheathing, and greaves to protect the lower legs. Helmets ranged from simple metal Boeotian hatlike helmets to complex Thracian models with cheek and nose protectors.

During this era, innovation in military technology was expressed in the development of siege engines. Building from the concept of the *oxybelēs*, a simple fixed bow, Greek and Hellenistic engineers developed advanced catapults using twisted sinews to increase power and range. Some of these machines were capable of launching 250-pound projectiles. Other innovations included the use of naphtha, or "flaming mud," and a solar-powered heat ray reportedly invented by Archimedes on behalf of the Syracusans in 212 B.C.E.

What was not invented could be borrowed. After capturing eighty battle elephants from King Porus at the Battle of the Hydaspes River, Alexander acquired one hundred more before returning to the west. Alexander's Hellenistic successors made elephants the fad weapon of the era. Able to frighten horses and terrify men, trample infantry and cavalry alike, and

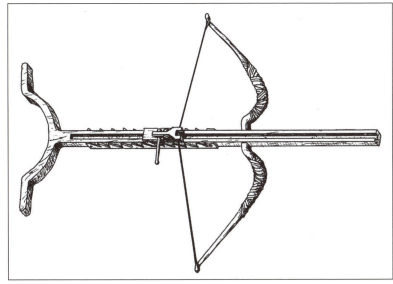

Kimberly L. Dawson Kurnizki

The gastraphetes*, or belly bow, developed by the Greeks around 400 B.C.E., was a significant advance in catapult technology. The operator would lean forward with his abdomen, pinning the weapon against the ground to force a slide backward.*

even demolish wooden fortifications, elephants could charge at fifteen miles per hour. At that speed, however, they were hard to stop, and they often tended to run amok, trampling friend and foe alike.

A more successful borrowing was the cataphract, a rider and steed covered completely in chain mail or scale armor. Human cataphract armor could contain as many as fifteen hundred scales and might weigh nearly ninety pounds, while the horse armor usually consisted of large aprons of scales tied around the animal's body. Originating in ancient Iran, the cataphract was widely adopted by the Hellenistic Seleucid Empire in Persia and by the Parthians, who used it victoriously against Roman forces in 53 B.C.E., with the defeat of Marcus Licinius Crassus at the Battle of Carrhae.

MILITARY ORGANIZATION

Although Greece is revered as the cradle of democracy, Alexander the Great was the undisputed ruler of the Macedonian Empire and its army. Parmenio and a few other well-regarded generals were Alexander's close advisers. Under this level were commanders, the selection of whom was based on personal relations, familial ties, and political status. Because conveying orders during battle could be difficult, instructions were given to subordinates during frequent prebattle general staff meetings, so these commanders met personally with Alexander on a regular basis.

To reinforce emotional cohesion within fighting units, men were grouped according to geographic origin. Even officers were usually selected from the same districts as the common soldiers. In addition, a hierarchy of relative positions of honor encouraged bravery and prowess in battle. The most prestigious unit was the *hetairoi*—the companions. Organized into regional squadrons made up of two hundred to three hundred soldiers and led by Alexander himself, the companion cavalry had originated in the horsemen of the Macedonian nobility, but membership later became based on skill, or *techne*, and character, *aretē*. This premier cavalry unit was always placed to the right of the line of battle, the place of highest honor in the Macedonian array. The Thessalian heavy cavalry, serving Alexander because he was *tagos*, or military leader, of Thessalia as well, deployed on the left flank.

Immediately to the left of the hetairoi were the noble-born royal guard. They were followed by the elite *hypaspistai*, or shield bearers, three subunits of one thousand foot soldiers each, made up of the best fighters selected from all the regiments. Then came six or seven battalions of foot soldiers, or *pezhetairoi*, each with perhaps fifteen hundred men. The order of the battalions was based on their past fighting performance. Place in line and even within cavalry, or *hipparchy*, lines reflected ranks of honor, spurring each man and each unit to outperform their fellow warriors.

The army of Alexander also included native Macedonian light infantrymen, ranking generally above mercenaries and consisting of javelineers, archers, and slingers. Macedonian control over the gold and silver mines of northern Greece provided the pay for thousands of additional mercenaries from various nations, so Thracians were hired as *peltastai*, or shield-bearing skirmishers, archers were recruited

from Crete, and spearmen were hired from Phrygia. These mixed troops provided added strength and flexibility throughout Alexander's conquests. Greek mercenaries were also used in the Macedonian expeditionary army, although these forces were mostly employed for garrison duty in the conquered provinces.

Later Hellenistic warlords often named individual units according to the colors of their shields to encourage unit pride and solidarity. For example, until after the Battle of Pydna in 168 B.C.E., when the Antigonid kingdom was crushed by Rome, units within the phalanx of the Antigonid armies had been designated as *Chalkaspides*, or bronze shields, and *Leukaspides*, or white shields.

DOCTRINE, STRATEGY, AND TACTICS

Iphicrates, a Greek general in the early fourth century B.C.E., likened the army to a human body, with light armored troops as its hands, the cavalry as its feet, the phalanx as its chest, and the general as its head. This organic integration is evident in the later armies of the Alexandrian and Hellenistic empires. Preferring professional troops over the part-time warriors of antiquity, Alexander the Great polished the skills of his men and units to perfection. He then developed an early form of combined-arms warfare in which each specialized unit could function as part of a synchronized whole. Alexander continued to use the modified Macedonian phalanx but combined its use with decisive cavalry attacks, subterfuge, intimidation of the enemy, swift retaliation against traitors, and the adoption of the new military technology of siegecraft.

Alexander's battle tactics were planned to force the enemy into hurried and perhaps rash countermoves. His attacks generally consisted of a bold advanced right flank and a refused center made up of battalions of phalangites, with their long, staggered arrays of spear points pinning down the enemy infantry. Meanwhile, a fierce assault by the heavy horse companions, usually led by Alexander in person, would engage an extreme flank of the opposing forces, folding them back against the center in an ac-

ALEXANDER'S CAMPAIGN AGAINST PERSIA, 334-331 B.C.E.

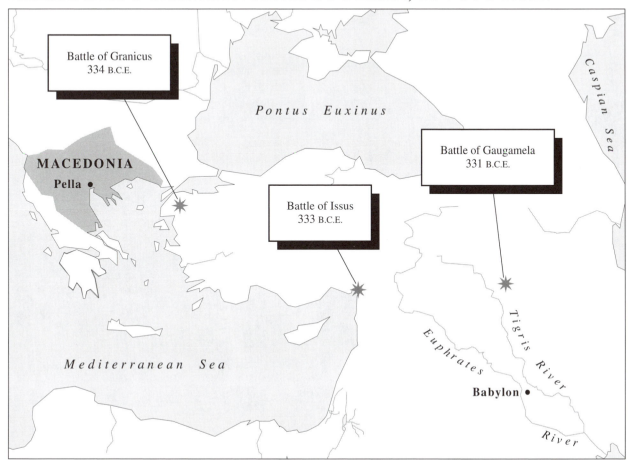

Battle of Granicus
334 B.C.E.

Pontus Euxinus

Caspian Sea

Battle of Gaugamela
331 B.C.E.

MACEDONIA
Pella ●

Battle of Issus
333 B.C.E.

Mediterranean Sea

Euphrates

Tigris River

Babylon ●

River

tion likened to a hammer hitting an anvil. The intensity of this initial charge was intended to break the spirit of the enemy. Victory often depended in large part on undermining the morale of an opponent, and toward this end, Alexander often employed unexpected maneuvers to surprise opposing forces. Generally ignoring the idea that favorable terrain was necessary to ensure victory, Alexander often chose apparently unsuitable ground from which to attack, a deceptive tactic intended to keep the enemy off balance. Another common tactic he used was to engage the enemy when his troops were fatigued by long marches or lack of reinforcements.

The Greek concept of *metis*, cunning intelligence or deception, was traditionally controversial in warfare, as it seemed to conflict with the ideal of forth-

right, noble battle. However, the ancient Greeks of Homer's epics had utilized it, and Alexander had no scruples in using deception, feints, and intelligence-gathering activities whenever possible. The Alexandrian and Hellenic armies often moved troops by night or behind lines of battle. Feints were used to divert the enemy's attention, and false information could be provided to known spies.

Alexander rarely used his elite cavalry directly against infantry, sometimes skirmishing along the flanks of the enemy to buy time while his infantry moved into position, as he did at the battle against the Malli. The Macedonian phalanx itself, usually sixteen men deep, could be transformed into a hammer-head formation of fifty or more ranks or unfolded into a wider and shallower line of battle.

The Hellenistic World, 185 B.C.E.

ROME

ILLYRA

Pella

MACEDONIA

GREECE

Athens

Sparta

Byzantium

BITHYNIA

GALATIA

PERGAMUM

LYCIA

Sinope

Karasi

PONTUS

CAPPADOCIA

Antioch

Seleucia

Edessa

Trapezus

ARMENIA

Artaxata

MEDIA-ATROPATENA

Seleucia on the Tigris

Susa

SELEUCID EMPIRE

Persepolis

PARTHIA

Hecatompylos

Pontus Euxinus

Caspian Sea

Aral Sea

Maracanda (Samarqand)

Bactria

GRECO-BACTRIA

GEDROSIA

Pura

Indian Ocean

Alexandria

PTOLEMAIC EGYPT

Mediterranean Sea

When facing elephants in battle for the first time at the Battle of the Hydaspes River, Alexander divided his force into two units. The first boxed in the enemy's cavalry, forcing them into close quarters with their own elephants. When the Macedonian archers focused their fire on the elephants, the enormous creatures ran amok, trampling the Indian cavalry. After the elephants were finally exhausted, Alexander ordered his phalanx to advance in tight formation. Any enemy troops fleeing this advance ran into the remainder of Alexander's army, commanded by General Craterus. This maneuver destroyed two-thirds of the Indian army.

Alexander also besieged fortified cities, as he did in 332 B.C.E., at the coastal city of Tyre. Having constructed a mole, an armored dock allowing siege engines to attack from a sea or river, the Macedonians poured into the city over bridges from siege towers based on the mole. They were met by tridents, nets, superheated sand, flaming missiles, and crows—giant fishing poles with hooks large enough to catch soldiers trying to scale walls. Eventually a two-pronged attack succeeded: Alexander led an assault to the seaward base of the city wall, while another contingent of Macedonians breached the wall and charged into the city. At the end of the seven-month siege, approximately seven thousand Tyrian men had been killed in battle. Another two thousand were hanged after the battle, and all of the city's women and children were sold into slavery. In the later Hellenistic period larger, more complicated siege engines were invented, and yet most sieges were broken in traditional ways, through reliance on human attacks, surprise, and the use of traitors rather than sustained mechanical assaults.

Use of the Macedonian-style phalanx persisted into the Hellenistic wars against Rome, but failure to defend exposed flanks (as at the Battle of Cynoscephalae) and rash decisions leading to breaks in formation (as at Pydna) allowed the Roman troops to prevail at critical points in history. While the phalanx remained on battlefields throughout the Hellenistic period, wars had evolved into more complex operations, involving naval combat and siegecraft, cataphracts and elephant corps. Eventually, the limited availability of Greek conscripts in the east led to dependence on untrustworthy mercenary forces, while western Hellenistic armies were continuously weakened by internecine or barbarian wars. Local manpower and generalship decreased, paving the way for Roman supremacy.

That being said, the Romans were excellent absorbers of the best of other cultures. They adopted many elements of the Greek and Hellenistic world, ensuring that the techniques and tactics of the Alexandrian and Hellenistic armies would survive, at least in part, within the legions of the Roman Empire.

ANCIENT SOURCES

Because no one can go back in time to witness historic events, scholars of history in the present must rely on accounts recorded by eyewitnesses of the original events. Lacking such accounts, any sources originating close to the time of the events in question become the next best thing. Most contemporary accounts from the time of Alexander the Great have been lost. Only a handful of original fragments and the works of later, but still ancient, writers who based their histories on primary sources still exist.

Among the best ancient sources on Alexander are Plutarch's *Life of Alexander* from his series *Bioi paralleloi* (c. 105-115; *Parallel Lives*, 1579) and works by Arrian (c. 89-155 C.E.), including the *Anabasis Alexandri* (early second century C.E.; *The Campaigns of Alexander*, 1893). Although he wrote nearly four centuries after Alexander's death, Arrian is an important historian because he based his work on the writings of several of Alexander's contemporaries, including Ptolemy, Callisthenes, and Aristobulus—works now all lost to time. Arrian's writings also contain the most complete account of military rather than biographical aspects of Alexander, in contrast to Roman historian Quintus Curtius Rufus, who wrote his ten-volume biography of Alexander the Great in the mid-first century C.E. Of those original ten books, eight still exist in at least partial form, but Curtius Rufus focused his work on Alexander's character rather than on solid factual detail.

BOOKS AND ARTICLES

Bar-Kochva, Bezalel. *The Seleucid Army: Organization and Tactics in the Great Campaigns.* New York: Cambridge University Press, 1976.

Green, Peter. *Alexander to Actium: The Historical Evolution of the Hellenistic Age.* Berkeley: University of California Press, 1990.

Heckel, Waldemar. *Macedonian Warrior: Alexander's Elite Infantryman.* Illustrated by Christa Hook. New York: Osprey, 2006.

Lendon, J. E. *Soldiers and Ghosts: A History of Battle in Classical Antiquity.* New Haven, Conn.: Yale University Press, 2005.

Mayor, Adrienne. *Greek Fire, Poison Arrows, and Scorpion Bombs: Biological and Chemical Warfare in the Ancient World.* Woodstock, N.Y.: Overlook Press, 2003.

Sabin, Philip, Hans van Wees, and Michael Whitby, eds. *Greece, the Hellenistic World, and the Rise of Rome.* Vol. 1 in *The Cambridge History of Greek and Roman Warfare.* New York: Cambridge University Press, 2007.

Sheppard, Ruth, ed. *Alexander the Great at War: His Army, His Battles, His Enemies.* New York: Osprey, 2008.

Sheppard, Si. *Actium 31 B.C.: Downfall of Antony and Cleopatra.* New York: Osprey, 2009.

FILMS AND OTHER MEDIA

Alexander. Feature film. Warner Bros., 2004.

Alexander the Great and the Catapult. Documentary. History Channel, 2006.

Antony and Cleopatra: Battle at Actium. Documentary. Discovery Channel, 2004.

The True Story of Alexander the Great. Documentary. History Channel, 2004.

Helen M. York

CARTHAGINIAN WARFARE

Dates: 814-202 B.C.E.

MILITARY ACHIEVEMENT

Carthage, a historic city on the north coast of Africa, traditionally was founded in 814 B.C.E. by Phoenicians. Historically, the military achievements of Carthage, a maritime trading power, have been measured by its naval and land conflicts with Rome, the emerging power on land. This deadly hegemonic contest, however, was not the only formal measure of Carthage's military achievements. Long before its fateful clashes with Rome in the Punic Wars (264-146 B.C.E.), Carthage had made its military presence forcefully known throughout the western Mediterranean, Southern European, North African, and West African regions from the eighth to the third centuries B.C.E. This strategic presence was based on a powerful professional navy with a significant troop-transport capacity that sustained land forces that protected Carthage's home and overseas territories, important trade routes, and wide-ranging commercial fleets. Carthage's strategic ability to move significant military forces throughout the western Mediterranean region would, for a period of time, deter Rome both politically and militarily from challenging Punic control of Sardinia and Sicily.

The land and naval expeditionary forces of Carthage ranged widely in the Atlantic and the Mediterranean, resulting in the occupation of Corsica, Spain, Sardinia, Sicily, and territories of North Africa. This first phase of Carthage's expansionism (264-237 B.C.E.) was characterized by a strict civilian control by the Council of Elders of senior army and navy commanders and their mercenary troops. During this period of civilian supremacy over political and military policy, Punic generals and admirals who were successful in battle were rewarded, and those who were not were either exiled or killed.

During the twenty-three years of the First Punic War, Rome had 400,000 casualties. At the same time,

Carthage suffered major defeats in the Battles of Mylae (260 B.C.E.), Ecnomus (256 B.C.E.), Adys (256 B.C.E.), and Panormus (250 B.C.E.). Carthage won a major battle at Tunis in 255 B.C.E., led by the Spartan general Xanthippus, who defeated the Roman consul Regulus and forced the latter's retreat from Africa. At the Battle of Drepana (249 B.C.E.), the Punic naval commanders Adherbal, Carthalo, and Himilico defeated a large Roman fleet under admiral Claudius toward the end of the First Punic War. Despite this victory, Carthage's surrender at the Aegates Islands (241 B.C.E.) ended the First Punic War. The defeat resulted in a severe loss of Carthaginian territory, including Sicily, Corsica, and Sardinia. Carthage also suffered large reparations, a vastly reduced battle fleet, and a weakened land army.

Rome, a weaker naval power, owed much of its success in the First Punic War to its acquisition of a new naval technology: the *corvus*, a nautical grappling hook. This device was simply a long, spiked gangplank mounted on the bow of a Roman warship and dropped onto the deck of a Carthaginian ship, securing the two ships together and allowing a Roman contingent to board and capture the opposing vessel. The corvus effectively ended Carthage's naval supremacy and had a long-term negative impact on Carthage's national security and overseas military operations.

The second phase of Carthaginian expansionism occurred from 237 to 202 B.C.E. The military achievements and the very survival of the Carthaginian Empire during this time rested on the strategic leadership and tactical genius of its talented military commanders, the Barcid family. The commanders—Hamilcar Barca (c. 270-228 B.C.E.), Hannibal (247-182 B.C.E.), Mago (died c. 203 B.C.E.), Hasdrubal (died 221 B.C.E.), Hanno (fl. third century B.C.E.), and Maharbal (fl. c. 216 B.C.E.)—would train the physically tough and hard-fighting indigenous and mercenary troops through the force of their personalities, charisma, and personal courage. This period also signaled the masterly control of the political and military policies of Carthage by these strong-willed and militarily gifted generals.

In 247 B.C.E. the Council of Elders' appointment of Hamilcar Barca as the military commander of Sicily began a dynamic new phase in the military history of Carthage. After the end of the disastrous First Punic War, the Barcid clan began to question the competency of the mercantilist faction of the Council of Elders to conduct political policy and wage war against Rome. This fierce internal struggle within the Council of Elders between the mercantilist faction and the Barcid clan and among other Punic interest groups would have long-term consequences.

The end of the First Punic War found Carthage without sufficient bullion to pay its mercenary army adequately, which revolted and attacked Carthage and its surrounding provinces. Hamilcar Barca was appointed by the Council of Elders to put down the revolt and moved quickly to defeat the rebellious mercenary forces. In the summer of 237 B.C.E., Hamilcar and his sons Hannibal, Mago, and Hasdrubal landed in Spain. After eight years of military campaigning, Hannibal subjugated important Spanish territories in preparation for the coming military conflict with Rome. He was the first in a dedicated group of highly trained and dedicated Punic military commanders who would practice strategic endurance, exercise tactical brilliance, and exert complete control over Carthage's political policy in the grand military conflict with Rome. In the winter of 229-228 B.C.E. Hamilcar died and his son-in-law Hasdrubal took over in Spain. After Hasdrubal was assassinated in 221 B.C.E., Hannibal came to power in Spain and in Carthage and strengthened the Punic army of 50,000 foot soldiers, 6,000 cavalry, and 200 battle elephants. In 218 B.C.E. Rome declared war against Carthage in response to Hannibal's defeat of Rome's ally in Spain, the city-state Sarguntum.

In late 218 B.C.E., Hannibal descended victoriously into Italy's Po River Valley with 20,000 soldiers and 6,000 cavalry. He had designed a major trap for the two Roman generals Scipio Africanus (236-184 or 183 B.C.E.) and Tiberius Sempronius Longus, who were meeting at Scipio's camp near Trebia, and routed the Roman forces. In June, 217 B.C.E., Hannibal designed another large ambush at Lake Trasimeno and killed 20,000 soldiers in the army of Gaius Flaminius. In August, 216 B.C.E., the co-consuls Lucius Aemilius Paulus (died 216 B.C.E.) and Gaius Terentius Varro (fl. c. 216 B.C.E.) arrived at Cannae with more than 87,200 soldiers. Hannibal's army of 50,000 men was prepared for battle. With losses of 47,000 infantry and 2,700 cavalry, and with 19,000 prisoners, the Roman army was decimated in what became known as the first battle of annihilation in history.

However, the military achievements of Hannibal and Carthage came to a final end with his military defeat by Scipio Africanus at the Battle of Zama in 202 B.C.E.

TURNING POINTS

247 B.C.E.	Hamilcar Barca is appointed Carthaginian military commander, marking the emergence of Carthage as a major military threat.
237 B.C.E.	Hamilcar begins a Spanish military campaign, in preparation for ultimate war with Rome.
221 B.C.E.	Hamilcar's son Hannibal takes command of the Carthaginian military.
218 B.C.E.	Hannibal leads a force of war elephants, cavalry, and foot soldiers across the Alps to trap and defeat the Romans at Trebia.
216 B.C.E.	Hannibal issues Rome its greatest defeat in battle at Cannae.
202 B.C.E.	Scipio Africanus defeats Carthage at the Battle of Zama.
146 B.C.E.	The Third Punic War ends; Carthage's threat to Rome's domination is defeated.

WEAPONS, UNIFORMS, AND ARMOR

There is little historical evidence relating to the weapons, uniforms, and armor used by the Carthaginian army and navy. The polyglot army that Hannibal fielded in the Second Punic

BATTLES OF THE SECOND PUNIC WAR, 218-202 B.C.E.

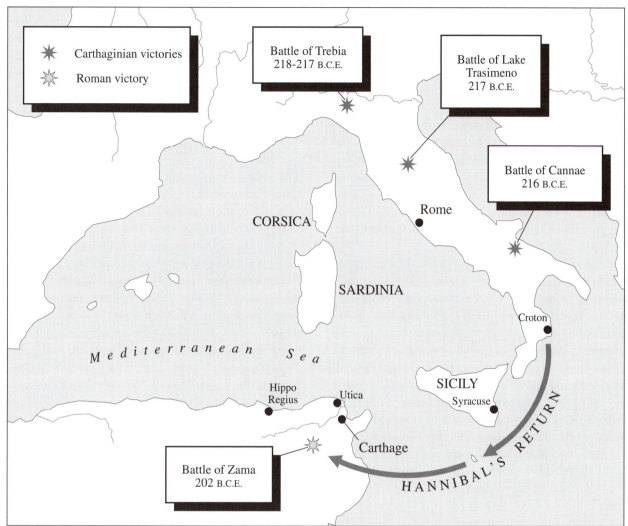

War was a unique mixture of Africans, Spaniards, Celts, Numidians, and Libya-Phoenicians, along with Greeks, Persians, and Egyptians. Hannibal's army was international in its racial and ethnic composition and was extremely loyal in its dedication to its supreme military leader. Hannibal used his heavy and light infantry divisions as maneuver units to unbalance enemy forces and his heavy and light cavalry divisions as his main strike force on the battlefield to annihilate the enemy forces.

The weapons, armor, and uniforms of Hannibal's infantry reflected the rich diversity of its fighting sol-diers. The famous African heavy infantry were for-midable, tenacious, and highly trained fighters from northern and western Africa. They wore a variety of colorful uniforms and clothing and were heavily armed with long and short battle swords, bows and arrows, and lances, as well as an assortment of other exotic weapons, which they used with deadly effi-ciency in battle. The African heavy infantry, which proved itself at the Battle of Cannae (216 B.C.E.), wore chain mail and carried shields for protection.

Hannibal recruited the courageous and tough-fighting Spanish infantry, heavy and light, from the

Iberian tribes of Spain. The Spanish light infantry were armed with javelins, darts, slings, and wooden shields, whereas the Spanish heavy infantry were dressed in chain mail and armed with javelins, as well as the noted heavy steel sword later adopted by the Roman heavy infantry. The Celtic light infantry were recruited from the Po River Valley in Italy and were armed with swords. They wore no armor and fought nude or half naked. Finally, the proud and sagacious Libya-Phoenicians were recruited from the Carthaginian elite classes, wore chain mail armor, and expertly used the battle weapons of the Greek hoplite. The Libya-Phoenicians formed the elite backbone of Hannibal's Carthaginian army in Italy, and they would prove their mettle repeatedly in countless battles and campaigns.

The heavy and light cavalry forces in Hannibal's army were also a polyglot mixture of nationalities, races, and languages. The cavalry corps were Hannibal's strategic strike force and implemented his orders on the battlefield with both precision and decisiveness. The elite heavy cavalry were composed of a small number of Carthaginians and Libya-Phoenicians, highly expert fighters on or off their battle horses and drilled in every conceivable cavalry maneuver. The Spanish heavy infantry comprised the bulk of Hannibal's heavy cavalry force, and they dressed in helmet and mail armor and were armed with short and long lances, short swords, bucklershields, and greaves (armor for the leg below the knee).

The magnificent light cavalry force comprised the Numidians, a North African people famous throughout the Mediterranean region for their outstanding mobility and expert fighting abilities. In battle, the Numidians wore their famous leopard skins and used swords, short javelins, and lances to maneuver expertly around and through their enemies, seeking a fatal weakness before striking. Finally, Hannibal used African battle elephants both to anchor his lines and to launch, along with heavy and light cavalry, combined-arms shock assaults to disorient and defeat the enemy on his front and rear. It has been argued that Hannibal also used his elephants along his route of march to impress and frighten European tribes to join his army.

The battle-hardened Carthaginian army constantly changed its weapons systems, military uniforms, and body armor after each successful battle with the Romans. This exchange of military technology and weapons systems was an integral component of Hannibal's war in Italy and proved decisive in allowing his forces to fight against Rome.

MILITARY ORGANIZATION

The military organization of the Carthaginian army stands unique in the history of the ancient world. Carthaginian leaders had decided early on that a standing professional army recruited from the general population of eligible men would ensure neither national security nor the worldwide advancement of Carthage's foreign economic policy interests. After enduring a period during which Punic generals and admirals sought to control the state's political policy, Carthage's Council of Elders ruled that the recruitment of trained mercenaries from the western Mediterranean region and elsewhere would be sufficient to meet military requirements in case of war.

The traditional military organization of the Carthaginian army was the Greek hoplite phalanx. Carthage inherited this military tactical system from the Phoenician cities of Tyre and Sidon, and it was a prominent tactical system in most ancient militaries, including that of Rome. However, Hannibal fundamentally altered the hoplite system to gain flexibility and tactical maneuverability in battle. His changes were designed to ensure maximum coordination and communication between the main strike force, the cavalry, and the main maneuver force, the infantry.

The importance of decisive battlefield communications, rapid logistical support, accurate military intelligence, and sound battlefield leadership was constantly communicated to officers and soldiers. As the historical record indicates, Hannibal tried to maximize surprise and shock against the enemy, attacking the enemy in difficult geographical areas, making the enemy fight up hilly terrain, or driving the enemy cavalry from the field of battle in order to launch attacks against the remaining enemy on his front or rear. In this context, Hannibal developed and trained an effective corps of officers, known for their toughness, wisdom, bravado, and discipline.

DOCTRINE, STRATEGY, AND TACTICS

The strategic political doctrine of the Carthaginian Empire was based both on satisfying its national security interests and on maintaining its worldwide commercial relations and trade routes. After the negative outcome of the First Punic War, Carthage's strategic doctrine took into account the empire's depleted resource base, its weakened battle fleet and naval troop transport capability, and its severe manpower limitations in any future conflict with Rome. Carthage had a military manpower base of 100,000 to 120,000 fighting men for its army and navy and a 30,000- to 35,000-man cavalry force, out of an estimated total population base of 700,000 citizens. In contrast, Rome and its allied states had a strategic military manpower base of 700,000 foot soldiers and 70,000 cavalry forces, and, for combat operations, Rome could deploy within a year more than 250,000 foot soldiers and a 23,000-man cavalry force. Based on these comparative manpower data, a war of attrition was out of the question for Carthage.

For this reason, the Barcid clan reasoned that any future war with Rome would have to be fought in Italy, in order to break the wills of the Roman Senate and the Roman people. This position, advocated by Hannibal, argued that Carthage could prevent Rome from launching major invasions of Carthage, Spain, or other important overseas territories only by launching aggressive combat operations in the heart of the Roman state. The Barcid clan also

reasoned that Carthaginian military land forces executing a major land war against Rome and contiguous territories could not expect military reinforcements from the sea while facing overwhelming Roman land armies. In this specific context, the Carthaginian forces would need to inflict serious manpower losses on the Roman army while minimizing their own losses until military reinforcements could arrive from either Carthage or Spain.

At a deeper level, Rome's increasing land and naval power operations in the western Mediterranean

Hannibal's army crosses the Rhone River in 218 B.C.E. on its way to invade Italy. Hannibal made the most famous use of war elephants with his crossing of the Alps in this Italian campaign.

CANNAE, 216 B.C.E.

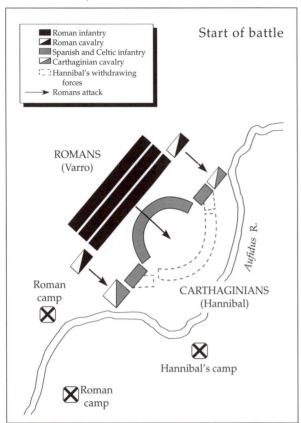

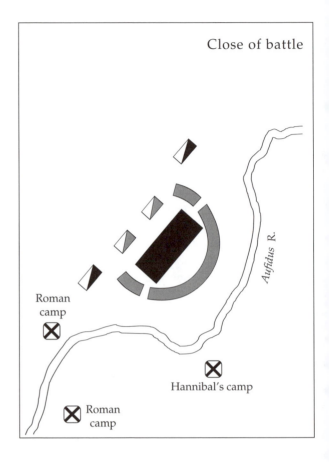

region proved a challenge to Carthaginian military strategy. Carthage could no longer adequately control sea lanes for military and commercial purposes; transport troops to danger spots; supply, reinforce, or extradite troops from overseas bases; or protect Carthage and Africa from Roman raids and invasion. For the Punic military and naval planners, the lack of robust naval forces to deter the powerful Roman navy had a profound impact on subsequent strategic military planning and tactical operations.

The implementation of Carthage's strategic military doctrine in the light of Rome's military resources and manpower preponderance was not easy. Hannibal's rise to power injected a new strategic dynamic factor, namely Hannibal's military genius and leadership capabilities, into Roman and Carthaginian foreign security relations. On the ground, Hannibal's offensively oriented strategy was based on the fol-

lowing principles: to win battlefield victories and encourage the defection or the neutrality of Rome's allies and, if militarily decisive in battle, to force Rome to negotiate a compromise peace on Carthaginian terms.

On the battlefield, Hannibal's operational doctrine was to execute the war against Rome using Rome's own material resources, instead of those of Carthage. Hannibal's decision to engage Rome in its own territory and use its resources was consistent with Punic strategic military doctrine against fighting wars of attrition. The objective was to fight a war for victory in Italy and, at the very least, to achieve a negotiated settlement, which would leave Carthage and its territories free of Rome. The implementation of this tactical doctrine required Hannibal to utilize a variety of military factors to engage, fight, and defeat the much larger and better-equipped Roman army in

Italy for more than fifteen years. Among the tactics he employed were successful battlefield maneuvers, strategic and tactical surprise, psychological warfare, mastery of the geographical terrain, and military intelligence.

However, Hannibal's war strategy was ultimately unsuccessful. Rome's military manpower and preponderance of material resources, combined with its improved military generalship, very powerful battle fleets, and large land forces, proved strategically overwhelming. The direct result was the inevitable dissolution of the Carthaginian Empire.

ANCIENT SOURCES

Ab urbe condita libri (c. 26 B.C.E.-15 C.E.; *The History of Rome*, 1600), by the ancient Roman historian Livy (59 B.C.E.-17 C.E.), is one of the primary reference sources that classical and modern scholars have used to "reconstruct" the great political, economic, and military struggle between the mature African power, Carthage, and the rising Italian power, Rome. Livy's critical analysis of the Punic Wars was based in the prevailing Roman worldview, and in his writings Livy painted both Hannibal and Carthage in less than friendly terms. He provides the student of Carthaginian warfare, however, with some insights into the character, intensity, and implications of Hannibal's military engagements with Rome from a Roman point of view.

Polybius (c. 200-c. 118 B.C.E.), a Greek historian taken as a prisoner to Rome in 168 B.C.E., wrote a series of histories of Rome and nearby countries from 220 to 146 B.C.E. (*The General History of Polybius: In Five Books*, 1773). His work contributed to the development of historiography as a significant area of inquiry away from previous leanings toward didacticism. Tiberius Catius Asconius Silius Italicus (25 or 26-101 C.E.), a Latin epic poet and politician, authored a seventeen-volume epic on the Second Punic War, entitled *Punica* (*Punica, with an English Translation*, 1934). Appianos, also known as Appian, a second century C.E. Greek historian, authored *Romaica* (*Appian's Roman History*, 1912-1913), a history of Rome and its conquests, including that of Carthage.

A more modern work that provides an interesting analysis of the origins of the First and Second Punic Wars using ancient sources exclusively is B. D. Hoyos's *Unplanned Wars: The Origins of the First and Second Punic Wars* (1997). Hoyos uses Roman historical writers such as Polybius, among others, to look deeply into the origins of the conflict between Carthage and Rome. The tightly argued historical analysis reexamines both ancient evidence and recent findings about the origins of the Punic Wars and the major personalities and events of the great struggle.

BOOKS AND ARTICLES

Bagnall, Nigel. *The Punic Wars*. London: Hutchinson, 1990.

Bradford, Ernle. *Hannibal*. New York: McGraw-Hill, 1981.

Campbell, Duncan B. *Ancient Siege Warfare: Persians, Greeks, Carthaginians, and Romans, 546-146 B.C.* Illustrated by Adam Hook. Botley, Oxford, England: Osprey, 2004.

Cornell, Tim, Boris Rankov, and Philip Sabin, eds. *The Second Punic War: A Reappraisal*. London: Institute of Classical Studies, University of London, 1996.

De Beer, Sir Gavin. *Hannibal: Challenging Rome's Supremacy*. New York: Viking, 1970.

_____. *Hannibal: The Struggle for Power in the Mediterranean*. London: Thames and Hudson, 1969.

Gabriel Richard. "Carthage, 814-146 B.C.E." In *The Ancient World*. Westport, Conn.: Greenwood Press, 2007.

Hoyos, Dexter. *Truceless War: Carthage's Fight for Survival, 241 to 237 B.C.* Boston: Brill, 2007.

_____. *Unplanned Wars: The Origins of the First and Second Punic Wars.* Berlin: Walter de Gruyter, 1998.

Kern, Paul Bentley. "Early Sieges and the Punic Wars." In *Ancient Siege Warfare.* Bloomington: Indiana University Press, 1999.

Lazenby, J. F. *Hannibal's War: A Military History of the Second Punic War.* Warminster, England: Aris and Phillips, 1978. Reprint. Norman: University of Oklahoma Press, 1998.

Stephenson, Ian. *Hannibal's Army.* Stroud, Gloucestershire, England: Tempus, 2008.

Wise, Terence. *Armies of the Carthaginian Wars, 265-146 B.C.* Illustrated by Richard Hook. Botley, Oxford, England: Osprey, 1982.

FILMS AND OTHER MEDIA

Annibale. Feature film. Euro International Film, 1959.

Carthage. Documentary. Films for the Humanities, 1990.

Carthage: The Roman Holocaust. Documentary. RDF Media, 2004.

Decisive Battles: Cannae. Documentary. History Channel, 2005.

Hannibal: Rome's Worst Nightmare. Television film. British Broadcasting Corporation, 2006.

Michael J. Siler

ROMAN WARFARE DURING THE REPUBLIC

Dates: 753-27 B.C.E.

MILITARY ACHIEVEMENT

According to tradition, the city of Rome was founded on the banks of the Tiber River in 753 B.C.E by Romulus, one of the twin sons of Mars, the Roman god of war. At the time of its founding, Rome's proud future still lay far in the distance. A dynasty of foreign kings from neighboring Etruria eventually settled at Rome and dominated the institutions of the city. Although this early history is uncertain, Rome's levy seems to have relied on the wealthy, because they could afford their own equipment for battle. Armed like Greek hoplites, Roman soldiers fought with thrusting spears, and, using a Greek formation—the phalanx—they stood shoulder to shoulder, with shields locked together.

After expelling the last of the Etruscan monarchs in 510 B.C.E, the Romans installed a Republican government, dominated by the Senate, and kept the Greek style of fighting. About a century later, however, some changes were introduced during a long war with Veii, an Etruscan stronghold north of Rome. In need of more soldiers, the Romans began recruiting more broadly. These new recruits, unable to afford full protective armor, adopted the *scutum*, a long Italic shield, in place of the hoplite's round buckler. Moreover, the Romans introduced pay for military service and, for the first time, provided at public expense a horse for every new member of the cavalry.

The Roman victory over Veii was followed by defeat on the Allia, a stream about 11 miles north of Rome. There, in around 390 B.C.E., Gallic warriors overwhelmed the Republic's forces, capturing and plundering the city before moving on. The conquering Gallic chieftain Brennus uttered the harsh words "Vae victis," meaning "Woe to the vanquished!" This disaster revealed Rome's military weaknesses

and stirred reform. No longer fighting as a single compact body, the Romans came to employ a looser formation, composed of small units, or maniples. After abandoning the thrusting spear, Rome's soldiers also came to adopt a throwing spear.

Eventually Rome's influence managed to spread beyond the neighboring communities of Latium and into southern Italy. Greek cities, established there centuries earlier, called on Pyrrhus of Epirus (r. 297-272 B.C.E.) to stop the advance. With his war elephants, Pyrrhus defeated Rome's forces at Heraclea (280 B.C.E.) and Ausculum (279 B.C.E.) but also suffered enormous casualties. He exclaimed that another victory such as his last would be the ruin of his army. After Beneventum in 275 B.C.E. he withdrew from Italy, never to return. By 264 B.C.E Rome controlled all of the Italian peninsula except the Po valley in the north.

Rome then turned to Sicily, vying for control of the island with Carthage, a powerful city on the North African coast. During the First Punic War (264-241 B.C.E.), Rome mobilized large fleets for the first time. Although Romans were inexperienced at sea, Rome's invention of a grappling hook and boarding bridge allowed soldiers to cross over to enemy ships and fight on their decks like infantry. With a final naval victory in 241 B.C.E., Rome expelled the Carthaginians from Sicily.

A generation later, the Second Punic War (218-201 B.C.E.) revived old grudges. With an eternal hatred of Rome, the Carthaginian general Hannibal (247-182 B.C.E.) planned to win the war through a bold surprise invasion of the Italian peninsula. Hannibal made a winter crossing of the Alps to enter Italy and gain victories at Trebbia (218-217 B.C.E.), Trasimeno Lake (217 B.C.E.), and Cannae (216 B.C.E.). However, Rome sent forces against his base in Spain and eventually confined him to the "toe," or south-ernmost tip, of Italy. After sixteen years in enemy territory, Hannibal finally withdrew to Africa, where he was crushed at Zama (202 B.C.E.) by Scipio Africanus (236-184 or 183 B.C.E.). Hannibal escaped the battlefield and urged his countrymen to surrender. Carthage lost some of its African territory to Rome's allies, and Spain was eventually organized as Roman territory.

Hannibal's alliance with Philip V (238-179 B.C.E.) of Macedonia led to two Macedonian Wars, in which Roman troops crossed the Adriatic Sea and at last secured victory at Cynoscephalae in 197 B.C.E. Although Macedonia survived and Greece was declared free, Rome's influence came to dominate the whole area. Once involved in the eastern Mediterranean, Rome's forces also accepted the challenge of Syria's Antiochus III (242-187 B.C.E.), also known as Antiochus the Great. After victory at Magnesia in 190 B.C.E., the Republic refused to annex any new territory, but it now arranged the affairs of Hellenistic Asia as it wished.

At Pydna (168 B.C.E.) the Republic defeated Philip's son, Perseus (c. 212-c. 165 B.C.E.). Macedonia was eventually organized as a Roman province, and its governor was made responsible for Greece. Moreover, Egypt was treated like a dependency. When Antiochus IV (c. 215-164 B.C.E.) invaded the Nile Delta, a Roman ambassador is said to have drawn a circle around the Syrian king and commanded him to order a retreat before stepping out of it. The Third Punic War (149-146 B.C.E.) resulted in the complete destruction of Carthage in 146 B.C.E, and the city's remaining territory became the province of Africa. Thus with the defeat of Carthage and Hannibal's allies, the Republic had destroyed its greatest enemies. Although more wars lay in the future, Rome's long-term dominion was ensured.

WEAPONS, UNIFORMS, AND ARMOR

The ancient sources present a reasonably clear picture of the Republic's military affairs as it emerged from the struggle with Hannibal. All Roman citizens between the ages of seventeen and thirty-six were liable for service. The maximum length of service was likely sixteen years for infantry and ten for cavalry, but in normal circumstances a soldier would probably serve for up to six years and then be released.

The number of the main infantry division, the legion, is given as 4,200 soldiers, but in emergencies it could be higher. The legion was drawn up in three lines of *hastati*, *principes*, and *triarii*, with the youngest and poorest forming the *velites*. As lightly armed skirmishers, the velites carried a sword, javelin, and small circular shield. The hastati and principes, in contrast, were heavily armed. Protected by the long Italic shield, they relied upon a short Spanish sword, or *gladius*, and two throwing spears, or *pila*. Like the

North Wind Picture Archives via AP Images

Soldiers of the Roman Republic, bearing spears, swords, shields, and standards with the initials SPQR, for "Senatus Populusque Romanus," or, "the Senate and People of Rome."

hastati and principes, the triarii were also heavily armed, but they carried a thrusting spear, or *hasta*, instead of the pilum. All soldiers wore a bronze breastplate, a bronze helmet, and a pair of greaves, or shin guards. In order to be distinguished from a distance, the velites covered their helmets with wolfskin, and the hastati wore three tall feathers in their helmets. To preserve a degree of exclusiveness, wealthy recruits wore shirts of ring mail, whether serving among the hastati, principes, or triarii.

MILITARY ORGANIZATION

The supreme magistrates of the state, the two consuls, usually served also as generals of the army. Elected to serve for one year, each consul traditionally commanded two legions. His authority, called imperium, was absolute beyond the walls of the city. The fasces, a bundle of rods and axes bound together by red thongs, symbolized the consul's power of life and death. After victory, the consul was decked with laurel and borne before the general by twelve attendants, or lictors, proceeding in single file.

The general's senior officers included the military tribunes. With six in each legion, all tribunes were required to have significant military experience and to meet stringent property qualifications. Usually most, if not all, were elected. They had some important military responsibilities. As elective officers, they more often tended to the welfare of the soldiers. By the early second century, it was also customary for the general to be accompanied by legates. Appointed by the Senate on the general's advice, these were often ambitious young men from prominent families, who had little military experience.

The real strength of Rome's military was the centurions, career officers who, as one contemporary observed, held their ground when bested and stood ready to die at their posts. There were sixty centurions in each legion, with two in each of thirty maniples. Selected by the tribunes, the centurions were organized into a hierarchy with a well-defined order of promotion. Every centurion's ambition was to serve as primus pilus, senior officer of the first maniple, because the holder of that title was recognized as the best soldier of the legion and given a seat on the general's war council.

In addition to infantry, the legion had three hundred cavalrymen. They wore linen corselets and relied on strong circular shields and long spears. They were divided into ten units, or *turmae*. Each of these had three decurions, and the most senior of the three always exercised command. Allied contingents, recruited from throughout Italy, also campaigned with Rome's citizen army. In fact, there was at least one legion of allies, if not more, for every legion of citizens. Known as *socii*, they were organized and equipped like Romans. They were also commanded by Roman citizens called *praefecti*. An elite corps, the *extraordinarii*, was selected from the best of the allies, horse and foot. The rest were divided into *alae*, right and left wings, reflecting their positions on the army's flanks. The great numbers of the socii especially contributed to the might and effectiveness of Rome's forces.

DOCTRINE, STRATEGY, AND TACTICS

After assembling with their arms, the soldiers would be ordered to pitch camp. It resembled a city, complete with a forum and tents arranged in neat rows. The *via principalis*, or "first street," ran past the tents of the senior officers, and the *via quintana*, or "fifth street," paralleled the main boulevard. During the time of the Republic, these camps were usually temporary. Because commanders always employed the same plan, every soldier knew the camp's layout and could find his way around, even in the dark. In addition to soldiers and officers, the camp also housed animals, equipment, baggage, and sometimes plunder taken from the defeated enemy. Moreover, there were hosts of camp followers. In 134 B.C.E., for example, numerous traders, soothsayers, and diviners, as well as two thousand prostitutes, were cast out of a camp near Numantia in Spain.

Yet the camp remained an integral part of Republican strategy. As an entrenched fortress, it provided a base for attack and a safe retreat in the event of defeat. The guarding of its gates therefore required discipline. Those who fell asleep during the night watch

TURNING POINTS

753 B.C.E.	The city of Rome is said to be founded on the banks of the Tiber River by Romulus, one of the twin sons of Mars, the Roman god of war.
c. 390 B.C.E.	Gallic warriors overwhelm the Republic's forces, capturing and plundering the city of Rome.
241 B.C.E.	In the final naval victory of the First Punic War, Rome expels the Carthaginians from Sicily.
202 B.C.E.	Rome defeats Carthage at the Battle of Zama.
168 B.C.E	The Roman Republic defeats Macedonian king Philip V's son, Perseus, at Pydna, eventually organizing Macedonia as a Roman province.
146 B.C.E.	Rome defeats Carthage in the Third Punic War, destroying its greatest enemy and ensuring its long-term dominion.
60 B.C.E.	The First Triumvirate is formed.
27 B.C.E.	Augustus establishes the Roman Empire.

were usually stoned to death. This harsh discipline extended to the field of battle, where a maniple, giving ground without good reason, could be, literally, "decimated." A tenth part of its men, selected by lot, would be clubbed to death, while the rest would be ordered to sleep outside the camp's fortifications on an unprotected spot. In contrast, there was also a system of military decorations to reward exceptional bravery. The general praised heroic soldiers before the assembled army and gave them prizes. To the first man mounting the enemy's walls, for example, he conferred a crown of gold.

On breaking camp, procedure had to be followed. On the first signal, the soldiers took down their tents. On the second, they loaded the pack animals. On the third, their march began. When attack was not expected, all moved in one long train, the extraordinarii leading the way. In times of danger, a different marching order prevailed. The hastati, principes, and triarii formed three parallel columns. When the enemy appeared, the maniples turned to the left or to the right, clearing the baggage trains and confronting the enemy from whichever side necessary. Thus in a single movement, the army placed itself in good battle order.

When engaging the enemy, the legion approached in three lines: first, the hastati; second, the principes;

third, the triarii. Each line consisted of ten maniples, drawn up with gaps between them, equal in width to the maniples. These gaps usually alternated in each row, like dark spaces on a checkerboard. Thus the gaps in the first line adjoined the maniples in the second line. Likewise, gaps in the second line adjoined maniples in the third.

Traditionally, the battle followed a more or less schematic plan. Forming a light screen, the velites opened with a hail of javelins and retired to the rear through the gaps. Then the hastati, closing the gaps in the first line, offered a united front against the enemy. After surging forward in unison and striking with their swords, the soldiers soon recoiled, rested, and tried again. If the assault continued to fail after many attempts, the hastati retired through the gaps in the line of the principes, who next advanced and attacked in the same manner. If the principes also failed, then they retired through the gaps in the line of the triarii, who proceeded to the final trial of strength, reinforced by survivors from the first and second lines. The Romans thus refused to expose all their forces to a frontal assault, keeping part of them in reserve, while the rest engaged the enemy.

On the whole, Roman strategy aimed at the destruction of the enemy in pitched battle. This strategy sometimes employed flexible tactics. In 169 B.C.E., for example, the Romans borrowed a formation from the gladiatorial arena. In this formation, called the "tortoise," or *testudo*, several ranks locked their shields together and formed a sloping roof over their heads. They advanced to the lowest part of the enemy's wall, where some of the Romans then mounted the roof of shields. After moving up its slope, they occupied the high end, where they fought face to face with the wall's defenders. Finally overwhelming their opponents, the victorious Romans crossed over into the enemy city and captured it.

Under a strong general, the storming and plundering of a city proceeded by well-defined stages, announced by signals. First the troops slaughtered. Next they looted. Finally they disposed of their spoils, with the profits distributed equally among all the soldiers. More often, however, the general made little attempt to restrain them. They held the power of life and death, and they did whatever they wished to the inhabitants of a captured city. In these cases, of course, every soldier looted for himself, and everything he laid his hands on became his private property.

Saluted as *imperator* by his troops, the successful general looked forward to a triumph, the most distinguished reward conferred by the Senate for military achievement. This ceremony celebrated important victories and was granted only under certain conditions, such as extraordinarily numerous enemy casualties and significant expansion of Roman territory. The triumph was a magnificent procession in which the victorious general, with laurel wreath on his brow and ivory scepter in his hand, mounted a chariot drawn by white horses and paraded through the streets of Rome. Before him were the spoils of conquered cities and captive leaders imprisoned in chains. After him followed his troops in military array, enjoying unusual license and singing bawdy songs. The procession formed upon the Campus Martius, the field of the war god Mars, and entered the city through the Triumphal Gate. It then ascended the Capitol, where the general offered sacrifice and dined with Jupiter, the king of the gods and goddesses. The entire population participated with unbounded jubilation in this ceremony of great pomp and circumstance. After all, the general was, at least temporarily, a god-king. However, as a reminder, a slave would be stationed near the general throughout the parade, occasionally whispering in his ear, "Remember! Thou art a man."

REFORMS OF THE LATE REPUBLIC

Although late second century B.C.E. Roman legions again met defeat, eventually Gaius Marius claimed victory for the Republic, in Africa over King Jugurtha (c. 160-104 B.C.E.) of Numidia and in northern Italy over the Teutons (102 B.C.E.) and the Cimbri (101 B.C.E.). While holding an unprecedented series of consulships in 107 and from 104 to 100, Marius encouraged military reform, and he has been credited by some with the conversion of Rome's citizen militia into a standing professional force. Marius undoubtedly played an important role in the evolution of Rome's military.

As in past crises of state, Marius opened the ranks to the *capite censi*, citizens who failed to meet prescribed property qualifications for military service. He likely viewed this measure as a temporary emergency action, but later generations followed his example. Immersed in wars both foreign and domestic, Marius's successors abandoned all restrictions on liability for service and recruited more troops than ever before. Because most of these soldiers came from poor families, the State equipped them at public expense. So variations in arms and armor soon disappeared.

Marius also made fundamental changes in tactical organization, preferring the cohort to the maniple as the basic unit within the legion. Marius's new cohort consisted of three maniples, one drawn from each line: hastati, principes, and triarii. As a result, his cohort was a microcosm of the old legion. The First Cohort consisted of the three maniples situated on the extreme right of the old lines. The last cohort, the Tenth, moving from right to left, consisted of the three maniples on the extreme left.

Marius's new legion drew up for battle in three lines. There were four cohorts in the first line, three in the second line, and three in the third. The cohorts likely had a standard size, which under the Empire was 480 men. Thus the new legion seems to have had a strength of 4,800 men, organized into ten cohorts and thirty maniples. The velites were apparently abolished. Eventually the Roman army incorporated contingents raised outside Italy. These new contingents carried their national weapons and were called *auxilia*. Some came from independent allies, others came from forced levies, and still others were paid as mercenaries.

In the press of battle, standards, banners on long poles, served as a rallying point. Marius gave preeminence to the *aquila*, or eagle, as the legion's chief standard. The legion had previously used a variety of standards, including the eagle, wolf, minotaur, horse, and boar, among others. Yet by the Republic's close, the eagle shared importance only with the standards of the hastati and principes, which consisted of slender poles decorated with circular bosses. The primus pilus, the best soldier in the legion, acted as *aquilifer*, or eaglebearer. To lose or surrender the aquila was, of course, a great disgrace for the entire legion.

Along with these changes, Marius modified the pilum. The iron tip of Rome's heavy spear was joined to its wooden shaft by two iron rivets. Marius replaced one of these with a wooden pin, and on striking a target the shaft now snapped off. The spear could no longer be picked up and thrown back at its owner. Moreover, Marius wished to reduce the great numbers of pack animals, because they slowed the army's march, so he required his troops to carry equipment and rations on forked poles flung over their shoulders. As the general's beasts of burden, the legionaries came to be called "Marius's Mules."

WARS OF THE LATE REPUBLIC

In Marius's later years, violence spread across the Italian peninsula, with serious repercussions for the Republic. Weary of Rome's stern ascendancy, the Italian allies rose in revolt. Fearful but wise, Rome promised citizenship to all who laid down their arms. Although the Social War (91-88 B.C.E.), as it was called, soon ended, the riot of its daily warfare created an angry generation whose sons found lodging in Rome's legions, filling them with a spirit of apathy and callousness. These soldiers cared little for the Republic and were loyal only to the general who paid them.

Almost inevitably, civil war followed the Social War. As one of its leaders, Marius died in 86, before destroying all of his opponents. His archenemy, Lucius Cornelius Sulla (138-78 B.C.E.), survived to conduct a great bloodbath and hold untrammeled authority until his own death. Under these chaotic conditions, only small military gains were made abroad. Yet when Mithridates VI of Pontus seized Asia Minor and invaded Greece, he was defeated by Pompey the Great (106-48 B.C.E.), who annexed Syria and Palestine, thereby enlarging Rome's Asiatic dominion.

Only a few years later, bold adventures began to unfold in Gaul. Julius Caesar (100-44 B.C.E.) embarked on a war of conquest against warrior Celts and their powerful priests, the Druids. With his small force, Caesar opposed the large Celtic armies and eventually defeated the Gallic tribes, organizing their territories as a province. At the same time Caesar accelerated the gradual professionalization of the Roman army.

Caesar followed tradition by relying upon the cohort and the centurion, although his military tribunes were mostly young men with political charges. Yet Caesar's legates, ten in number, played an essential role in his command structure. Acting as subordinate commanders, some commanded legions and auxiliary forces, while others managed the camp and secured the surrounding region. Perhaps even more important, Caesar's battle order responded dramatically to topography. He exploited flank attacks, for example, and often held troops in reserve for the decisive onslaught. Caesar thus helped to liberate Roman warfare from the traditional scheme of advance and assault.

Like a great Hellenistic king, Caesar raised siege towers, built bridges to span fierce rivers, and dug elaborate entrenchments around enemy bases. His formidable artillery included giant catapults, which fired heavy stones, and smaller *scorpions*, which fired arrows with extraordinary accuracy. Apart from his tactical expertise, Caesar's personal qualities also invited his success as a commander. More often than not, his decisiveness and instinct compensated for his reckless daring.

Despite the continued Roman military success, by 49 B.C.E. the Republic was again divided by civil war. Caesar crossed the Rubicon and swept through Italy into Greece, where he defeated Pompey. Embroiled in Rome's affairs, the Pharaoh of Egypt soon fell to Caesar's arms as well. Then Pharnaces (r. 63-47 B.C.E.), son of Mithradates the Great, took his turn, losing at Zela (47 B.C.E.). To underscore the rapidity of this victory, Caesar employed three short words, "Veni, vidi, vici," meaning, "I came, I saw, I conquered." Other civil war battles followed in Africa and Spain. Caesar prevailed in all and returned to Rome with unprecedented power, as dictator for life. However, by the Ides of March, 44 B.C.E., he lay dead, murdered by conspirators.

Through civil war Caesar's heir, Octavius (63-

14 B.C.E.), claimed unrivaled supremacy. He then adopted a new name, Caesar Augustus, and, ruling as Rome's first emperor, he replaced the citizen militia of the Republic, which had become increasingly unmanageable and restless, with a smaller professional force. Legionaries eventually served for twenty-five years, enjoyed promotion through the ranks, and received generous cash payments on discharge. Except for a special corps, they were stationed in the frontier provinces, at a safe distance from the imperial capitol. Augustus's reign thus signaled a new epoch in Roman political and military history, as well as the end of the Republic in 27 B.C.E.

In conclusion, the military institutions of the Republic proved extremely durable and successful. With great adaptability, the Romans learned from their opponents, borrowing weaponry and improving tactical structure. Rome's forces were also guided in a few critical moments by generals of genius. Yet the most fundamental reason for the Republic's success lay in its manpower, fueled by the populations of Italy, which allowed the Romans to ignore defeats. Thus Rome's military evolved from obscurity into a remarkable institution, which eventually dominated the ancient Mediterranean and shaped one of history's longest-lived empires.

ANCIENT SOURCES

Most historians contemporary with the Republic discussed military affairs, yet few of these scholars were actually eyewitnesses to councils of war and victories on the battlefield. However, there are two notable exceptions. First, the Greek author Polybius (c. 200-c. 118 B.C.E.) saw the Roman army in action against fellow Greeks, and later he seems to have accompanied a Roman general on military campaign. In his *Histories* (first appearing in English as *The General History of Polybius: In Five Books*, 1773), Polybius gives an important description of the Roman army as it emerged from the struggle against Hannibal. Second, Julius Caesar provides a valuable narrative of the Roman army at war. He recounts his own activities as general in Gaul, Germany, and Britain throughout a period of almost ten years. Caesar's *Comentarii de Bello Gallico* (51-52 B.C.E.; *Commentaries*, 1609) explores a wide range of the Republic's military institutions and activities as they existed in the first century B.C.E.

BOOKS AND ARTICLES

Bishop, M. C., and J. C. N. Coulston. *Roman Military Equipment: From the Punic Wars to the Fall of Rome*. London: Batsford, 1993.

Campbell, Duncan B. *Siege Warfare in the Roman World, 146 B.C.-A.D. 378*. Illustrated by Adam Hook. Botley, Oxford, England: Osprey, 2005.

Chrissanthos, Stefan G. *Warfare in the Ancient World: From the Bronze Age to the Fall of Rome*. Westport, Conn.: Praeger, 2008.

Dando-Collins, Stephen. *Caesar's Legion: The Epic Saga of Julius Caeser's Elite Tenth Legion and the Armies of Rome*. New York: Wiley, 2002.

Erdkamp, Paul, ed. *A Companion to the Roman Army*. Malden, Mass.: Blackwell, 2007.

Fields, Nic. *The Roman Army of the Punic Wars, 264-146 B.C.* Botley, Oxford, England: Osprey, 2007.

Gabriel, Richard A. "Republican Rome, 500-28 B.C.E." In *The Ancient World*. Westport, Conn.: Greenwood Press, 2007.

Gilliver, Kate, Michael Whitby, and Adrian Goldsworthy. *Rome at War: Caesar and His Legacy*. Botley, Oxford, England: Osprey, 2005.

Keppie, Lawrence. *The Making of the Roman Army from Republic to Empire*. Totowa, N.J.: Barnes and Noble Books, 1984.

Rich, John, and Graham Shipley, eds. *War and Society in the Roman World*. London: Rout-
    ledge, 1993.

Rosenstein, Nathan Stewart. *Rome at War: Farms, Families, and Death in the Middle Republic*.
    Chapel Hill: University of North Carolina Press, 2004.

Sage, Michael M. *The Republican Roman Army: A Sourcebook*. New York: Routledge, 2008.

Salvatore, John Pamment. *Roman Republican Castrametation: A Reappraisal of Historical
    and Archaeological Sources*. Oxford, England: Tempus Reparatum, 1996.

Santosuosso, Antonio. *Soldiers, Citizens, and the Symbols of War: From Classical Greece to
    Republican Rome, 500-167 B.C.* Boulder, Colo.: Westview Press, 1997.

Sekunda, Nicholas. *Republican Roman Army, 200-104 B.C.* Illustrated by Angus McBride.
    Botley, Oxford, England: Osprey, 1996.

FILMS AND OTHER MEDIA

Legions of Rome: Gallic Wars. Documentary. Kultur Video, 2007.
Legions of Rome: Punic Wars. Documentary. Kultur Video, 2007.
Rome. Documentary series. BBC/HBO/RAI, 2005-2007.
Rome: Power and Glory. Documentary. Questar, 1998.

Denvy A. Bowman

Roman Warfare During the Empire

Dates: 27 B.C.E.-476 C.E.

Military Achievement

The imperial Roman army was arguably one of the most impressive fighting forces the world has ever known. Its military campaigns greatly expanded the territory of the Roman Empire. In the first century C.E., Rome began the conquest of Britain, and in the second century, it conquered Dacia, modern Romania, and parts of modern Jordan and Iraq. The Roman army also defended the Empire against a wide range of enemies along its frontiers, including the Caledonians in northern Britain, various Germanic tribes, the Sarmatians, the Parthians, the Sāsānian Persians, and desert peoples in North Africa. Roman soldiers were highly skilled in pitched battle, siegecraft, and military engineering. In the course of their campaigns Roman troops built military roads, bridges, and large permanent camps, many of which eventually became cities in Europe, the Middle East, and North Africa.

Weapons, Uniforms, and Armor

At the beginning of Augustus's reign as emperor in 27 B.C.E., Roman legionary infantrymen wore a simple round helmet with a horsehair tail at the top as well as a chain mail shirt known as a *lorica hamata*. The latter consisted of interlocking metal rings and provided good protection but was, however, very heavy and took a long time to manufacture. Later in Augustus's reign infantrymen began to use a new type of helmet, of Gallic origin, which was more closely fitted to the skull and included neck and cheek guards. In addition, possibly due to a major loss of military equipment in the German defeat of three legions in the Battle of Teutoburg Forest (9 C.E.), the Roman infantry began to use a new type of breastplate known as the *lorica segmentata*. This armor consisted of horizontal metal bands covering the chest and abdomen as well as vertical metal bands protecting the shoulders. This could be manufactured much more quickly than mail armor and was very flexible. However, the fittings that held the bands together were easily damaged; as a result, this type of armor was in constant need of repair. Early imperial infantrymen also wore greaves, or shin guards, on their legs as well as leather strips called *pteurages* that were attached to their body armor and provided protection for their thighs and upper arms.

The principal weapon of early imperial legionary infantrymen was a short sword called a *gladius*, which was modeled after that of the Spanish Celts and used for hand-to-hand combat. Infantrymen also carried a javelin, or *pilum*, which was hurled at the enemy from a distance, as well as a thrusting spear known as a *hasta*. The large semicylindrical shield, or *scutum*, was probably of Celtic origin and derived from flat oval shields. By the first century C.E. its upper and lower curved edges had been removed, giving it a more rectangular shape. Legionary infantrymen were also equipped with a dagger, which, like the gladius, was of Spanish origin.

Roman officers of the early Empire wore the same Gallic-type helmets worn by the infantry and a variety of body armor, including mail shirts, cuirasses that were modeled after the human torso, or scale shirts known as *loricae squamatae*. The latter consisted of overlapping metal scales arranged in horizontal rows and fastened to a foundation of linen or hide. This type of armor was easy to make and repair and, when polished, gave the wearer an impressive appearance. However, it was not very flexible, and its wearer was vulnerable to a sword or spear thrust from below.

Under the early Empire, troops of the *auxilia* used equipment that was generally inferior to that of the legionaries; however, they began to receive better-quality equipment during the reign of the emperor Trajan (c. 53-c. 117 C.E.). The infantry wore a variety of helmets as well as leather tunics covered with metal plates or mail, and used narrow, flat, sometimes oval shields. Their principal weapons were the hasta and the *spatha*, a long sword that became the dominant form of sword throughout the Roman army by the early third century. Cavalrymen wore iron helmets that covered the entire head except for the eyes, nose, and mouth. They wore either mail or scale body armor and used the same weapons as did the infantry of the auxilia cohorts. Although they did not use stirrups, they were firmly anchored on horseback by the four projecting horns of their saddles.

During the crisis of the third century C.E. the Roman Empire experienced increased invasion and internal chaos but lacked a centralized military supply system. Armies were consequently forced to salvage equipment from battlefields or to obtain it on their own from other sources, which, in turn, led to an end to uniformity in the appearance of soldiers. During this period, the lorica segmentata was gradually abandoned, and soldiers increasingly made use of mail shirts as well as an improved form of scale armor. In this type of armor, which did not require a foundation, the scales were ringed together vertically as well as horizontally. The scales were therefore locked down, and the wearer was much less vulnerable to a thrust from below. Moreover, the older Gallic helmet was replaced by a new helmet of Sarmatian origin, the *spangenhelm*, which consisted of several metal plates held together in a conical shape by reinforcement bands. This helmet, which included cheek, neck, and nose guards, was used by both infantry and cavalry. In addition the scutum was replaced by a large-dished oval shield covered with hide or linen. Cavalry units used a similar type of shield that featured the insignia of the bearer's unit.

In the late third century C.E., the emperor Diocletian (c. 245-316 C.E.) established a series of state-run arms factories, or *fabricae*, in an attempt to remedy the supply problem. However, these factories failed to restore uniformity in military equipment due to the fact that a wide range of barbarian peoples were serving in the Roman army by this time and used their own native weapons. In the fourth century the fac-

tories did mass-produce a new type of helmet of Parthian-Sāsānian origin, known as a ridge helmet, because it consisted of two metal halves held together by a central ridge. During this period, soldiers also received monetary allowances for the purchase of clothing, arms, and armor. By the late fourth century C.E., the army came to include increased numbers of barbarians who had little need for armor and therefore little desire to purchase it for regular use. Instead, soldiers relied primarily on large circular shields for protection. When an army was on the march, its armor was carried in wagons and was normally used only during an actual pitched battle.

The Roman army also used various types of artillery both in battle and when conducting a siege. These included a device known as a *tormenta*, which fired arrows, javelins, and rocks, as well as larger *ballistae* and catapults that hurled larger arrows or stones.

MILITARY ORGANIZATION

During most of its history, the basic unit of the Roman army was the legion, which consisted only of Roman citizens and during the time of the early Empire numbered about 5,000 men. Each legion was organized into ten infantry cohorts, one of which consisted of five centuries of 160 men each, while the remaining nine cohorts were each composed of six centuries of 80 men each. The centuries were grouped into maniples, each consisting of two centuries. During the first to third centuries C.E., each legion also included a cavalry detachment of 120 men. The command structure of the legion consisted of the fifty-nine centurions, who commanded the centuries; five tribunes, each of whom commanded two cohorts; a prefect of the camp; a tribune of senatorial rank; and the legions' commanders, the legates.

The legions were supported by units known as auxilia, which consisted of troops recruited from subject peoples. These included infantry cohorts of 480 men divided into six centuries, and cavalry detachments (*alae*) consisting of sixteen troops (*turmae*) of thirty-two riders each. In the late first century C.E. these were enlarged to cohorts of ten centuries and alae composed of twenty-four turmae; the new

Roman Empire, c. 117 c.e.

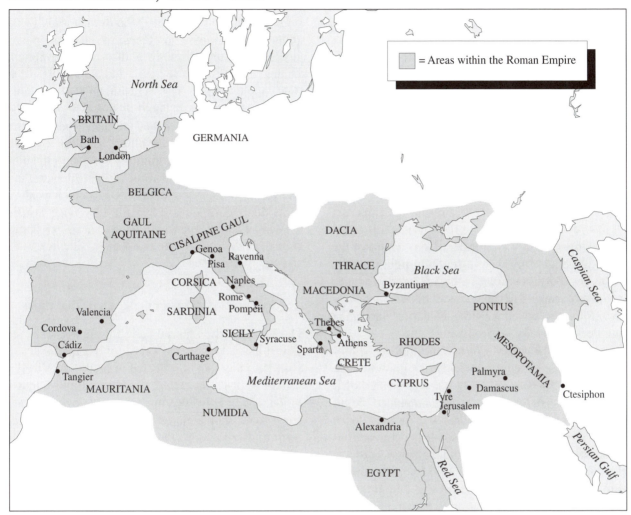

cohorts and alae each theoretically numbered 1,000 men but were actually somewhat smaller in number. There were also mixed units, known as *cohortes equitatae*, consisting of one infantry cohort and four troops of cavalry, and units known as *numeri*, which were not grouped as cohorts or alae but retained their own ethnic characteristics in terms of organization and weaponry. In addition to infantry and cavalry units, the auxilia included specialized troops such as archers and slingers.

The early imperial army also included certain elite units based in Rome. The most important of these was the Praetorian Guard, which was created by the emperor Augustus (63-14 B.C.E.) and originally consisted of nine cohorts. It supervised public life in the capital, escorted the emperor, and eventually came to play a major political role by occasionally helping to determine the succession to the imperial throne. The emperor was also protected by an elite personal cavalry unit known as the *equites singulares Augusti*. In the fourth century, the emperor Constantine the Great (c. 275 to 285-337 C.E.) disbanded both of these units because they had supported his rival Maxentius (died 312), and replaced them with a new bodyguard of German cavalry, the *scholae Palatinae*.

In the late second and third centuries C.E., the imperial army underwent some notable changes. The emperor Lucius Septimius Severus (146-211 C.E.) increased both the pay and the size of the army, adding new auxilia units as well as three new legions. One of these was stationed near Rome, serving as a reserve unit and ensuring that Severus remained in power. In 212 C.E. Severus's son, the emperor Caracalla (188-217 C.E.), extended Roman citizenship to most of the Empire's population; this action essentially ended the distinction between legions and auxilia. At the start of the third century crisis (235-284 C.E.), the Empire lacked reserve forces that could deal with invasions by German tribes. As a result, the emperors of this period formed reserve field armies that could readily respond to such invaders. The cavalry of the early imperial army were essentially light cavalry, but by the fourth century the army included two types of heavily armored cavalry, known as *cataphractarii* and *clibanarii*, which were modeled after Sarmatian and Persian cavalry respectively.

In the fourth century, Constantine the Great established a single large mobile field army known as the *comitatus*. This was led by two newly created officers, the *magister peditum*, who commanded the infantry, and the *magister equitum*, the commander of the cavalry. Constantine thus established a clear division between the field army and the frontier troops, the *limitanei*, who during this period were organized into legions of 1,000 men. However, due to the inability of this single field army to respond to simultaneous attacks on various parts of the frontier, Con-

stantine's successors divided the comitatus into a number of regional field armies.

In the late fourth century, the Roman army faced mounting manpower shortages, which became particularly acute following a disastrous campaign against the Persians (363 C.E.) and a major defeat at Adrianople (378 C.E.). As a result, units of limitanei were transferred to the field armies. Moreover, the Romans permitted individual German tribes to settle within Roman territory as allies, or *foederati*, who were obliged to provide military service to the emperor. However, the field armies fell into decline, and individual military commanders and other wealthy individuals consequently organized private armies known as *bucellarii*, which continued to exist after the fall of the western Roman Empire in 476 C.E.

Doctrine, Strategy, and Tactics

During the early imperial period Roman leaders believed that it was Rome's destiny to rule the entire world, a view that is reflected in book 6 of Virgil's (70-19 B.C.E.) *Aeneid* (c. 29-19 B.C.E.; English translation, 1553). However, during this same period they came to recognize major factors that limited further territorial expansion. One of these was the sometimes formidable resistance by enemies such as the Caledonians, the Germanic tribes, and the Parthians and Sāsānians. Moreover, some territories open to conquest, such as the Arabian deserts to the far southeast, were of little economic or strategic value. Finally, the empire simply did not possess the military manpower or resources to expand indefinitely. Augustus stationed most of the legions on the frontiers and recommended to his successors the basic strategy of defending Rome's existing frontiers rather than conquering additional territory.

Despite Augustus's recommendation, emperors of the first to third centuries C.E. did not completely abandon the policy of expansion. Notable examples of this policy can

Turning Points

70 B.C.E.	The Romans besiege Jerusalem, taking the city's population captive and leveling its buildings to the ground.
9 C.E.	Roman legions are defeated by the Germans at the Battle of Teutoburg Forest.
73	The Romans employ ramps and siege towers in the Siege of Masada.
122	Construction of Hadrian's Wall begins in Britain.
c. 400	Cavalry replaces infantry as the most important element in Roman armies.
476	The weakened western Roman Empire finally falls.

be seen in the conquests of Britain, Dacia, and certain Middle Eastern territories, and in Septimius Severus's campaigns in Mesopotamia and northern Britain. In addition, Roman emperors and their generals sometimes carried out preemptive attacks or reprisals in order to eliminate potential threats to the Empire. However, for the most part Roman emperors developed and adhered to a strategy of defense of the Empire's frontiers. In doing so, they gradually established defensive zones, or limes, along the frontiers. The central feature of such zones was a military road running along the actual frontier. At various intervals along such roads the Romans built various defensive fortifications, including large legionary camps, smaller forts, watchtowers, and fortified ports along rivers. In the first and second centuries emperors sometimes implemented a policy of "forward defense," in which Roman forces took control of adjacent enemy territory and built roads, watchtowers, and forts in order to monitor enemy activity and discourage possible attack.

Sometimes the Romans built continuous defensive barriers in the limes in order to prevent barbarian entry into imperial territory as well as to define the Empire's actual boundaries. These include three barriers built in the second century: Hadrian's Wall and the Antonine Wall in northern Britain, as well as a 240-mile-long wooden palisade built to protect the strategic area between the upper Rhine and Danube Rivers. Such fortifications consisted of a ditch, an embankment, and a rampart, with smaller forts and military camps of varying size built at intervals along the wall. A military road was built along the entire wall for the purposes of communication and moving troops in the event of an enemy threat.

During the early imperial period, frontier provinces were guarded by armies composed either of legions and auxilia or simply of auxilia cavalry and infantry units. The northern frontiers consisted of three regions: northern Britain and the Rhine and Danube frontiers, each of which was threatened by warlike barbarian peoples. Rome's eastern provinces lacked natural geographical barriers and were therefore vulnerable to attack from the Parthians and, beginning in the third century, the Sāsānian Persians. During the reign of Augustus, the Rhine and North African fron-

tiers were considered the most dangerous in the Empire. However, as these frontiers were stabilized, their garrisons were reduced, and those on the Danube and eastern frontiers were gradually increased during the first to third centuries.

During the third century crisis, frontier defenses collapsed and emperors consequently developed a new strategy of imperial defense. During this period Germanic tribes and Sāsānian armies frequently penetrated the limes and sometimes moved virtually at will within Roman territory. They sometimes posed a threat to cities located in interior areas away from the frontiers. The inhabitants of such cities consequently began to build defensive walls around them; in the late third century the emperor Aurelian (c. 215-275 C.E.) began construction of a wall around Rome itself. Moreover, third century emperors began to develop a strategy of "defense in depth," which featured less emphasis on frontier forces and greater use of mobile field armies that centered on heavy cavalry units. Such armies were stationed in cities away from the frontier and then sent to intercept and defeat invaders. Moreover, in an attempt to deal with a shortage of manpower, some barbarians (*laeti*) were allowed to settle in Roman territory and entrusted with defense of part of the frontier; they were also required to provide recruits for the army.

In the fourth century, Constantine the Great and his successors made increased use of mobile field armies. During this period, some emperors also attempted to strengthen the frontier defenses. Under Diocletian, frontier defenses were rebuilt, and new forts were built along the Danube and eastern frontiers and in North Africa. Valentinian I (321-375 C.E.) strengthened defenses on the Rhine and the Danube and directed preemptive attacks against barbarians along both frontiers. However, by the late fourth century the Empire was confronted with mounting manpower shortages as well as growing barbarian pressure on the frontiers. The manpower shortage resulted in understrength garrisons on the Rhine frontier being grouped together at a few vital points. In the fifth century C.E. Germanic invaders simply bypassed such strongpoints, which led to a complete collapse of the Rhine frontiers and, ultimately, to the end of the western Roman Empire.

ROMAN EMPIRE, C. 400 C.E.

ARMENIA

SĀSĀNIAN EMPIRE

Edessa
Antioch
Emesa
THE EAST
Damascus
Jerusalem

PONTUS
Caesarea
Heraclea
Nicomedia
Nicaea
Pergamum
Smyrna
ASIA

Black Sea

Constantinople

Cyprus
Tyre
Caesarea

Nile River

Alexandria
Memphis

EGYPT

RHODES

THRACE
Nicopolis
Adrianople
Dyrrhacium
MACEDONIA

Aegean
Sea

Athens

Crete

DACIA

Danube River

Danube River

Cyrene

Berenice

Mediterranean Sea

Adriatic Sea

Taranto
ROME
Reggio
Syracuse

Salzburg
Aquileia
ITALY
Ravenna
Bologna
Milan
Genoa
Rome
Naples
Cosenza
Palermo
Carthage
Sicily

Tripoli

Rhine River

Cologne
Mainz
Chalôns

GAUL

Narbonne

Corsica

Sardinia

AFRICA

Paris
Orleans

BRITAIN
London

SPAIN
Valencia
Merida
Cadiz

Cartagena

Atlantic
Ocean

☐ = Areas within the Roman Empire

The principal tactical objectives of a Roman commander were to move his army safely and swiftly and ultimately to defeat the enemy in open battle. A Roman army was most vulnerable when on the march, and therefore it had to be arranged in an order of march that would enable it to deal effectively with an enemy attack. Moreover, army commanders had to provide maximum protection for the baggage train because if enemy forces captured it and began looting, soldiers might break ranks in order to retrieve their belongings and consequently place the entire army in peril. In order to ensure safe and rapid passage through enemy territory, Roman troops often built roads and bridges. Moreover, at the end of each day's march they built temporary marching camps for protection. These camps were surrounded by earthen ramparts and ditches and were disassembled the following morning before the army resumed its march.

When preparing for battle, Roman commanders sought to gather information about the enemy and to position the army in a manner best suited to the terrain on which it would fight. In battle, the Roman army was normally deployed in three parts, including a center or main body with flanking forces to its right and left that could be used to encircle the enemy. The legions were the most important component of the army. By the second century C.E. their basic battle formation was a solid phalanx consisting of several ranks of legionaries; however, the legion's subdivisions of cohorts, maniples, and centuries gave it great flexibility in battle.

A Roman army normally began a battle with an artillery salvo designed to demoralize and disrupt the enemy. Next archers and slingers fired on the enemy, and the infantry hurled javelins. This was followed by a great shout from the Roman lines that was intended to frighten the enemy. If the enemy then fled, the Roman cavalry was sent in pursuit; the advance cavalry units moved rapidly to make sure that the enemy retreat was not a tactical deception, while the remaining cavalry advanced carefully in battle formation. If the enemy attacked, the front ranks of the legions held firm while other ranks hurled javelins, and archers fired arrows upon the attackers; the cavalry was sent to meet any enemy flank attacks. How-

ever, if the Roman army made the initial move, it directed its attack against the weakest point in the enemy position. Auxilia units carried out the initial assault. They were followed by the legions, who advanced in a "tortoise," or *testudo*, formation, with their shields locked together in the front, at the sides, and overhead in order to protect the legionaries from enemy javelins or arrows. After the enemy position was broken, hand-to-hand combat followed until the enemy either surrendered or fled. If the enemy did flee, Roman troops first searched the immediate surroundings to avoid falling into an ambush, and then the cavalry was sent in pursuit of the enemy.

When conducting sieges of enemy fortresses or cities, Roman armies first set out to confine the enemy within their defenses by means of a series of fortified positions. The defenders were surrounded by a ditch and earthen rampart as well as a system of forts. Once this was constructed, the Romans set out to penetrate the enemy's defenses and force them to surrender. In some cases, as in the Siege of Masada (73 C.E.), the Romans built a high approach platform or ramp, which they would use to move a large siege tower close to the enemy wall. Archers positioned at the top of the tower could then fire on the defenders below; sometimes siege towers also were equipped with battering rams that were used to break through the enemy wall. Another method was to approach the enemy position under cover of a movable protective structure and then attempt to undermine the wall. If these methods did not work, the Romans would launch a frontal assault on the weakest point in the enemy defenses. This was preceded by a major artillery bombardment. The legionaries would then approach under cover of a testudo and scale the walls. After the top of the walls was secured, enemy cities were then sacked.

During the late imperial period, Roman warfare changed considerably. By the fourth century, most military action consisted of small-scale skirmishes involving small detachments of troops. However, in large-scale battles Roman commanders still sought to defeat barbarians such as the Goths by means of a decisive infantry clash in which the Roman infantry was deployed in a phalanx formation. When the enemy approached, they came under fire from archers deployed behind the phalanx; this might slow or even halt the enemy advance. If it did not, both sides would shout a battle cry, or *barritus*, and the enemy would resume their advance. The Roman archery fire continued, while Roman infantrymen in the rear ranks hurled their javelins and moved forward to support the troops in the front ranks. After the enemy made contact with the Roman phalanx, the two sides pressed upon each other until one side lost heart and gave way. The cavalry then pursued the soldiers of the defeated army; it was in this last stage of battle that the largest number of casualties were inflicted.

Roman infantry employed the same tactics against enemy cavalry attacks. However, such attacks were relatively rare since it was difficult for cavalrymen to make their horses charge up against tightly packed infantry positions. If the infantry held firm, they could easily repel such attacks.

During the fifth century C.E., cavalry replaced infantry as the most important element in Roman armies. They generally used one of two different attack formations: a wedge, or rhomboid, formation, which was effective when carrying out elaborate maneuvers or seeking to pierce enemy formations, and a square, or oblong, formation, which was used when carrying out a full-scale charge. During the late imperial period, Roman cavalry used both skirmishing and shock tactics. In the former, the cavalry rode up to an enemy formation and fired their arrows; if the enemy held firm, they would fall back and attack again. If the enemy broke ranks, they then charged and engaged in close combat. *Foederati* and other German cavalry in the late Roman army used shock tactics in which they simply charged, sometimes with the support of mounted archers, and attempted to defeat the enemy in close combat.

ANCIENT SOURCES

The noted Roman historian Cornelius Tacitus (c. 56-120 C.E.) wrote a number of works that offer valuable insights into early imperial warfare. These include a biography of his father-in-law, a governor of Britain, that describes Rome's military campaigns in that province. Tacitus also wrote *Ab Excessu Divi Augusti*, also known as *Annales* (c. 116 C.E.; *Annals*, 1598), an account of events in the Empire in the period from 14 to 68 C.E., and the *Historiae* (c. 109; *Histories*, 1731) on the period from 68 to 96 C.E., of which only the portions on the period from 69 to 70 C.E. have survived. The Jewish historian Flavius Josephus (c. 37-c. 100 C.E.) wrote a history of the Jewish revolt of 66-70, which includes descriptions of the Roman army in action.

Arrian (c. 89-155 C.E.), a governor of Cappadocia under the emperor Hadrian, wrote a first-hand account of a campaign that he conducted against the Alani in 134. He also wrote the *Ars Tactica*, a manual on the training of cavalry. Pseudo-Hyginus, an obscure figure who probably lived during the second century C.E., wrote *De Munitionibus Castrorum* (second century C.E.; *Fortifications of the Camp*, 1993), a discussion of the planning and construction of Roman military camps. The fifth century Roman military theorist Flavius Vegetius Renatus wrote *De Re Militari* (383-450 C.E.; *The Fovre Bookes of Flauius Vegetius Renatus: Briefelye Contayninge a Plaine Forme and Perfect Knowledge of Martiall Policye, Feates of Chiualrie, and Vvhatsoeuver Pertayneth to Warre*, 1572; also translated as *Military Institutions of Vegetius*, 1767), a treatise in which he called for a restoration of traditional military drill and training, and in doing so discussed various aspects of the Roman army in earlier periods.

Ammianus Marcellinus (c. 330-395 C.E.), an officer who served in the Roman army in the 350's and 360's, wrote a history of the Roman Empire that continued Tacitus's account from 96 to 378 C.E. However, only the books on the period from 353 to 378 C.E. have survived; these are a major source for political and military events of this period. The *Notitia Dignitatum* (c. 395 C.E.) is an illustrated manuscript that lists the officers of the late fourth century army, as well as their units and where each was stationed.

BOOKS AND ARTICLES

Campbell, Brian. *War and Society in Imperial Rome, 31 B.C.-A.D. 284*. New York: Routledge, 2002.

Campbell, Duncan B. *Siege Warfare in the Roman World, 146 B.C.-A.D. 378*. Illustrated by Adam Hook. Botley, Oxford, England: Osprey, 2005.

Chrissanthos, Stefan G. *Warfare in the Ancient World: From the Bronze Age to the Fall of Rome*. Westport, Conn.: Praeger, 2008.

Cowan, Ross. *Roman Battle Tactics, 109 B.C.-A.D. 313*. Illustrated by Adam Cook. Botley, Oxford, England: Osprey, 2007.

Dixon, Karen R., and Pat Southern. *The Late Roman Army*. New Haven, Conn.: Yale University Press, 1996.

Erdkamp, Paul, ed. *A Companion to the Roman Army*. Malden, Mass.: Blackwell, 2007.

Fields, Nic. *The Roman Army of the Principate, 27 B.C.-A.D. 117*. Oxford, England, Osprey, 2009.

Goldsworthy, Adrian. *Roman Warfare*. London: Cassell, 2000.

Le Bohec, Yann. *The Imperial Roman Army*. Translated by Raphael Bate. London: Routledge, 1994.

Luttwak, Edward. *The Grand Strategy of the Roman Empire from the First Century A.D. to the Third*. Baltimore: Johns Hopkins University Press, 1976.

Mattern, Susan P. *Rome and the Enemy: Imperial Strategy in the Principate*. Berkeley: University of California Press, 1999.

Santosuosso, Antonio. *Storming the Heavens: Soldiers, Emperors, and Civilians in the Roman Empire*. Boulder, Colo.: Westview Press, 2001.

Simkins, Michael. *The Roman Army from Caesar to Trajan*. Botley, Oxford, England: Osprey, 1993.

_____. *The Roman Army from Hadrian to Constantine*. Botley, Oxford, England: Osprey, 1991.

Whitby, Michael. *Rome at War, A.D. 293-696*. Botley, Oxford, England: Osprey, 2002.

FILMS AND OTHER MEDIA

Ancient Rome: The Rise and Fall of an Empire. Television docudrama series. BBC One, 2006.

The Fall of the Roman Empire. Feature film. Paramount Pictures, 1964.

The History of Warfare: The Roman Invasions of Britain. Documentary. Cromwell Productions, 2009.

Legions of Rome: Roman Invasions of Britain. Documentary. Kultur Video, 2007.

Rome. Documentary series. BBC/HBO/RAI, 2005-2007.

Rome: Power and Glory. Documentary. Questar, 1998.

Thomas I. Crimando

CELTIC WARFARE

Dates: c. 500 B.C.E.-900 C.E.

POLITICAL CONSIDERATIONS

If any word is symbolic of the Celtic culture, it is "periphery." By the fifth century B.C.E., while civilizations battled for position along the Mediterranean basin, one rising civilization to the north stood apart. Hugging the fertile lands on the northern side of the Alps, the Celts flourished. Though lacking a centralized authority or literacy, the militant Celts spread. Power centers clustered around chieftains in defensive hill forts developed into *oppida*, or settlements,

and the Celts expanded. They were known for their splendid vessels, jewelry, weapons, and armor, and the fine metalwork of Celtic craftspeople became the basis for trade routes that spread throughout Europe, even to Carthage. Although their expansion north was limited by Germanic tribes, at the height of their expansion the Celts' territory in the east included areas of modern Atlantic Spain, France, and, by the first century B.C.E., England and Ireland. In the west, much of the area north of the Balkan Mountains, and even a tenuous colony in what is now Turkey, was under their control.

The Celts' lack of a centralized authority, combined with some chieftains' lust for Roman luxuries, led to their downfall. They were expelled from Italy by 191 B.C.E., and Julius Caesar utilized fear of the Gauls to launch an invasion into Gaul in 58 B.C.E. The area was pacified by 51 B.C.E. Although Caesar had made punitive expeditions into Britain in 55 B.C.E., it was not until 43 B.C.E. that Rome reached its farthest conquest in Britain. As further expansion was not profitable for Rome, a wall was built in 121 C.E. under the direction of the Roman general Hadrian to minimize the attacks of the Celtic Picts. Ireland, meanwhile, was largely ignored, allowing the Celtic culture to thrive there. Although Rome may have leveled the hill forts, traces of Celtic culture remained among the Britons. This culture, once converted to Christianity, replaced militaristic fervor with the fervor to convert. Thus a culture turned a geographic characteristic

North Wind Picture Archives via AP Images

A Celt depicted in battle with a Roman on the column of Roman emperor Antoninus.

CELTIC EUROPE, 60 B.C.E.

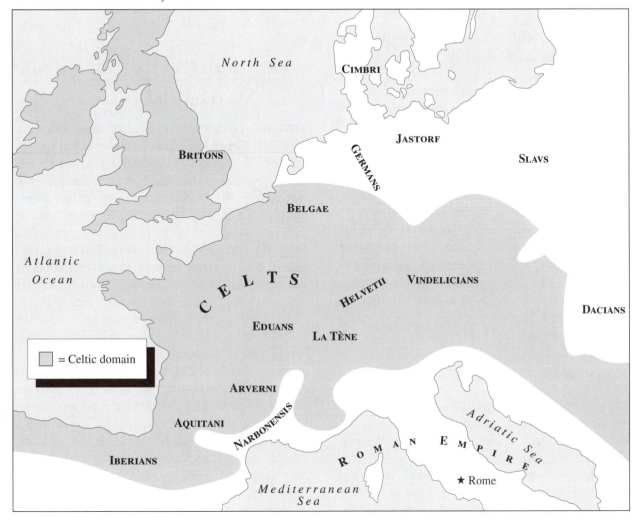

into something that allowed its survival: specifically, the periphery.

MILITARY ACHIEVEMENT

Although the Celts' expansion was a necessity for the acquisition of more farmland, it also led them into conflict with growing powers. Their military expansion allowed them to build a massive breadth of empire. Early victories staved off encroachment on Celtic lands by Mediterranean civilizations. However, the Celts were almost victims of their own suc-

cess; their lack of unified organization led to a slow defeat and retreat of lands.

Early Celtic victories began around 400 B.C.E. The Celts had pushed into the Po Valley. The Etruscans called for Roman emissaries, but the Celts felt the Romans took the Etruscan side and, in 387 B.C.E., declared war on Rome. They subsequently sacked Rome and left the city only after a huge ransom was paid, a slight that Rome never forgot.

Less than one hundred years later, the Celts raided Thrace and Macedonia from 298 to 278 B.C.E. They threatened Delphi. This invasion and final repulsion were likened by contemporary Greek historians to a victory rivaling that against the Persian king Xerxes almost two hundred years earlier. Celtic plundering, however, continued until 212 B.C.E.

In Spain, the Celtiberians conflicted with Carthage beginning in 237 B.C.E. By the Second Punic War (218-201 B.C.E.), they served as mercenaries for Carthage. The Celts, who had lost land to Rome in 225 B.C.E., fought and then supported Hannibal's army in 218 B.C.E.

With Carthage defeated, Rome moved against the Celts. Julius Caesar invaded Gaul in 58-54 B.C.E. After a rebellion led by Vercingetorix in 52 B.C.E., this was the zenith of Celtic power in Gaul. By 51 B.C.E., Gaul had been pacified. Britain was invaded in 47 B.C.E. Total resistance to Rome in the Po Valley remained until 49 B.C.E. In Spain, military resistance ended in 19 B.C.E. Although some Celtic pockets survived—in Ireland, Brittany, Wales, and Scotland—the lack of a centralizing unity and threats from Vikings weakened the culture.

WEAPONS, UNIFORMS, AND ARMOR

It was the iron of the Celts that allowed their incredible expansion. Once Celtic societies became proficient at the smelting of iron, the Celts rose to proficiency with the metal. The main weapon of the soldier was his iron sword, complemented by a spear. These were quite ferocious weapons, as pointed out in the first century B.C.E. by Roman historian Diodorus Siculus:

> Their swords are as long as the javelins of other peoples and their javelins have points longer than their swords. . . . Some of their javelins . . . are forged . . . so that the blow not only cuts but also tears the flesh, and the recovery of the spear tears open the wound.

Although bows, slings, and throwing clubs were also used, they were not typical. Celts were also highly regarded in their use of war chariots and cavalry.

For armor, the main item used was a shield. Most shields were made of leather and wood, although bronze ornamentation was sometimes added. In battle, many Celts wore bronze helmets and neck rings, or torcs. Although some Celts entered battle wearing tunics made of iron chain mail, the majority of Celts fought naked. The reasons for this nakedness are unknown, but it is believed to have been part of some ritual.

MILITARY ORGANIZATION

The Celtic culture was centered on the military. Indeed, the Greek geographer Strabo described the whole Celtic nation as "war-mad" and "quick for battle." He went on to state that the Celts "tend to rush to war all together, without concealment or forward planning," and "They are willing to risk everything they have with nothing to rely on other than their sheer physical strength and courage." War was necessary, for the Celts maintained a social structure based on the warrior elite; during boastful feasts, the warriors would regale one another with their exploits, seeking increased social position.

Celtic warfare had its own unique aspects—headhunting, for example, and a reliance on the reckless headlong charge to break an enemy line. Warriors fought for personal glory. In this quest for glory for the individual warrior, formal discipline was nonexistent, but the tactic worked often enough to justify the Celts' faith in it. Indeed, one last item that set the Celts apart was the willingness of their women to engage in battle. Roman historian Ammianus Marcellinus wrote the following in the fourth century C.E., on observations of the Celts during 63 B.C.E.-14 C.E.:

> A whole troupe of foreigners would not be able to withstand a single Gaul if he called his wife to his assistance who is usually very strong . . . and . . . she begins to strike blows mingled with kicks, as if they were so many missiles sent from the string of a catapult.

DOCTRINE, STRATEGY, AND TACTICS

The warrior code of personal glory and victory seemed to define much of the Celtic doctrine in battle. Victory at any price, any cost, seemed to be the almost manic approach of many Celts in battle.

Much of the strategy used by the Celts in battle centered on psychological warfare. Before fighting began, the Celts would cry out their victory and prowess in battle while demeaning those who stood against them. The naked warriors, sometimes covered in war paint, would all shout at once, creating a cacophony that unsettled enemies who were used to noises having some type of significant purpose in battle.

The Celts' most common tactic in battle, a ferocious headlong assault that was almost blind in its fury, unnerved many a foe. Although the emphasis on the individual in the Celtic army prevented coordinated action, the unpredictability of the Celts' seemingly deranged attacks prevented a strong defense. This form of frontal assault, combined with the armaments of sword and shield, was able to deal effectively with Mediterranean armies organized on the model of the Macedonian phalanx. The Celts also used cavalry, and they gained notoriety for their skill with horses. By the second century B.C.E., however, their use of the war chariot dropped off in continental Europe.

FINAL ROMAN CAMPAIGN AGAINST GALLIC TRIBES, 52 B.C.E.

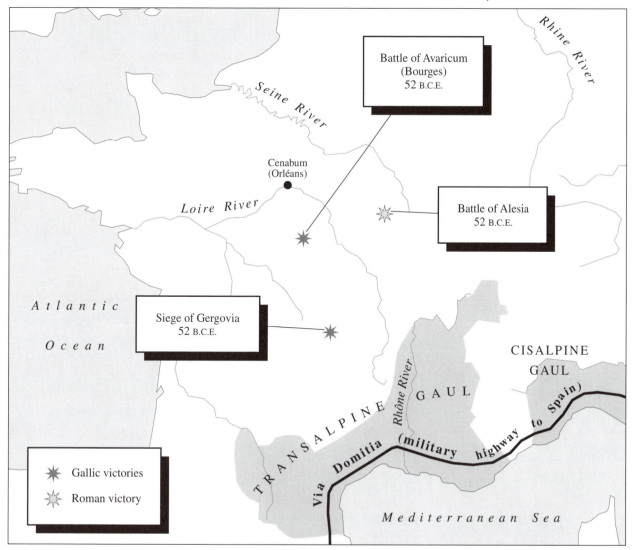

ANCIENT SOURCES

A difficulty arises when one consults ancient sources for information on the Celts. Because the Celts did not develop a written language of their own, all writing concerning them was left by those who fought against them, and readers should thus be aware of possible bias in these accounts. Of all the authors to address the Celts, perhaps the most famous and readable ancient source is Julius Caesar. His work on the conquest of Gaul, *Comentarii de bello Gallico* (52-51 B.C.E.; *The Gallic Wars*, in his *Commentaries*, 1609), is a document written by an ambitious general to build his own personal power and esteem. Of the various other authors who wrote about the Celts, from Greek to Roman, their actual exposure to the Celts was limited. Authors ranging from Athenaeus (fl. c. 200 C.E.) to Diodorus Siculus (c. 80-c. 20 B.C.E.) and Strabo (64 or 63 B.C.E.-after 23 C.E.) relied on sensational and fantastic stories to build the mystery of a culture that was completely foreign to them, a culture that had threatened and struck fear into both civilizations.

BOOKS AND ARTICLES

Cunliffe, Barry. *The Ancient Celts*. New York: Oxford University Press, 1997.

_____. *The Celts: A Very Short Introduction*. New York: Oxford University Press, 2003.

Haywood, John. *Atlas of the Celtic World*. New York: Thames and Hudson, 2001.

Kruta, Venceslas. *Celts*. London: Hachette, 2005.

Lang, Lloyd. *Celtic Britain*. New York: Charles Scribner's Sons, 1979.

Litton, Helen. *The Celts: An Illustrated History*. Dublin: Wolfhound Press, 1997.

Sullivan, Karen. *Glorious Treasures: The Celts*. London: Brockhampton Press, 1997.

FILMS AND OTHER MEDIA

Boudica. Feature film. Independent Television, 2003.

Caesar: Conqueror of Gaul. Documentary. History Channel, 2005.

The Celts. Documentary. History Channel, 1997.

Decisive Battles: Boudicca, Warrior Queen. Documentary. History Channel, 2004.

Druids. Feature film. Lolistar, 2001.

Andrew Reynolds Galloway

BERBER WARFARE

Dates: c. 1000 B.C.E.-1000 C.E.

POLITICAL CONSIDERATIONS

The term "Berber" was first coined by foreign conquerors in an attempt to classify a large population who resided in the Maghreb region of North Africa. Some scholars believe that "Imazighen" was the self-referential term. The exact identification of who constituted the Berber people during this period becomes difficult to determine given the wide use of this appellation and the complicated ancestry of those it attempts to describe. In the words of one of the foremost modern Berber scholars, Elizabeth Fentress, "at best we can define Berbers as Mediterranean." The term "Berber" is also used to refer to the Afro-Asiatic language group, with its many variants and dialects. At one point this language group constituted one of the major forms of verbal communication in North Africa.

The Berber population was not contained in one nation and was embroiled in numerous intertribal and international conflicts. Throughout the period from 1000 B.C.E. to 1000 C.E., Berber tribes, kingdoms, and mercenaries were both allies and enemies of Carthage and Rome, the Muslim invaders, and each other. To confuse the situation further, this duality was common during the major military conflicts. Sorting through this tangle can be daunting, but the task is made easier if it is understood that the term "Berber," when applied in a historical context, may refer to just a single kingdom, tribe, or mercenary band rather than to an entire population. The varied political situations that erupted into warfare led directly to the Berbers' identity as warriors.

MILITARY ACHIEVEMENT

The Berbers' actions on hundreds of battlefields across the ancient world, from the coasts of North Africa to Italy and Spain, earned them a reputation as accomplished and fierce fighters. Both Carthage and Rome courted Berbers during their long feud, drawing them into all three of the Punic Wars. Berbers again were a serious political and military consideration during the Vandal conquest and occupation of North Africa. Berber cavalry and infantry formed the backbone of resistance during the Muslim invasion of North Africa in the seventh century C.E. as well as alternately serving as a conquering force for Islam.

As the Berber population was not contained in one nation and was embroiled in numerous intertribal and international conflicts, only a summation of some of the most important engagements follows. The Berber kingdoms of Numidia (present-day Algeria and part of Tunisia) allied with the North African Phoenician city of Carthage (formed c. 814 B.C.E.). During the First Punic War (264-241 B.C.E.), Numidian soldiers and cavalry were in the ranks of the Carthaginian armies allied against Rome and its forces. Berber soldiers made up a large element of the discontent during the Revolt of the Mercenaries (241-238 B.C.E.), which was sparked over payment issues stemming from the First Punic War.

During the Second Punic War (218-201 B.C.E.), Masinissa, the chief of the Massyli tribe in Numidia, formed an alliance with Carthage against Rome. He commanded cavalry against Rome on a battlefield in Spain. In 206 B.C.E., however, he switched sides, allying with Rome in exchange for larger territory. At the climactic Battle of Zama (202 B.C.E.), Masinissa's cavalry was a decisive factor in the crushing Carthage defeat. In 151 B.C.E., open warfare broke out between Numidia and Carthage, ending in defeat for Carthage. Sensing weakness, Rome initiated the Third Punic War (149-146 B.C.E.). Once again, Numidian cavalry were part of the army that leveled Carthage in the final year of that war.

A descendant of Masinissa, Jugurtha, fought alongside Scipio Africanus the Younger in the Spanish siege of Numantia. In an attempt to consolidate his kingdom, Jugurtha attacked another Numidian king in 118 B.C.E., who sought and was granted Roman aid. The end result was the execution of Jugurtha in 105 B.C.E.

In 429 C.E. the Vandals crossed the Strait of Gibraltar into North Africa on a mission of conquest. Once again, Berbers assisted and repelled this latest foreign incursion, and they weathered the Vandal occupation until that empire's ultimate decline. Striking out from conquered Egypt, Muslims clashed with Berbers between 642 and 669 C.E. Although there remained pockets of resistance, the majority of the Berber population converted to Islam. It is estimated that eighty thousand Berbers fought on behalf of the Muslims at the Battle of Poitiers/Tours in 732 C.E. This would become the foundation for the Islamic empires of the Almoravids and Almohads of the later centuries.

WEAPONS, UNIFORMS, AND ARMOR

Perhaps the most effective weapon in the Berber arsenal was the horse. It is estimated that this living weapon of war was introduced to the Berber homeland around 1200 B.C.E. The Berber warriors quickly evolved into highly skilled horsemen. The Berber Garamantes, in the period predating the Roman excursions in North Africa, were noted as using horse chariots. These seem to have been used for purposes of shock and awe, as archery platforms, or perhaps as status symbols. Later accounts do not mention these chariots in use.

According to accounts left by their opponents, the Berber horsemen rode bareback (although it is likely they used saddlecloths). There was also amazement that the Berbers seemed to guide their horses without reins; in fact, they utilized the *bozal*, a rope or leather bridle to which a lead-rein is attached with a metal bit. The ability of the Berbers to marshal massive numbers of mounts was considered extraordinary. According to a report from Greek geographer Strabo, "Horse-breeding is followed with such exceptional interest by the [Berber] kings that the number of colts every year amounts to one hundred thousand."

Of course the horse was simply the conveyance for the warrior, who had to exploit the opportunity provided by his steed. The preferred missile weapon of the Berbers was the broad-bladed javelin, usually cut to a length of five feet. A short sword, often appropriated from a fallen Roman foe, was generally carried as a secondary offensive weapon and a defensive measure against other cavalry blades. Historical documentation also cites Berber horsemen equipped with short spears. Berber infantrymen were similarly armed with spears, swords, javelins, and the occasional bow.

For protection, a small, rounded leather shield was carried into battle, although in the later medieval period this was replaced with a much larger shield made from the hide of a kind of antelope known as the *lamt*. While larger, the lamt shield remained light. According to tradition, the lamt hide was cured in milk, and the shield was so effective that a saber blow would rebound or become stuck, while arrow holes tended to make only insignificant impressions in the thick surface.

As Berber troops hailed from various tribes rather than a single nation and were often employed as mercenary auxiliaries, there is no single distinctive Berber uniform from this period. It is probable that Berber warriors simply wore their "civilian" garb in battle, which often consisted of a goat-skin cloak and long, flowing unbelted tunics. Another distinctive article of clothing associated with the Berber is the hooded cloak called the *burnus*, which may have been inspired by the Roman legionnaire garment, the *sagum*. Berber warriors with exposed heads could be identified on the battlefield through another means: An ancient tribal custom, practiced into the medieval period, was to shave part of the head before going into battle.

MILITARY ORGANIZATION

Berber gatherings began at the level of the *ikhs*, a group of extended family headed by the eldest male member. The population of a Berber village often included several of these groups, and a Berber tribe comprised a dozen or more villages in a defined geographic area. The smaller of the tribes remained under the familiar system of elder rule, whereas the larger tribes spawned monarchs, some of which were led by kings with dynastic ambitions.

In times of need, warring Berber tribes would put aside their differences and muster into a coalition called a *leff* or *soff*. Such coalitions had political considerations; members pledged offensive assistance to other members or promised aid in defense against rival leffs.

The two most significant early Berber kingdoms were Numidia (present-day Algeria and part of Tunisia) and Mauritania (near present-day Algeria and Morocco). The kings of Numidia and Mauritania raised armies of slaves, freemen, and mercenaries through the time-proven system of taxation. Also in these kingdoms, an aristocratic class developed. Similar to medieval knights, the men of this highborn class became the elite cavalry. The kings could call their tribal subjects to their banners, but the subjects' availability to serve was hindered by agricultural considerations, such as harvesting and sowing. Ultimately, the kingdoms of Numidia and Mauritania were both destroyed by Roman imperial designs.

During the third century, under Emperor Diocletian's reforms, the Romans made a concerted effort to assimilate Berber forces into the Roman military machine. Large numbers of Berbers served with the Romans as *foederati*, semiautonomous allies. The Berber cavalrymen were arranged into relatively vaguely defined squadrons rather than into precise unit designations. These squadrons were led by the Berbers' own leaders, who were then overseen by the Roman generals, who commanded them on the field and on the march. This seems to have been the system typically used when large groups of Berbers were employed as mercenaries.

DOCTRINE, STRATEGY, AND TACTICS

Berber military doctrine remained fairly consistent during this period. There was a marked preference for ambush and guerrilla-style hit-and-run strikes over complex, large-scale maneuvers or siege warfare. Generally, the Berber troops were lightly armored and equipped and were extremely mobile. Roman opinion of the Berber warriors was that they were fierce and swift, but they were also unreliable and poorly armed.

Berbers were experts in guerrilla warfare against larger, better-equipped foes. The favored stratagem was to lead the enemy forces into an ambush on favorable ground by means of feigned retreat, then, once they arrived at a prearranged fixed position, spring the trap. A reserve, usually mounted, would often be kept at a distance and would then surge forward to envelop the enemy from all directions.

Mounts, such as horses, remained an important element in the Berbers' military operations. David Nicolle, a scholar of Berber warfare, gives an illuminating example of Berber ingenuity:

> In the later centuries, with a greater use of camels, the eastern Berber tribes would make these beasts kneel in a big circle as a barrier against cavalry, whose horses tended to fear the camels. Other animals could also be roped together as an inner barrier, while calthrops were scattered outside. Some warriors defended the living perimeter using spears as pikes, while javelin throwers stood between the camels. The best cavalry took up position some way away.

ANCIENT SOURCES

Strabo, the Greek geographer and historian, wrote of the Berber society in his seventeen-volume *Geōgraphica* (c. 7 B.C.E.; *Geography*, 1917-1933). Book 5 of Pliny the Elder's *Naturalis historia* (77 C.E.; *The Historie of the World*, 1601; better known as *Natural History*) contains a valuable cache of information about North Africa and Carthage. Sallust, one of the most shameless pillagers of North Africa, wrote the monographs *I bellum catilinae* (c. 42 B.C.E.; *The Conspiracy of Catilline*, 1608) and *Bellum iugurthinum* (c. 40 B.C.E.; *The Jugurtha War*, 1608), which shed light on this little-known historical event. Appian's *Romaica* (second century C.E.; history of Rome) contains information on the Second and Third Punic Wars and an appendix, which has survived only in part, on the Numidian War. Some information on Berber culture is also contained in the fifth century B.C.E. works of the preeminent classical scholar Herodotus. A book commonly attributed to Julius Caesar, but likely written by another Roman officer, titled *De bello Africo* (49-45 B.C.E.; *Commentaries of the African War*, 1753), deals with the battle between Caesar and Pompey in North Africa and provides details on the role of King Juba of Numidia and the Battle of Thapsus in 46 B.C.E. A fifth century bishop, Victor of Vita, in the small North African province of Byzacene, left behind his work *Historia persecutionis Vandalorum* (fifth century C.E.; *The Memorable and Tragical History, of the Persecution in Africke*, 1605), a rare eyewitness account.

MEDIEVAL SOURCES

Procopius of Caesaria's two-volume *De bello Vandalico* (550; *Vandall Wars*, 1653, in *The History of the Warres of the Emperour Justinian*) covers the Byzantine general Belisarius's campaign against the rebuilt and Vandal-held Carthage. Ibn Abd el-Hakem's work *Kitāb Futūḥ Miṣ wa-al Maghrib wa-akhbārihā* (ninth century; *The History and Conquest of Egypt, North Africa, and Spain*, 1922) book 5, deals with the Muslim conquest of Spain and North Africa in the ninth century C.E. Aḥmad ibn Yaḥyā al-Balādhurī's *Futūḥ al-buldān*, which was translated into English in 1916 as *The Origins of the Islamic State*, contains a great amount of information on the Berbers, including brief discussion of the Muslim advance into North Africa. Even though it was written centuries after the events, Abū al-ʿAbbās Aḥmad ibn Muḥammad ibn ʿIdhārī al-Marrākushī's book *al-Bayān al-mughrib* (eighth or fourteenth century) is also a valuable, if incomplete, resource.

BOOKS AND ARTICLES

Brett, Michael, and Elizabeth Fentress. *The Berbers*. Malden, Mass.: Blackwell, 1997.

Falola, Toyin. *African History Before 1885*. Vol. 1 in *Africa*. Durham, N.C.: Carolina Academic Press, 2000.

Gabriel, Richard A. *Empires at War*. Vol. 2. Westport, Conn.: Greenwood Press, 2005.

Montagne, Robert. *The Berbers: Their Social and Political Organization*. London: Frank Cass, 1973.

Nicolle, David. *The Desert Frontier*. Vol. 5 in *Rome's Enemies*. New York: Osprey, 1996.

Oliver, Roland, and Brian M. Fagan. *Africa in the Iron Age, c. 500 B.C. to A.D. 1400*. New York: Cambridge University Press, 1994.

Santosuosso, Antonio. *Barbarians, Marauders, and Infidels: The Ways of Medieval Warfare*. Boulder, Colo.: Westview Press, 1998.

FILMS AND OTHER MEDIA

The Road Behind, the Road Ahead: A Berber Story. Documentary. Zennia Studio, 2008.

Carthage: A Journey Back in Time. Documentary. Cromwell Productions, 2006.

The Dark Ages. Documentary. History Channel, 2007.

Legions of Rome: Punic Wars. Documentary. Kultur Video, 2007.

Maghreb: Back in the Middle Ages. Documentary. Customflix, 2007.

The Romans in North Africa: A Journey Back in Time. Documentary. Cromwell Productions, 2006.

Michael Coker

TRIBAL WARFARE IN CENTRAL AND EASTERN EUROPE

Dates: c. 500 B.C.E.-800 C.E.

POLITICAL CONSIDERATIONS

The tribes in central and eastern Europe that fought against the Roman Empire for the most part preserved their independence, and from the fifth century C.E., the combined effect of these tribes was to bring about the destruction of the Roman Empire of the West and also to weaken severely the Roman Empire of the East, making it far more susceptible to attack from the Turks, which led to its own military and then political decline. Prior to their defeat of the Romans, the tribes served to unite the Romans, who feared them greatly. The fact that the tribesmen were victorious against Roman armies in battle spread panic and terror to many Roman households, and this led many Roman generals to try to establish their political reputations through fighting against the German tribes. Although the tribes moved, by the fourth century C.E. the Vandals were between the Viadua and the Vistula rivers, the Visigoths were in modern-day Romania, north of the Danube, the Ostrogoths were in southern modern-day Ukraine, and the Huns were further east.

MILITARY ACHIEVEMENT

The Germanic tribes, as well as the Goths and Huns, transformed warfare during the first five centuries C.E., managing to defeat significant strong and well-equipped Roman armies by using their superior mobility in traveling to and also on the battlefield. This allowed a number of tribes to overwhelm and defeat Roman forces many times, the first major occasion being at the Battle of the Teutoburg Forest in 9 C.E., when a Germanic force wiped out three Roman legions. This defeat ended any serious attempt by the Romans to annex Germany or to get supportive tribes to form into a pro-Roman German confederation.

The tribes often combined in their military efforts, and gradually, with the decline of the central power in Rome, they conducted incursions into Roman territory. This continued through to the Battle of Adrianople in 378 C.E., when a Gothic army, using similar tactics, managed to destroy the forty-thousand-strong Roman army of the Emperor Valens in a confrontation some 150 miles northwest of Constantinople. The defeat led to a transformation of Roman military tactics, with the Romans starting to rely much more heavily on cavalry. Even with such changes, however, the Romans were still encountering major problems. In 451 C.E., the Roman emperor Aetius managed to ally with the Visigoths and defeat the Hun army of Attila at the Battle of the Catalaunian Plains, near Châlons, in modern-day France, but although they carried the day on the battlefield, the Romans were unable to drive home their victory, and Attila continued to pose a major threat to his adversaries until his death two years later.

The Germanic tribes formed a large, mobile military force that swept through areas of northern Europe in a way quite unlike that of armies before them. Instead of being solely a force of soldiers, the tribes brought with them their women and children; they formed vast convoys of wagons, chariots, horsemen, and people traveling on foot. By night they would draw their wagons together in a ringed or stockade fashion called a *Wagenburg* to provide the necessary defense for all the tribespeople; in battle they established similar formations. The Romans noted that during their battles with some of the Germanic tribes, the tribes' women and children would bang drums and gongs from within the stockade, both to inspire their own soldiers and to frighten those of the other side.

It was under Julius Caesar, during his wars in Gaul in 58-51 B.C.E., that the Romans first came to notice the strong fighting spirit of the German tribes. Caesar, who was much more adaptable than most of his contemporaries, and many of his Roman predecessors, in accommodating his fighting style to the terrain, immediately saw the value of the Germans. While the Romans relied heavily on the mass formations of their infantry—the legions attacking slowly and steadily—Caesar noticed the effectiveness of the Germans' style of attacking a single point in their opponents' battle line in a lightning charge. This led Caesar to start using Germans in his own army, and they served to good effect against the Gauls.

The Romans continued using large numbers of non-Romans as auxiliaries in their armies, and eventually the Roman cavalry was largely made up of these auxiliaries, recruited often from areas outside the empire itself. As a result, by the third century C.E. large numbers of Goths were serving as cavalry in the Roman forces, and by the late fourth century, many Roman cavalry units were made up entirely of Goths. This incorporation of Goths into the Roman army helped to alleviate the Roman weakness in lack of cavalry in many battles, but because many of the Roman generals were seriously worried about the loyalty of these cavalry units, they occasionally did not use the units to best effect.

It was the Goths' crushing defeat of Emperor Valens at the Battle of Adrianople in 378 C.E. that signaled a major change in the nature of the battles fought by the Byzantines. Until then they had, like their predecessors, relied heavily on tight infantry formations, but they saw that they had to change and incorporate large numbers of cavalry, especially heavy cavalry, into their armies. It was not long before the heavy cavalry came to constitute a substantial part of the Byzantine forces—the cavalry being formed from their own soldiers, not just those of their allies, as had been the case for centuries before.

Although the Byzantines adapted, the Roman armies of the Western Empire did not do so, and this meant that the western Romans often had to ally with potential enemies, such as King Theodoric I of the Visigoths, who fought alongside the Roman emperor Aetius in 451 in the Battle of the Catalaunian Plains. This battle against the Huns saw the infantry essentially as spectators, with the fighting being done by large cavalry units, and it was the cavalry charge by Attila that nearly carried the day and did result in the death of Theodoric. However, the Huns were outnumbered and forced to withdraw with heavy losses, giving eventual victory to the Romans and Visigoths. With each of the victors worried about the other gaining too much of a military advantage, the victory was not pressed, and Attila was able to lead the rest of his forces away and continue over the next two years to harry his opponents.

Although the Romans and the Visigoths formed an alliance, in 410 the Visigoths had managed to invade Italy and sack Rome under King Alaric I, and in 455, Genseric, king of the Vandals, also managed to sack Rome. Rome had barely recovered when it was sacked again in 546 by Totila, king of the Ostrogoths; this assault led to a major decline in stature from which the city did not begin to recover until more than one thousand years later with the increase in papal authority.

WEAPONS, UNIFORMS, AND ARMOR

Significant advances were made in weaponry during the tribal warfare that took place from the fourth century B.C.E. to the eighth century C.E. Throughout this period, the use of cavalry and also light infantry dramatically transformed the fighting, and as a result the emphasis started to be very much on minimal heavy weapons, strong morale, and weapons that were effective against Roman infantry.

The shields that the tribes carried in battle tended to be round—in contrast to both the rectangular curved shields of the Romans and the rectangular or nearly rectangular ones used by many of the Gauls. That said, some rectangular shields of the period have been recovered from burial sites and peat bogs in modern-day Germany and Denmark. The major difference between the Germanic shield and the Roman one was that the Germanic shield was specifically designed to be light, and it was used largely for deflecting opponents' weapons; the Roman shield, or

DOMAINS OF EUROPEAN TRIBES, C. 500 C.E.

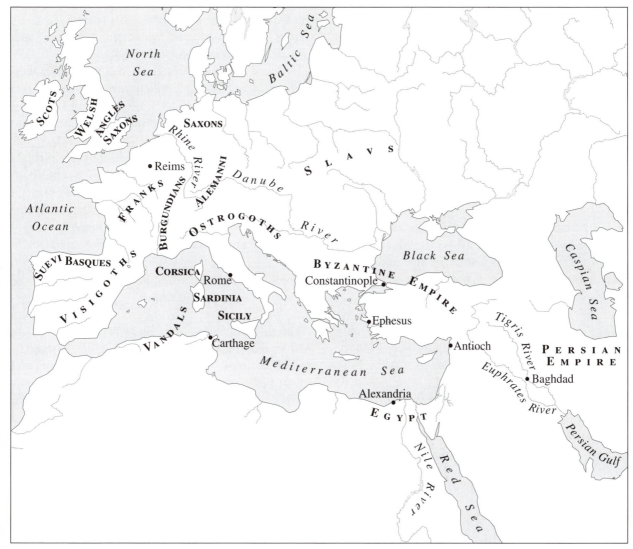

scutum, in contrast, could be used to cover most of the parts of the body. The Germanic shield also had on it a metal protuberance known as a boss, which was used in charging at Roman lines.

As the Germanic soldiers had to move quickly, their armor was much more limited than that used by the Romans, often being made from leather rather than metal or consisting of iron plates rather than the breastplates so commonly worn by the Romans. Of the tribes, the Visigoths are thought to be the major group that gradually adapted to use heavier armor,

and this was often when they were fighting as allies of the Romans. Germanic chiefs did wear some armor, but few of their ordinary soldiers did so—in fact, some went into battle naked to show their strength and prowess. Archaeologists, however, have discovered some mail armor from 200 B.C.E. in a peat bog in modern-day Denmark, and many helmets have survived from the Germanic soldiers—these being used, it would seem, as much to designate rank as for protection in battle.

The great advantages of the Germanic and Gothic

infantry lay in both where the soldiers could strike on a battlefield and their strength as individual warriors. They trained extensively in the use of the large sword and axes, which were usually swung at their opponents rather than used to thrust or stab, the traditional Roman fighting styles. Most often the swords and battle-axes were used one-handed; little archaeological evidence exists of the use of the larger two-handed sword of medieval Europe. Many of these soldiers would also be armed with several spears, which they would generally throw before engaging the enemy, a process that gradually led to their using Roman-style javelins with great effect.

The cavalry were also armed with spears or lances, and it was not unknown for soldiers to ride into battle with a number of spears that they threw at the ranks of their opponents prior to charging the enemy lines

with their horses. Caesar praised the use of the cavalry by the Germans and went as far as recruiting many of them to complement his forces; these soldiers were armed with lances or javelins and also two-edged slashing swords.

For most of the tribes, the horses themselves were generally unprotected, even though they served very much as part of the attack, the horses being flung against the tight formations of Roman infantry. Like the infantry, as the emphasis was very much on suddenness of attack and the advantage of mobility, the cavalry of the Germanic and Gothic tribes tended not to be heavily armored. In later battles against the Byzantines, however—especially after the Byzantines themselves started deploying heavy cavalry— the Germanic tribes began using horse armor.

MILITARY ORGANIZATION

The full nature of the military organization of the tribes that formed the Germanic, Gothic, Visigothic, Lombard, and Hun forces is not known with any degree of certainty. This is because the only descriptions of the tribes' armies that are available come from Romans who saw masses of people attacking their soldiers and were generally unable to discern how the individual units of their opponents worked. Obviously, the sheer numbers of tribal peoples who were able to be mustered at short notice to fight the Romans, and also presumably each other, indicate that there had to have been a sophisticated method of recruitment, training, and deployment. It is also probable that the system of government of the tribes underwent change and development during this long period—as it did in Rome and other places that are well documented.

The surviving evidence suggests that the method used by the German tribes was not dissimilar to that utilized by the Anglo-Saxons in early medieval England, about which much more information is available. The Romans described the overall ruler of a Germanic tribe as a "king," but that probably reflects their interpretation of a supreme ruler. It is possible that the position of ruler was hereditary in some areas and for some periods of time, but the concept of di-

North Wind Picture Archives via AP Images

A German warrior shown with a Roman general.

rect succession of father to son over a long period of time seems unlikely given the evidence to the contrary.

The "king"—the historian Tacitus uses the term *rex*—was therefore probably a chief who was elected from a meeting of the chiefs, and he ruled, and led his soldiers in battle, during his period in office, which could be for life, although some rulers were overthrown. The power of this chief therefore rested on his prestige, his personality, and his ability to persuade others. Even on a battlefield his orders were not necessarily routinely obeyed, although generally they were, as the soldiers were fighting for a common purpose. Under the supreme chief there were local chiefs and also village chiefs.

For the raising of armies, and also for administration and the collection of taxes, the villages were combined administratively into a grouping called a "hundred." There would therefore be chiefs of individual villages who would be answerable to the leader in charge of the hundred, who would provide about one hundred soldiers for the keeping of law and order. In times of crisis, or when the tribes were planning to attack, it seems likely that the Germanic hundred would be capable of putting between five thousand and six thousand soldiers into battle. Their chief, with his advisers, would be responsible for leading them on the battlefield.

DOCTRINE, STRATEGY, AND TACTICS

For many of the early German tribes, the primary tactic was to use shock troops—mainly cavalry, but also fast runners on foot—to attack a particular point in the opponents' front line. This would, if successful, lead to the formation of a wedge that would split the forces of the opponents—usually the Romans—and cause panic. The Goths and the Huns later developed this tactic further with cavalry attacks, feigned retreats, and the like. The German leaders had to develop their battle plans carefully beforehand, as their armies were not as well disciplined as those of the Romans and could easily be outmaneuvered by clever Roman commanders. This meant that the charging of the troops at the start of a battle had to be sufficiently fierce to push the battle in their favor quickly. In longer battles, when the sides were evenly balanced, the victories would tend to go to the Romans—which explains why most of the Germanic tribes chose either to attack when they had a vast numerical advantage or to ambush their opponents.

In those instances when large Germanic or other tribal armies fought the Romans, the tribes drew up careful plans, usually with the aim of enticing the Romans further into their territory and setting up an ambush. The destruction of three Roman legions at the Battle of the Teutoburg Forest in 9 C.E. is the most famous example of the success of such tactics. Even when extensive planning had taken place, however, speed was a crucial element for the Germanic tribes in battle.

Thus the most important part of the strategy of the Germanic tribes remained the soldiers who would form a wedge into the opponents' battle lines. The Romans labeled these the *cunei*, following from the Latin term *cuneus*, which, it is believed, came from the term *caput porcunum* (head of a hog). The term stems from the tribes' use of a standard in the shape of the head of a hog or boar that would he held aloft to indicate the direction of any attack. Imbued with some religious significance, this would serve as a battle standard, the capture of which was similar to the capture of Roman standards.

ANCIENT SOURCES

The ancient sources of information on the Germanic tribes—the Goths, Visigoths, Vandals, Lombards, and Huns—are invariably Roman accounts. These vary tremendously in their coverage and analysis. The earliest significant account is *Comentarii de bello Gallico* (52-51 B.C.E.; *The Gallic Wars*, in his *Commentaries*, 1609), Julius Caesar's work on the Gallic Wars, in which the great Roman general relates how he succeeded in capturing Gaul. Caesar achieved his success after he managed to win over some Germans to his side with money and other inducements. He is complimentary about the fighting strengths of the Germans, as he not only fought against them but also fought on the same side as them.

De origine et situ Germanorum, also known as *Germania* (c. 98; *The Description of Germanie*, 1598), by the Roman historian Tacitus, also details the Germanic tribes, discussing their traits and their everyday lives. All the information from Tacitus is secondhand, however, as the author himself never went to Germany, and recent historians have cast doubt on some of his ideas about links between tribes. It has been supposed that Tacitus drew information from Pliny the Elder's *Bella germaniae* (c. 47 C.E.), as well as from other published accounts and tales told by soldiers and merchants.

BOOKS AND ARTICLES

Barrett, John C., Andrew P. Fitzpatrick, and Lesley Macinnes. *Barbarians and Romans in North-West Europe, from the Later Republic to Late Antiquity.* Oxford, England: British Archaeological Reports, 1989.

Davidson, H. R. Ellis. *The Sword in Anglo-Saxon England.* Rochester, N.Y.: Boydell Press, 1994.

Fields, Nic. *The Hun.* New York: Osprey, 2006.

Halsall, Guy. *Barbarian Migrations and the Roman West, 376-568.* New York: Cambridge University Press, 2007.

MacDowall, Simon. *Germanic Warrior.* New York: Osprey, 1996.

Randers-Pehrson, Justine Davis. *Barbarians and Romans: The Birth Struggle of Europe, A.D. 400-700.* Norman: University of Oklahoma Press, 1983.

Todd, Malcolm. *Everyday Life of the Barbarians: Goths, Franks, and Vandals.* London: B. T. Batsford, 1972.

Whitby, Michael. *Rome at War, 293-696 C.E.* New York: Osprey, 2002.

Wilcox, Peter. *Germanics and Dacians.* Vol. 1 in *Rome's Enemies.* New York: Osprey, 1994.

FILMS AND OTHER MEDIA

The Fall of the Roman Empire. Feature film. Paramount Pictures, 1964.

Gladiator. Feature film. Dreamworks Pictures, 2000.

Teutons, Goths, Vandals, and Huns: The Tribes That Made Europe. Documentary series. SBS, 2003.

Justin Corfield

THE ANCIENT WORLD

WORLD

EASTERN, CENTRAL, AND SOUTHERN ASIA

CHINA
ANCIENT
Dates: c. 1523 B.C.E.-588 C.E.

MILITARY ACHIEVEMENT

Chinese tradition holds that throughout most of its history, China has relegated warfare and military matters to a secondary role within society. From the earliest dynastic records onward, the Chinese have deliberately differentiated *wen* (cultural or civil) and *wu* (martial) matters. The perfectly ordered society is one in which literate culture triumphs over mere force, and military matters are disdained. Civilized Chinese need not use brute force to maintain internal peace or repulse external aggression. Instead, cultural superiority and demonstrated moral virtue suffice in the pursuit of peace.

Despite these ideals, China's early history revolved around conquest and the centralization of the state. Every major dynasty was founded through warfare, and once unified, China guarded its frontiers with military force and sought to expand its territory at the expense of southern and western neighbors. Inevitably, each dynasty in turn fell as a result of warfare.

The Shang (Chang) are the first historically identifiable ancestors of the Chinese. Chengtang (Ch'eng T'ang) is credited with founding the dynasty, following his decisive victory over Emperor Jie (Chieh) of the Xia (Hsia) Dynasty in 1523 B.C.E. at the Battle of Ming Jiao (Ming Chiao). In a recurring pattern of Chinese historiography, the victorious commander's success is attributed to his moral superiority and his opponent's wretchedness.

Accordingly, the Shang fell as a result of Emperor Zhou Xin's (Chou Hsin) overall bad character and practice of mutilating pregnant women and murdering innocents with abandon. King Wu (the Martial King) led the Zhou into a decisive battle at Muye (Mu-yeh) in 1027 B.C.E. According to the *Shiji* (*Shih*

Chi) annals, the Zhou were vastly outnumbered, confronting a Shang army of 700,000 with a lilliputian force of 300 chariots, 3,000 Tiger Guards, and 45,000 foot soldiers. Despite the Shang's overwhelming numbers, the Zhou routed them in a matter of hours. Following an initial charge of one hundred infantry, the chariots were deployed to the astonishment of the Shang troops, who reportedly had never encountered such a mass attack. After their king fled, the Shang forces "inverted their weapons" and gave up the fight. After the death of King Wu, his brother, the duke of Zhou, acted as regent for his young nephew. During his regency, the Zhou domain expanded eastward and purportedly brought fifty states under Zhou control.

The Zhou policy of decentralized rule in its peripheral territories eventually led to its decline in 722 B.C.E., when an alliance of disgruntled vassals and a nomadic tribe killed the Zhou king. Despite moving the capital farther east to avoid further incursions, the Zhou never fully recovered, inaugurating nearly five hundred years of unremitting violence and warfare.

The remaining half of the Zhou dynastic age is subdivided into two sections: the Chunqiu (Ch'un Ch'iu) or Spring and Autumn period (c. 770-476 B.C.E.) and the Warring States period (c. 475-221 B.C.E.). This was an age characterized by the growth of powerful independent states, shifting alliances, and open warfare. Beside a dozen major states, innumerable smaller states existed, some no more than a town surrounded by a thick earthen wall and a few square miles of marginal territory. As Zhou power declined, the major states asserted increasing independence, until, by the Warring States period, their rulers had assumed the title of king. New technologies, including the long sword, crossbow, and iron implements, allowed the larger states to conquer and control surrounding territories.

Around 307 B.C.E. King Wu Ling of Zhao (Chao) took a cue from the nomadic tribes to the north and introduced the deployment of cavalry. Faster and far more mobile than the war chariot, cavalry revolutionized Warring States conflicts and prompted a change in Chinese uniforms: In place of their traditional long robes, Chinese soldiers now adopted the short tunics and trousers of their northern neighbors. Infantry also took on greater importance, as wars spread into the mountainous terrain and marshy valleys of the Chang (Yangtze) region.

Final unification occurred in 221 B.C.E. when the Qin (Ch'in) systematically defeated its rivals and imposed centralized control over the region. The Qin victory has been traced to two important factors: the strict and ruthless policies of Legalism, which brought Qin subjects under the iron hand of the state, and a highly efficient military structure in which cavalry, iron weapons, and massed infantry overwhelmed their opponents. Following unification, the Qin ordered the confiscation of their opponents' weapons, which were subsequently melted down and molded into twelve statues at the new capital. Old states were abolished, the country was divided into thirty-six commanderies headed by a civil governor and military commander, and prominent families moved to the capital. Once in power, the First Emperor Qin Shihuangdiiqin Shihuangdi (Ch'in Shih huang-ti; 259-210 B.C.E.) secured his northern borders and took control of the southern coast near Guangzhou (Canton).

Upon Shihuangdi's death in 210 B.C.E., the Qin Dynasty immediately fell into chaos, and by 206 B.C.E., the Han Dynasty had been established. Despite constant invasions from the north by the nomadic Xiongnu (Hsiung-nu), the Han managed to retain control of the country, and under the leadership of Wu Di (Wu Tii, 156-87 B.C.E.), the Martial Emperor, greatly expanded their territorial holdings. Between 136 and 56 B.C.E., twenty-five major expeditions were sent, fourteen to the northwest and west, three to the northeast, and eight to the south. In one case, a force of more than 300,000 launched an attack on the Xiongnu (133 B.C.E.). To safeguard his conquests, Wu Di established garrisons along the military routes and sent more than 2,000,000 Chinese to the northwest as colonists. One legendary encounter is reported to have occurred in 42 B.C.E. While on an expedition in the northern district of Sogdiana, a Chinese force purportedly engaged a group of Xiongnu accompanied by Roman legionaries. The Chinese victory is attributed to the use of the crossbow, the arrows of which apparently easily penetrated Roman armor and shields.

By 190 C.E., the Han had begun its decline, and in 194 General Cao Cao (Ts'ao Ts'ao; 155-220 C.E.) had

TURNING POINTS

1600-1066 B.C.E.	The Shang Dynasty rules in China.
1200 B.C.E.	The chariot is introduced to China from the northwest and is later adapted for use in siege warfare.
1066-256 B.C.E.	The Zhou (Chou) Dynasty rules in China.
5th cent. B.C.E.	The crossbow is developed in China, providing more power, speed, and accuracy than the composite bow.
307 B.C.E.	King Wu Ling of Zhao, inspired by steppe nomad tribes to the north, introduces the use of cavalry in China.
221-206 B.C.E.	The Qin (Ch'in) Dynasty rules in China.
206 B.C.E.-220 C.E.	The Han Dynasty rules in China.
220-280	The Wei, Shu, and Wu Dynasties rule in China during Three Kingdoms period.
265-316	Western Jin (Chin) Dynasty rules.
4th cent.	The use of stirrups is introduced in China, allowing cavalry armor to become heavier and more formidable.
317-420	The Eastern Jin Dynasty rules.
386-588	The Southern and Northern Dynasties rule concurrently in China.

emerged victorious in the ensuing civil war. Upon his death, however, the southern states refused to recognize the central authority of the upstart Cao Cao family, and the Han Empire was quickly divided into three major regions, inaugurating yet another 400-year period of almost-constant warfare.

Following the breakup of the Han, three kingdoms emerged. The Wei (220-265) dominated the north and moved into Korea, Shu-Han (221-263) in the southwest subdued several indigenous tribes, and the southern Wu (222-280) expanded as far as Vietnam. In 265, following the conquest of the Shu-Han and the Wu, a Wei general announced the creation of a new dynasty, the Jin (Chin), which would survive until 420. Southern China would then experience a succession of four southern dynasties, lasting into the sixth century. Meanwhile, a series of northern tribes ruled Northern China until 386, when the northern Wei successfully defeated the last kingdom and secured rule until 533.

WEAPONS, UNIFORMS, AND ARMOR

Weaponry evolved considerably over the period from 1500 B.C.E. to 500 C.E. During the Shang Dynasty, metallurgy had advanced to the point that nobility was primarily armed with bronze weapons, whereas commoners fought with arms made of wood, stone, or animal bones. Among the common weapons found in grave sites are bronze-tipped spears, probably the earliest known weapons in Chinese history; daggers; the composite reflexive bow and arrow, with the bow both longer and more powerful than its Western counterpart; and the *ge-* (*ko-*) halberd, a battle-ax with a curved bronze blade horizontally mounted atop a long wooden shaft approximately 43 inches long. Used primarily to hook and then slash one's opponent, late variations added a spear to the tip, a hooked blade behind the first, and another to the butt.

The war chariot also played a central role in early Chinese warfare. First introduced to China from the northwest in 1200 B.C.E., the chariot evolved from a symbol of royal power and prestige to a vehicle adapted to the exigencies of siege warfare during the Warring States period. Typically, a chariot team con-

sisted of three men: the driver in the center, a warrior armed with a *ge*-halberd on the right, and an archer to the left. Each would be accompanied by a platoon of foot soldiers armed with spears. Whereas Shang chariots were used primarily as elevated, mobile command posts for royalty, their Zhou counterparts were employed extensively in battle. States were judged by the number of chariots they could field, and battle records routinely reported the numbers captured. The *Zuo Zhuan* (*Tso chuan*, c. 475-221 B.C.E.; *Tso chuan*, 1872) attributes 4,900 chariots to the large Jin state, whereas the much smaller Zhu (Chu) boasted 600 chariots.

As the Warring States period progressed, the chariot was adapted to the emergence of armored infantry and new siege warfare tactics. To ward off infantry, knife blades were added to wheel hubs. Furthermore, whereas previous armies had routinely avoided fortified cities rather than expending manpower on their capture, the newly significant role of cities as economic and political centers now warranted aggressive assaults. Accordingly, chariots were outfitted with large shields, towers, battering rams, movable ladders, and multiarrow crossbows. In defense, towns employed a bewildering array of iron and wooden caltrops, collapsible fences, sharp iron stakes, "mined" moats, and a variety of long axes, halberds, firelances, and hammers. Vessels containing water, iron, sand, and human excrement were also available to hurl upon the heads of besiegers.

Swords do not appear until the middle of the Chunqiu, or Spring and Autumn, period, when they were probably adopted from steppe nomads. The earliest were fashioned from bronze, with iron swords becoming widespread during the Qin Dynasty. Although long, double-edged swords are mentioned as early as the seventh century B.C.E., most would appear to have been relatively short and used principally for thrusting rather than slashing. By the Warring States period, they had become standardized as the *jien* (*chien*), a double-edged sword with a blade measuring approximately 2 feet, eventually reaching a length of 3 feet during the Han Dynasty.

Clearly the most important innovation in early Chinese warfare was the crossbow. Developed in China sometime in the fifth century B.C.E., the new weapon was more powerful and far more accurate than the composite bow. The standard crossbow consisted of a wooden stock, a bow of laminated bamboo, and an intricately designed bronze trigger mechanism. The mortised stock supported the bow and included both a channel for the arrow and a pistol grip. Trigger mechanisms were complicated devices containing three moving pieces on two shafts that could hold a very heavy-tension load while firing easily and delivering a bolt with greater impact than that of a high-velocity rifle. By removing two pins, the mechanism could be dismantled in case of capture, and the Chinese would guard the secret of its construction well into the Han Dynasty. The earliest

bows could be hand-cocked, whereas the later, more powerful versions required either leg strength or a rope tied to the waist. By the time of the Qin Dynasty, crossbows had evolved into repeating models, those which could fire two bolts simultaneously, and larger, winch-powered versions mounted on carts and chariots.

The first Chinese armor appeared during the Shang Dynasty as simple, lacquered leather breastplates secured with leather thongs. Leather continued to be used as late as the sixth century C.E. By contrast, the first helmets were bronze and highly decorated. The construction of Zhou armor became more detailed, with body armor composed of small rectangu-

Robin Chen

Much that has been learned about Qin armor of the third century B.C.E. *is known from the life-size terra-cotta figures unearthed near the first emperor's tomb.*

lar pieces strung into rows and fastened with leather thongs, a process known as lamellar construction. Individual pieces and the rows themselves were then lacquered and colored.

A great deal about Qin armor is known from the life-size terra-cotta figures unearthed near the first emperor's tomb. Several styles of armor are noted, including short mail jackets of lamellar construction designed to cover the entire upper body; lamellar chest protectors; lamellar armor for charioteers, which includes both neck guards and armor extending to the wrists with plates to protect the hands; and that of the cavalry, shorter than the others and missing shoulder guards. Under the armor, each warrior wears a long-sleeved robe reaching to the knees, along with a heavy cloth bundle at the neck. Short trousers are also discernible.

Not until the time of the Han Dynasty was iron used for certain types of armor. Most armor consisted of plates arranged in the lamellar construction, designed to protect the neck, front, back, and thighs. One such suit contained 500 plates and weighed nearly 22 pounds. By the late Han Dynasty, authors begin referring to brilliant dark armor, which may suggest a suit made of decarburized steel, although none have been recovered as yet.

Robin Chen

Close-up of a Qin soldier and horse from the terra-cotta excavations.

Infantry typically appeared without armor and were generally equipped with little more than a shield and helmet. Most infantrymen wore a simple tunic, trousers, and leather shin guards. Helmets varied from the simple head-covering tied under the chin to heavier versions with straight earflaps. Iron helmets began to appear during the Warring States period but did not become prevalent until the Han Dynasty. Cavalry were furnished with a helmet, a mail jacket with a high collar and flared bottom, and a chaplike protector for the front of the leg.

Horse armor, or barding, appears in some of the earliest histories, but no evidence exists for its use until the end of the Han Dynasty. By that time, the cavalry had become an integral part of warfare, and as the cavalryman's armor improved, measures were also taken to ensure the safety of the horse. Early barding was of a single piece, protecting the top and underside of the horse's neck down to the chest, with some also covering the underside of the belly. As it evolved, barding became five separate pieces: head mask, neck guard, chest and shoulder guards, side armor, and rump armor. Lamellar construction was again used, with materials varying based on period and geographic region. After stirrups were introduced in the fourth century, the armor for cavalrymen and horses became heavier and more formidable.

Shields varied according to usage, with those carried by charioteers slightly longer than the *ge*-halberd, and those for the infantrymen somewhat shorter. Built on wooden frames, shields were made of either leather or lacquered cloth stretched across the front. Occasionally the leather was fortified by bronze and in some cases painted with patterns and designs. Iron shields appeared alongside iron weapons and the crossbow, although in relatively small quantities until the Qin and Han Dynasties.

MILITARY ORGANIZATION

Shang Dynasty military organization is open to a great deal of speculation. Given the paucity of reliable literary sources, scholars are dependent on archaeological evidence and speculation concerning the actual role of chariots in early warfare. It is clear that Shang social structure centered on clan units designated as *zu* (*tsu*). Most scholars believe that the zu represent military units assigned to protect the walled towns in which they resided. The zu chief functioned as the local military leader; the same arrangement applied to the royal capital, with the king acting as military leader for the kingdom. Each zu may have numbered one hundred members of the nobility, all under the command of the chief or king. A standing army consisting of selected zu members maintained order during peacetime, and all members were subject to mobilization when necessary. In such cases, ten zu were combined to form an army of 10,000. Oracle records suggest that infantry and archers alike were organized into companies of one hundred warriors. Three such companies constituted a regiment, deployed as left, middle, and right companies.

Under the Zhou Dynasty, the chariot emerged as the most important factor in organizing the military. Later tradition holds that each three-man chariot team was accompanied by a platoon of twenty-five infantry, arranged into five squads. Five companies of four chariots were further organized into brigades, then into platoons of 25, divisions of 2,500, and armies of 12,500. Command originated with the emperor, who often led many campaigns himself. A variety of commanders served under him; unfortunately, little is known concerning their functions. Included are such ministers as the Director of Horses, the Runner of Horses, the Commandant, and the Commander. None, however, appear to have been entrusted with full command over imperial forces.

Apart from local variations, this organizational structure held throughout the Spring and Autumn and Warring States periods. However, whereas warfare in the former was conducted by the nobility following strict codes of honor and chivalrous behavior, the latter was marked by increasing violence and retributive combat. As war intensified, the need for manpower increased dramatically, with forced conscription becoming the norm. Although only a single male from each family was required to serve during the Spring and Autumn period, every male became subject to military levy during the Warring States period.

Qin armies were filled through the conscription of peasants into local militia units available for immediate call-ups. Every male between the ages of seventeen and sixty served as either a warrior or a laborer. The Han modified this policy, filling its ranks with conscripts, volunteers, and convicts. Every male between the ages of twenty-three and fifty-six was required to serve two years, one in training, the other in active service at a garrison. Following their stint, soldiers joined the local militia until age fifty-six.

Both the Qin and Han used increasingly sophisticated armies combining infantry, chariots, crossbowmen, and cavalry. The first Qin emperor implemented the use of mounted crossbowmen and their coordination with the composite bow. These combined armies allowed the Chinese to deploy small independent units, as well as traditionally organized larger armies, in the field.

Although the nobility continued to fill the highest command positions, junior officers began to emerge from the general rank and file, being chosen on the basis of ability. Advancement was based on merit, with an elaborate system of differentiated pay relative to one's seniority and rank. Officers were assigned as a particular need arose. Titles and roles related specifically to the campaign, with several generals assigned to each to avoid possible coups.

The Han military was organized into three principal units: a standing garrison at the capital, a task force on the march, and a permanent frontier defense. Once mobilized in an emergency, the military was organized into divisions led by the generals, regiments led by colonels, companies led by captains, and platoons led by commanders. Although local variations would appear in the chaos that followed upon the collapse of the Han, this basic organizational structure as established by the Qin and Han continued to prevail.

The size of Chinese armies has been notoriously difficult to calculate, particularly for the earliest Shang and Western Zhou periods. As noted above, the war between the Zhou and Shang was said to have been fought by a Shang army of 700,000 and a Zhou force of 300 chariots, 3,000 Tiger Guards, and 45,000 foot soldiers. By the Spring and Autumn period, when warfare had become highly ritualized and was dominated by aristocratic charioteers, field armies typically numbered in the thousands but would appear to have rarely exceeded 10,000. As the scale of war increased in the Warring States period, the size of armies grew dramatically. In order to lay siege to fortified cities and to conduct wars that often took years to complete, hundreds of thousands of men were required. According to one contemporary account, the typical army consisted of "one thousand chariots, ten thousands of cavalry, and several hundred thousand armored warriors." The smallest of the warring states fielded armies of more than 300,000; the largest, such as Qin, commanded more than 1,000,000. Likewise, Han expeditions numbering from 50,000 to 300,000 were routinely sent out to quell rebellions and punish nomadic invaders.

DOCTRINE, STRATEGY, AND TACTICS

Throughout the Shang and early Zhou periods, warfare was violent and fought in the Homeric style.

Chariots served as transport or observational platforms, and warriors fought with spears, axes, and composite bows. If the military classic the *Taigong* (*T'ai Kung*, c. third century B.C.E.; *Tai Kung's Six Secret Teachings*, 1993) is to be trusted in its account of the Zhou triumph over the Shang, total warfare was to be fought by utilizing every conceivable method and resource necessary to achieve victory. The state's resources and all customary means of production

North Wind Picture Archives via AP Images

A Chinese Tiger Guard with weapons.

CHINA DURING THE WARRING STATES AND HAN DYNASTY, 475 B.C.E.-221 C.E.

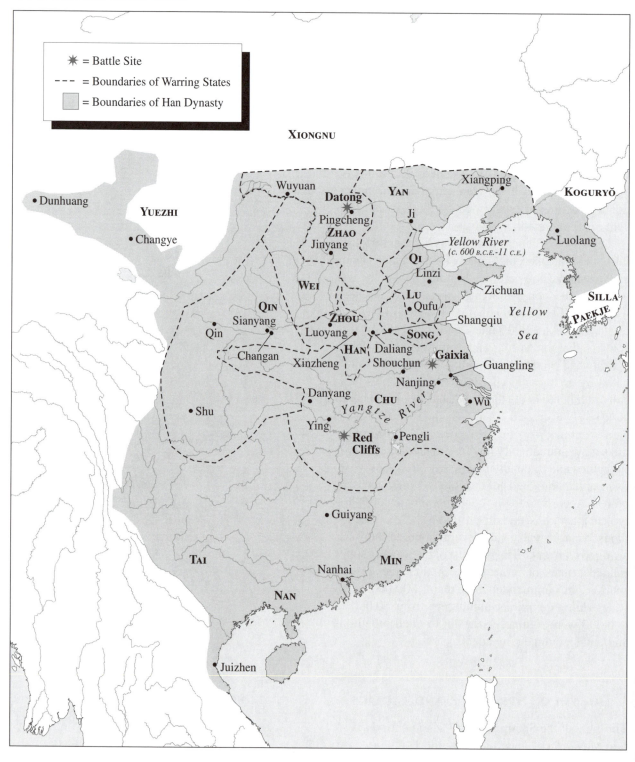

= Battle Site

- - - = Boundaries of Warring States

= Boundaries of Han Dynasty

XIONGNU

Dunhuang

YUEZHI

Changye

Wuyuan

Datong

YAN

Xiangping

KOGURYŎ

Pingcheng

Ji

Luolang

ZHAO

Jinyang

Yellow River
(c. 600 B.C.E.-11 C.E.)

QI

Linzi

Zichuan

WEI

LU

Qufu

*Yellow
Sea*

SILLA

PAEKJE

QIN

Sianyang

ZHOU

Shangqiu

Qin

Luoyang

SONG

Changan

HAN

Daliang

Gaixia

Xinzheng

Shouchun

Guangling

Nanjing

Danyang

CHU

Wu

Shu

Yangtze River

Ying

**Red
Cliffs**

Pengli

Guiyang

TAI

MIN

Nanhai

NAN

Juizhen

were to be employed in the campaign's execution. Strategically, the capable general would analyze the entire situation before engaging the enemy, gauging such factors as terrain, methods of attack and counterattack, escape routes, and techniques for psychological warfare. The *Taigong* advocates employing subterfuge and deception as the most effective means of securing victory. Among other tactics, the successful campaign would utilize feints, false attacks, and limited encounters to confuse and disorient the enemy before the main attack. In prosecuting the war, the best strategies would promote confusion within the enemy's ranks through aggression, misinformation, and speed. The humane treatment of prisoners would encourage others to surrender.

A new era of warfare began in the Spring and Autumn period. This was the great age of chivalry, in which honor and virtue dictated both strategy and the conduct of warfare. Fighting was ideally a game played between members of the nobility, mounted in chariots and accompanied by platoons of foot soldiers. During the heyday of chariot warfare, gentlemen studied the arts of charioteering, archery, and virtuous conduct. Actual combat followed an excessively strict code of conduct calling for bravery, valor, and honor. War was to be pursued with moderation and respect for the opponent. For instance, the duke of Song (Sung) waited for his enemy to cross a river and arrange his battle forces before launching his attack. Following his humiliating defeat, the duke justified his action by referring to the sage, who "does not crush the feeble nor order the attack until his enemy has formed his ranks." In another instance, "Yen Hsi shot a man in the eyebrow and retired, saying 'I have no valor. I was aiming at his eye.'"

Such sentiments were forgotten during the Warring States period. However, even as the violence escalated, strategists continued to advocate deception and speed as the primary means of securing victory. Siege warfare introduced new strategies and tactics, as massive armies sought to wrest control of fortified cities from their occupants, who in turn deployed new technologies designed to repulse the aggressors. In this regard, the Mohists became the undisputed masters of defensive warfare in ancient China.

Bingfa (c. 510 B.C.E.; *The Art of War*, 1910), by Sunzi (Sun Tzu; fl. c. 500 B.C.E.), is certainly the most famous text from this period. A general in the service of Wu, Sunzi had the primary objective of obtaining victory without combat. He argued that a more comprehensive victory could be forged by using diplomatic means, breaking up alliances, and thwarting the enemy's own strategy. In general, one should gain victory at the least cost possible, for both oneself and the enemy. "Thus attaining one hundred victories in one hundred battles is not the height of excellence. Subjugating the enemy's army without fighting is the true height of excellence." Failing that, he emphasized the manipulation of the enemy through the use of terrain, psychology, and the employment of both unorthodox and orthodox methods. Sunzi believed that "warfare is the way [*dao/tao*] of deception," advancing where least expected and attacking where the enemy is least prepared. Although he advocated unorthodox methods such as flanking movements and circular thrusts, Sunzi also insisted that orthodox measures could be effective, if they were employed in an unorthodox manner.

While specific tactics and strategies evolved and adapted to new technologies and the changing face of war, the fundamental principles espoused by Sunzi and other classical theoreticians continued to hold sway. From the Warring States period to the chaos following the fall of the Han, Chinese warfare emphasized the doctrine of maneuverability. Beginning with the fundamental organization of armies into flexible, self-reliant units of five, military maneuvers sought to exploit enemy weaknesses through speed, deception, and misdirection. Every strategist sought to manipulate the enemy into disadvantageous positions by using surprise, by exploiting climatic and topographical factors, and by psychologically and physically destabilizing the enemy to gain temporary, context-specific advantages.

Thus, even as the Han adapted the cavalry, they devised new strategies to defeat it. In 99 B.C.E., Li Ling defeated a cavalry of 30,000 using only 5,000 infantrymen. Behind a line of infantry armed with shields and pikes, Li Ling positioned archers with powerful multiple-firing crossbows. The nomadic horsemen continually charged unsuccessfully. Zhuge

Liang (Chu-ko Liang, 181-234), who served as adviser to the founder of the Shu-Han Dynasty (221-263), was a brilliant mathematician, mechanical engineer, and military strategist who both used and wrote a commentary on Sunzi's *The Art of War*. Said to have never fallen in battle, Zhuge became one of China's most celebrated heroes, was named a Confucian saint in 1724, and was immortalized in Luo Guanzhong's (Lo Kuan-chung; c. 1320-c. 1380) fourteenth century historical novel *San kuo chi yen-i* (*Romance of the Three Kingdoms*, 1925). Subsequent generations of tacticians continued to revere and employ the stratagems formulated by Sunzi and his contemporaries.

ANCIENT SOURCES

The most important primary sources fall into two basic categories. The first are the numerous histories compiled throughout this period. These include the *Shujing* (*Shu ching*), or *Book of History* (1918), which purports to cover the years 2357-627 B.C.E.; the *Chunqiu* (*Ch'un ch'iu*), translated as *Ch'un ts'ew* in 1872 and also known as the *Spring and Autumn Annals*, chronicling the period from 722 to 481 B.C.E.; the *Zuo Zhuan* (*Tso chuan*), or *Tradition of Zuo*, a commentary that carries Zhou history down to 468 B.C.E.; and the first official Chinese history, the *Shiji* (*Shih-chi*, 104 B.C.E.; *Records of the Grand Historian of China*, 1961), compiled by Sima Qian (Ssu-ma Ch'ien, c. 145-90 B.C.E.).

The second principal resource consists of several military texts brought together during the Song (Sung) Dynasty (960-1126 C.E.) and placed in a collection known as the Seven Military Classics. Each provides varying degrees of detail concerning the art of warfare, military strategy, and organization, along with references to the types of weapons used. As traditionally arranged, the Seven Military Classics consist of Sunzi's *Bingfa*, the *Wuzi* (*Wu-tzu*, c. 400 B.C.E.; *Wu-tzu*, 1993), *Sima Fa* (*Ssu-ma Fa*, c. fourth century B.C.E.; *The Methods of the Ssu-ma*, 1993), *Lei Weigong Wen Dui* (*Lei Wei-kung Wen Tui*, c. 600 C.E.; *Questions and Replies Between T'ang T'ai-tsung and Li Wei-kung*, 1993), the *Wei Liaozi* (*Wei Liao Tzu*, c. fourth century B.C.E.; *Wei Liao-tzu*, 1993), the *Huang Shigong San Lüe* (*Huang Shi-kung San Lüeh*, c. first century C.E.; *Three Strategies of Huang Shih-kung*, 1993), and the *Taigong*.

BOOKS AND ARTICLES

Gabriel, Richard A. "China, 1750-256 B.C.E." In *The Ancient World*. Westport, Conn.: Greenwood Press, 2007.

_____. "Chinese Armies: The Shang and Zhou Periods, 1750-256 B.C.E." In *The Great Armies of Antiquity*. Westport, Conn.: Praeger, 2002.

Gabriel, Richard A., and Donald W. Boose, Jr. "The Chinese Way of War: Chengpu, Guiling, Jingxing." In *The Great Battles of Antiquity: A Strategic and Tactical Guide to Great Battles That Shaped the Development of War*. Westport, Conn.: Greenwood Press, 1994.

Graff, David A. "Ch'in Shih-huang-ti." In *The Reader's Companion to Military History*, edited by Robert Cowley and Geoffrey Parker. Boston: Houghton Mifflin, 1996.

Kierman, Frank A., Jr., and John K. Fairbank, eds. *Chinese Ways in Warfare*. Cambridge, Mass.: Harvard University Press, 1974.

Lewis, Mark Edward. *The Early Chinese Empires: Qin and Han*. Cambridge, Mass.: Belknap Press of Harvard University Press, 2007.

Needham, Joseph. *Military Technology: Missiles and Sieges*. Vol. 5 in *Science and Civilisation in China*. Cambridge, England: Cambridge University Press, 1994.

Peers, C. J. *Ancient Chinese Armies, 1500-200 B.C.* Illustrated by Angus McBride. Botley, Oxford, England: Osprey, 1990.

_____. *Imperial Chinese Armies, 200 B.C.-A.D. 589*. Illustrated by Michael Perry. Botley, Oxford, England: Osprey, 1995.

Sawyer, Ralph D., trans. and comp. *The Seven Military Classics of Ancient China*. Boulder, Colo.: Westview Press, 1993.

Twitchett, Denis, and John K. Fairbank, eds. *The Ch'in and Han Empires, 221 B.C.-A.D. 220*. Vol. 1 in *The Cambridge History of China*. Cambridge, England: Cambridge University Press, 1986.

Yates, Robin D. S. "Making War and Making Peace in Early China." In *War and Peace in the Ancient World*, edited by Kurt A. Raaflaub. Malden, Mass.: Blackwell, 2007.

FILMS AND OTHER MEDIA

First Emperor of China. Documentary. Razor Digital Entertainment, 2006.

Red Cliff. Feature film. Beijeng Film Studio, 2008.

Jeffrey Dippmann

NOMADIC WARRIORS OF THE STEPPE

Dates: To c. 500 C.E.

MILITARY ACHIEVEMENT

The most significant of the steppe warrior societies included the Scythian, Xiongnu (Hsiung-nu), Yuezhi (Yüeh-chih), Śaka, Sarmatian, Avar, Hun, and White Hun. Some, such as the Yuezhi, were Indo-European peoples, and others, such as the Huns, were Turko-Mongolian peoples. Population growth was marked by competition for pasture lands in the north and by irrigation networks to the south. Nomadic societies looked to towns for trade but at other times were tempted to raid their accumulated produce and crafts. Until the emergence of cannons and muskets, the settled communities were easy prey for the mounted nomad warriors.

Scyths spread their nomadic influences across the Eurasian continent from Mongolia in the east to the Russian grasslands in the west. Believed to be Iranians from Turkistan who had refused to succumb to the settled existence of the Persian state to the south, some of the Scyths moved into the plains north of the Black Sea, displacing the Cimmerians in the Russian steppes after 750 B.C.E. From that base they attacked the fleeing Cimmerians, who penetrated the Assyrian lands to the south. Under a leader named Madyas, the Scyths subjugated the Medes about 628 B.C.E. Although the Medes rebelled and turned the Scyths northward, the Scyths were the first of the mounted nomad warriors to threaten the classical cultures south of the Black Sea. With iron implements forged by craftsmen from the Urals, the Scyths created the first recognized northern Eurasian empire, with territory extending from the Danube to Mongolia. Although divisions within their ranks were common, their federations remained threats to all the nearby communities for centuries. Although the Scyths who remained in Turkestan when the others moved across the Volga were called Śakas by the Persians, they were of the same Iranian nomad stock.

Steppe nomads were not always on the offensive. In the sixth century B.C.E. Cyrus the Great (c. 601 to 590-c. 530 B.C.E.) of Persia invaded Scythian Parthia, in the area of present southern Turkmenistan, before leading an army through the deserts of Gedrosia, in present Baluchistan, to defeat the Amyrgian Śakas of the mountains. Later his armies overran the Uzbek steppes between the Amu Dar'ya and the Syr Dar'ya Rivers. Along the latter Cyrus constructed a town named Cyropolis, later known as Khudzhand and Leninabad. To protect his territories he constructed seven forts to guard against the aggressive Śakas. In September, 529 B.C.E., the Massagetae Scyths defeated Cyrus even though other Scythian mercenaries had been recruited against these Śaka tribes east of Khiva. In 512 B.C.E. Darius the Great (550-486 B.C.E.) attacked and defeated the Tigrakhanda Śakas, also called the "Pointed Hat Śakas," of the Aral Sea region, capturing their chieftain. Other Śakas to the north and east were out of the range of Darius's conquests. Hence, Darius established twenty satrapys, or provinces, in his lands, including Bactria, Śaka, and Khorezm-Sogdia.

Farther west, Scythian ruler Ateas (died 339 B.C.E.) led his forces to challenge the Macedonian forces of Philip II (382-336 B.C.E.) in 340 B.C.E. but was killed the following year in battle against the Macedonians, after which the Scythians were absorbed by the Sarmatians, another Iranian nomad people of the Russian steppes. By 350 B.C.E. the Sarmatians were already governing the Pontic steppes, where they founded Kamenskoye, present Dniprodzerzhyns'k. Like the Scyths, these mounted nomads wore coats of mail and depended more on the lance than on the bow. By the late third century the Sarmatians had forced the Scyths south toward the Crimea and occupied the Russian steppes west of the Volga.

The Scyths of Central Asia, however, continued to menace the wealthy oases and towns to the south.

Macedonian leader Alexander the Great (356-323 B.C.E.), after conquering Persia, had failed to extend his rule over the nomads of that region. On the south bank of the Jaxartes River he founded a frontier outpost, Alexandria Eschate, but in 329 B.C.E. rebellious Śakas in Sogdiana threatened his new frontier town. Alexander then launched a campaign of terror enabling him to regain command of most of Sogdiana, including Maracanda, present Samarqand. The Scyths in Parthia seceded from Alexander's successors in the third century B.C.E., and during the Seleucid civil wars nomad strength was revived. More Scythian nomads from the northern steppes invaded Parthia to aid the local nomads led by Arsaces (fl. third century B.C.E.), who established an independent state with Nisa as its capital.

Farther east, a Turko-Mongolian people had begun attacking the Chinese empire as early as the ninth century B.C.E. Like the Scyths, these were nomadic, mounted warriors whose aggressiveness later caused the Chinese to construct the Great Wall. They were probably the ancestors of the Xiongnu, the earliest of the famous Huns. At any rate the Chinese were to adopt a more mobile style of warfare better suited to defense against these mounted neighbors. Only by the second half of the third century B.C.E. did these Xiongnu unite under a leader called the Shanyu (Shan-yü). Under Shanyu Duman (Shan-yü Tuman, died c. 210 B.C.E.), they moved into western Gansu (Kansu). Duman's son and successor, Mao Dun (Mao-tun), fought several wars with the Chinese and then turned westward in 177 B.C.E. to complete the conquest of western Gansu from the Yuezhi, driving the remnants into the Gobi Desert. However, the Xiongnu had been compelled to sign a treaty with China's Han rulers in 198 B.C.E., the beginning of Chinese ascendancy over the nomads. Han emperor Wu Di (Wu Ti, 156-87 B.C.E.) attacked the Xiongnu of the Ordos west of China and ended the payment of tribute to the horde in 133 B.C.E. Within twelve years China overcame the Xiongnu in Gansu and initiated Chinese set-tlements there. Han troops then attacked the Xiongnu in Mongolia. By 48 B.C.E. the Xiongnu presence had disintegrated in Mongolia, and the southern branch recognized Chinese hegemony to inhabit the Ordos region as subjects.

Meanwhile, after 140 B.C.E. Śaka nomads had overwhelmed the Bactrian kingdom of Heliocles I (r. 150-140), bringing an end to the Greco-Bactrian state. They themselves were being pushed south by the Yuezhi. Chinese sources place them in Xingjiang province, present eastern Turkistan, as early as the fifth century B.C.E.. The Yuezhih, also called Tochari, were an Indo-European people dwelling in Gansu (part of Xinjiang), just south of the Gobi Desert, by the early second century B.C.E. In approximately 177 B.C.E. they were driven from that region to the Ili Valley by chief Mao Dun of the Xiongnu and twelve years later were forced south by the Wu Sun (Wusun), ancestors of the Sarmatian Alans and vassals of the Xiongnu. Part of the Yuezhi formed a confederacy and moved south to the Tibetan mountains. Most, however, occupied territories between the Amu Dar'ya and Syr Dar'ya Rivers in Sogdia, driving Śaka tribes south into Khorāsān and Bactria. The Yuezhi established their capital at Kienshih, previously known as Maracanda and Samarqand. In 138 B.C.E. the Chinese Han emperor Wu Di dispatched an ambassador to the Fergana Valley to secure the Yuezhi's assistance against the Xiongnu. However, the embassy came to nothing, because the Yuezhi were more interested in the southern lands. Hence the

TURNING POINTS

1000 B.C.E.	Cimmerians first produce bronze battle-axes.
900 B.C.E.	Scyths and succeeding steppe warriors master the use of bows while on horseback.
6th cent. B.C.E.	The lance is first used by the Alans and Sarmatians, and the chariot is first used by various tribes in battle.
4th-3d cent. B.C.E.	The use of protective bone breastplates is regularly adopted.
2d cent. C.E.	The use of armor spreads from the Ukraine to Manchuria.
451	Attila the Hun invades Roman Gaul.

Yuezhi invaded Bactria between 141 and 128 B.C.E., after which the region was renamed Tocharistan. One branch of the Yuezhi, the Kushāns, moved into the Sistan and Kabul river valleys and crossed the Indus River in 50 C.E. to establish the Kushān Dynasty in northwestern India. Nevertheless, a Yuezhi state continued to exist into the next century in Bactria.

In 380 C.E. a chieftain named Toulun led his Mongolian people, called the Juan-juan, westward from China. These warriors defeated the Xiongnu to establish a large steppe empire. About a generation later Toulun adopted the title of "khan" or "khagan." The Juan-juan were eventually overwhelmed, however, by the Toga Turks, who controlled northern China in the fifth century. The remaining Juan-juan migrated to the Yenisei region in Siberia to launch the Avar Empire that spread westward through the steppes. That empire lasted until it was overthrown by the Altai Turks under a leader named Tuman or Duman, who took the title Khan of the Blue (or Celestial) Turks. Meanwhile, the western tribes of the Avars migrated to the Russian-Ukrainian steppes, eventually invading Eastern Europe to threaten the Byzantines for two hundred years.

The Huns emerged in fourth century B.C.E. Mongolia. Although little is known about them for several centuries, they most probably descended from the Turkic Xiongnu. After they had established control of Inner and Outer Mongolia, a rift occurred in their ranks by the year 44 C.E. Some of the Huns formed a new confederation and moved the nation into what is now Kazakhstan. By 48 C.E. the eastern branch further split into northern and southern factions, and the former were conquered by Mongol tribes called the Xianbi (Hsien-pi). Those in the south became confederates of the Chinese emperor and resided south of the Great Wall in Shansi. These southerners, under Liu Cong (Liu Ts'ung, died c. 334), eventually overthrew the Chinese emperors and became rulers of North China by 318. However, by 348 this Hun or Xiongnu Empire in China had collapsed.

The western Huns took their federation farther west, across the Volga, in 374, defeating first the Sarmatian Alans and then the Ostrogoths. All of the Goths were pressured to leave the steppes for Roman East Europe, and the Huns then followed them, terri-

fying the inhabitants with their mounted archers. The Roman historian Ammianus Marcellinus (c. 330-395 C.E.) described them as "skilled in unimaginable ferocity." In 432 the Romans were compelled to pay tribute to the Huns. When the Romans later balked at further exactions, Attila (c. 406-453), the Hun chieftain, led the Huns farther into the Roman world, as the emperor ceded vast lands to them south of the Danube River. Early in 451 Attila moved his nation into Roman Gaul. After crossing the Rhine, he set Metz ablaze but failed to take the fortified town of Orléans. He was stopped to the west of Troyes by a Frankish-Roman confederacy under Aëtius (died 454) in 451. A year later the Huns ravaged Milan and Pavia in Italy before retiring northward, following the promise of tribute by the bishop of Rome. After the death of Attila in Pannonia in 453, no new leader could manage to hold the nation together. The forced allies revolted and killed Attila's eldest son. Another son, Dengizich (died 469), at first directed the Huns back toward the steppes but then altered course to attack the Eastern Roman Empire. The Huns were defeated, Dengizich was killed, and his head was placed on exhibit in the circus of Constantinople in 468.

In Central Asia another horde, called the Ephthalite or White Huns, moved south from the Altai Mountains to the Aral Sea region of Turkestan in the mid-fifth century. This horde occupied Sogdiana, Transoxiana, and south to Bactria. Later in the fifth century they attacked Khorāsān, killing the Sāsānian king Peroz. Subsequently the White Huns took Merv and Herat, eventually replacing the Yuezhi and Kushāns in Bactria, Kandahar, and Kabul. They were stopped, however, when they attempted to conquer the Punjab. Sources describe these White Huns as barbarians eschewing all the elements of settled civilization. Like their counterparts in the West, they seem to have passed out of history in the same era.

WEAPONS, UNIFORMS, AND ARMOR

Paleolithic grave sites reveal the use of knives and spear points. Those of the Andronovo population of 1750 to 800 B.C.E. show flint arrowheads and bronze weapons. However, such evidence may indicate more of a hunting than a military culture. The Okunev peoples, who engaged in metalworking in the Altai Mountain region in the era from 1800 to 1500 B.C.E., may have been the first Siberians to develop metallurgy, especially bronze casting, for military enterprises, although armed horsemen arose much later. The Cimmerians had produced bronze battleaxes by 1000 B.C.E. Early in that first millennium sword-length daggers with hollow handles were typically found in grave sites. The first militant horsemen appeared in north Central Asia at about this time.

With the rise of organized warfare, the dominant weapon in the steppe was the bow and arrow. The Scyths and their successors in the steppes surpassed all other peoples in their ability to fire with accuracy from both sides (50-60 meters) while galloping on horseback at great speed. After dismounting they could fire also with amazing agility while running at full speed. Their arrows were usually of sharp bone points, shot from composite bows made from different materials, usually with a wooden core backed with sinews and bellied with horn. The length of the bow was 140 to 160 centimeters, and the string was permanently attached to one end. Such bows were found in graves from the fourth century B.C.E. Characteristic of the Scythian bow was its short length and double-curved nature. They were made by professional craftsmen, not by the steppe warriors themselves. Much later the Huns improved the composite bow, which was copied by the Romans.

Among other common steppe weapons was the lance, used since the sixth century B.C.E. The longest one was extended 10 feet and its weight was such that the user held it with two hands while on horseback. First used by the Alans and Sarmatians, it was still employed by the Huns one thousand years later. The lasso, used to entangle an opponent before hand-to-

HUNNIC MIGRATIONS, C. 484

hand combat, was a device employed by the Alans, the Sarmatians, and later the Huns.

As for armor, the steppe warriors for centuries fought without breastplates, until they were first worn by nobles. Gradually, the practice of wearing protective cuirasses made from bone or horn began to be regularly adopted. By the fourth or third centuries B.C.E. bone breastplates were found in use from evidence in burial mounds of the lower Ob River, although bone lamellae from as early as the eighteenth century B.C.E. have been discovered in the Cis-Baikal region. From 100 B.C.E. to 100 C.E. scale armor was introduced by steppe warriors in the Altai region and in Western Siberia.

The Xiongnu wore leather and bone armor and sometimes even bronze. Iron scales were used in Tuva as early as the second century B.C.E. Within a century, chain mail had appeared among the Sarmatians in the Kuban Basin. Use of armor spread from the Ukraine to Manchuria by the second century C.E. By the early fifth century the nobles among the Huns wore a metal thorax that covered the sides as well as the breast. By this time the same Huns wore helmets that protected even the nose, a device that may have been Sāsānian in origin. In the East, tribes wore such helmets by the beginning of the modern era. To decrease their weight, shields were made of wicker and supported by leather; they were made smaller for use on horseback and larger for use on foot. As for dress, common to the both the Scyths and Huns were wide trousers, gripped tight at the ankles to facilitate horse riding. The sleeves of the loose robes were also wound close to the wrists. Ammianus wrote that the Huns wore "ratskin" and linen tunics until they "rotted away on their bodies."

Library of Congress

Mounted Hunnic warriors on a raid carry a collection of weapons, including spears, swords, maces, and bows and arrows.

MILITARY ORGANIZATION

Steppe warriors were ruled by khagans, or khans, who exercised total authority over their troops. Organization was primitive, but the warriors gave allegiance to the tribal nobles who administered the wishes of the khagan. Military federations were formed, reformed, disintegrated, and overwhelmed. Armies depended upon the charismatic appeal of the leader and, upon his death, civil wars usually erupted among the followers of each son until the strongest was able to meld together a new federation. Grave sites confirm the existence of class among the warriors, and the elites were the first to wear armored protection. Armies also included women warriors, who may have constituted between 15 and 18 percent of the fighting forces. Most steppe warriors of the early centuries had no known military organization, similar to that of the medieval Mongols, yet the Huns were organized into right and left provinces, each of which was under a king who governed his army commanders. They in turn supervised the chiefs of either one thousand, one hundred, or even ten soldiers.

Most, however, were simply organized into hordes, living off the conquered lands by pillaging. As they moved over long distances, their allegiances were fragile, often breaking down over competing grazing rights or plunder.

DOCTRINE, STRATEGY, AND TACTICS

Nomad military success depended upon speed, surprise, and psychology. The rapid advance of the cavalry would be highlighted by volleys of arrows from the horsemen followed by hand-to-hand fighting by scattered bands who appeared to fight in disarray, but whose intent was to destroy any unity among the opposition. Often, when fighting other steppe tribes, the strategy of feigned flight was successfully employed. Sometimes steppe warriors fled quickly when encountering opposition and then suddenly reversed direction to attack again with amazing speed. There was no strategy employed to attack fortified positions, because, in most cases, warriors' accuracy with bows was sufficient to overcome the defenders. In many cases, combat was accompanied by "howling" typical of the Avars, Magyars, Huns, and others. Another psychological weapon was the well-advertised practice of scalping their defeated foes, whose heads were used for drinking vessels during victory feasts. From the Scyths in the West to the Xiongnu in the East, the steppe warriors were known for their swift, unexpected raids for plunder. If pursued, they would lead their opponents into an open field, where they could not be pinned down and where their horses could work to the best advantage. The nomads would employ volleys of arrows to exhaust their foes before engaging them in hand-to-hand combat.

As early as the fourth millennium B.C.E. the skill of horse riding may have existed in the region of modern Kazakhstan. The horse culture became so pervasive among the steppe peoples that the warriors, men and women, spent a great portion of their lives on horseback, eating, fighting, negotiating, and even sleeping. Such traits were common throughout the long history of nomadic peoples, whether Turk, Mongol, or Indo-European. Early steppe horsemen wore neither metal stirrups nor spurs, and they directed their horses with whips. Surely, however, the Avars used the stirrup with great success in their attacks on Eastern Europe. The early warriors used few saddles, though pillow saddles stuffed with deer hair were discovered in graves at Pazyryk. At the same site was evidence of earmarks to discern ownership of horses, and by the second century C.E., the Sarmatians were branding horses. From the era of the Scyths, steppe peoples castrated their male horses to better manage their herds.

Grave sites and burial mounds also reveal the use of chariots for carrying war booty from battle, as well as for fighting. Such practice was true of the Scyths (Śaka), Sarmatians, Xiongnu, Alans, and Huns from the sixth century B.C.E. Two-wheeled chariots drawn by steppe horses provided formidable fighting forces. The custom of burying chariots in the graves of rulers was common in Mesopotamia, the steppe cultures of Eurasia, and China. By 900 B.C.E. steppe warriors had mastered the art of attacking with bows and arrows while on horseback. When on march the warriors consumed fermented horse milk, horse blood, and sometimes a mixture of the two, as well as horse meat and cheese. It is said they even tenderized the meat by pounding it under their saddles.

ANCIENT SOURCES

Ancient sources on the earliest history of steppe warfare depend more on the findings of modern archaeologists than upon the ancient writers. Nevertheless, valuable information still rests upon classic works such as Sunzi's (Sun Tzu) *Bingfa* (c. 510 B.C.E.; *The Art of War*, 1910), which deals in part with the Chinese wars with the Xiongnu nomads. The military exploits of the Scyths, Massagetae, Cimmerians, and even the Amazons are fully described by the Greek historian Herodotus (c. 484-424 B.C.E.), especially in chapter 4 of his *Historiai Herodotou* (c. 424 B.C.E.; *The History*, 1709).

The Roman historian Ammianus Marcellinus (c. 330-395 C.E.), who was born a Greek and later served as an officer in the Eastern Roman armies, wrote a history describing the plight of the Roman Empire in its struggles with the barbarians, including the Huns and Avars. He did not know the Huns directly but relied upon Gothic intermediaries, ending his account in the 390's. The sixth century Gothic historian Jordanes tells much about the Huns from his knowledge of the writings, which survive only in fragments, of the Roman philosopher Helvidius Priscus (died c. 70-79 C.E.).

BOOKS AND ARTICLES

Beckwith, Christopher I. *Empires of the Silk Road: A History of Central Eurasia from the Bronze Age to the Present*. Princeton, N.J.: Princeton University Press, 2009.

Brentjes, Burchard. *Arms of the Sakas and Other Tribes of the Central Asian Steppes*. Varanasi, India: Rishi, 1996.

Cernenko, E. V. *The Scythians, 700-300 B.C.* Botley, Oxford, England: Osprey, 1983.

Chaliand, Gérard. *Nomadic Empires: From Mongolia to the Danube*. Translated by A. M. Berrett. New Brunswick, N.J.: Transaction, 2004.

Davis-Kimball, Jeanine, Vladimir A. Bashilov, and Leonid T. Yablonsky, eds. *Nomads of the Eurasian Steppes in the Early Iron Age*. Berkeley, Calif.: Zinat Press, 1995.

Fields, Nic. *The Hun: Scourge of God, A.D. 375-565*. Illustrated by Christa Hook. Botley, Oxford, England: Osprey, 2006.

Frye, Richard N. *The Heritage of Central Asia: From Antiquity to the Turkish Expansion*. Princeton, N.J.: Marcus Weiner, 1996.

Grousset, René. *The Empire of the Steppes: A History of Central Asia*. Translated by Naomi Walford. New Brunswick, N.J.: Rutgers University Press, 1970.

Hildinger, Erik. *Warriors of the Steppe: A Military History of Central Asia, 500 B.C. to 1700 A.D.* New York: Sarpedon, 1997. Reprint. Cambridge, Mass.: Da Capo Press, 2001.

Karasulas, Antony. *Mounted Archers of the Steppe, 600 B.C.-A.D. 1300*. Illustrated by Angus McBride. Botley, Oxford, England: Osprey, 2004.

Kelly, Christopher. *Attila the Hun: Barbarian Terror and the Fall of the Roman Empire*. Toronto: McArthur, 2008.

Man, John. *Attila: The Barbarian King Who Challenged Rome*. New York: T. Dunne Books/St. Martin's Press, 2005.

Mänchen-Helfen, Otto J. *The World of the Huns: Studies in Their History and Culture*. Edited by Max Knight. Berkeley: University of California Press, 1973.

Smith, John Masson, Jr. "Nomads." In *The Reader's Companion to Military History*, edited by Robert Cowley and Geoffrey Parker. Boston: Houghton Mifflin, 1996.

Szabó, Christopher. "The Composite Bow Was the High-Tech Weapon of the Asian Steppes." *Military History* 22, no. 9 (December, 2005): 12.

FILMS AND OTHER MEDIA

Attila. Feature film. Embassy Pictures, 1954.

Attila. Television miniseries. Alphaville Films, 2001.

Genghis Khan: To the Ends of the Earth and Sea. Feature film. Shochiku Films, 2007.

Mongol: The Rise of Genghis Khan. Feature film. New Line, 2007.

John D. Windhausen

INDIA AND SOUTH ASIA
ANCIENT
Dates: c. 1400 B.C.E.-500 C.E.

POLITICAL CONSIDERATIONS

Compared with those of other ancient civilizations, the interstate relations and warfare of India were the weakest aspects of Indian political affairs. Much of the role of fighting was traditionally assigned to the *kṣatriya* warrior caste. This caste, similar in some ways to the knights of medieval Europe, had its own traditions and customs, similar to the European concept of chivalry. The art of fighting was extolled and ancient epics glorified war, with legends such as the *Rāmāyaṇa* seeing men fighting demons. However, India appears to have displayed little skill in military matters. Generally peaceful and docile, the people of ancient India were not able to offer much resistance to hordes of invaders from the north. Even medieval Hindu kingdoms could not create lasting empires, maintain strong alliances, or sustain large military forces. Ancient traditions, cumbersome pedantic theories, and outmoded military techniques hampered the progression of military science. None of these burdened the invaders of India. War was accepted as an essential state activity, and condemnation of it was rarely voiced in Indian literature. The quintessential Jain-Buddhist doctrine of ahiṃsā, or nonviolence, was never interpreted as a condemnation of war until the Mahatma Gandhi (1869-1948) took up the banner in the twentieth century. Even Aśoka the Great (c. 302-c. 232 B.C.E.), the only monarch to repudiate war, as well as most Buddhist kings, accepted the use of warfare as necessary to achieve the cultural unit of Bhāratavarṣa, the ancient name of India—a dream constantly challenged by invaders of Indian soil.

MILITARY ACHIEVEMENT

The military history of South Asia coincides with the influx of Indo-European invaders, who, hardened by migrations from the steppes of Eastern Europe,

TURNING POINTS

c. 1800-1000 B.C.E.	Aryan invaders conquer India, mixing with earlier cultures to produce a new Hindu civilization in the area of the Ganges River Valley.
c. 1000-600 B.C.E.	Aryan Hindu civilization comes to dominate most of northern and central India while smaller states wage war for control in the South.
326 B.C.E.	The Indian king Porus employs war elephants against the forces of Alexander the Great at the Battle of the Hydaspes River, seriously disrupting the Macedonian phalanx.
c. 321 B.C.E.	Chandragupta Maurya expels Alexander's forces from India and establishes the Mauryan Dynasty.
4th cent. B.C.E.	The *Arthaśāstra*, an influential treatise on Indian politics, administration, and military science, is reputedly written by the prime minister Kauṭilya.
c. 274 B.C.E.	Aśoka the Great, grandson of Chandragupta Maurya and a military genius in his own right, solidifies the strength of the Mauryan Empire.
320 C.E.	Chandragupta I establishes the Gupta Dynasty, recalling the glory days of the Mauryan Empire and employing a feudal system of decentralized authority.

INDIAN KINGDOMS AND EMPIRES, 400 B.C.E.-500 C.E.

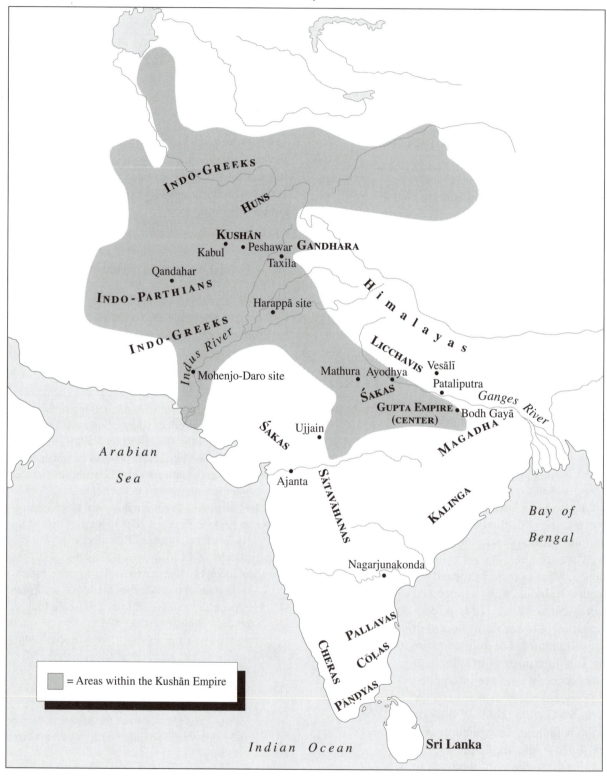

INDO-GREEKS

HUNS

KUSHĀN
• Kabul   • Peshawar   GANDHARA
• Taxila

• Qandahar

INDO-PARTHIANS
• Harappā site

INDO-GREEKS

Indus River

H i m a l a y a s

LICCHAVIS
• Vesālī
• Mohenjo-Daro site   Mathura • Ayodhya
• Pataliputra

ŚAKAS   *Ganges River*

GUPTA EMPIRE • Bodh Gayā
(CENTER)

Arabian   ŚAKAS   • Ujjain   MAGADHA
Sea

• Ajanta   SĀTAVĀHANAS   KALINGA

Bay of
Bengal

• Nagarjunakonda

= Areas within the Kushān Empire

PALLAVAS
CHERAS   CŌLAS
PAṆDYAS

Indian   Ocean   **Sri Lanka**

entered the Indus Valley and made contacts with the indigenous, dark-skinned Dravidians. The innate aggressiveness, superior military technology, iron weaponry, and horse-drawn chariots of the steppe nomad warriors successfully overwhelmed the local population. However, little is actually known of the conflicts between the two cultures. Archaeological finds present scant evidence of military conflict. Integration of the Indus Valley seems to have been achieved by means other than military absorption. The synthesis of the two cultures resulted in a Hindu civilization after 1400 B.C.E. in which small states pursued incessant warfare for dominance. Against this background developed the *Vedas*, the most ancient and sacred writings of Hinduism, which give tantalizing clues to military events of the Vedic period.

The post-Vedic era, however, produced reliable histories describing military events and weaponry in South Asia. The format of war that continued well into the modern era had its birth around 400 B.C.E. Between 600 and 400 B.C.E. a patchwork of feudal tribal states consolidated into sixteen republics, *mahajanapadas*, four of which in the eastern Gangetic Valley—Kosala, Kasi, Magadha, and Vrjji—gained ascendancy. Magadha emerged victorious under Chandragupta Maurya (r. c. 321-297 B.C.E.), who founded the Mauryan Empire and expelled the forces of Alexander the Great (356-323 B.C.E.) from India. The Mauryan Empire achieved its grandeur under Chandragupta's son, Bindusāra (r. c. 297-272 B.C.E.), and grandson, Aśoka. Of these, Alexander, Chandragupta, and Aśoka represent the first great military geniuses of Indian history. Although the art of warfare that Chandragupta learned from the Macedonians helped him solidify India under the banner of the Mauryas, dramatic developments in warfare remained static for approximately 2,200 years. Aśoka even renounced war and its effects in favor of Buddhist pacifism, although later Buddhist monarchs such as Harṣa of Kanauj (c. 590-647 C.E.) and Dharmapāla of Bihār and Bengal (r. c. 770-810 C.E.) pursued their political aims as ruthlessly as their Hindu neighbors.

Between 200 and 180 B.C.E. Mauryan power steadily declined, setting the stage for invasions by the Scythians, Parthians, and Yuezhi, with ensuing warfare and chaos. Dynasties rose and fell, with the Scythians, or Śakas, establishing a foothold in North India between 80 and 40 B.C.E. that was held by the efforts of the Andhra king. At the dawn of the Christian era the Andhra Dynasty controlled central India, and the Śakas the Indus Valley. South India, although independent, was engulfed in constant warfare between the Cōla, Pandya, and Chēras kingdoms.

The first two hundred years of the Christian era continued as a period of confusion throughout Hindu India with no significant developments in design or employment of weaponry. Between 1 and 50 C.E. an offshoot of the Śaka, the Kushān, entered the Punjab and carved out a vast empire under Kaniṣka (fl. c. 78-103) between 78 and 103 C.E. It was a short-lived attempt at empire building. Upon Kaniṣka's death, Śaka authority was usurped by satraps and feudal lords who maintained a state of confusion for ninety-seven years. During this period wars in South India were marked by copious bloodshed, violence, ferocity, and treachery, while in the north warfare was a sport of the monarchs, rarely a struggle for existence. Northern wars usually had limited objectives and were less savage than wars elsewhere in the world.

During the third and fourth centuries, kingdoms continued to rise and fall with no major power appearing on the scene. The Kushān Dynasty lingered into the mid-third century, and the Andhra Dynasty in the south collapsed and was replaced by the Pallava Dynasty of warrior kings, who dreamed of expansion. In 300 C.E. another Chandragupta, claiming descent from the founder of the Maurya Dynasty, consolidated the central Ganges, crowned himself Chandragupta I (r. 320-c. 330), or "King of Kings," and established the glorious Gupta Empire in 320 C.E. He conquered territory almost equal to that governed by Aśoka, but he employed a feudal decentralized authority. The golden age of the Gupta Empire was reached by the third emperor, Chandragupta II (r. c. 380-415), who added Vikramaditya to his name. With the approach of the Middle Ages, Ephthalite, or White Hun, invasions from the north challenged the now-weakened Guptas, who proved helpless against them. The Ephthalites established a kingdom in the Punjab and Rajputana between 500 and 530 C.E. but held sway for only twenty years. A patchwork of warring Hindu states ensued, with violent wars waged for territorial control.

The first five hundred years of the Christian era, then, were characterized by partially successful attempts at reestablishing Mauryan and Gupta glory, but ancient militarism did not result in a permanent empire. Only the Mauryans and Guptas exhibited the genius of empire building. The remainder of Indian history is a maelstrom of invasions and petty struggles toward creating a recognized cultural unit of Bhāratavarṣa.

WEAPONS, UNIFORMS, AND ARMOR

Although the military history of South Asia coincides with the influx of Aryan invaders, Stone Age weaponry in the form of celts (axes), knives, and arrowheads have been discovered. Between 3500 and 3000 B.C.E. Mesopotamia and Egypt utilized weapons of copper which, a few hundred years later, were hardened with tin to usher in the Bronze Age throughout the Near East and Indus Valley cultures. The subsequent Iron Age enhanced the manufacture of weapons. In major cultural centers a highly developed art of war with land and water transport, chariots, cavalry, and iron-steel weaponry ensued. Primitive military organization and combat techniques began to surface. By the sixth century B.C.E. continuous warfare records reveal the more sophisticated military trends.

The Aryans who entered India in the second millennium B.C.E. proved formidable adversaries, skilled in warfare and bronze metallurgy as seen in spear, dagger, arrowhead, mace, and sword specimens found in the mounds of Mohenjo-daro. The most significant improvement during the early historic period, then, was the use of metal for implements of war. Metallurgical skill permitted the working of malleable metal, a skill that produced highly sophisticated weaponry to ensure conquest of the Indus River Valley.

The primary weapon was the bow and arrow, which was used from the Stone Age until the end of the Middle Ages. Four to five feet in length, the bow

was constructed of bamboo, horn, wood, or metal. Its strings were made of *sana* fiber, hemp, skin, or animal hide. An invaluable weapon, its effective range was 100 to 120 yards, fewer if heavy, antielephant arrows were used. It was carried into battle on the left shoulder or carried aloft in the left hand. So great was its importance in ancient times that a code of rules regarding archery was ennobled as a subsidiary *Veda*, the *Dhanur Veda*. The title of *Dhanurdhāra*, or "master of the bow," was the highest accolade paid to a warrior, and the stringing of the bow was often a test of strength as with Prince Rama in the *Rāmāyaṇa*.

Arrows, fabricated from deer horn or iron, were barbed, crescent-shaped, needle-pointed, and dentiform, or serrated, and they were carried in a quiver made of hide, basket-work, or metal plates. The quiver was slung on the back and tied in front by a cross-belt. Fire-arrows and other incendiary missiles, often used against elephants, were disapproved by *smrti* writers. The *Arthaśāstra* (300 B.C.E.-300 C.E.; *Treatise on the Political Good*, 1961) of the Indian philosopher Kautilya (fl. 300 B.C.E.), a treatise on Indian polity from the Mauryan period, stressed the value of birds and monkeys to carry fire to enemy rooftops. Arrows tipped with metal and poison were used but were also condemned in religious texts.

Warriors also used a variety of hacking, stabbing, and felling weapons in the form of pikes, lances, spears, and battle-axes, as well as an assortment of swords, daggers, and javelins. The javelin, or *śela*, used by the infantry was highly praised, and a special long lance, the *tomara*, was used by warriors mounted on horses or elephants. Swords were double-edged, thick and heavy, and always borne in the hand. Sabers, on the other hand, were short-bladed, curved, single-edged, and worn on the left side. The *mushṭika*, a dagger of varied shape and form, was especially favored by the warriors. Siege machinery in the form of artillery, battering rams, and ballistae for hurling rocks, boiling oil, melted rosin of the *sal* tree (*kalpala*), and fire-tipped darts became common during the Mauryan period.

Besides traditional weapons, charioteers and infantry used a *nāgapāśa*, or lasso, to snare the enemy, as well as a boomerang that returned to the spot from which it was thrown.

Hindu warriors wore protective armor for head, torso, and legs, usually fabricated from leather reinforced with metal. Helmets, which had generally appeared by the Middle Ages, as well as breastplates and greaves, to protect the leg below the knee, were made entirely of bronze and iron. Prior to the Middle Ages warriors had depended on the thick folds of a turban to protect the head. To protect hands and arms from bowstring friction, leather guards were used. A wooden or wicker shield covered with buffalo or rhinoceros hide was carried in the left hand on the left arm. Archers without shields were protected by a front rank of oblong or circular shield-bearing javelin throwers. By the Middle Ages coats of mail were common protective gear for both man and beast.

Around the sixth century B.C.E. two decisive war machines appeared, namely the chariot, which developed after the Persian invasions, and the war elephant, which was considered as valuable as the chariot.

Elephants were outfitted with a housing, or howdah, covered with cloth or carpet and bells around the neck and rump. Lower-ranked warriors armed with bows and other missiles were seated in the howdah. According to the Greek historian Megasthenes (c. 350-c. 290 B.C.E.), who was sent as a representative to the royal court of India, three archers and a driver rode on each elephant.

Primary reliance was placed upon the chariot, or *śaṭangaratha*, a two-wheeled, open vehicle similar to those used in other ancient cultures. Drawn by horses, the chariot became a decisive fighting instrument in Indian warfare. Chariot wheels were occasionally outfitted with scythe-like blades projecting from the axles, making the chariot a most dangerous weapon. Sanskrit literature describes chariots ornamented with precious materials and armed with an array of weapons. Large numbers were used in battle. Battalions of 405 infantry, 81 chariots, and 243 horses are commonly described in Sanskrit literature.

The Indian prince Porus is defeated by Alexander the Great at the Battle of the Hydaspes (327 B.C.E.), during the ancient Vedic period of Indian history.

Cavalry armed with lances and short swords dominated the warfare of North India, whereas infantry was most important in South India, because southern geography and climate did not support the raising of sufficient horses for large cavalry units. Most of the superior horses of southern India were used for chariots. Although cavalry gave way to more disciplined and maneuverable infantry in Asia, India continued to rely heavily upon cavalry. India generally lagged behind other civilized cultures in military development. Its major contribution to military technology was the stirrup, which provided lancers stability in the saddle and was used by the Indian army as early as the first century B.C.E.

MILITARY ORGANIZATION

The Hindu army consisted of various categories of warriors but its backbone of seasoned hereditary troops were the *Kṣatriya* professionals. Its ranks were filled by southern mercenaries from Chēra, Karnata, and other areas; troops that generally protected caravans or trading posts of *śreṇi*, or merchant guilds; troops supplied by subordinate allies; army deserters; and wild guerrilla tribesmen. All castes were incorporated into the army, but *Kṣatriya* represented the warrior par excellence. Brāhmans held high military ranks, whereas the lowest two castes, Vaiśya and Śūdra, fought as auxiliaries. Warriors were arranged according to the clans and districts to which they belonged. During the Vedic period, all free men were subject to military service, but this obligation vanished as caste rules solidified. After the Mauryan period general conscription was rare.

The army was divided into four sections, the whole forming a *caturangam*: elephants, chariots, cavalry, and infantry. Elephants, the first line of defense, were trained with extreme care and utilized as battering rams, to frighten horses, to trample troops underfoot, and to ford rivers. Although they were difficult to wound, they were protected by infantry. However, there was constant danger that elephants could easily be unnerved by fire and panic. When Porus used them at the Battle of Hydaspes in 326 B.C.E., he used between 85 and 200 elephants to shield his infantry and then used his cavalry, which Alexander the Great drove back on the elephants who were, in turn, driven back on the infantry. In spite of these occasional disasters, elephants were used well into the nineteenth century by later Muslim monarchs.

The cavalry, long considered indispensable, were the shock troops in the time of Porus. However, gradually they were less and less used, and by medieval times they proved to be a weak element in Indian armies. The mounts were often wretched, failed to cover great distances, and proved vulnerable to mounted invaders from the northwest. They were not relied upon to any great extent. Chariots, on the other hand, were major fighting units in the Vedic period. They were used widely in Mauryan armies but by Gupta times, the light two-horsed car had evolved into a larger, more cumbersome transport vehicle.

The strength of the army rested in the infantry. In most Indian kingdoms an elite corps was pledged to protect the king to the death. Generally, however, they represented a miscellaneous horde of men that fell upon an enemy without any method or concerted plan. Each recruit usually provided his own mount and also received a stipend for himself and for the upkeep of his horse. Undisciplined mercenaries often deserted. Some reference is made to armies having mutinied in face of the enemy until pay was received. Yet the infantry, numerically the army's largest contingent, represented its main strength and was relied upon heavily.

Thousands of noncombatants also accompanied the fighting force to battle. They were especially evident in disorderly camps pitched during campaigns. Soothsayers, astrologers, dancers, prostitutes, acrobats, quacks, merchants, cooks, fakirs, religious mendicants, entire families of the fighting men, and royal family, wives, and concubines often slowed the pace of the army. The *Arthaśāstra* speaks of physicians and veterinarians attached to the army to care for man and beast.

The size of the Hindu army usually was enormous. In ancient and medieval times, according to various sources, the army engaged 600,000 to 900,000 men, although these figures are clearly exaggerated. The king led his army personally into battle. Under him were a number of superintendents with a *senāpati*, or general, at the head of all military affairs. The Mauryan army, according to Megasthenes, was organized under a committee of thirty with subcommittees that controlled infantry, cavalry, chariot, elephant, navy, and commissariat elements. Captains from feudal nobility served under the general. Standards identified all regiments, divisions, and squadrons.

DOCTRINE, STRATEGY, AND TACTICS

Three reasons are given in the *Arthaśāstra* for pursuing war: *dharmavijaya*, or victory for justice or virtue; *lōbhavijaya*, or pursuit of booty and territory; and *āsuravijaya*, or incorporation of territory into that of the victor and political annihilation. The Mauryan kingdom waged wars for glory and homage rather than wealth and power. The Guptas, on the other hand, stressed political annihilation and incorporation of territory. However, *dharmavijaya*, or victory for justice, was the ideal that Hindu kings were expected to pursue. War, however, became a sport of kings, profitable and always serious. Defeat was usually expunged by suicide. Dravidian South India, never fully influenced by Aryan culture, waged wars of annexation. Captives and noncombatants were treated with ruthlessness, but the ideal of *dharma-vijaya* was still present.

War was considered a religious rite, the highest sacrifice of a warrior. Battle was preceded by purification rituals, and astrologers determined the time and day for battle. The *Arthaśāstra* advised the employment of elephants and infantry in the center; light infantry, chariots, and cavalry on the wings; and archers behind spearmen. Emphasis was placed on single combat between selected warriors, but mass encounter of rank and file proved decisive. Morale was provided by leaders; if a leader was slain, the army generally fled. Elite *Kṣatriya* warriors were expected to fight to the death. Prisoners were treated honorably, usually released upon payment of ransom or after ransom was fulfilled by labor. Massacre was deprecated in Sanskrit literature.

The king and his nobles, the *rājanya*, fought from chariots. Infantry marched along with charioteers to the accompaniment of martial music that inspired them toward victory. Laying siege was considered dangerous and was rarely pursued. Generally a town was attacked and starved into capitulation.

Armies met each other face to face, approaching in parallel lines, infantry in the center, with chariots and cavalry on the flanks. Swarms of archers and slingers approached in the foreground, raining harassing fire with shouts and clashing of arms. The usual objective was to outflank an enemy, because the ten to thirty ranks of infantry were deemed vulnerable. Until 700 B.C.E. chariots provided the striking force, and the infantry provided a solid base around which more important groups could operate. Little organization was present, because the primary objective was to reach a suitable battle site and overwhelm the enemy. When charioteers struck terror in the enemy, the battle resulted in a rout. Usually each side converged and fought for an hour or more until one side would sense defeat. After 1000 B.C.E. more order, discipline, and organization entered the military system.

India generally lagged behind other civilized cultures in military theory, strategy, and tactics up to the dawn of the common era. Although training and discipline were well known to the Hindus, they found it difficult to impose military fundamentals upon the troops. The *Arthaśāstra* of Kauṭilya became the primary guide for military organization, tactics, ethics, and doctrine well into the medieval period.

ANCIENT SOURCES

Early Indian literary sources such as the *Rigveda*; the *Mahābhārata* (c. 400 B.C.E.-200 C.E.; *The Mahabharata*, 1834), including the *Bhagavadgītā* (c. fifth century B.C.E.); and the *Manusmṛti* (compiled 200 B.C.E.; *The Laws of Manu*, 1886) describe the power of weaponry, the religious duty of war, the importance of strong leadership, and the ethical aspects of waging war. The comprehensive Mauryan *Arthaśāstra* of Kauṭilya, composed between 300 B.C.E. and 300 C.E., looked upon war as a "continuation of polity by other means," as a legitimate last resort for achieving the aims of government and not to be embarked upon lightly. Although earlier literature had stressed a warrior's *dharma*, or duty, the motive of the *Arthaśāstra* was the establishment of a great empire. Around 500 C.E. the *Śiva Dhanur Veda*, of unknown authorship, stressed the skills of archery and military science in general. Its importance is seen in the application of the term *Dhanur Veda* to all writings on the art of war. There are also many battles, albeit largely men and monkeys against demons, in the *Rāmāyaṇa*, but it still contains some important military concepts. The major non-Indian source is Arrian, the *Anabasis Alexandri* (early second century C.E.; *The Campaigns of Alexander*, 1893), which contains detailed descriptions of the Indian commander Porus at Hydaspes.

BOOKS AND ARTICLES

Basham, E. L. *The Wonder That Was India: A Survey of the History and Culture of the Indian Subcontinent Before the Coming of the Muslims.* New York: Grove Press, 1954.

Bhakari, S. K. *Indian Warfare: An Appraisal of Strategy and Tactics of War in Early Medieval Period.* New Delhi: Munshiram Manoharlal, 1981.

Bull, Stephen. *An Historical Guide to Arms and Armour.* London: Cassell, 1991.

Mitra, Rajendralala. *Indo-Aryans: Contributions Towards the Elucidation of Their Ancient and Mediaeval History.* 2 vols. Delhi, India: Indological Book House, 1969.

Nicolle, David. *Fighting for the Faith: The Many Fronts of Medieval Crusade and Jihad, 1000-1500 A.D.* Barnsley, England: Pen and Sword Military, 2007.

Nossov, Konstantin S. *War Elephants.* New York: Osprey, 2008.

Spaulding, Oliver L. *Warfare: A Study of Military Methods from the Earliest Times.* 1925. Reprint. New York: Barnes and Noble Books, 1993.

FILMS AND OTHER MEDIA

In the Footsteps of Alexander the Great. Documentary. British Broadcasting Corporation, 2005.

George Hoynacki

THE MEDIEVAL WORLD

THE MEDIEVAL WORLD

THE ROMAN LEGACY

BYZANTIUM

Dates: 312-1453 C.E.

POLITICAL CONSIDERATIONS

In 312 C.E. Constantine the Great (c. 272 to 285-337) won a key battle at the Milvian bridge outside Rome that ensured his domination over rivals in the Roman Empire. The victory relied on Roman divisions who counted numerous Christians among them, and Constantine announced that his victory had been blessed by heaven when he saw a cross in the sky with the words, "By this sign you shall conquer." Constantine built a new eastern capital, in addition to the one in Rome. This city, Constantinople (modern Istanbul), was built on the old Greek colony of Byzantium, and historians regard its establishment as a capital in 324 as the beginning of the Byzantine Empire. At this time Constantine also legalized Christianity and ordered its organization, although the pagan religion was not outlawed until 385.

The early Byzantine Empire still regarded itself as part of the Roman Empire, and its legions were formed in the Roman way. In its early centuries the Empire concerned itself with the increasing Germanic, Slavic, and Hunnic invasions into the Danubian region and the western portions of the Empire, where a co-emperor remained in Rome until 476. From the east the Byzantines also faced incursions of the Persian Empire. Unlike Rome, Constantinople was able to resist the German invasions mainly due to its fabulous defense system, created by its early emperors. In contrast to the modern city of Istanbul, which spans two continents, Europe and Asia, old Constantinople was confined to the southwestern tip of a peninsula on the European side of the Bosporus Strait linking the Black Sea and the Sea of Marmara. Constantinople was bounded by the Sea of Marmara, the Bosporus, and, to the north, the Golden Horn, an inlet on the Bosporus. In the fourth and fifth centuries Byzantine emperors constructed a series of impenetrable walls, whose ruins can still be seen, across the land side from Marmara to the Golden Horn. An additional sea wall was built around the Sea of Marmara and the Bosporus to the Golden Horn, and a large boom blocked the entrance to the latter. The Byzantines, with a majority Greek population, would in fact, after the seventh century, be considered Greeks. They were the best sailors in the Mediterranean. Just as their wall held off land armies until the Fourth Crusade of 1204 and the Ottoman Invasion of 1453, their navies protected the city from sea attack.

In addition to foreign wars, the Byzantines fought civil wars against pagan generals opposed to the new Christian order and against heretical Christians associated with the old Hellenistic centers, such as Antioch and Alexandria. By the time of Justinian I (483-565),

TURNING POINTS

324	Roman emperor Constantine builds a new eastern capital at Constantinople.
527-565	Emperor Justinian reigns, definitively codifying Roman law, waging war against the Germans and Persians, and changing the nature of the Empire from that of a constitutional to that of an absolute monarchy.
610-641	Heraclius reigns, Hellenizing the Byzantine Empire and introducing the theme system of Byzantine provinces ruled by military governors.
1096-1204	The First through Fourth Crusades are waged by Christians seeking to protect the Byzantine Empire and to recapture the Holy Land from Muslims.
1453	Constantinople is captured by the Ottoman Turks, ending the Byzantine Empire.

the religious wars had died down, but the emperor himself had almost lost his throne in the Nika Uprising of 532, which began after a fight between fans of competing chariot teams. The steadfastness of Justinian's wife, Theodora (c. 497-548), a commoner, saved the throne. Justinian continued with a glorious career, building the magnificent church of Santa Sophia, definitively codifying Roman law, and waging war against the Germans and Persians. In the last, however, he ultimately failed. Although his commander-in-chief Belisarius (c. 505-565), one of the four great generals of antiquity, regained much land in North Africa and Spain and won significant battles against the Persians, he did not restore the old Roman Empire, and those lands gained were lost just a few years after Justinian was succeeded by his nephew, Justin II (r. 565-578).

Justinian changed the nature of the Empire from that of a constitutional to that of an absolute monarchy. The emperor now bore the title "autocrat." In the early seventh century, under Heraclius (c. 575-641), the Byzantine Empire became Hellenized, with Greek replacing Latin as the official language. Although citizens of the Byzantine Empire still called themselves Romans, they were now really Greek. Heraclius also fought against the Persians in the field, winning victories that exhausted the empire's resources. In the years from 632 to 670 the Muslim Arabs, storming out of the Arabian desert and filled with religious zeal inspired by the recently deceased prophet Muḥammad (c. 570-632), easily conquered the Near Eastern and North African lands even while they fought among themselves for leadership of the faithful. The resentment of the Christian dissidents who still lived in those regions and who were tolerated by the Muslims played an important part in these defeats.

From the north the Byzantine Empire contended with the Slavic invasions of the sixth and seventh centuries that culminated in the creation of the first Bulgarian empire on both sides of the Danube. The next four centuries witnessed periods of peace and alliance alternating with wars between the Greeks and Bulgarians. During this period the Byzantine emperors established the "theme system" of Byzantine provinces ruled by military governors. During times of war the peasants of the theme manned the Byzantine army and navy. The themes of the sea embraced the islands and hence were the major contributor to the navy.

Beginning in 711 the Byzantine Empire went through its most critical internal struggle until its downfall—a period of civil war over Iconoclasm. Iconoclasts were religious dissidents who wanted to remove religious pictures and icons from the Christian service, and one of their proponents, Leo III (c. 680-741), became emperor. Even though he won important victories against the Arabs and Bulgarians, his Iconoclast views were unpopular. At the end of the century Byzantine ruler Irene (c. 752-803) restored the veneration of icons and was later made a saint in the Christian church.

In 867 Basil I (c. 812-886) established the 189-year Macedonian Dynasty (867-1056), which brought the Byzantine Empire to new heights. In the tenth century the dynasty repulsed an attempt of the Bulgarian king Simeon I (died 927), claiming to be the Byzantine emperor, to seize the capital and the throne. In 1018 Basil II (c. 958-1025) defeated the Bulgarians and incorporated their empire into his own.

However, within forty years the Macedonian Dynasty had ended for lack of a male heir, and a series of intrigues and bloody rivalries among the noble families ensued, which gave the term "Byzantine" its pejorative connotation. The conflicts of this period led to the losses of southern Italy to Norman adventurers at the Capture of Bari (1071) and of Asia Minor to the Seljuk Turks (Battle of Manzikert, 1071). Furthermore, in 1054 during the height of the struggles, the Christian church had split into Eastern and Western branches. In response Emperor Alexius I (c. 1048-1118) of the Comnenus Dynasty (1081-1118) asked Pope Urban II (c. 1042-1099) to send some Western knights to Constantinople as military assistance to heal the breach by helping the Greeks reconquer Asia Minor. The pope embraced the enterprise, with a grander vision of expanding the Christian community, calling for the First Crusade (1095-1099).

Alexius initially welcomed the knights but was unhappy to see the throngs of peasants who also took up the cross and came on crusade. Furthermore,

The Roman emperor Constantine, who in 312 B.C.E. established a new, eastern Roman capital at Constantinople, which became the seat of the Byzantine Empire.

when the Crusaders conquered the Arab land, they would not agree to hold it as Alexius's vassals but instead set up their own feudal hierarchy under Godfrey of Bouillon (c. 1060-1100), the Crusade leader who became the king of Jerusalem. When the Muslims reconquered the Crusader states, and Western Christians launched the Second (1145-1149) and Third Crusades (1187-1192) led by kings, the Greeks became less hospitable. After the failure of the Third Crusade, the spirit declined even in the west. In the meantime there had been a family rupture in the Byzantine Angelus Dynasty (1185-1204). Alexius III (r. 1195-1203) had overthrown and blinded his brother Isaac II (r. 1185-1195; 1203-1204) and had him im-

prisoned with his son, Alexius IV (r. 1203-1204). In 1202 a new group of Crusaders had gathered at Venice for another attempt to retake the Holy Land. However, the project did not have enough funds to begin. The Crusaders relied on the doge of Venice to give them the needed resources in exchange for the conquest of the merchant city-state of Zara, which had recently broken away from the Venetian empire. Because of the destruction of this Christian city, Pope Innocent III (1160 or 1161-1216) abandoned the enterprise. Isaac II's son Alexius IV escaped from Constantinople and promised to finance the Crusaders further if they could help him reestablish his father's claim to the Byzantine throne. The Crusaders agreed

BYZANTINE EMPIRE AT JUSTINIAN'S DEATH, 656 C.E.

FRANKS

Atlantic Ocean

VISIGOTHS

Córdoba

AVARS

LOMBARDS

BULGARS

ILLYRICUM

THRACE

Ravenna

OSTROGOTHS

CORSICA

Rome • **ITALY**

SARDINIA

Brindisi

Thessalonika

Athens

Constantinople

Nicaea

ASIA MINOR

Smyrna

Black Sea

Trapezius

Antioch

GHASSĀNID ARABS

SICILY

Carthage

V A N D A L S

Tripoli

Mediterranean Sea

CRETE

RHODES

CYPRUS

Jerusalem

Alexandria

EGYPT

Red Sea

= Domain of empire

to the diversion, invaded Constantinople, expelled the blind emperor's brother, and put Isaac back on the throne with his son as co-ruler. Alexius IV, however, was unable to honor his commitment to supplying the Crusaders. Furthermore, a popular uprising in the city turned against Isaac and Alexius in favor of another member of the family. After realizing that Constantinople was an even better and easier prize than Jerusalem, the Crusaders and their Venetian allies seized the city and established themselves as rulers of the empire. Baldwin of Flanders (1172-1205), sponsored by the Venetian doge, became Baldwin I of Constantinople, and he distributed the themes among his followers as vassal fiefs.

This Latin Empire (1204-1261) continued for only fifty-seven years, but the damage it did continued until the end of the Byzantine state in 1453. While Western rulers established a dozen new states in the themes of the empire, other rulers established independent realms as well. The great medieval Slavic empires—Serbia, Bulgaria, and Croatia—flourished in this age. There were several independent merchant cities, such as the Italian and Hungarian enclaves of Venice and Dubrovnik, as well as the Ottoman sultanate, which appeared in the thirteenth century and within two hundred years had steadily engulfed all of the Christian states, culminating in the conquest of Constantinople in 1453.

MILITARY ACHIEVEMENT

The key to Byzantine endurance was its magnificent defense system, beginning with the walls of Constantinople and the boom at the entrance of the Golden Horn. Added to this was the best navy in the region, which was used primarily as a defensive force. The Greeks also effectively employed both peasant infantry and noble cavalry. However, throughout its history the empire alternated between periods of military victory and defeat. It reached its heights during the reigns of Justinian and Heraclius and later during the Macedonian Dynasty, but constant civil and religious wars, popular uprisings, and internal rivalries and intrigues revealed its weaknesses and flaws. The Greeks suffered at various times major defeats at the

hands of the Slavs, Arabs, Turks, Normans, Crusaders, pagan Patzinaks, and other adversaries.

WEAPONS, UNIFORMS, AND ARMOR

The most spectacular and renowned weapon of the Byzantines was Greek fire, a paraffin mixture whose exact formula remains unknown. When set aflame it could not be doused by water. Greek fire was especially effective in naval warfare when the Greeks catapulted balls of the flaming wax onto enemy ships, spreading general panic. In the last years of the empire, it was shot through tubes using a form of gunpowder. Individual sailors and soldiers carried small amounts of Greek fire in a type of hand grenade that exploded on contact. Greek fire was also used in land warfare and dropped from the walls of besieged cities against soldiers trying to scale the defenses.

At the height of the Byzantine Empire, from the sixth to eleventh centuries, the cavalry was the mainstay of the Byzantine land forces. The heavy cavalry, known as *cataphracts*, dressed in mail covering their bodies in the Persian fashion and wore steel helmets. Their weapons included swords, daggers, bows that were also borrowed from the Persians, and lances. They protected their horses with breast and frontal armor. Light cavalry and light infantry also used the bow, which was employed on long attacks. Some light infantry carried lances. Heavy infantry wore mail, as did their cavalry counterparts, and fought with swords, spears, battle-axes, and shields.

In the navy there were several classes of warships, known as *dromons*. Battleships of different sizes had sails and several banks of oars with an average crew of two to three hundred men. Seventy of the crew were marines who fought both on land and ship-to-ship. The remainder were rowers and sailors. Cruiser-type ships, *pamphyli*, were lighter, swifter, and more maneuverable, having only two banks of oars. They also fought in set battles. A special pamphylus stood as the admiral's flagship. Light ships with one bank of oars served for reconnaissance and carrying dispatches. Byzantine ships had ramming rods, which the lighter maneuverable vessels used very effectively.

MILITARY ORGANIZATION

The first Byzantine army was Constantine's Roman army, which followed the organization of the late third and early fourth centuries. These were divided into the border divisions, or *limitanei*, composed of the peasants of the region; the mobile units, or *comitatensis*, who fought in the field; and the guards, or *palatini*, the best troops. Under the emperor the highest ranks were prefects and two commanders-in-chief, or *magistri militum*, the senior for the cavalry and the junior for the infantry. However, when on independent campaign, either commander led mixed cavalry and infantry. At the end of the fourth century Emperor Theodosius the Great (346 or 347-395) settled the original commanders in Constantinople and added three more in the provinces. The commanders then operated independently, subject only to the emperor. Justinian added one more. The generals, or *dux*, of the provincial armies served under the commanders and had administrative and supervised judicial bureaus headed by chiefs, *princips*, from the imperial bureaucracy.

In principle the state subjected all Byzantine males to conscription. In practice landowners could pay to keep their peasants out of military service, and the draft affected mostly the urban population. The sons of soldiers were also regularly recruited. In fact most of the military was filled with volunteers, including foreigners and mercenaries called allies or *foederati*. Generals also maintained, at their own expense, troops called *bucellarii*, who took an oath to their leaders as well as to the emperor, thus presenting a danger to the throne. Nevertheless by Justinian's time the bucellarii had increased so much that they formed a major part of the army. The Roman army continued, with divisions composed of soldiers from regions such as Asia Minor, Thrace, and Armenia, and was held in special esteem. In the sixth century the cavalry replaced the infantry as the main force, and the financial difficulties caused by Justinian's ambitious wars and projects, together with a threat from the Russian steppe in the form of the pagan Avars, reduced the mercenary forces and increased conscription.

Heraclius introduced the theme system as a military measure to strengthen the provincial armies. Theme governors known as *strategoi*, literally generals, and division leaders, or *comes*, replaced the infantry and cavalry commanders-in-chief. Each theme provided an army *thema*, the equivalent of an army corps, divided into two or three division-strength *turmai*, about five thousand troops, commanded by *turmachs* serving both as army generals and civilian administrators in their provincial district. Smaller units included *moirai* (brigades), *tagmata* (regiments), *banda*, *pentarchies*, *pentakontarchies* (companies of forty men), and *dekarchies* (platoons of about ten men). Banda contained five pentarchies and pentarchies contained five pentakontarchies. Banda officers included *drungarii* and *kometes*. *Komes* commanded pentarchies and *pentakontarchos* the pentakontarchies. In addition special troop *kleisurai* (literally "mountain passes") commanded by *kleisuriarchs* guarded frontiers subject to invasion. If these districts became themes, the theme organization was applied. *Akritai*, the legendary frontier warriors of the Byzantine folk epics, at times fought beside the kleisurai and at other times independently. Higher officers were usually of noble rank. Each bandon had its own baggage train and accompanying noncombatants, such as slaves, servants, and physicians. The train brought engineering equipment, for building bridges and field camps, as well as siege equipment.

Apart from the theme armies there were special corps assigned to the capital. They included four cavalry tagmata named *scholarii*, *excubitores*, *hikanatai*, and *arithmos*, sometimes called *vigla*. *Domestici* commanded the first three, and a drungarius led the latter, the imperial guard. However, the real protectors of the emperors were the *hetairia*, or retinue, which had a large number of mercenaries and was led by the *hetairiarchos*. There was also an infantry tagmata, the *numeri* commanded by a domesticus, and additional infantry troops. The Constantinople soldiers fought with the emperor except for a battalion under the domesticus of the walls that always remained to protect the city.

From the sixth century the highest army commander was the strategos of the Theme of the East, and the next in rank was the domesticus of the scholarii. In the tenth century, after the emperors no longer regularly led the army in battle and the number of themes had increased, the scholarii domesticus became the commander-in-chief of the entire army. The army strength of the Byzantine Empire varied over time, but at its maximum it was about 150,000. Although military pay was small, soldiers' rights as peasants on theme land made up for the deficiency.

After the eleventh century the losses in Asia Minor and the Balkans brought about the decline and finally the end of the theme system. Citizens could purchase exemptions from the conscription, and the number of mercenaries increased to include Slavs, Arabs, Turks, Mongols, "Latins," Germans, and Caucasians. The elite Varangian corps of the Comnenus Dynasty was composed of Anglo-Saxons. The fortunes of the empire became more precarious. In a 1204 battle with Crusaders, the mercenary army, which had not been paid, refused to fight. By the last years of the Byzantine Empire, under the Paleologus Dynasty (1261-1453), the regular organization had dissolved and the army was a patchwork of troops, mainly mercenary soldiers.

Although the Byzantine army had evolved from that of the Romans, the Byzantine navy was created afresh. The Roman fleet was hardly more than a coast

BYZANTINE EMPIRE, C. 1250

guard, and even up until the time of Justinian, the navy had played only a supplementary role. However, during the height of the empire the navy was a key part of the Byzantine military, especially in the empire's defense. The threat of the Arabs forced the Greeks to increase the size of the navy and to integrate it into the theme system. The fleet commander-in-chief was the strategos of the *carabisiani*, named after the *carabos*, a type of ship. Under him were one or two drungarii, with the responsibility of admirals although the equivalent rank in the army is similar to a modern colonel—a discrepancy stemming from the higher position of the army in the empire. Sailors came from the coastal regions and islands, the best being the Cibyhrrhaeots, from the Pamphylian city of Cibyra in southern Asia Minor. In the eighth century the Muslim caliphate moved inland to Persia and lessened the threat from the sea, after which the imperial navy declined. Because of a renewed Muslim threat in the Mediterranean in the following century, the Macedonian Dynasty paid more attention to the naval fleet. They added a third theme of the sea and established naval stations in the European themes. After the crisis of the eleventh century, the navy, as did the army, suffered a steady and eventually irreparable decline.

DOCTRINE, STRATEGY, AND TACTICS

Byzantine commanders paid detailed attention to military science. The Greeks, including emperors themselves, wrote manuals and commentary of military affairs, for example the *Strategikon* (before 630; *Maurice's Strategikon*, 1984), attributed to Flavius Tiberius Mauricius (c. 539-602), a Byzantine emperor who reigned from 582 to 602, which gives detailed information on the differences in strategies between the Persian and the Roman soldiers, as well as the intricacies and differences in their weapons and their uses. The *Taktika* (compiled c. 905; tactics) of the emperor Leo VI (866-912) was another well-studied text. The commanders studied the character of the enemy and the nature of the region for battle

and applied their findings in the preparation and execution of both offense and defense. Surprisingly, the Greeks, who throughout history had been renowned for their seamanship, did not pay as much attention to naval science.

Special emphasis was laid on defense, and the Greeks used attack as their main strategy only in siege operations. Byzantine defense followed the frontier tactics of the late Roman Empire; the Greeks built fortified camps and small forts and posted troops at strategic passes and areas from which the enemy might invade. They fortified interior towns and cities and erected a chain of warning signals throughout the empire. If enemy forces succeeded in invading past the border defenses, the infantry would fall in behind them and block their retreat, while light infantry harassed their troops until the theme commander could assemble support from neighboring provinces in sufficient number to attack. In battle heavy cavalry, the main force of the army, attacked in mass formation. Light cavalry fought in quick sorties, made harassing raids, and carried out reconnaissance.

Byzantine military manuals carefully laid down the rules of field operations, but the commanders were also expected to show innovation and independence. The guiding principle in battle was to minimize casualties. Among the stratagems used to gain victory with the least loss were intelligence and espionage, negotiation, delaying tactics, ambushes, moving troops for their protection, and feigning retreat. Training, discipline, and experience enabled the Greeks to use these doctrines effectively. The Greeks knew the value of esprit de corps, rewarding special service and recognizing valor. The emperor and commanders appointed orators to emphasize the glory of courage, arousing the spirit and enthusiasm of the troops for God, Christianity, the emperor, and the Empire. Religion played a major part in the life and spirit of the troops. Greek wars were holy wars. Solemn masses were celebrated on the battlefield. Every day began with morning prayers, and the Greek battle cries were "God is with us" and "The cross is victorious."

MEDIEVAL SOURCES

There exists a large body of primary sources for the Byzantine Empire, many of which have been translated into English and published. Among the best known are the sixth century Byzantine historian Procopius's *Anekdota, e, Apokryphos Historia* (c. 550; *Secret History*, 1674), an account of the reign of Justinian I and Theodora; Michael Psellus's (1018-c. 1078) *Chronographia* (English translation, 1953) on the eleventh century; and princess Anna Comnena's (1083-c. 1148) *Alexiad* (English translation, 1928), an account of reign of her father, Alexius I, which includes Comnena's impressions of the Crusaders and the war with Patzinaks. Although these are general histories, they contain valuable information on the Byzantine military. Procopius, who was secretary to the general Belisarius, also wrote the official court histories of Justinian, which included accounts of his wars. Information about the military hierarchy of the early centuries is found in the *Notitia Dignitatum* of the fifth century and John of Lydia's (fl. sixth century) *De Magistratibus* (after 554; *On the Magistracies of the Roman Constitution*, 1971) of the sixth. Descriptions of the wars of Heraclius are found in the poetry of George Pisides (fl. seventh century).

There are a number of seventh and eighth century chronicles of the Byzantine Empire. Those of the monk Theophanes the Confessor (c. 752-c. 818) and the patriarch Nicephorus are valuable. The tenth century historian Joseph Genisius wrote about the end of the Iconoclast struggle and the first years of the Macedonian dynasty. Leo Diaconus (fl. tenth century) recounted in his history the military achievements of the emperors Nicephoras II Phocas (r. 963-969) and John I Tzimisces (r. 969-976). The chronicle of Byzantine historian John Scylitzes (fl. eleventh century) covers the years 811 to 1057. Some non-Byzantine sources important to this period include *Provest' Vremennykh Let* (twelfth century; *Russian Primary Chronicle*, 1930), partly attributed to Nestor (c. 1056-1113), and the Latin *Antapodosis* (tenth century; *Antapodosis*, 1930) of Liutprand of Cremona (c. 922-c. 972). The emperor Constantine VII (905-959) wrote on a number of subjects, including the themes. Two military manuals of this period are the *Taktika* of Leo VI and the *Sylloge Tacticorum* (compiled tenth century; *Sylloge Tacticorum*, 1938). For the eleventh century, in addition to Psellus and Comnena, there is also the *Strategicon* of Cacaumenus, a Byzantine general. John Cinnamus and Nicetas Choniates wrote on the twelfth century. For the crusades there are many Western works with tangential reference to Byzantine military affairs. Important historians of the last years of the Byzantine Empire include George Pachymeres (1242-c. 1310), Nicephorus II Phocas, and the emperor John VI Cantacuzenus (1292-1354), all of whom wrote before the fall of the empire in 1453. Those who wrote after the fall include Laonicus Chalcocondyles (c. 1423-c. 1490), Ducas (fl. mid-fifteenth century), Critobulos of Imbros (fl. fifteenth century), and George Sphrantes (fl. fifteenth century), whose description of the fall of Constantinople is a standard account.

BOOKS AND ARTICLES

Bartusis, Mark C. *The Late Byzantine Army: Arms and Society, 1204-1453*. Philadelphia: University of Pennsylvania Press, 1997.

Bradbury, Jim. "The Byzantine Empire and Eastern Europe, 400-1453." In *The Routledge Companion to Medieval Warfare*. New York: Routledge, 2004.

Dawson, Timothy. *Byzantine Cavalryman, c. 900-1204*. Illustrated by Giuseppe Rava. Botley, Oxford, England: Osprey, 2009.

_____. *Byzantine Infantryman: Eastern Roman Empire, c. 900-1204*. Illustrated by Angus McBride. Botley, Oxford, England: Osprey, 2007.

Haldon, John F. *The Byzantine Wars: Battles and Campaigns of the Byzantine Era*. Charleston, S.C.: Tempus, 2001.

_____. *Byzantium at War: A.D. 600-1453*. Botley, Oxford, England: Osprey, 2002.

_____. *Warfare, State, and Society in the Byzantine World, 565-1204*. London: UCL Press, 1999.

_____, ed. *Byzantine Warfare*. Burlington, Vt.: Ashgate, 2007.

Heath, Ian. *Byzantine Armies, 1118-1461*. Illustrated by Angus McBride. Botley, Oxford, England: Osprey, 1995.

Hyland, Ann. *The Medieval Warhorse from Byzantium to the Crusades*. Conshohocken, Pa.: Combined Book, 1996.

McGeer, Eric. "Byzantine Siege Warfare in Theory and Practice." In *The Medieval City Under Siege*, edited by Ivy A. Corfis and Michael Wolfe. Rochester, N.Y.: Boydell Press, 1995.

_____. *Sowing the Dragon's Teeth: Byzantine Warfare in the Tenth Century*. 1995. Reprint. Washington, D.C.: Dumbarton Oaks Research Library and Collection, 2008.

Nicolle, David. *Romano-Byzantine Armies, Fourth-Ninth Centuries*. Illustrated by Angus McBride. Botley, Oxford, England: Osprey, 1992.

Regan, Geoffrey. *First Crusader: Byzantium's Holy Wars*. Stroud, Gloucestershire, England: Sutton, 2001.

Treadgold, Warren T. *Byzantium and Its Army, 284-1081*. Stanford, Calif.: Stanford University Press, 1995.

FILMS AND OTHER MEDIA

Byzantium. Documentary. Discovery Channel, 1997.

Byzantium: The Lost Empire. Documentary. The Learning Channel, 1997.

Civilizations in Conflict: Byzantium, Islam, and the Crusades. Documentary. United Learning, 1998.

Fall of Byzantium: May 29, 1453. Docudrama. Zenger Video, 1989.

The Fall of Constantinople. Documentary. Time-Life, 1970.

Justinian: The Last of the Romans. Documentary. A&E Home Video, 1997.

The Siege of Constantinople. Documentary. Ambrose Video, 1995.

Frederick B. Chary

THE FRANKS AND THE HOLY ROMAN EMPIRE

Dates: 482-918 C.E.

POLITICAL CONSIDERATIONS

During the last days of the Roman Empire, the Western European landscape was divided among various Germanic tribes, remaining bastions of Roman administrative rule, and surviving Roman military settlements, or *laeti*. The Franks alone were divided into at least four subgroups that competed for control with various Gallo-Roman magnates whose cities and surrounding territories comprised lands sufficient for them to be called *sub reguli*, or "sub-kings," in the sources. It is little wonder that any military commander with enough drive and power to stitch together an identifiable fabric from this crazy quilt of disarray would be hailed as more than just another king. Such a man was Clovis I (c. 466-511), a king of the Sicambrian Franks who created something approaching a unified Gaul at the point of his lance. Although this first Francia would be a heterogeneous kingdom, it would suffer from two major flaws that were principally Frankish in origin: the practice of partible inheritance among royal sons, which divided lands and encouraged disunion and often outright civil war, and the eventual usurpation of royal power by the chief executive officer of the king, the major domo, or "mayor of the palace." The former flaw acted as a check on Frankish expansion and the latter eventually led to a change of dynasty from the ruling house of the Merovingians to that of the House of Charles, or Carolingians.

Although Clovis was named consul by the eastern emperor Anastasius (c. 430-518) after gaining control of most of Gaul, this title was imperiled upon his death in 511. Clovis's four sons each received an equal portion of his holdings and spent the next fifty years battling for his inheritance. No sooner had it all fallen into the hands of the surviving son, Chlotar I (c. 497-561), than he died, redividing the kingdom once again among his own four sons, who showed even less inclination toward cooperation than had the preceding generation. Gaul was torn by incessant civil war for yet another fifty years. With the execution of the matriarch queen Brunhilde in 613, Chlotar II (r. 613-629) introduced a brief period of effective Merovingian rule.

At this point, an office originally intended to relieve the kings of burdensome daily administrative duties began to encroach on royal prerogatives. The position of major domo had been created to oversee supplies and the smooth running of the royal estates. During the turbulent civil wars, the office came to be occupied by key magnates of the realm who could bring military power to the side of their king. By the mid-600's, the Merovingian kings had begun to place more military authority in the hands of the mayors. By 687 the mayor Pépin of Herstal (r. 687-714) had defeated his rivals and solidified his rule over all Franks. Pépin's illegitimate son, Charles (688-741), later known as Charles Martel, or the Hammer, furthered the power of the position by seizing control in a palace coup in 714. The stage was now set for a contest between the king and the mayor for mastery of Francia. However, there was no contest. The later Merovingian kings, long characterized by French historians as *rois faineants*, or "fainting kings," were unable, or unwilling, to contend seriously for power. By 752 Charles Martel's son, Pépin III (714-768), known as Pépin the Short, had sent the last Merovingian to a monastery and assumed the throne as the first Carolingian king with the blessing of the Pope.

This move inaugurated an efflorescence of Frankish power under Pépin and his legendary son, Charles (742-814), known as Charlemagne, or, literally,

Charles the Great. During this period the Franks reassembled a large portion of the old Roman Empire—Gaul, Italy, and extreme northern Spain—and conquered most of Germany as well. In 800 Pope Leo III crowned Charlemagne as Holy Roman Emperor, reviving the concept of a Roman Empire and solidifying the division between the Roman Empire in the west and the Byzantine Empire in the east. By the time of Charlemagne's grandsons, and the Treaty of Verdun in 843, however, the issue of partible inheritance had once again divided the Frankish Empire and diluted its power. This fact, coupled with the in-

CAROLINGIAN EMPIRE

creasing pressure of Viking invasions, brought an end to any dreams of unity as the newly emerging concept of feudalism further subdivided the West.

MILITARY ACHIEVEMENT

The Frankish legacy is one of military conquest. Clovis's accession to the Frankish throne in 482 came at a time in which there was no one overarching military presence in northern Gaul. Therefore, with a fairly small contingent of troops, Clovis was able, in 486, to conquer the Kingdom of Soissons, a sub-Roman territorial remnant under the command of the patrician Syagrius (c. 430-486), the last Roman governor in Gaul. By 491 Clovis had absorbed Paris and campaigned victoriously against Thuringian settlements in eastern Gaul. The incursion of the Alemanni into Frankish lands in 496 provided Clovis with opportunities for leadership over all the northern Franks. He used this leverage to good effect with a decisive victory that same year over the Alemanni at Tolbiac, southwest of Cologne. Although Clovis's subsequent conversion to Christianity somewhat eroded his Frankish coalition, he was still able to intervene in Burgundy, come to terms with the Alan laeti in Armorica, in present-day Brittany, and finally secure his Rhineland borders. In 507 he moved on the biggest prize: the Visigothic kingdom of southern Gaul under Alaric II (r. 484-507). In the late spring and early summer of 507, Clovis's forces crushed the Visigoths at Vouillé, killing Alaric II and opening the way for the conquest of the south. Clovis took most of the key cities in the south and the Visigothic royal treasury but could not take the province of Septimania. He finished his career of expansion from 508 to 511 by incorporating holdout Frankish subgroups in the north, notably at Cambrai and Cologne.

The sons of Clovis were mostly concerned with one another's patrimony, but they did cooperate long enough to effect the conquest of Burgundy in 534, at the prompting of the queen mother, Clotilde, herself a Burgundian princess. After the old queen died in 544, the remaining brothers gave themselves over to internecine strife. Matters only worsened with the succession of the four sons of Chlotar in 561. Only an occasional raiding campaign into Lombard, Italy, broke the monotony of civil war.

After unity was restored under Chlotar II in 613, two major developments occupied the Frankish military: the extension of control into Austrasia, the territories east of the Rhine, and the growth of the positions of the major domos, or mayors of the palace. By the 660's, the mayors of Neustria (central France) and Austrasia were openly influencing the choice of Frankish kings. In 687 Pépin of Herstal, the Austrasian mayor, was able to defeat his Neustrian rival and proclaim one king with one mayor for all of Francia. As he passed this on to his son, Charles Martel, the Franks found themselves governed by the mayor much more than the king. This was the situation when the Saracens, under leader ʿAbd al-Raḥmān (died 732), encountered the Franks near Poitiers on October 25, 732. Charles Martel, the mayor, formed his men into a defensive infantry position, and the Muslim forces, mostly foot soldiers with some cavalry, broke on the Frankish shield wall.

In the ensuing years, as the Carolingians made their rule officially royal, Pépin the Short conquered central Italy for the Pope, the so-called Donation of Pépin of 756. Charlemagne subdued northern Italy in 774 and ultimately Saxony, at the end of a bitter decades-long campaign. Frankish military power had won a realm extending from the Spanish March to the Elbe River and from the plains of Hungary well into central Italy.

Throughout this period the Franks evolved from a fragmented Germanic tribe to become the single strongest military force in Europe. By incorporating into their fighting forces the strengths of the various peoples they conquered, the Franks became so powerful that the Pope, when threatened in the 750's with Lombard invasion and Byzantine control, intentionally sought an alliance with them. By the end of Charlemagne's reign in 814, the Franks were supreme on the continent. Only the old malaise of a divided empire and the new threat of recurrent Viking raids, which challenged even the most formidable military of the era, brought an end to Frankish power. After 918 the local military agreements collectively known as feudalism would fragment both the land and the military might of Francia, as it did most of Europe.

WEAPONS, UNIFORMS, AND ARMOR

The disparate nature of Frankish armies worked against any uniformity in their appearance. The concept of "personality of the law," wherein each man was judged by his ethnic background, had military applications as well. Whether Frank, Saxon, Sarmatian, Alan, Gallo-Roman, or from some group less well known, the individual soldier would be expected to wear into combat that which conformed to his own tastes, abilities, and national dress. Any uniformity in dress or equipment would have derived from a soldier's military function, such as cavalry, infantry, or siege operator. Even after Charlemagne's rule took on the characteristics of a centralized empire, the use of territorial levies precluded uniforms. Because there was no government issue of battle dress or equipment, there could be no uniformity assured.

Despite these variations, the typical infantryman in a Frankish army most likely carried a spear and a shield. The spear could be of two types; the *hasta*, or *lancea*, was a thrusting spear for close engagement, whereas the *angon* was a shorter, barbed throwing spear with an iron housing extending down from the head to encase almost the entire length of the weapon. The typical length of the lance was about 8 feet, although longer ones are known. The angon, generally no longer than 6 feet, also could be used for thrusting, but its long, narrow shaft made it more suited for throwing. The theory behind the angon was that once it impacted the enemy's shield, its weight could not be cast off due to its barbed head, thereby pulling down the shield. Battle descriptions also tell of Frankish warriors stepping on the trailing angon shafts in order to deprive their opponents of their shields. Should the angon penetrate the opponent's body, its barbed spearhead ensured maximum damage when removed. The angon's long metal casing prevented the easy hacking away of the shaft and created quite a problem for the victim.

Frankish shields appear to have been round, or occasionally elliptical, and of 32 to 36 inches in diameter. A metal stud in the center permitted the soldier to strike his opponent with a punching motion, giving the shield offensive as well as defensive possibilities. The shield was usually made of wood, rimmed with iron or, in lesser instances, wicker covered by hides.

Swords seem to have been fairly rare in the Frankish world, as they were throughout early medieval Europe. Those that did exist were of two types: the long sword and the *scramasax*. The long sword was a double-edged weapon of 30 to 36 inches in length. Because its center of gravity was somewhat closer to the tip of the blade, it was better suited for cutting rather than thrusting motions, which may explain why the long sword made the transition from foot to mounted combat. The short sword, or scramasax, a single-edged weapon, ranged in length from 8 inches to a more formidable 16 inches. Its obvious use was for close combat, and its lethal impact could be enhanced by the judicious use of poison in its blood-gutter groove.

A favorite weapon of the Frankish infantryman, particularly in the early years of the period, was the *francisca*. This small ax, with a 16-inch haft attached to its 7-inch single-edged head, weighed only about 2.5 pounds, making it suitable for both striking and throwing. When thrown, the francisca could have an effective range of up to 39 feet on three in-air rotations; sources mention the Franks engaging their opponents in this way. In hand-to-hand combat, the francisca also worked much like a heavy tomahawk or hatchet.

TURNING POINTS

482	Clovis I accedes to the Frankish throne.
507	Clovis defeats the Visigoths at Vouillé and unifies Gaul.
687	Pépin of Herstal wins the Battle of Tertry, solidifying rule over all Franks, and unifies the office of Mayor of the Palace.
714	Pépin's illegitimate son, Charles Martel, seizes control over Frankish kingdom in a palace coup.
800	Charlemagne is crowned Holy Roman Emperor by Pope Leo III.
843	The Treaty of Verdun divides the Frankish Empire.
918	Feudalism disintegrates the Frankish Empire as Saxons and northern raiders infiltrate.

Although some sources claim that the Franks were without bows and arrows, evidence in Frankish graves indicates otherwise. Double-curved bows and arrowheads of more than 2.5 inches in length are suggested by the archaeology of the age. Frankish prelate and bishop Gregory of Tours (539-594), describing a particularly arrogant Frankish count, noted the count's habit of entering church with his quiver slung over his shoulder.

Body armor included the helmet, or *galea*, usually a variation on the simple iron cap, often without a nasal piece. The better-attired warriors would also have a *brunia*, or leather tunic covered in either ring-mail or mail of iron plates that overlapped like scales. Even as late as Charlemagne's day, the high cost of these pieces of equipment made them rare; the brunia itself could cost the equivalent of six cows in the early 800's. Consequently the vision of Frankish armies with little or no body armor has taken hold. The heterogeneous nature of the Frankish forces meant that some of their early armies contained elements of Roman laeti, who were frequently outfitted in mail. By the time of Charlemagne, the heavy cavalry, or *caballarii*, were protected by the brunia, whereas the *lantweri*, or general levy, would be less heavily armed.

MILITARY ORGANIZATION

Despite the general impression of early medieval warfare as undertaken by ignorant armies, the military organization of this period in Francia was quite complex. When Clovis began his career of conquest he assembled warbands of Frankish sub-kings, the armed retainers of Gallo-Roman magnates, descendants of Roman garrisons, armed colonists, or laeti, from late Imperial days, and barbarian allies. Each of these components could be expected to contribute their distinctive abilities. For example, the Alan laeti of Armorica were noted for their cavalry, the Gallo-Romans for their siegecraft, and the erstwhile Roman garrison personnel for their archery and missile weapons expertise. The end result would be an army capable of a combined-arms approach to war, as well as one that conceivably could be avail-

Charlemagne, crowned Holy Roman Emperor in 800, united the Frankish kingdoms and solidified the division between the Roman Empire in the West and the Byzantine Empire in the East.

able nearly year-round. The army of the first great Merovingian king, Clovis I, bore a much greater resemblance to a late Roman force than to a barbarian, tribal army.

The major addition to this system, introduced in Francia during the time of Clovis's warring grandsons (c. 560-590), was the introduction of levies.

Based on a double heritage of Frankish and Roman custom, each king could call out his populace in time of war. The Franks had held that all able-bodied men owed military service and had developed a procedure for bringing this into effect. It was called the *campus Martius*, which could mean either "field of Mars" or "Marchfield." It is assumed this was originally an early spring muster of all available fighting men, but the sources indicate that it eventually became a muster of combatants at any time of the year. Warriors

DIVISION OF CHARLEMAGNE'S EMPIRE

were to bring their own equipment and supplies, because pillaging was restricted until the army reached enemy territory.

The Roman tradition was one of each landowning group supplying a man from their land to serve in the army. This was called *praebitio tironum*, and it meant that the Roman populace was accustomed to regularly furnishing troops to the government. Once again these soldiers were financed and thus equipped and provisioned by those satisfying the praebitio. The sixth century grandsons of Clovis simply accessed an old notion when they began calling up levies of troops for their incessant civil wars.

There were, however, distinctions among the levies, of which there appear to have been two types. Local levies, only affecting the *territorium* of certain cities, did not include the poor or those whose absence from farming or commerce would cause disruption to the flow of society. The city would make the determination as to who would be called up and who would be excused. General levies, on the other hand, were just that: a general call to arms of every able-bodied man. Even general levies were restricted to the areas under direct threat. The general levies, owing to the low level of military fitness among the troops, were not particularly helpful. As the Frankish presence expanded throughout Gaul and into Germany and Italy, so did the concept of local and general levies.

By late Carolingian times, the Franks had virtually re-created the old Roman praebitio tironum. Charlemagne's edict of 806 required men of a certain level of landholding to fight and those of lesser landholdings to pool their responsibility with others to share in the provision of a warrior. A man whose small landholding was not enough for him to serve personally, but who joined with others to furnish a warrior and supplies, was said to have done his military service. All this could be seen to offer great numerical potential for Frankish armies. Yet out of a possible thirty-five thousand horsemen and some hundred thousand foot soldiers available to Charlemagne, his usual victorious army numbered from fifteen to twenty thousand, at the most. Given the shrunken state of early medieval armies, however, this was more than enough to dominate.

DOCTRINE, STRATEGY, AND TACTICS

The issue of doctrine, strategy, and tactics to a large degree revolves around the question of how "Roman" or how "barbarian" armies in Frankish Gaul were. Once again the heterogeneous nature of Frankish forces provides a clue to the mixed viewpoints of Frankish commanders and their armies. Much of the military action in the period from 482 to 918 appears reactive and circumstantial, and thus more "barbarian," as if devised to conform to events rather than some far-sighted, state-driven strategic plan. Clovis, for example, is said to have invaded the Visigothic south because he felt angry that the Arian Visigoths should occupy an Orthodox land.

Despite this alleged barbarianism, there are certain strategic considerations that can be seen in the Frankish campaigns. Clovis seems to have intentionally sought territorial expansion and executed a systematic campaign of besieging cities after his decisive victory in the open field at Vouillé. His sons and grandsons, however, appear to have begun and finished campaigns with little more than a grand raiding objective in mind. It would not be until the era of Pépin the Short and Charlemagne that the Franks would reattain a strategic view of conquest and the reduction of rebellious peoples. With that as their objective, the Franks invested their energies in the capture of key cities, using a type of scorched-earth policy to deny the strongholds their subsistence.

The Franks seem to have been somewhat deficient in siege warfare, at least until they incorporated into their empire those who had inherited knowledge of Roman siegecraft. Generally the Franks took fortified strongholds by deceit, which required abilities of a different sort. Although there is scant mention in source literature of them doing so, Franks do appear to have been able to construct many types of siege engines. They were, however, capable of circumvallation—building walls to deny the besieged city any outside contact. Frankish supply trains consisted of large wagons and carts, called *basternae*. So thorough could be the Frankish investment that the Avars, having fortified their strongholds for a 791 Frankish cavalry attack, simply gave up when they saw Charlemagne's approaching army with all its supplies in tow.

Frankish battle tactics included the basic barbarian charge, called the "wedge," which, in formation, was sometimes likened to the blunt snout of a wild boar, an animal generally revered by the Germans for its ferocity. As the charge was made, the Franks would let their franciscas and angons fly and would generally count on breaking the enemy's resolve in one rush. With the incorporation of other peoples and tactics in their armies, the Franks also supplemented thier cavalry with Alans, a warlike people from the steppes northeast of the Black Sea. With their practiced wheeling maneuvers, the Alani rendered the Frankish army a more diversified and dangerous fighting force. When faced with a stronger foe, the Franks would form a shield wall with their infantry and allow the enemy to beat itself into submission on it.

Toward the end of the Frankish period, as cavalry grew in prominence, the Carolingian armies were still dominated primarily by infantry. Even the advent of the stirrup did not give the horseman the leverage he would have two centuries later when the cantle enabled him to deliver a lance blow without being driven over the rump of his mount. Lances were used, as were the long swords, by the Carolingian cavalry in a downward thrusting manner.

MEDIEVAL SOURCES

Although sources are not lacking for the period from 482 to 918, many are flawed as reliable sources of information. A common problem is brevity; for example, the Viking invasions are frequently dismissed with a terse "this year the heathen ravaged." There is also a fundamental problem of worldview. The sources of the early medieval period more frequently recount facts than convey causation. They describe what happened, but not why. Despite an abundance of detail about an event, the lack of analysis often hinders a holistic understanding of the event. Information about weapons, tactics, and military matters must be gleaned from chance comments offhandedly dropped into narratives. It is revealed, for example, that as Count Leudast strode into church, he wore a mail shirt, had a bow and arrow, a javelin, and a cuirass, but his sword is mentioned only when, much later in the story, he is called to defend himself. When descriptions are offered, they can be maddeningly vague.

Nevertheless, the sources available for interpretation do include some gems of Western historiography. They begin with Gregory of Tours' (539-594) *Historia Francorum* (c. 594; *The History of the Franks*, 1927), which covers the history of the Franks to 591. A work that provides an overlapping but slightly different view is the *Liber Historiae Francorum* (1973), translated by Bernard S. Bachrach from an earlier Latin text, as well as *The Fourth Book of the Chronicle of Fredegar* (1960), translated by J. M. Wallace-Hadrill, both of which take the Frankish saga up to the time of the Carolingians. A Lombard viewpoint covering many of the same events is offered by Paul the Deacon's (c. 720-c. 799) *Historia Langobardorum* (c. 786; *History of the Lombards*). Eastern views on Frankish warfare are available in small doses in the works of the Byzantine historians Agathias (c. 536-c. 582), whose work is contained in Averil Cameron's *Agathias* (1970), and Procopius of Caesarea's (between 490 and 507 and after 562) *Polemon* (c. 551; *History of the Wars*, 1960).

A Byzantine view on the Carolingian military is found in the *Tactica* of the emperor Leo VI (866-912), once again not translated into English. The greatest of the Carolingian personalities, the Holy Roman Emperor Charlemagne, is described in Einhard's *Life of Charlemagne*, translated by Sidney Painter. Because Einhard served in Charlemagne's court, he presumably had firsthand knowledge of his subject's governance.

A vast and disparate field of supplemental study is that of the lives of the various saints from the period. Once again, it is the accidental rather than the intentional inclusion of material that repays the search.

BOOKS AND ARTICLES

Bachrach, Bernard S. *Armies and Politics in the Early Medieval West*. Brookfield, Vt.: Ashgate, 1993.

_____. *Merovingian Military Organization, 481-751*. Minneapolis: University of Minnesota Press, 1972.

Bradbury, Jim. *The Routledge Companion to Medieval Warfare*. New York: Routledge, 2004.

Contamine, Philippe. *War in the Middle Ages*. Translated by Michael Jones. Oxford, England: Basil Blackwell, 1984.

Elton, Hugh. *Warfare in Roman Europe, A.D. 350-425*. Oxford, England: Oxford University Press, 1996.

Nicolle, David. *The Age of Charlemagne*. Illustrated by Angus McBride. Botley, Oxford, England: Osprey, 1984.

_____. *Carolingian Cavalryman, A.D. 768-987*. Illustrated by Wayne Reynolds. Botley, Oxford, England: Osprey, 2005.

_____. *Poitiers, A.D. 732: Charles Martel Turns the Islamic Tide*. Illustrated by Graham Turner. Botley, Oxford, England: Osprey, 2008.

Reuter, Timothy. "Carolingian and Ottonian Warfare." In *Medieval Warfare: A History*, edited by Maurice Keen. New York: Oxford University Press, 1999.

Schoenfeld, Edward J. "Charlemagne." In *The Reader's Companion to Military History*, edited by Robert Cowley and Geoffrey Parker. Boston: Houghton Mifflin, 1996.

_____. "Otto I (the Great)." In *The Reader's Companion to Military History*, edited by Robert Cowley and Geoffrey Parker. Boston: Houghton Mifflin, 1996.

Wood, Ian. *The Merovingian Kingdoms, 450-751*. New York: Longman, 1994.

FILMS AND OTHER MEDIA

Charlemagne. Television Miniseries. Acorn Media, 1994.

The Dark Ages. Documentary. History Channel, 2007.

Burnam W. Reynolds

THE ANGLO-SAXONS

Dates: c. 500-1100 C.E.

POLITICAL CONSIDERATIONS

With the end of Roman rule over the British Isles occurring with the withdrawal of the remaining legions by order of Emperor Constantine in 410 C.E., the local populations of Britain were left to govern themselves until the Angles and Saxons arrived forty years later. The indigenous people of Britain were left without recourse to Rome for assistance. As a result of their successful invasion, the Anglo-Saxon peoples filled the political and social vacuum left by the implosion of the Roman Empire. Through their many kingdoms, the Anglo-Saxons established the political, social, and economic systems referred to collectively as the feudal system. Rather than being governed by the familiar system of oligarchy that would develop later, with its single king and numerous lords, dukes, and earls, Anglo-Saxon England had a complicated set of sometimes conflicting allegiances between local manor lords, known as *princips*; regional powers, or kings; and seven overlords (kings of East Anglia, Kent, Lindsey, Mercia, Northumbria, Sussex, and Wessex), who held the allegiance of the regional kings in their area.

A freeman, a person who owned land and slaves, ruled over a small village and could move up in a number of ways. If freemen gained wealth, they could become *thegns*. Thegns could attain higher status through birth (with the laws of primogeniture passing down the possession of large amounts of land) but also through service to the regional king. The companions (*gesiths*) obtained their wealth and status by service to the king. In time, this latter group of royalty became manor lords and other vassals. These vassals became the landed aristocracy; their interests were primarily local. They evolved into magistrates and interpreters of the king's law. The basic fact of political life, however, was that one freeman's power grew through his gaining the fealty of less powerful freemen. Successful thegns could expand their influence by alliances with other vassals, through conquest of other thegns, and through intermarriage. This extended to kingship as well. During the sixth and seventh centuries, a king's claim to his throne was usually based as much on the patronage he had built as on patrilineal descent and succession. In fact, patronage could lead to a more secure claim in the long run, as fictitious claimants to the throne were often numerous and having the backing of one's vassals was a good way to ensure a long reign. It was not until Alfred the Great's reign over Wessex and Kent during the tenth century, just a century before the Norman Conquest, that a monarchy, with the backing of the Church and the military, brought about a more unified state.

The sheriff coordinated the links between political divisions known as the kingdom, shire, and hundred. He was responsible for justice and collected fees and fines for the crown. The shire had its own system, functioning under inflexible legal procedures. A smaller subdivision, the hundred (a term of Germanic origin), had military implications: It supported one hundred warriors and their families. King Canute I the Great (r. 1016-1035), a Viking, reinstated the laws of Edgar (962-963), Anglo-Saxon laws designed to ease common grievances. Canute said that non-noble freemen, or peasants (*ceorles*), were the basis of Anglo-Saxon society and referred to them as "trustworthy." Even serfs, the lowest element of society, had a *wergeld* (a monetary value, literally, "man worth"). Although a serf was totally dependent on his lord, the lord could not, theoretically, abuse him. The serf could marry, could not be sold, and had to pay for the land he held subject to his producing food for the nobility.

MILITARY ACHIEVEMENT

Warfare was a constant part of life in Anglo-Saxon England. Whether it was, as during the fifth through eighth centuries, warfare between vassals in quests for greater power, or, as during the ninth through eleventh centuries, warfare against an ever-increasing threat from the Vikings, in many important ways warfare defined the parameters of Anglo-Saxon life. That said, characterizing the military arrangements of the entire Anglo-Saxon era is impossible, because it was constantly changing and took different forms in different shires, vassalages, and kingdoms. Early vassalage relationships revolved around warriors seeking out leaders who gave them the greatest chance for advancement.

Although the Venerable Bede puts the Anglo-Saxon conquest in 449 C.E., it was actually a process that began prior to Bede's date and took more than sixty years before it was completely successful. As late as 516, Britons defeated the Anglo-Saxons at Mount Badon, but by that time the Anglo-Saxons controlled much of the southeastern section of the island. The changes taking place were not just military, though; in 597, the Anglo-Saxon king of Kent, Æthelbert, invited Augustine to establish a monastery at Canterbury, beginning a very quick conversion of the island to the newly introduced religion. It did not take long for the new religion to impact warfare. In 642, Oswald, the king of Northumbria, fought Penda, the king of Mercia, in battle at Oswestry, dying in battle and gaining martyrdom in the eyes of the Church. However, religion was not always the cause of conflict. The desire for military power was always present among the Anglo-Saxon kings. In 685, Ecgfrith, the king of Northumbria, invaded Scotland, only to be defeated by an army of Picts under the leadership of his cousin. Henceforth, Anglo-Saxon power would remain confined to England.

In 789, a Viking attack in Dorset marked the beginning of nearly three hundred years of continual raids and warfare between the Vikings and Anglo-Saxons. However, the Anglo-Saxon kings did not present a united front. In 829, Egbert, king of Wessex, already the most powerful king in southern England, conquered Mercia and forced Northumbria

into submission. It would be Egbert's grandson, Alfred, who consolidated the monarchy into a single institution over all of England. However, Anglo-Saxon hegemony was anything but sure. By the late 860's, the Vikings had stepped up the level of the conflict, going from small raiding parties to a large invading army, taking York in Northumbria, and killing both the kings of Northumbria and East Anglia. By 871, the Viking army had engaged the armies of Wessex, under the leadership of their king Æthelred (or Ethelred) and his brother Alfred. Æthelred was killed, and Alfred became king. In 878, the Vikings took Wessex, forcing Alfred into hiding for eight years. By 886, Alfred had signed a treaty with the Vikings to divide England into two kingdoms, one Anglo-Saxon and one Viking. Peace between the two groups lasted until 937, when King Æthelstan of Wessex retook York from the Vikings. Ten years later, the Vikings attacked Wessex once again. At the mammoth Battle of Brunanburh, Æthelstan of Wessex won a crushing defeat against the invading army.

In 1013, another Viking invasion army landed, under the command of the Danish leader Sweyn Forkbeard. Taking London, he forced the Anglo-Saxon king, Æthelred, to flee. Sweyn died the following year, seemingly opening the door for Æthelred to return, but he died two years later. The successor to the Anglo-Saxon throne, Edmund Ironside, made a truce with Canute, resulting in a divided kingdom again. However, Edmund died shortly thereafter, leaving Canute as king of all England. In 1042, Edward the Confessor became king of England, beginning a period of increasing Norman influence.

When Edward died in January, 1066, the succession was in question. Harold Godwinson Harold, earl of Wessex, became king (Harold II) but faced claims from William, duke of Normandy, and Harold Hardrada, king of Norway. In September, 1066, Harold Hardrada invaded England, defeating Harold II's forces at the Battle of Fulford Gate, taking York, but later that month Harold II killed Harold Hardrada at the Battle of Stamford Bridge, sending his army back to Norway. While Harold II was dealing with Harold Hardrada in the north, William of Normandy landed on the southern coast of the country, setting the stage for the cataclysmic Battle of Hastings. On October

14, 1066, William's Norman forces defeated Harold II's Anglo-Saxon armies. Harold and many of his nobles were killed, and the Norman Conquest brought an end to the Anglo-Saxon era.

WEAPONS, UNIFORMS, AND ARMOR

The Anglo-Saxons employed a wide range of weapons, depending on their purpose, including spears, axes, missile weapons, swords, mail armor, nail armor, helmets, and shields. Spears and javelins were light, with long shafts and barbs on the tip. One would aim the device at the enemy and shoot the blade in his shield to limit the shield bearer's movements. The thrusting spear (winged) was stronger, could be thrown a greater distance than the javelin, and would penetrate mail and padding.

Most warriors carried a single-edged knife called

a *scramasax*. This was the symbol of a freeman; it served in everyday work as well as war, appearing in several varieties. The small hand ax (*francisca*) was an attack instrument used for close quarters. It had a heavy blade and did not travel fast. The intended could catch it and throw it back against the initiator of combat. Less favored, at least early on, were the bow and arrow, whose major purpose was to hammer down the opponent's shield. The sling, although primarily a hunting tool, was used to attack unprotected parts of the body, such as the head. Later in the period, swords began to serve as a mark of status and became the most prized weapons, especially those with well-decorated hilts. The pummel diverted an opponent's sword. Neither opponent wished to hit the other's sword, fearing that his own weapon could be broken or dulled. Swords could be used to breach armor, but their main purpose was to incapacitate the enemy by breaking bones and destroying internal organs. Shields made of linden, alder, or poplar wood were almost universally carried.

Although not all soldiers could afford it, the most common form of body armor was mail, which was made by putting small links of iron together into sheets and then creating mail shirts that extended just below the waist and were short-sleeved. Later in the period, mail shirts became longer, reaching the knees and elbows. As the mail could stop the cutting edge of weapons but not the blunt crushing effects, a padded garment was usually worn beneath the mail shirt. Mail coifs, or headpieces, covered everything but the face.

THE BRITISH ISLES, C. 885

MILITARY ORGANIZATION

After the beginning of the ninth century, the threat of invasion by the Vikings was an increasing reality for Anglo-Saxon kingdoms. Military service had always been a part of the vassalage arrangement, but its particular forms varied greatly. By the beginning of the Viking raids, the forms of military service became more standard. Although there were still professional soldiers in service of the king and a good number of mercenaries, the basic military unit became the *fyrd*, or army, which was constituted by drawing one man for each small-to-medium-sized unit of land. The particular arrangements were set out in the land-grant agreements that a thegn would have with his sponsoring lord, but normally each thegn was required to provide one *fyrdsman*.

Later, naval service was introduced on a similar basis. Larger areas, called ship-sokes, were required to provide sixty *sokesmen*, or warrior seamen, and to pay for the construction and maintenance of a warship. During peacetime, fyrdsmen had to serve four months out of the year in order to keep a sizable military force on hand in case of raids and to act as a police force. By the early eleventh century, Canute I had created a small, elite band of soldiers called *huscarls*. Although their relationship was still based on the feudal obligation, these professional soldiers lived at the king's court and received pay for their services. Huscarls were well armed and heavily armored. As they constituted a small standing army, huscarls continued in service during peacetime, performing nonmilitary duties such as collecting taxes and witnessing royal charters.

Doctrine, Strategy, and Tactics

The fyrds' strategies, like their composition, evolved over the Anglo-Saxon period. However, some general comments are possible, especially about the later period of conflict with the Vikings and the Normans, about which more information is available. After the time of Alfred, when a truly national force became a reality, the English army consisted of various forces from the eolderdoms, shires, hundreds, private sokes, and personal forces of the king and nobles. Naval forces would have been similarly derived, including the king's warships, private warships provided by eolderdoms, and ship-sokes.

The Battle of Hastings offers a case study in the ultimate form of the strategy and tactics of Anglo-Saxon warfare. The front line of the English army consisted of the king's huscarls. These were the elite warriors of the day and would have been able to blunt any advance by Norman cavalry. However, many of them were cut down by Norman spears, and this shortened their lines, as they did not want to allow lesser soldiers to weaken their lines. When the fyrdsmen failed and began to flee, the huscarls closed ranks around the king, until Norman infantry and knights broke their ever shrinking lines, killing King Harold and ending the Anglo-Saxon era at the same time.

Ancient Sources

There are a large number of primary sources on Anglo-Saxon England, most prominently the Venerable Bede's widely published *Ecclesiastical History of the English People* (731; English translation, 1723).

In addition, the Knýtlinga saga details Canute's invasion of England in 1015-1016. Asser's *Vita Ælfredi regis Angul Saxonum* (893; *Asser's Life of King Alfred*, 1906) and *Annales Cambriae* (c. 1200; *Annales Cambriae (The Annals of Wales)* in *The Anglo-Saxon Chronicle*, 1912) cover wide swaths of life in Anglo-Saxon England, which largely revolved around warfare. The seventy-three-line poem "The Battle of Brunanburh," which details the 937 English victory under King Æthelstan over a Norse-Celtic army, is contained in the *Anglo-Saxon Chronicle*, held at Corpus Christi College, Cambridge.

Books and Articles

Campbell, James. *The Anglo-Saxon.* New York: Penguin Press, 1991.
Giles, J. A. *Bede's Ecclesiastical History of England.* Whitefish, Mont.: Kessinger, 2007.

Harrison, Mark. *Anglo-Saxon Thegn A.D. 449-1066*. New York: Osprey, 1993.

Hindley, Geoffrey. *A Brief History of the Anglo-Saxons*. Philadelphia: Running Press Books, 2006.

Pollington, Stephen. *The English Warrior from Earliest Times till 1066*. Norfolk, Hockwald-cum-Wilton, Norfolk, England: Anglo-Saxon Books, 1996.

Scragg, Donald, ed. *Edgar, King of the English, 957-975*. Rochester, N.Y.: Boydell Press, 2008.

FILMS AND OTHER MEDIA

Beowulf and the Anglo-Saxons. Documentary. Arts Magic, 2006.

The Dark Ages. Documentary. History Channel, 2007.

A History of Britain: The Complete Collection. Documentary. British Broadcasting Corporation, 2008.

King Arthur. Feature film. Touchstone Pictures, 2004.

Kings and Queens of England, Vol. 1: From the Dark Days of Anglo-Saxon Times to the Glorious Reign of Elizabeth I. Documentary. Kultur Video, 2006.

Living in the Past: Life in Anglo-Saxon Times. Documentary. Kultur Video, 2006.

Arthur Steinberg and Steven L. Danver

The Lombards

Dates: c. 500-1100 C.E.

Political Considerations

Taking their name from the Latin, *Langobardi*, the Lombards included a series of Germanic tribes that originated in northern Europe and moved south, invading Italy in 568 and establishing the kingdom of Italy from 568 until 774, when they were overwhelmed by the Franks. The name subsequently became associated with the region of Lombardy in modern-day northern Italy.

The origins of the Lombards are described in the seventh century book *Origo gentis Langobardorum* (seventh century; origin of the Lombard people), which was used by the eighth century writer known as Paul the Deacon for his *Historia gentis Langobardorum* (after 796; *History of the Langobards*, 1907). These books state that the Lombards originated in parts of southern Scandinavia—as is seen in the nature of their gods—but owing to the pressure of the population on scarce land, they moved south into modern-day Germany. The Greek geographer Strabo (64 or 63 B.C.E.-after 23 C.E.) noted that they were living near the mouth of the Albis River (River Elbe), which is borne out by archaeological evidence.

Military Achievement

It is clear that from the time of the Roman emperor Augustus (r. 27 B.C.E.-14 C.E.), the fierce fighting spirit of the Lombards was well known to Romans, with further information coming from the Roman historian Velleius Paterculus. It has been suggested that the Lombards had made a treaty with the Romans that kept them out of the Battle of the Teutoburg Forest in 9 C.E. They started consolidating their military strength, and by the mid-second century, the Lombards were living along the west bank of the River Elbe, through to the Rhineland, and focusing on expanding the lands under their control, which gradually came to threaten the power of the Roman Empire.

Their main military achievements were that they were able to take advantage of the weakness of Byzantine Italy, invading in 568 under King Alboin (r. 565-572), who had succeeded to the throne after a power struggle. Alboin had led the Lombards to victory over the Gepids, an eastern Germanic tribe, and his success caused the Romans to enlist his help in defeating King Totila of the Ostrogoths, a victory that took place in 552.

It was after this that Alboin recognized the weakness of the Romans, and he allied with the Saxons and invaded the Italian peninsula, taking Venice and then advancing into Liguria, taking Tuscany. His forces were never strong enough, however, to take fortified cities such as Rome and Ravenna, and Alboin's victory led to his ruling much of Italy for three and a half years, until he was assassinated in 572. In spite of this, the Lombards remained in control of much of Italy until 774, when Charlemagne led the Franks against them on the pretext of coming to the defense of the papacy.

Weapons, Uniforms, and Armor

In the first century C.E., the Lombards, in common with most of the other Germanic tribes, were armed with swords, axes, spears, and shields—wielding their long swords (*spatha*) like their axes, to cut and harry opponents rather than to stab and slash as the Romans did, although many wore daggers (*scramasaxes*) as well. Archaeological evidence indicates that the scabbard was often attached to a belt slung over the shoulder and then secured to the belt around the waist. The shield, usually relatively small and round, made from bronze rather than wood—and with a spike (*umbo*) on it—was used to take blows from the opponent and was good for combat in which the numbers were evenly matched or the Lombards were more numerous than their enemy. In close combat, or when the Lombards were outnumbered, their shields were not as good as the Roman shields, which protected more of those who bore them.

The use of horses by the Lombards is an issue debated by historians, with the Lombard law issued by King Aistulf stating that all wealthy Lombard warriors should have a horse, and those who were unable to afford a horse should be able to use a bow and arrow. The Ostrogoths were known to deploy dismounted archers, and this was probably the case with the Lombards as well.

As to horses, certainly the royal bodyguards and retainers had their own horses, and when fighting the Franks the Lombards used horses more often in battles. In May, 2008, archaeologists working on a sixth century site at Testona, near Turin, uncovered the grave of a twenty-five-year-old Lombard warrior who had been buried with his horse. The skeleton of a hunting dog was also found nearby. Although there was heavy reliance on horses, it seems that, like the Anglo-Saxons, the Lombards used their horses largely for getting to battlefields and around battlefields, with much of the fighting taking place on foot, although some fighting on horseback was inevitable. Certainly a surviving letter from Lupus of Ferrières to Bishop Pardulus of Lyon in 849 noted that the writer was unable to carry out his duties as an infantryman and cavalryman, suggesting that Lombard fighters were trained in fighting both on foot and on horseback.

Although chiefs wore some armor (often only breastplates), for much of their period in Italy the Lombards, who relied heavily on their speed and mobility on the battlefield, did not do so. However, a gilded copper repoussé helmet plaque from the late sixth century depicting King Agilulf does show guards to a king wearing armor in plates—possibly iron or leather, and with helmets that have plumes on their tops. Some carvings of Lombard civilians show them wearing tunics with belts, in the Roman fashion, but it appears that warriors wore much heavier tunics, sometimes protected by leather pads, and also trousers that were tied up with leggings.

MILITARY ORGANIZATION

Regarding the military organization of the Lombards, it is known that certain families owed their position in society to their being related to the bodyguards of the king; these bodyguards were well trained and fought as a cohesive unit in small engagements. By the eleventh century, the men in this unit were often dressed in chain mail and were influenced in their military planning by their battles with the Normans.

In larger battles the Lombards relied on numbers of less well-armed men drawn from villages, either as volunteers or as conscripts. In the periods of the barbarian invasions, these warriors were involved in regular fighting and could form themselves into effective fighting units with ease. As time progressed, however, and the Lombards came to control much of Italy, their military organization became more relaxed; this is what allowed them to be overwhelmed so easily by the Franks.

DOCTRINE, STRATEGY, AND TACTICS

Before the sixth century, the Lombards formed themselves into large raiding parties and skirmished extensively with the rival Germanic tribes. However, for the invasion of Italy they had to form a much stronger military unit in order to be able to defeat their opponents. In battle, they relied heavily on mobility, and often a large proportion of the soldiers were cavalry—Lombard leaders tending to downplay the importance of archers. This battle strategy often involved the Lombards charging their opponents, with the aim of forming a wedge in the enemy lines.

As the Lombard kings changed from being invaders to being rulers who governed large areas in Italy, the tactics in battle changed, with more and more Lombards fighting on foot. By the eleventh century, the Lombards had started to adapt to new military tactics, and in battle they tended to revert to the Norman tactics of a shield wall for the infantry, with the cavalry, backed by archers, sent against their opponents.

MEDIEVAL SOURCES

There are a number of sources on the Lombards, the most well known being that by Paul the Deacon, *Historia gentis Langobardorum*, which in turn drew heavily on the *Origo gentis Langobardorum* from the seventh century. Other information comes from a range of contemporary accounts, such as that in the *Codex Gothanus*, which dates from about 830. Further descriptions come from Frankish, Norman, and other accounts by the Lombards' adversaries.

BOOKS AND ARTICLES

Christie, Neil. *The Lombards: The Ancient Longobards*. Malden, Mass.: Blackwell, 1995.

Halsall, Guy. *Warfare and Society in the Barbarian West, 450-900*. London: Taylor and Francis, 2003.

Nicolle, David. *Italian Medieval Armies, 1000-1300*. New York: Osprey, 2002.

Pohl, Walter, ed. *Kingdoms of the Empire: The Integration of Barbarians in Late Antiquity*. Leiden, Netherlands: E. J. Brill, 1997.

FILMS AND OTHER MEDIA

Barbarians 2: Lombards. Documentary. History Channel, 2007.

Justin Corfield

THE MAGYARS

Dates: c. 500-1100 C.E.

POLITICAL CONSIDERATIONS

During the period from 500 to 1100, the Magyars, or Hungarians, underwent immense political and social transformations. Prior to their settlement in the Carpathian basin in 895 or 896, the Magyars lived a nomadic lifestyle on the southern steppes of modern-day Russia and Ukraine. Traditionally, the Magyars were said to have consisted of seven tribes, and though each tribe had its leaders, the tribes were held together in some form of tribal confederation. Around the middle of the ninth century, the Hungarians moved farther west between the Dnieper River and the lower Danube, known as Etelköz.

Pressure from another nomadic group from the east known as the Pechenegs forced the Magyars into the Carpathian basin, where they eventually established themselves as overlords of the native population. The arrival of the Magyars into the Carpathian basin is traditionally termed "the Conquest" in Hungarian historiography. Initially, the Magyars continued the practice of conducting raids, some of which ranged as far as Iberia and Italy. However, exposure to the settled peoples of the Carpathian basin, combined with a series of serious defeats at the hands of Otto I the Great in the west (Augsburg, 955) and Byzantine and Bulgarian forces in the south (Arcadiopolis, 970), ended the practice. The last decades of the tenth century and the first decades of the eleventh saw a series of wars for supremacy among the Magyars themselves. Stephen I (István; r. 997-1038), with the help of knights brought in the entourage of his Bavarian wife Gisella, defeated the other Magyar tribal leaders, and established the dominance of the Árpád clan. Stephen also set the Hungarians on the course of becoming a Western-oriented kingdom based on Catholic Christianity.

MILITARY ACHIEVEMENT

The Magyars established themselves within the Carpathian basin during the Conquest, and from there they staged raids across western and southeastern Europe. After the civil wars, the Árpáds under Stephen gained supremacy over the other tribes and created a Western-oriented kingdom. Stephen's victory over the other Magyar tribes fashioned a viable state that eventually became fully integrated into Europe.

The Magyars conducted raids against Bavaria, Moravia, and Bulgaria while they still lived east of the Danube in the 880's and 890's. The Carpathian basin was, therefore, not unknown to them. In 895-896, the Magyars came under attack by a neighboring nomadic group called the Pechenegs. By 899, the Magyars began the first of the great raids on western Europe when Arnulf of Carinthia paid them to conduct raids on his enemies in northern Italy. With each year, the Magyars raided farther into western Europe, crossing the Rhine for the first time in 911 and raiding Burgundy in 913. Almost yearly raids sent the Magyars as far as the Iberian Peninsula, where in 942 they attacked both Andalusia and Galicia. The period of raids came to an end, in part, because of two significant defeats inflicted on the Hungarians. In 955, a Magyar army crossing Bavaria was destroyed by Otto I at Augsburg, and in 970, a Magyar army suffered an equally significant loss to the combined Bulgarian and Byzantine army at Arcadiopolis.

Following these defeats came a series of civil wars in which the descendants of Árpáds established primacy over the other Magyar tribes. The main actors in the rise of the Árpáds were Prince Géza (died 997) and his son Stephen, or István, who was crowned king of Hungary in 1001. Stephen had married Gisella, the daughter of the duke of Bavaria, and several German knights in her entourage lent their service to the rising Stephen. After Stephen I's death in 1038, the new kingdom underwent a series of wars for the throne. During the course of these wars, the German emperor invaded three separate times in attempts to put his protégé on the throne. The kingdom withstood the crisis, but German intervention was a continuing threat until 1077, when László I (r. 1077-1095) came to power. A stabilization of the kingdom occurred under László, who fended off an invasion from the east by the nomadic Cumans. László also added Croatia to the crown through conquest in 1091.

WEAPONS, UNIFORMS, AND ARMOR

The primary weapon of the Magyars was the recurved composite bow. The importance of the bow is seen in Regino of Prüm's testimony about the Magyars: "They seldom use swords, but they kill thousands with arrows." The bow is called composite because it was constructed using several materials, such as wood, sinew, and horn. In addition, the bow itself could consist of up to five different joined pieces: the handle, to which were attached the two arms, which in turn would have pieces of hardwood attached to their ends (the "horns"). All these pieces were connected using a tongue-and-groove structure. The foundation material of the bow was most often a soft wood, such as birch, and softened, degreased sinews were attached to the front (the side away from the archer) with a glue made from fish innards. On the back of the bow (toward the archer) was glued horn. The sinew and the horn provided the relatively short bows (40-47 inches, roughly 100-120 centimeters) with great strength. The "horns" provided leverage with which the archer could bend the bow even further. The bow was recurved because prior to being strung, it rested in a slight "C" shape toward the front at approximately a 35-degree angle, and only when strung would the curve be in the normal direction (toward the archer). The arrows were typically of willow, birch, or cottonwood and were around 20-24 inches (50-60 centimeters) long. The arrowheads were typically of iron and were rhomboid in shape, with a slight spine running the length. The composite

recurved bow had maximum effective ranges of 500-600 feet (150-200 meters).

Though by far the most important, the bow and arrow were not the only weapons used by the Magyars. For close combat, a short lance appears to have been common, and there is some evidence of the use of mace and ax. The Magyars also used the slightly curved single-edged saber, though its presence seems to have been limited to the more prominent members of society. In the tenth century the saber was replaced among the Magyar elite by the double-edged sword. As for defensive armor, most warriors wore only leather armor, although aristocrats covered the leather with either bone or iron plate.

MILITARY ORGANIZATION

The organization of the Magyar military experienced significant transformation during the time period in question. These changes were directly the results of the transition of Hungarian society to one based on landownership and the development of a Western-style monarchy. Before the rise of the Árpád Dynasty, the Hungarians were organized into a tribal alliance of seven tribes. Some historians have held that the army consisted of the retinues of the tribal and clan leaders and that the common freeman would therefore not have participated in warfare. However, consensus now generally holds that the population was divided between free and servile, and all free males (the overwhelming majority) would take part in war. The Hungarian army during the era of the tribal alliance was divided into units of tens, hundreds, thousands, and tens of thousands. It is difficult to determine how many fighters there were among the Magyar tribes, but scholars have estimated their numbers to be approximately twenty thousand at the time of the Conquest.

The tenth and eleventh centuries saw a great transformation in the military system of the Hungarians. First Géza, then his son, Stephen, used foreign immigrant knights as their retinue. These German and Italian knights formed the elite units in the army and were completely separate from the native, Magyar units, which were still essentially mounted archers.

VIKING, MAGYAR, AND MUSLIM INVASIONS, NINTH CENTURY

After Stephen took control in the civil wars of the first part of the tenth century, the Hungarian military was reorganized. The organizational center of the army was the castle, which had its own lands and subjects to support it. This territory was known as the "castle county" and was headed by a royal official called an *ispán*. At the same time, the base of power became landownership, and common free Magyars were allowed to settle on the land of the more powerful magnates in exchange for their labor service. In this way they became subjects of their new lords and excluded from the army. Some of the warriors, however, were settled on the castle lands and continued to serve in the army under the command of their ispán.

DOCTRINE, STRATEGY, AND TACTICS

Warfare provided the Magyars with a significant source of income, and Magyar campaigns were frequently raids in force with the purpose of obtaining plunder. Captives provided a significant source of income for the Magyars, as they were sold into slavery. The Magyars also commonly sold their military services to the highest bidder. Thus, in 881 Svatopluk I of Great Moravia paid the Magyars to attack the eastern Franks. In 894, the situation was reversed, and the Franks hired the Magyars in their conflict against Svatopluk. In the following year, the Magyars again served Svatopluk against the Franks.

The tactics of the Magyars were those common to other steppe nomads and centered on lightning raids, showers of arrows to disrupt the enemy, and the feigned retreat. At the beginning of engagement, the Magyars would release volleys of arrows from horseback into the enemy's ranks in an attempt to disrupt them. The Battle of Ennsburg in 907 is a clear example of the use of the feigned retreat by the Magyars. After a failed invasion of Hungary, the Bavarians sought refuge behind defensive earthworks. The Magyars drew them from behind their defenses by simulating a retreat, and the Bavarians soon found themselves surrounded by other Hungarian forces that had been well hidden and were quickly destroyed. Similarly, the Magyars defeated a Bulgarian-Byzantine coalition in 934 when a feigned retreat allowed the Hungarians to surround and destroy the Byzantine heavy cavalry. However, the feigned retreat was successful only if the enemy forces lost battle discipline while pursuing the apparently retreating Magyars. At the Battle of Merseburg (933), neither volleys of arrows nor feigned retreat was successful in breaking the ranks of the Bavarian forces, and the Magyars quickly withdrew from the battlefield rather than risk combat with the still-closed ranks of the Bavarians.

The military reforms of Stephen took time to complete, and the Hungarian military was not fully Westernized until the thirteenth century. As a result, Hungarian tactics frequently relied on the mounted archer and feigned retreat through the eleventh century. For example, it seems likely that the Magyar tribal leader Ajtony and his army fell victim to the tactics of feigned retreat and encirclement by Stephen's forces at Nagyősz in 1008.

MEDIEVAL SOURCES

The main literary sources regarding the pre-Conquest Magyar life and military affairs come from Muslim geographers or from Byzantine authors commenting on the steppe peoples. Unfortunately, several of the key works regarding the Magyars still await translation into English. The earliest Muslim source is the work of the Persian geographer Ahmad al-Jayhāni, who served in the Saminid court in the tenth century. Jayhāni's work is no longer extant, but portions of it can be found in Ibn-Rustah's *Kitāb al-a'lāq al-nafisah* (c. 903-913; French translation, *Ibn Rusteh: Les Atours précieux*, 1955). Portions of Jayhāni's work are also found in that of the later Persian geographer Gardizi. The relevant portions of Gardizi's *Zayn al-akhbār* (c. 1050-1053) have been translated by Arsenio P. Martinez in "Gardizi's Two Chapters on the Turks," which appeared in the journal *Archivum Eurasiae Medii Aevi* in 1982. Gardizi described the Magyars as conducting frequent raids against neighbors primarily to obtain slaves to sell to the Byzantines.

Byzantine authors provide the most detailed descriptions of Magyar warfare. Unfortunately, the relevant portions of the most important work, Leo VI the Wise's *Tactica* (c. 895-908; tactics), has yet to be translated into English. Constantine VII Porphyrogenitus's *De administrando imperio* (c. 948-952; *On the Administration of the Empire*, 1967) described the political associations of the Magyars, whom Constantine termed "Turkos."

For the transformations that occurred with the supremacy of the Árpáds, the early laws of the kingdom are very useful: *Decreta regni mediaevalis Hungariae* (1000-1526; *The Laws of the Medieval Kingdom of Hungary*, 1989 and ongoing). The chronicle composed by Simon de Kéza, *Gesta Hungarorum* (1282-1285; *The Deeds of the Hungarians*, 1999), provides a picture of the myth of the Conquest as it had developed by the thirteenth century. In his account, Simon depicts the Hungarians as the descendants of an earlier steppe people—the Huns.

BOOKS AND ARTICLES

Engel, Pál. *The Realm of St. Stephan: A History of Medieval Hungary, 895-1526*. New York: I. B. Taurus, 1999.

Horváth, András Pálóczi. *Pechenegs, Cumans, Iasians: Steppe Peoples in Medieval Hungary*. Budapest: Covina, 1989.

Karasulas, Antony. *Mounted Archers of the Steppe, 600 B.C.-A.D. 1300*. New York: Osprey, 2004.

Kristó, Gyula. *Hungarian History in the Ninth Century*. Szeged, Hungary: Szegedi Közép-korász Műhely, 1996.

Róna-Tas, András. *Hungarians and Europe in the Early Middle Ages: An Introduction to Early Hungarian History*. Budapest: Central European University Press, 1999.

Sugár, Peter. *A History of Hungary*. Bloomington: Indiana University Press, 1994.

FILMS AND OTHER MEDIA

The Conquest (*Honfoglalás*). Feature film. Korona Film/Magyar Televízió, 1997.

Cameron Sutt

THE VIKINGS

Dates: c. 700-1066 C.E.

POLITICAL CONSIDERATIONS

The Vikings were Swedish and Danish/Norwegian. Viking homelands were made up of kingdoms divided into districts. Farmers, merchants, the rich, and the king all theoretically had equal voices in the *thing*, a political assembly, and in the hearing of land disputes and criminal cases. In reality, wealth and power led to greater influence in gatherings with few formal procedures. Sometimes the only justice was the feud or trial by ordeal. When justice seemed impossible, slighted merchants could take matters into their own hands.

Viken was an area located near Oslofjord, and the Vikingar were merchants disgruntled by tariffs levied by their rulers on goods passing across Danish waters. Rather than acknowledge their subordinate status, they went to sea as traders. Swedes sailed to Russia, the Islamic Caliphate, and Byzantium. Danes and Norwegians sailed to Iceland, Greenland, North America, and Europe.

Despite Charlemagne's establishment of the Carolingian Empire, European kingdoms were weak and disunited by feuds and rivalries—and ripe for exploitation. The modern nation-state was centuries away, and a kingdom often consisted of a town and however much of the hinterland the sovereign could hold. Besieged at Paris, Frankish king Charles III (the Simple) gave Normandy to the Viking Rollo on condition that Rollo become Christian. The Scandinavians were absorbed by the dominant French culture.

Danish Vikings ruled half of England from late in the ninth century into the eleventh century. In the Danelaw, Scandinavian lords governed under Danish law. By 1014 England was virtually under Danish rule. Knud (also Knut or Canute), known as Canute the Great, became English king in 1016, marrying Ethelred II's widow as well. By 1033 Vikings controlled England, Normandy, southern Sweden, and Denmark, the lands surrounding the Baltic Sea that provided entry to the waterways that led to Europe and Arab lands. In 1066 the Norwegian king Harold III Hardrada was defeated at Stamford Bridge, leading to the Norwegian consolidation of their gains and the end of Viking expansion.

Vikings extorted and stole and became Normans and Irish and English and Byzantines. In the North Atlantic they extended the European frontier. They influenced languages, cultures, and political institutions. They revitalized towns and commerce, making commercial centers of York, Kiev, and other towns.

MILITARY ACHIEVEMENT

The first Viking raid in Britain was at Lindisfarne in 793. Within five years thereafter, the Vikings had raided in Northumbria, Wales, Ireland, the Isle of Man, the Isle of Iona, and islands off France's Aquitaine. Thus began a 250-year reign that terrorized Europeans, ending the period between the sixth and eighth centuries when Europeans experienced little external invasion and leaving Europe at the conclusion a more cohesive area with a broader awareness of a larger world.

Vikings had been for the most part farmers and traders. When they began trading in Europe they noticed that many European locations were wealthy and poorly defended, and by the eighth century trade was secondary for the Vikings, done only if the Europeans were too well armed for the Vikings to plunder with impunity. The eighth century was also a time of European disarray, a consequence of the Fall of Rome in the fifth century, and the Carolingian Empire was powerful in France and Germany but not in the rest of Europe, where Charlemagne lacked the numbers to resist the Vikings. Between 790 and 840 the Vikings used the advantage of the shallow draft

VIKING RAIDS, 790-850

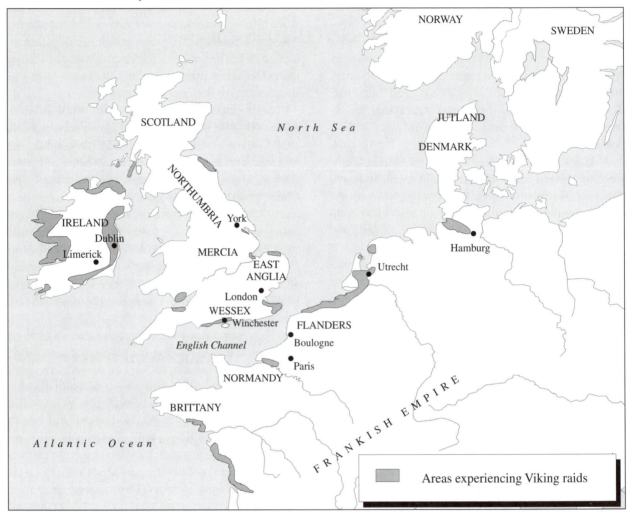

of their longships to strike coastal towns and monasteries quickly, looting and departing before the locals could react. They hit coastal England and France first, moving along the rivers on later forays.

Between 841 and 875 the raids became more frequent, faster, larger, and more intense. From initial forays of three ships they grew to forays of more than three hundred ships at a time, and the Vikings plundered, killed, enslaved, and burned before departing. In 843 they wintered on foreign soil for the first time, settling in Aquitaine and never leaving it. The Danish Great Army in East Anglia established winter quarters in 873-874.

Attacks after 841 shifted to the Mediterranean. In 844 a Viking fleet hit Nantes, Toulouse, Gijon, Lisbon, and Seville before being defeated and forced back to Aquitaine. After that, another fleet hit North Africa, France, and Spain before being defeated in Italy. Vikings as permanent residents were a political threat, leading many rulers to attempt to bribe them to leave. The Vikings at this time established their Great Army, thousands organized into smaller bands that fought on their own, sometimes with each other.

From 876 to 911 the Vikings and the Great Army plundered but also began colonizing their English and French bases as well as establishing settlements in Ireland, Russia, Iceland, and other lands they raided from England and France. In 911 Charles the Simple ended the raids by giving the Vikings Normandy. The Viking Rollo became a duke and Christianized, a vassal of the French king and the ruler of Normandy. Normans expanded to Italy and Sicily, pushing out Byzantines, Lombards, and Muslims. They established the Kingdom of Naples and Sicily, friendly to the pope and a counter to other Italian nobles.

Vikings also raided Persia and North Africa. They were in Iceland and Greenland and touched North America. With only a handful of people (Scandinavia had a population of barely one million in all), they controlled territory with millions of inhabitants.

WEAPONS, UNIFORMS, AND ARMOR

The most common Viking weapon was an ax that could be thrown or swung. The "bearded ax" had a curved blade. An adept fighter could decapitate an ox with a single blow using this weapon.

Viking spears, which were either thrust or thrown, had iron blades on wooden shafts, usually ash; they ranged from six to ten feet long. The iron blades took various shapes, from long spikes to broad leaves. A skilled spearman could reportedly throw two spears at once or catch one in flight and throw it back on target.

Swords were expensive and represented high status. They were double-edged and about thirty-five inches long. Early Viking sabers were single-edged; strips of wrought iron and mild steel were twisted and forged together, and than a hardened edge was added. Scabbards were of wood bound in leather. Later swords had homogeneous steel blades. Because weapons symbolized wealth and status as well as battle-readiness, they were often decorated with twisted wire or inlays in copper, bronze, and silver.

Wealthy Viking warriors wore expensive chainmail hauberks or byrnies, tunics reaching below the waist; these were worn over heavy cloth padding. Average fighters wore leather armor, metal plates attached to leather or cloth backing, or padded leather shirts topped by iron breastplates. Reindeer hide was more effective than mail as armor.

The helmets Vikings wore were made of iron, some of a solid piece hammered into a cone or bowl shape, others of various pieces of iron riveted or tied together with leather. The nosepieces were of iron or leather, and some face guards protected the eyes. Cheek guards were uncommon. Helmets were most likely worn only by the leaders, because they were extremely hard to make; average fighters wore hide caps. Horned helmets were not part of the Viking armory because such headgear would be unbalanced and heavy in battle while offering no protection. Horned helmets probably were used ceremonially by pre-Viking chieftains.

The typical Viking shield was circular, about three feet across. It was wooden, with a central hole for an iron handgrip riveted to the back of the shield boards. An iron boss over the hole protected the hand. Leather covered the shield, and the rim was bound with either leather or metal. Some shields were painted in simple patterns or with scenes of heroes and moments from

TURNING POINTS

793	Vikings sack Lindisfarne Abbey in northern England.
843	Vikings sack Dorestadt and Utrecht.
845	Charles the Bald, king of the Franks, pays Vikings money to retreat.
886	Last Viking siege of Paris.
891	The Vikings suffer a rare defeat at Louvain.
911	Rollo receives county of Normandy from the French king.
930	Vikings settle Iceland.
954	English expel the last Viking king from York.
1013	Danish king Sweyn I Forkbeard defeats English king Ethelred I, forcing him into exile.
1016-1035	Sweyn's son Canute rules both England and Denmark.
1066	Norwegian king Harold Hardrada is defeated at Stamford Bridge in England; William of Normandy defeats English at Hastings.

mythological stories. Around 1000, the continental kite-shaped shield, which better protected the bearer's legs, came into use among the Vikings.

The Vikings' longships used sails and oars. The builders employed overlapping planks split from trees with mallet and wedge, riveted the planks with iron, and caulked them with tarred, twisted horsehair or other animal fur. The ships ranged in length from about 60 feet to 120 feet, and both bow and stern had the same shape, allowing them to change direction without turning around. Steering was accomplished through the use of a starboard oar, not a rudder. The average speed of the longships was 10-11 knots. With frightful figureheads and red-painted sails to intimidate foes, a longship with sixty armed Vikings aboard was a fearsome weapon.

MILITARY ORGANIZATION

The early Viking formation was the *hird* (a medieval term for hearth), the lord's retinue or household or court, which consisted of the men who lived in the lord's domicile and had sworn loyalty to him—in effect, his knights. They were often countrymen attracted by the reputation of the lord for generosity or bravery, but some were more mercenary, professionals in search of the best opportunity for gain. By the thirteenth century the hird developed ranks comparable to the continental squire, man-at-arms, and knight. The hird in time of war served as the core of the army.

The country was divided into units called *hafna*, each of which had to provide a mark of gold toward the arming and manning of a ship. The ship would have a crew of forty to sixty *lithsmen*, each supplied with a spear, a helmet, and a shield. Each ship had a single mail shirt, and bows with arrows were provided at one per six benches. There may have been a rotation in service similar to that of the Saxon *fyrd*, because full-time duty would have been onerous on the estates, even with the professionals in the retinue.

During the eleventh century, the Viking military became more professional. In 1012, during the attack of Sweyn I and Canute against England, forty-five ships separated from Sweyn's fleet and promised to defend Æthelred's (Ethelred's) land in return for food and clothing. After disbanding the army, Canute maintained a standing army of forty ships. The lithsmen were professionals, unlike the draftees of the earlier age. Lithsmen received eight marks a year per oar. The system lasted until the reign of Edward, when the Danish influence faded. The Danish ships sailed away with their wealth.

Canute established the *tinglith*, or *huscarl*, which formalized the *hird*. The difference between the tinglith and the hird was that the tinglith was supported only by the king through taxes and fees on towns, which sometimes provided *butsecarles* in lieu of fyrd service. The butsecarles were mercenaries who served in garrison to safeguard a town while its men were on the fyrd.

Viking armies consisted of *drengs*, or young warriors, and *thegns*, or older crewmen. The *merkismathr* was standard-bearer (an important post because the standard was believed to have magical properties). The king's deputy was the *stallari*, or marshal. The king's retinue in the eleventh century consisted of about ninety men along with associated hangers-on and menials. The retinue broke out into *hirdmenn*, those who shared the hearth, and *gestir*, guests who received half hirdmenn pay. Gestir lived apart from the household with their own leader. They were the king's police, tax collectors, and enforcers of justice. Hirdmenn were the handpicked elite, loyal to king and the other hirdmenn—Viking knights, in a sense.

DOCTRINE, STRATEGY, AND TACTICS

Vikings had no standing army for most of the period, and their discipline was slight. There were no set fighting formations, but loyalty to the lord helped the force remain cohesive. Weapons training began with hunting, games, and raiding at an early age. The ambitious would-be warrior sought the best retinue, there to earn wealth, weapons, and fame. War became necessary as a way of keeping the retinue satisfied and keeping the warriors from shifting to rival retinues.

The principal battle method was the strong blow

An artist's depiction of a tenth century Viking raid carried out in Norse longboats.

that could break through the enemy's armor and crush bone and flesh. Where space permitted, the battle-ax was commonly used. The broad axes of the late tenth and eleventh centuries required two hands to wield, so warriors carrying these weapons were shieldless; they would hide behind the front line of fighters until, at the opportune moment, they raced into the open and attacked enemy fighters.

Through the eleventh century Vikings were foot soldiers. Their horses were small and inferior to those of the lands they attacked. Leaders sometimes had horses for rapid movement to the battle, where they dismounted to fight.

Vikings preferred to hit and run, but when forced to stand and fight they formed a shield-fort, the *skjaldborg*, preferably on a hill or with marshes on the flanks. A bodyguard stood close by the commander. The Vikings' foes drank ale or mead to fortify their courage before taking on the skjaldborg.

The battle began with the Vikings throwing a spear across the enemy line to dedicate the soon-to-be-slain foe to Odin, the chief Norse god. A rain of spears, arrows, and other missiles followed. If the two sides still were not ready to quit, one attacked the other. A wedge of twenty to thirty warriors, the *svinfylking* (boar formation), charged and either broke the enemy or initiated a general melee. When the two sides collided with thrusting spears, swinging axes, and ramming shields, neither wanted to back off. The side that broke away and turned to run left itself open to slaughter by the pursuers.

The maniacal warriors known as berserkers may have worn the skins of wolves or bears and may have fought in groups. Berserkers believed themselves protected and given supernatural powers by Odin; they drank ale infused with hallucinogenic mushrooms and attacked with no regard for any wounds they received. They often bit the edges of their shields in battle. Some scholars have speculated that berserkers tended to be psychopaths.

It was uncommon for Vikings to engage in sea battles, and those they fought took place close to shore. Ropes tied the longships in a line facing the opposing fleet. After an exchange of arrows and other missiles, hand-to-hand fighting ensued as each crew sought to board the opposing ship. The goal was to capture, not destroy, the opposing ship, as it represented a significant investment in money, time, and resources.

MEDIEVAL SOURCES

Medieval Scandinavia lacked the literary tradition of the Islamic and Christian areas. Contemporary sources on the Vikings are mostly Anglo-Saxon or Frankish cautionary tales written between the thirteenth and fifteenth centuries. They include chronicles, sagas, skaldic epics, laws, and runic inscriptions. Runic inscriptions are the exception, being written at the time of events they describe. They are normally only a few lines long, and they are scattered both geographically and chronologically. Runic sticks are few, but rune stones are more common, with 140 in Denmark.

The other types of source are all foreign. Most of them are written in Latin in the context of a military or religious conflict with the Vikings. Annals are the chronological yearbooks written by a country's clerics about internal and foreign policy. Among them are the *Annals of the Frankish Empire*, which reports that in 808 Godfred, king of the Danes, fortified his southern border in defense against Emperor Charlemagne of the Frankish Empire. The *Annála Uladh* (entries from 431 to 1540; *Annals of Ulster*, 1895) of January, 840, mention the first foray by the Vikings: They plundered and took bishops, priests, and scholars captive, putting others to death. These annals date from the fifteenth century, but scholars regard them as reliable reports of the Viking activity in the Christian world during their era.

Also important is the *Anglo-Saxon Chronicle*, a collection of documents on Anglo-Saxon England to 1154. Some are secondary sources based on legend, but there are also firsthand accounts of Viking conquest and plundering not covered elsewhere. *Povest vremennykh let* (*The Russian Primary Chronicle*, 1930) dates from the eleventh century to the twelfth century.

Travelogues and biographies usually mention the Vikings only in passing. *Chronicon Roskildense* (c. 1138-1140; Roskilde chronicle) and *Gesta Danorum* (1514; *The History of the Danes*, 1894, 1980-1981), the latter by Saxo Grammaticus, are the two oldest histories of Denmark. Both are modeled on the work of Adam of Bremen, whose *Gesta Hammaburgensis ecclesiae pontificum* (c. 1075; *History of the Archbishops of Hamburg-Bremen*, 1959) contains, in its fourth book, *Description of the Islands in the North*, an account from Danish king Sweyn II, making it an important source for the period from 870 to 1080. The biography of Saint Ansgar deals with his missionary work in Denmark and Sweden in the ninth century. Arab travelogues include that of Ahmad ibn Fadlan, who met the Vikings on the Volga River in the tenth century. The Spanish Arab Ibn-Rustah recorded a tenth century visit to Hedeby in *Kitāb al-a'lāq al-nafisah* (c. 903-913; French translation, *Ibn Rusteh: Les Atours précieux*, 1955). Other travelers who wrote about the Vikings include Ohtere and Wulfstan.

Sagas are high medieval Icelandic tales about Norse notables. They provide information about ships, fleet sizes, and other elements of Viking society. Snorri Sturluson's *Heimskringla* (c. 1230-1235; English translation, 1844) is the progenitor of the Scandinavian skaldic (bardic) epics.

Occasional medieval legal texts have laws traceable back to the Viking era. Among them is the *Gulatinglov*, the model for Icelandic law. It dates from before 930 but was written in the twelfth or thirteenth century.

BOOKS AND ARTICLES

Durham, Keith. *Viking Longship*. New York: Osprey, 2002.

Durham, Keith, Mark Harrison, and Magnus Magnusson. *The Vikings: Voyagers of Discovery and Plunder*. New York: Osprey, 2008.

Heath, Ian. *The Vikings*. New York: Osprey, 1985.

Santosuosso, Antonio. *Barbarians, Marauders, and Infidels: The Ways of Medieval Warfare*. Boulder, Colo.: Westview Press, 2004.

Siddom, J. K. *Viking Weapons and Warfare*. Stroud, Gloucestershire, England: Tempus, 2003.

Sprague, Martina. *Norse Warfare: The Unconventional Battle Strategies of the Ancient Vikings*.

FILMS AND OTHER MEDIA

Erik the Viking. Feature film. KB Erik the Viking, 1989.

Ivanhoe. Feature film. Metro-Goldwyn-Mayer, 1952.

The Long Ships. Feature film. Avala Film, 1964.

The Norseman. Feature film. Charles B. Pierce Film Productions, 1978.

Prince Valiant. Feature film. Constantin Film Produktion, 1997.

Prince Valiant. Feature film. Twentieth Century-Fox, 1954.

The Thirteenth Warrior. Feature film. Touchstone, 1999.

The Vikings. Documentary. Public Broadcasting Service/WGBH, 2000.

The Vikings. Feature film. Brynaprod, 1958.

The War Lord. Feature film. Court Productions, 1965.

Warrior Challenge: Vikings. Documentary. Public Broadcasting Service/Thirteen/WNET New York, 2003.

John H. Barnhill

ARMIES OF CHRISTENDOM AND THE AGE OF CHIVALRY

Dates: c. 918-1500 C.E.

POLITICAL CONSIDERATIONS

Most historians agree that warfare in the Middle Ages cannot be studied in isolation. By its very definition, war—organized violence by groups against other groups—reflects the societies involved and, in turn, shapes them. This dynamic was especially true in the high medieval period, when military needs fueled administrative developments in finance, organization, recruitment, supply, and the tools of government itself. Before then, however, the very deterioration of such structures would limit the forms that warfare could take. Larger cultural issues would likewise play off of, and be played upon, by war. The Christian Church spent centuries trying to restrain or redirect the violence of its newest converts, the Germanic peoples. In time, however, the Church would find itself inextricably entangled in violent endeavors. On the secular side, the cult of chivalry developed first as the expression of a new, knightly identity; once in place, this new ethos sometimes had its own power to shape the contours of battle.

Although scholarly ideas about its dominance and character are undergoing continual revision, the network of feudal relations that lay across most of Europe in this period was the hallmark of medieval politics and war. In summary, these arrangements were coming into being even during the reign of Charlemagne (r. 768-814), but their evolution was speeded by the breakup of his empire and of effective central government, coupled with foreign invasions by Vikings and Magyars. By the end of the first millennium, the Western European population's overwhelming need for protection had caused feudalism to be cobbled together in varying ways across the former Carolingian lands. The typical model of feudalism appeared thus: Men in need (vassals) would approach someone (a lord) capable of protecting them because of his already collected followers. In officially entering this lord's entourage, the vassals would swear faithfulness or fealty to that lord. The price of protection for the vassal was his own service in the lord's retinue, or mesne, as it was later called. Other obligations later became standard, but military service was the original and fundamental one. These early vassals depended on the lord for upkeep, and in the absence of a money economy, the institution of the fief evolved. Usually in the form of land, the fief provided the economic component of feudal relationships; with it, the vassal had the wherewithal to report with all the panoply of war: horse, armor, weapons, and supplies for campaign.

Military historians have recognized for some time that feudalism did not accurately describe all the means whereby medieval armies came together. The idea of the "nation-at-arms" still compelled many to answer a summons. This was as true of the Anglo-Saxon *fyrd* before 1066 as it would be 150 years later when King John (1166-1216) of England summoned even the most recently liberated serfs to repel French invaders. On the continent, King Louis VI (1081-1137) in 1124 gathered more of his vassals together to face a German attack than he had ever commanded as a feudal lord. In addition, money was never truly absent; its role in recruiting and maintaining armies continued throughout the High Middle Ages. Thus, military historians see less incongruity than do legal historians in the use and prevalence of contracts to engage soldiers in the late medieval period.

It would be difficult to overstate the reciprocal influences on each other of the Church and medieval warfare. At first, though, the Church saw little success in its efforts to curtail the violence of its members. Before the year 1000, it had already proposed

(*Continued* p. 262)

HOLY ROMAN EMPIRE, C. 1190

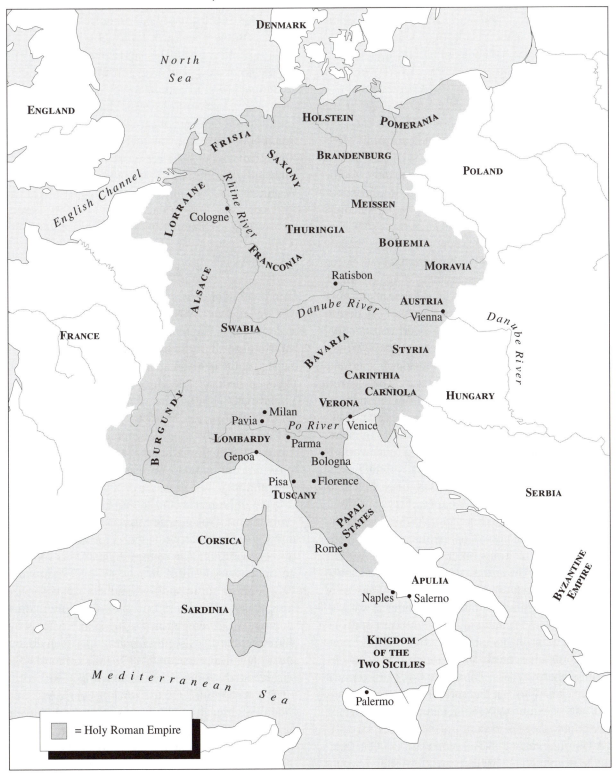

DENMARK

North Sea

ENGLAND

HOLSTEIN

POMERANIA

FRISIA

BRANDENBURG

POLAND

SAXONY

English Channel

LORRAINE

MEISSEN

Rhine River

Cologne

THURINGIA

BOHEMIA

FRANCONIA

MORAVIA

ALSACE

Ratisbon

AUSTRIA

Danube River

Vienna

Danube River

FRANCE

SWABIA

BAVARIA

STYRIA

CARINTHIA

CARNIOLA

HUNGARY

BURGUNDY

VERONA

Milan

Pavia

Po River

Venice

LOMBARDY

Parma

Genoa

Bologna

Pisa

Florence

TUSCANY

SERBIA

CORSICA

PAPAL STATES

Rome

BYZANTINE EMPIRE

APULIA

Naples

Salerno

SARDINIA

KINGDOM OF THE TWO SICILIES

Mediterranean Sea

Palermo

= Holy Roman Empire

the idea of the Truce of God. The Truce endeavored to set certain days aside as inappropriate for any violence: Days of religious significance obviously dominated this agenda, thereby "officially" making large parts of the yearly calendar off-limits for warfare. The Peace of God quickly followed, which insisted that certain groups, primarily the unarmed populace such as clergy, women, children, and peasants, were also off-limits. Although both movements had limited success, constant appeals indicate how often they were violated by combatants. Such calls on the conscience of medieval warriors went unheard for the most part, but the many gifts to the church by soldiers testify to the soldiers' uneasiness about their profession.

When Pope Urban II (c. 1042-1099) preached in 1095 that Europe's knights could actually earn redemption instead of condemnation by going on armed pilgrimage to Jerusalem, he struck a more responsive chord than he had anticipated. The success of the First Crusade (1095-1099) guaranteed that generations of Europe's knights would "take up the cross" both as penance for their violent misdeeds and as a novel continuance of their profession. The Church would rail against Christians who killed Christians in wars, including even those simulations of war, tournaments, which were condemned in numerous councils. Against infidels and heretics, however, warfare was deemed more than licit; it was divinely approved. As the later Crusades not only failed to achieve similar success but also went terribly awry, as did the Fourth Crusade (1198-1204) at Constantinople, the Church found its military involvement more problematic. The Church got further involved in the development of the knightly caste, as it sanctioned some of the trappings of chivalry. The vigils that preceded formal dubbing ceremonies as well as the oaths taken by new knights seemed to confirm that the Church had indeed domesticated its most troublesome sons. Such an appearance was deceptive, though, because chivalry always remained more a secular creation than an ecclesiastical one.

In fact it ought to be remembered that chivalry was the province not only of a secular group but also of a knightly caste that was not alone on Christendom's battlefields. In the early 1100's writers such as Ordericus Vitalis (1075-c. 1142) remarked that the absence of fatalities among knights came from a mutual Christian desire to hold violence in check. This idea of brotherhood among foes continued throughout the Middle Ages. The national orders of chivalry of the fourteenth and fifteenth centuries regularly welcomed foreign members who displayed the requisite chivalric virtues. Although chivalry might restrain lethal tendencies among knights, however, it hardly mattered when aristocratic warriors met their social inferiors. With ransoms or honor rarely at stake, this combat was far more vicious and far more deadly.

MILITARY ACHIEVEMENT

The conviction that the Middle Ages was above all the Age of Cavalry is primarily a legacy of the great military historians of the nineteenth and early twentieth centuries. For them, this was the military contribution, and a questionable one at that, of the Middle Ages to history. The British historian Sir Charles Oman (1860-1946) wrote of the "complete superiority of heavy cavalry" and drew a compelling picture of the massed charge of horsemen with their couched lances. Although this image continues to be propagated in film and general histories, even very good ones, military historians have revised their view of the role of heavy cavalry to one of more limited importance. Some suggested that the end of cavalry's dominance originally seemed to lie in the successes of the Swiss pikemen of the 1300's. Others focused on the Hundred Years' War (1337-1453), in which the longbow supposedly played the more decisive role. This interpretation, however, has since evolved to place more emphasis on the combined use of forces by the English to cripple the French charge. Other historians credit the Flemish infantry, who withstood the French in the opening years of the 1300's. The motion picture *Braveheart* (1995), even though it transposed the actions of Bannockburn (1314) and Stirling Bridge (1297), validated, with some dramatic license, those who credit the Scots with teaching the English the value of foot soldiers.

Historians of the Angevins and Anglo-Normans have demonstrated the pivotal role of infantry, or dismounted knights, at multiple battles. Although the mounted knight was a hallmark of the Middle Ages, he was not the period's definitive warrior.

As a result of this improved understanding of medieval combat, a better appreciation of the military achievement of the Middle Ages is possible. Rather than seeing an epoch of heedless courage and pell-mell charges that appear as an endless cycle of fruitless violence, late-twentieth century historians have come to appreciate the sophisticated answers of medieval commanders to problems that were peculiarly their own. At first, the emphasis on cavalry grew quickly because of the need to counter the mobility of Viking, Magyar, and Muslim raiders. Other military issues came into play, however, as the new feudal blocs began to compete with each other. This competition drove innovation: in tactics, weaponry, fortification, and behind the lines, in the very creation and provisioning of armies. The crucible of invasions and internal fighting honed the overall military practice of Christendom so that it was able for centuries after 1095 to field armies far away in the Middle East. The experiences of Crusader forces sharpened European armies, as veterans returned with an appreciation of the successes to be gained by discipline and practice. Although Europe would effectively give up crusading after 1291, other conflicts, especially the Hundred Years' War, would further the development of military establishments. Amending the thesis of historian Geoffrey Parker on a "Military Revolution" in the early modern period, medievalists have traced the outlines for earlier changes that might account for Europe's later military preeminence.

The Saxon Dynasty came to power in 918 in the Germanic territories of Charlemagne's former empire. Reviving not only Charlemagne's imperial title but even some of his political and military power, this dynasty managed to withstand the double threats to any medieval government: internal factiousness and external invaders. The victory of Otto the Great (912-973) at the Battle of the Lechfeld (955) confirmed their success. By the end of the medieval period—a date open to much dispute—an entirely different military and political situation prevailed. The nation-

state was replacing the feudal system, permanent armies appeared by the 1470's, and Charles VIII's (r. 1483-1498) invasion of Italy in 1494 showed that old styles of warfare no longer applied against national armies wielding powerful gunpowder weapons.

Weapons, Uniforms, and Armor

Two weapons especially dominated the personal medieval arsenal: the sword and the spear. The latter was undoubtedly the most popular weapon employed, but the former was the most prized. The expense and time involved in the manufacture of swords restricted their availability and thus contributed to their importance as status symbols. Not surprisingly, those who could afford a mount also owned swords, and the sword became associated with cavalry and medieval society's elite. The long sword tended to be between 75 and 100 centimeters in length with a blade of up to 6 centimeters in width, double-edged, and counterweighted by an enlarged pommel behind the hilt. A fuller, or groove, ran much of the length of the blade's center, removing some of the weapon's weight without sacrificing any strength; the result was a sword that averaged 1.5 kilograms in weight. Some time before the tenth century, blacksmiths began to taper the blade so that it began a gradual narrowing immediately from the cross-guard. This development helped shift the blade's center of gravity closer to the hand, making the sword even more manageable. The importance attached to swords ensured their preservation across generations of owners and thus led to an increasing number of them available in the later Middle Ages. At one muster in England in 1457, swords were second only to bows in the number of weapons brought.

The innovations in gunpowder and armor in the later medieval period caused rapid changes in sword design. As the transition from chain mail to plate armor became more widespread after 1350, the emphasis in sword design moved from slashing to perforating. Blades grew shorter and stiffer, because the point was now the offensive part of the weapon.

For both infantry and cavalry, however, the spear

was the weapon that lay most often at hand. In the wake of some efforts at standardization by the Carolingians, spears for both branches averaged 2 meters in length, but both archaeology and contemporary art evidence a wide variety of spearheads. The basic similarity testifies that for infantry and cavalry alike it was a thrusting weapon. If the Bayeux tapestry's representation is true-to-life and not an effect of the weaving, spear shafts were rather flimsy even late in the eleventh century.

The medieval cavalry's switch to sturdier lances came with its implementation of "mounted shock

MAJOR SITES IN THE HUNDRED YEARS' WAR, 1337-1453

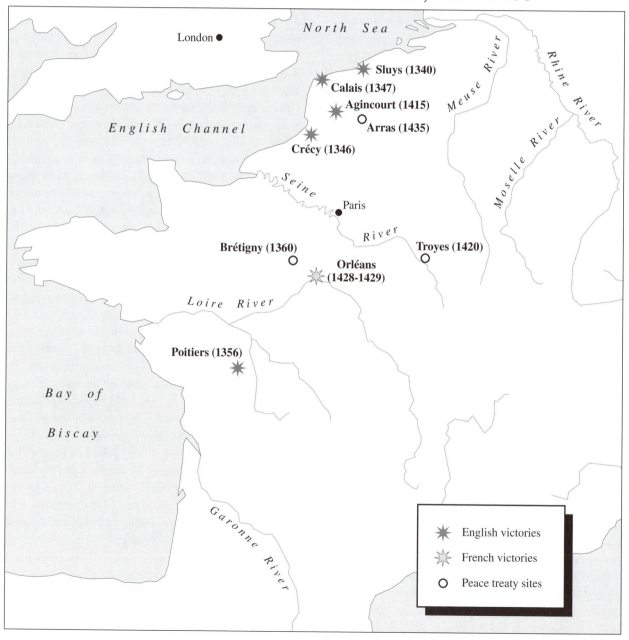

combat." This form of attack is the archetypal view of medieval combat: The horse-borne warrior, lance couched under his armpit, charges his enemy. The combined weight of the knight and his horse are thus concentrated in the irresistible point of the lance. At least, contemporaries saw it this way. Byzantine princess and historian Anna Comnena (1083-c. 1148) suspected that the walls of Babylon would not withstand a charge by the Frankish Crusaders she witnessed passing through Constantinople in 1095. Popular poems such as the French epic *Le Chanson de Roland* (eleventh century; *The Song of Roland*, c. 1100) painted a far more graphic, if exaggerated, picture, making reference to a knight charging his foe, cutting through his bones, and tearing the whole spine from his back.

The necessary prerequisite to such mounted combat is the stirrup, which holds the rider on his horse, and this small piece of equipment has created quite an industry among scholars trying to date its first appearance in Europe. The old assumption that mounted shock dominated the entire medieval period was unseated in 1951 when D. J. A. Ross contended that references to such assaults came no earlier than the late eleventh century *chansons de geste* such as that of Roland. Lynn Townsend White, Jr., challenged this argument a decade later when he tried to date the stirrup (and shock combat) as early as the 700's. A bevy of historians, among them Bernard R. Bachrach and David Charles Nicolle, arose to counter White's assertion, and, on the whole, their arguments have focused on the early twelfth century as the moment when mounted shock combat became the primary cavalry tactic of Christendom. To date, their contentions have carried the field.

Infantry weapons, such as the spear, remained mostly unchanged until the late medieval period. However, there were experimental modifications. King Philip II (1165-1223) of France and his retinue at Bouvines (1214) faced mercenary foot soldiers who endeavored to pull the king and his knights from their horses with hooked spears that caught their chain mail links. Unhorsed, the knights were threatened by the soldiers' daggers, which could reach unarmored areas, such as the groin or armpit. In the 1300's and 1400's the Flemish and Swiss levies

began utilizing pikes in regular formations that achieved repeated victories against cavalry. Other alterations of the spear resulted from combinations: spear and ax became the halberd; the billhook had a curved blade on the side of a lance.

There was no shortage of other handheld weapons. The Vikings often used axes in battle, as did the Anglo-Saxons. The Bayeux tapestry may show one of the earliest representations of a mace, which had by the twelfth century become a popular weapon in tournament melees and on the battlefield. The dagger, like the sword, evolved in form to whatever shape was most effective at penetrating the weak points of armor.

Armies of the High Middle Ages understood the value of missile weapons and relied upon a variety of them. Slings were still used as late as the thirteenth century, especially in the form of staff slings, which propelled the missile more forcefully. For the early part of the period, short bows and composite, or Turkish, bows predominated. The latter were adopted by Christians from their Muslim foes, particularly in Spain, where the Christians even went so far as to emulate Muslims in the use of horse archers. In the Crusader kingdoms, warriors turned to native horse archers willing to fight for their new masters. The composite bow was less popular to the northwest, perhaps because the wetter climate affected the glue that held the bows together. Short bows were used by the Normans, including William the Conqueror (c. 1027-1087), who saw no dishonor in personally using the weapon. William took a great many archers with him to England, where they proved their worth by the attrition they caused in the formations of Harold II (c. 1022-1066).

The best-known bow of the Middle Ages is the Welsh longbow. Averaging 1.8 meter in length, with an exterior strip of sapwood and an interior strip of heartwood to increase its spring, the longbow was able to propel "cloth-yard shafts" from 365 to 400 meters. At 200 meters, the longbow's arrows could penetrate chain mail. After facing this formidable weapon in the thirteenth century, the English reacted by recruiting large numbers of Welshmen proficient with the bow to serve in their continental armies. The longbow had its heyday during the Hundred

Years' War, playing a large role in British victories at the Battles of Crécy (1346), Poitiers (1356), and Agincourt (1415). However, the longbow was one weapon among several that the English used wisely in conjunction with others to assure victory. The longbow's use continued with English armies until the fifteenth century, when the government simply found itself unable to ensure that there were enough bows, arrows, and archers to fill the usual complements.

The counterpart of the longbow was the crossbow, which was known throughout the period but grew in usage as siege warfare became a larger component of campaigning. From that function, it developed also into a weapon of field armies. Its potential for lethality resulted in official bans of its use by the Church in the late eleventh century and 1139. The repeated bans also testify to the fact that medieval soldiers did not give up such a weapon easily. After 1200, the Church finally approved the crossbow's use against non-Christians. Nonetheless, Christians often used it against other Christians. English king Richard I (1157-1199) was so fond of using crossbows that he was erroneously credited with introducing the weapons to the French. Experimenters improved the bow across the Middle Ages, constantly increasing its power and range while attempting to decrease the time necessary for reloading. The original wooden bow and stock became a composite bow by the 1200's and would be made entirely of steel by the 1400's. Stirrups, ratchets, and levers were all added to ease the task of drawing the bow's string back to the trigger. Load times varied between 12 and 35 seconds, but the tremendous power was sufficient to puncture even the plate armor of the later Middle Ages. The advantages of the crossbow, power combined with a low level of training necessary for accuracy, would be the same ingredients that in the later fifteenth century would enable the gun to displace the crossbow on the battlefield.

Apart from personal weapons, successful armies also employed a siege train, a collection of raw materials, prefabricated weapons, and personnel who could build and operate such pregunpowder artillery. The importance of such weapons is reflected in the complaint that the so-called artists of war, knights, had

been replaced by the new specialists: engineers, miners, crossbowmen, and artillerists.

The siege weapons handled by the new specialists worked by one of three means. The onager was a survivor from antiquity in which a single beam, inserted through a horizontal braid of animal tendons or hair, was pulled back into firing position. This torsion weapon was less powerful than its classical predecessors and was immensely heavy; one reconstruction weighed nearly 2 tons. The ballista of the Romans was probably a two-armed torsion weapon, but the term referred in the Middle Ages to a tension weapon that was essentially an oversized crossbow on a stable platform. Lever machines were the third variety of pregunpowder artillery. The use of lever artillery originated in China and spread via Byzantium and the Islamic lands. Lever artillery relied on either traction power or a counterweight. In the former case, a crowd of operators hauled downward on ropes attached to one end of the lever-arm, causing it to swing on a pivot and release its projectile in a high arc. This was the *petraria*, or stone thrower. The trebuchet was the pregunpowder giant; it replaced the human hauler with a fixed counterweight that allowed truly impressive weights to be launched. Projectiles typically weighed between 50 and 75 kilograms, with a range of approximately 200 meters.

Given the impressive arsenal that both the well-to-do knights and common soldiers carried into battle, there is little wonder that medieval combatants also invested in sophisticated personal armor. The simplest, most efficient form of armor remained the shield, in use since ancient times. In the tenth century, the shield was still evolving, from a round shape to that of an elongated kite. The new shape better protected the legs of horsemen without adding too much weight. In addition, infantry could jam the shield's lower point into the ground for more stability when creating the formation called a "shield-wall." Although the shield would later be shortened, this triangular shape remained standard until the best plate armor made shields themselves redundant.

Armor itself underwent several changes throughout the medieval period. The primary body armor before 900 had been a leather jacket with metal scales attached. By the eleventh century this form of armor had grown more complex; the Bayeux tapestry shows coats of chain mail on most of the Normans. Made up of thousands of interlocked rings, this hauberk was probably worn over a padded undergarment both to prevent chafing and to soften opponents' blows should some of the links be broken and forced inward. This form of armor, with continued improvements, would dominate Europe and the Crusader kingdoms for several centuries. Extra pieces of mail would be added for the lower legs, the back of the neck, the lower face, feet, and hands. The helmet evolved from a conical shape with only a nasal guard to the "great helm," an enveloping, metal defense for the entire head. As missile weaponry evolved, plate armor became widely adopted. Steel, which had been tested especially against crossbows, began to be combined with chain mail and later replaced it. Eventually, knights would wear form-fitting plates that covered not only all major parts of the body but also protected complex joint areas such as the knees, elbows, and even fingers. Apart from such armor's protective benefits, its gleaming qualities also appealed to those who could afford it.

Because medieval warriors were usually responsible for outfitting themselves, there would be little use of standardized uniforms until the late Middle Ages, when powerful rulers and some cities would either provide or require them. Before that point, the emphasis fell more on individual insignia and costume. Although the Bayeux tapestry shows some painted shields, the earliest evidence for heraldic decoration comes from the reign of Stephen, king of England, also known as Stephen of Blois (r. 1135-1154). During his day, the Clare family began consistently to display its gold and red bands, and Geoffrey of Anjou (Geoffrey Plantagenet, 1113-1151) his two lions, which would in changed form become the English royal insignia. Although the participants in the Third Crusade (1187-1192) would adopt national identifiers such as differently colored crosses for the French, English, and Flemish, the real shift from personal to corporate designations came later. Wealthy cities such as Tournai were outfitting contingents in uniform livery in 1297 and again in 1340. Men from Wales and the adjoining marches wore green and white costumes and hats when serving on the Con-

tinent in the mid-1300's. As revenues increased, princes also began to outfit notable units within their forces; thus, French kings Charles VII (1403-1461) and Louis XI (1423-1483) contributed to the distinctiveness of their Scots Archers in the fifteenth century. The dukes of Burgundy would do likewise before their finances and power failed.

A turning point in medieval warfare came with the widespread adoption of gunpowder weapons. The first known recipe in Europe for gunpowder comes from 1267 in the works of Roger Bacon (c. 1220-c. 1292), more than two centuries after its first mention in Chinese texts. Within sixty years the first evidence for cannons appears in the illustrated margins of medieval texts, followed by their confirmed use at Puy-Guillaume (1338) and then against Lille (1341). Within twenty years, evidence of gunpowder artillery spread from Italy to Scandinavia and from Russia to England. The most dramatic example of the new technology was the bombard. With a weight of around 16,000 kilograms and firing balls of 380 kilograms, the largest of these giants could breach almost any wall with only several well-placed shots. On the battlefield, however, the effect of early cannons was more limited. They may have been used at Crécy in 1346 merely for the shock effect of the noise they made. The adoption by the early 1400's of smaller calibers made cannons more accurate, and a roll call of distinguished victims began.

Even though the overall battlefield effect of cannons remained negligible, the sudden vulnerability of elite warriors, the quick obsolescence of old defenses, and the new demands on military budgets spelled the end of chivalric warfare.

MILITARY ORGANIZATION

Medieval warfare, at its most proficient practice, was a sophisticated affair, marked by careful preparations, skillful analysis of risk and reward, and the use of multiple branches of service. This thesis, however, has been only recently accepted by a wide audience holding a more traditional image of feudal armies as violent mobs. The historian Oman claimed in 1885

Library of Congress

A fourteenth century English knight. In the late Middle Ages the cult of chivalry developed as the expression of a new, knightly identity, an ethos that sometimes shaped the contours of battle.

that medieval troops were neither disciplined nor unified, and this idea has been long held. The conviction that chivalric ideals were "inimical" to battlefield discipline and organization appeared repeatedly in encyclopedia articles and surveys of military history throughout the twentieth century. It was supposed that knights, ever desirous of increasing their personal glory, turned battles into giant melees of individual combats. However, closer attention to the original sources by recent scholars has shown otherwise.

Well before battle got under way, medieval knights reported to a muster less as individuals than as members of a group. At the very least, they came as part of a lord's retinue, following his banner and perhaps wearing colors or insignia indicating their corporate identity. By the 1300's, even individual knights typically reported with a coterie of aides. In fourteenth century France this group, often called a lance, consisted of two men; in the 1400's the standard composition was three. These units could then be organized as necessary into larger units called by multiple terms: banners, *conrois*, *échelles*, *batailles*, or battles. Such units were then spread in compact ranks across the perceived battlefield. The widespread use of these terms across Europe and in all vernaculars indicates such tactical units had a long history in medieval warfare.

Vernacular literature also reveals that these units stayed together compactly in battle rather than being dispersed enough to allow the individual combats supposedly characteristic of war in the Middle Ages. The *chansons de geste* (literally "songs of war") repeatedly describe the ranks of armies as being drawn up so tightly that objects thrown amid them would not have reached the ground. Latin prelate William of Tyre (c. 1130-1185) provides a particularly instructive example, describing a Crusade in 1180 to relieve the fortress of Darum. Partly out of fear and partly from lack of training, the crusading knights crowded so compactly together that their ability to launch an attack was hampered. Nonetheless, this dense group forced its way through the Muslim lines with steady pressure, rather than a dramatic charge. Their success was a testament more to their organization and discipline than to their reckless courage.

DOCTRINE, STRATEGY, AND TACTICS

A legacy of late nineteenth century medieval studies has been an appreciation of the quality of medieval military strategy and tactics. Until that time, medieval historians had been heirs to the military tradition of the decisive battle. Such historians often had been frustrated by the study of medieval military efforts, because they saw a quite random pattern of violence marking medieval campaigns. The historians could not find the decisive, battlefield resolution that they assumed was the natural goal of any expedition. The repetitive medieval cycle of raid and counterraid appeared only as senseless violence. The appearance was only made worse by the fact that medieval commanders had, in the fifth century Roman military theorist Flavius Vegetius Renatus's treatise *De Re Militari* (between 383 and 450 C.E.; *The Fovre Bookes of Flauius Vegetius Renatus: Briefelye Contayninge a Plaine Forme and Perfect Knowledge of Martiall Policye, Feates of Chiualrie, and Vvhatsoeuuer Pertayneth to Warre*, 1572; also translated as *Military Institutions of Vegetius*, 1767), a reputable guide to the tactics and strategy of late fourth century Rome. Numerous copies of this work in both Latin and native dialects survive as evidence of its popularity. There is also narrative evidence that commanders such as Geoffrey of Anjou consulted Vegetius's work for instruction on building incendiary devices. At the end of the Middle Ages, the dukes of Burgundy turned to Vegetius for counsel in building new siegeworks. Although the actual influence of Vegetius has been questioned, his work nonetheless served to introduce generations of medieval leaders to larger strategic issues.

One thing that medieval commanders understood quite well on their own was the utter uncertainty of battle. It was to be avoided not from fear, but from a sound recognition that far better means lay at hand to force an opponent to the bargaining table. The Latin kings of Jerusalem avoided battle as a policy, because the price of failure would be too high. In 1187 Guy de Lusignan (1129-1194) gambled at Hattin, and Saladin's (1138-1193) resulting victory left the rest of the kingdom incapable of defense. The destruction that attended so many raids was actually part of the

medieval "science of war." Far more than daredevil heroes or wanton destroyers of countryside, good commanders such as William the Conqueror and Richard I conducted strategic raids that had the cumulative effect of enfeebling the opponent at the least risk to one's own army. Richard's case is all the more dramatic; in nearly thirty years of campaigning, he fought only one pitched battle by his own choice.

There were, of course, times to seek battle, as evidenced by William the Conqueror at Hastings (1066), Frederick II (1194-1250) at Cortenuova (1237), and the French in the great battles of the Hundred Years' War. Each demonstrates a different aspect of strategy. The French doubtless felt they had met Vegetius's criteria for offering battle; they had superiority of numbers, and the foe was in pitiful condition. Their defeats at Crécy, Poitiers, and Agincourt served to reinforce the lesson of fickle fortune. Frederick II gambled in 1237 by dividing his forces, but he did so as a ruse; by convincing the Milanese that he was retiring for the winter, he engineered a devastating ambush. Under different conditions William worked to provoke Harold to battle in 1066, primarily because he could not hope to hold his invasion force together indefinitely. Many other battles, however, occurred in more accidental fashion; even though a clash was intended, Bouvines took place on a Sunday in 1214 because Otto IV's forces overtook those of Philip II more quickly than was expected.

Although anything might transpire when battle did occur, a few themes appear amid the varied actualities. Although many other elements of medieval warfare are often emphasized, knights and their potential charge remained the central concern in battles. The actual, successful delivery of such a charge as both initiation and conclusion of a battle seems to have been a rare occurrence. Of more concern were the reserve or flanking units of cavalry, which many commanders kept ready. This very disposition belies the contention of some scholars that once battle was joined, the possibility of giving orders disappeared in the chaos. The prebattle arrangement of forces varied over the years. From the eleventh through early thirteenth centuries, commanders formed several long shallow lines composed mostly of infantry but often augmented by dismounted knights. Its primary role was to withstand the opponent's charge. In protected positions, or even in front of this first line at the very start, archers would add their missile fire so as to disrupt the enemy assault. Variations on this line would appear. The Knights Templar had a "crown" formation they adopted for defense; the Flemings at Bouvines and the Scots a century later at Bannockburn withstood charges in circular formations. As the Flemings and later the Swiss fielded large numbers of infantry in the 1300's, they utilized massive arrangements of squares and wedges with no real cen-

ter. Where the defending force was not wholly composed of infantry, the concern was to break the foe's charge or at least engage it until a counterattack came from reserve or flanking units. Once a formation broke, the pursuit naturally involved the mounted units; even here, the pursuers had to take care they were not being drawn out of their formation and into an ambush by a feigned retreat. In all cases, the charging knights constituted a minority on the battlefield but remained uppermost in the minds of leaders and combatants.

MEDIEVAL SOURCES

In the area of military affairs, and most especially combat, medieval sources present a number of intersecting problems. The authoritative writers of the age were churchmen, men unlikely to have witnessed combat, particularly if they were monks. Some, such as William of Tyre or Ordericus Vitalis, are noteworthy for having obviously sifted through their informants' accounts to give posterity as full and accurate a narrative as possible. However, the details of battle often did not concern such writers; they were more interested in the miraculous than the human aspects of battle. Thus they told more of the saints who appeared in the melee than of the actual tactics employed. Moreover, because the lesson to be drawn from a military event was far more important, ecclesiastical writers tended to treat numbers with some license. Medium-sized hosts numbered 300 so often as to defy belief, whereas truly large armies appear in multiples of 100,000, numbers quite beyond the administrative capabilities of any medieval government. Further complications arose when clerics adapted terms from antiquity to refer to peculiarly medieval items.

Such problems can be occasionally resolved, however, by relying also on secular, typically vernacular sources. The documents written for the military elite help us by using more precise language. Even the fanciful world of the *chansons de geste* can be instructive if carefully culled. Such songs had a practiced, knightly audience in mind who would have little appreciated an inaccurate picture of the realities of battle, apart from the superhuman accomplishments of the heroes. The *Histoire de Guillaume le Maréchal* (c. 1225; the story of Guillaume le Maréchal) often reads like the *chansons* but rather is a biography that has been found correct in many questionable details. Many of the poem's events were clearly witnessed in person. Firsthand accounts include those of Ambroise d'Évreux (fl. c. 1190), who was at Arsuf with Richard I; Jean (or John) de Joinville (c. 1224-1317), who was at Mansurah; and Jean le Bel (c. 1224-1317), who was in Scotland. These sources provide details on tactics, strategy, and weaponry, as well as a picture of the actual experience of the medieval warrior in combat. There were moments of both fear and courage.

Finally, there is the pictorial record. The Bayeux tapestry is a uniquely rich source. Numerous medieval manuscripts, even many that do not deal specifically with military topics, abound with decorated letter forms and illustrations of combat in the margins. Awareness of the dates of such manuscripts allows scholars to refine theories on the use of certain weapons and armor. Similarly, the carvings in churches and monasteries reveal much about medieval armaments. The seals of many feudal lords are also instructive, although only for the weapons of the elite.

Where details of armaments can be discerned in these smaller figures, though, the dating is quite precise.

BOOKS AND ARTICLES

Abels, Richard P., and Bernard S. Bachrach, eds. *The Normans and Their Adversaries at War: Essays in Memory of C. Warren Hollister*. Rochester, N.Y.: Boydell Press, 2001.

Bowlus, Charles R. *The Battle of Lechfeld and Its Aftermath, August 955: The End of the Age of Migrations in the Latin West*. Burlington, Vt.: Ashgate, 2006.

Bradbury, Jim. *The Routledge Companion to Medieval Warfare*. New York: Routledge, 2004.

Contamine, Philippe. *War in the Middle Ages*. Translated by Michael Jones. Oxford, England: Basil Blackwell, 1984.

DeVries, Kelly. *Guns and Men in Medieval Europe, 1200-1500: Studies in Military History and Technology*. Burlington, Vt.: Ashgate/Variorum, 2002.

_____. *Medieval Military Technology*. Lewiston, N.Y.: Broadview Press, 1992.

France, John. *Western Warfare in the Age of the Crusades, 1000-1300*. Ithaca, N.Y.: Cornell University Press, 1999.

Funcken, Liliane, and Fred Funcken. *The Age of Chivalry*. 3 vols. Englewood Cliffs, N.J.: Prentice-Hall, 1983.

Harari, Yuval N. *Special Operations in the Age of Chivalry, 1100-1550*. Rochester, N.Y.: Boydell Press, 2007.

Nicholson, Helen J., and David Nicolle. *God's Warriors: Crusaders, Saracens, and the Battle for Jerusalem*. Botley, Oxford, England: Osprey, 2005.

_____. *Medieval Warfare: Theory and Practice of War in Europe, 300-1500*. Basingstoke, England: Palgrave Macmillan, 2004.

Nicolle, David. *Arms and Armour of the Crusading Era, 1050-1350*. London: Greenhill Books, 1999.

_____. *Fighting for the Faith: The Many Fronts of Medieval Crusade and Jihad, 1000-1500 A.D.* Barnsley, England: Pen and Sword Military, 2007.

Strickland, Matthew, ed. *Anglo-Norman Warfare*. Woodbridge, England: Boydell Press, 1992.

Verbruggen, J. F. *The Art of Warfare in Western Europe During the Middle Ages*. Woodbridge, England: Boydell Press, 1997.

Walsh, Michael J. *Warriors of the Lord: The Military Orders of Christendom*. Alresford, England: John Hunt, 2003.

FILMS AND OTHER MEDIA

Braveheart. Feature film. Icon Entertainment, 1995.

Charlemagne. Television miniseries. Acorn Media, 1994.

The Dark Ages. Documentary. History Channel, 2007.

Henry V. Feature film. BBC/Curzon/Renaissance, 1989.

In Search of History: The Knights Templar. Documentary. History Channel, 2005.

Knights and Armor. Documentary. History Channel, 2002.

Steven Isaac

CRUSADING ARMIES OF THE WEST
Dates: 1095-1525 C.E.

POLITICAL CONSIDERATIONS

The engine driving the Crusades began with Pope Urban II (1042-1099) in 1095 at the Council of Clermont, when he called for Christendom to rise in defense of the Holy Land. The pope had responded to Byzantine emperor Alexius I's call for assistance against Islamic encroachment in areas Christianity deemed important as part of an effort to seal the 1054 rift between Catholicism and the Orthodox Byzantine East. Beginning at Clermont, the pope called for the Holy Land's rescue and the restoration of the "Truce of God." Following his cue, clergy throughout Europe began preaching sermons and delivering calls to liberate Jerusalem and the Holy Land from Islam, spurring nobles to take up arms and undertake the long, arduous journey. Additional inducements, such as the forgiveness of sins and eternal glory, convinced many to go. An additional political motive behind the Crusades was to divert the nobility from fighting with each other. This peace, both in the Holy Land and in Europe, would serve to strengthen the Church's authority.

When the First Crusade began in 1095, the Byzantine military had declined and its forces were composed of mercenaries throughout Europe. Despite the internal decay, the Byzantine military remained a force worthy of consideration. It would provide supplies, siege columns that proved extremely useful in siege operations, and medical units that marched in the field with the fighting troops. The Byzantines also used the Varangian Guard, descendants of the early Viking settlers in Rus who had followed two Byzantine monks, brothers Cyril and Methodius (later made saints), down the Dneiper River in the ninth century and whose mission was to convert the uninformed to Orthodoxy.

Library of Congress

Crusaders under English king Richard I reach the holy city of Jerusalem.

MILITARY ACHIEVEMENT

The First Crusade did not succeed, at least in part because of a lack of planning and experience. Participants and their motives varied and the prospective glories were exaggerated in order to gain general support for the ventures. Seven Crusades between 1096 and 1254 marked Crusader-Islamic relations and left a negative imprint on relations between the Islamic world and Chris-

272

tian Europe. Also, internal problems plagued the Crusader force; while some wanted to conquer Jerusalem, other Crusaders wished to create a fiefdom for themselves. In time, the disorganization dissipated, but distance and supplies made short shrift of any gains. Many small "Crusader kingdoms" collapsed as quickly as they came into existence from 1098 until the fall of Acre in 1291, and enthusiasm diminished with each Crusade. However, as new militant orders were created, the Crusaders finally developed a semblance of central authority and armies to combat the Islamic forces. The Crusaders, led by European nobility, had knights, archers, battle columns, squares, archers, and footmen. Each nobleman could furnish a force, but not equal to that of the combined Islamic forces, who knew how to dress for warfare in the region.

WEAPONS, UNIFORMS, AND ARMOR

As the Crusades were waged over numerous centuries, the types of weaponry used by both sides were vast. Often, the weaponry used was haphazard and makeshift. Crusaders who were not of high social rank used whatever weapons they could get their hands on, from pikes to rudimentary clubs, which could be fashioned easily from nearly any piece of wood. The cudgel was essentially a club with metal pieces attached to it, so as to inflict more damage. A step above the cudgel were crude axes. Likewise, the maul, essentially a large sledgehammer, could do significant damage. Taking some skill on the part of the weaponsmith were the mace and the ball-and-chain. These blunt weapons could inflict significant damage, but like all weapons of this sort, they were used by the lower-class Crusaders in hand-to-hand combat.

Those Crusaders who were of higher birth had access to better weaponry. Their blunt weapon of choice was the war hammer, which came in blunt and sharpened versions. Although the evolution of weaponry during these centuries was slow, one technological innovation that had an important impact was the crossbow, which appeared in the eleventh century.

The fact that it could be loaded with arrows prior to the battle rather than during the heat of combat made it especially useful. Small daggers were useful as secondary weapons but were not especially effective. The Knights Templar were well known for their effective use of the lance. The weapon that knights were probably best known for, however, was the sword. (The stereotypical long sword, however, did not appear until almost the end of the Crusade era.)

The swords and knives used by the Muslims had many different types of blades, most of them curved, giving them greater speed in their use. Scimitars, sabers, and tulwars were three typical types of blades used by Muslim defenders, but, like the weapons of the Crusaders, the variety of the Muslims' weapons was nearly infinite.

Large-scale weapons were used to lay siege to cities. Many of them were too large to transport over long distances and thus were often built of local materials very close to the cities they were used to attack. A ballista was a large, arrow-shooting machine that could hurl heavy arrows several hundred yards. Different catapults, such as the mangonel and the trebuchet, hurled rocks at city walls. Siege towers were built and then pushed against city walls, allowing soldiers to climb stairs within the tower's interior, protecting them from city defenders. More crudely built, battering rams were used to break through city gates. In defense, garrisons poured boiling liquids—oil being the most effective, if the most expensive—from the tops of the walls, inflicting immense pain on those trying to scale the walls.

Only wealthy soldiers would have been able to afford any type of armor. Commoners used makeshift shields and other rudimentary methods to protect themselves as best they could. True armor was one way in which knights were identified. Chain mail, one of the earliest forms of armor, was used in conjunction with a shield and a helmet. However, with the development of better weaponry, such as the crossbow, mail armor became increasingly ineffective, and plate armor appeared near the end of the Crusades. Though cumbersome, it could protect the knight against most weapons and made other types of protection, such as shields, unnecessary.

TURNING POINTS

1095-1099	During the First Crusade, initiated by Pope Urban II, European crusaders, fighting to protect the Holy Land for Christianity, capture Jerusalem.
1145-1149	The Second Crusade, unsuccessfully led by the kings of France and Germany, is prompted by Muslim conquest of the principality of Edessa in 1144.
1187-1192	The Third Crusade succeeds, especially through the efforts of English king Richard I, in restoring some Christian possessions.
1198-1204	The Fourth Crusade, initiated by Pope Innocent III, captures Constantinople and damages the Byzantine Empire.
1217-1221	The Fifth Crusade, organized to attack the Islamic power base in Egypt, succeeds in capturing the Egyptian port city of Damietta but ends in defeat when the crusading army attempts to capture Cairo.
1228-1229	In what is sometimes referred to as the Sixth Crusade, the excommunicated Holy Roman Emperor Frederick II sails to the Holy Land and negotiates a reoccupation of Jerusalem.
1248-1254	The Seventh (or Sixth) Crusade is led by Louis IX of France and follows a course similar to that of the Fifth Crusade.
1269-1270	Eighth (or Seventh) Crusade is organized by a now-elderly Louis IX, who dies upon landing in Tunisia, leading to the breakup of his army.
1270-1272	Edward I, the son of Henry III of England, decides to press on alone to Palestine after the French abandon the Eighth Crusade and achieves some modest success with a truce before the ultimate fall of Acre, the last bastion of the Crusader states, in 1291.

MILITARY ORGANIZATION

The reasons for joining a crusading army involved the feudal class system as well as political, economic, and social factors. The feudal system defined every human's station in life. Society resembled a pyramid, with the king sitting at the apex, the nobility below him, and the great masses at the bottom. The king was the absolute ruler of the state, aided by his nobility. His knights of the sword governed without restraint and with the Church's collusion. The rationale for the existence of various classes was to defend the kingdom.

Kings, nobles, and knights controlled the workings of society but had a responsibility to provide soldiers when called upon. Feudal nobility and royalty hired mercenaries if they were unable to draft enough local soldiers, and such soldiers served regardless of faith and background. With increased births and the expansion of the noble classes, more heirs existed than positions available. As a result, many nobles did not acquire estates; the options were that the eldest received the estate (primogeniture), the second male became a warrior, and the third joined the Church. Many of those denied estates had to join the Crusades to make their fortunes. The lower classes served the needs of the nobility, whose duty was to defend them. Peasant classes had few rights and many obligations to their lords. They surrendered much of their produce, cared for animals, and had to endure the humiliation of the "first night," during which the noble could enjoy carnal relations with the newly married woman before her husband did. Such a custom, which could not be resisted, caused despair and offered no hope for the future. This hopeless status provided the impetus for many peasants to take up the Cross and join the Crusades.

Women's positions were even more confining and problematic. At the time of the First Crusade women of noble birth could marry, enter a convent, or walk to Jerusalem, the latter option providing an alternative to the confines of their roles in Europe. The long, arduous trip offered some hope of a less restricted life, but even that option was removed when, in the aftermath of the bloody failure of the First Crusade in 1096, the pope declared that no women, children, or old people would be allowed to go on later Crusades.

With the need for additional well-trained troops, the Knights of Saint John of Jerusalem (known as the Hospitallers)—whose membership comprised men of noble birth and those who had taken vows of poverty, chastity, and obedience to the Church—were founded in 1080 as a hospital in Jerusalem. After the Crusaders were finally able to take Jerusalem in 1099, they were transformed into a military-religious order, and their experience in the region helped the Crusaders. They maintained medical and hospital facilities for the pilgrims and had military obligations, as the Church charged them with the defense of pilgrims in the Holy Land. They received donations of castles and other significant properties in the Holy Land and in time had to fight in their defense. The Knights of the Temple, or Knights Templar, were another military crusading order. They were chaste, subject to rigid discipline, and imbued with feudalism. They actively participated in the seizure of Jerusalem. After their formation in 1119, they bore the major burden of retaining Jerusalem for Christianity. They protected pilgrims, had small empires, formed

the largest army in the east, and maintained castles and fortifications. Although their existence survived the end of the Crusades, they soon fell out of favor both with European royalty and with the pope, because of their great wealth. The pope would eventually, in 1314, abolish the Knights Templar for fear that they were acquiring too much wealth and power. Other orders appeared, but their contributions were smaller than those of the Knights Hospitaller and the Knights Templar. The Brethren of the Sword, the Knights of Calatrava, the Knights of Santiago, the Brethren of Santa Maria, and the Knights of Our Lady of Montjoie all made contributions, but to differing degrees. They demonstrate, however, the universal attraction of joining the Crusades, coming from as far away as Spain. Such orders, with small contingents, generally left the region after collecting their booty.

Despite the tenuous relations between Rome and

EUROPE AND THE BYZANTINE EMPIRE DURING THE CRUSADES

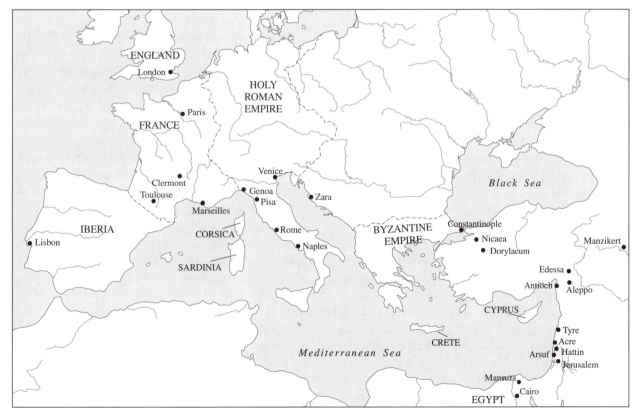

Constantinople, the Byzantines had shared a common enemy with the European Crusaders: the expansionist forces of Islam. Providing a safe route to Jerusalem led to constant warfare with the Seljuk Turks and others. Specialized units of Byzantine cavalry aided the Crusaders. They captured Antioch in 1137, forcing the Christians to pay homage to the Byzantine emperor. A year later, a combined force of Franks and Byzantines compelled the emir of Shaizar to yield. Shortly afterward, Byzantine forces accompanied the Franks in their struggle against the Saracens. In 1163-1164, the Byzantine navy transported the Franks on their Egyptian venture, but as competition between the Franks and the Byzantines became more obvious, this was the last engagement of a combined force against Islam.

DOCTRINE, STRATEGY, AND TACTICS

The Crusades were intended to purify Christendom against pagans, heretics, and the excommunicated. The driving ideology was that all disagreements between Christian lords should be put aside, and the nobles' efforts directed toward a more important enemy, the Muslims, who had held the Holy Land for more than three hundred years and who were making it difficult for Christians to make pilgrimages to the land where Jesus walked. The problem of the Muslims was not just confined to the Levant, though. At the time, Turks were at the gates of Europe and the Byzantine Empire was only a weakened shadow of its former self. Pope Urban II's call to free Jerusalem of the Muslim infidels provided long-sought opportunities under the guise of religious zeal and sacrifice. Individuals of every social, political, and economic class, many of whom were unprepared for the journey, assembled at various points through Europe and moved toward the Mediterranean Sea. On the way, the Crusaders pillaged for food and murdered in the name of God. Whole Jewish communities were eliminated solely for religious reasons. Rome, viewing Jewish and Muslim believers equally as infidels, made no effort to quell the Crusaders' European slaughter.

The Crusades, and the ideology behind them, flowed from the Papacy. The nobles who partici-

pated received indulgences for the forgiveness of sins, temporal privileges, and often immunity from civil jurisdiction. The Papacy itself stood to gain from the Crusades as well. At the time, papal jurisdiction did not extend outside Europe, and the establishment of the Crusader kingdoms certainly expanded the power of the Western, or Roman, Catholic Church into regions that had previously been under Eastern, or Byzantine, jurisdiction. The Knights Templar and the Hospitallers formed the largest portion of the crusading army remaining in the east. Their expressed devotion resulted in large donations and recruits for the Outremer (literally, "overseas"—the name for the Crusader kingdoms of the Middle East). They soon became the largest landholder in the area. Their self-declared responsibilities required them to patrol the vast regions seeking pilgrims in trouble. The quest for power was also a large part of the ideologies that drove many individual Crusaders and a number of the religious orders that were founded during this time. City-states, like the maritime cities in Italy, also saw the potential to gain power through participation in the Crusades. By 1204, papal leadership was for the most part dispensed with, as German and French princes pursued Crusades of their own accord. Still, Crusades went on until the fifteenth century, when the Turks were allowed to take Constantinople and Europe withdrew from the Middle East.

In time, the Crusaders, through the assistance of these orders, learned how to prolong the conflict between themselves and Islam. They allowed the creation of soldier-monks to protect the Christians on their pilgrimage to Jerusalem. Since they were involved in a "just war," the pope did not condemn the actions of his armies. Rather, European conduct became known and when the Franks arrived at Jerusalem, the Muslims and Jews united to fight for the city, which fell on July 15, 1099.

After capturing the city from the Muslims, the Jewish and Muslim populations were massacred. The Crusaders then established four major kingdoms, the Kingdom of Jerusalem with Godfrey of Bouillon proclaiming himself as king, County of Edessa, Principality of Antioch, and County of Tripoli. Throughout the region the Crusaders established other fiefdoms, in none of which were non-

Christians well treated. These events strengthened the opposition to the Crusades and provided Islamic fervor to fight. In 1009, Fāṭimid caliph al-Ḥākim destroyed the Church of the Holy Sepulchre, and by 1039 it was rebuilt mainly because the Muslims realized the profit of having Christian pilgrims in the region. Whether Turks, Mamlūks, ʿAbbāsids, Moors, Seljuks, Fāṭimids, Ayyūbids, or Syrians, they did not forget the Crusaders' conduct. Their professional armies were larger and better trained, had better archers, had more sophisticated strategies, were more adaptable to the climate and food, had public support, and had time on their side. While the European nobility eventually tired in their ventures, Muslims retained the vigor of fighting the "infidel" in their own land.

Eventually a Kurd, Saladin, became the commander of Islamic forces after the fall of the Fāṭimids, and he established a new dynasty, the Ayyūbids. He had military talent and was appointed commander of all Muslim forces. He united the Muslims in Egypt and, in 1187, recaptured Jerusalem in the Battle of Hattin. Under Muslim rule, Jewish and Christian populations were respected. After Saladin, the Crusaders lost their initiative and did not mount another credible campaign against the Muslims. By the thirteenth century, the few remaining principalities in Crusader control had fallen to the Egyptian Mamlūks. With the fall of Constantinople to the Ottoman Turks in 1453, Christendom gave up its religious and political influence in the region.

MEDIEVAL SOURCES

As interest in the Crusades has been nearly constant over the centuries, there is no dearth of published sources written by the Crusaders themselves. Mostly written by those of nobility, among the most accessible are those of William, archbishop of Tyre (c. 1130-c. 1190), who wrote *Historia rerum in partibus transmarinis gestarum* (*History of Deeds Done Beyond the Sea*, New York: Da Capo Press, 1973). Philippe de Mezières (c. 1327-1405) wrote *Le Songe du vieil Pelerin* (the dream of old Pelerin; London: Cambridge University Press, 1969). John M. Sharp edited and Frances Hernandez translated *The Catalan Chronicle of Francisco de Moncada* (El Paso: Texas Western University Press, 1975). The nine thousand lines of verse that constitute *The Chronicle of Morea* tell the tale of Frankish Crusaders during the Fourth Crusade. Edited collections include Elizabeth Hallam's *Chronicles of the Crusades: Eye-Witness Accounts of the Wars Between Christianity and Islam* (London: Weidenfeld and Nicolson, 1989) and D. C. Munro's 1902 *Letters of the Crusaders*. Primary sources looking at the Crusades from the Muslim side include Ibn Kalanisi's *The Damascus Chronicle of the Crusades* and Amin Maalouf's *The Crusades Through Arab Eyes* (London: Al Saqi Books, 1984).

BOOKS AND ARTICLES

Cowdrey, Herbert E. J. *Popes, Monks, and Crusaders*. London: Hambledon Press, 1984.

Kedar, B. Z. *Crusade and Mission: European Approaches Toward the Muslims*. Princeton, N.J.: Princeton University Press, 1984.

Nicholson, Helen, and David Nicolle. *Crusaders, Saracens, and the Battle for Jerusalem*. New York: Osprey, 2005.

Nicolle, David. *The Crusades*. New York: Osprey, 2001.

_____. *Knights of Jerusalem: The Crusading Order of Hospitallers, 1100-1565*. New York: Osprey, 2008.

_____. *Teutonic Knight: 1190-1561*. New York: Osprey, 2007.

Riley-Smith, Jonathan. *The Oxford Illustrated History of the Crusades*. New York: Oxford University Press, 2001.

Wise, Terence. *Armies of the Crusades*. New York: Osprey, 1978.

FILMS AND OTHER MEDIA

The Crusades. Feature film. Paramount Pictures, 1935.

The Crusades: Crescent and the Cross. Documentary. History Channel, 2005.

Crusades: Quest for Power. Documentary. History Channel, 2003.

Kingdom of Heaven. Feature film. Twentieth Century-Fox, 2005.

Soldier of God. Feature film. Anthem Pictures, 2005.

Arthur K. Steinberg and Steven L. Danver

THE MEDIEVAL WORLD

WORLD

THE MIDDLE EAST
AND AFRICA

ARMIES OF MUHAMMAD AND THE CALIPHATE

Dates: 622-1060 C.E.

POLITICAL CONSIDERATIONS

The armies inspired by Islam unified the fractious Arabian Peninsula in the Riddah Wars (Wars of Apostasy) during the eight years before Muhammad's death in 632 and the subsequent rule of his father-in-law, Abū Bakr, the first *khalīfat rasul al-Lah* (successor to the messenger of God, often rendered as "caliph"). From 636 to 714, relatively small but disciplined armies conquered a large portion of the Byzantine Empire and the entire Sāsānian Persian Empire, both exhausted by twenty-seven years of continuous mutual warfare. The Arabic language, which previously had no written grammar, became the language of religion, scholarship, law, and commerce over wide areas of western and southern Asia and northern Africa. Islam, a revealed faith centered in the isolated cities of Mecca and Medina (the latter formerly called Yathrib), became one of the world's largest religions.

Three distinct caliphates ruled a more or less united, and expanding, Dar-al-Islam (literally "home" or "abode," a division of the Islamic world) from 632 until about 909. Abū Bakr, the consensus choice to lead the fledgling Muslim community, oversaw collection of notes from Muhammad's revelations, which would become the Holy Qur'ān, and organized the command structure of a disciplined army. Three more *rashidun* (rightly guided) caliphs, from Muhammad's inner circle, were chosen by consensus of the *shūrā*, elders of the Muslim community. The second caliph, ʿUmar ibn al-Khaṭṭāb, adopted the title *amīr al-muʾminin*, commander of the faithful. The two titles were used interchangeably, but over time, "caliph" was commonly the title of the highest ruler, while "emir" (or "amir") was sometimes a subordinate office. ʿUthmān ibn ʿAffān followed ʿUmar, who

was followed in 656 by Muhammad's cousin and son-in-law, Alī ibn Abī Talīb.

ʿAlī's caliphate was challenged by Muʾāwiyah ibn ʿAbī Sufynā, a son of Mecca's Banū Umayya clan, wealthiest of the Quraysh (Arabic *Quraš*). Muhammad's Banū Hāshim clan were Quraysh, although lower on the social scale. Years of *fitna*, wars between Muslims, ended in 661, when Muʾāwiyah established the caliphate's first hereditary dynasty, with its capital in Damascus. Adherents of ʿAlī, who had been pushed into what is now central and southern Iraq, became the nucleus of the Shia branch of Islam. ʿAbbāsid caliphs (claiming descent from Muhammad's uncle, al-ʿAbbās) took power in 750 after another fitna, nearly exterminating the Umayyads, and established a new capital, which became Baghdad. One Umayyad prince, ʿAbd al-Rahmān ibn Muʾāwiyah ibn Hishām, established himself in 756 as emir in fractious al-Andalus (southern Spain), where his descendants would claim the title of caliph in 929.

Little effort was made to convert the inhabitants of conquered territory. Arabs, like Jews, considered themselves the chosen people of God's revelation. In the second sura (chapter), the Qurʾān enjoins believers to fight against unbelievers "until idolatry is no more and al-Lah's religion reigns supreme" but also asserts, "There shall be no compulsion in religion." The first caliphs had little experience and less interest in the details of administration, which was left to clerks, judges, and administrators among the conquered peoples. Umayyad caliphs made sharp distinctions between Arabs, *mawali* (non-Arab converts to Islam), and *dhimmi* (non-Muslim subjects). The finances of the Umayyad caliphate depended heavily on the *jizya*, a tax paid by nonbelievers.

Social and political distinctions between different Arab identities persisted for centuries in military ri-

MUSLIM EMPIRE IN 760

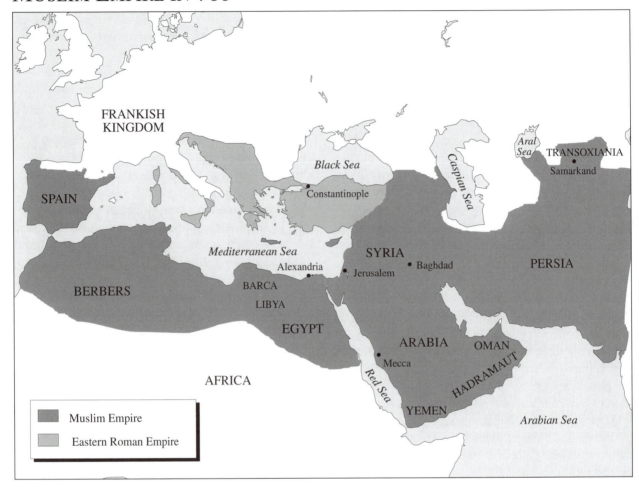

valry in newly acquired territories on three continents. Yemenis and southern Arabs competed with northern Arabs, while Arabs long settled in Syria (al-Shamiyyun) were resented by those remaining in the Hijaz of the Arabian Peninsula. Berbers in western North Africa, once converted to Islam, became rival claimants to power. One result of rapid conquest is that Arabia itself lapsed into tribal disunity as an isolated backwater of the growing empire. As early as 813, Iranians and Turks from beyond the Amu Dar'ya (Oxus River) dominated the armies of the ʿAbbāsid caliphs.

The Dar-al-Islam ceased to be a single caliphate, even formally, by 909. The Fāṭimid Dynasty of Ifriqiya (modern Tunisia) formally established the first Shia caliphate, eventually extending from Tunisia to Egypt and Palestine. The Umayyad caliphate of Córdoba, established in 929, broke up into competing *taifa* states after 1031. By the 1080's, successive Berber religious revivals known as *al-Murabitun* (Almoravids) and fifty years later *al-Muwaḥḥidūn* (Almohads) built their own empires in the Maghreb of North Africa and al-Andalus. In Baghdad, Seljuk Turks intervened between 1055 and 1060 on behalf of the weakened ʿAbbāsid caliphs, against the efforts of Buyid princes to establish Shia rule and ally with the Fāṭimids. In 1058, the authority of the caliph was delegated to the Turkish general Tughril (or Toğrül) under the title of sultan. By the early 1100's, political disintegration into a series of autonomous feudal estates left the sultanate vulnerable to the invading Frankish Crusades.

MILITARY ACHIEVEMENT

Muḥammad's first accomplishment was to survive military confrontation with the future generals of Islamic conquest, his Meccan adversaries of the Quraysh clan. These battles began as traditional *razzia*, or raids against caravans. A successful ambush by a few hundred Muslims in March of 624 at Badr was followed in March, 625, by Meccan revenge in a battle at Uhud. In March, 627, an army of ten thousand Quraysh marched on Medina and was repulsed at the Battle of the Trench. A combination of tribal diplomacy, domination of trade routes, growing wealth, and the allegiance of Bedouin warriors allowed Muḥammad to secure the capitulation of Mecca in January, 630, without battle.

Significant conquests outside the Arabian Peninsula began in 636, four years after the Prophet's death, under the second caliph, ʿUmar I. After defeating a Roman and Armenian force of thirty thousand at the Battle of Jabiya-Yarmūk on August 20, 636, the armies of Islam dominated Syria and Palestine. Jerusalem was surrendered after a seven-month siege in 638. Generous terms, allowing non-Muslims to pay the jizya (a tax on non-Muslims) and practic their own religion and laws, left little motive to die fighting Islam. Alexandria, with impregnable walls and a garrison of as many as fifty thousand Roman soldiers, was surrendered by its patriarch in 641, following a five-month siege, to Muslim commander ʿAmr ibn al-ʿĀs. The Eastern Roman Empire lost close to 80 percent of its territory in five years.

In 637, the Iranian capital of Ctesiphon fell after a battle with thirty thousand Sāsānian soldiers near al-Qādisiyya, on the west bank of the Euphrates River, near the present location of Baghdad. The Sāsānian Empire ended after the Battle of Nihawand in 642. Muslim influence reached and passed the Oxus River (Amu Dar'ya) into central Asia.

The first Umayyad caliph made a determined effort in 672-679 to take Constantinople, sending a fleet of as many as one thousand ships into the Sea of Marmara, after seizing a number of Aegean islands. Extensive use of the incendiary weapon "Greek fire" to destroy the caliph's ships, together with the walls built by Emperor Theodosius II, defeated the siege. The Theodosian walls were 5 yards thick, rose 12 yards high, and were constructed of brick and granite. In 717, Caliph Süleyman (or Sulaymān) ibn ʿAbd al-Malik tried again, with an army of eighty thousand, including the elite *ahl al-Sham* of Syria; Khorāsāni from northern Iran; cavalry from Persia, Iraq, Arabia, and Egypt; and infantry from as far away as the Oxus River and Ifriqiya. In addition to a fleet in the Sea of Marmara, Süleyman's brother Maslama brought an army to the plains west of Constantinople, against the walls built by Anastasius I.

TURNING POINTS

622	In a journey known as the Hegira, the Islamic prophet Muḥammad (c. 570-632) flees from Mecca to Medina to avoid persecution.
632-661	Muḥammad is succeeded after his death in 632 by the four legitimate successors of the Rāshidūn caliphate.
680	The forces of Muḥammad's grandson Ḥusayn are ambushed and massacred at the Battle of Karbalā, marking the beginning of Shia as a branch of Islam.
mid-8th cent.	Islam becomes the dominant religio-political power structure of the Middle East, from the Atlantic to the Indian frontier, including the Mediterranean coast and Spain.
1095	The Crusades are launched by Christian warriors seeking to reclaim the Holy Land for Christianity.
1187	Jerusalem is captured by Saladin from the Crusaders.
1260	Baybars I, the Mamlūk sultan of Egypt, defeats the Mongol hordes at Nabūlus.
1453	Muslim Turks besiege and capture Constantinople, extinguishing the Byzantine Empire.

The siege ended after eleven months, the caliphal army decimated by cold weather, shortage of food, disease, and a surprise attack by Bulgarians.

Mu'awiya sent an army commanded by 'Uqbah ibn Nāfi' into the Maghreb of western North Africa in 670. After initial success, 'Uqbah died in 682 in Ifriqiya fighting a Berber chieftain named Kusayla, supported by remaining Greco-Roman soldiers and a substantial Jewish population. The Muslim fortification of Qayrawan (Kairouan or Kirwan) fell in 684; for the next twenty years, forty thousand troops under Hasān ibn an-Nu'mān al-Ghassānī fought to retake the Maghreb. A Jewish woman known as Kahina of the Aurès led resistance after the death of Kusayla. Emir Hasān's soldiers captured Carthage in 690, but resistance was not fully ended until 704. A new vizier of Barqa and Ifriqiya, Mūsa ibn Nuṣayr, had employed diplomacy and Muslim 'ulama to secure Berber allegiance. By then, the caliphate had been through another fitna. After the death of Mu'awiya's son Yazīd and his son Mu'awiya II, another branch of the Umayya, the Marwanids, fought Arabs from the Hijaz region (including Mecca and Medina) in 684, ending with the Umayyad caliphate still ruling.

A convert from one of the Berber tribes, Tāriq ibn Ziyād, was given command in 708 of Tangier, and in 711 he launched the invasion of the Iberian Peninsula, where a Visigothic aristocracy ruled a disarmed population of Iberians, Romans, and Jews. A single battle in July near the Guadalete River and the town of Sidonia (Shaduna) eliminated King Roderick and a good part of the Visigothic nobility; Tāriq lost at least three thousand men. Eight hundred men under Mughith al-Rumi, apparently a Roman convert, took the undermanned fortifications of Córdoba, while Tāriq found Toledo nearly deserted. Tāriq was joined in 712 by Mūsa ibn Nuṣayr, with an additional eighteen thousand Yemeni soldiers. Sevilla resisted for three months in late 712; Merida was defended for more than five months in 713, including a charge by Visigothic cavalry and infantry, which badly damaged the besieging forces. At the end of 714, the entire land south of the Pyrenees, called al-Andalus by the new conquerors, was nominally subject to the caliph in Damascus. However, independent wālis resisted rule from emirs in Córdoba, even indulging in alliance with Aquitainian Christians. An incursion by Emir 'Abd Allah al-Ghafiqi ('Abd al-Raḥmān) into Aquitaine was repulsed by Charles Martel, the Frankish king, at Tours in 732. A Berber revolt in 739 preoccupied caliphal armies in Spain and Africa for many years. By 795, Charlemagne's Spanish March had fostered small Christian kingdoms in the northern part of what became modern Spain, benefiting from alliance with wālis dissatisfied with the new Umayyad emirate established in 756.

WEAPONS, UNIFORMS, AND ARMOR

The armies that emerged from the Arabian Peninsula fought mainly with sword and spear, often wearing felt armor and carrying shields of various leathers. Helmets were rare, although chain mail and iron helmets were not unknown. Armored infantry were generally placed in the front ranks to protect those with lighter or no armor. Javelins were sometimes used prior to physical contact. At the Battle of al-Qādisiyya in 637, a Muslim army fought thirty thousand Sāsānians with darts, arrows, spears, swords, and battle-axes.

Bedouin lances—one 5 cubits in length, another 11 cubits—were the main cavalry weapon. (A cubit was defined as the length of a man's forearm.) Horse-mounted cavalry were equipped with shields, hauberks, and helmets and were armed with swords on baldrics; horsemen also carried a packing needle, five small needles, linen thread, an awl, scissors, and a horses's nose-bag and feed basket. Leather loop stirrups were known but despised as a sign of weakness and therefore seldom used. When Muslim conquest reached Khorāsān at the close of the seventh century, iron stirrups were adopted, spreading back across Mesopotamia and Africa.

Under the Umayyad caliphs, cavalry were supplied with lances, maces, swords, and the khanjar daggers. Berber cavalry, who fought first against the Muslims, then became fierce soldiers of Islam, were wearing the imama (a turban over a metal cap) and coats of light mail under leather.

Iranian (Persian) and Turkish armies from central Asia, which came to dominate the later years of the

THE ʿABBĀSID CALIPHATE, C. 800

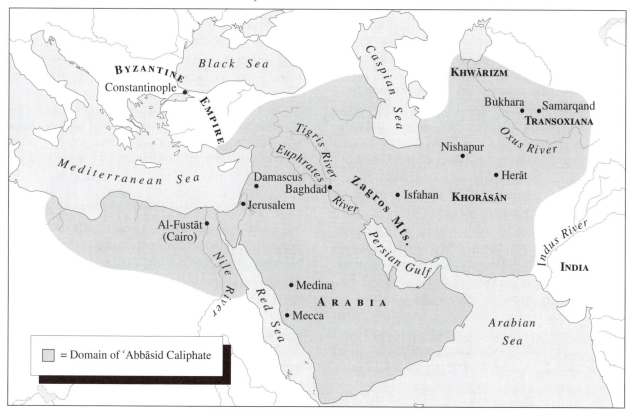

caliphate, were predominantly cavalry, featuring armored archers shooting from horseback. Horses were protected by bards of felt, and riders were equipped with lamellar cuirasses, hauberks, arm covers, lances, and leather shields of Tibetan origin. Maces, battle-axes, and single-edged short swords were also used, and full-size swords were slightly curved.

MILITARY ORGANIZATION

Muḥammad and Abū Bakr organized the Muslim armies into disciplined formations, contrary to previous Arab custom. Troops were drawn up in lines of battle with a center (qalb, literally heart), right wing (maymana), and left wing (maysara). Many fought in tribal units, with their own banners. As in Byzantine armies, archers were deployed primarily to protect infantry flanks from enemy cavalry attacks.

Distinctions between infantry and cavalry were blurred, since infantry was transported on horses and camels, while cavalry often dismounted, fighting on foot. Warhorses were rare and carefully conserved, led to battle, and mounted only when fighting began. Horses were a high priority for tribute from newly acquired territory. While camels were not used in battle, they allowed the infantry greater maneuverability in choosing the time and place to give battle.

For the first few decades, successive caliphs kept their armies apart from the conquered population, building garrison towns such as al-Kufa, Basra, Qayrawan, and al-Fustat. Jabiya, the principal military camp of the Bilad al-Sham, was larger than the city of Damascus, which it secured. Muslim soldiers were enrolled in a roster called the *diwan*, with a salary according to a fixed pay scale, initiated by the second rashidun caliph, ʿUmar. Under the caliphate of Muʾawiya (661-680) the diwan reached forty thousand names but was thereafter closed, enrollment becoming a privilege rather than a routine record of enlistment.

Regional armies were organized or designated in territories that became part of the Dar-al-Islam, both the region and the army known as a *jund*. The soldiers were Arab settlers, supported by tax revenue from their area. Junds were assigned for Damascus, Jordan (with the capital at Tiberias), Palestine (capital at Jerusalem), Ascalon, and Homs. Later junds were designated for Qunnasrin (including Antioch, Manbij, and Aleppo). The original jund established in Egypt included south Arabian or Yemeni tribes, principally the Azd, Himyar, Kinda, and Lakhm. Junds were also designated in al-Andalus. The original leadership were *ahl al-Raya*, or "people of the standard," drawn from the Quraysh and the *ansar*, companions of the Prophet. Parcels of land known as *khittas* were allotted to each tribal group. Soldiers in the jund were enrolled in the diwan, and received monthly pay called *ata*. Inevitably, the junds became power centers on which caliphs, rebels, or challengers relied to uphold the current ruler or overturn him, to sustain the unity of the Dar-al-Islam, or to secede from caliphal authority. In the late ninth century, junds were largely replaced by the Turkish *ghulams*.

DOCTRINE, STRATEGY, AND TACTICS

Speed and maneuverability accounted for many of the early Arab victories over larger, better armored and well-established armies, trained to hold fixed positions or move en masse. Offensive moves called *karr wa farr*, repeated attack and retreat, were employed not only against Byzantine and Sāsānian forces but also against Visigothic Hispania, which became Muslim al-Andalus. At the Battle of Jabiya-Yarmūk in 636, a feigned retreat on the third day of fighting by Āmir ibn ʿAbdullāh ibn al-Jarrāh's troops drew Armenian general Vahan's infantry in pursuit, opening space for Khālid ibn al-Walīd's soldiers to drive a wedge between Byzantine infantry and cavalry, ending the battle in a rout. The armored cavalry of Tāriq ibn Ziyād similarly opened a wedge in the Visigothic line near the Guadalete River in July, 711. Repeated

THE FĀṬIMIDS, C. 1040

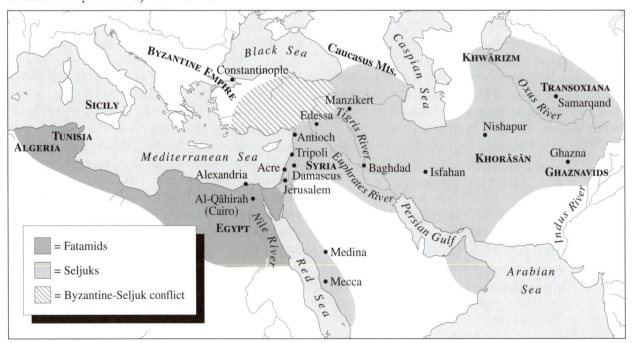

= Fatamids
= Seljuks
= Byzantine-Seljuk conflict

charges failed to dent the Sāsānian cataphracts at al-Qādisiyya in 637, and Iranian war elephants panicked Arab cavalry horses. After experienced elephant fighters arrived on the third day, sending the elephants crashing back into the Sāsānian line, Persian discipline broke down. With limited room to maneuver, the defenders were driven into the Euphrates River.

Medieval Sources

Prior to the emergence of Islam from the Arabian Peninsula, there was little tradition of either scholarship or written literature in the Arabic language. Perhaps the most comprehensive Muslim scholarship roughly contemporary to the history of Muḥammad and the Caliphate is Abū Jaʿfar Muḥammad ibn Jarīr al-Ṭabarī's *Taʾrīkh al-rusul wa al-mulūk* (872-973; *The History of al-Ṭabarī*, 1985-1999, 39 volumes). Individual volumes include *Muḥammad at Mecca* (volume 6) and *The Conquest of Iraq, Southwestern Persia, and Egypt* (volume 13). Al-Ṭabarī was already well known for an exhaustive multivolume commentary on the Holy Qurʾān, completed about 903 C.E. A later reference is Ibn Khaldūn's *Muqaddimah* (1375-1379; *The Muqaddimah*, 1958; also translated as *An Introduction to History*, 1967). While much of the material is secondary, it offers the most detailed primary material on the history of the Mahgreb.

Offering a rare glimpse from the nearly illiterate lands north of the Pyrenees is the *Annales regni Francorum* (741-829; *Royal Frankish Annals* in *Carolingian Chronicles*, 1970), which includes reference to the Spanish March. While most Byzantine manuscripts from this period have not been preserved, Theophanes' *Chronographia* (815; *The Chronicle of Theophanes*, 1982) draws on many lost sources, and it along with Nikephoros's *Breviarium historicum* (787; *Short History*, 1990) are both available in English translation.

Books and Articles

Donner, Fred McGraw. *The Early Islamic Conquests*. Princeton, N.J.: Princeton University Press, 1981.

Kaegi, Walter Emil. *Byzantium and the Early Islamic Conquests*. New York: Cambridge University Press, 1995.

Kennedy, Hugh N. *The Armies of the Caliphs: Military and Society in the Early Islamic State*. New York: Routledge, 2001.

Lewis, Bernard. *Islam and the Arab World: Faith, People, Culture*. New York: Knopf, 1976.

Lewis, David Levering. *God's Crucible: Islam and the Making of Europe, 570-1215*. New York: W. W. Norton, 2008.

Nicolle, David. *Armies of the Muslim Conquest*. New York: Osprey, 1993.

_____. *Poitiers, A.D. 732*. New York: Osprey, 2008.

Nicolle, David, and Angus McBride. *The Armies of Islam, 7th-11th Centuries*. New York: Osprey, 1982.

Films and Other Media

Islam: Empire of Faith. Documentary. Public Broadcasting Service, 2000.

Muḥammad: Messenger of God (in North America as *The Messenger*). Documentary. Moustapha Akkad, 1976.

The Story of Islam. Documentary. ABC News, 1983.

Charles Rosenberg

ARMIES OF THE SELJUK TURKS

Dates: c. 900-1307 C.E.

POLITICAL CONSIDERATIONS

In 750 the ʿAbbāsid Dynasty had succeeded the Umayyad Dynasty as rulers of the Muslim world. However, by 1050 ʿAbbāsid authority was greatly reduced; this decline further splintered the followers of Islam. Into this leadership void stepped the Seljuk Turks, and for nearly a century and a half they were the dominant Muslim dynasty ruling abroad in Armenia, Persia, Iraq, and Syria.

Close to a century earlier, a tribal leader named Seljuq (also known as Selchuk or Seljuk) had moved and settled this nomadic band from the region north of the Aral Sea into Central Asia. Around 1040 this tribe, which had been previously identified as part of the larger group of Oghuz Turks, became known as the Seljuqs or Seljuks. Two brothers, Toghrïl Beg and Chaghrï Beg, grandsons of the Seljuq namesake, successfully united various tribes into a Seljuk army, which they led to victory over the Ghaznavid Dynasty (which spanned eastern Iran, central Afghanistan, and modern-day Pakistan) at the Battle of Dandanqan. This decisive victory signaled the end of the Ghaznavid Dynasty and heralded the rise of the Seljuk Turks.

In 1055 the Seljuk Turks seized Baghdad in a bloodless coup. An ʿAbbāsid caliph was left to rule as titular ruler, but the Seljuks were the true political force for the next three generations. In 1067 they were raiding lands claimed by their Christian rivals, the Byzantine Empire. Toghrïl Beg's nephew, Alp Arslan, led the Seljuks to a decisive victory at the Battle of Manzikert in 1071. This one-sided win opened the way for mass Turkish migration into Anatolia. In this same year, Seljuk forces occupied the holy city of Jerusalem.

Alp Arslan was killed the following year in a bizarre duel with an enemy commander, often called an assassination. His son Malik Shāh I, along with the grand vizier Niẓām al-Mulk, brought a short-lived period of stability, organization, and cultural flourishing to what had come to be called the Empire of the Great Seljuks. In theory the "Great Seljuks" were to be masters of all the Seljuk sultan lines, but this was seldom the case. Sultanates operated in territories in Persia and Syria, and a fiercely independent Seljuk state was founded by Süleyman after his capture of the Byzantine city of Nicaea in 1078. This became the sultanate of Rum—the Arabic word for Rome was Rum, and this was a fitting designation as the region had once been in Roman/Byzantine possession.

THE GHAZNAVID EMPIRE, C. 1030

288

SELJUK TURKS, C. 1090

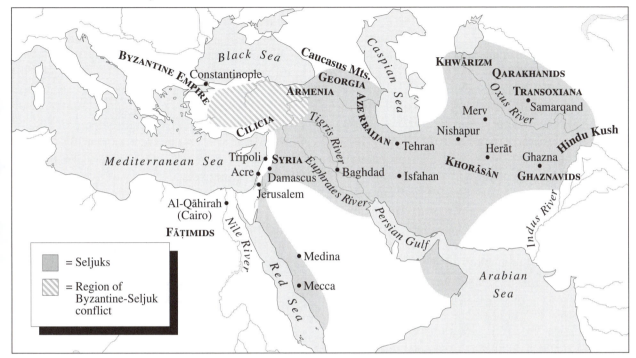

Religious differences between sects brewed dissent among the nations of Islam. These theological disputes sparked the creation of the Assassins, a militant Islamic sect that was responsible for the death of Niẓām al-Mulk in 1092.

Political infighting also hastened the dissolution of the empire. It was common practice to carve up a deceased ruler's property and dole out separate kingdoms to the surviving sons in grants called *iqtāʿ*. This ever-increasing collection of disparate emirs and lesser sultans continuously undermined Seljuk central authority. The weakness in this system was especially apparent upon Malik Shāh's death in 1092, when his brother and four sons began to squabble over the inheritance.

In 1095 the First Crusade began, and several key Seljuk cities, including Nicaea and Jerusalem, were lost in 1099. Throughout the rest of the Crusades, divisions between the kingdoms led to some Seljuks supporting the Crusaders. By 1200, Seljuk influence had been checked in all but the Anatolia region. The loss at the Battle of Köse Dag in 1243 to the Mongols

reduced the surviving Seljuk kingdoms to a tributary state of the Mongol Dynasty. Finally, in 1307 Sultan Ghiyath ad-Din Mesud II (Masʿūd II) and his son were killed, ending the once-powerful dynasty. The remnants would be absorbed into the Ottoman Empire, which would endure until the end of World War I.

MILITARY ACHIEVEMENT

At the Battle of Dandanqan in 1040 the Seljuks triumphed over the Ghaznavid Dynasty. This gained them a wide swath of land in Iran and central Asia that laid the foundation for their future empire. In 1050, without a battle, the Seljuks gained the important political and military post of Baghdad. Although they were technically subservient to the ʿAbbāsid Dynasty, they were the power behind the scenes. Five years later, at the Battle of Pasinler, the Seljuks won their first significant victory over the Byzantines and their Georgian allies. In the aftermath the Byzantine emperor, Constantine IX Monomachus, was forced to treat with the Seljuk as victors. In 1067 the Seljuk general Kilic Aslan II sacked the Byzantine city of Caesarea (also known as Kaisaria), turning it into the capital of a smaller emirate. This further increased the Seljuk holdings and was another chink in the armor of the Byzantine Empire.

The most significant military achievement for the Seljuk Turks was victory over the Byzantium army just over two decades later, in 1071, at Manzikert. The Byzantines lost the bulk of their professional army in this engagement, and their emperor, Romanus IV Diogenes, was captured and ransomed. This effectively ceded Asia Minor to the invading Turkish bands, who may not have been obedient to the Seljuks but further weakened the Byzantine Empire nonetheless. The ability of the Byzantines to mount future campaigns was greatly crippled, as ceding so vast a territory cost the empire dearly in levies of manpower and other resources. The date of the battle, August 19, 1071, was forever after known by the Byzantines as "the dreadful day." In 1176, at the Battle of Myriocephalon, the Byzantine emperor Manuel I Comnenus suffered another severe setback at the hands of the Seljuks while trying to recover lost territory in Anatolia. This further reinforced the notion of the Turks' supremacy on the battlefield against their Byzantine rivals.

WEAPONS, UNIFORMS, AND ARMOR

The Seljuk Turk fighters could accurately be called steppe light cavalry. The main component of any Seljuk force was mounted archers. Horses were such an important aspect of the Seljuks' battlefield philosophy that on extended campaigns each rider brought at least one spare horse to have in reserve. The territorial reserves, the "irregulars," were also generally mounted.

These riders bore composite bows of horn or bone fed by quivers containing thirty to fifty arrows. While the bow was certainly the preferred weapon, missile weapons such as javelins were also used. Bows were scarce among the irregulars; swords and spears were

the weapons used most frequently by those in this fighting element. The Seljuks' primary stopping power was in the bow, but, like any mounted troops, they were prepared to engage in hand-to-hand combat. Swords and maces served as secondary weapons.

In order to maintain a mobility advantage, the Seljuk Turks were unarmored or at best lightly armored. Usually a horse archer carried only a small, rounded shield, usually brightly colored. Some mounted and foot troops were known to wear captured mail, but generally some form of lamellar armor was employed.

The Seljuks appear to have employed no signature uniforms. The chieftains reportedly wore wide-skirted topcoats, cut diagonally with a flap called a *muqaylab*. Normal tribal clothing, frequently dyed in a bright shade, was worn by other Seljuk forces. Belts, made of leather or overlapping plates, were a key component of these warriors' battle clothing, used for keeping close at hand such equipment as replacement strings and bows and secondary weapons. In the Seljuk culture, belts were common gifts to mark favor.

MILITARY ORGANIZATION

The Seljuks relied mainly on the military organization of their predecessors, with a few notable differences. Under their rule a more feudal system was established, each province raising and absorbing the cost of a contingent. A ruler (usually someone with a hereditary claim), called the *amīr al-mu'minīn* (the English word "emir" is derived from this title), was given the revenue for a particular province. A portion of this revenue was expected to be gifted back to the local sultan as a tribute. In times of war the emir was to bring to the fold a certain number of fighters. Some of these would be *askars*, the forces of regular professional soldiers who served as the bodyguards of the emirs; the men who made up the askars were referred to as *askaris*. The sizes of askars varied by province or district; an account from the First Crusade lists two thousand askaris hailing from one particular wealthy region.

Mercenaries supplemented these corps of regulars. For manpower, the emirs turned to the varied Turkmen tribes, which were headed up by their own leaders, called *beys*. These mercenaries were the bulk of the Seljuk military; when rallied and merged with the regulars, these combined armies could be more than 100,000 strong.

DOCTRINE, STRATEGY, AND TACTICS

At the heart of the Seljuk military manifesto was the bow. One outside observer remarked, "The Turks, indeed, who themselves continually seek to develop their skills with bows and arrow, pressed without ceasing." Hunting and intertribal warfare provided ample opportunity for the Seljuks to hone their skills in the use of this vital weapon from a very young age. These large composite missile weapons, when partnered with men on swift horses, gave the Seljuks a decided advantage against the slower, more heavily armored Byzantine and Crusader foes.

The Seljuk Turks were expert light cavalry and, until the emergence of the Mongols, the supreme horseback archers. A typical Seljuk encounter would involve a spirited charge like the one described in this contemporary account: "The Turks began, all at once, to howl and gabble and shout, saying with loud voices in their own language some devilish word which I do not understand . . . screaming like demons." After unnerving the enemy with such a disconcerting outburst, they would attempt an envelopment while keeping far enough away not to engage in hand-to-hand fighting. Again, a contemporary account captures this particular stratagem and its potential devastation:

It was like an earthquake with howling, sweat, a swift rush of fear, clouds of dust and not least hordes of Turks riding all around us. Depending on his speed, resolution and strength, each man sought safety in flight. The enemy chased them, killing some, capturing some and trampling others under the horses' hooves. It was a terribly sad sight, beyond any lamenting or mourning.

If their opponents held together, the Seljuks would continue to pepper them with arrows from distances that astonished their enemies. One stated, "After we had set ourselves in order the Turks came upon us as from all sides, skirmishing, throwing darts and javelins and shooting arrows from an astonishing range." When the Seljuk archers were pressed, or when they were attempting to execute a more complex plan, they would break and feign retreat. If their unwary foes tried to pursue, they would find it just as dangerous as standing their ground, as the Seljuks would turn and, from their mounts, fire a hail of arrows.

While the bow was the cornerstone of their offensive, the Seljuks recognized the need to close for melee, as this contemporary account shows:

[The Turks] surrounded our men and shot such a great number of arrows and quarrels that rain or hail never darkened the sky so much and many of our men and horses were injured. When the first bands of Turks had emptied their quivers and shot all their arrows, they withdrew, but a second band immediately came from behind where there were but more Turks. These fired even more thickly than the others had done. . . . The Turk, seeing that our men and horses were severely wounded and in great difficulties, hung their bows instantly on their left arms under their armpits and immediately fell upon them in a very cruel fashion with maces and swords.

MEDIEVAL SOURCES

The *Itinerarium peregrinorum et gesta regis Ricardi* contains an invaluable primary account of the Third Crusade (1187-1192) and provides a very good descriptive account of the Crusaders' clash with the Seljuks in 1191. William of Tyre, an archbishop and chronicler of the Crusades and the Middle Ages, left behind several works of interest to those studying this period and looking for a firsthand account of Seljuk Turk warfare. His account of the Crusades is bundled into the *Recueil des historiens des Croisades*, a large collection of period documents.

Matthew of Edessa, another period chronicler, provides information on the Battle of Harran (1104) as well as on the political climate of the day. The eleventh century *History* produced by Armenian historian Aristakes Lastivertsi contains a wealth of information about the events of that time, including the Seljuk invasions and the Battle of Manzikert in 1071.

BOOKS AND ARTICLES

Asbridge, Thomas. *The First Crusade*. New York: Free Press, 2005.

Contamine, Philippe. *War in the Middle Ages*. Translated by M. Jones. Hoboken, N.J.: Wiley-Blackwell, 1991.

Jones, Archer. *The Art of War in the Western World*. Champaign: University of Illinois Press, 2000.

Turnbull, Stephen. *The Ottoman Empire, 1326-1699*. New York: Osprey, 2003.

Wise, Terrance, and Gerry A. Embleton. *Armies of the Crusades*. New York: Osprey, 1978.

FILMS AND OTHER MEDIA

Byzantine Era. Documentary. CreateSpace, 2009.

Byzantium: The Lost Empire. Documentary. Koch Vision, 2007.

Crusades: Crescent and the Cross. Documentary. History Channel, 2005.

Kingdom of Heaven. Feature film. Twentieth Century Fox, 2006.

Michael Coker

THE OTTOMAN ARMIES

Dates: 1299-1453 C.E.

POLITICAL CONSIDERATIONS

Anatolia was a politically diverse crossroads in the thirteenth century. The Ilkhans, the descendants of the Mongols, lost their grip on power in Iran; the Byzantine Empire was besieged by the Franks from the west and the Turks from the east. A serious power vacuum developed in the region. A wide array of smaller states formed in this period. Close to a dozen Turkish emirates emerged throughout Anatolia, the Italian trading republics of Venice and Genoa established a presence along the coasts, and various other groups attempted to control what was left.

Out of this situation one group emerged to dominate the rest. The founder of this new state was Osman. He carved out an independent center of power near the Byzantine Empire and after years of raiding and building up a political network, the Ottomans, or *Osmanlılar* (those who are associated with Osman), became a force to be reckoned with. They developed a *ghazi* ethos (an Islamic ideology of fighting for the faith) but also an inclusive policy of recruiting military talent of any faith. The Ottomans found a fertile ground for their raids in 1354, as they crossed into the Balkans. There they discovered a politically disunited patchwork of states that were eventually brought into the Ottoman fold. With a foothold in Europe, the Ottomans dominated both sides of the Aegean.

Slowly the majority of the other regional powers were subordinated to the Ottomans. At the dawn of the fifteenth century, the Ottomans faced a new challenge from the East: the Turkic commander Tamerlane (also known as Timur, 1336-1405). The Ottomans faced him at the Battle of Ankara (1402) and were soundly defeated. The Ottoman sultan Bayezid I (r. 1389-1402) was captured, and the Ottoman state was thrown into chaos. Between 1402 and 1413, contending Ottoman princes and former Ottoman vassals fought to fill the power vacuum as Tamerlane's empire quickly evaporated.

Slowly the Ottomans were able to reestablish rule over their old territories and solidify their state again. During the reigns of Murad II (r. 1421-1451) and Mehmed II (r. 1451-1481), the Ottoman Empire reconsolidated and began to expand. Those former vassals who had asserted their independence were brought to heel, and the empire was stronger than ever before. With the defeat of the Byzantines and the capture of Constantinople in 1453, the Ottomans established a position as the preeminent power in the eastern Mediterranean.

MILITARY ACHIEVEMENT

The Ottomans were able to establish an empire centered on the Aegean, controlling western Anatolia and southeastern Europe in the fourteenth and fifteenth centuries. They unified a host of disunited states into a strong political entity. Despite defeat at the hands of Tamerlane and brief vassalage thereafter, the Ottomans became the dominant power in Anatolia, the Balkans, and the Aegean.

The Ottoman armies in this period consolidated power in most of Anatolia by defeating their principal Turkish rivals: the emirates of Aydin, Menteshe, Karesi, Saruhan, Hamit, Germiyan, Teke, and Karaman. While accomplishing this, they inflicted a series of defeats upon the Byzantines at Bursa (1326), Iznik (1331), and Edirne (1361), culminating with the capture of Constantinople (1453). While the Ottoman armies were establishing dominance over Anatolia, they also took the opportunity to become the premier power in the Balkans. After the fall of the

of the period was the capture of Constantinople in 1453, which eliminated the Byzantines, made the Ottomans masters of the Aegean, and positioned them to become a world power.

Frederick Ungar Publishing Co.

The death of Ottoman sultan Mehmed II in 1481. His sack and control of Constantinople in 1453 marked the beginning of the Ottoman Empire.

Serbian Empire in 1355, the Ottomans slowly established suzerainty over the Serbian and Bulgarian successor states with major victories at Maritza (1371) and Kosovo (1389), thereby becoming the dominant Balkan power of the period. Ottoman forces were also successful against various Crusader armies sent against them, winning the day at Nicopolis (1396), Varna (1444), and Kosovo (1448). The Ottomans also had substantial success against the Venetians at Thessalonica (1430). The definitive military success

WEAPONS, UNIFORMS, AND ARMOR

The Ottoman army was initially reliant upon a cavalry force that was used to engage in plundering raids. These forces were typically lightly armed and armored, with an emphasis on speed. They frequently armed themselves with war hammers, maces, short swords, sabers, javelins, and spears. Early Ottoman armies often wore leather lamellar armor into battle. Later, as the Ottomans came into contact with the Byzantine, Crusader, and Serbian armies, they began to adopt more substantial armor and heavier weapons. Heavy mail and plate armor was utilized frequently, which differentiated the Ottomans from most of the early Islamic armies. In addition to carrying on the Turko-Mongolic tradition of armaments, the Ottomans borrowed from the Byzantines and other European powers.

The Ottomans were known to use heavy guns during sieges as well as on the battlefield. Despite conflicting accounts of the use of artillery against the Karamans (1388), at Kosovo (1389), and at Nicopolis (1396), definitive evidence shows artillery in the Ottoman armies by 1420 and widespread use by 1440. For sieges, the heavy guns were frequently used, and these were often cast on the spot. Some of the cannons were enormous; according to certain sources, some of the cannonballs shot at the walls of Constantinople in 1453 weighed in excess of 1,900 pounds.

Ottoman armies also gradually began to utilize handheld firearms in the form of the harquebus (*tufenk*). The *janissaries* were massed among the *araba*, a series of linked wagons similar to the *Wagenburg* (a Bohemian defensive line of wagons) and used large volleys to suppress cavalry charges. These weapons were confined mainly to the janissaries and became prevalent only at the end of the fifteenth century.

MILITARY ORGANIZATION

The earliest organization of Ottoman forces was a predatory confederation drawn from nearby tribes, allies, and renegades; however, as Ottoman territorial control expanded, organizational principles were enforced. Two organizational systems were in place during this period. The first represents the initial attempt by the Ottomans to organize their army into something other than a raiding band. The second is the beginning of the form that the Ottoman army would assume in the sixteenth and seventeenth centuries.

Some of the first regular troops employed by the Ottomans were known as the *müsellem* (tax-free), which were the earliest organized cavalry units, and the *yayas*, the earliest infantry forces. These groups were given land grants in return for their service. They were organized using a decimal system. This was the first structure given to the Ottoman army. However, the loyalty of these freedmen raised concerns for the Ottoman sultans and encouraged the creation of a new structure.

With the effective establishment of an Ottoman state, the principle of military slavery was enforced in the form of the Kapıulu corps. This force was made up of military slaves who were theoretically the property of the Ottoman sultan. The two principal branches of the Kapıulu were the janissaries and the *sipahis*, a cavalry force.

As the army grew, a specialized infantry force was utilized. The *yeniçeri* (the janissaries) were first drawn from prisoners of war and later from a special levy (*devshirme*) on the Christian subjects of the empire. The janissaries adopted gunpowder weapons early in the fifteenth century, particularly the harquebus, which was used with great effect in

this period. This force was organized into *ortas*, or regiments, typically containing between one hundred and three thousand troops.

The *azab* corps were established in the early fifteenth century and were drawn from rural Anatolia. Utilized principally as an infantry force, they also performed a naval function later. The azabs continued as a second-line infantry force in the Ottoman army until some time in the sixteenth century.

The sipahis (sometimes rendered "spahis" in English) were cavalry forces drawn from the notables of Anatolia. Many of these forces received nontransferable land grants, *timars*, from which they drew their income and gathered their own forces in times of war. These forces were armored and generally heavily

F. R. Niglutsch

Turks surrender Varna to the Russians.

armed. "Sipahi" was also a term used for a unit from the six cavalry divisions of the Ottoman palace, which served as the bodyguard of the Ottoman sultans. These forces, along with the janissaries, formed the backbone of the Ottoman army after about 1400. There was a well-known rivalry between the sipahis and the janissaries.

In addition to these forces, the Ottomans employed various elements from vassals in the Balkans and Anatolia, particularly the Serbs. The Christian vassals of the Ottomans brought infantry forces that were often referred to as *voynuks*. These troops performed garrison duty along the Ottoman frontiers in the Balkans and joined the Ottoman army in major campaigns.

Additionally, Ottoman armies began to include units of miners and sappers who were needed to reduce the many fortifications that Ottoman armies encountered on campaign. An initial lack of these forces had hindered the Ottomans against Byzantine and Crusader fortifications. Later these forces became adept at using gunpowder and mining operations.

DOCTRINE, STRATEGY, AND TACTICS

The Ottoman armies employed a wide array of tactics against the various opponents they faced as they consolidated power. The earliest Ottoman armies were little more than raiding bands. They relied on speed and subterfuge for success, and especially upon the time-honored nomadic strategy of feigned retreat and counterattack. These forces essentially wore other forces down by attrition rather than by using field tactics to win set battles. These forces were all but ineffective against fortified positions.

Ottoman armies from the beginning and throughout the period made frequent use of light cavalry raiders, or *akıncıs*. These forces began to appear in the Balkans around 1400. Later they were drawn from Ottoman vassals such as the Crimean Tatars and the Walachians; they constantly harassed opposing armies and softened up border defenses. They kept the borders of the Ottoman Empire in a nearly constant state of war, which meant that the Ottomans' opponents had to be constantly concerned about raids. Hence, many opponents of the Ottomans in the Balkans built elaborate border fortresses. During battles, these light cavalry forces attempted to draw the enemy in toward the Ottoman strong point and the entrenched janissaries.

One of the Ottomans' most enduring tactics was the use of a fortified center on the battlefield as a rallying point. These points were often strengthened using field fortifications, such as trenches or palisades of sharpened stakes. Later the arabas were used by the Ottoman armies while on campaign as mobile strong points containing a concentration of cannons and muskets. These strong points also functioned as command centers, often housing the Ottoman sultan and his cavalry bodyguard as well as the janissaries. These formations were particularly effective against cavalry forces and led to Ottoman victories at Nicopolis (1396) and Kosovo (1448).

CONTEMPORARY SOURCES

Sources for the earliest years of the Ottoman army are scant. The Ottoman army began as a raiding confederacy and kept no real records. Of the extant sources from this period, the majority are from the perspective of the Ottomans' adversaries. The Ottoman sources of the period are also problematic, because they are laced with legends and figures from previous periods; as a result, contemporary events are difficult to disentangle—and even these sources were often written after the events they relate. Another issue is that few of these sources have been translated into English.

By the end of the fourteenth century, there were better accounts of the Ottoman military. Those available in English include Konstantin Mihailović's *Pamiętniki janczara* (fifteenth century; *Memoirs of a Janissary*, 1975), which offers a unique look into the Ottoman army from the perspective of one of the janissaries. It provides great detail about the rigors and the lifestyle of the janissaries. *The Crusade of Varna* (2006; part of the Crusade Texts in Translation series) gives extensive information about the Crusade of Varna (1444) from the perspectives of all parties involved, including the Ottomans, the Hungarians, the French, and others. A section in this work, the anonymous "The Holy Wars of Sultan Murad Son of Mehmed Khan," provides an Ottoman perspective on this conflict. *The Siege of Constantinople: Seven Contemporary Accounts* (1972) gives great detail on the 1453 siege from the Byzantine and Genoese perspectives.

BOOKS AND ARTICLES

Bartusis, Mark C. *The Late Byzantine Army: Arms and Society 1204-1453*. Philadelphia: University of Pennsylvania Press, 1997.

Chalkokondyles, Laonikos. *Laonikos Chalkokondyles: A Translation and Commentary of the Demonstrations of Histories*. Translated by Nikolaos Nikoloudis. Athens: Historical Publications St. D. Basilopoulos, 1996.

Doukas. *Decline and Fall of Byzantium to the Ottoman Turks*. Prepared by Harry J. Magoulias. Detroit: Wayne State University Press, 1975.

Imber, Colin. *The Ottoman Empire, 1300-1650*. New York: Palgrave, 2002.

_____, ed. *The Crusade of Varna*. London: Ashgate, 2006.

Inalcik, Halil. "Osman Ghazi's Siege of Nicea and the Battle of Bapheus." In *The Ottoman Emirate, 1300-1389*, edited by Elizabeth Zachariadou. Heraklion: Crete University Press, 1993.

_____. *The Ottoman Empire: The Classical Age, 1300-1600*. Translated by Norman Itzkowitz and Colin Imber. London: Weidenfeld and Nicolson, 1973.

Kaldy-Nagy, Gyor. "The First Centuries of Ottoman Military Organization." *Acta Orientalia* (Budapest) 31 (1977): 147-183.

Melville-Jones, J. R., trans. *The Siege of Constantinople: Seven Contemporary Accounts*. Amsterdam: Hakkert, 1972.

Mihalović, Konstantin. *Memoirs of a Janissary*. Translated by Benjamin Stoltz. Historical commentary and notes by Svat Soucek. Ann Arbor, Mich.: Joint Committee on Eastern Europe, American Council of Learned Societies, by the Department of Slavic Languages and Literatures, University of Michigan, 1975.

Nicolle, David. *Armies of the Ottoman Turks, 1300-1774*. New York: Osprey, 2001.

_____. *Crusade of Nicopolis, 1396*. New York: Osprey, 1999.

Robinson, H. R. *Oriental Armour*. London: Herbert Jenkins, 1967.

FILMS AND OTHER MEDIA

Ottoman Empire. Documentary (Eastern Traditions Series). Wolf Productions, 2005.

The Ottoman Empire. Documentary. Films Media Groups, 1996.

Ottoman Empire: The War Machine. Documentary. A&E Home Video, 2006.

James N. Tallon

WEST AFRICAN EMPIRES

Dates: 400-1591 C.E.

POLITICAL CONSIDERATIONS

In the period from 400 to 1591, West Africa saw the rise and fall of the indigenous kingdoms and empires of Ghana, medieval Mali, and Songhai. Although many other petty states and kingdoms arose in West Africa during this time, only Ghana, Mali, and Songhai achieved the status of full-fledged and long-lived conquest states and expansionist empires, for which contact-era Islamic and European documentary histories are available.

Ghana's emergence as the first of the West African empires ultimately set the stage for subsequent developments identified with the establishment of the kingdoms of Mali and Songhai. In each instance the intensification of trade along the trans-Saharan trade network was a critical factor underlying the expansion, influence, and institutionalization of the military orders of the day. In fact, much of the wealth generated to support the maintenance of professional armies—documented by various Islamic writers to have ranged between 40,000 and 200,000 soldiers each—was derived directly from the military and po-

lice protections afforded foreign travelers and merchants on the trans-Saharan trade corridor. With the advent and spread of the Islamic faith out of North Africa in the eighth century, new forms of commercial, religious, social, cultural, and military interaction transformed the social and political landscape of West Africa. In some instances, as with the reign of Mansa Mūsā I of Mali (1312-1337 C.E.), Islamic influence transformed the organizational structure of the empire and the administration of justice and launched the religious wars of the Islamic jihad. Subsequent kings and kingdoms either waged war under the doctrines of the Islamic tradition or sought to eradicate the Muslim tradition altogether, setting the stage for much of the military history of the kingdoms of Mali and Songhai until the emergence of the European slave trade and the introduction of firearms. These latter developments in turn fueled a long-standing pattern of internecine warfare that ultimately depopulated entire towns and regions subject to West Africa's colonial-era encounter with European merchants, militarists, and slave traders.

TURNING POINTS

700-1000	Ghana emerges as the dominant kingdom and military power of the western Sudan.
1230	The kingdom of Mali is founded by a Mandinka prince after the defeat of the Susu kingdom.
1450	Songhai incorporates the former kingdom of Mali and comes to control one of the largest empires of that time.
1468	Songhai armies invade Timbuktu, execute Arab merchants and traitors, and sack and burn the city; thereby heralding a period of anti-Islamic sentiment in West Africa.
1591	Songhai is conquered by a Moroccan army consisting primarily of European mercenaries armed with muskets, the first to be used in West African warfare.

MILITARY ACHIEVEMENT

Military achievement during this period centered on the emergence and mobilization of professional armies and cavalry forces; the formalization of military protocols, organizational structures, propaganda, and tactics; and the adoption of new military technologies, fortifications, and weaponry. Whereas the primary achievements ascribed to the kingdom of Ghana center on the fact that it was the first of the western Sudanese empires to establish large pro-

Africa, c. 1000-1500

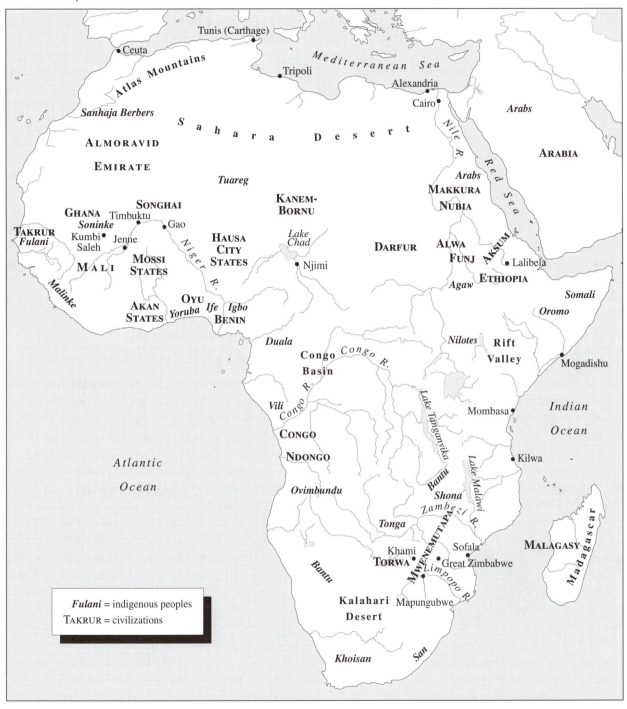

Ceuta

Tunis (Carthage)

Mediterranean Sea

Tripoli

Alexandria

Cairo

Arabs

Atlas Mountains

Sanhaja Berbers

S a h a r a   D e s e r t

ALMORAVID

EMIRATE

Tuareg

KANEM-BORNU

Nile R.

Arabs

MAKKURA

NUBIA

Red Sea

ARABIA

SONGHAI

Timbuktu

Gao

GHANA

Soninke

Kumbi
Saleh

Jenne

TAKRUR
Fulani

**HAUSA
CITY
STATES**

*Lake
Chad*

DARFUR

ALWA

FUNJ

AKSUM

Lalibela

**MOSSI
STATES**

Niger R.

Njimi

Agaw

ETHIOPIA

MALI

Malinke

**AKAN
STATES**

OYU
Yoruba

Ife

Igbo

BENIN

Somali

Oromo

Duala

**Congo
Basin**

Congo R.

Nilotes

**Rift
Valley**

Mogadishu

Vili

Congo R.

CONGO

NDONGO

*Indian
Ocean*

Mombasa

Lake Tanganyika

*Atlantic
Ocean*

Ovimbundu

Bantu

Shona

Zambezi R.

Lake Malawi

Kilwa

Tonga

MWENEMUTAPA

Sofala

MALAGASY

Khami

TORWA

Great Zimbabwe

Limpopo R.

Madagascar

Bantu

Mapungubwe

**Kalahari
Desert**

Khoisan

San

Fulani = indigenous peoples
TAKRUR = civilizations

fessional armies for the maintenance of law and order over a vast territory, the medieval kingdom of Mali in turn contributed to the formal development and mobilization of cavalry forces in the thirteenth and fourteenth centuries in order to command the battlefields of the savanna and sahel regions of West Africa. Both within and beyond the context of indigenous warfare, the kingdoms of Songhai and Benin, among others, further advanced indigenous armaments, protective armor, fortifications, tactical mobilizations, and, ultimately, the adoption of firearms.

The combined impact of the Islamic faith and the deployment of cavalry forces on the military culture of the era were most forcefully felt during the reign of the Malian king Mansa Mūsā I. Mansa Mūsā undertook the military expansion of Mali and the concomitant control and taxation of the trans-Saharan trade in salt, gold, ivory, ebony, pepper, and kola nuts. His primary contribution was the military incorporation of the Middle Niger River region into the kingdom of Mali through the use of cavalry forces and professional armies. In addition, his conquests ultimately led to the control and incorporation of the important mercantile centers and cities of Timbuktu and Gao, the trans-Saharan trading town of Walata, and the salt mines of Taghaza to the north. During Mansa Mūsā's reign the territory of Mali was doubled in size, and the capture and control of the primary salt- and gold-producing areas of the region secured the empire's wealth and stability. So famous were the cavalry exploits of Mansa Mūsā's day that one of the more notable art forms of this time consisted of relatively large terra-cotta figures of mounted cavalry troops replete with padded body armor, backpacks, elaborate helmets with chin straps, and a variety of weapons including swords and javelins. Ultimately, Mansa Mūsā's conquests and his organization of an imperial form of government transformed Mali from a regional to an international presence, with Malian ambassadors posted in Morocco and Egypt.

The kingdom of Songhai provides another prominent body of documented achievements in the use of light cavalry for the purposes of territorial gain and empire building. Malian and Songhai battle formations, or *mandekalu*, entailed the use of light cavalry forces bearing padded armor, spears or javelins, and imported swords. Such forces were highly effective in combat with enemy soldiers within the range of the savanna; however, these same cavalry forces were far less effective in the forested areas to the south of the Niger River or within tsetse-fly-ridden regions where horses were vulnerable. This was clearly the case for the Mandekalu horse warriors of the Mali Empire, whose realm was largely restricted to the West African sahel and savanna woodlands through much of the period extending from 1100 to 1500 C.E. Following on the heels of the cavalry were the infantrymen, who typically bore full armor, iron-tipped spears, and poisoned arrows.

Ultimately, the development of sophisticated military organizations, advanced strategies and tactics, effective diplomacy, and weaponry of the kingdoms of Mali, Songhai, and successor states of West Africa was such that these kingdoms largely dictated the conditions of European and Arabic commerce in West Africa well into the eighteenth and nineteenth centuries.

WEAPONS, UNIFORMS, AND ARMOR

The earliest indigenous forms of combat relied largely on the deployment of shock weapons, including short-handled wood, stone, and iron-tipped thrusting spears; javelins; iron swords; protective headgear; and bamboo shields. The use of these weapons provides a clear indication that hand-to-hand combat was a key strategy both in the sahel and savanna and in the jungle-shrouded landscapes that contained the West African kingdoms. As did the armies of other societies engaged in jungle or desert combat before the advent of firearms, those of the West African kingdoms employed thrusting spears and other shock weapons. To this ensemble of shock weapons were added projectiles, or "missile weapons," in the form of the hunting bow and iron-tipped arrow, which was a critical innovation for those infantry that accompanied the cavalry corps late in Ghana's military history. Much of this early weaponry constituted the warriors' toolkit for centuries to come. Primary innovations centered on the transition from stone-tipped wooden arrows and spears, and bows and arrows, to iron-tipped projectiles in these same categories. The slingshot has also been documented among the weaponry utilized in combat within and between the West African kingdoms. The addition of North African, Spanish-Moorish, and German steel sabers and swords to the growing arsenals of West African weaponry indicates the growing international status and wealth of West African armies.

The kingdom of Mali eventually standardized its warriors' battle regalia and uniforms, as did the kingdoms of Ghana, Songhai, and Benin. In addition, Malian rulers introduced the so-called Honor of the Trousers. According to the twelfth century Arab author al-ʿUmarī (1301-1349), who chronicled the history of the Mali Empire, "Whenever a hero adds to the list of his exploits, the king gives him a pair of wide trousers, and the greater the number of a knight's exploits, the bigger the size of trousers. These trousers are characterized by narrowness in the leg and ampleness in the seat." Combat insignia and ethnic accoutrements were also characteristically donned by warriors, and the role of insignia, such as feathers inserted into headgear, was intended to signify rank and status within the battle formations. Fifteenth century Bini swordsmen were depicted in brass castings wearing an elaborately standardized protective armor that included armored helmets, spiked collars and breastplates, massive curvilinear swords, and war hammers.

MILITARY ORGANIZATION

According to one Muslim history of West Africa, the Songhai military, known as the Tarikh al-Fattash, was organized under the aegis of three full-time commanders or generals. The *dyini-koy* or *balama* was the commander of the army, the *hi-koy* was the admiral of the war-canoe fleet, and the *tara-farma* was the full-time commander of the cavalry forces of the empire. Each of these commanders and his respective subordinates was identified by his uniform, clothing, and insignia.

West African kings typically rose to power through either inheritance or demonstrated success as a military leader, conqueror, or facilitator of a coup. All military organization and support in West African kingdoms was directly subject to the order and mandate of the ruling king in his capacity as commander in chief. The organizational culture of each kingdom's armies varied according to the nature of the military mobilization. Slaves or other captives often served a critical support function during major military operations. Although professional armies were often renowned for their cavalry corps, they often included tens, if not hundreds of thousands, of infantrymen, backed by slaves who facilitated the

A mounted warrior of the Bornu, where cavalry was a dominant aspect of the savanna kingdom's military.

WEST AFRICA, 15TH-16TH CENTURIES

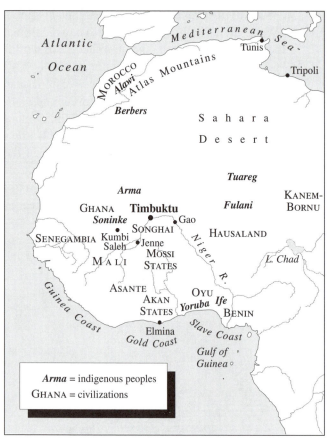

Arma = indigenous peoples
GHANA = civilizations

tion. The earliest recorded wars and military mobilizations of the Ghanaian peoples centered on the protection of the all-important salt trade. However, the nature of war and weaponry in West Africa evolved in response to the growing significance of iron for tools and weapons, the capture of war captives for the slave trade, and the mining of gold for commercial exchange with Arab and European merchants. Ultimately, the protection of the kingdom and its long-distance trade networks and merchants led to the formalization of professional armies and the formation of special military units within the kingdom. Despite this changing relationship between the king and his soldiers, Ghana is thought to have depended largely on civilian reserves for the mobilization of standing armies. The later kingdom of Mali expanded the role of the professional soldier and created large standing armies as well as highly disciplined cavalry forces. The kingdom of Songhai clearly epitomized the changing nature of military practice: Songhai's unceasing pattern of territorial and political expansionism served to justify the role and status of its formally institutionalized military.

Throughout the course of West African history, religious doctrine served to define and redefine the nature and transformation of military doctrine, political organization, and, ultimately, conquest interactions with neighboring states. Whereas Ghana was the dominant power of the western Sudan from 700 to 1000, the Islamic domination of North Africa and the growing role of Islam in West Africa provided a catalyst for the intensification of professional soldiering and the protection of trade with Arab merchants. Given the growing penetration of Islamic thought and culture in West Africa, the military took on a police function where trans-Saharan trade was concerned. During this period, although the protection of trade remained of paramount concern, the advent of the Islamic jihad, or holy war, signaled the beginning of wars devoted to spreading the Islamic faith and eliminating infidels, or nonbelievers. With the rise of Mali, the military took on an expansionist function, conquering the city of Gao and consolidating control over the salt and

movement of cargo and supplies necessary to the deployment of troops in long-distance engagements. The combination of infantry, cavalry, and naval corps proved a highly resilient and organizationally effective military method for maintaining the long-term stability of the West African kingdoms of Mali and Songhai.

DOCTRINE, STRATEGY, AND TACTICS

The doctrines, strategies, and tactics that characterized West African warfare varied considerably through time, reflecting cultural and technological influences that affected the region through the course of nearly twelve hundred years of human interac-

gold trade. The heavily Islamic character of Mansa Mūsā's reign reflected a long-standing pattern of Islamic influence and status. On one hand the adoption of the Islamic tradition in Western African kingdoms increased social and cultural cohesiveness over a vast geographic region and brought about a new era of prosperity. On the other hand, the scorched-earth policy of empire building and the role of the jihad ultimately fed the decline of the kingdom of Mali and, subsequently, that of Songhai.

MEDIEVAL SOURCES

Early Arab and Muslim accounts of the culture, society, technology, militarism, and urban settings of the West African kingdoms are among the most authoritative and complete. Such accounts include those of the eleventh century Arab geographer al-Bakri (died c. 1094), who describes ancient Ghana in *The Book of Routes and Kingdoms*; and Mahmud al-Kati, a Muslim scholar who authored the *Tarikh al-Fattash*, or *History of the Sudan*, which was largely incorporated into the accounts of Ibn Mukhtar in his publication of the *Tarikh al-Fattash*. Among the most important historians of later periods of the kingdoms of Mali and Songhai are Ibn Baṭṭūṭah, a fourteenth century Muslim traveler, and al-Ḥasan ibn Muḥammad al-Wazzān al-Zaiyātī (c. 1485-c. 1554), also known as Leo Africanus, who wrote about his travels in *History and Description of Africa and the Notable Things Contained Therein* (1526).

BOOKS AND ARTICLES

Brooks, George E. *Landlords and Strangers: Ecology, Society, and Trade in Western Africa, 1000-1630*. Boulder, Colo.: Westview Press, 1993.

Connah, Graham. *African Civilizations: Precolonial Cities and States in Tropical Africa, an Archaeological Perspective*. New York: Cambridge University Press, 1987.

Conrad, David C. *Empires of Medieval West Africa: Ghana, Mali, and Songhay*. Rev. ed. New York: Chelsea House, 2009.

Davidson, Basil. *African Kingdoms*. New York: Time-Life Books, 1971.

_____. *West Africa Before the Colonial Era: A History to 1850*. London: Longman, 1998.

McKissack, Patricia, and Fredrick McKissack. *The Royal Kingdoms of Ghana, Mali, and Songhay: Life in Medieval Africa*. New York: Henry Holt, 1994.

Martin, Phyllis M., and Patrick O'Meara, eds. *Africa*. 3d ed. Bloomington: Indiana University Press, 1995.

Mays, Terry M. "At Tondibi in 1591, Firearms and Stampeding Cattle Heralded the Fall of a Once-Great Empire." *Military History* 18, no. 3 (August, 2001): 18.

Mendonsa, Eugene L. *West Africa: An Introduction to Its History, Civilization, and Contemporary Situation*. Durham, N.C.: Carolina Academic Press, 2002.

Oliver, Roland, and Anthony Atmore. *Medieval Africa, 1250-1800*. New York: Cambridge University Press, 2001.

Phillipson, David W. *African Archaeology*. Cambridge, England: Cambridge University Press, 1985.

FILMS AND OTHER MEDIA

The Forts and Castles of Ghana. Documentary. Image Entertainment, 2003.

Ruben G. Mendoza

ETHIOPIA

Dates: c. 300-1543 C.E.

POLITICAL CONSIDERATIONS

The military history of Ethiopia is closely tied to political and commercial relations of the highland regions to those in the surrounding lowlands. It is also tied to the caravan trade in Nubia and to sea-based trade along the Red Sea coast, and thus to the Arabian Peninsula. Related to these geopolitical factors are religious ones: first the fourth century spread of Christianity into areas dominated by animistic and pagan religious practices, and later the seventh century introduction of Islam in the lowlands. The areas to the east, north, and west of the Ethiopian highlands retained a lively Christian religious tradition and came to view themselves as isolated island bastions of Christianity surrounded by a sea of Islam.

The formation of states in the Ethiopian highlands, financed by thriving commerce, dates back to several centuries before the common era. These states were increasingly influenced by Arabian culture and later by commercial ties with the Ptolemaic Dynasty subsequent to the Alexandrian imperial period in the late fourth century B.C.E. down to the emergence of the Roman Empire. The interplay of commercial wealth with the growth of numerous political states gave rise to a constant competition between the food-growing regions of the Ethiopian highlands and the commercial settlements along the Red Sea coast. Warfare increased in scale and importance during this period, as competition among local elites for the profits of trade drove them into violent confrontation. By the first century C.E., the powerful state of Aksum, centered in the Tigrayan highlands, emerged as the dominant player in the commercial contest, but Aksum acted more as a monitor over a feudal system of trade than as a monolithic state. Aksumite Ethiopians gradually expanded their dominance over the southwestern littoral of the Red Sea, attempting to dominate even the caravan trade to the north. They also established a considerable presence on the Arabian side of the Red Sea. Trade with the Roman Empire was considerable, and with the success of Christianity in that empire, it was only a matter of time before Aksumites also began to embrace the Christian faith in the third and fourth centuries. Tradition maintains that during the fourth century Christianity was more firmly established by the shipwrecked Syrian Frumentius (fl. c. fourth century). Frumentius later became bishop and successfully evangelized much of the Aksumite kingdom, which maintained a largely peaceful domination of Ethiopia and neighboring regions until its displacement from the Arabian coast by Persians in the mid-sixth century. The Aksumite kingdom was further weakened in the seventh and eighth centuries by the spread of Islam throughout Arabia, into North Africa, and along the lowland regions of the Eritrean and

TURNING POINTS

1st cent. B.C.E.	Aksumite Ethiopians emerge as dominant players in the control of Red Sea trade.
7th cent.	Aksumite kingdom is weakened by the spread of Islam throughout Arabia and North Africa.
1314	Emperor Amda Tseyon comes to power in Ethiopia, expanding and solidifying the Solomonid Dynasty.
1529	Muslim leader Aḥmad Grāñ defeats forces of Lebna Dengel at the Battle of Shimbra-Kure, opening southern Ethiopia to Islamic rule.
1541	Portuguese musketeers arrive to help defend Ethiopia, ending Islamic threat two years later, under the emperor Galawdewos.

Somali coasts. The Aksumite Empire, deprived of its links to the Mediterranean and to lucrative trade, could no longer maintain large armies, nor rely on sea-based or caravan trade. In growing isolation from the rest of the world, the Aksumites moved south into the mountainous interior of the Abyssinian highlands, where they dominated Agau-speaking agriculturalists, assimilating much of the local population through intermarriage, cultural transplantation, and religious conversion. Still, Agau-speaking peoples fought back in peripheral areas that the centralized but by now weakened Aksumite state could not control during the tenth and eleventh centuries.

The cross-fertilization of Aksum with the Agau produced a new dynasty, the Zagwe, whose most celebrated figure was the emperor Lalibela (r. c. 1185-1225), who was Agau by bloodline but thoroughly assimilated into the Aksumite Christian culture. Lalibela was unable to hold the fractious and feudal empire together, however, and was eventually defeated by the Shewan rebel and Christian leader Yekuno Amlak (fl. thirteenth century) after a series of battles that culminated with Lalibela's death. Yekuno Amlak declared himself emperor and, to bolster his legitimacy, claimed to be a descendant from the line of King Solomon and Queen of Sheba of the Old Testament. He quickly consolidated the existing empire and subdued neighboring Muslim areas. In the early thirteenth century, Emperor Amda Tseyon (r. 1314-c. 1344) expanded and solidified the Solomonid Dynasty over the divided feudal system. He established military garrisons throughout the highlands, areas difficult to govern even in the best of times, given their remoteness and inaccessibility. He also encouraged Christian evangelization. The order instituted by Amda Tseyon increased both the economic activity and wealth of the area, as he extracted tribute from his locally appointed administrators and feudal lords. Amda Tseyon attacked Ifat, a Muslim

ETHIOPIA, C. 1500

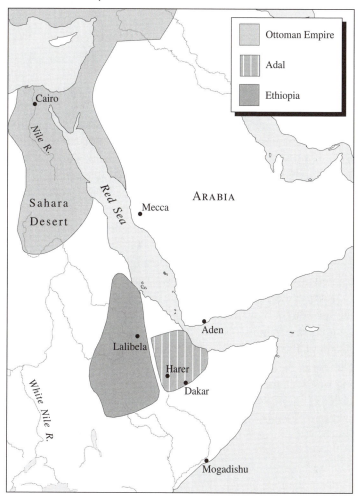

area that had earlier provided tribute. When troubles in the empire called his attention elsewhere, however, the Ifat Muslims responded by declaring a holy war in 1332. Amda Tseyon responded vigorously and with great military brilliance. Against the highly mobile Muslim units, he used his army effectively to isolate and attack the weakest Muslim units, fielding decoy columns to keep the Muslim-federated troops off-balance and always on the defensive. Eventually he thoroughly routed the Muslim forces and substantially expanded the extent of his empire. Subsequent Ethiopian kings built on his success by fostering Christianity as a unifying force in an otherwise feudal economic system. However, not all Muslims in the empire converted, and thus they remained a group susceptible to mobilization when outside Muslim forces intervened.

From the fifteenth to the sixteenth century, the greatest threat to Ethiopia proved to be the Islamic peoples of the northern and eastern lowlands and the Oromo peoples to the south. Under the reign of Lebna Dengel (fl. sixteenth century), Islamic rebellions were put down, but increasing pressures were placed upon the lowland grazing grounds of both Somali and Oromo peoples to the south and east. The Somalis and Oromos gradually migrated into Muslim upland areas under Lebna Dengel's control, precipitating constant turmoil in these areas. Muslims eventually responded with the jihad of Muslim leader Aḥmad ibn Ibrāhīm al-Ghāzī, known as Aḥmad Grāñ (1506-1543), "the left-handed," who trained a disciplined group of warriors in the art of highly mobile warfare, made more deadly by the introduction of firearms obtained from the Ottoman Turks. Aḥmad Grāñ's smaller fighting force defeated the larger but disunited armies of Lebna Dengel at the Battle of Shimbra-Kure (1529), opening much of the southern part of the Ethiopian Empire to Islamic rule.

Lebna Dengel died in 1540, still in control of the highland region of his country. His appeal to Portugal eventually paid off, when in 1541, about 400 Portuguese musketeers disembarked and made their way to Abyssinia's support. With this firepower, Ethiopian forces won their first victory over the forces of Aḥmad Grāñ, who, stung by defeat, turned to the Ottoman Turks for additional support, which was granted. With nearly a thousand Turkish mercenaries armed with muskets and cannons, Aḥmad Grāñ defeated the Ethiopian-Portuguese forces in 1542. Subsequently, however, under the emperor Galawdewos (r. 1540-1559) the Ethiopians shifted to hit-and-run warfare, and eventually Aḥmad Grāñ was killed in 1543, thus ending the Islamic threat to Ethiopia. The gradual rise of the largely animistic Oromo peoples along the periphery of the Ethiopian Empire in subsequent years further insulated Ethiopia from direct contact with Islamic forces.

MILITARY ACHIEVEMENT

Throughout the history of Ethiopia, military activity tended in its tactical and technological dimensions to lag behind that of other regions. Although Ethiopia was not known for its military innovation, military leaders of both the Ethiopian state and of rebel groups along its periphery were quick to adopt tactics and methods of warfare suited to their immediate needs. Their tactics were further reinforced by changing economic conditions over time. When the central state was stable and encouraging to economic growth and commerce, more revenues were available to maintain larger armies. Tactics for maintaining control of an expanding state included the garrisoning of soldiers in hinterland regions. The interconnection of military policy with that of religious evangelization was critical to the expansion of his empire during the reign of Amda Tseyon.

Two ancient Ethiopian warriors spar with each other.

Appeals by contending forces to external assistance and to the latest weaponry were hallmarks of warfare in the region during the sixteenth century, as each side sought to increase its firepower.

WEAPONS, UNIFORMS, AND ARMOR

The spear was the principal traditional weapon of the Ethiopian warrior. For defense, warriors carried shields. Uniforms consisted of full and colorful pants and long-sleeved shirts. Caps and capes of cloth or fur were worn for warmth in the cool of the highland regions. Rebel and Muslim armies in the lowlands also fought with spears and sabers, although their dress was much lighter, befitting the hotter and dryer conditions of the desert lowlands. Only in the early sixteenth century were firearms and cannon introduced into the warfare of the region, typically with the deployment of mercenary forces familiar with the new technologies. Rebel forces in the lowland regions used camels for transport and cavalry.

MILITARY ORGANIZATION

Military organization varied significantly throughout Ethiopian history. Feudal and clan warfare marked by temporary and shifting alliances of small militialike forces were perhaps the most common and persistent manifestations of warfare during most of the period from the fourth to the sixteenth centuries. During periods of expansion of the central state such as those of the Aksum Dynasty from 300 to 500 and the Solomonid Dynasty of the fourteenth and fifteenth centuries, larger armies were maintained. During periods of central governmental weakness, the various isolated areas broke down along lines of feudal lordship, as did the armies. Under stronger emperors, greater unity of command and control over the military forces were in evidence.

DOCTRINE, STRATEGY, AND TACTICS

As in the area of military organization, so in the areas of military doctrine, strategy, and tactics, a great deal of variation is exhibited in Ethiopian military history, and this variation was itself the result of changing circumstances and necessity. For example, when Amda Tseyon was faced with full rebellion in the predominantly Muslim areas of his country in 1332, he deftly used his military forces in a highly mobile warfare that prevented the rebels from ever mounting a successful counterattack in force. By gradually defeating smaller units apart from any main body of forces, the emperor was able to win victory over otherwise fairly mobile rebel forces. By forswearing a conventional positional strategy and by using superior numbers, Amda Tseyon bested the rebels in their one potential advantage, mobility.

Similarly, Aḥmad Grāñ, by using hit-and-run tactics, largely crippled Lebna Dengel's forces during the jihad of 1527 to 1543. The Ethiopian forces, though far superior in number, fought a more conventional and positional war strategy that proved unable to match Aḥmad Grāñ's highly motivated and carefully trained forces, who were armed with some firearms and under a clear chain of command. Dengel's forces, though larger, were divided by feudal loyalties, proving no match for Aḥmad Grāñ's better-trained and better-led army. When Portuguese muskets arrived to tip the balance slightly against Aḥmad Grāñ, he sought further outside support and firepower, regaining the advantage. Under Emperor Galawdewos, Ethiopian forces shifted strategy and, like Amda Tseyon before them, employed hit-and-run tactics, thus turning Aḥmad Grāñ's own tactics against him. This plan eventually succeeded because Aḥmad Grāñ was fighting on unfamiliar ground, whereas the Ethiopians were defending their own mountainous territories. With this strategy, the Ethiopians caught Aḥmad Grāñ alone with only a small force and were thus able to trap and kill him. Clearly, Ethiopian military figures were capable of assessing the threats and forces they faced and of adapting their strategies and tactics to the demands of changing situations.

Ancient Sources

The history of East Africa is based in several different types of sources: African oral tradition; African, Arabic, and European writings; archaeological artifacts such as the stelae at Aksum and the inscription of King Ezana of Aksum (c. 325 C.E.); and local histories such as a collection of writings in Kiswahili on the history of the East African coast, including the "Kilwa Chronicle" and the "History of Pate." For the ancient period, oral tradition forms an important source of information—if one that must be approached carefully to filter out bias and in combination with other sources to fill gaps. Local historians transcribed some of these oral histories and offered their own contemporary observations.

Classical accounts of ancient Ethiopia can be found in the third book of Herodotus's *Historiai Herodotou* (c. 424 B.C.E.; *The History*, 1709); *De bello Africo* (49-45 B.C.E.; *Commentaries of the African War*, 1753), attributed to Julius Caesar but possibly by a Roman soldier; various passages of Strabo's *Geōgraphica* (c. 7 B.C.E.; *Geography*, 1917-1933); book 5 of Pliny the Elder's *Naturalis historia* (77 C.E.; *The Historie of the World*, 1601; better known as *Natural History*); the *Periplus maris erythraei* (first-third centuries C.E.; *The Periplus of the Erythraean Sea*, 1912); and book 1 of *Polemon* (c. 551 C.E.; *History of the Wars*, 1960), by Byzantine historian Procopius of Caesarea.

A sense of what East Africa and the region that came to be known as Ethiopia were like during the fourteenth century can be gained from reading book 4 of *Tuḥfat al-nuẓẓār fi gharaʿib al-amsar wa-ʿajaʿib al-asfar* (1357-1358; *Travels of Ibn Battuta*, 1958-2000, best known as the *Riḥlah*).

Books and Articles

Abir, Mordechai. *Ethiopia: The Era of the Princes: The Challenge of Islam and the Reunification of the Christian Empire*. New York: Praeger, 1968.

Adejumobi, Saheed A. *The History of Ethiopia*. Westport, Conn.: Greenwood Press, 2007.

Greenfield, Richard. *Ethiopia: A New Political History*. New York: Praeger, 1965.

Henze, Paul B. *Layers of Time: A History of Ethiopia*. New York: St. Martin's Press, 2000.

Keys, David. "Medieval Houses of God, or Ancient Fortresses?" *Archaeology* 57, no. 6 (November/December, 2004): 10.

Levine, Donald. *Greater Ethiopia: The Evolution of a Multiethnic Society*. Chicago: University of Chicago Press, 2000.

Marcus, Harold G. *A History of Ethiopia*. Updated ed. Berkeley: University of California Press, 2002.

Nicolle, David. *Armies of the Caliphates, 862-1098*. Botley, Oxford, England: Osprey, 1998.

Pankhurst, Richard. *The Ethiopians: A History*. Malden, Mass.: Blackwell, 2001.

Phillipson, David W. *Ancient Ethiopia: Aksum—Its Antecedents and Successors*. London: British Museum Press, 1998.

Films and Other Media

Ethiopia: The Kingdom of Judas Lion. Documentary. Ambrose Video, 1998.

Explore Ethiopia: Land of Sheba/Sanctuaries of Stone. Documentary. Esicma, 1995.

Robert F. Gorman

THE MEDIEVAL WORLD

WORLD

EASTERN AND SOUTHERN ASIA

CHINA
MEDIEVAL
Dates: 581-1644 C.E.

POLITICAL CONSIDERATIONS

After the collapse of the Han Dynasty in 220 C.E., China drifted into a period of political chaos during which it was controlled by a number of rival regional kingdoms. However, by the sixth century, Yang Jian (Yang Chien), also known as Wendi (Wen-ti; 541-604), a successful military commander, had won the support of the majority of the regional leaders in the north to reestablish a central authority that eventually brought most of traditional China under his control. By 589 the Sui (Sui) Dynasty (581-618) had set in motion a number of reforms that increased and stabilized the Chinese standard of living. Yang Jian instituted a new system of taxation that brought needed financial relief to most of the peasantry. He also constructed a series of regional granaries, which both lowered prices and ensured the equal distribution of food. This newfound prosperity was short-lived, however, because the emperor was assassinated by his eldest son, Yangdi (Yangti; 569-618). As emperor, Yangdi began a series of extensive civil engineering projects in an attempt to improve transportation and tie the vast empire together. He also started a series of military campaigns to gain control of the northern portion of the Korean Peninsula. Both actions greatly disrupted the economy and were especially hard on the peasant population. Violent political uprisings broke out in every corner of the empire, and Yangdi was finally assassinated by a group of his ministers in an attempt to quell the fighting and reestablish political order.

This internal dissent severely weakened the Sui Dynasty, and in 618 Li Yuan (Li yuan; 565-635), the duke of Tang, took advantage of the situation to establish the Tang (T'ang) Dynasty (618-907). Li Yuan's first action was to restore the traditional scholar gentry as the foundation of the government bureaucracy, returning the intellectual class to the study of Confucian philosophy and reinstating the national examination system as the entry into government positions. These actions produced a class of neo-Confucian scholars that would have a profound ethical impact upon China's civil and military services. Most important, this new intellectual class believed the major function of Confucian philosophy was to develop an individual moral code. This new philosophical system would impact Chinese society in important ways. The scholar gentry became very xenophobic and rejected all alternative worldviews as inferior. This narrow focus on a strict social structure stressed tradition and fought any political, economic, scientific, or technological innovation. The gentry's emphasis on individual moral growth clashed with the harsh realities of the martial arts and resulted in an antimilitary bias among the Chinese intellectual class.

Under both the Tang and Song (Sung) Dynasties (960-1279), China experienced widespread economic growth, which in turn gave birth to a Chinese golden age. This success was based upon the development of the agricultural potential of southern China, most significantly in the production of rice in the Yangtze (pinyin, Chang) River Valley. The future of China would now be determined by the link between the bureaucratic north and the agricultural south. To solidify this crucial relationship, the government constructed the Grand Canal, a magnificent civil engineering project that was, in its time, the largest human-made waterway in the world. The canal increased transportation throughout the country, both accelerating trade and creating a sense of unity. The maintenance and protection of the Grand Canal became a major focus of the Chinese military. In times of conflict, this waterway allowed the emperor to move troops swiftly to any trouble spot.

With China's great economic success came a softening of Chinese society, widespread political corruption, and a series of weak and incompetent emperors who eventually sapped the energy of the empire. In particular, the effectiveness of both the bureaucracy and the military was decreased, helping to create the conditions for the Mongol conquests at the beginning of the thirteenth century. These nomadic warriors first entered China at the invitation of the declining Song Dynasty. The emperor hoped that they would engage and destroy the Jürcheds and the Jin (Chin), two northern nomadic tribes that threatened to invade China. In 1234 the Jin were defeated by a Sino-Mongolian military alliance, but then, in direct violation of that agreement, the Song attempted to occupy the newly conquered land and extend their empire into the northern territories. This action shattered the alliance and set in motion the Mongol conquest of China and the establishment of the Yuan Dynasty (1279-1368).

The Mongols would have a significant impact upon Chinese history. They established their capital at Beijing and abolished the bureaucracy based upon Confucianism and the examination system. These actions were taken specifically to negate the influence of the scholar gentry. The Mongols eventually adopted many aspects of Chinese culture and aggressively promoted its literature and art. Despite this openness, the Mongols were never able to find a solution to the Sino-Mongolian ethnic rivalry. Most of the intellectuals from the gentry class considered the Mongols to be uncouth barbarians. This ethnocentricity was exacerbated by the gentry's resentment of the abolition of the state examination system, which blocked the gentry from gaining access to the highest levels of political power.

After the death of Kublai Khan (1215-1294), the Yuan Dynasty fell into a period of decline. There were essentially four reasons that this took place. First, the southern region was occupied by a large number of activists who had remained loyal to the Song Dynasty. As the Yuan declined, many of these disenchanted groups were emboldened to take political action that eventually resulted in an empire-wide

revolt. Second, Yuan military prestige also suffered a severe blow from two disastrous military expeditions against Japan in 1274 and 1280. Third, Yuan military failures were founded in the general weakness of the post-Kublai Khan government that was beset by deep-seated corruption within the political bureaucracy. By the middle of the fourteenth century, the Mongol government was far too weak to maintain its control over all of China. Fourth, the increase in peasant uprisings and the rise of secret revolutionary societies resulted in a series of disastrous insurrections that finally forced the Mongols to withdraw to their ancestral homeland.

By 1368 the Ming Dynasty (1368-1644) had been firmly established, and, from the very beginning, the new leadership made a concerted effort to reinstate the important Chinese institutions that had been suppressed by the Mongols. Most important, the Ming emperor restored the power of the scholar gentry. Confucianism once again became the dominant philosophical system and served as the basis for the renewal of the civil service examination system. In the first decades of Ming rule, the emperor began to develop a truly global perspective. China became a major force in Eastern trade, and by the 1400's it controlled the extensive and profitable Indian Ocean trade. China experienced an unprecedented age of economic growth that impacted every sector of Ming society. China at this time truly ruled the oceans of the world. From 1405 to 1433 no other civilization could match China's marine technology. During this time the great Ming imperial fleet made seven extensive voyages to every major port from the South China Sea to the east coast of Africa. Products from throughout the Eastern Hemisphere flowed into the markets of the empire. Most important, the latest geographic, medical, and scientific knowledge became available to the Ming Dynasty. However, as China was poised to become the first world empire, the emperor decided to adopt an isolationist policy and completely dismantled his great world navy.

This profoundly important historical act was the result of an intellectual battle between the newly established Confucian scholar gentry and a group of Mongolian technocrats led by the famous admiral Zheng He (Cheng Ho; c. 1371-c. 1433). This contro-

THE TANG EMPIRE, EIGHTH CENTURY

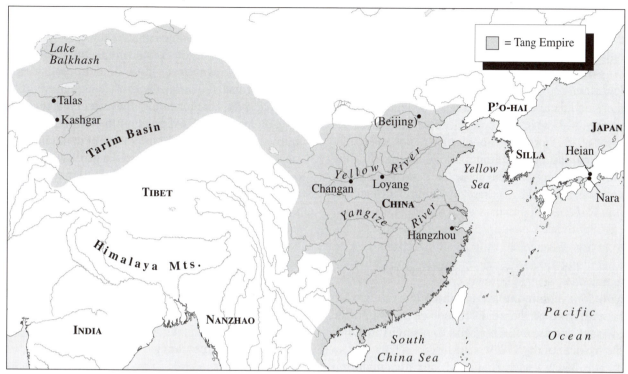

versy was fueled by a fifteenth century Chinese "postmodern" worldview based upon the scholar gentry's fear of the new scientific and technological class. The scholar gentry realized that this new group, with their knowledge and skill, could very well dominate the development of China's economic, defense, and social policies. These scholars were influenced by the strong Confucian ideal of isolationism and tradition, rejecting the idea of internationalism. Finally, the knowledge base upon which the scholar gentry entered government service was founded in their ancient classical texts. The new sciences of modern astronomy, navigation, and marine engineering were both foreign and threatening to this bureaucratic elite.

The gentry were victorious against the technologists because they successfully implemented a three-pronged attack. In their argument to the emperor they first appealed to the ethnocentric tendencies inherent to Chinese culture. The name "China" itself means "Middle Kingdom," and traditional Chinese thought

regarded the country as occupying the prestigious position in the center of the world. This view lent credence to the argument that China had nothing to learn from the world beyond its borders. Second, the gentry emphasized the superiority of classical knowledge, from which the traditional political philosophy of the Tian Ming (T'ien Ming), or "mandate of Heaven," the idea that an emperor was conferred directly from Heaven the right to rule, had evolved. Finally, because there still existed within Chinese society a profound hatred of the old Mongol regime, the Confucians were able to use the ethnicity of these technologists, most of whom were descendants of the Yuan Dynasty, against them to bring the emperor over to the gentry's side. Eventually, a decree came forth from the Ming Dynasty that China's navy would remain in port, and that future funding of this great fleet would be canceled. In just a few short years the most sophisticated navy in the world fell into decay and eventually disappeared.

At first glance, the Ming Dynasty would seem to

have survived its neo-isolationist policy, but in fact the opposite was true. By the mid-sixteenth century it was evident that the empire had entered a state of decline. A series of incompetent emperors created an environment of corruption that led to a drastic reduction in the effectiveness of the government. This widespread inefficiency had the greatest impact in the area of public works. Corrupt officials allowed the agricultural infrastructure of dikes and irrigation canals to fall into a state of disrepair, creating conditions that resulted in famine and starvation. The government lost its mandate of Heaven, and the countryside was ravaged by peasant uprisings. The resulting political chaos led to the fall of the Ming Dynasty.

MILITARY ACHIEVEMENT

Military events also played an important role in Chinese affairs during the era between the rise of the Sui Dynasty and the fall of the Ming Dynasty. Yang Jian, the founder of the Sui Dynasty, used his prestige as a great military leader to bring all of China under his control. Despite his military success, however, he was unable to establish a lasting peace. His new government was beset by revolts, and he reacted to this chaos by implementing an authoritarian style of government. His greatest threat came from the disaffected population in the south, where he sent his two most trusted generals to crush any resistance to imperial authority. The emperor then instituted a policy of forced labor, which concentrated on the construction of the Grand Canal and the restoration of more than 1,000 miles of defensive walls on the empire's northern borders.

Yang Jian's two major military problems were the constant threat of invasion from the northern steppe and the fear of rebellion. In an attempt to control the military, he issued a series of decrees that placed all army units throughout the empire under the direct control of local civilian officials. These loyal bureaucrats were also directed to confiscate all privately owned weapons and store them for possible military use.

Yang Jian also began an expansionist policy, and his primary goal was to return Vietnam to Chinese control. In 602 he sent an expeditionary force to Vietnam, where his army was devastated by both stiff resistance on the part of the Vietnamese and a deadly virus that killed hundreds of soldiers.

The emperor's son Yangdi used this disaster to organize and execute an assassination plot, which brought him to the throne in 604. The young emperor also had plans for extending the borders of the empire, and in 607 he led an army that marched westward against the T'u-yü-hun, a band of nomadic warriors that had recently negotiated a military alliance with the Koguryo, the most powerful dynasty in the northern Korean Peninsula. Fear that such an agreement would prove a threat to China, Yangdi initiated a military campaign against this potential rival. The Koguryo took advantage of the mountainous landscape of northern Korea, fortifying their towns and implementing a defensive strategy against the invading Chinese. Stifled by this tactical policy, the emperor's army fought a long, difficult, and unsuccessful campaign, and Yangdi returned home to find his empire in open rebellion.

Li Yuan, the duke of Tang, took advantage of this military disaster to increase his power in the area. In 617 he successfully negotiated an alliance with the Turks, who agreed to supply men and horses to the duke's army. Secure in this new military arrangement, Li Yuan moved against the Sui. After a disastrous military campaign in which his forces were soundly defeated, Yangdi died. The duke of Tang, upon hearing of these events, declared himself the new emperor of China.

Li Yuan adopted a military policy that proved to be very successful. The Tang Dynasty used the mountains in the west as a natural fortification against invasion from the central Asian steppe. The new emperor was also very generous to the Sui army, and he implemented the enlightened policy of granting both the enlisted men and officers from defeated armies positions in his armed forces. This policy not only increased the effectiveness of his military but also ended any possibility of a future military uprising by the Sui forces.

Li Shimin (Li Shih-min; 600-649), the duke's son, was also a major factor in the military success of the Tang. He was a great tactician and was famous for his use of cavalry. Concerned about his father's advancing age and emboldened by an important victory against peasant rebels in the Yellow River Valley, Li Shimin forced his father's abdication and assumed the Tang throne. He governed China for twenty-three years and became one of the most successful military leaders in Chinese history. He launched an ambitious plan to enlarge the territory of the empire, beginning this quest with an important victory over the Turks in 629, during the Sino-Turkic War (629-630). The success of this campaign so enhanced his international reputation that both the Persian and Byzantine Empires sent representatives to his court. Li Shimin continued to expand his empire, and by the time of his death in 649, the borders of China stretched from Tibet in the south to Lake Balkhash in the west. Tang military power continued into the next century. From 663 to 668 the Chinese fought and defeated the Japanese in the War of Kokuryo, uniting all of Korea under one rule, subject to China.

After he had secured the eastern border, the Tang emperor returned his attention toward the west. From 736 to 755 a series of successful campaigns extended the borders of the empire to the Pamir range, bringing the Tang to the frontier of Islamic civilization and placing these two great eighth century powers on a collision course. This Sino-Islamic crisis reached a flash point at the Battle of Talas River (751), a bloody confrontation that lasted for five days. The armies of Islam ultimately defeated the Chinese forces, ending Tang westward expansion.

This defeat marked the beginning of the Tang Dynasty's decline. Decades of military campaigns had taken a toll on Chinese society, and the losses in both revenue and productivity were significant. These problems led to widespread civil unrest, which devastated Chinese society. For more than one hundred years, the emperors and their bureaucracies had failed to return the empire to a state of normalcy, and by 884 the Tang Dynasty was shattered.

With the final collapse of the Tang Empire in 907, China fell into a chaotic intermediate period referred to as the time of the Five Dynasties (907-960). None of the dynasties was able to unify China, and order was finally restored in 960, with the establishment of the Song. Most historians refer to the Song as the

world's first modern state, and its emperors were traditionally antimilitary. The government, in constant fear of an armed takeover, made strong efforts to limit the army's power. The Song created a military model that placed their generals under the control of the civilian bureaucracy, resulting in the military's lowered prestige and appeal for the aristocratic class. In time, the military came to be dominated by the lower echelons of Song society, and by the middle of the eleventh century enlisted men were receiving one-tenth of their former wages. This lowered pay caused great economic hardship, and mutinies became commonplace.

The Song government was faced with significant financial difficulties. The population of China had reached 140 million, and vast amounts of money had been set aside for the construction of large-scale irrigation projects. The empire had to import the vast majority of its cavalry horses, which also cost a considerable amount of money. China's underfinanced military was grossly ill-equipped to meet the security challenges of the nomadic horsemen of central Asia. The Song bureaucracy responded to this problem by adopting a military philosophy based upon the concept of strategic defense. Money was allocated for the construction of massive fortifications that would frustrate the light horse cavalry tactics of the nomadic armies. The military theory that all defensive structures are eventually neutralized by an opposition force came to pass in the last years of the Song Dynasty. When the Song-Mongol military alliance broke down, the aggressive Mongol warriors quickly defeated the demoralized forces of the emperor and established the Yuan Dynasty. Between 1200 and 1405 the Mongols conquered Tibet, Russia, Iraq, Asia Minor, and southern and eastern Europe.

By the middle of the fourteenth century, the Yuan Dynasty began to decline. Years of famine gave rise to peasant unrest, and a secret religious sect known as the White Lotus spread anti-Yuan propaganda concerning the reestablishment of the Song Dynasty. In turn, the White Lotus also supported a peasant rebel organization known as the Red Turban movement. Fighting broke out between the Yuan forces in the south and the rebel armies. The success of these armies was primarily due to the fact that the Yuan had

THE SONG DYNASTY, C. 1050-1150

failed to keep the system of defensive walls under repair. The Yuan's nomadic heritage and military success were based upon swift cavalry movements, and a defensive mindset was totally alien to them. Eventually, the Mongols were able to defeat the rebel armies, but they were never able to regain complete political control of southern China.

From 1351 to 1368 the Mongols were involved in a series of military campaigns against Chinese forces in the south, in which they suffered a series of disastrous setbacks. The Mongols decided to abandon much of their territory and returned to their ancient homelands in the north. This strategic withdrawal marked the beginning of the Ming Dynasty (1368-1644).

The new Ming emperor and his intellectual elite modeled themselves after the Song Dynasty. Like the Song the Ming adopted an isolationist policy that kept the government's focus on protecting the homeland.

WEAPONS, UNIFORMS, AND ARMOR

The development of Chinese weaponry between 589 and 1644 reflected the dominant military philosophy

of the most prominent dynasties. The Sui, Tang, and Song military policies were oriented toward the defense of the "Middle Kingdom." This attitude was reinforced by Confucian philosophy, which questioned the ethical status of militarism. Finally, the emperors also feared the possibility of a coup d'état. These factors made the development of the infantry the major focus of these dynasties, and weapons development reflected this orientation. Every infantryman received training in the use of both the sword and the spear. The most important weapon in the early Chinese arsenal was the crossbow, which had a devastating impact on enemy ground forces. As tactics evolved, the crossbow became both more sophisticated and more specialized. The military developed different types of crossbows that were used against infantries and cavalries and finally a series of bows that propelled fire-arrows to aid in the penetration of defensive walls.

The most important weapon used in sieges was the catapult. This technology had existed since the time of the Han Dynasty, but it was perfected under the Song. Three basic types of stone throwers were utilized by the Song, ranging from small, highly maneuverable machines to large siege weapons that were used to destroy permanent fortifications. The Arabs also introduced the Chinese to the use of naphtha, an oil-based chemical mixture that burned on contact with water. This weapon was oriented toward naval warfare and proved devastating when wind conditions allowed its use.

The defensive, infantry-oriented philosophy of the Song changed with the onset of the Yuan Dynasty. The nomadic heritage of the Mongols emphasized constant movement. The most important weapon in the Yuan arsenal was the horse, a small, sturdy, and highly maneuverable Asian breed. A Mongol cavalryman was taught to ride by his mother at the age of three, and by the time he was ready for military service, he could both eat and sleep in the saddle. These mounted warriors were armed with a compound bow that had a force of 166 pounds and a killing range of 300 yards. Each warrior carried two bows and two to three quivers of arrows, some with small heads for distance and larger ones for close-in fighting. Both the rider and horse were protected by armor that consisted of a series of leather or iron strips and was quite effective against swords and spears.

The Ming made improvements to traditional weapons, such as the crossbow and catapults, and initiated significant progress in the use of gunpowder and explosive devices. Small handheld grenadelike projectiles became commonplace in Ming infantry units, and the shrapnel produced in the explosion of these bombs was quite deadly. The Ming also developed accurate rockets that were used to bring down wooden fortifications. These projectiles were usually launched from wheelbarrows, and their maneuverability made them a valuable addition to the Ming arsenal. The most significant development in weaponry during the Ming Dynasty was the construction of the Great Wall. China, because of its emphasis on defense, had a long history of using defensive walls as part of their arsenal. This strategy extends back to the Qin (Ch'in) Dynasty (221-206 B.C.E.) in the third century before the common era. As the result of both internal problems and foreign invasion, most of these walls became inoperable. Soon after the Ming came to power they began to construct a series of defensive walls to protect China from invasion from the north.

By the mid-sixteenth century China once again found itself threatened by a new Mongol army. To counteract this threat the Ming government began the construction of the Great Wall, actually a series of fortifications linked by a defensive wall. Ironically, China's main danger did not come from the central Asian steppe but from the sea. The European armies that entered China all possessed the technology to overcome this Great Wall.

MILITARY ORGANIZATION

The Sui based their military organization upon a military and social philosophy that emphasized the obligation of the social elite to provide service to the state. The military leadership of the Sui came from old, established, aristocratic families, and their traditional social values formed the foundation of the Sui military organization.

This orientation toward service continued during the Tang Dynasty but was tempered by the impact of Confucian philosophy. The Tang armed forces consisted of six hundred militia units that ranged in size from eight hundred to twelve hundred men. Control of the army was transferred from the old aristocratic families under the Sui to the scholar gentry that now ran the newly formed Ministry of the Army. The armed forces were divided into two basic groups, the infantry and cavalry, with sections divided into smaller units consisting of two hundred, fifty, and ten men. The Tang also developed a permanent cadre of professional officers, and the enlisted ranks consisted of men who rotated to duty for a specific number of months. This system was established so that soldiers could support themselves through agriculture, thus reducing the government expense of supplying the army. In times of great military danger, the Tang would also employ mercenaries to increase the size of its armed forces.

By the early eighth century, the cost of sending a large expeditionary force to a particular trouble spot became too expensive. The ministry created nine frontier commands and adopted the philosophy of a defensive army. By 737 the militia was replaced by a totally professional armed force, and these units were placed in the region of a powerful provincial official who would make decisions about their deployment. Each group constructed a fortified base of operations that served as a regional sanctuary in times of trouble.

The military strength of China began to decline under the Song Dynasty. The emperors were so fearful of a military uprising that they dissolved the successful organizational model that had evolved during the Sui and Tang Dynasties. They took control of the military decision-making process away from the generals and placed it under the tight control of the civilian government. Most important, the Song emperors used the enlisted ranks of the army as a social welfare program, providing employment for the poorest sectors of society. This system lowered the status of the military, and by the middle of the eleventh century the average enlisted man was receiving about one-tenth of his formerly allotted wages. This great inequity decreased the operational effectiveness of the army and eventually caused numerous mutinies.

The military organization under the Yuan Dynasty reflected the aggressive, loyal heritage of nomadic warriors, and was based upon the decimal system, with the smallest and largest units consisting of ten and one thousand men, respectively. Within the Mongol organization, each individual soldier occupied a unique position in the unit and was responsible to perform a specific task. The Mongol army was always divided into three operational units that controlled the left, right, and center of any military operation. All individuals within the Yuan armed forces were expected to carry out the necessary functions of a successful soldier. Both generals and enlisted men stood guard duty, and every member of the unit strictly obeyed the orders of his superior. Promotion was based upon skill, and it was quite common for a commoner to rise to the level of a great general. The martial qualities of bravery, discipline, and strength made the Mongols a very successful military organization.

The Ming military organization mirrored that of the Song. Its focus was directed primarily toward the defense of China and the control of the military. The government implemented a system that divided the country into military districts under the control of the civilian leadership. The logistics, supply, and training for the military were controlled by a Board of War.

DOCTRINE, STRATEGY, AND TACTICS

Military strategy and doctrine in the period between 581 and 1644 were profoundly influenced by the writings of China's great ancient military philosophers. These theorists were in turn influenced by the important philosophical systems that dominated ancient Chinese intellectual life. The four most important early schools of thought were Confucianism, Mohism, Daoism, and Legalism. Both the ethical codes and social models espoused by these philosophies formed the intellectual framework in which China's military theories were constructed.

Confucius (551-479 B.C.E.), who wrote prior to the Warring States period (475-221 B.C.E.), believed that China's social and political chaos was due to the fact that the nation was divided into competing regional states. He stated that the only solution to this situation was the development of a strong centralized government. A philosophically strong ruler supported by a Confucian bureaucracy would bring the peace and prosperity the Chinese nation so desperately needed. This would be a government based upon the development of personal morality. Later military theorists used this Confucian system to develop their doctrines, believing that the most important factor in preparation for war is the stability of one's own nation. The emperor must be a virtuous ruler whose actions have created a harmonious state. Before an emperor goes to war, he must have both the loyalty of his people and the "Mandate of Heaven" behind him.

The fifth century B.C.E. philosopher Mozi (Mo-tzu) challenged Confucianism with his Mohist philosophy of universal love, which rejected all offensive war as immoral. To attack one's neighbor would be in violation of this most basic principle, causing the ruler to lose the Mandate of Heaven. According to Mozi, the only justifiable war is a defensive one, conducted to protect the population.

These two opposing philosophical schools would have the deepest impact on the evolution of Chinese military doctrine. The Confucian emphasis on the development of a strong personal ethical code would always be in conflict with the aggressive nature of the martial arts. This would be the basis for placing the military under the control of the gentry-dominated bureaucracy. The Mohist stand against offensive war would lead to the development of a "Grand Defensive Strategy" that would greatly influence the development of training, tactics, and weaponry.

The philosophical foundation for tactical operations can be found in the writings of the Daoist military philosopher Sunzi (Sun Tzu; fl. c. fifth century B.C.E.). In keeping with the philosophical premise that the laws of nature were the ultimate reality, Sunzi developed a tactical doctrine that synthesized Confucian, Mohist, and Daoist beliefs. Sunzi, incorporating the Daoist concept of natural order, wrote that war is governed by five eternal elements. The correct application of all five by the military commander was necessary in order to carry out a successful campaign. Every military commander had to develop a plan of action that would take into consideration the moral law, weather, geography, the commander and his rules, and finally the military organization he was commanding. The success or failure of any military campaign depended upon all five of these factors operating in harmony with one another.

Finally the implementation of these theories under battlefield conditions was influenced by the philosophy of Legalism, which emphasized order and strength. Every successful leader, before he engaged the enemy, had to be assured that his orders would be executed without question and that his forces were always operating from a position of superior strength.

MEDIEVAL SOURCES

The vast majority of Chinese sources have yet to be translated into English, although some have been translated into French, German, and Russian. The most important medieval sources are three military manuals that were used by the Tang, Song, and Ming Dynasties. The earliest of these is Li Quan's (Li Ch'üan; fl. 759), *Shen chi chih ti T'ai-pai yin ching*, a manual that was utilized by the armies of the Tang Dynasty. The most respected source is the *Wujing* (*Wu-ching*), or "Five Classics," a collection of treatises written during the Song Dynasty giving detailed accounts of medieval Chinese military strategy.

Sunzi, the military theorist who wrote *Bingfa* (c. 510 B.C.E.; *The Art of War*, 1910), was active in military affairs during the Zhou (Chou) Dynasty and had a profound influence on later Asian military thought. He was largely unknown in the West until the eighteenth century and received widespread appreciation only in the twentieth.

The primary chronicle of the Yuan Dynasty is the *Yuan Shih* (1370), originally composed in ten volumes by Song Lian and Wang Wei, and revised and rewritten in 1934 by Ke Shaobin in 257 volumes as *Xin Yuanshi*. It contains not only the history of the conquests and the military in general but also includes biographies of most of the commanders throughout the Mongol Empire.

BOOKS AND ARTICLES

Graff, David A. *Medieval Chinese Warfare, 300-900*. New York: Routledge, 2002.
_____. "Yüeh Fei." In *The Reader's Companion to Military History*, edited by Robert Cowley and Geoffrey Parker. Boston: Houghton Mifflin, 1996.
Huang, Ray. "Ch'i Chi-kuang: The Lonely General." In *1587, a Year of No Significance: The Ming Dynasty in Decline*. New Haven, Conn.: Yale University Press, 1981.
Lorge, Peter. "War and Warfare in China, 1450-1815." In *War in the Early Modern World*, edited by Jeremy Black. Boulder, Colo.: Westview Press, 1999.

_____. *War, Politics, and Society in Early Modern China, 900-1795*. New York: Routledge, 2005.

McNeill, William H. "Ch'i Chi-kuang." In *The Reader's Companion to Military History*, edited by Robert Cowley and Geoffrey Parker. Boston: Houghton Mifflin, 1996.

Peers, Chris. *Imperial Chinese Armies, 200 B.C.E. to 1260 C.E.* Illustrated by Michael Perry. 2 vols. Botley, Oxford, England: Osprey, 1995.

_____. *Late Imperial Chinese Armies, 1520 to 1840 C.E.* Illustrated by Christa Hook. Botley, Oxford, England: Osprey, 1997.

_____. *Medieval Chinese Armies, 1260-1520*. Illustrated by David Sque. Botley, Oxford, England: Osprey, 1992.

_____. *Soldiers of the Dragon: Chinese Armies, 1500 B.C.-A.D. 1840*. Oxford, England: Osprey, 2006.

Roberts, J. A. G. *A History of China, Prehistory to c. 1800*. New York: St. Martin's Press, 1996.

Turnbull, Stephen. *Chinese Walled Cities, 221 B.C.-A.D. 1644*. Illustrated by Steve Noon. Botley, Oxford, England: Osprey, 2009.

FILMS AND OTHER MEDIA

Eternal Emperor: Emperor Wu Zetian in the Tang Dynasty. Documentary. Peninsula Audiovisual Press, 2007.

Khubilai Khan: Fall of the Mongol Hordes. Documentary. Atlantic Productions, 2005.

The Warrior. Feature film. Sony Pictures, 2001.

Richard D. Fitzgerald

JAPAN
MEDIEVAL
Dates: c. 600-1600 C.E.

POLITICAL CONSIDERATIONS

Two outstanding political institutions dominate most of Japanese history until 1867: the samurai warrior class and the shogun military dictators. It is not exactly clear when the first Japanese state appeared, but Chinese and Korean chronicles speak of a recognizable kingdom at least by the fourth century C.E. In the fifth and six centuries, powerful families and clans residing in the area of present-day Kyoto and Osaka became united into the Yamato Court, the first real political entity in Japanese history. These hereditary clans, known as *uji*, controlled the majority of the population: the peasants, or *be*, who were grouped in castelike fashion by occupation, residence, and family.

The *uji-be* system was modified in 645, but a characteristic feature of Japanese government at this time was the use of outpost soldiers, or *sakimori*, who guarded the borders. Sakimori protected strategic locations, such as outlying islands in the south and mountain passes in the north. An incipient standing army, these frontier guards were also sent on expeditions of various kinds, such as fighting the indigenous Ainu people in the northern territories. Although troops were initially provided by only the most powerful clans, by the eighth century each provincial governor was expected to provide a certain number (sometimes up to one-third of the male population aged sixteen to fifty-nine) of peasant-soldiers for three-year commitments. This policy was intended to break up the monopoly on military power held by the influential families.

However, the government, unable to control the activities of the remnants of the local uji clans in certain distant provinces, sent officials to these areas to oversee its interests and supervise the local administrations. The government also began granting land and tax exceptions to loyal subjects and to the younger sons and relatives of the court who, under the system of primogeniture, would not inherit their family's wealth.

A two-year smallpox epidemic beginning in 735 decimated the country, killing at least a quarter of the population and causing a severe labor shortage. As a result the government was economically unable to provide for a standing army, and landowners and aristocrats—as well as the officials previously sent by the government—began recruiting kinsmen to form bands of warriors to guard their own estates. Eventually, these blood ties lessened, but the permanent use of groups of such soldiers, called "samurai," or "those who serve," became a common way for landowners to protect and expand their holdings. The

TURNING POINTS

c. 750	Carbon-steel swords first appear in Japan.
1192	The samurai Minamoto Yoritomo establishes the first shogunate at Kamakura, bringing order to Japan after four centuries of feudal chaos and political vacuum.
1477-1601	Perpetual civil war is waged throughout the Sengoku, or "Warring States," period.
1543	Firearms are first used in Japan.
1575	Three thousand musketeers help General Oda Nobunaga win control of central Japan.
1600	After the Battle of Sekigahara, Japan is unified as Tokugawa Ieyasu establishes the Tokugawa shogunate, with its capital at Edo (present-day Tokyo).

relationship between these noble warlords, eventually termed "daimyo," or "great names," and their vassals became one of intense loyalty. The samurai themselves grew into a class of military elite, with leaders drawn from descendants from the imperial family.

Although it was nominally a monarchy, medieval Japan actually was not ruled by the reigning emperor. Since the mid-700's, true power had lain in the hands of the shogun, a military dictator who theoretically protected the emperor from revolutionaries or barbarous indigenous border tribes. Although emperors inherited their titles, shoguns were ambitious leaders who rose to power on the basis of individual military skill and political guile. These shogun warrior governments ruled Japan until the mid-nineteenth century.

Under the shogunate system, power was divided between court and regent, allowing social or political instability as each disputed matters of jurisdiction. Because the shogun ostensibly governed on behalf of the emperor, his control was never absolute. Often disgruntled daimyo warlords would have their own ambitions and might rebel. Some samurai were never even vassals of the shogunate to begin with and were reluctant to obey its commands. Occasionally emperors themselves would try to assert direct authority and start revolutions of their own. Of course, too, there were many disputes over shogunal succession, both from within the ruling families and from outsiders.

MILITARY ACHIEVEMENT

Much of Japanese history centers on the struggles of the various shogunates and the resulting countrywide conflicts. Civil war was rampant, brutal, and endemic.

The Sengoku, or Warring States, period was a particularly cruel time. Perpetual fighting went on for more than a century, from 1477 to 1601. By the 1580's two generals, Oda Nobunaga (1534-1582) and Toyotomi Hideyoshi (1537-1598), had succeeded in unifying Japan after fighting numerous battles against various clans and eliminating the last

Ashikaga shogun, Yoshiaki (1537-1597). After the assassination of Nobunaga by one of his own generals and the death of Hideyoshi, the country again fell into civil war. Tokugawa Ieyasu (1543-1616), Hideyoshi's successor, defeated a coalition of generals and warlords at the Battle of Sekigahara in 1600.

The Battle of Sekigahara is considered the most important Japanese battle in premodern times, ending the almost constant warfare that had preceded it and finally uniting the country. Ieyasu moved the Japanese capital to present-day Tokyo and established a reign of peace that lasted some 250 years. During this time of peace, the samurai evolved from warriors to government bureaucrats, administrators, scholars, and intellectuals. Though still an armed elite, the samurai warrior caste had, after a thousand years of struggle, finally been tamed in probably the greatest military achievement in Japanese history.

WEAPONS, UNIFORMS, AND ARMOR

SWORDS

The most famous Japanese weapon of this time is undoubtedly the Japanese sword, which had been made in the islands since the eighth century. More than two hundred schools of sword making could be found, each with its own distinctive style and characteristics. By the tenth century Japanese swords were considered the best in the world, a distinction that lasted until an 1868 imperial edict limiting their production.

Swords came in a number of sizes, weights, and lengths. During the Muromachi period of government (1338-1573), it became common for samurai to carry matching pairs of swords: a long *katana* sword with a blade about 2 feet in length and a short *wakizashi* sword with a blade about 16 to 20 inches in length. Only samurai were allowed to wear swords, tucked into sashes around the waist, in noncombat situations.

SPEARS

Although regular foot soldiers would often carry swords, usually of inferior quality, their primary weapon was the long spear. Spears of every possible length and weight could be found, but one popular type of spear was the *naginata*: a curved steel blade placed on a polished wood staff of about 5 or 6 feet in length. The naginata was particularly effective against mounted attacks. The straight *yari* was the most common type of spear, with a double-edged hardened steel blade placed at the tip.

BOWS AND ARROWS

Japan has always been famous for the art of archery, and for centuries the bow and arrow was the primary military weapon. Mounted archery was a favorite sport of the early imperial court, and troops of mounted archers played an important role in repelling the thirteenth century Mongol invasion led by Kublai Khan (1215-1294). Arrows were made of fine points of steel, and the layered bows were especially powerful. By the fifteenth and sixteenth centuries, units of foot soldiers would advance while firing their arrows in alternating rows. Although it was not especially accurate, this steady stream of arrows flying at the enemy often forced defenders to break ranks.

ARMOR

Although armor was used in Japan as early as 400, it was not until the ninth century that the distinctively Japanese style of armor known as *yoroi* first appeared. This style remained basically unchanged until the modernization of Japan in the mid-nineteenth century. Medieval Japanese armor was some of the most intricate and beautiful in the world. Squares of metal were laced together with leather straps, allowing for a great range of motion. This supple armor gave mounted archers and swordsmen the flexibility needed to ride and fight and also afforded foot soldiers solid protection against piercing lunges or deflected blows. Japanese iron helmets were works of art unto themselves, displaying everything from antler horns to flags to demon faces.

UNIFORMS

Uniforms were not standardized in Japan until the late sixteenth century. Each warlord or clan had its own distinctive crest or coat of arms. Individual samurai, too, were quite idiosyncratic in their choice of

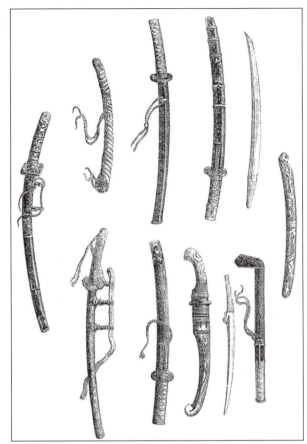

North Wind Picture Archives via AP Images

A collection of Japanese swords, which, from the tenth to the nineteenth century, were considered the best in the world.

dress. By the mid-sixteenth century, battles had become colorful. Samurai wore small flags, or *sashimono*, on the backs of their armor to indicate their affiliations, and the foot soldiers and conscripts of a particular daimyo began to wear similar kinds of dress.

MILITARY ORGANIZATION

Even as late as the Battle of Sekigahara in 1600 the Japanese system of military organization differed from the regimental models found in Europe. The main operational unit was the individual daimyo's army. Forces were placed in the field according to

North Wind Picture Archives via AP Images

A group of samurai warriors, a class that served as Japan's military elite throughout the medieval period.

sary to withstand cannon attacks, all wood castles quickly disappeared. Japanese gunsmiths never really designed siege guns to destroy castle walls. Thus, individual artillery units were also rare.

DOCTRINE, STRATEGY, AND TACTICS

The famous battles of the Gempei Wars (1180-1185) and the Japanese Civil Wars (1331-1392) established the strategies and tactics of Japanese warfare that would last for more than two hundred years. Typical military formations employed samurai armed with swords or bows and arrows, peasant foot soldiers armed with pikes, and the occasional mounted samurai cavalry charge. It has been said by some military historians that these battles, for the most part, were little more than mass confusion. Although elaborate and colorful formations were often staged before the battle, no strict patterns were followed in fighting. Struggles often degenerated into numerous one-on-one fights pitting individual soldiers against one another, each man simply trying to stay alive and attempting to decapitate the nearest foe.

family or warlord, and orders were given to each unit's individual leader, often without close coordination with the other field units. This lack of organized communication often caused severe logistical problems.

Unit specialization in the Japanese army was not particularly pronounced. Japanese armies generally consisted of foot soldiers and archers. Japanese horses tended to be small, making Japanese mounted attacks less effective than those of the European knights. Samurai often rode to battle but dismounted to fight; organized cavalry units, then, were not especially popular. Artillery units were also unusual. After Japanese daimyo learned that stone castles were neces-

This form of battle owed much to the samurai ethos of personal bravery and honor. For example, Daidoji Yuzan (1639-1730), in his book *Budo sho-shinshu*, translated as *The Code of the Samurai*, recommended that a true warrior "never neglects the offensive spirit" and that he should follow the proverb "When you leave your gate, act as though the enemy was in sight." According to the way of the samurai, the public demonstration of one's personal individual honor on the battlefield was more important than large-scale military or geographic objectives. In fact, some samurai even discouraged the study of military strategy altogether. In another famous treatise on the samurai way of life, the *Hagakure*, which translates literally as "in the shadows of leaves," and is often known as *The Way of the Samurai*, Yamamoto Tsunetomo (1659-1719) argues that "Learning such things as military tactics is useless. If one does not strike out by simply closing his eyes and rushing into the enemy, even if it is only one step, he will be of no use." Indeed, it could be argued from the perspective of a millennium's distance that these individual private battles were as much the real reason for fighting as anything else.

Japanese warfare before 1570, then, was a highly unstructured affair; troops underwent little training and few drills. Samurai leaders, too, paid little attention to a campaign's supposed military goals. In the mid-sixteenth century, however, all this changed. A century of protracted civil war had altered the political climate and power dynamics in Japan. The central government and the shogunate were now vastly weakened, and the daimyo sought to enlarge their individual domains by force of arms. War came to be defined as warlord against warlord, clan against clan. To maintain this constant state of siege and countersiege, larger armies were needed. As there were not enough samurai (never more than 5 or 10 percent of the population), more and more peasant troops had to be used. These *ashigaru*, or foot soldiers, made up increasing portions of each of the daimyo's forces.

By the 1580's Nobunaga had realized the need for major changes, and his initial successes were due at least in part to his new ways of military thinking. Previously, a general in command of a smaller army had been able personally to inspire his troops with his own charisma, persuasion, and bravery. Now, with 20,000- to 50,000-man armies often commonplace, a leader's method of training, tactics, and command control were as important as his swords-manship. Nobunaga, for example, realized the importance of uniforms and unit insignias for his troops, both to make identification during battle easier and to instill a sense of unit cohesion and identity.

Another major sixteenth century development was the introduction of firearms in 1543. The first guns brought to the country were Portuguese harquebuses, matchlocks, and muskets. Japanese daimyo immediately ordered their swordsmiths to start making copies. Within a few decades Japanese gunsmiths, working with high-quality Japanese copper, were some of the best in the world. Firearms became relatively inexpensive to produce and reliable to use. As early as 1549 Nobunaga bought five hundred matchlocks from a local daimyo and established the first musket brigade in a Japanese army. By the 1570's more than a third of all daimyos' armies had muskets, which became the most important weapon in the Japanese arsenal.

These new weapons forced major changes in tactics, as Nobunaga was quick to realize. Nobunaga pioneered the use of harquebus volley fire as a major

Tokugawa Ieyasu defeated a coalition of generals and warlords at the Battle of Sekigahara in 1600, unifying Japan.

offensive tool, and others followed suit. In response to the adoption of firearms, the infantry was reformed into structured formations and echelons, including second-line units held back as reserves, a notion not used effectively by the Europeans until the early seventeenth century. In skirmishes spearmen were placed to the rear and flanks of the infantry to protect against infiltrators, and musketeers guarded the infantry and spearmen from cavalry charges.

After a series of power struggles throughout the late sixteenth century, Ieyasu defeated a coalition of generals and warlords at the Battle of Sekigahara in 1600 and established peace in the land. At this point he issued an unprecedented series of decrees that would eventually remove firearms from the country. Gun manufacturing first was restricted to one location and eventually was abolished altogether. The decision to eliminate firearms had several possible motivations. First, there was a generally negative feeling at this time toward all things Western, including guns. Second, according to samurai ethics, it was considered cowardly to kill someone from a great distance without meeting him face-to-face on the battlefield. Third, swords and the art of their use held special symbolic and aesthetic meaning in the minds of the samurai, who apparently felt almost naked without them. Finally and most simply, the country did not seem to need firearms. After stabilization by the Tokugawa family, Japan effectively cut itself off from the rest of the world for the next two and one-half centuries. Ironically, it was American gunboats in the 1850's that reopened the door.

MEDIEVAL SOURCES

There are many surviving documents, books, images, and artifacts from medieval Japanese times that tell a great deal about the lives of the samurai, daimyo, shoguns, and emperors. For example, illustrated training manuals of the era include guides to musket marksmanship, fencing, hand-to-hand combat, and even ninja assassination techniques. Also, the extensive writings of individual warriors tell much about their personal lives and philosophies. For instance, the loneliness of the sakimori frontier guards is reflected in the *Man'yō-shū*, an anthology of sakimori poems collected around 800 C.E. and translated into English as *Collection of Ten Thousand Leaves* in 1967 by H. H. Fonda. The famous *Gorin no sho* (c. 1643; *The Book of Five Rings*, 1974), written by master swordsman and artist Miyamoto Mushashi (1584-1645), is still read for its timeless insights on the philosophy of martial arts. The intrigues of the court and the shoguns are documented in the genre of war tales writings, the most famous of which is the *Heike monogatari* (c. 1240; *The Tale of Heike*, 1988). This collection of traditional tales of the five-year Gempei Wars (1180-1185) is probably the best existing expression of the samurai code of bushidō, the virtue of martial loyalty.

BOOKS AND ARTICLES

Farris, William Wayne. *Heavenly Warriors: The Evolution of Japan's Military, 500-1300.* Cambridge, Mass.: Harvard University Press, 1992.

Friday, Karl F. "Oda Nobunaga." In *The Reader's Companion to Military History*, edited by Robert Cowley and Geoffrey Parker. Boston: Houghton Mifflin, 1996.

_____. *Samurai, Warfare, and the State in Early Medieval Japan.* New York: Routledge, 2004.

Kure, Mitsuo. *Samurai: An Illustrated History.* Boston: Tuttle, 2002.

Miller, David. *Samurai Warriors.* New York: St. Martin's Press, 2000.

Ratti, Oscar, and Adele Westbrook. *Secrets of the Samurai: The Martial Arts of Feudal Japan.* Edison, N.J.: Castle Books, 1999.

Sugawara, Mokoto. *The Ancient Samurai.* Tokyo: The East Publications, 1986.

_____. *Battles of the Samurai.* London: Arms and Armour Press, 1992.

Turnbull, Stephen. *The Samurai Invasion of Korea, 1592-98*. Illustrated by Peter Dennis. Botley, Oxford, England: Osprey, 2008.

———. *Samurai Warlords: The Book of the Daimyo*. London: Blandford Press, 1992.

———. *Strongholds of the Samurai: Japanese Castles, 250-1877*. Botley, Oxford, England: Osprey, 2009.

———. *Warriors of Medieval Japan*. Botley, Oxford, England: Osprey, 2005.

Varley, Paul. "Warfare in Japan, 1467-1600." In *War in the Early Modern World*, edited by Jeremy Black. Boulder, Colo.: Westview Press, 1999.

Varley, Paul, with Ivan Morris and Nobuko Morris. *Samurai*. New York: Dell, 1970.

FILMS AND OTHER MEDIA

Samurai Japan. Documentary. Cromwell Productions, 1997.

The Seven Samurai. Feature film. Toho, 1954.

Shogun. Television miniseries. NBC, 1980.

James Stanlaw

THE MONGOLS

Dates: c. 600-1450 C.E.

POLITICAL CONSIDERATIONS

Numerous steppe nomad empires existed in Eurasia throughout the medieval period. Prior to 1200 the Mongols had been merely one of many tribes in the steppes of Mongolia. Mongolia had long been a training ground for the horse archers that formed the cores of steppe nomad armies. Between 600 and 1206 C.E. several empires rose in Mongolia. The first was the early Turkic T'u-chüeh Empire of the early 600's. The Uighurs, who formed an empire from 744 to 840, were driven south by the Kirghiz of the Yenisei River, who held Mongolia until 920, when the Khitans established an empire over part of Mongolia and northern China that lasted until 1125.

Most of the information concerning these empires indicates that their armies consisted primarily not of infantry but of horse archers who relied on mobility and barrages of arrows to defeat their enemies, rather than on the shock tactics of European cavalry. Indeed, the most difficult battles for the nomads usually were those fought against other armies of horse archers, and not those fought against their sedentary opponents in China, central Asia, Europe, or Iran. Despite the long existence of these armies, it was not until the establishment of the Khitan Empire, also known as the Liao Dynasty (907-1125) of China, in southern Mongolia and northern China, that a true standardized military organization took cohesive form. After the fall of the Liao, the nomads of Mongolia still maintained their military predominance, yet not until the ascendance of Genghis Khan (who lived from between 1155 and 1162 to 1227) did they become the premier military power of the medieval period.

Genghis Khan drew upon the military formations of the Khitans and the Jürcheds (1115-1234), a Manchurian people who defeated the Khitans, as well as nomadic traditions and technology from the lands he conquered, to create an army that surpassed contemporary foes not only in fighting ability but also in strategy, tactics, and organization. The innovations he introduced continued throughout the Mongol Empire and were adopted by later leaders such as the Turkish conqueror Tamerlane (1336-1405), whose talents for military and administrative leadership allowed him to become the first central Asian leader to overthrow the Mongols. Although modifications of Mongol formations and equipment continued throughout the period following the Mongol Empire, it was not until the late fifteenth century that sedentary armies could match the achievements of the steppe nomads.

MILITARY ACHIEVEMENT

The Mongols' military achievements were impressive: The Mongols built, through mobility, superior discipline, and advanced strategies, the largest contiguous land empire of its time. Although the empire remained unified for roughly only seventy years after the death of Genghis Khan, its heritage was maintained by his successors, who included his grandson, Kublai Khan (1215-1294), and later successors such as Tamerlane.

Perhaps the most difficult achievement for Genghis Khan was the unification of the tribes of Mongolia. Once these tribes were united, Genghis Khan forged them into an army of unprecedented size and force. Although tribal confederations had appeared throughout history, none of them possessed the martial potency, discipline, and organization of the Mongols. Furthermore, the Mongols quickly learned to adapt those military methods of their opponents that they deemed effective, particularly siege warfare and the mobilization of resources.

The Mongol Empire at its height stretched from

the Pacific Ocean to the Carpathian Mountains. Its armies ranged even farther, invading Vietnam and reaching the Adriatic Sea in Europe. In the early 1220's Jebe (fl. 1200-1230) and Sabutai (c. 1172-1245), two of Genghis Khan's top commanders, led roughly twenty thousand men into modern Iran, across the Caucasus Mountains into the Russian steppe, and back to Kazakhstan without the benefit of modern communication systems or even maps. This feat is even more impressive considering that the troops fought numerous battles along the way without reinforcements. The organization of the Mongol military allowed the empire to wage offensive wars on several fronts, from China to the Middle East. Although the empire gradually expanded over decades across Asia, individual invasions were rapid and fierce.

Successors such as Tamerlane carried on the Mongol tradition. His campaigns consisted of continuous marching, from India into Siberia and the Middle East. Tamerlane was victorious over many of the top commanders of the late medieval era, including the Ottoman sultan Bayezid (c. 1360-1403), who struck fear into Europe, as well as Toqtamish (fl. c. 1380-1390), who had reunified the Golden Horde, a tribe of Mongols that sacked and burned Moscow in 1382.

WEAPONS, UNIFORMS, AND ARMOR

The average Mongol soldier's primary weapon was a composite bow. This multilayered bow was small enough to be used on horseback but possessed a range equal to, if not better than, that of the English longbow. Each Mongol warrior carried two or three such bows, often in a quiver attached to the saddle of his horse. For ammunition, each soldier carried approximately sixty arrows in multiple quivers, also of-

TURNING POINTS

553	The eastern T'u-chüeh Empire is founded in Mongolia.
c. 740-840	Uighurs destroy T'u-chüeh Empire and dominate Mongolia.
840-920	Kirghiz invade Mongolia and drive out the Uighurs, continuing to dominate the region.
920	Khitans drive out the Kirghiz and establish an empire in Mongolia and China.
1125	Jürcheds conquer northern China and drive out the Khitans, and Mongolia descends into tribal warfare.
1206	Genghis Khan is named ruler of the Mongols.
1213	Mongols invade China.
1236-1242	Mongols make conquests in Russia, Eastern Europe, Iran, and Transcaucasia.
1258	Mongols capture Baghdad and end the ʿAbbasid Caliphate.
1260	Mongols invade Syria and capture Damascus but are defeated by Mamlūks at Ain Jalut.
1261	A civil war between the Il-Khanate of Persia and the Golden Horde of Russia begins.
1272	Kublai Khan establishes the Yuan Dynasty.
1335	The Il-Khanate of Persia ends.
1368	The Yuan Dynasty ends in China, and Mongols are driven back to Mongolia, where a period of civil war ensues.
1369	Tamerlane becomes ruler of central Asia.

ten attached to the saddle. The arrows were divided into three categories. The first included arrows that could pierce the heavy armor of European knights when fired from the 80- to 160-pound draw of the Mongol bow. Arrows in the second class were lighter and had a greater range but little penetrating power. Arrows in the third group were signal, or whistling, arrows, which were used to communicate within armies as well as to frighten enemies. The Mongols possessed a variety of other arrowheads for specialized purposes.

The Mongols also carried other weapons, such as sabers and axes, and often short lances, more often used for flying banners than in battle. However, these lances also possessed a hook forged into the blade, which enabled the Mongols to ensnare and then to pull more heavily armored foes off their mounts.

The single most important weapon or piece of equipment used by the Mongols and other steppe nomads was the horse. The Mongol horse was small, roughly the size of a pony, yet durable, with incredible stamina. Each warrior possessed a string of horses, ranging from three to six, although some records report higher figures. The large number of horses allowed the warrior to remain mounted for the entire campaign; if one horse was killed, he had a replacement. More important, this arrangement allowed the Mongols to maintain their superior mobility: As one horse tired, a warrior could switch to another.

For the most part, Mongol warriors were unencumbered by heavy armor. They wore little armor, apart from hardened leather, or leather reinforced with lamellar plates, considerably lighter than even the finest chain mail. Chain mail was worn occasionally, but because the art of Mongol warfare depended on mobility, the extra weight of the mail was considered a hindrance. Heavy cavalry units armored their horses with lamellar cuirasses, which covered the horses' upper bodies. In the Il-Khanate of Persia, a Mongol dynasty that ruled in Iran (1256-1353), the Mongols switched from a light cavalry to a heavier force that naturally required more armor.

Although the Mongols did not have a specific uniform, they did cut their hair in a certain manner to identify themselves. Even those conscripted from the conquered would receive the Mongol coif, which consisted of a tonsure similar to that of a monk, with only a tuft of hair remaining in front and two braids trailing from the back.

MILITARY ORGANIZATION

The Mongols drew upon the Khitan military system to base the organization of their armies on the decimal system. The largest unit was the *tumen*, a division of ten thousand men. Contained within each tumen were ten *minggans*, or one-thousand-man units. These in turn were divided into ten *jaghuns*, or one-hundred-man units. The jaghun was the basic tactical unit. The smallest unit consisted of ten men and was known as the *arban*.

During larger campaigns, the Mongols often instituted a *tamna* force, in which a certain number of men from every unit, approximately two out of ten, were mustered to form an army. Once the campaign ended, these troops were allowed to return to their units. The conquered were also included in conscription, but they were usually required to serve in for-

THE MONGOL EMPIRE IN 1260

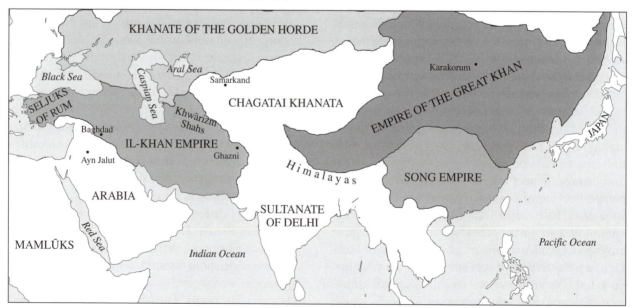

eign lands, in order to prevent rebellion. The most common method of preventing mutiny at a critical moment was simply to divide the new recruits into existing units. This arrangement prevented the new recruits from forming a cohesive and potentially disrupting force, and it helped to maintain the unit integrity of existing formations. Tamerlane, like Genghis Khan, divided members of recalcitrant tribes among various units in order to prevent mutiny.

DOCTRINE, STRATEGY, AND TACTICS

When the Mongols engaged an opponent's field army, they used a wide array of tactics to achieve victory. One such tactic, usually the opening one, was a barrage of arrows from a distance. Although this opening volley often inflicted little harm, it allowed the Mongols to see how the enemy would react. To remain in a position under constant fire probably became frustrating, especially for elite units. For massed infantry, often haphazardly armored, it became precarious.

From the Jürcheds, the Mongols adopted a troop composition of roughly 60 percent light cavalry and 40 percent medium-to-heavy cavalry. Army formations essentially consisted of five lines. The first three lines were light cavalry, and the last two were heavy cavalry. During battle the light cavalry released numerous barrages of arrows upon their opponents before retiring to regroup behind the heavy cavalry. After the opponent had become sufficiently disorganized, or after the Mongol commander decided to deliver the final blow, the heavy cavalry would trot forward in silence, accompanied only by the pounding of drums. Just before contact, the riders would release a terrific, collective scream, intended to frighten their opponents.

The key element in battle remained the Mongol barrage, or "storm," of arrows, after which the Mongols would base their ensuing actions on their observations of their enemy. They would opt either for an enveloping maneuver or for a continued arrow barrage, at a closer, more destructive range. Another tactic was the *mangutai*, or the so-called suicide attack. In this maneuver a select group of Mongols would harass the enemy lines, showering them with arrows at close range until the enemy finally broke ranks and charged. The Mongols would then flee, still firing their arrows by turning backward in their saddles, a technique known as the Parthian shot, perfected and made famous by Parthian warriors of ancient Persia. After the pursuing forces became strung out and disorganized, the majority of Mongol forces would then charge. Often these forces had been waiting in ambush along the flanks, or were in fact the mangutai troops, who had mounted fresh horses. The pursuing forces would be unable to withstand the cohesive force of the Mongol charge. This maneuver—the feigned rout—was an old steppe trick, one that the Mongols raised to perfection. In the encircling maneuver the Mongols often left a gap between their lines. Eventually, the encircled foe would detect the gap and attempt to escape through it, inevitably leading to a rout, during which the Mongols would pursue and cut down the fleeing soldiers.

The Mongols conducted the majority of their battles at a distance. They possessed a great advantage in the power of their bows and believed in the principle of massed firepower, coordinating their fire arcs through the use of banners, torches, and whistling arrows. Much like that of modern directed artillery fire, the effect of massed Mongol firepower could be devastating.

Mongol use of massed firepower also applied to sieges. At Aleppo in 1400, the Mongols arranged twenty catapults against one gate. The Mongol use of massed firepower—decades before the English use of massed longbow archers—reduced enemy armies, and with catapults and ballistae, demolished city defenses.

Other Mongol tactics included psychological maneuvers. The Mongols often lighted more campfires than normal to make their camps appear to be larger than they were. At times they also mounted dummies on their spare horses, so that their armies would appear from a distance to be larger than they were. Tamerlane contributed the trick of tying branches to the tails of his horses, so that enormous clouds of dust could be seen from a distance, deceiving his enemies. Merchants who served as spies spread rumors far in advance of the army. Furthermore, Mongols treated

Mongol warriors harass their enemies in battle.

with leniency cities that surrendered, whereas they crushed mercilessly those that opposed or rebelled.

In terms of strategy, the Mongols had a set method of invasion that varied only slightly from campaign to campaign. The Mongol army invaded in several, usually three, columns: a center force and two flanking corps. The flanking units, in some instances, went into neighboring territories before a rendezvous with the center army, as in the Mongol invasion of Hungary in 1241. Armies sent into Poland distracted the Poles, the Teutonic Knights, and the Bohemians from joining the Hungarians. A screen of scouts and outriders constantly relayed information back to the column. Their preplanned schedule and use of scouts allowed the Mongols to march divided, but to fight united. Furthermore, because their forces marched in considerably smaller concentrations, the Mongols were not impeded by columns stretching for miles.

They used their mobility to spread terror on many fronts at the same time; their opponents were rarely prepared to concentrate their forces against them.

The Mongols' use of many-pronged invasions also fit in with their preferred method of engaging the enemy. The Mongols preferred to deal with all field armies before moving deep into enemy territory. Because the enemy usually sought to meet the Mongols before they destroyed an entire province, reaching this goal was rarely difficult. Furthermore, the Mongols' use of columns and a screen of scouts enabled the gathering of intelligence that usually allowed the Mongols to unite their forces before the enemy was cognizant of all the different invading forces, thus better concealing their troop strengths. This arrangement also meant that an embattled force could receive reinforcements or, in the advent of defeat, could be avenged.

By concentrating on the dispersion and movement of field armies, the Mongols delayed assault on enemy strongholds. Of course, the Mongols took smaller or more easily surprised fortresses as they encountered them. The destruction of the field armies also allowed the Mongols to pasture their horses and other livestock without the threat of raids. One of the best examples occurred during Genghis Khan's Khwārizm campaign (c. 1220). The Mongols took the surrounding smaller cities and fortresses before capturing the principal city of Samarqand, in modern Uzbekistan. This strategy had two effects. First, it cut off the principal city from communications with other cities that might provide aid. Second, refugees from these smaller cities fled to Samarqand, the last stronghold. The sight of this streaming horde of refugees, as well as their reports, reduced the morale of the inhabitants and garrison of the principal city and also strained its resources. Food and water reserves were taxed by the sudden influx of refugees. Soon, what once had seemed a formidable undertaking became an easy task.

After conquering the surrounding territory, the Mongols were free to lay siege to the principal city without interference of a field army. Smaller forts and cities could not harry the Mongols, who either foraged or pursued other missions during the siege. Most important, the many Mongol columns and raiding forces had prevented the main city from effectively assisting its smaller neighbors without leaving itself open to attack. Finally, the capture of the outer strongholds and towns provided the Mongols more siege experience as well as raw materials in the form of labor either to man the siege engines or to act as human shields for the Mongols.

The Mongols also strove to destroy any hopes their opponents had to rally by harrying enemy leaders until they dropped. Genghis Khan first did this during his unification of Mongolia. In his first few encounters, the enemy leaders had escaped, which continually haunted him. After this lesson, the Mongols habitually hunted down opposing leaders. In Khwārizm Sultan ʿAlā al-Din Muḥammad (r. 1200-1220) died alone on an island in the Caspian Sea after being hounded by Jebe and Sabutai. Mongol units relentlessly pursued Jalāl ad-Dīn Mingburnu (r. 1220-1231), Muḥammad's son. Béla IV (1206-1270), king of Hungary, barely escaped the Mongols, led by Batu Khan (died 1255), in 1241, as his boat pushed off of the Dalmatian coast into the Adriatic Sea.

Constantly on the move to avoid the Mongol forces, an enemy leader was unable to serve as a rallying point for his armies, who were also required to keep moving in order to find him. In many reports, the enemy leaders were only a few steps ahead of the Mongols. This strategy also allowed the Mongols opportunities to acquire new intelligence on other lands, because fleeing leaders ran in the opposite direction of the Mongols. The pursuing Mongol forces could then wreak havoc in new territories. Local powers would keep their forces at home, instead of sending them to help their overlords. In many instances the Mongols would defeat local armies they encountered along the way while avoiding the strongholds, another example of the Mongol method of destroying field armies before laying siege. The most important aspect of these pursuit columns was their capacity for destruction and intimidation, which created a buffer between the currently occupied territories and those that recently had been subdued. Thus, the main army could finish its mission of subjugation while the surrounding environs were devastated and rendered harmless.

MEDIEVAL SOURCES

Medieval sources of information about the Mongol military are fairly rich, due to the fact that the Mongols covered a large territory. Most accounts were written by the conquered, or by individuals hostile to the Mongols. The one surviving Mongol source, *The Secret History of the Mongols* (c. 1240), is extremely important for the study of the Mongol military. It is the primary source for the unification of Mongolia under Genghis Khan, revealing his initial defeats and the lessons he learned from them. It also describes the organization and tactics of the Mongol army.

Finally, this work also provides the best description of the *keshik*, or the bodyguard of Khan. The keshik also served as a training school for officers.

The *Jāmi 'at-tawārīkh* by Persian physician, historian, and politician Rashīd ad-Dīn (1247-1318), and the *Tārikh-i jehān-gushā* (1252-1256; *A History of the World Conqueror*, 1958) by ʿAṭā Malek Joveynī, also known as ʿAṭā Malek Juwaynī, are among the most important Muslim sources. Both authors were members of the civil government under the Mongols, and their works reveal much about Mongol conquests, organization, and strategies. Rashīd ad-Dīn's work also is the source of Maḥmūd Ghāzān's (1271-1304) reforms for the Il-Khanate's military. In addition, numerous Arab authors and later ones from the Mamluk period (1250-1517) discuss the Mongol invasions, as well as more minute details of strategy and tactics. Arab author Ibn al-Athīr (1160-1233), a historian and scholar of Mosul and Baghdad, wrote *al-Kāmil fi at-tārīkh*, whose title means "the complete history."

Among European sources, the travel accounts of French Franciscan friar and traveler Willem van Ruysbroeck (c. 1215-c. 1295) and missionary Giovanni da Pian del Carpini (c. 1180-1252) stand out. Both individuals traveled to the court of the Khans, a few years apart. Their accounts contain much anecdotal and incidental information and vary greatly in tone. Shortly after the Mongol invasion of Hungary Pope Innocent IV in 1246 sent del Carpini to the Mongols in an effort to determine the Mongols' intentions for the rest of Europe. Thus, del Carpini's account is that of a diplomat and a spy who is very concerned with the future of Christendom. Del Carpini notes the weapons and composition of the Mongols' armor and provides a lengthy treatise on how the Europeans should combat the Mongols. Had Europe heeded del Carpini's words, its military systems would have more closely resembled those of the Mongols. Del Carpini clearly recognized the inadequacies of the unruly masses of European knights and men-at-arms against the disciplined Mongol forces.

The vast majority of the Chinese sources have yet to be translated into English, although some have been translated into French, German, and Russian. The primary chronicle is the *Yuan Shih* (1370), originally composed in ten volumes by Song Lian and Wang Wei, and revised and rewritten in 1934 by Ke Shaobin in 257 volumes as *Xin Yuanshi*. It contains not only the history of the conquests and the military in general, but also biographies of most of the commanders throughout the Mongol Empire.

BOOKS AND ARTICLES

Biran, Michal. *Qaidu and the Rise of the Independent Mongol State in Central Asia*. Surrey, England: Curzon, 1997.

Gabriel, Richard A. *Subotai the Valiant: Genghis Khan's Greatest General*. Westport, Conn.: Praeger, 2004.

Hildinger, Erik. *Warriors of the Steppe: A Military History of Central Asia, 500 B.C. to 1700 A.D.* New York: Sarpedon, 1997. Reprint. Cambridge, Mass.: Da Capo Press, 2001.

Hull, Mary. *The Mongol Empire*. San Diego, Calif.: Lucent Books, 1998.

Jackson, Peter. *The Mongols and the West, 1221-1410*. New York: Pearson Longman, 2005.

Kennedy, Hugh. *Mongols, Huns, and Vikings: Nomads at War*. London: Cassell, 2002.

Manz, Beatrice Forbes. *The Rise and Rule of Tamerlane*. Cambridge, England: Cambridge University Press, 1989.

Martin, H. D. *The Rise of Chingis Khan and His Conquest of North China*. Baltimore, Md.: Johns Hopkins University Press, 1950.

May, Timothy. *The Mongol Art of War: Chinggis Khan and the Mongol Military System.* Barnsley, England: Pen and Sword Military, 2007.

Morgan, David. *The Mongols.* 2d ed. Malden, Mass.: Blackwell, 2007.

Prawdin, Michael. *The Mongol Empire: Its Rise and Legacy.* London: Allen and Unwin, 1940. Reprint. New Brunswick, N.J. AldineTransaction, 2006.

Saunders, J. J. *The History of the Mongol Conquests.* London: Routledge and Kegan Paul, 1971. Reprint. Philadelphia: University of Pennsylvania Press, 2001.

Turnbull, Stephen. *Genghis Khan and the Mongol Conquests, 1190-1400.* New York: Routledge, 2004.

_____. *Mongol Warrior, 1200-1350.* Illustrated by Wayne Reynolds. Botley, Oxford, England: Osprey, 2003.

FILMS AND OTHER MEDIA

Genghis Khan: To the Ends of the Earth and Sea. Feature film. Funimation Productions, 2007.

Mongol: The Rise of Genghis Khan. Feature film. New Line Cinema, 2008.

The Storm from the East. Documentary. Films for the Humanities and Sciences, 1994.

Timothy May

INDIA AND SOUTH ASIA
MEDIEVAL
Dates: c. 500-1526 C.E.

POLITICAL CONSIDERATIONS

India's long history, with the exception of Aśoka's (c. 302-c. 232 B.C.E.) Mauryan rule between 269 and 232 B.C.E., has been one of constant internal strife and defensive warfare. Early Hindu literature considered war and duplicity as serious activities, extolling them as honorable duties of king and subject alike. A warrior caste, the *kṣatriya*, was dedicated to warfare, and the concepts of glory and honor were punctuated in works such as the *Mahābhārata* (c. 400 B.C.E.-200 C.E.; *The Mahabharata*, 1834); the *Manusmṛti* (compiled 200 B.C.E.-200 C.E.; *The Laws of Manu*, 1886); and the *Arthaśāstra* (300 B.C.E.-300 C.E.; *Treatise on the Political Good*, 1961). Prior to the Mauryan Empire and Aśoka's rule, war had been brutal and merciless. After the second century B.C.E., however, war was fought in a more humane manner.

Around 500 C.E., with the appearance in India of numerous invaders from Central Asia, where armies and fighting techniques were superior, Hindu warfare underwent a profound modification. War elephants, concentrated use of cavalry, and emphasis upon horses were integrated with Indian techniques to give the highly mobile invaders a distinct advantage over rigid Indian methods. Horses, which had not flourished in India, were hearty, strong, and durable in battle. The invaders' concentration upon cavalry with superior horses increased their mobility. With their entrance into the Punjab and their operation around trade routes, the invaders opened a new era in Indian warfare. Hindu principalities, for the most part, continued to engage in petty intertribal disputes.

The one thousand years between 500 and 1526 C.E. witnessed four critical periods characterized by internecine warfare and destruction. The sixth century introduced numerous invading hordes that opened India to centuries of defensive warfare. Muslim influence in the tenth century, in the form of the Ghaznavid Turks from Afghanistan, began an early influx of Islamic and Muslim influence that continued almost uninterrupted into the early sixteenth century. The most traumatic period was the fourteenth century with the Mongol invasions of Tamerlane (1336-1405) in 1398, which left North India devastated. Two hundred years later, a turning point in Hindu history occurred with the invasions of Turkic armies out of Kabul, Afghanistan, under Bābur (1482-1530) and the founding of the first Mughal Empire of India.

MILITARY ACHIEVEMENT

Petty squabbles and interprincipality rivalries for territorial control characterized the approximately one-thousand-year period from 500 to 1526 C.E. Attempts were made at creating unified empires, but these were short-lived. During the first half of the seventh century two figures emerged who vied for supremacy. North India was conquered by Harṣa (c. 590-c. 647) who, in attempting a southward expansion, was repulsed by Pulakeśin II (r. 609-642), the greatest of the Cālukyan monarchs. After the death of Harṣa, constant endemic warfare erupted between numerous rival dynasties and local kingdoms amid frequent foreign invasions by steppe nomad warriors and by Arabs whose militant religious zeal left an indelible mark on Indian history.

During the ninth century North India witnessed a fierce three-way struggle between three dynasties—the Prātihara of Rajputana, the Pāla of Bengal, and the Rāṣṭrakūṭa of the Deccan—that left general chaos

HARṢA'S EMPIRE, C. 640

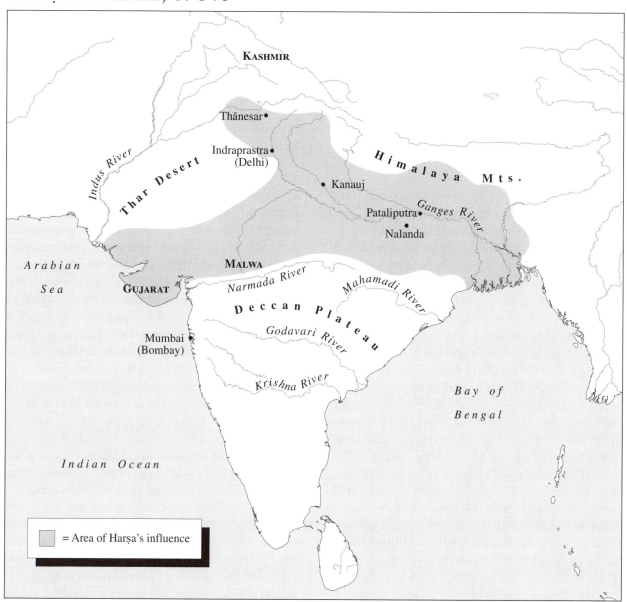

KASHMIR

Indus River

Thar Desert

Thānesar •

Indraprastra •
(Delhi)

Himalaya Mts.

• Kanauj

Pataliputra •

Ganges River

Nalanda

Arabian

Sea

MALWA

GUJARAT

Narmada River

Mahamadi River

Deccan Plateau

Godavari River

Mumbai •
(Bombay)

Krishna River

Bay of

Bengal

Indian Ocean

☐ = Area of Harṣa's influence

and disunity in its wake well into the tenth century. On the periphery of India a new power flexed its muscle in the form of the Central Asian Turks. Their Muslim emirate of Ghaznī in Kabul, Afghanistan, exploited the anarchy of the subcontinent by raiding northern Punjab. In the early years of the eleventh century, Maḥmūd of Ghaznī (971-1030), one of the most able military leaders of Asiatic history, exerted such pressure with his raids that Hindu princes swore allegiance to him. He weakened the power of Hindu states in North India and removed the Prātihara Dynasty of Kanauj, the greatest obstacle to the spread of Islam. These raids ceased in 1030, and the Turks turned to gaining control of Persia and Central Asia. Maḥmūd's successful attacks were a precursor of events to come later in the twelfth century. The

TURNING POINTS

500	Central Asian invaders appear in India, bringing superior fighting techniques and concentrated use of cavalry.
10th cent.	Ghaznavid Turks invade India from Afghanistan, introducing an Islamic influence that will continue almost uninterrupted until the early sixteenth century.
1398	Mongol invasions by Tamerlane devastate North India.
1526	The Asian Turk Bābur defeats Delhi Sultan Ibrahīm Lodī at the Battle of Pānipāt and establishes the Mughal Empire.

Hindu rulers continued their wrangling using the same unwieldy military tactics, having learned nothing from their defeat at the hands of the Turks.

Muslim invasions continued during the twelfth century, led by Maḥmūd's successor, Muḥammad of Ghor (died 1206), who completed the conquest of North India. Meanwhile, interdynastic war between the Cōla, Cālukya, and Hoysala Dynasties raged for hegemony of South India, and Tamil invasions of Ceylon added to the area's struggles. With Muslim conquests and the spread of Islam, North India fell under the domination of a foreign power, a foreign religion, and a foreign language. The Muslim Sultanate of Delhi and its offshoot, the Slave Dynasty, dominated the Indian scene throughout the thirteenth century. Quttbuddin Aibak (died 1210), Shams al-Dīn Iltutmish (r. 1211-1236), and Ghiyās al-Dīn Balban (r. 1266-1287) extended the Sultanate, ruled with great ability, and attended to the safety of the empire, which was constantly threatened by various Mongol hordes on its borders. Periods of stability existed but were punctuated by anarchic dynastic changes, Hindu rebellions, and endemic civil war between Turkish nobility and the Mongol raiders of India.

In 1296 the ruthless monarch ʾAlāʾ al-Dīn Muḥammad Khaljī (r. 1296-1316) conquered the Deccan to unite most of India under one rule. By the end of the century, however, the empire collapsed in 1398 under the relentless onslaught of Mongol forces led by Tamerlane. For two hundred years North India lived in utter chaos under the Mongol onslaught, while South India collapsed under the conflicts waged between various Hindu and Hindu-Dravidian dynasties as well as the assault of ʾAlāʾ al-Dīn Muḥammad Khaljī.

The rise of the new Hindu kingdom of Vijayanagar continued warfare with the Muslim Sultanate of Bahmanī during a large part of the fourteenth century. The Muslims were victorious, but Vijayanagar remained independent. The Sinhalese of South Ceylon, meanwhile, waged war with the Hindu Kalingas of the north, against whom they were generally successful.

After Tamerlane's disastrous invasion, the central Gangetic Valley and south-central and southwestern India fell under the control of turbulent Muslim rulers. The Hindus took advantage of the situation and emerged as leading powers in eastern and western India, most notably in Orissa and Mewar. Intermittent warfare continued between the two powers until two great events of the sixteenth century ended the chaos of the fourteenth and fifteenth centuries and changed the course of Indian history. In 1498 Portuguese traders arrived on the Malabar Coast and exposed India for the first time to European ideas and influence. Simultaneously the Central Asian Turk Bābur succeeded in occupying Kabul in 1504. He took advantage of the chaotic political environment to invade India, defeat the Delhi Sultan Ibrāhīm Lodī (died 1526) and establish the first Mughal Empire of India in 1526. Such an empire had not been seen since the days of the Guptas.

The medieval period in South Asia was dominated by three outside forces that revealed the inherent weakness of the Hindus against less numerous but better trained and equipped mounted invaders. Turkic Muslims, Central Asian Mongols, and European Portuguese traders exerted an influence that forever altered the course of history in India, a history dominated by superior military skill and prowess.

WEAPONS, UNIFORMS, AND ARMOR

Before the time of written records, wars were waged between tribal units using clubs, spears, and knives to vindicate offenses. Rarely were wars waged to acquire territory or gain some economic advantage.

During the ancient period in India battles were close-formation skirmishes fought by the *kṣatriya* warrior caste utilizing thrusting and throwing instruments. During the medieval age, from 500 to 1500 C.E., battles were dominated by heavy cavalry. The primary weapon of choice was the bow and arrow. The growing reliance upon cavalry and archers was due to technological advancements in archery and the introduction of the saddle and stirrup between 300 and 800 C.E., which provided stability for the rider and support for his sword, spear, and lance.

Weapons during the medieval age were generally the same as those used in ancient warfare. These included quivers (*bhastrā*) slung from a shoulder, broad-bladed swords (*khadga*), heavy broadswords (*niṣṭrimśa*), spears (*śakti*), javelins (*śūla*), reverse-curved swords, ancient slings (*gophaṇa*), curved throwing sticks (*vālāri kāmbi*), and sharpened throwing discs (*jah*) thrown horizontally or dropped vertically upon attackers.

Head and body protection included shields of leather, the preferred material, scale or lamellar helmets, and a "coat of a thousand nails" scale-lined and fabric-covered or padded about the torso. Heavier lamellar armor of thin plates, common in premedieval times, was rarely worn, especially in the humid, tropical south. For climatic reasons soft cotton quilted armor was preferred, and its use eventually spread to the Middle East and even to Europe. Asbestos cloth appeared in an assortment of fireproof clothing by the twelfth century. Some protective armor for arms and legs was also used.

Horse harnesses were primitive at best. A leather toe-stirrup had been known in India since the first century B.C.E. and continued to be used well into the eighth century C.E. Horse armor seems rarely to have been used in Indian warfare.

Years of civil strife left Indian armies poorly equipped. The infantry, made up of peasants, farmers, Jats, Gujratis, and various robbers, used bamboo staffs and, at best, rusty swords. The bow and arrow, much relied upon as a primary weapon, could not pierce the armor worn by Central Asian Turkic forces. The Hindu rajas relied heavily on herds of war elephants to demoralize enemy ranks and disperse cavalry. Turkic forces, however, used steel-clad warriors mounted on superb, agile horses. These were kept in reserve in the center of battle, behind the front line of attack, and were used to decide the final outcome.

Hindus generally expended their energy pursuing Turkic horsemen who harassed them with firepower, counterattacked, and forced them into hopeless flight and slaughter. The Turkic nomadic invaders used a composite two-piece bow considered the most fearful weapon on the battlefield. Hindus possessed noth-

CĀLUKYA AND CŌLA DYNASTIES, C. 1030

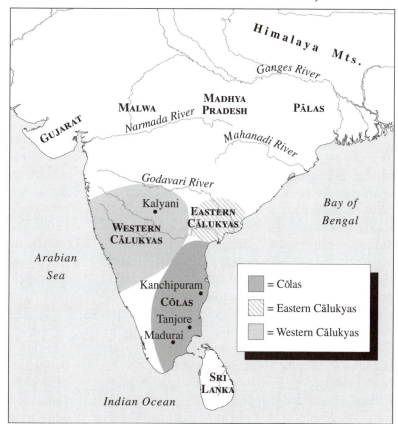

ing that matched the success of the composite bow. They used mounted bowmen as light troops to harass the enemy, whereas Turks used heavy armor-clad cavalry equipped with long spears in mass charges.

Military superiority gave the Turks the advantage over the Hindus. Turkish horses were superior in speed, endurance, intelligence, and dependability in hostile desert terrain. Turks used swift camels to carry provisions while living off the land, whereas Hindus used slow and burdensome pack-oxen. Thousands of years on the steppes and deserts of Asia had trained the Turks in stamina and strength.

The Muslim forces utilized various weapons de-

veloped by superior metallurgy around the tenth century C.E. Of these the curve-bladed steel scimitar proved supple, tough, sturdy, and capable of being honed to razor sharpness. Arab and Mongol forces possessed artillery against grenades, fireworks, and rockets of the Delhi Sultans. The arrival of Bābur's hardy, disciplined, and seasoned troops signaled the end of the disorderly and poorly equipped forces of the Sultans of Delhi. The introduction of muskets and artillery turned the tide against Hindu forces at the Battle of Pānīpat in 1526. Hindu rule in North India collapsed with the establishment of the first Mughal Empire of India, which lasted well into the nineteenth century. Gunpowder changed the course of warfare forever.

DELHI SULTANATE, 1236-1398

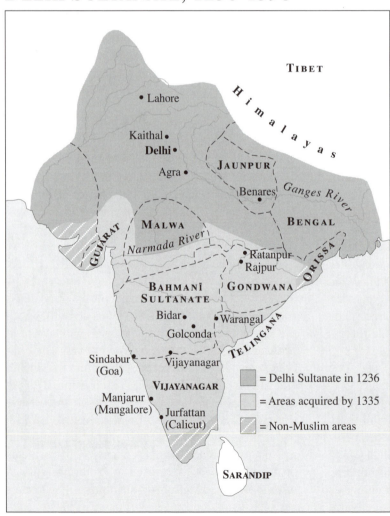

= Delhi Sultanate in 1236

= Areas acquired by 1335

= Non-Muslim areas

MILITARY ORGANIZATION

The organization of standing armies in India since the third century B.C.E. was based on an ideal extolled in classic religious texts. An army (senā) was commanded by a supreme commander (senāpati) over a four-tiered structure of infantry, cavalry, chariots, and elephants. Harsha's army consisted of 50,000 infantry, 20,000 cavalry, and 5,000 elephants. Support services and noncombatants complemented this huge, unwieldy army. Chariots, mentioned in the seventh century C.E., represented a continuation of the ancient form of warfare. The senāpati used a four-horse chariot surrounded by a bodyguard and officers (nāyaka). The ancient military organizational system continued well into the fourteenth century, when cavalry gained greater importance in confronting Muslim invasions. However, traditional Hindu ideals of military organization remained.

In South India there was a clear militarization of the state into military camps. The huge and effective fourteenth century Vijayanagar army was organized by a governmental department called the Kandāchāra and led by a *dandanāyaka*, or commander-in-chief. However, there was a notable absence of discipline among the military personnel.

Muslim invaders maintained a well-organized and effective army unlike anything they confronted in India. Muslim forces relied heavily upon superior leadership, seasoned troops of high quality, highly developed military science, and great metallurgical skill. Morale was of the highest nature, supported by a firm brotherhood and religious zeal that rationalized war and conquest in the name of religion. Primary goals were booty and destruction of heathen places of worship.

The backbones of the Delhi Sultan's army were cavalry and war elephants, the latter adopted from the Hindus. The effect of one elephant in battle was equal to that of 500 horsemen. Infantrymen were recruited slaves and individuals needing employment.

Bābur, descended from the Mongol leader Genghis Khan (between 1155 and 1162-1227), organized his Turkic army on that of Tamerlane (1336-1405). A first-rate military genius, Tamerlane had organized his fighting forces on a rational basis rather than one of ancient traditional practice, assuring him of unfailing success. He surrounded himself with loyal lieutenants whom he could safely trust with far-flung branch operations beyond his personal direction.

Muslim and Mongol organizational skills, complete mobility, and superior horses and weaponry overwhelmed Hindu forces governed by tradition and lack of discipline. Although Hindu rajas commanded close to one million men, lack of discipline made them vulnerable to highly structured outside forces.

DOCTRINE, STRATEGY, AND TACTICS

The *Arthaśāstra* remained the guide for military doctrine, strategy, and tactics well into the medieval period. After the Gupta monarch Skanda Gupta (r. c. 455-467) successfully repulsed the Ephthalite, or White Hun, invasion in 445 C.E., greater emphasis was placed on shock tactics and mobility of cavalry and archers. However, after Ephthalite leaders caused the collapse of the Gupta state early in the sixth century, Hindu armies again reverted to traditional use of inferior cavalry, war elephants, and less mobility in battle. Warriors continued to use quivers attached to the rear of a saddle. Chariot warfare declined, and shock-value use of war elephants increased. In the south, the Deccan army of the Vijayanagar kingdom used camel troops as mounted infantry. Certain troops long abandoned in most of Asia, such as slingers, were still maintained and used by Hindu rajas. Archers also remained a critical component of the army, guided by the *Dhanur Veda*, "science of archery," military manual.

Military tactics were heavily governed by the *Artharva Veda* (1500-1200 B.C.E.), one of the sacred writings of Hinduism. Archers shot from a kneeling position supported by spear, javelin, and shield-wielding infantry. Such immobility opened the army to ravaging attacks by extremely mobile Muslim and Mongol troops skilled in fighting on horseback. Elephants generally carried a driver, or *mahout*, and three to four warriors. In response, the use of large caltrops, iron-pointed triangular devices set in the ground to impede elephant and cavalry advances, was developed. Such Indian tactics were old-fashioned by the tenth century, but they continued into the thirteenth. Hindu pride prevented leaders from learning from their foreign adversaries. Hindus valued strength in numbers over speed and mobility, a doctrine that rapidly caused their defeat.

Pre-Islamic India was, however, well fortified, with walls built of stone, brick, or wood, and protected by slopes and bastions. Towers projected a short distance from the wall. Towns and villages of the seventh century had inner gates, wide walls of brick or tiles, and bamboo or wood towers. Six hundred years later the military architecture of Muslim and Hindu added the *chatri*, a ceremonial kiosk above the main gate to allow a monarch an observation post. Countersiege was highly developed, utilizing scaling ladders secured to mud-brick walls and iron plates to breach them. Elephants with iron plates on their foreheads were used as battering rams. A *pāshtīb*, or raised platform of sandbags, filled ditches between walls, and a *gargaj*, or movable wooden tower, reigned down firepower upon the enemy. Attacks were impeded by use of fire, smoke, and heated iron grills.

Turk, Muslim, and Mongol strategy revolved around hit-and-run tactics, the defeat and humbling of a raja into vassalship, the utilization of his kingdom as a base for further advances into India, and the eventual annexation of the territory. The strategy of nibbling away at border provinces allowed a deeper penetration of the subcontinent. Success was directly dependent upon a well-established line of communications with Central Asia, which provided fresh reinforcements and supplies to accomplish deeper penetration. Together with social solidarity, a broth-erhood of equality, lust for loot, and a fiery Islamic zeal against the infidel, the invaders quickly overcame Hindu resistance. Rapid movement necessitated a strong cavalry, which paralyzed Hindu armies with sharp decisive blows that frustrated their battle plans and evacuation.

Unlike Muslim solidarity, interclan and intercaste Hindu feuding and stress upon tradition in military affairs led directly to their final demise at the hands of Bābur's forces at the Battle of Pānipāt. Here Muslim firearms dominated the field of battle. The result was the complete collapse of Hindu resistance in 1526 C.E. and the formation of the first Mughal Empire in India.

MEDIEVAL SOURCES

The *Manusmṛti* (compiled 200 B.C.E.-200 C.E.; *The Laws of Manu*, 1886), which stressed glory and power, and the *Arthaśāstra* (300 B.C.E.-300 C.E.; *Treatise on the Political Good*, 1961), the primary treatise on Indian polity, laid the standards for war and peace well into the medieval period. The latter established principles of warfare, military organization, strategy, tactics, the role of king, military leaders, and warriors, as well as weaponry of war. In a theory of concentric circles, the core state was seen as surrounded by enemy states, and the aim of policy was to achieve a series of mutual alliances. Its emphasis was upon the reality of war rather than glory. The critical arm of the army, the archers, was governed and guided by the *Dhanur Veda*, written in approximately 500 C.E., an important manual on the science of archery.

Muslim military science and government of the thirteenth century was guided by the *Ādāb-ul-Mulūk wa-kifāyat al-mamlūk* (c. thirteenth century; translated in part in *Fresh Light on the Ghaznavids*, 1938), written by Fakhir-i Mudabbir (fl. twelfth-thirteenth centuries) for Sultan Shams al-Dīn Iltutmish. It covered governmental policies and served as a war manual, laying out guidelines for camping sites, battle formations, subterfuge, spying and scouting, night warfare, equipment and arms, and the care of man and horse alike.

BOOKS AND ARTICLES

Bhatia, H. S. *Mughal Empire in India: Their Political, Legal, Social, Cultural, Religious, and Military Systems*. New Delhi: Deep and Deep Publications, 2001.

Gommans, Jos J. L. "Warhorse and Gunpowder in India, c. 1000-1850." In *War in the Early Modern World*, edited by Jeremy Black. Boulder, Colo.: Westview Press, 1999.

Gommans, Jos J. L., and Dirk H. A. Kolff, eds. *Warfare and Weaponry in South Asia, 1000-1800*. New York: Oxford University Press, 2001.

Khan, Iqtidar Alam. *Gunpowder and Firearms: Warfare in Medieval India*. New Delhi: Oxford University Press, 2004.

Majumdar, Ramesh Chandra, H. C. Raychaudhuri, and Kalikindar Dutta. *An Advanced History of India*. London: Macmillan, 1950.

Marston, Daniel P., and Chandar S. Sundaram, eds. *A Military History of India and South Asia:*

From the East India Company to the Nuclear Era. Foreword by Stephen P. Cohen. West-port, Conn.: Praeger Security International, 2007.

Naravane, M. S. *Battles of Medieval India, A.D. 1295-1850*. New Delhi: APH, 1996.

Nicolle, David. *Medieval Siege Weapons: Byzantium, the Islamic World, and India*. Illustrated by Sam Thompson. Botley, Oxford, England: Osprey, 2002.

Nosov, Konstantin S. *Indian Castles, 1206-1526: The Rise and Fall of the Delhi Sultanate*. Illustrated by Brian Delf. Botley, Oxford, England: Osprey, 2006.

Oman, Charles. *A History of the Art of War in the Middle Ages*. London: Greenhill Press, 1991.

Sandhu, Gurcharn Singh. *A Military History of Medieval India*. New Delhi: Vision Books, 2003.

Sarkar, Jadunath. *Military History of India*. Calcutta, India: M. C. Sarkar and Sons, 1960.

Wise, Terence. *Medieval Warfare*. Botley, Oxford, England: Osprey, 1976.

FILMS AND OTHER MEDIA

Ancient India: A Journey Back in Time. Documentary. Cromwell Productions, 2006.

Story of India. Documentary. Public Broadcasting Service, 2007.

George Hoynacki

SOUTHEAST ASIA

Dates: c. 500-1500 C.E.

POLITICAL CONSIDERATIONS

Although little is known about the early history of the Southeast Asian region and the origins of its peoples are unclear, the neighboring civilizations of both China and India had major influences upon Southeast Asian history. As a result of the permeation of Indian culture in the fifth century, the Indian warrior class and methods of waging war were adopted by the new Southeast Asian empires. The migration of the Guptas led to the founding of the Funan Empire. The Pallava wave was the impetus for the empires of Angkor (Cambodia) and Śrivijaya; and the Pāla Dynasty of Bengal profoundly influenced the Javan culture. The desire for aggressive imperial expansion was also subsequently embraced in Southeast Asia, and constant raids and sieges among Southeast Asian empires mark the early history of the region.

Some of the kingdoms of the region were controlling empires based on agriculture rather than foreign trade. Others were ports where trade with other states was of prime importance. Certainly Funan has its origins in trade, but the shift of the Khmer people toward Angkor shows a move either toward greater self-reliance or away from places that were also clearly vulnerable to foreign attack.

The main aim of rulers throughout the region was to maintain their dynasties. Much of the region was dominated by Hinduism, and the Hindu rulers of Angkor, and also the kingdoms in Java, wished to extend the boundaries of their lands by conquest. Gradually, with the advent of Buddhism, rulers began to see themselves as working in a compact with their people, with the goal of bettering the lives of their subjects. If this could be achieved through military aggression, then war would result. If, instead, it could be done by major building projects, those would take priority.

The gradual conversion to Islam in island Southeast Asia, the Malay states, and for the Champa king-dom, was accompanied, once again, by a rise in trade and also a period during which members of ruling families of one state would marry somebody from another, leading to a series of alliances and reducing the numbers of wars, although these still took place.

MILITARY ACHIEVEMENT

The earliest information that exists on the warfare in the region comes from the small Indianized states on the Malay Peninsula, many of which were within the Funan Empire to the north, in the area of present-day Cambodia, and southern Vietnam. As the power of Funan faded, the Kingdom (or kingdoms) of Chenla arose. This was probably a federation of states that came together under a king at times of external invasion, but with constituent parts having much regional autonomy, a pattern that was followed elsewhere in the region at this time.

Militarily, this federal system was no match for unified states, and under Jayavarman II, the Kingdom of Angkor emerged in the 800's, taking over. A similar process took place in Champa (modern-day central Vietnam) and also later in modern-day Thailand. The first two were at this time Hindu monarchies, as were many of those in Java. In these societies, the rulers were warriors who served to represent the power of the state and defend its dignity against attack. Militarily they were successful at exerting their will over weaker neighbors, with clear evidence from surviving chronicles of many wars of aggression and also of depredations from their neighbors.

The growth and expansion of the Śrivijayan and Javanese Empires are strong examples of the common aggressive desire to expand, and the constant conflict between the two empires eventually led to the absorption of Śrivijaya within the dominion of the Majapahit kingdom, which controlled most of

Sumatra, the coastal regions of Borneo and Celebes, and the Lesser Sunda Islands.

By contrast, in mainland Southeast Asia, there was a balance of power for much of this period between the Burmans, Thais (or Tais), and the peoples from Angkor and Champa.

WEAPONS, UNIFORMS, AND ARMOR

The weapons used by most of the people in Southeast Asia in medieval times were Indian in style: bows, arrows, curved flat swords, broad short daggers, and long shields. In Śrivijaya, the unusual arrows had crescent-shaped heads, which could cut a head from a body or divide a bow in two. Battle scenes are depicted in many bas-reliefs in Java and Cambodia from the tenth century C.E. Although these images tell nothing of tactics, they are significant in revealing that only infantry took part in the melees, although chariots can be seen in subsequent victory processions. This was almost certainly an aspect of Javanese warfare; horses and elephants were mainly reserved for chiefs and high officers. Of note is the virtual absence of spears in Java, because only the strongest Indianization could have replaced this favorite local weapon with the bow. By contrast, in Angkor, the spear shared the primary place with the flat and curved sword. There were daggers, but no trace at this time of the kris, a typical Malay dagger invented around the fourteenth century. Shields varied in shape with most being oval or rectangular. Some soldiers were also depicted wearing a cuirass, protective armor covering the torso. Another local weapon, especially preferred by the jungle peoples, was the blowpipe, which probably fired some form of poisonous dart.

As a result of the Indian influence, elephants were used in battle and the King of Funan was reported as riding on an elephant as early as 245 C.E. Gradually more elephants were used in battle; one division of the army consisted of one hundred elephants, and a hundred men surrounded each elephant. In Cambodia, by the eleventh century, there was a sort of cage, called a *howdah*, on the back of the elephant. In it rode four men armed with bows, arrows, and lances.

The elephant's tusks might also be sharpened or lengthened with sword blades, and it might pick up enemy soldiers with its trunk or trample them underfoot. The standard battlefield role of war elephants was in the assault, to break up the enemy ranks, but elephants were also used in sieges, to push over gates and palisades or to serve as living bridges.

After the formation of the Majapahit Dynasty, however, weapons and warfare underwent significant changes in island Southeast Asia. The military dress completely evolved from the Indian to the East Javanese fashion. Weapons, notably axes, clubs, swords, and daggers, seem to have been Indian in design, though the curved swords are of a later type than those on the Central Javanese reliefs. The reappearance of the spear in these reliefs, while the use of the bow is confined to human heroes, suggests an increasing pressure to resume use of local types of weapons. Both swords and daggers have definitively Indian-type hilts, and the kris seems still to be absent from use. The kris may not have become popular until the fifteenth century, when Majapahit krises appear to be represented on a relief of a Javanese forge.

A Javanese inscription of 1323 speaks of "magically forged weapons," indicative of the belief that magic and proper worship and sacrifice to the gods would bring victory on the battlefield. Much importance was placed on the art of procuring talismans, incantations, or drugs, the knowledge of which was the education of every hero. Another piece of evidence concerning the character of Majapahit warfare is the reproduction through drawings of a battle array, a crayfish-type military formation in which the forces were distributed in order in preparation for an attack. The Javanese often gave up any idea of preserving their own lives in battle and would rush the enemy, committing indiscriminate slaughter and refusing to surrender alive.

As well as fighting on land, the Khmers and the Chams also fought at sea. They used galleys to attack each other, and the Chinese also launched a seaborne invasion of Champa. This was notable because the Chinese introduced artillery to overcome the Cham elephant attacks. After the Chinese had landed, they directed all their arrow fire against the Cham elephants and subsequently obtained victory. The bal-

SOUTHEAST ASIA, 8TH-9TH CENTURIES

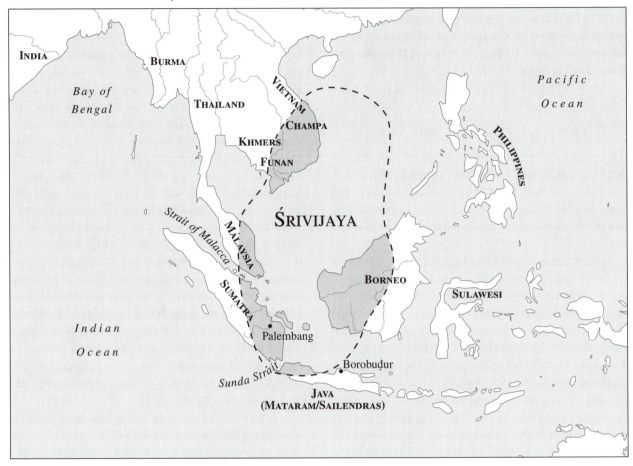

lista, first used by the Chams, also became incorporated into the Khmer equipment.

MILITARY ORGANIZATION

During its Angkor period (802-1431), the Khmer Empire, by force of arms, extended its commonwealth to encompass vast areas of Southeast Asia. The first attempts, in about 813, by a Cham general named Senāpati Par to test the united Khmer state were never more than raids, for Jayavarman II (c. 770-850) kept the empire firmly in his grasp. The strategies of the Chams, however, had been sharpened by their constant quarrelling with the Chinese on their northern frontier. As the Khmers and Chams

battled, the Khmers too learned of new strategies and weapons, and a fairly homogeneous art of war was established.

The Hindu concept of war as a religious sacrifice was fully recognized by the Khmers. Therefore, much like the Javanese, the Khmers associated the ancestor mountain god, Hinduized as Shiva, with military ventures and prayed for his aid on the battlefield. At about the same time in Champa, 1064, Rudravarman III, also made ornate gifts to the goddess of the kingdom to show his devotion.

The commander-in-chief of both the Khmers and Chams was usually a prince, often the king's brother. Of other officers there is little detailed knowledge, but it seems that they would begin in the Royal Guard and then ascend to captain roughly a thousand men for war. The officers were distinguished by the red parasols that they carried into battle. Moreover, as in Java, in the Khmer and Champa empires, the use of horses and elephants was confined to officers. Unlike the Indian custom, there was only one rider per elephant with a shield on his left arm. The number of horses was limited, as they were difficult to procure from China; therefore, there probably did not exist a cavalry division in either army. An accurate number of soldiers for either side is also difficult to ascertain. It seems that there were roughly 50,000 soldiers assembled on one side in the fourth century, a number that increased with time. By the eighth century, the royal guards alone numbered 5,000. On both sides, the infantry formed the greatest part of the militaries' strength.

According to Chinese texts, Cham weapons consisted of shields, spears, halberds, bows, and crossbows. The arrows of bamboo, however, were not feathered, but the points were poisoned. Cham sculptures also show swords and daggers. The lance, or spear, was the most common of the Khmer weapons, and cases of them were attached to the sides of the elephant platforms. By the twelfth century, the lance had largely replaced the sword to become the most distinctive of Khmer arms. The club, which was the weapon of the Khmer gate guardian, was relatively rare in the hands of warriors. Bows and arrows were also used for distance fighting. For protection the Chams had cuirasses made of plaited cane in addition to their shields. The Khmers used this armor as well, but in a more limited capacity; it seems it was used more for parades and than for actual fighting. The Khmers also fought bareheaded, though the Chams are shown in sculptured relief wearing a reversed flower headdress.

It is known that during the thirteenth century, the commanders of the Javanese army received an annual salary of twenty taels of gold, and the soldiers, 30,000 in number, also received fixed annual pay in varying amounts in gold. The reliefs of the temples of this time reveal little. An inscription of 1294, alongside reports in Chinese annals, tells much about the results of the fighting that took place in repelling the Mongol invaders and in establishing the Majapahit Dynasty, but almost nothing about the nature of the warfare.

DOCTRINE, STRATEGY, AND TACTICS

The Khmer and Cham empires also had considerable knowledge of fortification. The Cham capital was a mountain of bricks dominated by pavilions and towers reaching 70 or 80 feet. The Khmer capital of Angkor Thom was also built up of massive stone walls, which, in the twelfth century, replaced earlier defenses of moat and mound. Despite its seemingly impenetrable fortifications, in 1177 Angkor fell to an unexpected Cham naval attack. It was not only Champa that possessed a navy, however; the Khmers also practiced naval warfare. The Chams often employed fleets of more than one hundred vessels, which were almost exclusively barges propelled by rowers. The fleets on both sides operated in conjunction with armies that relied on boarding, not ramming. Both sides were armed with long spears and shields, and in one relief of the period, a Khmer barge is filled with archers. This suggests that the bow was used in naval warfare before the close combat began. Naval warfare was limited at this time, however, as navies could not venture far from a shore held by friendly forces, because of the need to frequently replenish fresh water supplies.

The ideal type of army exchange was to bring about a pitched frontal battle. In a battle such as this, once some important leaders had been slain or had run away, the defeated side usually fled to the sheltering jungle. Chinese accounts claim that the Cham soldiers fought in parties of five, and the members mutually helped one another. If one fled, the other four were liable to be punished with death. Once the battle was over and a victor clear, it was the custom for the conqueror to set up pillars to commemorate victory. A similar system operated in Java and in the Majapahit Empire.

Concerning the early Mon warfare and that of the Burmans of the Pagan Empire, these civilizations left no bas-reliefs illustrating their ways of war, and the spiritual practice of Buddhism did not condone the glorification of warfare in inscriptions. It can only be assumed that, because they were an Indianized people, the early Mons and Burmese adhered to Indian models of warfare. The capital of the Thai state was established at Ayutthaya in 1350 and, following this, the history of modern Siam is commonly traced. Although Siam ascended consistently in power and frequently kept its warlike neighbors of Japan, China, and India at bay, its history is plagued by centuries of quarrels between tribes, as the prominent provinces of Chiangmai, Ayudhya, and Sukhothai battled tirelessly for the semblance of a united kingdom under their respective rule. The second Siamese kingdom captured Angkor in 1352, after the Khmer kingdom had become weak and exhausted. In 1393 the Siamese took Angkor again, and in 1432 they captured it for the final time. Thus, although the Siamese had embraced Buddhism, they began to learn the ways of war from the dying Khmer Empire.

MEDIEVAL SOURCES

Few written sources exist regarding warfare in Southeast Asia during this period, and many of these are questionable. The earliest knowledge, extremely limited, comes from various Chinese sources beginning in the third century. This is often found in the form of accounts drawn from Chinese missions as well as pilgrims heading to India, especially the seventh century account of Xuanzang (Hsüan-tsang), the *Yijing (I-Ching)*. These often relate to economic vitality. Much knowledge comes from temple inscriptions in Cambodia and Myanmar, as well as monuments devoted to various kings, particularly in the Khmer and Pagan empires. Statues and bas-reliefs throughout the region indicate the nature of weapons and battle dress. There are also a number of annals that provide basic royal genealogies, especially from Cambodia, though these are often confused or incomplete. The dependencies of the Majapahit kingdom, for instance, are enumerated in Mpu Prapa ha's *Nagarakrtagama* (1365). Marco Polo recounts his twelfth century experiences in Southeast Asia in *The Travels of Marco Polo* (first transcribed in French in the fourteenth century as *Divisament dou monde*, or "description of the world," and translated into English in 1579). Some information has also been gleaned from sixteenth century Portuguese accounts of their early voyages in the region.

BOOKS AND ARTICLES

Charney, Michael W. *Southeast Asian Warfare, 1300-1900*. Leiden, Netherlands: E. J. Brill, 2004.

Coèdes, Georges. *The Indianized States of Southeast Asia*. Edited by Walter F. Vella. Honolulu: University of Hawaii Press, 1968.

Hall, D. G. E. *A History of South-East Asia*. 4th ed. New York: St. Martin's Press, 1981.

Jacques, Claude. *The Khmer Empire: Cities and Sanctuaries*. Bangkok, Thailand: River Books, 2007.

Quaritch Wales, H. G. *Ancient South-East Asian Warfare*. London: Bernard Quaritch, 1952.

Tarling, Nicholas. *The Cambridge History of Southeast Asia*. 2 vols. New York: Cambridge University Press, 1992.

Wolters, O. W. *Early Southeast Asia: Selected Essays*. Ithaca, N.Y.: Cornell University Southeast Asia Program, 2008.

FILMS AND OTHER MEDIA

Children of the Seven-Headed Snake. Documentary. FIP-Odysse-Ampersand, 1999.

Mekong: The Three Ancient Kingdoms of Cambodia, Thailand, and Vietnam. Documentary. Global Edu-tainment, 2008.

Aaron Plamondon

THE MEDIEVAL WORLD

THE AMERICAS

THE MAYA AND AZTECS

Dates: c. 1500 B.C.E.-1521 C.E.

POLITICAL CONSIDERATIONS

Warfare in Mesoamerica can be reconstructed only from the cultural remains that have been left behind in the portable art, sculpture, architecture, and documents of the ancient Maya and Aztecs. Although this incomplete record allows only a partial glimpse of the politics, military achievements, weapons, and strategies of these early people, archaeologists and historians have been able to reconstruct much of their ancient military and warfare history. The cultures and chronologies of the ancient Maya and Aztecs differed greatly, but many parallels can be drawn between their politics and warfare strategies.

THE MAYA

The ancient Maya were once thought to have been gentle stargazers; however, discoveries such as that in 1946 of the murals at Bonampak in Chiapas, southern Mexico, depict violent and bloody scenes of warfare and sacrifice. Because the Maya are a much older culture, there is less abundant information about their methods of warfare than those of the Aztecs. The ancient history of the Maya region is typically divided into three periods: the Formative (c. 1500 B.C.E.-300 C.E.), the Classic (250-900), and the Postclassic (900-1500). Whereas much of the contemporary knowledge of Aztec society stems from contact-period documents, the Maya population had already gone into severe decline by the time the Spanish conquistadores arrived in the Americas in the fifteenth and sixteenth centuries. Nonetheless, it is known that the Maya engaged in extensive civil war, often capturing the kings and other elite officials of competing city-states. It has been said that militarism and conquest were instrumental in creating and perpetuating a ruling elite and political centers. The success of an individual ruler was measured by his successful taking of captives, as depicted in much of the art and sculpture of the ancient Maya. Hieroglyphic texts often refer to the conquests of kings, and naked and defeated captives are frequently depicted below the feet of triumphant captors. Early conflicts were generally not waged over long distances; instead, small-scale warfare was limited to local polities. As conflict grew over limited resources, warfare remained localized but became endemic. Captives became a necessary element in the inauguration of a new king, at the dedication of a new building, or for other sacred events; this need continued to motivate the Maya to invade neighboring polities. The intent of Mayan warfare was not to expand territory but to increase the prestige and power of the successful raiders.

THE AZTECS

The Aztecs, wandering barbarians, arrived late in Mesoamerica, settling at the site of Tenochtitlán in 1345 C.E. Over the next century, they assembled inexhaustible armies that marched hundreds of miles from the Valley of Mexico to confront and defeat rival cultures. Although they were a dominant power for only slightly more than one hundred years (1400-1521 C.E.), they were able to create an empire, maintain extensive economic trade routes, and appropriate the military organization, arts, and cultures of their subjects, incorporating them into their own civilization.

Religious fervor drove the Aztecs into constant war to capture political prisoners for sacrifice to their gods. Gory images of war captives with their hearts gouged out have been inextricably tied to the Aztecs.

MILITARY ACHIEVEMENT

THE MAYA

The greatest military achievement for the ancient Maya was the successful capture and sacrifice of a

ANCIENT MESOAMERICA

Gulf of Mexico

Pacific Ocean

Chichén Itzá
Cobá
Tulum
Copán
Dzibilchaltún
Uxmal
MAYAN AREA
Tikal
Altar de Sacrificios
Palenque
Izapa
OLMEC AREA
San Lorenzo
Monte Albán
San José Mogote
ZAPOTEC AREA
Cholula
El Tajín
AZTEC AREA
Teotihuacán
Tula
Tenochtitlán

king from a neighboring and competing polity. Although this was a relatively rare event, it was depicted with both hieroglyphic text and images on the monuments of the victorious king. This visual and textual propaganda legitimized the power of the ruling king and often had profound effects on the cities of both the victor and loser. For example, in the first millennium C.E., when the king of the less powerful center of Quiriguá captured the ruler of the dominant center of Copán, Quiriguá was able to catapult itself into a more powerful position, while Copán went into a minor decline in authority and influence. The defeat of a ruler was an exacting blow to any city, and it placed the losing city in a state of flux. According to tradition, a new ruler could not be put in place until the preceding ruler had died, and in some cases, captured rulers were kept alive in order to weaken the power of the competing polity.

THE AZTECS

Military achievement for the ancient Aztecs was measured by the expansion of territory through intimidation of enemies in battle or simply the threat of battle. After the Aztecs had successfully moved into a new area, they became reliant on local leaders to successfully maintain their domains. Rather than install their own leaders in newly conquered areas, at the expense of their own human resources, the Aztecs would allow local leaders to remain in their positions under Aztec power. The Aztecs allowed the vanquished to maintain their traditional systems of trade and markets, while at the same time extracting some of the local resources as tribute. This system of loose military alliances allowed the Aztecs to spread their forces across a much broader region. The Spanish noted at the time of contact that the Aztecs were a fierce people, with a skilled military that lacked a fear of battle. Although there are few monuments dedicated to the successful military achievements of individuals, extensive records of tribute were documented, indicating the territory that was maintained and the resources that were extracted. Successful soldiers were highly valued and were rewarded for their valor with the special recognition of promotions and distinctive uniforms.

WEAPONS AND ARMOR

WEAPONS

Due to the fragmentary archaeological record, it is unlikely that a conclusive inventory of the weapons, uniforms, and armor of the ancient Maya and Aztecs will ever be cataloged. However, depictions in art and documents from the pre- and postcontact periods do give insight into the more common and important weapons of warfare employed by these cultures.

North Wind Picture Archives via AP Images

An Aztec warrior, carrying a wooden sword with stone blades and a decorated shield and dressed in cotton armor and an animal-head helmet.

Projectile weapons, used at a distance to strike at an enemy, include the bow and arrow, the sling, the dart, and the all-important atlatl. The atlatl, or spear-thrower, allowed the user to launch darts at greater distances than hand-thrown darts could be thrown. Depictions of the atlatl indicate that it had been used since the Classic period (250-900 C.E.). Atlatls were often ornately decorated with low-relief carving and even gold. The few existing examples are about 2 feet long, with a hook at one end where the barbed darts were attached. In some cases, loops were affixed to the other end of the weapon and used as finger grips. Many of the more extravagant atlatls were probably used only in ceremonies but were nonetheless extremely effective weapons in war. Spanish accounts attest to this potency, asserting that the darts could penetrate any armor and deliver a fatal wound. Experimental archaeology has confirmed that an experienced atlatl thrower could hurl a dart up to a distance of 243 feet and that atlatls allowed up to 60 percent more accuracy than did an unaided spear.

The bow and arrow was another commonly used weapon in Mesoamerica. Bows measured up to 5 feet in length, and bowstrings were often made of animal sinew or deerskin. Arrows used in war had heads made of obsidian or fishbone and included barbed, blunt, and pointed styles. There is no indication that either the Maya or the Aztecs put poison on their arrow tips, but apparently both used fire-arrows to shoot at buildings. Experiments indicate that traditional arrows could be shot to ranges between 300 and 600 feet and that skilled archers could easily penetrate quilted cotton armor.

Slings made of maguey fibers, from agave plants, were used to catapult rounded, hand-shaped stones at adversaries. Stones were often collected in advance and apparently could be thrown more than 1,300 feet. Slings were often used with bows and arrows and could be extremely effective for penetrating the heavy Spanish armor.

Weapons used in close combat included the thrusting spear, which was actually most productive for slashing and parrying. Depictions from contact-period drawings indicate that the weapon was approximately 6 to 7 feet in length, with a roughly triangular head that was laced with closely set stone blades forming an unbroken cutting edge. The Aztecs also had one-handed and two-handed wooden swords, with obsidian or flint blades adhered into grooves along the edge of the weapon. According to the Spanish, these blades were more effective than Spanish swords. Other weapons included wooden clubs, sometimes with a circular ball on the end that was most forceful on downward blows. Axes, blowguns, and knives were also known in Mesoamerica but were more likely used in hunting than in warfare.

DEFENSIVE ARMOR

Shields, helmets, and armor were used in Mesoamerica as defensive weapons. Shields were usually made of hide, wood, palm leaves, or woven cane with cotton backing. They were decorated with feathers, paint, gold, silver, and copper foils and were round, square, or rectangular in shape. A shield's decorations were often reflective of the status and caliber of its user. The shield's primary use was as protection from projectiles; it probably was not very effective against clubs and swords.

Armor was made of a quilted cotton consisting of unspun cotton placed between two layers of cloth and stitched to a leather border. The thickness of the armor protected wearers from darts and arrows and was better suited than metal to the heat and humidity of Mesoamerica. Soldiers wore various styles of jackets and pullovers, which protected their upper bodies and thighs. Lower legs were protected with cotton leggings, although few weapons targeted this area of the body. War suits of feathers and fabric, or feathered tunics, were worn by higher-ranking warriors over their cotton armor. Some helmets were made of wood and bone and decorated with feathers, whereas others were made out of the heads of wild animals, such as wolves, jaguars, and pumas, placed over a wooden frame. The soldier's face could be seen in the gaping mouth of the animal's open jaw.

MILITARY ORGANIZATION

THE MAYA

The Maya's military organization appears to have been much less formalized than that of the Aztecs. However, those involved in conquest appear to have been afforded high status in society. Warriors, with their ability to seize captives, played a critical role in bringing power to a king and his city. Considered members of the elite class, they wore elaborate regalia and participated in rich ceremonies when they brought captives back to their king. Warriors also participated as ballplayers in the ball game that reenacted the ritual capture and eventual sacrifice of important rulers and elites from other sites. Although ballplayers and warriors were frequently depicted on portable art, they are almost never identified as individuals in texts. Kings, however, were recognized and regularly depicted as warriors, and the military prowess of their warriors was broadcast as their own success. Battles were generally short, limited in geographic scope, and usually timed around significant historical events. This system of warfare, unlike that of the Aztecs, afforded the Maya the luxury of not needing to maintain a huge standing army.

THE AZTECS

Aztec society was highly stratified, and military ranking was intimately tied to this overall social organization. The ruling nobles were placed in positions of higher rank, based on their birthright and social status, whereas the commoners often earned their military status through their skills in warfare. Most commoners paid their dues to society through the production of goods for tribute and labor, and many of them served in the Aztec military. All those who assisted the military were given extensive training in the use of weapons and the taking of captives, although those of higher status were provided with more thorough instruction. Soldiers who successfully took multiple captives were rewarded with promotions and uniforms signifying their accomplishments. Appropriate jewelry, hairstyles, body paint, and other insignia were also indicative of a soldier's status, and higher-ranking individuals were given privileges such as the rights to consume human flesh in public, to have mistresses, and to feast in the royal palaces.

DOCTRINE, STRATEGY, AND TACTICS

All Mesoamerican cultures were limited by the lack of efficient transportation beyond human foot traffic. Although Mesoamerican cultures did have knowledge of the wheel, the harsh environment limited their ability to use it effectively. Draft animals were not introduced to the area until after the contact period. Transportation difficulties limited the cultures' abilities to control regions and their resources from long distances. The Maya and the Aztecs each developed different systems to maintain their political control over competing cities.

THE MAYA

The most effective method through which the Maya gained control over a competing city was either that of a royal marriage or that of a conquest, which was often the preferred choice. Ancient monuments at several Mayan cities depict both such events. Many sites, including the major city of Tikal, exhibited earthen walls along their boundaries as a form of protection from these battling neighbors, although they often proved ineffective. Numerous depictions in both text and art indicate that kings would send elite soldiers to raid smaller, less powerful polities and to capture and bring back important personages as prisoners. Low-ranking captives were often put into slavery or other service, while higher-ranking officials were displayed to the public and eventually sacrificed. These raids were important to validate the power of new polities and were frequently reenacted in the ritual ball game, an event held in elaborately built ball courts. The triumphant city would host the ball game as a ritual competition, after which the losers would be sacrificed. The Maya, believing in the cyclical nature of time, often planned their raids and reenactments to coincide with meaningful anniversaries of past events.

Hernán Cortés and his troops ended an indigenous rebellion in Cholulu just prior to the Spaniards' sacking of Tenochtitlán and the fall of the Aztec Empire.

THE AZTECS

The Aztecs instituted a system in which local rulers of conquered areas were allowed to remain as heads of these areas, which were then required to produce and transport goods as a form of tribute to their conquerors. The Aztecs decided that, rather than leave behind their own garrisons to maintain controlled areas and extract large amounts of resources, they would instead lower the costs of administration and leave the control of conquered areas in the hands of local officials. Although this policy meant that Aztecs could not extract the maximum amount of goods from these conquered areas, it freed up soldiers and officials to continue their expansion into more distant areas. Campaigns were often scheduled around practical factors, including agricultural and seasonal cycles, such as the rainy season. This schedule often limited the ability of the Aztecs to run year-round crusades, and they had to depend on the local politicians to maintain their power.

The rulers of the Aztec Empire kept the local rulers of their loose alliance in line by continually intimidating them and engaging in warfare. Those who did not comply were harshly punished, and members of neighboring cities were often used to aid in these raids. Aztecs often pitted traditional adversaries against one another, and the threat of impending attack often allowed them to coerce loyalties without ever having to do battle. The Aztecs often used spies to gain military intelligence. Individuals were sent into rivals' territories dressed in their clothing and speaking their language. Spies were useful for obtaining strategic information about their foe's fortifi- cations and preparations but were often caught or turned against their own. Although the overall mili- tary strategy of the Aztecs was fraught with prob- lems, their system allowed them to maintain the larg- est political domain in all of Mesoamerica.

CONTEMPORARY SOURCES

Maya

Although the Maya codices do not deal with the topic of Mayan warfare and the contact- period documents deal with a culture in severe decline, some recent volumes have begun using the Maya's own texts and documents to look at aspects of elite society, including war and con- quest. In Linda Schele and Peter Mathews's *The Code of Kings: The Language of Seven Sacred Maya Temples and Tombs* (1998), the authors decipher the ancient hieroglyphs on the monu- ments and buildings of seven Classic-period sites to reveal what the ancient Maya had to say about themselves. In it, there are numerous discussions of warfare between major cities, includ- ing war tactics, sacrifice, the ballgame, and war imagery. Matthew Restall's *Maya Conquista- dor* (1998) retells the Spanish encounter with the Maya from the Maya point of view. Using documents written by the Maya at the contact period, Restall allows the Maya to retell what the conquest was like. This book allows the reader to see that these brutal interactions with the Spanish fit into the Maya's cyclical worldview, and that they continued to deal with outsiders the way they had for hundreds of years. Both of the volumes offer an innovative and inside view of the native perspective of warfare and conquest. For a more traditional look at the contact pe- riod, a classic document is the 1941 translation by Alfred M. Tozzer of the original *Relación de las cosas de Yucatán* (1566; English translation, 1941); also known as *Yucatan Before and After the Conquest* (1937) by Bishop Diego de Landa, available in the papers of the Peabody Mu- seum of American Archaeology and Ethnology at Harvard University. This significant docu- ment provides great insight into the contact period from the perspective of a Spanish bishop attempting to save the souls of the Mayan natives. In it, he describes the expeditions of the conquistadores in Yucatán, as well as Mayan culture and warfare, with information obtained from native informants and his own observations.

Aztecs

When the Spanish encountered the Aztecs in 1519, they discovered an empire that covered much of Mexico. Numerous contact-period documents describe the process of the Spanish con- quest: the individual battles and the eventual taking over of Aztec society and its empire's trib- ute. Various chronicles, including *Historia de las Indias de Nueva-España y Islas de Tierra Firme: Mexico* (1579-1581; *The Aztecs: The History of the Indies of New Spain*, 1964), by Diego Durán; *Obras Historicas* (1891-1892), by Fernando de Alva Ixtlilxóchitl; *Crónica Mexicana* (1598), by Fernando Alvarado Tezozómoc; and *Relaciónes Originales de Chalco Amequemecán* (c. 1620), by Domingo Chimanlpahín, describe Aztec military campaigns, dy- nastic relationships, and political and military strategies of assassination, bribery, and manipu- lation. These documents also reveal that Aztecs were more concerned in warfare with acquiring goods and services from a region than with occupying the territory themselves. *Historía Verdadera de la Conquista de la Nueva España* (1568; *The Discovery and Conquest of Mexico, 1517-1521*, 1844), considered the classic volume on the Spanish conquest, was written by

Bernal Díaz del Castillo (1496-1584), a conquistador under Hernán Cortés who witnessed and documented wartime events, including more than one hundred battles, and the imprisonment of the Aztec king Montezuma II (c. 1480-1520).

BOOKS AND ARTICLES

Aguilar-Moreno, Manuel. "Warfare." In *Handbook to Life in the Aztec World*. New York: Facts On File, 2006.

Clendinnen, Inga. "Aztecs." In *The Book of War*, edited by John Keega. New York: Viking, 1999.

Culbert, T. Patrick, ed. *Classic Maya Political History: Hieroglyphic and Archaeological Evidence*. Cambridge, England: Cambridge University Press, 1991.

Fash, William L. *Scribes, Warriors, and Kings: The City of Copán and the Ancient Maya*. Rev. ed. New York: Thames and Hudson, 2001.

Foster, Lynn V. "Warfare." In *Handbook to Life in the Ancient Maya World*. New York: Facts On File, 2002.

Hassig, Ross. *Aztec Warfare: Imperial Expansion and Political Control*. Norman: University of Oklahoma Press, 1995.

_____. "Peace, Reconciliation, and Alliance in Aztec Mexico." In *War and Peace in the Ancient World*, edited by Kurt A. Raaflaub. Malden, Mass.: Blackwell, 2007.

Pohl, John. *Aztec, Mixtec, and Zapotec Armies*. Illustrated by Angus McBride. Botley, Oxford, England: Osprey, 1991.

_____. *Aztec Warrior, A.D. 1325-1521*. Illustrated by Adam Hook. Botley, Oxford, England: Osprey, 2001.

Pohl, John, and Charles M. Robinson III. *Aztecs and Conquistadores: The Spanish Invasion and the Collapse of the Aztec Empire*. Botley, Oxford, England: Osprey, 2005.

Sharer, Robert. *The Ancient Maya*. 6th ed. Stanford, Calif.: Stanford University Press, 1994.

Townsend, Richard. *The Aztecs*. London: Thames and Hudson, 2000.

Wise, Terence. *The Conquistadores*. Illustrated by Angus McBride. Botley, Oxford, England: Osprey, 1980.

FILMS AND OTHER MEDIA

Apocalypto. Feature film. Icon Entertainment, 2006.

In Search of History: The Aztec Empire. Documentary. History Channel, 1997.

In Search of History: The Maya. Documentary. History Channel, 1997.

Lost Kingdoms of the Maya. Documentary. National Geographic, 1993.

Jennifer P. Mathews

THE INCAS
Dates: c. 1200-1500 C.E.

POLITICAL CONSIDERATIONS

The Incas were one of many South American tribes engaged in a power struggle in the Andean highlands from the thirteenth century through the middle of the fifteenth century. Prior to this time, this region had been occupied by many different tribes. Between 500 and 1000 C.E. the Tiahuanco and Huari cultures, for example, developed large urban settlements and organized state systems. During the years from 1000 to 1456, however, the region encompassing modern Colombia, Ecuador, Peru, and Chile experienced a process of fragmentation that resulted in the development of small, regional states. Although warfare between different tribes was common, no one group was clearly dominant. The Incas were just one of the many tribes involved in warfare in the southern highlands near modern Bolivia. They were not especially strong at this time and had to form alliances to survive. The Chanca and Quechua tribes in the Apurímac Basin and the Lupaca and Colla tribes in the Titicaca Basin presented the biggest threats to the Incas, who, until the fifteenth century, dominated only a small area near Cuzco.

MILITARY ACHIEVEMENT

Under the leadership of the Incan warrior Pachacuti (c. 1391-1471), the Incas defeated the Chanca tribes in a battle at Cuzco in 1438. According to legend, the boulders on the battlefield became warriors who fought for the Incas. After this victory, Pachacuti became emperor, and the Incas began to expand their territory by conquering other tribes. Under Pachacuti the Incas emerged as the strongest military power in the southern highlands, and their territory stretched as far south as the Maule River in modern south-central Chile. Unlike other peoples, however, the Incas did not loot and abandon vanquished tribes, but rather they incorporated these former foes into their own military. The Incas conquered the western Titicaca Basin and nearly all of the Urubamba, Apurímac, and Mantaro Basins during the twenty-five years following their defeat of the Chancas. The military and logistical support provided by the vanquished tribes enabled the Incas to control the territory of the southern highlands and to begin expanding their territory through conquests along the northern coast. The defeated Chancan tribes, now fighting for the Incas, began conquering the northern tribes, which formed a part of the Chimú Empire.

The Incas attacked and defeated the Chimú tribes after Topa Inca Yupanqui (r. 1471-1493), Pachacuti's son, led attacks as far north as Ecuador before returning south along the coast. He extended the Incan Empire and maintained his father's policy of incorporating the vanquished tribes into the military. His son, Huayna Capac (r. 1493-1525), succeeded him as emperor and solidified the empire by conquering smaller areas throughout Ecuador, expanding Incan territory as far north as Colombia and establishing boundary markers to the Angasmayo River. Huayna Capac made Quito the northern capital of the empire, which spanned 2,500 miles. The Incas called their empire Tahuantinsuyu, meaning "the land of the four quarters." The Incan territory was divided into four regions and subdivided into more than eight provinces.

WEAPONS, UNIFORMS, AND ARMOR

The Incas had an advanced Bronze Age technology in the fifteenth century that served as the foundation of the military force. The sling was the deadliest projectile weapon. Other effective weapons included bows and arrows, lances, darts, a short variation of a sword, battle-axes, spears, and arrows tipped with

An Inca-style battle scene in which warriors wear helmets and quilted tunics and wield swords, axes, and spears in hand-to-hand combat.

copper or bone. The weapons used by the Incan lords were decorated with gold or silver. For protection military leaders wore casques, or helmets, made from wood or the skins of wild animals and decorated with precious stones and the feathers of tropical birds. Soldiers wore the costume of the province from which they came; their armor consisted of a wooden helmet covered with bronze; a long, quilted tunic; and a quilted shield. The soldiers, who jogged at a pace of about 3 miles per hour and traveled nearly 20 miles per day, carried only their own supplies, while an army of soldiers was responsible for carrying baggage on their backs. Garrisons were housed in fortresses, whereas detachments occupied storehouses, which consisted of magazines filled with weapons, grain, and ammunition. Sacsahuamán, the site where the Incas defeated the Chancas, was the only fortress garrisoned by the Inca people. Sacsahuamán was only one of many Incan fortresses; others included Paramonga, a fortress constructed like a mountain of adobe bricks that had once been a part of the Chimú kingdom. These storehouses provided the army with food and clothing, thus avoiding the necessity to pillage villages as the army traveled across the country.

MILITARY ORGANIZATION

The Incan military was highly organized and consisted of nearly 200,000 soldiers. The military served as a public service organization that brought food and materials from one region of the country to another and trained specialists who contributed to the growth of the empire. In order to prepare future soldiers, military training took place on a bimonthly basis and began with boys as young as ten years old, who took part in physical activities such as wrestling, weight lifting, and sling shooting. This training enabled the Incan commanders to determine which soldiers could be used as specialists, such as builders, stonemasons, bridge experts, and assault leaders. Village elders reported on the progress of the boys, whom the military drafted as either warriors, carriers, or craftsmen. Short-term service drafting ensured an ample supply of young men in each district. The periods of service depended upon climatic conditions, and not all men returned to civilian life. The commanders ordered the most outstanding soldiers, those who were the bravest, the most disciplined, and the most adept at fighting, to remain permanently in the military.

The organization of the army was similar to that of the decimal system utilized by the Romans. Although the commanders were usually members of the Incan royal family, many ascended from the ranks because of their extraordinary ability and devotion to the emperor. One of the demands placed upon the commanders, who had to deal with the logistical problems of the roads and supplies, was to calculate the most efficient way to move their military across the country. Because the strategy was to fight only if absolutely necessary, the commanders had to ensure a deployment of soldiers superior to that of the enemy and would not waste manpower by sending too many. On important occasions, the emperor personally assumed command of a campaign. Topa Inca Yupanqui, for example, took personal command of an effort to expand the empire by overseeing the extension of the main highways, a task too difficult for an army commander to handle alone. Soldiers were required to participate in battles as far away from their homes as possible in order to avoid fraternization and to allow them to experience the vastness of the country and the grandeur of the empire. Because the purpose of the military was both to defend and to extend Tahuantinsuyu and to serve the Sun God, individual glory in battle was not valued by the Incas.

DOCTRINE, STRATEGY, AND TACTICS

The primary aim of the Incan military was to spread the worship of the Sun and to seek harmony through the integration of so-called barbarians—who lacked military discipline, worshiped false gods, and practiced human sacrifices and cannibalism—into the Incan culture. The Incas believed, therefore, that their conquests were justifiable and were motivated by a desire to improve the quality of life of their vanquished tribes. The Incas traveled with the purpose of disrupting the lives of Peru's inhabitants as little as possible. Specialized engineering corps designed and constructed the travel routes, which extended through the mountains and along the coastal desert. The same corps of engineers also constructed giant suspension bridges where necessary. Different armies followed each route, and they eventually met

before advancing. Because the idea behind the creation of Tahuantinsuyu was to spread universal peace, the Incas often showed mercy to the vanquished tribes and pursued peaceful resolutions whenever possible.

The principal strategy utilized by the Incas to defeat their enemies was to destroy harvests and inflict famine. War, however, was often the only option. The slingers, due to their accuracy, began the attack on a fortress. Their sling bolts easily pierced the Peruvian helmets worn by their enemies. Feints were

THE INCA EMPIRE, 1493-1525

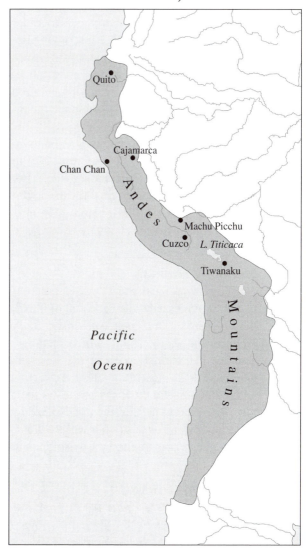

often used to draw defenders away from the center of an attack. Soldiers assembled human pyramids to attack the higher walls of enemy fortresses; the pyramid shape enabled the soldiers to attack quickly with their maces. The skin of the captured leaders was often made into drums used at festivals celebrating Incan victories. After killing the leaders, the Incas ripped out their intestines, dried the bodies as carefully as possible, fitted the abdominal skin over a bentwood frame, and finally placed the skin on a carrying frame. Although these drums were not very musical, they served as amusement for the Incas and as a warning of the fate of those who dared to resist the Incan emperor. Most leaders, however, surrendered and were incorporated into the Incan system of government. The Incas roped their prisoners together and sacrificed a few to the Sun God. Most of the prisoners, however, were detained long enough to ensure that they would cooperate with the Incas and contribute to the empire. The only prisoners who endured slave labor were the ones assigned to maintain the Incas' standards for roads and villages.

The evolution of the Inca Empire was an ongoing process, as each succeeding Incan emperor tried to continue the military plans of his predecessor. After each conquest, the Incas allowed time for the settlement of the new territory before pursuing the next one. This interval also gave the vanquished time to assimilate the Incan culture and to prepare to fight in the name of their new god. The receptions given to Incan sovereigns in the capital after a conquest rivaled Roman triumph celebrations in pomp and ceremony. Dressed in the colorful costumes of their provinces of origin, the people greeted their victorious ruler, who was borne aloft in a golden chair raised on the shoulders of his nobles, as he passed beneath arches erected along the route to the Temple of the Sun. Alone in the temple, because attendants were not permitted to enter, the sovereign, barefoot and stripped of his regal costume, gave thanks for his victory. A large celebration followed in which music, dancing, and bonfires commemorated the addition of a new territory. The Inca Empire, in reality, was a confederation of tribes with the Incas in control of a common government, a common religion, and a common language. A council of rulers ruled each of the tribes, which pledged its allegiance to the emperor, who, as a descendant of the Sun God, was considered divine. The conquered tribes maintained their individual cultural identities, but they paid Incan labor taxes; payment ensured that every individual received fulfillment of all of his or her basic needs. Although the inhabitants of each conquered town spoke their native languages, the Incas also imposed the Quechua language on them in order to enable communication among the different peoples.

MEDIEVAL SOURCES

El Inca Garcilaso de la Vega (1539-1616), the son of an Incan princess and a Spanish explorer, provides a detailed account of the Incan civilization both before and after the arrival of the Spaniards in his *Los Comentarios Reales de Los Incas* (1609-1617; *The Royal Commentaries of the Incas*, 1688), which remains one of the most complete and accurate available sources of information about the Incas. In the first part of this book, completed in 1609, Garcilaso de la Vega chronicles the development of the Inca Empire and discusses the political and social status of the Incas, as well as their legends, traditions, customs, and methods of warfare. The second part, written in 1617, describes the wars of the Spanish conquest, in which Garcilaso de la Vegas's father was a primary figure. "El Inca" bases the second part of his history on the stories told to him by soldiers and conquerors who fought alongside his father.

BOOKS AND ARTICLES

Burland, C. A. *Peru Under the Incas*. London: Evans Brothers, 1967.
D'Altroy, Terence N. "Militarism." In *The Incas*. Malden, Mass.: Blackwell, 2002.
Davies, Nigel. *The Incas*. Boulder: University Press of Colorado, 1995.

Guilmartin, John F. "Incas." In *The Reader's Companion to Military History*, edited by Robert Cowley and Geoffrey Parker. Boston: Houghton Mifflin, 1996.

Julie, Catherine. "War and Peace in the Inca Heartland." In *War and Peace in the Ancient World*, edited by Kurt A. Raaflaub. Malden, Mass.: Blackwell, 2007.

Kaufmann, H. W., and J. E. Kaufmann. *Fortifications of the Incas, 1200-1531*. Illustrated by Adam Hook. Botley, Oxford, England: Osprey, 2006.

Lanning, Edward P. *Peru Before the Incas*. Englewood Cliffs, N.J.: Prentice-Hall, 1967.

McEwan, Gordon F. *The Incas: New Perspectives*. Santa Barbara, Calif.: ABC-CLIO, 2005.

MacQuarrie, Kim. *The Last Days of the Incas*. New York: Simon and Schuster, 2007.

Stern, Steven J. *Peru's Indian Peoples and the Challenge of Spanish Conquest*. 2d ed. Madison: University of Wisconsin Press, 1993.

FILMS AND OTHER MEDIA

Great Inca Rebellion. Documentary. National Geographic, 2007.

The Incas. Documentary. Public Broadcasting Service, 1980.

The Incas Remembered. Documentary. Monterey Home Video, 1986.

NOVA: Secrets of Lost Empires—Inca. Documentary. Public Broadcasting Service, 1997.

The Royal Hunt of the Sun. Feature film. National General Pictures, 1969.

Michael J. McGrath

NORTH AMERICAN INDIGENOUS NATIONS

Dates: c. 12,000 B.C.E.-1600 C.E.

POLITICAL CONSIDERATIONS

Among the southeastern and southern North American chiefdoms of the Mississippian period (900-1540 C.E.), there were cities designated as "peace towns" and "war towns," which were occupied alternately during times of peace and war. There were also chieftains who bore the same designations and alternately led their people during these times. The "Red Chief" led in times of war, and the "White Chief" in times of peace. This system continued through to the early eighteenth century, when the Chickasaw of northern Mississippi, who were in periodic conflict with the Choctaw and their English allies, would turn leadership over to their Red Chief and remove their people to the red towns when hostilities loomed. It is assumed that this elaborate tradition of response to war and peace was in place long before the European contact.

Apparently, there was no effort on the part of Native American groups in the South and Southeast to develop what could be called empires. The chiefdoms controlled large areas that included many towns, but distance was an important factor in the amount of control a small group of native nobles and priests could have over a large territory. The Natchez of western Mississippi, near the city now bearing that name, along the Mississippi River, were probably the best and most advanced example of centralized control over people. The Great Sun was the absolute ruler, presiding over a tightly controlled class system that included four distinct classes: the Great Sun and his immediate family, the Nobility, the Honored Ones, and the Stinkards, or agricultural peasants. It is unlikely, however, that the total Natchez population ever exceeded 5,000 or 6,000, and the territory controlled by the central government was, by modern standards, extremely small. Some distance had to be maintained between chiefdoms to prevent encroachment upon one another's territories. These buffer zones also served as hunting territory.

Other politically advanced chiefdoms were groups later known to the Europeans as the Chickasaw, Choctaw, Seminole, Timucua, Quapaw, Catawba, Tunica, Caddo, Shawnee, Chitimacha, Calusa, Tuscarora, Pamlico, and Powhatan. This Mississippian, or "temple mound," group of cultures extended from Virginia to Oklahoma and from the Ohio River to the Gulf and Atlantic coasts. The Mississippian peoples also extended some distance up the Mississippi River into Wisconsin. At the peak of their development in the late fifteenth century, they probably included no more than one-half million people. They, like most of the Native American groups, periodically fought small battles with each other, but the fighting was mainly precipitated by encroachments into hunting territories, or misunderstandings stemming from language differences. For instance, the Chickasaw often drove the Kickapoo out of their hunting grounds in present Tennessee and Kentucky, east of the Tennessee River. The Cherokee and the various Muskogean peoples—the Chickasaw, Choctaw, those who later made up the Creek Confederation, and the Seminole—were generally hostile to each other because the Cherokee, who had arrived in the Southeast in the twelfth or thirteenth century, spoke an Iroquoian language. The Muskogeans all spoke closely related dialects of the Muskogean language.

One of the most politically advanced groups in the East and Northeast was the Iroquois Confederacy, a United Nations-type alliance that had been organized by the sixteenth century. An increase in separate tribal identities had begun in the fourteenth century, perhaps as a male response to the increasing

NATIVE PEOPLES OF EASTERN NORTH AMERICA, C. 1600

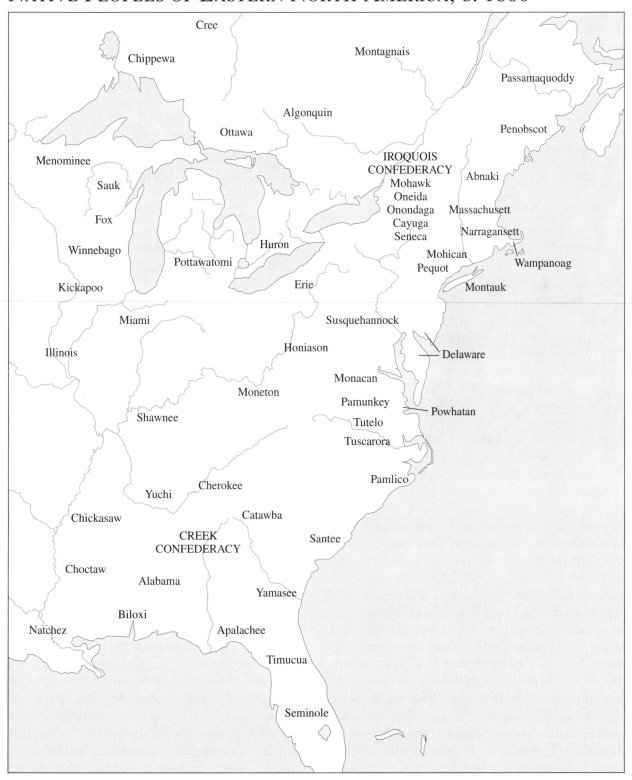

North Wind Picture Archives via AP Images

West Indian natives and Spanish explorers clash at Columbus's settlement at La Navidad.

importance of women in food production, with the spread of maize agriculture in the Northeast during this time. Male prestige, which had previously resulted from the successful hunting and auspicious bravery during the hunt, declined, and men roamed farther from home for longer periods of time, encroaching on the territories of others with whom they engaged in violence, all in search of prestige. Another view involves the trade in prestige items such as copper, obsidian, sea shells, and exotic furs. As male prestige suffered among the Iroquois, raiding to obtain these items by force brought about increased warfare between related groups that had once traded peacefully. By the time of European contact, the Iroquois Confederacy was responsible for a somewhat

peaceful coexistence between formerly hostile tribes in the East Lakes region, New England, and southern Canada. These tribes often joined forces to fight their hostile western and southern neighbors.

Another significantly developed political entity were the Anasazi, who were a fundamentally agricultural people occupying a large area of Colorado, Arizona, New Mexico, and Utah. They built great pueblos in such places as Chaco Canyon and Mesa Verde in the Four Corners region. Some believe that the far-flung Anasazi confederation was destroyed in the thirteenth century by raids conducted by Utes, Apaches, Navajos, and Comanches who had been driven out of adjacent habitats by a great and prolonged drought that impacted almost all of western

North America during what was called the Little Ice Age. During this time, crops failed and the courses of rivers changed. The successors to the Anasazi, known as the Pueblo peoples, an amalgam of the raiding groups, occupied, and continue to occupy, villages consisting of great adobe apartment complexes. These peoples were not, however, part of any large confederation, but rather were more like bands who often fought with one another for a variety of reasons, many trivial.

Along the coast of British Columbia, reaching into southern Alaska and Washington state, lived tribes such as the Tlingit, who were highly developed both socially and politically. These tribes maintained some degree of peace by engaging in the periodic practice of the potlatch, the ceremonial act of giving a great deal of a group's material possessions to another group, which was expected to reciprocate appropriately within a reasonable time. Northwestern tribes did, however, engage in frequent combat with their neighbors over hunting and gathering territory and perhaps in response to raids for obtaining women.

The archaeological record reveals that during the early fourteenth century there were hostilities between Native Americans who lived along the river valleys of the Dakotas and those who occupied the river valleys of Kansas and Nebraska. The southern group, probably responding to drought conditions, moved northward, forcibly encroaching upon the Dakota group. At the Crow Creek site on the Missouri River in South Dakota, more than five hundred scalped and mutilated bodies were unearthed from a shallow mass grave at one end of a defensive trench. Evidence indicates that this massacre occurred around 1325. Many other such occurrences have been documented by archaeologists.

It is certain that warfare did exist between Native American groups during the prehistoric period, though it was almost always on the small scale of war parties, perhaps the size of squads or platoons. Battles were seldom fought for the purpose of territorial conquest, but rather in response to encroachments into hunting territory, over misunderstandings due to language differences, for theft of prestige items, or in raids to obtain slaves or wives.

MILITARY ACHIEVEMENT

Because no written historical record exists for North America north of the Valley of Mexico before 1500 C.E., warfare between groups of Native Americans cannot be documented with any precision. There are some oral sources but most information derives from archaeological evidence, which does point to violent conflicts. Many towns were fortified with palisades, bastions, and defensive trenches that would have been unnecessary had there not been real or potential enemy incursions.

WEAPONS, UNIFORMS, AND ARMOR

The weapons of prehistoric Native American warfare would have been essentially, if not exactly, the same weapons as those used in hunting. These would have included the throwing and thrusting spear, dart, bow and arrow, hand ax, war club, hand pick or tomahawk, knife, accoutrements such as the atlatl (spearthrower), detachable projectile points, body armor, shields, quivers, and knife sheaths.

The spear was probably one of the earliest Native American weapons, arriving with the earliest immi-

TURNING POINTS

c. 400	The bow and arrow is introduced in eastern North America.
c. 700	Triangular projectile points are developed.
c. 1200	Destruction of southwestern Anasazi culture, possibly by raiding Ute, Apache, Navajo, and Comanche tribes.
c. 1300	An increase in separate tribal identities develops in response to increasing importance of agriculture and clearer definition of gender roles.
c. 1500	The Iroquois Confederacy, an alliance of separate tribes formed to fight hostile western and southern neighbors, is established in the Northeast.

grants across the Bering Strait land bridge fourteen thousand or more years ago. The evolution of its use in North America is believed to have roughly paralleled that in Eurasia. The spear was originally used as a thrusting instrument in the early Paleolithic period (c. 12,000 B.C.E.). It then progressed to the throwing spear by the late Paleolithic period (c. 8000 B.C.E.). The earliest evidence of the atlatl comes from the Fort Rock Cave in Oregon and dates to approximately 6500 B.C.E. At the Five Mile Rapids site east of The Dalles, Oregon, on the Columbia River, two atlatl spurs, which engage the tip of the spear at the throwing end, were discovered and found to be contemporaneous with the Fort Rock Cave atlatl. There are two basic types of atlatl: the compound, with the spur as a separate piece attached to the body of the atlatl, and the simple, which combines the two into one piece. The simple atlatl appears to have appeared somewhat later than the compound. By the late Woodland period (c. 400 C.E.), the simple atlatl and spear, or the shorter dart, were in use, along with the bow and arrow. They appear to have been used as a weapon until about the end of the Woodland period (c. 700 C.E.) in both the South and Southeast. The spear continued to be used after this time in the Great Plains and in the West.

The spear point was made of a variety of lithic materials. In the West, flint and basalt were used. Slate, being easily chipped, was common in the Northeast, whereas chert and flint were utilized in the South and Southeast, as well as the Great Plains. Horn was also known to be used. These points were hafted into a groove at the end of the shaft and secured with sinew and glue.

The spear was constructed from hard, straight woods such as hickory and oak in the East; yew and sometimes cedar in the West; and spruce, especially Sitka spruce, in the Northwest. Atlatls were often constructed of horn, such as that of the bighorn sheep, as well as wood. They had stone weights attached to their handles that enabled effective balance of the weapon in the hand of the thrower. The atlatl-thrown spear was a very effective weapon, but it was neither as effective nor as easily portable as the bow and arrow. During the temple mound period in the South and Southeast, the spear became a ritual item.

The bow and arrow appears to have been the principal weapon used during the period one thousand to twelve hundred years before European contact with native North Americans. Only the projectile points, or arrowheads, of spears have survived through time to the present day; the organic parts have been lost to decay. There are exceptions, however, in cases where weapons were deposited in dry caves. The time when the bow and arrow were introduced, and its diffusion throughout North America, remains a matter of dispute. Most archaeologists date its inception in the fourth or fifth century C.E. However, a few would put the introduction of this technology in about 500 B.C.E., and still fewer as far back as 4000 B.C.E. The earliest sites have been reported, and highly disputed, to be in the southern half of the Canadian Shield region, which includes Labrador and the southern taiga of eastern Canada. Some have suggested that bow and arrow weapons were diffused throughout this region through contact with Paleoeskimo (Inuit) peoples as early as 1500 B.C.E. At some pre-Dorset sites (1050 to 550 B.C.E.) in the eastern Arctic zone of North

Scalping Knife

Deer-shank Tomahawk

Two types of Mohawk weapons.

America, the region that includes Baffin Island, small, chipped, stone projectile points have been found and interpreted to be arrowheads.

In the lower and middle Columbia River region of Washington and Oregon, small projectile points inferred to be arrowheads date as early as 550 B.C.E. Sites in the Willamette Valley of Oregon and Saint Lawrence Island, Alaska, place the bow and arrow in use as early as 50 B.C.E. If these inferences are true, the bow and arrow may have diffused from Asia to the Paleoeskimo (Inuit) cultures of the North American Arctic. It is known that there were strong lines of communication between prehistoric Inuit peoples. At the time of European contact, their languages, from those of eastern Siberia to those of eastern Greenland, were fairly uniform. Therefore, the bow and arrow could have diffused southward along both the Pacific and Atlantic coasts.

From these northwestern and northeastern locations, weapons technology moved into the Great Basin and the West Lakes regions by about 100 C.E. From these locations, diffusion into the East Coast and Southeast regions, the Colorado Plateau, and California occurred by about 400 C.E. It was probably another few hundred years (525-950 C.E.) before the bow and arrow reached the bulk of the Great Plains region.

Before the introduction of the horse by Europeans in the early sixteenth century, bows were commonly from 1.5 to 2 meters in length and were fired from a vertical position. Later the bowman on horseback used a much shorter bow and fired from a horizontal position. In the western and northern Great Plains, bows were often wrapped with sinew, which has elastic qualities. Because sinew-wrapped bows were prone to lose their tensile strength with exposure to high humidity, the craftsman would wrap the bow with rattlesnake skin, which is nonporous. Horn bows were also sometimes wrapped in a similar manner. Some bows resembled a curved lath, or rod, that was tapered in thickness from about 2.5 centimeters at the grip to about 1.5 centimeters at the tip. Other, compound, bows were elliptical in shape, bending outward from the grip; when strung, they bent gracefully in compound curves.

Bowstrings were fashioned from the tough shoulder sinew of the large male bison or elk. The sinew was separated into strands, soaked in water and a glue probably made from reduced vegetable and hoof materials, and finally twisted into a heavy cord. One end of the cord was always attached to one end of the bow, whereas the other end was attached to a notch on the other end only when the warrior was ready to string the bow for use. This allowed the bow to maintain its elasticity and tensile strength. The bowman often carried a spare string.

Arrows were made from essentially the same wood material as were bows. The length of arrows varied throughout North America. The Omaha, for instance, traditionally made arrows the length of the distance from the pit of the left elbow to the tip of the middle finger and back over the hand to the wrist bone, an average of 63 to 64 centimeters. Arrows were fletched with feathers—usually three—and some of the feather fletching extended a full one-third of the shaft length. The feathers had to be large enough to split, so the feathers of turkeys, prairie chickens, owls, chicken hawks, eagles, and vultures were preferred. The feathers, after splitting, were often tied to the shaft at both ends with sinew, allowing the middle section to be free from the shaft. The shafts were grooved from the fletching to the tip, and the design of the grooving varied from tribe to tribe. The purpose of this grooving has been lost through time, but some Native Americans of seventeenth and eighteenth centuries claimed that the grooves made the arrow fly a straighter course; some claimed they were bleeding channels, others claimed they kept the arrow from warping, and still others claimed they were occult symbols that ensured accuracy.

The notch on the arrow that fit on the bowstring was at the feather end of the arrow. This end was made a bit bulbous to facilitate a better grip with the thumb and index finger. The string was pulled with the other three fingers.

The arrowheads of war arrows were perpendicular to the bowstring, so that the arrows would easily pass between the ribs of the enemy. Hunting arrowheads were parallel to the string, so that they would pass through the ribs of game. Some reports claim that there was essentially no difference between hunting and war arrows, except that the arrowhead on the war arrow was longer for more effective penetration. Arrows were often distinctly decorated among the tribes and among individuals. This decoration facilitated retrieval by the owner and also emphasized tribal distinctiveness.

Arrowheads took many forms even in the early periods of bow and arrow usage. By the late Woodland period, points were side notched and corner notched on the hafting, or attaching, end and these were of varying lengths to suit various purposes, such as hunting and warfare. The war arrowhead was the longest and most slender. Toward the end of the Woodland period and the beginning of the Mississippian, or temple mound, period, the triangular-shaped point became increasingly prominent.

These points were crafted by chipping and flaking any of several substances. Chert, flint, and obsidian were the most common materials; all are varieties of quartz. Chert, a poor-quality flint, was used when better qualities of raw materials were not available. Most arrowheads were made of good-quality flint. Flint, composed of extremely fine-grained sediment, has a concoidal fracture that easily lends itself to accurate chipping or pressure-flaking. Obsidian, or natural glass, is a volcanic rock and was available only in parts of the Rocky Mountains and the Cascade-Sierra Nevada ranges of the far West. Obsidian produced a super-sharp edge and could be easily sharpened when it became dull.

The arrowhead was hafted to the tip of the arrow shaft with sinew and glue. A notch was cut in the tip of the shaft, and the head was wedged into the notch. In the case of the war arrow, the head was sometimes detachable. It was loosely hafted to the shaft, and no sinew or glue was used. The head was simply wedged into the notch. If the arrow's victim attempted to pull the arrow out, the arrowhead would remain and increase the severity of the wound.

The bow and arrow was a very effective weapon of war. An arrow could be projected up to 500 meters and, in the hands of a skilled marksman, was extremely accurate at distances of 100 meters or more. The penetrating power of an arrow shot from a bow with a 40-pound pull had more penetrating potential than did a bullet shot from a Colt .45, and it was more accurate at long distances.

Bows were usually carried in highly decorated bow cases, and arrows were carried in equally elaborately decorated quivers that were slung over the shoulder and hung almost horizontally near the waist. Quivers were generally made of soft animal skins, such as that of the river otter.

In the Great Plains and in eastern North America, prehistoric bows often had a long flint blade or knife hafted to one end. These were used as bayonets in hand-to-hand combat. The Omaha called these weapons *mindehi*, which means "bowtooth."

The war club was a common weapon throughout North America. In very early times it was probably similar to the simple hand ax, made of ground sandstone with a groove near the top to permit it to be hafted onto a short wooden handle and lashed together with rawhide. During the temple mound period in the East and South, the war club was made of either stone or bone. The stone head, sometimes rounded, sometimes pointed, was hafted to a wooden handle with rawhide. Willow was a choice wood because it could be split on the hafting end and was pliable enough to wrap around the hafting groove. The whole assembly was wrapped with wet rawhide that shrunk tight while drying. A bone war club was a one-piece item made from one of the long bones of a large animal, the socket forming the rounded head of the club.

The Nootka of the Pacific Northwest often made their war clubs from whale bones. These war clubs were straight or slightly curved with a hole drilled in the handle end to facilitate a wrist thong. They were ornate objects, and intricate carvings of various designs are known. During the years of first European contact, war clubs of the Northwest were valuable trade items and carried great prestige.

Knives were bifacial instruments made of flaked or chipped flint or obsidian in most of North America. Ground or chipped slate knives have been found among the archaeological remains in the sub-Arctic Northeast. Some flint knives were as many as 75 centimeters in length and could be classified as short swords. Most, however, were considerably shorter and were hafted onto wooden handles in the manner of projectile points. The knife was often kept in a sheath made of leather, ornately decorated with shell and beads, and worn tucked in the waist belt. The knife, like the war club, was very effective in close combat.

A type of armor was sometimes worn by warriors in battle. Some of it was constructed of bent wooden laths that were drilled and sewn together with rawhide. Armor was also made of the thick leather of buffalo or elk, folded several times and worn as a vest that covered the entire torso. This same material was used by warriors in the Northwest to make thigh and shin guards. It was very difficult to penetrate, even with arrows and thrusting spears. Shields were also carried into battle. They were generally made of wood, covered with leather, and painted with various designs that were believed to have magical powers to protect the warrior.

It is not known whether the Native American warrior wore distinctive dress or a type of uniform that set him apart from the nonwarrior, because such items have not survived to the present day. At the time of European contact there was no indication that a particular type of uniform set any tribal warrior apart from others. It might be inferred, though, that someone wearing only a loincloth but carrying all of his weapons, body armor, and a shield could be identified as prepared to fight. European observers in all parts of North America often reported that, except for chiefs and shamans, all the men seemed to be dressed similarly.

MILITARY ORGANIZATION

It does not appear that any Native American group in prehistoric times had a standing army or even a warrior class. Warriors were able-bodied young men who, when called upon to engage in violence, left their normal duties as farmers, hunters, and craftsmen and assumed the role of warrior.

Most violent encounters between groups seem to have been conducted by small bands of warriors numbering no more than twenty or thirty. Oral tradition indicates that battles started with an ambush and concluded with hand-to-hand combat. It is true that some groups displaced others from their traditional territories. The traditions of the Shawnee tell of their former home somewhere in central Tennessee, and it is believed that they were displaced to the north of the Ohio River by pressures from some of the Southern tribes during the fifteenth or sixteenth century. Choctaw and Chickasaw migration legends claim that these peoples originally came from somewhere to the west of the Mississippi River. These removals, though, could have resulted just as easily from environmental conditions as from warfare. It would not have taken a vast army to cause the removal of small groups from their traditional homes. Persistent attacks by small raiding parties, which could not be successfully rebuffed or answered by counterraids, would have been enough pressure to force migrations. There is no record until after European contact of large military assemblages descending upon an enemy.

DOCTRINE, STRATEGY, AND TACTICS

Little or nothing is known of prehistoric military doctrine or strategies, and what is known of tactics is simple. Some of the tactics would have come from hunting, involving moving silently before the attack. The shock of ambush with bows and arrows, usually followed by close fighting with clubs and knives, seems to have been the favorite tactic used in hostile encounters. The strategies and tactics used by Native Americans after European contact, involving large numbers of warriors, probably were not traditional and could easily have been due to European influence.

MEDIEVAL SOURCES

Native Americans north of Mexico, prior to European contact, had no written languages; therefore, no information except the archaeological record remains. Apart from some Viking and Welsh legends, which may or may not have any historical foundation, there is little in the Native American legends to provide details on the military history of the region before 1500.

Castañeda de Nágera (fl. sixteenth century), chronicler for Francisco Vásquez de Coronado (1510-1554), recorded what he witnessed in the Southwest from February, 1540, until the fall of 1542. Alvar Nuñez Cabeza de Vaca (c. 1490-c. 1560) traded along the Gulf Coast in 1535 and left a journal describing his trade in bows and arrows. El Inca Garcilaso de la Vega's (1539-1616) chronicles of the 1539 to 1543 expedition of Hernando de Soto (c. 1496-1540) through the South offer a glimpse of Native American warfare at the close of the prehistoric period.

BOOKS AND ARTICLES

Ballentine, Betty, and Ian Ballentine, eds. *The Native Americans: An Illustrated History*. Atlanta: Turner, 1993.

Cressman, L. S. *Prehistory of the Far West: Homes of Vanished Peoples*. Salt Lake City: University of Utah Press, 1977.

Fagan, Brian M. *Ancient North America: The Archaeology of a Continent*. New York: Thames and Hudson, 1991.

Fiedel, Stuart J. *Prehistory of the Americas*. New York: Cambridge University Press, 1992.

Lewis, Thomas M. N., and Madeline Kneberg. *Tribes That Slumber: Indians of the Tennessee Region*. Knoxville: University of Tennessee Press, 1958.

Mann, Charles C. *1491: New Revelations of the Americas Before Columbus*. New York: Knopf, 2005.

Stewart, Hilary. *Indian Artifacts of the Northwest Coast*. Seattle: University of Washington Press, 1973.

Sutton, Mark O. *An Introduction to Native North America*. Boston: Pearson, 2008.

FILMS AND OTHER MEDIA

Broken Arrow. Feature film. Twentieth Century-Fox, 1950.

Bury My Heart at Wounded Knee. Feature film. HBO, 2007.

Crazy Horse. Film. Frank von Zernick, 1996.

Dances with Wolves. Feature film. TIG, 1990.

Five Hundred Nations. Documentary. Tig Productions, 1995.

Geronimo: An American Legend. Feature film. Columbia Pictures, 1993.

The Great Indian Wars. Documentary. Centre Communications, 2005.

Last of the Mohicans. Feature film. Twentieth Century Fox, 1992.

The Trail of Tears: Cherokee Legacy. Documentary. Rich-Heape, 2006.

Ulzana's Raid. Feature film. Universal, 1972.

Charles Mayer Dupier, Jr.

THE MEDIEVAL WORLD

FROM MEDIEVAL TO MODERN

HANDARMS TO FIREARMS

Dates: c. 1130-1700 C.E.

NATURE AND USE

Firearms are a Chinese invention for which the earliest evidence dates to 1130. By that time the Chinese were using gunpowder in primitive flamethrowers made of bamboo, wood, or metal tubes. Within another century they had developed gunpowder projectile weapons that fired lances, arrows, and probably balls. Beyond these early weapons, however, development of firearms did not proceed much further in China. Although most historians agree that thirteenth century Mongols brought gunpowder to Europe, where its first definitive mention is dated to 1267, there is no consensus on whether the Mongols also brought Chinese gunpowder weaponry to the West.

An English illustration from 1326 shows the earliest known gunpowder weapon in Europe during a siege. The first certain use of gunpowder weaponry in Europe occurred in 1331 during a siege of Friuli in northeastern Italy. A French source for the Battle of Crécy (1346) states that the English fired three cannons at crossbowmen in the French army as they advanced toward the English lines, but many historians do not accept the report's accuracy. At the English siege of Calais following their victory at Crécy, there is good documentation for the use of small cannons called *ribaulds*, but these cannons had only a small role in the siege. Over the next twenty years cannons increased greatly in size. During his 1377 siege of Odruik in the Netherlands, Philip II, duke of Burgundy (1342-1404), used cannons called bombards, which were capable of firing 200-pound stone balls. This occasion was the first known instance of cannon fire breaching walls. Philip was the strongest early advocate of gunpowder weapons, encouraging experimentation with different sizes, gunpowder mixtures, and metals. Soon bombards weighing twenty tons and firing 1,000-pound balls were bringing sieges to quick conclusions across Europe.

DEVELOPMENT

FIFTEENTH CENTURY

By 1410 gunpowder weaponry had captured the attention of an unlikely commentator on military affairs, Christine de Pizan (c. 1365-c. 1430), a native of Italy who lived most of her life at the French court. Her *Le Livre des fais d'armes et de chevalerie* (1410; *The Book of Fayttes of Arms and of Chivalry*, 1489) discusses at length the use of the cannon as a siege weapon, recommending that the defenders of a fortification use twelve cannons using stone balls and ten pieces of mechanical artillery. Christine estimated the need for 1,500 pounds of gunpowder along with 200 stone balls and argued that attackers would need a much larger arsenal: forty-two cannon shooting

TURNING POINTS

1331	First known use of gunpowder weaponry occurs at the Siege of Friuli in Italy.
1377	Cannon are first used successfully to breach a wall at the Siege of Odruik, the Netherlands.
1420	Hussite leader Jan Žižka makes innovative and effective use of firearms, with the *Wagenburg*, a defensive line of wagons and cannons.
1525	Spanish Square formation of pikemen and harquebusiers is perfected at the Battle of Pavia.
1631	Gustavus II Adolphus's military reforms prove their value at the Battle of Breitenfeld.

200-pound balls, along with many mechanical artillery pieces and smaller firearms. Attackers would also need 30,000 pounds of powder, 1,100 stone balls, and 500 pounds of lead for the smaller pieces, because working stone into balls small enough for these weapons was difficult and time-consuming. Christine also advocated mounting cannon on ships for war at sea.

The fact that Christine's work makes little mention of gunpowder weapons in battle suggests that, at least in France, they were not yet being widely used. In Flanders, ribaulds were placed on carts and used as field artillery. The first battle in which they had an impact was Beverhoudsveld (1382) in the Netherlands. The militiamen of the city of Ghent had some two hundred carts with several ribaulds apiece in the

North Wind Picture Archives via AP Images

A hand-cannon of the fifteenth century, fired from the shoulder or from a rest such as a wall with a lit match.

battle against the count of Flanders. Concentrated ribauld fire against the count's men as they charged caused them to panic and flee. These carts were difficult to move, and later the same year Ghent was defeated when its forces charged the enemy only to find that the ribauld carts could not keep up, depriving them of supporting fire at the crucial moment.

The solution was the development of handguns small enough to allow their bearers to move with the rest of the army. The first evidence for such weapons is found in an illustration from around 1400, which shows a soldier holding in one hand the breech end of a long narrow tube that rests on a tripod at the muzzle while he applies a burning stick to the touchhole. This device appears to be so clumsy that it was most likely used not in the field, but rather as a siege weapon. Walls provided a base on which to steady the weapons, and hooks attaching them to the walls absorbed much of the force of the recoil. Recoil was a serious problem in early handguns, which required two hands to use: one to hold either the burning stick or the match that appeared around 1420, and the other to hold the piece. Consequently early handguns were butted up against the middle of the user's chest, often resulting in a broken breastbone. The first hook guns probably were used in the Hussite Wars (1419-1434), an anti-Catholic revolt against King Sigismund of Bohemia (1368-1437). To counter the knightly forces of Sigismund, Hussite leader Jan Žižka (c. 1360-1424) devised the *Wagenburg*, a defensive line of wagons on which were placed men with firearms. Between the wagons, cannons were stationed. Men on horseback presented a large target for the gunpowder weapons in use, inaccurate as they were. These weapons had the additional advantage of frightening the horses with their smoke and noise. Even after Žižka's death, the Wagenburg continued to help the Hussites to victory over German knights. German efforts to replicate the Wagenburg failed, but Hussite hook guns appeared in Germany, where the German word for them is regarded as the source for the word "harquebus," used as the name for the first effective firearm.

The harquebus was a product of several German innovations that had been made by 1460. Corned, or granulated, powder provided greater explosive power than had earlier powder and produced higher muzzle velocities. Gunsmiths found the right compromise between ballistic performance and weight by using barrels of about 40 inches in length. Another major innovation was the match: a piece of string soaked in saltpeter that burned slowly but with a tip hot enough to touch off gunpowder. The match replaced the burning stick, which was both clumsy and unreliable. The match, however, created the same problem for its users as had the burning stick: It had to be held in a hand and touched down into the chamber to fire the powder, leaving only one hand to hold the piece. The solution was the matchlock, which brought together springs, a trigger, and a clamp for holding a smoldering match. When the trigger was pulled, the burning tip was thrust into the powder and touched it off. The shoulder stock, borrowed from

The harquebus, popular by the sixteenth century, had a matchlock firing device that allowed for more reliable firing.

the crossbow, reduced the impact of the recoil. The users of the matchlock device found that although overly coarse powder failed to be ignited by the match, overly fine powder created too forceful a recoil. The solution was the placement of a small pan behind the chamber of the barrel, into which fine powder was placed. Coarse powder was then put in the chamber. The match touched off the fine powder in the pan, blowing flame through a hole into the chamber, igniting the coarser powder there, and firing off the ball.

The harquebus's impact on the battlefield was slow to appear. Compared to longbows, the early harquebus performed poorly in its reliability, rate of fire, and accuracy. It found its first niche as a siege weapon, replacing the crossbow. Firearms were useful weapons for the militiamen who guarded the city walls across Europe. They did not require much training to be used effectively on walls, and the artisans and merchants who made up the urban militias could afford them. The earliest mentions of the har-

quebus appear in the weapons inventories of cities.

For a brief time, the use of the harquebus as a defensive weapon on walls reduced the advantage that heavy cannons had provided besiegers, but gunpowder artillery continued to improve more rapidly than did firearms. A problem with early cannons was the poor quality of cast iron used to make them, which resulted in pieces frequently bursting and killing gunners and bystanders. A solution was the use of bronze. Europeans were familiar with casting bronze bells, and that technology was easily transferred to the making of weapons. The use of bronze allowed founders to manufacture long-barreled pieces with small muzzles, which were capable of using iron or lead balls. Under Charles VII (1403-1461), the French led the way in developing high-quality cannons. The final years of the Hundred Years' War (1337-1453) saw dramatic improvements in the royal artillery train. Charles's masters of artillery organized a system of manufacturing cannon, procuring gunpowder and shot, and hiring gunners that

R. S. Peale and J. A. Hill

The Battle of Pavia (1525) between forces of French king Francis I and Holy Roman Emperor Charles V.

played a significant role in reducing English-held locations in Normandy and Gascony. In the war's last major battles, Formigny (1450) and Castillon (1453), the French placed their guns all along the line of battle, routing the English. The king also promoted experimentation to improve the gun carriage, leading to the creation of the carriage with high wheels and long tail that defined gun carriages until the nineteenth century. Using an artillery train of around eighty bronze cannon on mobile carriages, Charles VIII (1470-1498) had great success in reducing Italian fortifications during the initial phase of the Italian Wars of 1494-1559. In the Battle of Fornovo (1495) the French artillery also played a role as a field weapon.

SIXTEENTH CENTURY

During the wars in Italy after 1494, field armies began to include harquebusiers. At the Battle of

Cerignola (1503) in the French-Spanish War over Naples, the Spanish commander Gonzalo Fernández de Córdoba (1453-1515) devised a way to make effective use of harquebusiers by digging trenches in front of their lines. This action transformed the battlefield into a fort and imitated a siege, a situation in which the harquebus had long proven itself. Harquebus fire raked the French forces as they approached the Spanish trenches. Over the next twenty years the Spanish infantry was victorious as long as it had the time to dig entrenchments and the French and their Swiss mercenaries relied on frontal assault. At the Battle of Pavia (1525) the combination of harquebusiers and pikemen in the army of Holy Roman Emperor Charles V (1500-1558) formed without entrenchments and defeated the French. This infantry formation, in which pikemen and harquebusiers provided mutual support, was known as the Spanish Square.

During the Dutch Wars of Independence (1566-1648), Maurice of Nassau (1567-1625) made his infantry more effective by extensive drilling, which had special success in improving his handgunners' firepower. He broke down the process of loading and firing a matchlock firearm into forty-two steps; each step had a word of command shouted by the sergeant. Drill books showing the steps and providing the words of command spread across Europe. Gustavus II Adolphus (1594-1632) of Sweden built upon the Dutch system, emphasizing drills and increasing the rate of fire from firearms by providing a cartridge with a ball and a measured amount of powder. Intent on increasing firepower for his forces, he also introduced a light piece firing a 3-pound ball that could be moved with the infantry on the battlefield, thereby providing support fire for the infantry in a way that heavier cannon could not do. For Gustavus II Adolphus, the purpose of firepower was to create opportunities for shock forces to carry the attack into the ranks of the enemy. Pikemen continued to be a significant part of the European infantry until the development of the bayonet by 1700 combined shock and firepower in each soldier.

Books and Articles

Arnold, Thomas F., ed. *Renaissance at War*. London: Cassell, 2001.

Chase, Kenneth. *Firearms: A Global History to 1700*. New York: Cambridge University Press, 2003.

Cooper, Jeff. *Fighting Handguns*. Los Angeles: Trend Books, 1958. Reprint. Boulder, Colo.: Paladin Press, 2008.

DeVries, Kelly. *Guns and Men in Medieval Europe, 1200-1500: Studies in Military History and Technology*. Burlington, Vt.: Ashgate/Variorum, 2002.

_____. *Medieval Military Technology*. Peterborough, Ont.: Broadview Press, 1992.

Diagram Group. *The New Weapons of the World Encyclopedia: An International Encyclopedia from 5000 B.C. to the Twenty-first Century*. New York: St. Martin's Griffin, 2007.

Hall, Bert. *Weapons and Warfare in Renaissance Europe*. Baltimore: Johns Hopkins University Press, 1997.

Lugs, Jaroslav. *Firearms Past and Present: A Complete Review of Firearms Systems and Their Histories*. 2 vols. London: Grenville, 1973.

Parker, Geoffrey. *The Military Revolution*. Cambridge, England: Cambridge University Press, 1988.

Pauly, Roger. *Firearms: The Life Story of a Technology*. Westport, Conn.: Greenwood Press, 2004.

Films and Other Media

Tales of the Gun. Documentary series. History Channel, 1998.

Frederic J. Baumgartner

KNIGHTS TO CAVALRY

Dates: c. 1000-1600 C.E.

KNIGHTS

Although the roles of knights and cavalrymen are often confused, the two are actually different. Knights were mounted warriors who fought as an aggregate of individuals; cavalry were tactical bodies of horsemen who fought as a cohesive unit. Knights, who dominated the battlefields of central and western Europe from the eleventh to the fourteenth centuries, were identified by their horses, armor, and weapons. Although it was not a violation of the knightly code for knights to fight on foot, knights generally fought on horseback, wearing armor, and engaged in hand-to-hand combat using couched lances, broadswords, and other shock weapons, such as maces. Knights' proper opponents were other knights, not the ill-disciplined and badly armed infantrymen who accompanied medieval armies.

The usual knightly tactic was the frontal charge, with the horsemen forming up in a line and riding toward the enemy's line, reaching a full gallop some 30 to 40 yards before colliding with the enemy. Unless one foe was badly inferior in number or morale, allowing the line to be broken, hand-to-hand combat ensued in the melee after the two lines collided, where individual combatants were nearly identical in equipment, strength, and training. The knights spent little time drilling together. Imbued with the old Germanic tradition that the best warrior led the others into battle, the knights competed to be the first into battle, making it difficult for commanders to coordinate simple tactical moves such as flanking maneuvers before the knights rode off to charge the enemy.

For all of their deficiencies, knights proved their mettle against Byzantine and Muslim forces, and for nearly 250 years after the Battle of Hastings (1066) they were all but invulnerable to the weapons used by European infantrymen. At the Battles of Courtrai (1302) in the Franco-Dutch War and the Morgarten (1315) in the First Austro-Swiss War, however, Flemish and Swiss pikemen demonstrated that the proper choice of terrain allowed resolute foot soldiers to defeat French and Austrian knights respectively. By then the use of powerful crossbows and longbows also put knights at greater risk of death on the battlefield at the hands of commoner bowmen. The combination of archer and dismounted knight used by the English throughout the Hundred Years' War (1337-1453) proved deadly effective against French knights. Men-at-arms responded to their new vulnerability by using plate armor for themselves and their horses, which were more likely than their riders to be killed in battle. Plate armor presented several problems. It was too expensive for the less wealthy nobles, so that the

TURNING POINTS

1302	Flemish pikemen defeat French knights with advantageous choice of terrain at Courtrai.
1420	Hussite leader Jan Žižka stymies German knights during the Hussite Wars with his *Wagenburg*, a defensive line of wagons and cannons.
1503	Spanish infantry using Spanish Square formation of pikemen and harquebusiers defeat French knights at Cerignola.
1544	At Cerisolles, French knights fighting in the traditional style play a major role in gaining victory over the Swiss, the last battle in which they are to do so.
1562	The caracole maneuver is first executed by Huguenot pistolers against Catholic forces at the Battle of Dreux.
1631	Disciplined cavalrymen combine firepower and shock tactics at Breitenfeld.

Medieval knights face a massed infantry pike formation, against which, in their heavy armor astride their large, unwieldy horses, they became less and less effective.

near equality in knightly equipment that had marked the previous era disappeared. Its weight required larger and more costly warhorses, which were slower and less maneuverable, allowing the men-at-arms to do little more than a straight-ahead charge. Despite defeat by the Swiss infantrymen in numerous battles throughout the fifteenth century, culminating at Nancy (1477) in the death of Charles the Bold (1433-1477), the duke of Normandy, armored horsemen remained a potent element, especially in the French army.

IMPACT OF GUNPOWDER WEAPONS

The development of gunpowder weapons after 1325 did little to change warfare for 150 years. Their first niche was in siege warfare. During the Hussite Wars (1419-1434) in Bohemia, Hussite leader Jan Žižka (c. 1360-1424) successfully brought the siege to the battlefield using the *Wagenburg*, which copied a fort by placing firearms and small cannon on wagons

drawn up in a defensive line. Žižka's Wagenburg stymied the German knights who were his enemy in the war, but the tactic did not spread beyond Bohemia. The new weaponry, including both firearms and artillery, was too inaccurate, slow to reload, and clumsy to use on the battlefield to be effective against men-at-arms, although its ability to pierce plate armor increased knightly casualty rates.

During the Italian Wars of 1494-1559, which began in 1494 when French king Charles VIII (r. 1483-1498) led an army of 8,500 horsemen across the Alps, the men-at-arms continued to have a significant place in battle. At Seminara (1495) the French men-at-arms crushed the Spanish and Italian horsemen and then routed the enemy infantry by attacking its flank and rear. Faced with the need to reform his army after its crushing defeat, Ferdinand II of Aragon (1452-1516) decided to concentrate on the infantry, introducing the combination of firearms and pike that became known as the Spanish Square. This formation demonstrated its potential against the French men-at-arms at Cerignola (1503), when well-entrenched infantrymen using harquebuses and pikes held off their charge and killed the French commander with a harquebus ball as he rode toward their line. The men-at-arms had their victorious moments, most notably at Marignano (1515), where they had a major role in the French victory over the Swiss. The last battle in which French men-at-arms using their traditional fighting style had a significant role in gaining victory was Cerisolles (1544) in northern Italy. Their foe, a Spanish and German force serving Holy Roman Emperor Charles V (1500-1558), placed too much faith in the ability of harquebusiers to withstand a cavalry charge without support from pikemen. The harquebusiers could not sustain fire strong enough to halt the men-at-arms as they charged through the balls into their ranks.

France was the last place in Europe where knights continued to be used as a major part of the army. This tradition reflected the attitude of the French nobles, who regarded fighting on horseback as their God-given right. The Spanish had never developed much of a force of armored horsemen because their principal foe through the Middle Ages had been the light cavalry of the Moors and because Spanish agriculture was incapable of breeding many of the heavy horses the knights required. The English had been using armored men as heavy infantry since conquering Wales in the thirteenth century. English ability to deploy armored men on horseback was severely limited by the lack of heavy horses. The Italians had used men-at-arms as their principal fighting force until 1494, but one consequence of the Italian Wars of

Frederick Ungar Publishing Co.

French king Henry II is mortally wounded in a joust the year of the treaty between France and Spain that ended decades of war between the two countries.

1494-1559 was a rapid decline in that system. A city such as Venice would keep some armored horsemen under arms until late in the sixteenth century, but this practice was more for the appeasement of its noble class than for any practical value the knights had on the battlefield.

The Pistol

The final challenge to the traditional man-at-arms appeared in Germany. German knights had continued to appear in war until 1540. Then, within a decade, the pistoler replaced the knight. The wheel-lock mechanism for the pistol was developed about 1505 in either Germany or Italy, but it evolved into the pistol first in Germany. By 1518, Holy Roman Emperor Maximilian I (1459-1519) had banned weapons small enough to be concealed in one's sleeve. The production of the wheel lock was a time-consuming task that required much smaller tolerances than the matchlock used in the harquebus did. Because the wheel lock had to be sturdy enough for use in a weapon, it was very expensive. Cost probably was the principal reason the pistol did not become a weapon for foot soldiers, although some wheel-lock muskets were made.

The nobles, who still insisted on their right to fight on horseback, found that the pistol could be effective from horseback, especially if they carried three or four of them, which could be loaded in advance, placed in slings or in their boots, and fired in rapid succession. The wheel-lock pistol was badly inaccurate at any distance beyond a few paces and only more so when fired from a moving horse. However, a horseman firing three or four pistols rapidly could have some hope of hitting a foe. The pistol was a one-handed weapon, which allowed the rider a free hand to control his horse. Although there had been mounted harquebusiers in most European armies since 1500, the sparking match of the harquebusiers' two-handed weapons frightened their horses, and the harquebusiers usually dismounted to fire. Pistols offered many benefits: Pistolers could shed much of their armor, making their mobility the key to what success they had; their horses could be smaller and cheaper; and it required less training to use a pistol than a lance.

Mounted pistolers first appeared in the war between Charles V and the Lutheran princes in Germany (1546-1555). When they served in Charles's army that fought the French for control of Lorraine (1553-1554), the French called them *reîtres*. The French men-at-arms were astonished when a force of reîtres little larger than their own band defeated them at Saint-Vincent in Lorraine (1553). The forces of Spanish king Philip II (r. 1556-1598) had great numbers of reîtres at the Battle of Saint Quentin (1557). Their speed played a major role in the deadly pursuit of the routed French forces. French king Henry II (r. 1547-1559) then recruited eight thousand reîtres for the French army. In the French Wars of Religion that followed Henry's accidental death while jousting (a further blow to the traditional style), the Protestant army had the larger number of reîtres, because most were Lutherans.

The Caracole

In the Battle of Dreux (1562), between the Protestant Huguenots and the Catholics, the Protestant pistolers for the first time executed the tactic known as the caracole. The reîtres rode toward their enemy's line in successive ranks, fired their pistols a few yards from the foe as they wheeled their horses about, and returned to the rear of their formation to reload and wait their turn to repeat the maneuver. The caracole had success against an infantry force armed only with shock weapons, but it was ineffective against a well-equipped force of harquebusiers, who had greater range. The caracole was more successful against the men-at-arms because reîtres could rely on greater speed to keep clear of their shock weapons. In 1568 Marshal Gaspard de Tavannes (1509-1573), the royalist Catholic commander, ordered that each company of horsemen would ride together in the formation it would take on the battlefield, so that men would become accustomed to holding their positions, a clear statement of the change from the knight to the cavalryman. The pistolers formed up in depth, while the knights charged in a line one or two ranks deep. To be effective in their deep formation, reîtres required more organization, drill, and training than did knights. Cohesion in their units was more crucial to what success they had on the battlefield. François

The values—and limitations—of the caracole maneuver were demonstrated in the Battle of Dreux in 1562.

de La Noue (1531-1591), a Protestant captain, noted with distaste in his *Discours politiques et militaires* (1587; *The Politicke and Militarie Discourses*, 1588) that pistolers could defeat noble men-at-arms if they kept tight order and discipline.

By the time Henry IV (r. 1589-1610) became the French king, the pistol had largely replaced the lance in France. Henry regarded shock tactics as necessary, and he had his horsemen charge into the ranks of the enemy with swords after they had fired their pistols. The greater discipline in Henry's cavalry units made them effective in hand-to-hand combat. During the Dutch Wars of Independence (1566-1648), Maurice of Nassau (1567-1625) ordered his horsemen to abandon the lance entirely. When Gustavus II Adolphus of Sweden (1594-1632) went to war with Poland (1617-1629), he found that his pistolers lacked the discipline and training to counter the powerful Polish lancers, who still fought largely in the traditional style. The scarcity of firearms in eastern Europe meant that horsemen there had not increased the weight of their armor and thus were still mobile and effective. Although he allowed his horsemen to fire a pistol as they closed on the enemy, Gustavus reemphasized shock tactics using the sword. However, he also demanded that his horsemen drill extensively so that they would fight as a cohesive unit. In battles of the Thirty Years' War such as Breitenfeld I (1631), he demonstrated the success of his ideas and completed the transition from knight to cavalry.

Books and Articles

Baumgartner, Frederic. "The Final Demise of the Medieval Knight in France." In *Regnum, Religio, et Ratio*, edited by Jerome Friedman. St. Louis, Mo.: Sixteenth Century, 1988.

Delbrück, Hans. *The History of the Art of War*. Translated by Walter Renfroe. 4 vols. Westport, Conn.: Greenwood Press, 1985.

Ellis, John. *Cavalry: The History of Mounted Warfare*. New York: Putnam, 1978. Reprint. Barnsley, England: Pen and Sword, 2004.

Eltis, David. *The Military Revolution in the Sixteenth Century*. London: I. B. Tauris, 1995.

France, John. "Men of War: Cavalry." In *Western Warfare in the Age of the Crusades, 1000-1300*. London: UCL Press, 1999.

Gillmor, Carroll. "Cavalry, Ancient and Medieval." In *The Reader's Companion to Military History*, edited by Robert Cowley and Geoffrey Parker. Boston: Houghton Mifflin, 1996.

Gravett, Christopher. *Real Knights: Over Twenty True Stories of Battle and Adventure*. Illustrated by John James. New York: Enchanted Lion Books, 2005.

_____. *Tudor Knight*. Illustrated by Graham Turner. Botley, Oxford, England: Osprey, 2006.

Hall, Bert. *Weapons and Warfare in Renaissance Europe*. Baltimore: Johns Hopkins University Press, 1997.

Hyland, Ann. *The Warhorse, 1250-1600*. Stroud, Gloucestershire, England: Sutton, 1998.

Morillo, Stephen. "The 'Age of Cavalry' Revisited." In *The Circle of War in the Middle Ages: Essays on Medieval Military and Naval History*, edited by Donald J. Kagay and L. J. Andrew Villalon. Rochester, N.Y.: Boydell Press, 1999.

Sinclair, Andrew. *Man and Horse: Four Thousand Years of the Mounted Warrior*. Stroud, Gloucestershire, England: Sutton, 2008.

Urban, William L. *The Teutonic Knights: A Military History*. London: Greenhill, 2003.

Films and Other Media

Knights and Armor. Documentary. History Channel, 2004.

Tales of the Gun: Early Guns. Documentary. History Channel, 1998.

The Works: Guns and Ammo. Documentary. History Channel, 2008.

Frederic J. Baumgartner

GALLEYS TO GALLEONS

Dates: To c. 1600 C.E.

THE MEDIEVAL GALLEY

The history of medieval naval warfare is the history of the galley. Since ancient times, battles at sea have taken place largely on the decks of ships and were fought much like land battles, with hand-to-hand combat. Medieval naval battles usually followed a similar pattern. First, smaller, more maneuverable ships would pin down the enemy fleet. Then the larger, more heavily armed galleys would attack, initially firing missiles and then ramming or grappling the enemy vessel in order to board it. Blasts of lime were often fired to blind the enemy and were then followed by volleys of stones. One of the most dreaded tactics was to fling onto the enemy ship what was known as Greek fire, a substance that, once ignited, was inextinguishable in water. Crossbows, lances, bows and arrows, and, by the late Middle Ages, guns and cannons served as well at sea as on land. However, the ship itself was the most powerful weapon, often determining the outcome of a naval battle. The warship at sea was likened to the warhorse on land and, like the warhorse, the warship was bred for fighting.

Equipped with sails for distance and oars for maneuverability, the medieval galley was ideally suited for the purpose of war. Medieval variations on the classical galley were many. The *dromon*, developed by the Byzantines, was a large galley that utilized one or two tiers of oars, a square sail set on a single mast, and a stern-hung rudder. In times of war, the dromon could carry troops, weapons, supplies, and cavalry horses, as well as engage in sea battles when necessary. The beam of the dromon permitted mounted cannons in the bow of the ship, which could be fired directly ahead of the vessel. A variation on the dromon was the Italian galley, which had one level of oars with two or three oarsmen to each rowing bench, a total of approximately 120 oarsmen. The Italian galley was manned by about fifty soldiers and typically had a large catapult mounted on a platform on the front deck.

The galleas was another variation on the galley. Developed by the Venetians, the galleas had a gun deck, oars, and two to three masts. The triangular lateen sails, adopted from those of the Arab dhows, permitted the galleas to sail nearly straight into the wind, impossible with square sails. Sailors armed with crossbows and lances could fight on the ships' decks.

TURNING POINTS

674-678	Greek fire, a flammable liquid, is used by the Byzantines against Arab ships during the Siege of Constantinople.
mid-13th cent.	The cog, with high sides that offer protection against other vessels, is developed in Northern Europe.
mid-14th cent.	The carrack, an efficient sailing ship with multiple masts, becomes popular in Atlantic and Mediterranean waters.
1501	The development of gunports allows a ship's heaviest guns to be mounted on its lowest decks, stabilizing its center of gravity.
1571	The Battle of Lepanto II, fought between the Ottoman Turks and the Christian forces of Don Juan de Austria, is the last major naval battle to be waged with galleys.
1588	The English employ galleons to individually attack the larger ships of the formidable Spanish Armada, defeating the Spanish and revolutionizing naval tactics.

The last major naval battle in which galleys were employed was the Battle of Lepanto II, fought off the coast of southwestern Greece on October 7, 1571, between the Ottoman Turks, under the command of Ali Paşa (died 1616), and the Christian forces, under the command of Don Juan de Austria (1547-1578), half brother of King Philip II of Spain (1527-1598). The Turks' 273 ships (210 were galleys) and the Christians' 276 ships (208 were galleys) faced off in long lines across from one another, with the Christian forces hemming in the Muslim forces. Don Juan skillfully placed his most heavily armed galleys in the center of the line and his smaller, more maneuverable galleys on the outside, where they could dominate the flanks. The massive and heavily armed Christian galleys eventually triumphed over the lighter and less armed Arab ships, giving naval supremacy to the Christian forces in the Eastern Mediterranean. The Battle of Lepanto was the last major naval battle in which galleys were employed, and it was the first major naval battle in which guns and gunpowder played the decisive role. From this point on, guns and cannons would be increasingly important in naval warfare.

Although the galley was the vessel of choice in the Mediterranean Sea for more than four millennia, it was a typically unstable ship, particularly in rough waters. Maneuverability during battle was provided by oars, rather than by the sails, which had to be lowered during battles to prevent the enemy from tearing or setting fire to them. Despite their shortcomings, however, various forms of galleys continued to be employed in the Mediterranean until 1717 and in the Baltic Sea until 1809. In an effort to produce a more seaworthy craft, medieval shipbuilders turned to other designs for seagoing vessels.

Frederick Ungar Publishing Co.

A sixteenth century galley, forerunner of the galleon, in an engraving by Raphael.

THE COG

Developed in Northern Europe as a trading vessel, the cog was one step closer to the first true full-rigged ships, which relied on sails, rather than oars, for both distance and maneuverability. The cog was clinker-built, of overlapping planks. It had a broad beam, a rounded bow and stern, fore- and aft castles, and a single square sail hoisted on a yard. The castles were constructed primarily as high platforms for lookouts and archers and were useful in sea battles. Lower, oar-driven ships found it nearly impossible to conquer a taller ship due to its sheer height and to the superior positioning of its archers and fighting men. The cog was maneuvered by a rudder, attached like a hinge at the center stern and manipulated by a tiller.

This steering system was a great technological advance, and it remains the basic means of control on ships.

The principal purpose of the cog was for commerce, but when enemies or pirates threatened, the cog became a warship. In 1234 and again in 1239, the Baltic German city of Lübeck, a central member of the Hanseatic League, sent a fleet of cogs against the king of Denmark when he threatened to take over the city. After pirates invaded the Mediterranean in 1304,

the Genoese and Venetians began to use cogs in their navies. A psalter dating to 1330 depicts two cogs in a battle, with the soldiers engaged in hand-to-hand combat across the decks of the ships.

In naval battles the primary goal was not the sinking of the enemy's ship; in fact, it would have been considered foolish to sink a vessel that had been so expensive to construct. In 1340, during the Hundred Years' War, King Edward III of England (1312-1377) sailed in a cog to lead an English fleet of 250 vessels into battle against the French fleet anchored at Sluys, off the coast of Flanders. Although outnumbered, Edward was able to defeat the French fleet and capture 190 French ships. His chronicler estimated that Edward saved 200,000 florins in shipbuilders' wages.

By the fourteenth century cogs sailed the throughout the Mediterranean and the northern European seas. The cog was not without its shortcomings, among which were its inability to keep cargo dry and its insufficient leeway to allow navigation in shallow waters. As trade, exploration, and military challenges increased, so too did the need for more capable and seaworthy vessels.

F. R. Niglutsch

An engraving of the Christian fleet's defeat of the Muslim Ottomans at the Battle of Lepanto, the last major naval battle in which galleys were employed.

THE CARRACK

From the fourteenth to the seventeenth century, a larger vessel called the carrack was the predominant trading vessel in Europe. The carrack combined the square sails of the northern ships with the lateen sails of the Mediterranean ships, along with three masts, a stern rudder, and very high fore- and aft castles, producing a vessel noted for its large cargo capacity and its ability to traverse great distances. Improvements in maps and charts greatly improved navigation, especially in the Mediterranean. Written sailing instructions called portolan charts described coastlines, ports, and dangerous sailing areas, and also provided information regarding the availability of supplies for seafarers.

These charts aided sailors by mapping coastlines, marking locations of cities, and stating sailing distances.

Although primarily used in trade, the carrack was also employed in war. The English carrack HMS *Mary Rose* was built in 1510 as a ship of war. Like other warships of its day, the *Mary Rose* had gunports with large guns mounted in its hull. Although the date of the first ship gunport is debated, it was most likely first developed by a Brest shipbuilder named Descharges in about 1501. The *Mary Rose* may have been the first of King Henry VIII's (1491-1547) ships to be equipped with gunports, perhaps installed when the *Mary Rose* was renovated in 1536. The guns on board the *Mary Rose* were cast of iron and bronze, with the heaviest guns mounted on the lowest deck in order to stabilize the ship's center of gravity. The *Mary Rose* carried a variety of guns, from smoothbore barrel guns to oddly bored scatter guns. The low placement of the gunports, however, combined with the sheer weight of its eighty guns, led to the sinking of the *Mary Rose* when it was sent against the French on July 19, 1545, in a battle off Spithead, taking its crew and its captain, Roger Grenville, as well as the vice admiral, Sir George Carew, down with her.

Frederick Ungar Publishing Co.

A galleon called a man-of-war, or combatant warship, from the sixteenth century.

THE GALLEON

The development of the galleon marked the turn from medieval to modern naval warfare. Designed in the sixteenth century by the admiral in charge of the Elizabethan navy, Sir John Hawkins (1532-1595), the galleon surpassed all previous ships. It was an adaptation of the carrack, eliminating the high forecastle to produce a ship with a lower profile and therefore with far better performance, particularly when sailing into the wind. This improved carrack design reached Spain about seventeen years after its introduction in England, and the result was the develop-

ment of the Spanish war galleon. Within forty years, the galleon replaced the carrack as both the primary trading vessel and warship. For three centuries, the galleon ruled the world's seas.

Galleons differed from carracks in more than the absence of the high forecastle. On the aft was typically a quarterdeck instead of a deck-mounted aft castle. Gunports lined one or both of the main decks, and special, smaller decks served as fighting platforms. A galleon's hull was longer, narrower, and sleeker than that of a carrack. The result was a ship designed for speed, maneuverability, seaworthiness, and, especially, warfare.

By the late sixteenth century, commercial and religious rivalry between Catholic Spain and Protestant England brought the two countries to the brink of war. Spain, confident of its maritime supremacy, made the first move. In May, 1588, the Spanish Armada, assembled by King Philip II of Spain and under the command of the duke of Medina-Sidonia, Alonso Pérez de Guzmán (c. 1550-1619), sailed out of Lisbon harbor en route to the Low Countries to pick up the prince of Parma and his forces. Their goal was to invade England. The Spanish fleet consisted of 130 ships of varying sizes and types, the majority of which were galleons. Meanwhile, the English prepared for the Spanish invasion by dividing the English navy between Plymouth, with 94 ships under Charles Howard of Effingham (1536-1624), and Dover, with 35 ships under Lord Henry Seymour.

After heading into the English Channel, the Spanish positioned their ships in a crescent formation, which the smaller English ships could not break. The English turned this to their advantage by attacking the larger Spanish ships individually at close firing range. When the Spanish fleet anchored at Calais on July 27 to wait for the prince of Parma and his forces, the English sent in small fireships to attack the anchored Spanish vessels. The Spanish were forced to cut their lines and sail out into the bay, where they were met by the combined forces of Howard and Seymour. The Spanish Armada retreated to Spain with only 67 of its original 130 ships.

The difference between the Spanish loss and the English victory lay in the strategy of each. The Spanish relied on the traditional warfare technique, used since ancient times, of coming alongside and boarding enemy ships to engage in hand-to-hand combat. The English, however, did not attempt to board the enemy ships, but rather attacked them downwind at close range, disabling as many as possible. This was an important turning point in naval history. The naval tactics that were first employed by the English against the Spanish Armada continued in use in naval warfare from that point forward.

BOOKS AND ARTICLES

Gardiner, Robert, ed. *The Age of the Galley: Mediterranean Oared Vessels Since Pre-Classical Times*. London: Conway Maritime Press, 1995.

Guilmartin, John Francis, Jr. *Galleons and Galleys*. London: Cassell, 2002.

_____. *Gunpowder and Galleys: Changing Technology and Mediterranean Warfare at Sea in the Sixteenth Century*. Rev. ed. Annapolis, Md.: Naval Institute Press, 2003.

Hanson, Neil. *The Confident Hope of a Miracle: The True History of the Spanish Armada*. New York: Doubleday, 2003.

Keen, M., ed. *Medieval Warfare: A History*. Oxford, England: Oxford University Press, 1999.

Kirsch, P. *The Galleon*. London: Conway Maritime Press, 1991.

Konstam, Angus. *The Armada Campaign, 1588: The Great Enterprise Against England*. Westport, Conn.: Praeger, 2005.

_____. *The Renaissance War Galley, 1470-1590*. Illustrated by Tony Bryan. Botley, Oxford, England: Osprey, 2002.

_____. *Sovereigns of the Sea: The Quest to Build the Perfect Renaissance Battleship*. Hoboken, N.J.: J. Wiley and Sons, 2008.

_____. *Spanish Galleon, 1530-1690*. Illustrated by Tony Bryan. Botley, Oxford, England: Osprey, 2004.

Lewis, A. R., and T. J. Runyan. *European Naval and Maritime History, 300-1500*. Bloomington: University of Indiana Press, 1990.

Unger, R. W., ed. *Cogs, Caravels, and Galleons*. London: Conway Maritime Press, 1994.

FILMS AND OTHER MEDIA

Great Ships: The Sailing Collection. Documentary. History Channel, 1996.

Sonia Sorrell